Re-examining the Cold War
U.S.-China Diplomacy, 1954–1973

Harvard East Asian Monographs, 203

Re-examining the Cold War

U.S.-China Diplomacy, 1954–1973

edited by

Robert S. Ross and Jiang Changbin

Published by the Harvard University Asia Center
and distributed by Harvard University Press
Cambridge (Massachusetts) and London, 2001

Printed in the United States of America

The Harvard University Asia Center publishes a monograph series and, in coordination with the Fairbank Center for East Asian Research, the Korea Institute, the Reischauer Institute of Japanese Studies, and other faculties and institutes, administers research projects designed to further scholarly understanding of China, Japan, Vietnam, Korea, and other Asian countries. The Center also sponsors projects addressing multidisciplinary and regional issues in Asia.

⊗   Library of Congress Cataloging-in-Publication Data

Re-examining the Cold War : U.S.-China diplomacy, 1954-1973 / edited by Robert S. Ross and Jiang Changbin.
    p. cm. -- (Harvard East Asian monographs ; 203)
    Includes bibliographical references (p.) and index.
    ISBN 0-674-00524-4 (acid-free paper) -- ISBN 0-674-00526-0 (pbk. : acid-free paper)
    1. United States--Foreign relations--China. 2. China--Foreign relations--United States. 3. United States--Foreign relations--1945-1989. 4. Cold War. I. Ross, Robert S., 1954- II. Jiang, Changbin. III. Series.

E183.8.C5 R38 2001
327.73051--dc21

                                                          2001026485

Index by Mary Mortensen

    Printed on acid-free paper

Last figure below indicates year of this printing
10 09 08 07 06 05 04 03 02 01

Acknowledgments

WITHOUT THE ASSISTANCE and contributions of friends and colleagues, this volume could not have been published. The editors are grateful to Anthony Saich, who, as Representative of the Ford Foundation in China, understood the significance of this project and generously supported it throughout its course. We also deeply appreciate the contribution of our many translators, who worked hard to convey, in Chinese and in English, the complexities of U.S.-China diplomacy. Chen Xiaoping tracked down many elusive citations and helped to standardize the translations of Chinese- and English-language documents.

Thanks also go to John Ziemer, Executive Editor of the publications program at the Asia Center, who supported publication of the manuscript from the beginning, to Linda Howe, who guided the book through the publication process, and to Nancy Hearst, whose careful attention to detail is reflected on every page.

Contents

Preface

Jiang Changbin

THE PUBLICATION OF THIS BOOK is a major development in scholarly cooperation between the United States and China. The research presented in the following chapters reflects over five years of collaboration by Chinese and American scholars in a spirit of scholarly exchange and mutual learning.

From their elementary school textbooks, Chinese youngsters have learned about such American documents as the Declaration of Independence and the Emancipation Proclamation, so that there is widespread respect for early American history within Chinese intellectual circles. Nonetheless, modern China-U.S. relations have not always been harmonious. On the contrary, in the twentieth century there were frequent clashes between the United States and China. One reason for this difficult history is the differences in the social customs, cultural traditions, and values of the two countries and in their status in the international community. But a further important factor has been the lack of mutual respect and equal exchange between all levels of their respective societies, especially between their scholarly communities.

China and the United States first established contact in 1784, when the American clipper ship *Empress of China* arrived in Chinese waters. Since then, the history of China-U.S. relations has gone through roughly four complete stages. The first was from 1784 to 1844, when the two sides initiated and developed the foundation of commercial ties. The second, from 1844 (marked by the conclusion of the Sino-American Treaty of Wangxia) to 1899, was a period characterized by U.S. commercial expansion in China.

The third began in 1900, when the United States participated in the occupation of Beijing by the Eight Allied Troops during the Boxer Rebellion, and ended in 1949 with the establishment of the People's Republic of China. During this period, the United States carried out political, military, economic, religious, and cultural expansion in China. The fourth and final stage, from 1949 to 1972, was characterized by extreme conflict and tension over the Taiwan issue.

Now the relationship is in a fifth stage, which began with the initial steps toward normalizing relations in 1972. This stage is the most important for both China and the world. Bilateral relations between China and America are not only of momentous significance to the development of both countries in the twenty-first century, they also affect general trends in the development of the international system. It is the obligation of the scholarly communities in both countries and of all concerned citizens to promote the constructive development of Sino-U.S. relations.

Chinese and American scholars have taken the lead in promoting U.S.-China cooperation. In the 1980s Harry Harding and Yuan Ming presided over collaborative research on Sino-U.S. relations from 1945 to 1955. Their achievements resulted in the publication of a special volume of papers in both English and Chinese versions.[1] Since then, many new Chinese and U.S. research materials have become available, providing favorable conditions for ongoing research. In 1995, when Robert Ross was Fulbright Professor at the China Foreign Affairs College, we agreed that the John King Fairbank Center for East Asian Research at Harvard University and the International Strategic Research Center of the Central Party School should continue such cooperative research. The two institutes quickly established a program to promote collaborative research between China and the United States on the period from 1955 to 1971. The research focused on four major issues: tension across the Taiwan Strait in the 1950s; the Vietnam War; the impact of the global setting on the bilateral policies of the United States and China; and the impact of Chinese and U.S. domestic conditions on their respective foreign policies.

In October 1996, the paper writers and commentators representing the two sides held the first research workshop in Beijing.[2] Following the conference, the original papers were revised by the authors, edited by the two project directors, and published in Beijing in 1998.[3] The participants also agreed that it was necessary to carry out further research on Mao Zedong's diplomatic thinking and the foreign policy-making process during the early years of the People's Republic of China. In addition, they agreed that research on the Sino-American ambassadorial-level talks at Warsaw and on the second Taiwan Strait crisis in 1958 should be included in the volume of papers. In May 1998, the second research symposium was held at the John King Fairbank Center for East Asian Research. The papers prepared for this workshop were likewise revised and edited. This English-language collection represents a broad overview of the work presented at the two conferences. These papers have also been published in China.[4]

The United States is the largest developed country in the world, and China the largest developing country. Whether the relations between the two countries are good or bad, they will undoubtedly have a great impact on the security and stability of the international community. At the beginning of a new century, it is important for scholars in both countries to strengthen exchange and dialogue. For that reason, the Fairbank Center for East Asian Research and the International Strategic Research Center are determined to develop a third round of cooperation. We hope that this project will also result in a volume of collaborative research and will contribute to greater U.S.-China understanding.

I am grateful to William C. Kirby and Ezra Vogel for their support of our project and to the Ford Foundation for its encouragement and generous support. Without their assistance, the project and this book would not have been possible.

Contributors

ROBERT ACCINELLI is a professor of history at the University of Toronto and the author of *Crisis and Commitment: United States Policy toward Taiwan, 1950–1955*.

ROSEMARY FOOT is Professor of International Relations and the John Swire Senior Research Fellow at St. Antony's College, University of Oxford. Her latest book is *Rights beyond Borders: The Global Community and the Struggle over Human Rights in China*.

STEVEN M. GOLDSTEIN teaches at Smith College, where he is the Sophia Smith Professor of Government.

GONG LI is Professor of International Relations, International Strategic Research Center, Central Party School of the Chinese Communist Party. He has written several books on Sino-American relations, including *Mao Zedong yu Meiguo* (Mao Zedong and the United States).

JIA QINGGUO is Professor and Associate Dean of the School of International Studies, Peking University. He received his Ph.D. from Cornell University in 1988 and has published extensively on U.S.-China relations, relations between the Chinese mainland and Taiwan, Chinese foreign policy, and Chinese politics. He is Vice President of the China Association for Asia-Pacific Studies.

JIANG CHANGBIN is Professor and Director of the International Strategic Research Center, Central Party School of the Chinese Communist Party. His research focuses on Russian studies and U.S.-China relations. His most recent publications are *Sidalin Zhengzhi Pingzhuang, 1879–1953* (Critical and political biography of Stalin, 1879–1953) and *Zong Duizhi Zouxiang Huanghe: Lengzhan Shiqu zhong Zhong Mei Guanxi zai Tantao* (From confrontation to détente: A reexamination of Cold War U.S.-China relations, 1955–1971), co-edited with Robert S. Ross.

WILLIAM C. KIRBY is Edith and Benjamin Geisinger Professor of History and Director of the Harvard University Asia Center. A historian of modern China, he examines China's economic and political development within an international context. Among his publications are *Germany and Republican China, State and Economy in Republican China*, co-edited with Man-houng Lin, James Chin Shih, and David A. Pietz, and *A World Transformed: A Global History of the Twentieth Century* (forthcoming).

LI JIE is Professor in the Department for Research on Party Documents, Central Committee of the Chinese Communist Party. His most recent book, co-authored with Pong Xianshi, is *Mao Zedong he Chaoxian Zhanzheng* (Mao Zedong and the Korean War).

RONALD W. PRUESSEN is Chair of the Department of History at the University of Toronto and a specialist in the history of twentieth-century U.S. foreign policy. He is the author of *John Foster Dulles: The Road to Power, 1888–1952*. His research for the second and concluding volume of this biography has included an examination of German-American and Chinese-American relations in the 1950s and the United States' postwar experiences with "globalization."

ROBERT S. ROSS is Professor of Political Science, Boston College, and Associate, John King Fairbank Center for East Asian Research, Harvard University. His publications include *The Great Wall and the Empty Fortress: China's Search for Security*, with Andrew J. Nathan, and *Engaging China: The Management of an Emerging Power*, co-edited with Alastair I. Johnston.

MICHAEL SCHALLER is Professor of History at the University of Arizona. He has written several books on U.S. relations with East Asia, including *Altered States: The U.S. and Japan since the Occupation.*

ROBERT D. SCHULZINGER is Professor of History and Director of the International Affairs Program at the University of Colorado at Boulder. Among his many books are *A Time for War: The United States and Vietnam, 1941–1975* and *U.S. Diplomacy since 1900.* He is editor-in-chief of the journal *Diplomatic History.*

ZHANG BAIJIA is Research Professor of the Party History Research Center, Central Committee of the Chinese Communist Party. He has written several books on Chinese foreign policy and Party history, the most recent of which is *Zhongguo Gaige Kaifang 20 Nian Shi* (Twenty years of China's reform and open door).

Re-examining the Cold War
U.S.-China Diplomacy, 1954–1973

Introduction

Robert S. Ross

IN RECENT YEARS, as scholars have gained increasing access to Chinese and American diplomatic archives, they have uncovered new information about U.S.-China relations that has revised and expanded current understanding of the sources of U.S.-China Cold War conflict. The first stages of research and writing following the gradual opening of American archives focused on U.S.-China relations during the late 1940s and early 1950s.[1] Some of the most important extensions of this research involved a series of collaborative studies undertaken by Chinese and American scholars. Drawing on newly available materials in their own respective national archives, they prepared research papers, which they then presented to their colleagues from the other country. These collaborative projects produced important work on the origins and escalation of U.S.-China conflict during the early years of the Cold War, revealing the constraints on policymakers, the limits to cooperation, and the effects of policy mistakes and misperceptions.[2]

Seeking to build on this important work and to take advantage of recently expanded access to U.S. archival materials, the John King Fairbank Center at Harvard University and the International Strategic Research Center at the Central Party School of the Chinese Communist Party Central Committee, with the generous support of the Ford Foundation, developed a collaborative research project—the first of its kind between an American research institution and China's Central Party School—to examine U.S.-China relations from the mid-1950s to the onset of U.S.-China rapprochement in the late 1960s and early 1970s. Our explicit objective was to encourage Chinese and American scholars who were actively engaged in using their own national archives to write research papers on this later period of U.S.-China Cold War conflict. The Chinese participants were all scholars at research institutions who had access to official archives and had used these archives in the past. The American, Canadian, and European participants were diplomatic historians and international relations specialists whose ongoing research entailed the use of various U.S. archives and recently released American documents. The organizers made no attempt to select participants with similar historical or analytical perspectives or to impose a common interpretive framework. We simply asked first-rate scholars engaged in archival research to address important issues in U.S.-China Cold War history.

The project convened two conferences, the first in Beijing in 1996, the second in Cambridge, Massachusetts, in 1998. At each conference, the researchers presented their work to all project participants. The ensuing conference discussions allowed them to reconsider their papers in light of the research and findings of other scholars. After the conferences, the participants carried out significant revisions and continued to revise to incorporate material from more recently released documents. Selected papers from both of these conferences have been collected in this volume. Taken together, they offer new information, new insights, and new perspectives on a critical period of U.S.-China relations.

Policymaking and U.S.-China Interactions

The research presented here highlights similarities in Chinese and American approaches to bilateral diplomacy and perceptions of each other's policymaking motivations. Much of the literature on U.S.-China relations posits that each side was motivated either by its own ideologically informed interests or by ideological assumptions about its counterpart. The more recent Western literature on the U.S.-China conflict, however, tends to stress the importance of pragmatism and perceptions of Sino-Soviet conflict in the development of the Eisenhower administration's "wedge strategy."[3] The contributions to this volume strengthen this perspective on U.S. policy toward China and support a similar understanding of Chinese policy. Rather than devise inflexible policies against an allegedly implacable foe, U.S. and Chinese policymakers developed responsive and tactically adaptable foreign policies, which they could adjust in response to changing international circumstances and their own changing assessment of their counterpart's policies. Equally important, as these studies also reveal, both Beijing and Washington assumed that the immediate policy objectives of their counterparts were similarly motivated by pragmatic national security considerations rather than by the ideological considerations their respective revolutionary or anticommunist rhetoric would suggest.

During the two Taiwan Strait crises of the 1950s, Chinese leaders tracked U.S. policy toward Taiwan and revised their own in response to shifting U.S.-Taiwan relations. Substantiating earlier Western analyses of Chinese behavior,[4] these studies show that Chinese leaders, including Chairman Mao Zedong, believed that improved U.S.-Taiwan security relations would reinforce Taiwan's separation from the mainland and make unification even more difficult. They regarded the 1954 negotiation and signing of the U.S.-Taiwan defense treaty and U.S. consideration of Taiwan for membership in a regional security organization as overt challenges to China's most important foreign policy objective. Beijing similarly appraised the 1957 U.S. deployment of Matador missiles and consolidation of U.S. military operations on Taiwan. In each case, Chinese leaders considered the use of force a necessary demonstration of their determination to resist U.S. policy moves and halt the development of closer U.S.-Taiwan relations.

Even at the height of the 1954–55 crisis, Chinese and American leaders acted with considerable caution to avoid direct hostilities. Mao Zedong personally oversaw Chinese military activities to ensure that there would be no U.S. casualties, even ordering the People's Liberation Army (PLA) to delay its seizure of Dachen island to avoid engaging U.S. forces. Similarly, during the 1958 crisis, fearing that Chinese troops would kill U.S. soldiers and provoke U.S.-China hostilities, Mao gave orders that the PLA should not shell U.S. vessels. On the U.S. side, Eisenhower and Dulles, equally interested in avoiding extreme measures and maintaining tactical flexibility, tried to deter Chinese actions without expanding the U.S. commitment to Taiwan. In 1954 they considered committing the United States to the defense of Jinmen and Mazu but decided against it, and in 1958 they tried to persuade Chiang Kai-shek to abandon the islands to PRC forces. Eisenhower and Dulles also had to manage domestic political pressure urging escalation and check

Chiang Kai-shek's more belligerent objectives, while developing a brinkmanship policy that maintained a necessary degree of ambiguity in U.S. policy.

During the first and second Indochina wars, Washington and Beijing displayed similar concern about any escalation of U.S.-China conflict and exercised similar tactical caution. Chinese leaders consistently pursued two objectives: first, protecting Chinese border security, and second, avoiding war with the United States. During the 1954 Geneva Conference they worked for a cease-fire to the first Indochina war because they feared that if the negotiations broke down, the United States would intervene, and the war might spread to China's borders. During the second Indochina war, they regarded expanded U.S. intervention following the Tonkin Gulf incident as a threat to Chinese security. As U.S. bombing escalated, Mao believed that war with the United States was highly possible. Beijing canceled its consumer-oriented Third Five-Year Plan to concentrate on defense; it also launched a military aid program to help North Vietnam defeat the United States and deter U.S. escalation of the war against China. At the same time, however, throughout the domestic political chaos and ideological struggles of the Cultural Revolution, Beijing also manipulated its aid to North Vietnam to minimize the possibility of U.S. retaliation. Chinese support troops entered North Vietnam in secret not because Beijing believed Washington would not detect them, but because it wanted to assist the United States in maintaining diplomatic flexibility.[5] Beijing managed its response to U.S. violations of Chinese airspace with similar caution: at first it ordered the PLA Air Force not to fire on U.S. jets; then it ordered retaliation but not pursuit of U.S. aircraft across the border into North Vietnam. Finally, using various diplomatic channels, Zhou Enlai and Foreign Minister Chen Yi tried to ensure that Washington received China's signals defining its moderate policies but also the limits to Chinese tolerance.

The Johnson administration was equally concerned about aiding its ally, South Vietnam, while at the same time minimizing the possibility of war with China. U.S. government agencies conducted numerous analyses of PRC activity to determine the conditions under which Chinese forces would engage the U.S. Army directly. U.S. policy toward China paralleled that of China toward the United States: Washington escalated its involvement in the Vietnam War to check the strategic expansion of its adversary, yet encouraged South Vietnam to limit escalation to avoid war with this same adversary. White House officials, including President Johnson, correctly believed that bombing North Vietnam would not provoke the Chinese to direct participation in the war, but, fearing Chinese military retaliation, Johnson resisted advice that he allow deployment of U.S. ground forces north of the 17th parallel.

As these examples of U.S. and Chinese caution reveal, neither country based its diplomacy on rigid ideological precepts. Conflict management informed the policies of both countries during the two Taiwan Strait crises and the Vietnam War. But China also relied on tactical flexibility during more peaceful periods and adjusted its policy toward the United States according to its assessment of the international situation and current U.S. policy. Following the Korean War, Mao argued to the Chinese Politburo that divisions between the United States and its allies offered Beijing an opportunity to develop relations with Washington. But when Washington proceeded to strengthen its position on containment, China altered course. It attempted to compel Washington to reconsider its Taiwan commitment through its use of force and its instigation of the 1954 Taiwan Strait crisis. Once China had made its own position clear, it adopted conciliatory measures to see whether its strategy had been effective. Seeking improved U.S.-China relations—in part to divide the United States from Taiwan and compel Taiwan to come to terms with Beijing—China proposed an international conference on Taiwan and direct U.S.-China talks. China's subsequent posture at the Warsaw talks reflected this shift to a less belligerent U.S. policy. Zhou Enlai's statements in 1955 and 1956 in favor of the "peaceful liberation" of Taiwan, along with his and Mao's public support for mainland-Taiwan negotiations for a "third period of cooperation," also aimed to reduce U.S. hostility toward China, to divide Taiwan and the United States, and to pressure Taipei to negotiate.

China's next policy adjustment, in 1958, was a direct outcome of its assessment of the preceding peace offensive. Beijing concluded that its peace offensive had failed: Washington had actually strengthened its strategic relationship with Taiwan as well as with Japan. Meanwhile, Beijing concluded that Washington was using the Warsaw talks to feign a reasonable policy toward China while in fact constraining PRC options. Mao believed that the Soviet launching of *Sputnik* had placed the United States on the defensive and shifted global momentum to the socialist bloc, so that the "East Wind prevailed over the West Wind." To Mao, these trends suggested that heightened U.S.-China tension might actually benefit Chinese diplomacy. It was time to return to "struggle." China thus abandoned its peace offensive and once again deployed force to pressure the United States into revising its Taiwan policy, this time by provoking the 1958 Taiwan Strait crisis. Afterward, this cycle of alternating strategies continued. Mao now promised that after unification, Taiwan could keep its own way of life and the "three principles of the people," and that it would not have to reduce the size of its armed forces.

Research on the Taiwan Strait crisis of 1958 also throws light on the connections between China's Taiwan policy, the 1958 crisis in Lebanon, and the Great Leap Forward. Mao had decided to use force in the Taiwan Strait in response to developments in U.S.-Taiwan relations. The optimal timing would have been while the United States was involved in the Lebanon crisis: China's initiative would support Middle East opposition to U.S. intervention in Lebanon and take advantage of U.S. preoccupation with Lebanon to press for advantage in the Taiwan Strait. Mao began mobilizing troops, preparing to provoke a Taiwan crisis in the midst of the crisis in Lebanon. When the Lebanon crisis ended earlier than expected, he nonetheless pressed ahead, determined to pressure the United States into reconsidering its commitment to Taiwan. An added benefit of the crisis in the Strait, although not a principal motivating factor of Chinese policy, was its anticipated contribution to mobilizing the peasantry for the Great Leap Forward.[6]

Clearly, the leaders in both countries were calculating and cautious policymakers trying to maximize their own national security. Despite an adversarial relationship, frequent crises, and the war in Indochina, they assumed that their counterparts were not ideologues bent on aggression and conflict and that they could develop policy that would elicit a predictable response.[7] Chinese leaders were convinced that the United States developed day-to-day policy on the basis of its national interests and could change it in response to changing international circumstances, including alterations in Chinese policy. Even in the midst of the ideological extremism of the Cultural Revolution, Chairman Mao believed that a combination of retaliation against U.S. violations of Chinese airspace, restraint, and diplomatic signaling could limit U.S. escalation of the war in Vietnam and lessen U.S. interest in engaging Chinese forces. Moreover, Mao understood that changes in American security circumstances would encourage the United States to seek improved relations with China, and thus he signaled Chinese interest in U.S.-China rapprochement.

American policymakers considered the role of ideology in Chinese foreign policy, but they attached greater weight to traditional Chinese security interests and rational decision making. Although they perceived a potential threat and were on constant alert for the next crisis and a possible renewal of hostilities, during the crises in the Taiwan Strait and throughout the Vietnam War, U.S. policymakers regarded China not as an ideological power driven by loyalty to Soviet leadership or to revolutionary goals, but as an independent actor, pursuing realpolitik objectives, that would react to changing international circumstances. During the Vietnam War, U.S. policymakers, including President Johnson, continued to believe that cautious management would minimize China's perception of threat and elicit corresponding caution. Even during the height of the Cultural Revolution, when American leaders were preoccupied with Mao's ideological extremism and revolutionary foreign policy, they relied on realpolitik assumptions in their analysis of likely Chinese responses to U.S. policy. They knew that Mao considered China's domestic enemies more threatening than its foreign enemies, and they were aware that Chinese leaders felt themselves unprepared for war amid such domestic instability. Washington thus concluded that Beijing would avoid conflict and reciprocate U.S. restraint.

Despite their Cold War ideological perspective, their lack of information about Chinese politics, and the absence of diplomatic relations with China, U.S. policymakers and analysts correctly analyzed PRC policymaking, trends in Sino-Soviet relations, and Chinese interests in Taiwan and Vietnam. Similarly, Chinese leaders correctly assessed U.S. interests and managed U.S.-China conflict to avoid unnecessary and unintended escalation. These assumptions—of rationality and mutual interest in conflict control— also encouraged communication and signaling between Washington and Beijing. As the United States escalated its bombing of North Vietnam, Beijing sent, and Washington received, signals conveying the limits to its restraint. Through various diplomatic and media channels, Premier Zhou Enlai warned that a U.S. extension of the ground war to North Vietnam would elicit PRC engagement of U.S. forces. Recalling Chinese intervention in the Korean War, American officials took these Chinese warnings seriously and integrated them into policymaking.[8] This mutual signaling produced a tacit agreement on escalation. In fact, the United States attached such importance to this agreement that policymakers advocating the resumption of bombing in 1966 argued in part that without it, Beijing would think Washington had compromised unilaterally by reducing the parameters of the war. U.S. policymakers wanted PRC reciprocity before they would give up a policy Beijing had accepted.

In the aftermath of the Korean War, the United States and China not only avoided significant policy errors, they also found ways to cooperate to defuse conflict escalation. Overall, from the mid-1950s to the end of the 1960s, the course of U.S.-China conflict was not very different from that of other traditional great power conflicts. Both sides used the customary foreign policy instruments and diplomatic tactics to try to influence their counterpart's policies and to achieve their own respective goals at minimal cost to other policy interests.

China and the United States also adopted similar "wedge" strategies, each seeking to use diplomatic and/or military pressure to drive a wedge between the other country and its ally. U.S. strategy, directed at the Soviet Union and China, was intended to compel Chinese leaders to come to terms with the United States and abandon their effort to reshape the East Asian strategic order. Washington carried out a policy of stringent economic and strategic containment of China in the expectation that Beijing would place intolerable demands on Moscow, thus causing the Soviet Union to distance itself from the U.S.-China conflict. Receiving insufficient Soviet support against unrelenting U.S. pressure, China would have no choice but to accommodate itself to U.S. interests.

China's "wedge strategy" in the 1950s attempted to distance the United States from Taiwan. Although China at times employed a "peace offensive" to weaken the U.S.-Taiwan alliance, it also believed that military pressure on Taiwan would place excessive demands on the United States and might compel Washington to reconsider its commitment, and thus the Kuomintang (KMT) to accommodate itself to PRC power and acknowledge PRC sovereignty. A key component of this strategy was China's attempt, during both crises in the Taiwan Strait, to prevent the United States from "drawing a line" between Taiwan and the mainland that would bolster its "two-China" strategy. Indeed, during the crisis of 1958, although China could have ousted KMT forces and taken Jinmen and Mazu without fear of U.S. retaliation, Mao ordered the PLA not to attack and to allow Kuomintang ships to resupply the troops on the islands. He even timed the shelling to assist Chiang Kai-shek in resisting U.S. pressure to abandon the islands. Rather than allow the United States to extricate itself from the mainland-Taiwan conflict and more easily pursue a "two-China" policy, Mao decided to retain the option of periodic attacks on the islands to raise the costs of U.S. policy. If successful, China's "wedge strategy" would pressure the United States to reevaluate its defense of Taiwan and compel the Kuomintang to concede PRC sovereignty over Taiwan.

Each side also employed various deterrence strategies. The United States tried to deter the PRC's continued use of force and escalation of hostilities during the 1954–55 Taiwan Strait crisis. It threatened Beijing with direct intervention and the prospect of its use of nuclear weapons. For its part, China also used the threat of intervention to deter the United States from escalating the war in Vietnam. Chinese leaders understood that China's position as North Vietnam's "rear area" was even more important to Hanoi than material aid. Although Beijing failed to deter the U.S. from bombing North Vietnam, the threat of a large-scale engagement with PRC forces deterred Washington from introducing ground forces into North Vietnam. Until the threat of Chinese intervention had weakened, in the context of U.S.-China rapprochement, China also prevented the United States from bombing Hanoi, mining North Vietnamese harbors, and pursuing North Vietnamese aircraft into Chinese territory. Chinese leaders understood the key importance—to PRC security as well as to the course of the war—of establishing the credibility of China's deterrence threat and signaled their determination to retaliate against U.S. escalation.[9]

Policy Objectives and U.S.-China Conflict

The contributions to this volume stress the cautious, pragmatic policies developed by China and the United States in an attempt to influence each other's behavior and successfully manage conflict in ways that would avoid direct confrontation, but they also emphasize the counterproductive trends in both countries. China and the United States both had a common attachment to unrealistic and destabilizing foreign policy objectives, which made any negotiated resolution of their conflicts all but impossible. Their pragmatic day-to-day policies in the service of extreme policy objectives contributed to avoidable crises and war.

Following the Korean War, the United States was strongly committed to the status quo in both Indochina and Taiwan. Although U.S. security did not depend on a strategic presence in either area, American credibility was now based on preserving the status quo. But instead of finding a way to preserve its credibility and minimize conflict with China, Washington believed that it had the capability to maintain its political preponderance throughout East Asia and coerce China into accepting the regional status quo. As a result, it pursued a stringent containment policy against China, including an economic embargo significantly more severe than the one it imposed on the Soviet Union, and, in contrast to its Soviet policy, it refused to accommodate itself to Chinese border security interests. It also refused to offer China any compromise on its Taiwan policy. In this context, the ambassadorial-level talks with China served U.S. interests because they helped to diffuse criticism of U.S. inflexibility at home and abroad.

America's overestimation of its capabilities and its destabilizing policy objectives were wedded to extreme assessments of the costs of compromise. During the 1950s, U.S. policymakers feared that China could transform one diplomatic or military success against the United States into a regionwide trend that would banish U.S. influence from East Asia. During the 1960s, in the context of emerging U.S.-Soviet détente and China's first nuclear test, American policymakers considered China a greater challenge to U.S. security than the Soviet Union. China possessed the most primitive military hardware and had just endured two years of economic catastrophe and widespread famine. Yet American leaders developed policy objectives on the premise that China had the ability not only to challenge U.S. objectives but to pursue regional expansion.

America's policy overextension contributed to the conflict over Taiwan and the escalation of the war in Vietnam. During the 1954 Strait crisis, Washington feared that Jinmen and Mazu, two small islands lying outside Chinese harbors, would be the first of the East Asian "dominoes" to fall, as China displaced American power throughout the region. In 1958, Washington feared that the loss of the islands would undermine KMT legitimacy, foster instability on Taiwan, facilitate PRC expansion, and call a U.S. presence in Asia into question. These concerns fueled the crisis and prompted the United States to "brandish" its nuclear weapons. American involvement in the Vietnam War similarly reflected only the most dire assessment of the costs of withdrawal from Indochina. A cautious military policy served unrealistic objectives, alarmist assessments of the costs of compromise, and overconfidence in U.S. capabilities. Secretary of Defense Robert McNamara considered the Vietnam War as a Chinese test of American will and capabilities, and believed that an American defeat in Vietnam would lead to

PRC successes throughout East Asia. At the same time, the strongly held assumption that only the total defeat of Chinese and Vietnamese objectives would protect U.S. security effectively silenced advocates of more limited U.S. objectives. In the end, America's long-term strategic intentions rather than its immediate military policies dictated the escalation and duration of the Vietnam War. Only when Washington reconciled itself to the limits of its own power and the need to accommodate Chinese power, and reconsidered its policy objectives, could the war finally end.

Beginning in the 1960s, as the essays in this volume reveal, Chinese foreign policy endured the burden of extremism. But in contrast to the United States, China's extremism was reflected in its diplomacy rather than in its policy objectives. Following on a period of cautious and pragmatic policy during the 1950s, China entered a period of foreign policy instability. As Sino-Soviet relations deteriorated in the wake of Moscow's failed proposal for Sino-Soviet military cooperation on Chinese territory and its cancellation of the nuclear-sharing agreement, Beijing found itself in heightened confrontation with both superpowers and isolated from much of the world. Wang Jiaxiang proposed that China break out of its isolation by reducing tension in its relations with the superpowers and India, and moderating its support for revolution in the Third World. Mao Zedong, however, resisted Wang's advice and silenced all advocates of moderation, determining that China would persist in its absolute opposition to the United States and the Soviet Union.

Chinese intransigence in the face of overwhelming strategic vulnerability exemplified Maoist "idealism." Mao held that U.S. and Soviet intentions threatened China's interest in secure borders and in developing an independent foreign policy. He was also concerned that an imminent large-scale war involving China had grown increasingly likely. But rather than try to manage international tension with diplomacy, he concluded that a peaceful international environment was not in China's interest. He was convinced that to prevent war, China should struggle against the superpowers and prepare for war. He was confident that Chinese belligerence could act as a deterrent because contradictions between the superpowers would keep them from attacking China and because Chinese diplomacy would draw strength through developing ties with the "intermediate zone"—countries in Europe and the Third World seeking independence from superpower domination. Even after escalation of the war in Vietnam and U.S. bombing of North Vietnam, Mao refused to reconsider his conviction that total struggle was necessary.

Beijing's decision to provide military aid to Vietnam reflected not only its perception of the U.S. threat to Chinese security but also Mao's strategy to "avoid war through fighting." He resisted any thought of supporting peace negotiations or U.S.-China détente, lest the United States underestimate PRC determination and expand the war to China's border, leading to Sino-American war. Mao was so alarmed by the American threat that he placed the Chinese economy on a war footing.

During the 1960s, the United States and China both held extreme views of the other's strategic, long-term objectives and potential threat to their respective security. One contributing factor was the acute attention each side gave to the other's ideological rhetoric. U.S. policymakers took more seriously and paid closer attention to Maoist revolutionary propaganda and the alleged successes and popularity of the Maoist economic model in the Third World than to China's actual military and economic capabilities. Chinese leaders likewise focused on U.S. anticommunist polemics and its ability to threaten China's territorial integrity, and were convinced that Washington might try to occupy all of Vietnam. Equally important, both countries possessed an exaggerated sense of their respective capabilities. The United States believed it had the ability to secure Chinese accommodation to a U.S. presence on China's borders and on Taiwan, while China believed it could withstand the pressure of intense conflict without allies. Thus, neither side would compromise. More than anything else, this mutual combination of a heightened perception of threat and overconfidence explains the protracted nature of the Sino-American conflict.

As the studies in this volume demonstrate, only when the United States and China reevaluated their respective capabilities and the potential threat they posed to each other could they consider rapprochement and bring the war in Vietnam to an end. In the late 1960s, policymakers in Washington developed a more skeptical attitude toward Chinese economic and military power. Whereas analysts during the 1950s had predicted that China was on the verge of becoming a regionwide military power, they now understood that Chinese hardware and manufacturing capabilities had yet to develop significantly and that Beijing confronted formidable obstacles to military modernization. Equally important, Washington reevaluated the "Maoist model of development." American leaders had feared that Maoism might not only provide economic support for Chinese military expansionism but also appeal to leaders throughout the Third World, posing an ideological challenge and offering an economic alternative to capitalist democracy. But during the Johnson administration, policymakers perceived that Maoism had failed to solve China's economic problems and that its revolutionary implications had alienated many Third World leaders. Once China's military, economic, and ideological power no longer impressed U.S. policymakers, their assessment of the cost of defeat declined and made reduced hostility toward China possible.

Coinciding with their revaluation of Chinese power, U.S. leaders also reevaluated American power and, thus, its objectives in Asia. During the Johnson administration it became clear that the United States lacked the ability to simultaneously maintain an independent South Vietnam and contain Chinese power north of the 17th parallel, engage in U.S.-China conflict over Taiwan, and prepare for Sino-American hostilities, while also contending with Soviet power and American domestic opposition to the Vietnam War. U.S. policymakers thus became reconciled to withdrawing from Vietnam, compromising on Taiwan, and accepting an expanded Chinese role in East Asia. In this context, Chinese support for North Vietnam and its threat to use force against Taiwan were no longer obstacles to U.S. concessions to Hanoi, withdrawal from Vietnam, or U.S.-China rapprochement.

Research on U.S.-China-Japanese relations indicates that American rapprochement with China was not motivated exclusively by the costs of superpower conflict and the war in Vietnam. As rapprochement between the United States and China developed and then expanded, the Nixon administration was quick to appreciate the many collateral benefits of cooperation, especially Washington's newfound leverage over Tokyo in U.S.-Japan trade conflicts. President Nixon relished the opportunity to use America's strategic relationship with China to heighten Japanese insecurity and coerce Tokyo to agree to U.S. trade demands. Indeed, Nixon suggested that by not forewarning Japanese leaders of Kissinger's 1971 visit to China and the plans for the U.S.-China summit, he had given Japan a "jolt," reducing Japanese complacency in its relations with the United States. Chinese leaders, however, were less confident that Japan would become more compliant once the United States and China had improved relations. In the midst of preparations for Kissinger's secret visit to Beijing, the Politburo advised Chinese negotiators to be wary of Japanese "militarism" and its efforts to expand into Taiwan.

As the Chinese contributions to this volume reveal, Beijing's interest in U.S.-China rapprochement was preceded by a similar reassessment. By the

end of the 1960s, Cultural Revolution extremism had so infused Chinese diplomacy that Beijing had alienated nearly every country in the world. The
burning of the British embassy in August 1967 marked the nadir. It exposed
the bankruptcy of China's attempt to establish an alternative coalition to
oppose the superpowers and persuaded Mao to allow foreign policy professionals to resume control over Chinese diplomacy. Moreover, when the
Soviet Union invaded Czechoslovakia in August 1968, warning that it might
also invade other wayward socialist countries, Mao's confidence in the U.S.-
Soviet conflict and in its own relations with ideologically appropriate "intermediate zone" allies to protect China now seemed highly exaggerated, and
the dual-adversary policy reckless. Increasingly alarmed by the Soviet threat,
Mao also realized that the United States was ready to accept defeat in Vietnam and posed a reduced threat to China. He read Richard Nixon's articles
and speeches carefully and thought it possible to consider improving U.S.-
China relations.

Rapprochement between China and the United States also affected China's Japan
policy. During the early stages of rapprochement, Chinese leaders viewed the alliance
between the United States and Japan, and U.S. efforts to bolster Japanese defense capabilities, as a grave threat to PRC security. Beijing relentlessly criticized the alliance
and Japanese defense policy. But once relations with the United States improved following the February 1972 summit, China no longer viewed the U.S.-Japan alliance as a threat. It now welcomed the alliance's role in containing Soviet
"hegemonism" and focused on its contribution to restraining the development of an independent and rearmed Japan. By the early 1970s, the U.S.-
China-Japan triangle was an active part of regional diplomacy and shifts in
triangular relations affected all three.[10]

Although both U.S. and Chinese policy reflected diplomatic extremism,
China had developed a radical diplomacy in pursuit of vital strategic objectives, while the United States had developed objectives that exceeded its security needs. Thus, Beijing's contribution to U.S.-China rapprochement was
to abandon, if not its objectives, then its isolationism and its demands for
immediate and complete U.S. capitulation on Taiwan, while Washington's
contribution was to compromise on its objectives in relation to both Taiwan
and South Vietnam. Washington could compromise because it had continued its strategic cooperation with Taiwan and South Vietnam to maintain its strategic commitments to its more important partners in East Asia,
including Japan. Indeed, American policymakers had never believed that a

U.S. military presence on Taiwan and in mainland Southeast Asia was an essential contribution to American security.[11] Ultimately, U.S.-China rapprochement was possible because the conflict of interests entailed immoderate and nonvital U.S. objectives that reflected not vital regional security interests but derivative U.S. interests in East Asia.

Domestic Factors and U.S.-China Relations

The major cause of prolonged high-level U.S.-China conflict was each side's exaggerated appraisal of its counterpart's threat and its own ability to pursue independent and noncompromising countervailing policies. A number of the contributions to this volume emphasize the role of domestic factors in promoting foreign policy extremism in China and the United States.

During the 1950s, China pursued a relatively moderate foreign policy. Although Mao was clearly in charge, foreign policy professionals and Mao's lieutenants also contributed. Until the end of the decade, China's foreign policy priority was to recover Taiwan and break out of diplomatic isolation, and it relied on traditional foreign policy instruments, including peace offensives and the use of force, adjusting its diplomacy according to international circumstances. All this changed completely in the early 1960s. The fundamental reason was Mao Zedong's assessment of China's domestic circumstances. In 1962, following reassurances from the United States that it would not support a Kuomintang attack on the mainland, Mao judged that the greatest threat to China was the prospect of Soviet-style revisionism and capitalist restoration. Although Mao had worried about Soviet penetration of China in the 1950s, he now judged it to be potentially a far greater threat than the American threat, not only in terms of foreign pressure on China but also of Soviet infiltration of Chinese politics and society. Just as Americans had penetrated KMT economic institutions in the 1940s, extensive Sino-Soviet cooperation in the 1940s and 1950s had allowed Moscow to penetrate CCP institutions. Soviet advisers had influenced the ideological outlook of Chinese cadres throughout the government and the Communist Party, encouraging them to promote Soviet-style revisionist economic policies. Mao suspected Chinese party and government officials of sympathy with the Soviet Union and of subverting the Chinese revolution. In August 1962 he began to actively oppose domestic policy initiatives that undermined his political objectives and socialist economic institutions.

In this context, Chairman Mao considered any proposal to moderate Chinese foreign policy a reflection of domestic revisionism. The architect of the moderate phase of Chinese diplomacy during the 1950s, he now regarded moderation as anathema. This was the attitude Wang Jiaxiang encountered when he proposed that Beijing ease tensions with the superpowers. Mao did not want to end Chinese isolation, he wanted to combat revisionism, and Wang's suggestions merely reinforced his opposition to the "right-deviationist wind." Wang's fate deterred other Chinese leaders from suggesting any change in foreign policy until 1969.[12]

Having decided that the U.S. threat was manageable, Mao concluded that the Soviet threat now posed the greatest immediate danger to Chinese security, but he had not anticipated the escalation of the war in Vietnam and large-scale U.S. intervention. U.S. bombing of North Vietnam meant that China now confronted grave security threats from both superpowers. By early 1965, Mao had concluded that the United States posed an immediate military threat to China, and he placed the country on a war footing. But Mao refused to reevaluate his foreign policy or consider diplomatic flexibility, since moderation toward either superpower would undermine his offensive against the greatest threat—capitalist restoration in China. Mao sought a foreign policy, consistent with his domestic ideological requirements, that would make China secure. The result was an unfounded confidence that a combination of constant and heightened preparation for war, cooperation with Third World countries, and ongoing superpower tension would deter the superpowers from attacking China, allowing him to devote his attention to the most dangerous foe: domestic subversion of the socialist revolution. Chairman Mao's preoccupation with the destruction of his domestic enemies was reflected in China's dual-adversary policy and the severity of the Sino-Soviet border crisis in 1969, when the Soviets threatened nuclear war.

U.S. China policy resulted, in part, from China's domestic politics, including pressure from both moderates and hard-liners. But if domestic politics could cause fundamental policy change in China, in the United States, until the Johnson administration, domestic politics reinforced policymakers' a priori inflexibility. During the 1950s, as America conducted its own search for domestic enemies, conservative members of Congress demanded a more belligerent China policy. Throughout the Taiwan Strait crisis of 1954–55, administration officials spent long hours with members of Congress trying to ease their opposition to White House efforts to avoid a larger war.

Congressional belligerence also made it difficult for the White House to moderate Chiang Kai-shek's saber-rattling. As the crisis in the Strait continued, domestic political pressure coalesced with the U.S. military's efforts to adopt more aggressive policies. During the Taiwan Strait crisis of 1958, the administration's attempts to moderate KMT policy and avoid hostilities with China were further complicated by congressional demands for a greater show of support for Taiwan. Although the administration's rigid Taiwan policy was not a result of congressional and military pressures—Eisenhower and Dulles had their own reasons to resist compromise—such pressures reinforced their instinctive belligerence toward China and exacerbated their frustration with its intransigence, helping to escalate U.S. military threats against the PRC.

Following the 1954–55 Taiwan Strait crisis, the Eisenhower administration also had to contend with those domestic critics who charged that its continued belligerence unnecessarily risked war with China. The administration wanted to avoid war with China, but it also wanted to maintain its uncompromising stance on Taiwan and its global isolation of China. Dulles thus employed the Sino-American ambassadorial-level talks to feign interest in compromise in an attempt to neutralize criticism from moderate politicians.

In the Kennedy and Johnson administrations, domestic politics and presidential personality also influenced policy. Despite high expectations that the Kennedy administration might develop a new China policy, the new president adopted his predecessors' inflexibility. The contrast between Soviet and Chinese diplomacy and China's bellicose rhetoric during the 1962 Cuban missile crisis fostered in Kennedy a personal hostility to China. He concurred in the widespread assessment that China presented a greater threat to world peace and American security than the Soviet Union, and he sided with India during the 1962 Sino-Indian conflict. Johnson shared Kennedy's concern as U.S. apprehension mounted after China tested a nuclear device in 1964.

Domestic politics also reinforced Kennedy's personal reluctance to undertake any shift in policy. He had won a narrow victory over Richard Nixon and had campaigned against the Republicans' weak foreign policy, including the so-called "missile gap." As president, Kennedy feared that he would become the target of charges that he was "soft" on China. Eisenhower still actively opposed any change in policy on the issue of PRC representation at the United Nations. These pressures deterred the White House from developing tactical initiatives that could have alleviated conflict between the United States and its allies over China policy. The Kennedy administration rejected the two-China solution to Chinese representation in the United Nations and offered Beijing conciliatory trade proposals whose conditions were humiliating enough to guarantee Chinese rejection.

By 1966, the Johnson administration had begun to reexamine the premises of U.S. China policy. It had developed a more realistic domestic appraisal of Chinese military and economic capabilities. Moreover, public and congressional opposition to improved relations with China had softened, and some influential members of Congress had even begun to call for improved U.S.-China relations. But Johnson feared criticism of any softening of U.S. China policy from conservatives, especially in the context of the ongoing war in Vietnam. In these circumstances, although the administration considered various options for ending the U.S.-China deadlock, it maintained the China policies of the Eisenhower and Kennedy administrations. And, in a tactic similar to Dulles's use of the Warsaw talks, he publicly implied interest in a new China policy simply to neutralize criticism from moderate members of Congress.

Under Maoism, the influence of domestic politics on foreign policy was especially disruptive. The contributions presented here underscore the omnipresent role of Chairman Mao in PRC policymaking. Even in the 1950s, when he accepted advice from colleagues and professionals, he retained total authority to make the final decision on all crucial matters, including instigating both Taiwan Strait crises and defining China's peace offensives. But in the 1960s Mao's dominance became all encompassing and destructive. He personally determined Chinese policy toward the superpowers and decided when to send material aid to North Vietnam and to introduce Chinese soldiers into the war. His lieutenants, including Lin Biao and Zhou Enlai, deferred to Mao's authority, never knowingly challenging his policy preferences. Thus, Mao single-handedly assessed the country's strategic environment and analyzed threats to Chinese security, which provides some explanation for China's extreme preoccupation with domestic enemies and its dual-adversary policy during this period.

But Mao was more than simply China's chief diplomatic strategist. During the 1950s and 1960s he was also a "hands-on" policymaker who paid close attention to policy details. He oversaw the planning and daily implementation of Chinese military operations during the Taiwan Strait crises. He participated in decisions about the content of Chinese aid to North Vietnam and the shipment of Soviet aid to North Vietnam across Chinese territory. He also carefully managed China's response to U.S. violations of Chinese airspace. Throughout this period, he read detailed reports on developments in the United States and oversaw internal dissemination of documents. When Chairman Mao did not oversee policy, Premier Zhou Enlai, his loyal lieutenant, did so with great attention to detail, while consulting with Mao on every tactical move.

Research on American diplomacy shows that U.S. presidents have consistently incorporated the advice of a wide range of foreign policy experts. In contrast to China's heavy reliance on the role of the chief executive in policymaking, during the Eisenhower administration U.S. decision making took place within a hierarchical institutionalized setting in which numerous agencies and specialists contributed to policy deliberations. The National Security Council stood at the apex of these institutions. It coordinated the role of government agencies, and it was the venue within which policy was debated and decided. During the Vietnam War, President Johnson, like Chairman Mao, considered the implications for U.S.-China relations of U.S. military activities in North Vietnam and made policy accordingly. He also actively participated in the detailed decision making on bombing Vietnam. But participating with Johnson in policymaking were broad-ranging specialists who had no counterparts in China under Mao Zedong's leadership. Although the process did not preclude costly foreign policy mistakes, including a prolonged and costly commitment to the South Vietnamese government, U.S. presidents did not obstruct the entire foreign policy operation or allow domestic divisions to engulf every facet of society.

China, the United States, and the Lessons of Cold War Conflict

Many of the factors that prolonged and exacerbated conflict between the United States and China in the 1950s and 1960s may also bedevil U.S.-China relations in the post–Cold War era. As the research presented in this volume suggests, understanding the nature and the course of the conflict may help policymakers in both countries avoid unnecessary and unintended confrontations in the twenty-first century.

Particularly striking is the resemblance between contemporary American discussions of China and American assessments of China in the 1960s. In the mid-1990s there is still a tendency in the United States to exaggerate China's military and economic capabilities and to call for containment of Chinese power, while overlooking China's many economic and social problems and technological deficiencies. Compounding the problem of perceptions of power is the role of ideology. One of the few remaining countries to be ruled by a Communist party, China is the prime target of ideological attention and rhetoric in the United States, and as such, it inspires exaggerated estimates of its intentions. Moreover, as in the 1960s, contemporary American views of China are shaped by comparisons between China and Russia. In contrast to Russia, whose fragile democratic system and relatively more cooperative diplomacy moderate criticism in the United States, China has developed a reputation as a "rogue state" that threatens international peace and world order, an image that further exacerbates the unease between the United States and China.

In circumstances reminiscent of the Kennedy and Johnson administrations, contemporary American domestic politics also limit Washington's ability to improve U.S. cooperation with China. Political opposition at home has inhibited post–Cold War administrations from adopting pragmatic conflict-reduction policies. Moreover, just as John Kennedy was constrained by his campaign rhetoric and his narrow election victory over Richard Nixon in 1960, Clinton's campaign promise to be tough on China and his narrow election victory over George Bush in 1992 restrained his foreign policy flexibility.

The contributions to this volume also suggest similarities between China's Cold War foreign policy and its contemporary foreign policy. The confrontation in the Taiwan Strait in 1996, in particular, recalls the earlier crises. The research presented here argues that Chairman Mao used force in 1954–55 and again in 1958 to respond to U.S. support for Taiwan's separation from the mainland and to compel Washington to reconsider. Similarly, in 1996, following Lee Teng-hui's visit to Cornell University in June 1995, China reacted to what it perceived to be growing U.S. support for Taiwan independence by conducting provocative military exercises and tests near Taiwan's ports.[13] Once again, one of China's objectives was to arouse international concern over the prospect of war over Taiwan and to pressure the United States to reevaluate its Taiwan policy. Another potential parallel is the role of U.S. arms transfers to Taiwan in U.S.-China crises. The U.S. transfer to Taiwan of Matador missiles contributed to the 1958 Taiwan

Strait crisis. Sales of advanced technologies to Taiwan in the twenty-first century could lead to similar conflict.

China's post-Mao flexibility toward Taiwan also recalls China's Taiwan policy in the 1950s. During the 1980s, under Deng Xiaoping's leadership, Beijing assured Taipei, as it had in the 1950s, that Taiwan could maintain its military and its distinct political and social systems after unification. Its 2000 "White Paper" on Taiwan offered similar assurances.[14] Clearly, Chinese policy in the 1950s was not as uncompromising as it appeared, nor was Deng's later "one-country, two-systems" policy as novel. In both the 1950s and 1980s, rather than consistently threaten the use of force, China promoted the "peaceful liberation" of Taiwan. Since 1949, when freed from domestic political imperatives, Chinese leaders have often pursued flexible tactics to achieve their long-term goal of unification.

The dynamics of U.S.-China-Japan relations during the early 1970s are also instructive for contemporary U.S. policy in East Asia.[15] When U.S.-China relations were uncertain, Beijing viewed the U.S.-Japan security alliance as a threat to Chinese security rather than as a restraint on Japan's military policy. But once U.S.-China relations improved after rapprochement, Beijing adopted a more positive perspective on the alliance. In the 1990s the triangular relationship has come full circle. At first, China was supportive of the alliance's contribution to its security and to regional stability, but as U.S.-China relations deteriorated in the context of heightened conflict over Taiwan and ongoing post–Cold War tensions, Beijing adopted an increasingly belligerent posture. China's assessment of the U.S.-Japan alliance has throughout been a function of U.S.-China relations, and its opposition to U.S.-Japan security cooperation has challenged regional stability. Moreover, just as in 1971, China remains concerned that a "militarized" Japan will seek to replace U.S. influence in Taiwan.

The chapters in this volume illuminate, in many ways, the sources of U.S.-China conflict and the complex circumstances of the Cold War. However, they also suggest two major conclusions. First, when Chinese and American policymakers have developed realistic assessments of their own country's capabilities and of mutual threats to national security, they have been able to contain conflict and avoid escalation of tension. Second, and more generally, when conflicts are a matter of pragmatic national interest considerations rather than ideological or domestic impulses, they can be managed, and even resolved, through negotiation. Indeed, although China and the United States have had, and continue to have, significant conflicts over security interests since 1949, none of their respective interests has required policies inherently threatening to the other's security. U.S.-China Cold War tension was not inevitable. In contrast to U.S.-Soviet Cold War relations, those between the United States and China have allowed for conflict management and fairly minimal great power tension, encouraging optimism about U.S.-China relations in the twenty-first century.

Chinese and American Research Traditions

China and the United States follow different practices in declassifying and allowing access to the materials in their national security archives. According to U.S. law, documents must be opened to the public within twenty-five years of the events they record. A committee composed of government officials and independent scholars determines any extension of confidentiality for selected records, and its decision is based solely on national security considerations, not domestic political considerations. Once the archives are opened, they are universally available without restriction, and all released documents can be fully cited in the notes of scholarly works.

In the People's Republic of China, the government is under no legal requirement to open national security archives. Government officials control access, basing their decisions on national security and domestic political considerations. Current political circumstances can influence which documents remain closed, but materials tend to be released following significant changes in Chinese foreign policy and domestic politics. Thus, the archives on the Maoist era were opened after Mao died, and those on the Deng Xiaoping era have become more accessible in the post-Deng era, although in both cases, not all documents may be available. In addition, access to those archival materials that are available is not universal but is offered only to select Chinese researchers who have been given "clearance." And even these privileged scholars often have access to only one of many archives—that of the party or the military or the foreign ministry, for example—rather than to all relevant collections. These practices might suggest that subsequent scholarship offers a distorted view of history, that outside scholars cannot evaluate Chinese scholarly work by examining the sources, and that archival materials cannot be fully cited in reference notes.

Western scholars are understandably frustrated by the limited and restricted access to post-1949 Chinese archives and suspicious of the quality and reliability of the resulting scholarship. Nonetheless, the Chinese government has made publicly available a large body of materials documenting the foreign policy activities of such senior leaders as Mao Zedong, Zhou Enlai, Liu Shaoqi, Chen Yi, Wang Jiaxiang, and Wu Xiuquan. In addition, many retired Chinese officials, including interpreters and ambassadors, have written memoirs that detail Chinese decision making and diplomacy. Despite the selective release of such documents and the bias in the memoirs (in China as in the West), these readily available materials are valuable primary sources that can be used to develop sophisticated studies of Chinese diplomacy.[16]

As the notes reveal, the Chinese contributors have relied heavily on important archival materials, including transcripts of Mao's meetings with foreign leaders, thus making available otherwise inaccessible information. They have also relied on openly published documents and on the memoirs of Chinese statesmen, just as the Western contributors have drawn heavily on the published documents in the *Foreign Relations of the United States* series and on memoirs. Despite the uneven availability of Chinese resources, PRC and Western scholars drawing on Chinese archival materials have made important contributions to our understanding of U.S.-China Cold War relations in books and articles that present, for example, a more well-developed historical narrative or a new interpretation of well-known events. The chapters in this volume also reflect the very different Western and Chinese practices of document citation. But differing political and scholarly cultures do not have to prevent scholarly collaboration or mutually beneficial scholarship. This collaborative project has attempted to pursue both.

CHAPTER ONE

The Two Chinas in the Global Setting
Sino-Soviet and Sino-American Cooperation
in the 1950s

William C. Kirby

THE DIPLOMATIC HISTORY of the Cold War in Asia has in recent years emphasized not the power-political and economic blocs that once defined "east" and "west" but the ambivalence, tensions, and rivalries within the allied camps. Thus, the wartime Chinese-American alliance descends immediately, in the postwar period, into a "partnership for disorder."[1] Stalin and Mao are "uncertain partners."[2] The United States, China, and the Soviet Union become, variously, "friends and enemies."[3] And Taiwan and Hong Kong enjoy at best "uncertain friendships" with the United States.[4] Somewhat lost in this history of discord are the alliances that defined the Asian Cold War in the first place.

Yet the alliances between the Soviet Union and China's new Communist regime on the one hand, and between the United States and the Nationalist government on Taiwan on the other, were the foundation of Chinese diplomacy in the 1950s. More important from the perspective of Chinese history, they did much to determine the nature of postrevolutionary China on both sides of the Taiwan Strait. Divided between Communist and Nationalist rule, China became incorporated into not one but two contending international systems. The "two Chinas" and the two superpowers entered into bilateral military, political, economic, and cultural relationships of greater depth and complexity than any of modern China's foreign relationships before or since. The new People's Republic of China (PRC) took the Soviet Union as its political and economic model; on Taiwan, Sino-American cooperation flourished as it had never done under the Republic of China on the mainland. Well after the end of these formal Sino-Soviet and Sino-American alliances, and indeed the Cold War itself, some traits of these partnerships have endured.

The formal relationships between states and parties in these alliances are increasingly well documented, as the papers presented in this volume attest.[5] Rather less attention has been given, however, to the "internal frontier" of Chinese foreign relations in the 1950s—the cooperative efforts with allied powers undertaken by the Communist mainland and Nationalist Taiwan, particularly in the area of economic relations—which this essay discusses. What was the historical basis for Sino-Soviet and Sino-American cooperation in the postwar period? What were the domestic aims and outcomes of the alliances of the 1950s? (Can one speak, in any sense, of a "primacy of domestic policy" in China's international partnerships?) What were the comparative strengths and limitations of these alliances? Why, by the end of the 1950s, did the Sino-Soviet alliance deteriorate, while the Sino-American partnership on Taiwan developed into the high point of Sino-American cooperation in this century? These are among the questions that this essay seeks to address.

Patterns in Sino-Soviet and Sino-American Relations before 1949

Sino-Soviet Relations

Of the two competing alliances across the Taiwan Strait, that between the PRC and the Soviet Union would surely have been the easiest to predict. The very existence of the Soviet Union, its rise to world power, and the spread of its doctrines and methods had a profound influence on Republican China and on the political world in which both the Nationalist and Communist parties matured.

The Soviet Union provided a forceful lesson in how to seize and hold political power. Thanks in significant measure to Soviet assistance and the weight of its example, the Party-State became the central arena of Chinese politics in this century. The Comintern, which in 1924 energized and reorganized the Guomindang, had earlier presided at the birth of the Chinese Communist Party. As the Chinese historian Xiang Qing puts it, "the founding of the Communist party of China was a direct consequence of Comintern intervention to establish a Chinese branch of the Communist International."[6] The opening and now partial publication of the Comintern archives in Moscow demonstrates anew that the history of the Chinese Communist Party—and therefore of the People's Republic of China—is inextricably entwined with the history of the Soviet Union.[7]

If the Soviet Union had a profound influence on the two great Chinese political parties, it also served as a model—in China and around the world—of economic development. Its belief in the "scientific" planning of an economy and the state ownership of industry, and its obsession with heavy industrial and military development as the key to state power would be shared by Nationalist and Communist regimes alike, and would make economic cooperation, when it came, all the easier. As soon as the Nationalist regime was established, it created a Reconstruction Ministry (*Jianshebu*) with a fifty-year plan to construct the nation's communications and industrial infrastructure. A National Reconstruction Commission (*Jianshe weiyuanhui*) then focused on electrification. In the mid-1930s, a National Resources Commission (*Ziyuan weiyuanhui*) took control of China's mineral and fuel resources and the running of state-owned industries. Under a "controlled" if not (as in the Soviet Union) fully planned economy, by the late 1940s two-thirds of China's industrial capital was under government ownership, following a postwar Five-Year Plan emphasizing military and heavy industrial development. Thus, important aspects of the "Soviet model" were already part of Chinese industrial policy.

The same could be said for foreign trade. By 1938, state industrial and military imports were almost entirely financed through a series of revolving barter/credit (*yihuo changzhai*) and counterpurchase (*fan goumai*) arrangements, by which industrial and military goods and services advanced in credit by the Soviet Union were repaid in raw materials by China. Under these arrangements the Soviet Union and China reached three major credit agreements in 1938–39, assisting China's war effort during years in which Western aid was minimal and foreshadowing the trading patterns of the 1950s.[8] Even for the Nationalists, then, the Soviet Union was a logical, if not yet politically compatible, partner for a China that wished, as a leading Nationalist planner put it, to follow "the socialist road."[9]

There were also, to be sure, less happy precedents from the pre-1949 period. A series of Sino-Soviet economic enterprises in China's northwest and northeastern border areas were examples less of bilateral cooperation than of old-fashioned Soviet-style imperialism. In theory joint ventures, these were as a rule Soviet-managed facilities on Chinese soil. Two examples of projects that came under joint Soviet-Nationalist government management were the Chinese Eastern Railway and the Dushan (Xinjiang) oil field. The former was the subject of the 1929 Sino-Soviet war and was later sold to the Japanese over Nanjing's protests; the latter was initially, like most Sino-Soviet ventures, an arrangement made directly with a Chinese provincial government that became a joint venture at the national level only after first being seized by the Nationalist regime in 1943, at a low point in Sino-Soviet ties.[10] The pattern remained after the Second World War. The 1946 Soviet proposal to place all Manchurian heavy industry under joint Sino-Soviet management was, according to the chief Soviet negotiator (in response to Chinese suggestions that joint management made economic sense in only a few industries), "not an economic question, but above all a political question," reflecting the Soviet Union's de facto political and military power in that part of China.[11]

A second, unhappy precedent was that of the legal status of Soviet citizens in China. The famous Karakhan Manifesto "to the Chinese nation" of July 1919, which stated the generous terms on which the Soviet state was prepared to renounce imperialism and its entitlements in China, made promises that were never to be fulfilled. Indeed, the Soviet Union would be the only power *not* to relinquish its extraterritorial privileges in China. In one guise or another, all Soviet citizens would be under extraterritorial jurisdiction until at least 1960.[12]

The lack of Soviet concern for Chinese sensitivities regarding national sovereignty was taken furthest with the separation of Outer Mongolia from China. Mongolia's separation had been a political fact of life since the 1920s, but the Nationalist regime resisted its legitimization until the very last moments of the Sino-Soviet treaty negotiations of 1945. Even so, Chiang Kai-shek's "sacrifice," as his negotiator Song Ziwen [T. V. Soong] called it, was offered "on the altar of perpetual friendship between China and the U.S.S.R.," and seemed bearable only if a treaty with the Soviet Union could avert the "national calamity" of Communist rebellion.[13] It didn't, and when Mao Zedong made his pilgrimage to Moscow in 1949–50 to renegotiate—but not to repudiate—the 1945 treaty, the loss of Mongolia was confirmed.[14]

Despite these tensions, by 1950 there were good historical reasons for a Sino-Soviet alliance that went beyond ideological affinity or strategic partnership. In economic development in general, and industrial development in particular, the Sino-Soviet relationship of the 1950s harkened back to Sun Yat-sen's grand plan to develop "the vast resources of China . . . internationally under a socialistic scheme, for the good of the world in general and the Chinese people in particular."[15] More immediately, Sino-Soviet cooperation was less a revolutionary break than a logical progression from the Nationalist government's nationalization of industry and foreign trade, the growing power of state-planning bureaucracies, and the series of Sino-Soviet agreements for joint industrial ventures and barter-credit exchanges.[16] For the 200,000 employees of the Nationalist industrial and planning bureaucracies who remained in the service of the PRC, the heyday of Sino-Soviet economic cooperation in the mid-1950s would be, for most, the culmination of their careers. Clearly the seeds of what Deborah Kaple has called "modern China's Stalinist roots"[17] were planted well before 1949.

SINO-AMERICAN RELATIONS

So much has been written about Sino-American relations in this period that one can be quite brief. With the defeat of Japan in 1945, the first Chinese-American alliance, which had begun with Pearl Harbor, achieved its grand objective. It also lost its raison d'être. U.S. relations with the Nationalist regime (not to mention with the Communists) deteriorated quickly in the postwar years as both sides realized how little, save for mutual enemies, they had in common.

Sino-American relations for most of the first half of the century had been without the major conflicts found, for example, in Sino-British, Sino-Soviet, and (especially) Sino-Japanese relations, nor had there been an experience of intense cooperation at the official level, as was the case in Sino-German and (in two periods) Sino-Soviet relations. Before the late 1930s the relationship was simply not of central importance to either government. Although non-state cultural and economic relations were strong, they produced no obvious effect on official relations.

American ambitions for a united, liberal, pro-American China bore no resemblance to the factionalized Guomindang dictatorship that had flirted with fascism before the war and had sunk into a corrupt malaise during it. When the United States relinquished its extraterritorial rights in China in 1943, it aimed to treat China as the "great power" the Americans hoped it would become. However, the policies by which the Chinese government expected to maintain "great power" status after the war—by militarizing and nationalizing the Chinese economy while stripping Japan of its modern industry through war reparations—emerged in opposition to stated American interests.

To be sure, during the war the Americans had sent mixed signals about their own level of commitment to postwar China. The economic agencies of the New Deal era were in general more supportive than the political leadership. The fact that the prospective leaders of China's postwar development received advanced training in the United States during the war did not, in the end, facilitate economic cooperation. The massive postwar reconstruction plans of the Nationalist government—the Three Gorges Dam project is the most famous—were all predicated on an intensification of American aid and investment that simply did not materialize. On the international issues of greatest importance to China, the United States gave but half-hearted support to the Nationalist government in its difficult negotiations with Moscow in 1945 and later opposed large-scale Japanese reparations for China. With the exception of one field of strategic interest to both sides—nuclear energy—the prospects for broad-ranging postwar cooperation were not bright even before the outbreak of the Chinese civil war, and as that war unfolded, they became nonexistent. By the time the China Aid Act of 1948 was passed by the U.S. Congress, its purpose was less to participate in postwar reconstruction than to allow the United States to abandon its doomed Nationalist ally more gracefully. As Chuxiong Wei has put it, it was medicine given belatedly to a dying man in order "to avoid the charge that the doctor had not tried to save the patient's life."[18]

By early 1949, when the Soviet Union appeared to be contemplating a Cold War division of China at the Yangzi,[19] the American abandonment of the Chiang Kai-shek regime seemed a certainty. At that time, to the degree that American officials could conceive of aid for Taiwan, it was a Taiwan separated from China, perhaps under United Nations trusteeship, and above all rid of Chiang Kai-shek and his regime.[20]

China and the Socialist World Economy of the 1950s

Given this situation, the question a historian studying the 1950s must ask is not why the People's Republic of China entered into such a close alliance with the Soviet Union, but—particularly given the withdrawal and then hostility of the United States—how it could have pulled out of it at the end of the decade. Certainly there were excellent reasons to work closely in all fields with what was now officially called the "elder Soviet brother."[21]

In foreign relations, recent scholarship makes it clear that the CCP was not a reluctant ally pushed into Soviet arms by a tactless Washington, which thereby lost its chance to accommodate the new PRC. Mao Zedong may have believed himself a Chinese patriot, but he also believed in "proletarian internationalism." He had shown himself, much more often than not, to be a loyal follower of Stalin, and in his first years in Beijing he would go to great lengths to prove that he was no "Tito" intent on pursuing an independent foreign policy. Although Mao may have sought to maintain a degree of flexibility in his policy toward the United States,[22] the Sino-Soviet alliance of 1950, as John Garver has shown, "virtually eliminated" the prospect of Chinese Titoism, and so helped the Americans to decide, however reluctantly, to reengage with Nationalist Taiwan.[23] Whatever the American response, the new alliance was going to happen. As Michael Sheng puts it, it was "the end result of a long process from the very beginning of CCP history."[24]

In military matters after 1950, despite later suspicions over the desirable level of cooperation,[25] only the Soviet alliance gave China a measure of security in the face of unremitting American hostility. And in economic development, since the task was now to build socialism in the country the CCP had won, only the U.S.S.R. had the experience, the will, and the capacity to help.

For much of its first decade, the People's Republic was a more attentive student of Soviet models in statebuilding—the construction of political, legal, educational, and cultural infrastructures—than the CCP had ever been of Comintern approaches to revolution.[26] As Lowell Dittmer has commented, "the post-revolutionary political apparatus superimposed following liberation was essentially identical to the Soviet structure upon which it was patterned. The elites who led these revolutions shared the same general ideological outlooks as well as the specific objective of modernization without the putative inequities of capitalism. They fully expected their developmental paths to converge in the course of socialist modernization and the eventual realization of socialism."[27]

As Dittmer has also noted, much of Western scholarship on Sino-Soviet relations during the PRC era has studied the conflicts between the two Communist powers, not their cooperation.[28] This is true also of post-1960s Chinese writing on the relationship,[29] though not, by and large, of Soviet histories and reminiscences on the 1950s, which have tended to stress the collaborative dimensions of Sino-Soviet relations.[30] In any event, cooperation began with great expectations. In 1949, even before the establishment of the PRC, a small army of Chinese and Soviet officials initiated a process of formal tutelage on Stalin's theory of the state, on policy toward nationalities, on the tax system of the U.S.S.R., on the role of party cells in factories and ministries, and so on.[31] In the winter of 1950, while Mao was negotiating the terms of the alliance with Stalin, Chen Boda was visiting the Supreme Party School, the prototype for Beijing's *Zhongyang dangxiao*; a Soviet labor union delegation was touring China; and a commission of Soviet urban planners was preparing to leave for Shanghai with the aim of turning it into a modern, socialist metropolis.[32] Exchanges of teachers and farm animals followed the next spring. By that autumn, the Chinese Central Committee was having its suits made in Moscow.[33]

On the economic front, Mao Zedong's desire to transplant the Soviet experience to China appears to have outpaced that of his comrades. When the Chinese Communist Party came to power, it was publicly committed to something called "New Democracy" (as distinct from "bourgeois" democracy), promising both a coalition government and a mixed economy lasting fifteen years or more. Perhaps the economic policy of the "Chinese NEP," as some conceived it, was simply a useful "united front" slogan during the civil war. Yet some senior CCP leaders—Liu Shaoqi, Chen Yun, Deng Zihui, and Bo Yibo—believed in it enough to promote an economy that would tolerate capitalism in a manner "specifically Chinese in form," promulgating policies that, when carried much further decades later, would be called "market" socialism.[34] So it came as a surprise to many, not only within but outside of the CCP, when in October 1953 Mao announced a new "general line for socialist transition" that put China on a distinctly Stalinist path of development. In fact, it seems that Mao had made this decision by 1950, and admitted only in 1958 that he had kept it a secret for purely tactical reasons.[35] Hua-yu Li suggests that, reliant as Mao was on Stalin for ideas, assistance, and indeed legitimacy, his was a "deeply rooted commitment to Stalinism"[36] in all its aspects. His economic program after 1953 was inspired above all by his reading, back in the 1930s, in Stalin's famous *Short Course*, a history of the CPSU and the stages of Soviet economic development. Mao's "general line" plagiarized Stalin's of 1929, a sign of both respect and submission by a junior partner in global communism.[37]

This commitment to Stalinism was not, as Deborah Kaple has suggested, simply the result of book learning—the studying in China of translated materials—though it surely matters that the materials translated were of the "high Stalinist" Fourth Five-Year Plan (1946–50).[38] It was to some degree already in practice in the model of economic development that guided China's northeast, under CCP control for most of the postwar period, where a large state sector emerged from former Japanese and "puppet" industries. CCP-Soviet economic cooperation in the northeast began with an "unofficial" 1946 trade agreement between the U.S.S.R. and the Communist-held territories. By May 1947, a permanent Soviet foreign trade and transport apparatus had been created in northern Manchuria. Soviet specialists then consulted on long-term plans for Manchuria's reconstruction, while also providing significant, immediate aid to the CCP war effort.[39] As defined by Zhang Wentian, the "northeast model"[40] of economic development that had emerged by 1948 followed both Nationalist practice and Soviet advice in stressing the rapid growth of defense and heavy industries according to state plan. In July 1951, with Soviet advice, the concept of nationwide planning was reintroduced with the PRC's first annual economic plan. By the end of 1951 the state sector accounted for 80 percent of heavy industry, 100 percent of oil production, 98 percent of iron and steel production, 82 percent of machine-tool building, 76 percent of electrical power, and 70 percent of the cotton textile industry.[41] Although even after 1953 China's planning system would not become as all-embracing as its Soviet counterpart, it more than sufficed to take China down the Stalinist road.

After the adoption of Mao's new "general line" and the beginning of the PRC's First Five-Year Plan in 1953, Sino-Soviet trade expanded enormously.[42] In industrial relations, the broad outlines of this cooperation as it developed through the 1950s are well known: the construction of over 150 industrial projects, mostly as "turnkey" (that is, fully finished) installations, which became the core of the Communist state industrial sector; the transfer of thousands of industrial designs; and the visit of perhaps 10,000 Soviet specialists to China and of over 50,000 Chinese engineers, trainees, and students to the Soviet Union. Millions of Soviet books were imported, and thousands translated. Soviet aid was simply massive, and, although it was not free, it was given on better terms than could then have been arranged through any other source—even if China had access (as it clearly did not) to alternative sources of credit, advice, and investment.[43] For the Soviet Union, itself still a net importer of capital goods in 1954, industrial exports to China competed with domestic demand and East European markets for the same goods.[44] Although Chinese foreign trade officials noted that the price of certain commodities differed from that of the world market, overall and over many years the financial calculations of Sino-Soviet trade were deemed "reasonable and fair,"[45] and this despite the fact that China, in importing capital goods from the Eastern bloc only, was in a "seller's market," and would normally have been forced to be a "price-taker." Soviet prices to China for certain commodities were higher than those for the same goods when exported to the West,[46] but as Feng-hwa Mah has shown, barter ratios for Soviet industrial equipment were "clearly to China's advantage as far as its industrial program" was concerned. Where else in the world could China get five tons of steel products for one ton of frozen pork or a steel-pipe factory for 10,000 tons of tobacco?[47]

Moreover, there is little evidence that Moscow used its bargaining power to achieve a comprehensive economic advantage.[48] Soviet technical assistance, for example, was never measured according to world market equivalents. Indeed, the concept of intellectual property was so alien to the Soviet bloc that scientific-technical documentation, including blueprints, was provided without direct compensation, as noted in the Sino-Soviet economic agreement of May 15, 1953. China was charged for the physical machinery, but the technology was basically free. For its part, the Chinese government was contracted to reimburse Moscow for only 50 percent of the estimated costs of Soviet technical advisers in China. And if the international value of the ruble was overstated in Sino-Soviet agreements, given the very low interest rates of Soviet credits (never more than 2 percent per annum) there can be little doubt that China fared very well indeed under the terms of a Sino-Soviet exchange in which each country became the leading trading partner of the other.[49]

Beyond bilateral ties, the Sino-Soviet exchange was only one part of a larger web of cooperative relationships with all the "brother countries" of the Eastern European bloc. China was now a member of one of what Stalin had called "two parallel world markets . . . confronting one another."[50] This attempt at a socialist world economy was an extraordinarily ambitious and complicated undertaking. It was handicapped, however, by the strong bias in the Soviet model toward autarky, which all members of the bloc then emulated at the national level, hence the building of huge iron and steel complexes in East Germany, Poland, Czechoslovakia, Hungary, Bulgaria, and Romania, as well as in the Soviet Union and China.[51] Beyond that, the use of trade to integrate centrally planned economies was particularly difficult in an environment in which domestic prices were insulated from international markets and currencies were effectively nontransferable or nonconvertible with each another, not to mention with the "hard" currencies of the West. Nevertheless (particularly after Stalin's death), determined efforts were made to promote specialization and trade within the bloc, and the negotiation of multilateral and bilateral trade agreements with the Eastern bloc nations became an integral part of Chinese economic planning.[52]

The creation of what Nikita Khrushchev imagined as "a single world system of socialist economy"[53] began with the negotiation of a set of bilateral commercial treaties defining the framework of trade and including provisions for most-favored-nation treatment, followed by bilateral trade agreements of varying duration and, finally, by the signing of specific contracts between the foreign trade corporations of the governments involved specifying quantities, prices, and delivery dates of individual products. For multilateral transactions—rare at first but facilitated by a "one price" rule for goods traded within the bloc—the Soviet State Bank served as a clearing house after 1957. [54] These ongoing negotiations brought together, on a regular basis, Communist elites from East Berlin to Beijing who had the challenging task of coordinating their international economic obligations with their national economic plans. Just as domestic five-year plans were subject to periodic (usually annual) adjustment, so the multiyear cooperative agreements between China and its Eastern partners were in fact renegotiated annually to bring them more in line with the realities of production in a given year.

The documents recording China's annual negotiations with the Soviet Union and the German Democratic Republic are now available to researchers.[55] These are, to be sure, extraordinarily tedious materials, but they give the historian new respect for the broad knowledge and attention to detail required of the diplomatic and trade representatives within the Eastern bloc: it is no easy thing to run the economy of half the world. Almost without exception they report exacting negotiations, particularly on the pricing of goods in rubles,[56] which frequently had to be settled at the highest level. Zhou Enlai, for example, was the arbiter of China's soybean exports to the GDR in 1957–58.[57]

But throughout the 1950s these negotiations also appear to have been marked by a sense of—how else to put it?—solidarity. The concept of "brother countries" was taken seriously, and the broader cause of building socialism appears to have been a factor facilitating compromise. The annual negotiations were thus frequently a means of adjusting commitments to take into account the difficulties of one or both parties.[58] In urgent cases, supplementary agreements were signed, as in 1953, when, in the wake of anticommunist riots in East Berlin, the PRC sent 50 million rubles worth of emergency foodstuffs to the tottering GDR. As Zhou Enlai wrote to his German counterpart, Otto Grotewohl, in a private letter, "In consideration of the friendship between the Chinese and German peoples and in order to overcome the current difficulties into which the American imperialists and the West German bandits have brought the German people, we see our assistance to the German people as our duty and as an honor."[59]

There was no pretending that the idea of a socialist world economy was exclusively, or even primarily, economic in origin. It was, according to a Soviet study of the PRC in 1959, "trade of a consistently socialist type, which is organically inherent to a rapid tempo of development . . . [by] socialist states which are united together by having the same type of socio-economic, political, and ideological bases and by having a unity of interests and goals."[60] As for the precise means of calculating economic value in socialist trade, the principle of "comradely mutual assistance" determined the use of "one or another variant of [financial] calculation among socialist states," according to a Soviet study of Sino-Soviet scientific and technical exchange.[61] In other words, if their politics were in alignment, the economics would take care of itself.

China's incorporation into the socialist world economy was not, of course, without tensions and problems. Many of these were of China's own making in attempting a First Five-Year Plan more audacious than the first Soviet Five-Year Plan. A significant readjustment after 1957 was inevitable.

In other realms, too, there were excesses from following Soviet examples too slavishly, for example, in the sciences, where Lysenkoism controlled the field of genetics even longer than in the Soviet Union,[62] and in architecture, where the great exhibition centers in Beijing and Shanghai remain pointed reminders of Stalinist taste. The most problematic exchanges with the Soviet Union were two that never happened. The Soviet Union first agreed to, and then canceled, an offer to provide China with technical assistance sufficient to develop nuclear weapons. A more bizarre source of tension was Khrushchev's proposal, during his first visit to China in 1954, that China send a million workers to Siberia to assist in the economic development of the Russian Far East. Mao Zedong—perhaps sarcastically—offered to send *ten* million. In the end, 200,000 went for temporary work.[63] At the same time, the several hundred thousand (mostly "White") Russians, who had lived in China since the Russian Civil War of 1917–21, were repatriated to the Soviet Union in three stages.[64] Socialist brothers, it appears, did not need to reside in close proximity. This was pointedly true in the case of Soviet specialists in China, who normally lived and ate in hotels, separated from the Chinese units to which they were assigned. Inevitably too, there were tensions between groups and individuals at the local level, more commonly, it seems, between Soviet advisers and Chinese than between East Europeans and Chinese.[65]

The cultural dimensions of the relationship are contradictory, perhaps because there was, in the Stalinist system employed by both the U.S.S.R. and the PRC, no purely "private" dimension to cultural relations. (Not until December 1956 did the first group of 21 Chinese tourists, traveling at their own expense, visit the Soviet Union, and even then they were on a state-organized tour.)[66] To promote a "shared socialist culture" was the job of governments, and more specifically of the Society for Chinese-Soviet Friendship, which by 1959 had opened branches in 23 Chinese provinces and cities. Through its auspices, between 1955 and 1959, nine million Chinese listened, with varying degrees of attentiveness, to 18,516 lectures and speeches, and 61 million Chinese visited 27,500 photo exhibits. Yet of the 756 Soviet books translated by the Society, of which over 100 million copies were published, how many were actually read, and by whom? Can one speak of the enduring impact of the 747 Soviet films shown in China and the 102 Chinese films shown in Russia? How did Russian audiences react to the many new translations of Lu Xun's work?[67] What was the longer-term impact of the technical and educational exchanges between the two Communist powers? Why, of the 551 leading scientific personnel in the Chinese Academy of Sciences as of 1962, were only six known to have trained in the Soviet Union?

We do not know the answers to these questions, but it seems far-fetched to attribute the fall of Sino-Soviet economic cooperation to the cultural realm, however broadly conceived.[68] Certainly, in economic terms this was, to borrow Steven Goldstein's phrase, "the alliance that worked."[69] Indeed, there were no overriding economic, technological, *or* cultural reasons to call an end to a complex of international relationships that, whatever else they accomplished, had helped the PRC to succeed where the Nationalists had only begun: in building the industrial, technological, and military capacity to be a great power.

One can read in the archives of China's economic relations with the Eastern bloc and never know of the tensions that would tear the bloc apart in the late 1950s and early 1960s. For these were not, fundamentally, economic tensions. Even after the Great Leap Forward and the Sino-Soviet split, China continued to sign bilateral agreements, albeit of ever lesser value, with other socialist nations and honored them into the 1960s and beyond. But if there is no exact date when China "withdrew" from the international socialist economy, there was perhaps a moment of no return. It was July 23, 1959, when, at the Lushan Conference, Mao Zedong unleashed his counterattack against Defense Minister Peng Dehuai, who, with several others, had found the courage to remonstrate with the Chairman over the failures of the Great Leap.

The Great Leap Forward was surely in part an economic and ideological assertion of independence on the part of Mao Zedong, but as an economic plan it was still recognizable as a variant of Stalinism (in its massive state investment in producer industries, for example, or in its "communization" of agriculture as a radical extension of collectivization). Nevertheless, it may well be that Peng believed, as Mao charged, that China was veering too far from the Soviet Union in this as in other areas. In any event, given the manner in which Mao forced the issue with his senior colleagues, collusion with the Soviet Union—which in some sense had been the national policy of the PRC—now constituted betrayal.

If Peng's was an act of protest, it was a secret, intraparty challenge apparently well within the bounds of Leninist discipline and CCP practice. Its resolution, too, fit the CCP's Leninist/Stalinist heritage: a purge, first in secret and then in public, of an allegedly conspiratorial faction, in this case of a "rightist opportunist" variety. Over the course of the next three years, as Mao broke with Khrushchev, as Soviet advisers were withdrawn, as tens of millions of Chinese perished in the aftermath of the renewed Maoist Leap, the Soviet system continued to shape Chinese politics, if not Chinese economics, but now in defiance of the Soviet Union.

Taiwan and the American World

For the People's Republic, economic and technological cooperation with the U.S.S.R. made great sense historically. The two great socialist powers, now at the high tide of the international communist movement, *wanted* to cooperate and had much to offer each other. Moreover, despite the stated aim of the new PRC government to be rid of the legacy of Nationalist rule, its industrial planning before 1959 was based on heavy industrial and national defense priorities similar to those of the Nationalist period, and for these the U.S.S.R. was an ideal partner. It was thus no accident that many individual projects developed under Sino-Soviet cooperation during the First Five-Year Plan of 1953–58 had been on the drawing board before 1949.

The economic development of Nationalist Taiwan, too, would be based in part on economic and policy continuities from the pre-1949 period. But no one could have imagined in 1949 how these would combine, over a decade of Sino-American cooperation, to take Taiwan in quite a different direction.

When Taiwan reverted to the Republic of China in 1945, it underwent a sudden decolonization under the leadership of individuals who were themselves outsiders to the island. Plans for its economic takeover were similar to those for all of occupied China: Japanese- and "collaborator"-owned enterprises would be nationalized and placed under the direct management of individuals appointed by the national and provincial governments. Taiwan's economy would be totally redirected from its former markets in the Japanese empire, and, like that of all provinces, "synchronized" (*peihe*) with the needs of the national economy on the Chinese mainland.[70] By the end of 1946 the state had taken ownership of the heights of economic power on Taiwan: the sugar, power, oil, aluminum, ship-building, and machinery industries. In the process, Taiwan was also brought into synchrony with the ills afflicting the postwar Chinese economy on the mainland, including its debilitating inflation. Although the eruption of popular dissent in the "2–28" incident of 1947 might indicate that conditions were particularly poor in postwar Taiwan, the fact is that Taiwan was less a "special case" than an area in which postwar plans were carried out to the fullest. To implement them, and to oversee the island's economic recovery, the Nationalist government sent a large number of its most talented young economic planners, who had been trained in the United States during the war. (They went to Taiwan thanks in part to the Soviet Union: many were slated for Manchuria, China's biggest industrial area, but the continued Russian presence, not to mention looting, in northeastern industries led to their reassignment.) By the time Chiang Kai-shek's regime retreated to Taiwan for good, it would have on its "bastion of national recovery" a fully rehabilitated industrial foundation and an enviable pool of national talent.[71]

This hardly guaranteed Taiwan's survival, however. Only the Americans could do that, and they did so in July 1950, less to save Taiwan for the Nationalists than to keep it from the Communists. In contrast to Sino-Soviet relations of the same period, there was precious little in the way of mutual admiration, trust, or shared values between Washington and Taipei in 1950. Once again (as in 1942) only a common enemy would lead the United States and Nationalist China—as American officials still called it— into an alliance.

It helped that institutions for Sino-American cooperation after 1950 did not need to be created from scratch. The fact that the Nationalist state still called itself the Republic of China (ROC) facilitated continuity in cooperation. The China Aid Act, that dose of medicine for the dying man on the mainland, permitted a form of life support for Taiwan, since programs funded under it, such as the work of the Economic Cooperation Administration (ECA, later reorganized as the Agency for International Development, or AID) and the Joint Commission on Rural Reconstruction (JCRR), continued on the island. Also preexisting (since 1948) was the ROC government's interministerial committee for administering American assistance, the Council on U.S. Aid (CUSA). Still in place, too, was the J. G. White Engineering Corporation of New York, which after 1945 was the leading foreign consultant to the ROC government for industrial rehabilitation projects, including many on Taiwan. It would become the unofficial project consultant to American aid administrators. The Economic Stabilization Board (ESB), which would play such an important role in the 1950s, was new in name in 1951, but was in fact a reorganization of the Executive Yuan's Financial and Economic Working Group.[72]

It helped, too, that there were obvious lessons to be learned—on both sides—from the debacle that had befallen the Nationalists on the mainland. The initial aim of American aid was not to make Taiwan prosperous or even, for that matter, capitalist but simply to make it stable. There were none of the grand, world-historical expectations that had accompanied American aid to China during the Second World War. Stability, not development, was the goal also of Chiang Kai-shek and his followers, seared by the memory of economic chaos and military defeat on the mainland, which they were determined somehow to reconquer. The assumption that economic stability was the precondition for everything else, as the recent mainland experience seemed to prove, was the one overriding goal on which American aid officials and their Chinese counterparts could agree.

Aid initially took the form of commodity imports to address shortages of basic goods (food and clothes, not the least) and gradually, in the process, to restore public confidence. These imports helped to offset the continued heavy military expenditures that caused chronic budget deficits; in other words, through civilian as well as military aid, the Americans helped to keep the Nationalist military alive. With the goal of "improving [Taiwan's] capacity for self-support,"[73] the United States aimed to make the ROC military increasingly self-reliant while providing for Taiwan's population and stabilizing the currency. At the same time, since one perceived lesson from the loss of the mainland was the need for agrarian reform—a still-constant fear being a revolution emanating from the countryside—the JCRR, with a staff of mostly American-returned agronomists, oversaw a major land tenure reform during 1951–53. Whereas over the same period, the direct Soviet role in land reform in the PRC was negligible, the Americans were deeply involved in the equally fundamental and more enduring reforms that took place on Taiwan.

The amount of funds devoted to these two categories of aid showed that what had been a small commitment when spread over China as a whole could be rather more effective when applied to an island of 8.4 million people. But there was much more aid once the PRC entered the Korean War and after the passage of the Mutual Security Act in 1951. Even then, such was the reputation of the Chiang Kai-shek regime in the U.S. Congress that aid was allocated on an annual basis only. It took the Taiwan Strait crisis of 1954 and the subsequent Mutual Defense Treaty to stimulate an ongoing program of assistance through AID. The statutory basis for aid was military need: only one-eighth of American assistance to Taiwan over the years 1951–65 would be recognized explicitly as "developmental assistance." But the amounts of nonmilitary aid were great in magnitude—an average of $80 million per year, or 6.4 percent of the ROC's gross national product over fifteen years—and given on generous terms (outright grants until 1955, and thereafter, low interest credits).[74] Equally important, perhaps, was the commonality of perspectives among American advisers and Chinese economic leaders about how this aid should be spent.

Unlike the disagreements that marked Sino-American economic negotiations in the 1940s, based in part on differing principles of economic life, and indeed, unlike the ideological dimension of Sino-Soviet disputes over economic rationality in the late 1950s, the sense that Taiwan was an important "front" in the global Cold War lent a hard-boiled pragmatism to Chinese planners and American advisers alike. To this may be added a sense of common professionalism among economic experts who were able to forge a working relationship under the political protection of both governments in the early 1950s. Thus, in pursuit of stability, American advisers supported rather than resisted the continued ROC government emphasis on infrastructural and industrial development in a protected economic environment. "Import substitution" was not simply a *Chinese* policy. Despite the fact that the government owned 80 percent of industry in 1953, there was no American insistence on a broad program of "privatization." When landlords were compensated in part with shares in state corporations, no one imagined the impact this would have on Taiwanese entrepreneurship. Americans no less than Chinese recognized the central role of state-owned enterprises (SOEs)—Taiwan Sugar Corporation was the island's largest earner of foreign exchange—and concentrated their advice on the improvement of accounting and management in SOEs, which were, after all, the major institutional recipients of American aid. Although American aid gradually created a greater space for private economic development on Taiwan (Wang Yongqing's Formosa Plastics began with a small AID grant, for example), it never aimed to challenge the dominance of the state.

The longstanding Nationalist commitment to the "scientific" planning of the economy through detailed, multi-year plans had been resisted by the

Americans in the 1940s. Now it was strongly encouraged, not least to force the Chiang Kai-shek regime to contemplate more than a temporary stay on the island. Indeed the First Four-Year Plan on Taiwan (1953–56) was initially called for by the American aid mission.[75] Subsequent Chinese requests for assistance through 1965 would be based on the priorities set in the Four-Year Plans of 1957–60 and 1961–65.

By almost any measure, the American advisory group in Taiwan had more substantial leverage than did the Soviet effort on the Chinese mainland. It was more unified organizationally under two authorities located in Taipei: AID and the Military Assistance Advisory Group (MAAG), in contrast to the hundreds of ministries, universities, and units that—albeit under the broad oversight of the Central Committee of the CPSU—sponsored Soviet advisers. It was more plugged in at the top levels of economic decision making. Soviet specialists worked as consultants (in setting up the First Five-Year Plan or in the later Twelve-Year Plan for Science and Technology, for example,) but they did not participate in administrative, managerial, or leadership positions in the Chinese economy.[76] In contrast, American aid officials became an informal part of a decision-making process on Taiwan in which economic policy was increasingly left in the hands of the economic, not Party, bureaucracy. The JCRR was of course "joint" by original design. At meetings of the Economic Stabilization Board, the AID mission was represented (not as a formal member). Americans participated, too, in the deliberations of the Council on U.S. Aid, the interministerial (indeed extraministerial) body that, thanks to the U.S. aid it was delegated to administer, enjoyed considerable administrative autonomy within the ROC government.

By the late 1950s, Taiwan had pursued, in a highly supported and protected environment, policies of military-economic development that were recognizable from the Nationalist years on the mainland. Indeed, given the initial emphasis on economic stabilization, followed by a vigorous program of import-substitution aided by a foreign patron, its policies bore a family resemblance to those of the PRC before 1958. But whereas the PRC had endeavored, in its First Five-Year Plan, to become part of the socialist world economy, Nationalist Taiwan, although part of the global military-political front that called itself the "free world," could hardly be said to be integrated into the international capitalist system.

It was then, in the late 1950s, while Mao Zedong was abandoning his Soviet partners for his "Great Leap Forward," that Taiwan, less publicly but with an equal degree of risk, initiated what we may now call its "Great Leap Outward." No one predicted the subsequent, stunning success of Taiwan's export-led growth and its attraction of foreign investment (where there had previously been virtually none). The liberalization of controls on industry and foreign trade over the years 1958–60 was certainly encouraged by the Americans, but it was adopted by the Chinese in part because American aid was about to end. That is, its timing was assisted by the American announcement that Taiwan would soon "graduate" from U.S. aid and be on its own. As perilous as many perceived the relaxation of economic controls to be, the prospect of economic self-reliance, even if gained by novel strategies, was a greater attraction.[77] Thus the new policies on Taiwan were similar to the mainland's Great Leap Forward in one way: as a Chinese declaration of economic autonomy, if not quite independence, from the foreign superpower.

Taiwan's new path was no triumph of neoclassical economics, and certainly not the triumph of "pro-business" as opposed to "pro-state" forces.[78] The state would continue to "govern the market" at home with an industrial policy designed to promote specific export industries; the economic bureaucracy would retain an important role in "guidance" planning; SOEs would continue to be protected and subsidized. But now the (largely) private, export-oriented economy was allowed to cohabit with, and indeed ultimately outgrow, the Nationalist state economy.[79] In the process, the economies of Taiwan and the United States became linked through trade and investment as they had never been in the period of direct American aid.

From the perspective of 1950, it would have been difficult to imagine that Sino-Soviet cooperation—which made sense in some form for *any* Chinese government—would founder so quickly, never to be revived, while Nationalist Taiwan would remain autonomous and become prosperous because of its integration into the competing American camp. The Sino-Soviet alliance was in some sense preordained by the tutelary role of the U.S.S.R. in international communism in general and over the Chinese Communist Party in particular. It began with grand dreams and clear blueprints, not just for "red factories" but for the path to the Stalinist society outlined in the famous *Short Course*. The U.S. alliance with the ROC on Taiwan was, by contrast, a second marriage of convenience between two wary partners, for which there was no grand design except survival.

Perhaps that is one conclusion: that no alliance could have withstood the expectations that accompanied Sino-Soviet partnership, not just for security and economic development, but for the path to a shared utopia. As the review of industrial and scientific cooperation between the communist powers suggests, there were no economic contradictions compelling enough to call it off; quite the contrary. The tensions ultimately lay elsewhere, above all in Mao Zedong's pretensions to ideological originality, which challenged the concept of "scientific" planning, undermined a founding assumption of the alliance (Soviet leadership), and led China into economic chaos and international isolation. More important from the point of view of Cold War history, this was a death blow to communism as an international movement. Yet before then, the Soviet Union had given its stamp, politically and physically, to the People's Republic, which today is still under the Leninist leadership of a president trained in the Soviet Union, and now confronts, in the reform of state industries, the most enduring material manifestation of that era.

Compared to the aspirations of the Sino-Soviet alliance, expectations of Sino-American cooperation on Taiwan could not have been lower. But for ROC officials, what was the alternative? This sobering thought surely facilitated cooperation, just as it made an ROC repudiation of the United States, then as now, unthinkable. But the onset of the Cold War in Asia also made the Americans more cooperative, much more generous, and rather less fussy about the economic and political deficiencies of their default ally. (Taiwan's later democratization is surely not the legacy of this period of American influence.) For both, the experience of failure in the 1940s was important. Above all the Cold War led Chinese and American economic officials and organizations to work closely together, on a regular basis, over many years, in a politically protected environment,[80] and far removed from the frenzied ideological struggles that would plague their counterparts on the Chinese mainland. In this context, Taiwan's Great Leap Outward, unlike Mao's Great Leap Forward, was not a leap in the dark.

CHAPTER TWO

The Changing International Scene
and Chinese Policy toward the United States,

1954–1970

Zhang Baijia

SINO-AMERICAN RELATIONS have never been simply a bilateral affair. During the years of mutual estrangement, developments in bilateral relations reflected the strong influence of a third party, either a great power, such as the Soviet Union, or a small nation, such as Vietnam, whose role can never be ignored, even when focusing on great power relations. At the same time, because the United States is one of two superpowers with global influence, the Chinese leadership must inevitably take it into account in developing overall foreign policy. In effect, China's policies toward the United States can be regarded as akin to guiding principles that reflect the leadership's strategic perspective on major international issues and the global political structure as well as China's national interest.

This essay explores the evolution of China's policies toward the United States through three historical stages: from the end of the Korean War to 1958, from 1958 to 1967, and from 1968 to 1970. Each stage represents a different combination of three important factors: Beijing's assessment of the overall international situation, the guiding principles it derived from this assessment, and the foreign policy it developed, on the basis of those guiding principles, toward specific countries or particular issues.

The New and Tentative Period in China's U.S. Policy
(1954–1958)

From 1954 to the first half of 1958, the People's Republic of China assessed its strategic environment and developed the principles that would guide and shape its foreign policy, including that toward the United States, in the late 1950s and the mid-1960s. From its establishment in 1949, the PRC found itself in confrontation with the United States. Viewed against a U.S.-Soviet Cold War backdrop, the U.S.-China conflict reflected three distinctive factors: America had sided with the Nationalist government during the Chinese civil war, and the Chinese Communist Party viewed American imperialism as its primary external enemy; after the emergence of the PRC, the United States not only refused to extend diplomatic recognition to the new Chinese government, it adopted a China policy of containment and isolation, which led to China's decision to "lean to one side" and align itself with the Soviet Union; and finally, the PRC and the United States were at war on the Korean peninsula.

After the Korean War ended, in June 1953, China entered a period of intensive internal economic development. During this period of relatively stable domestic and international conditions, the Chinese leadership adopted a long-term perspective on the country's interests and focused its resources on rapid establishment of the socialist system. Under Mao Zedong's leadership, China implemented important political, economic, and cultural policies. Subsequent changes in the international environment, however, required a more active foreign policy.

Three influential trends emerged during the mid-1950s. First, the Cold War between the socialist camp and the capitalist camp continued unabated, but as each side adjusted its tactics, the dynamic of U.S.-Soviet relations shifted from one of escalating tension in the immediate aftermath of the Second World War to one of alternating tension and relaxation. Second, internal problems developed within each of the two camps as both superpowers faced the challenge of trying to control their respective allies. Third, national liberation movements struggling against imperialism and colonialism expanded, and Indochina and the Middle East became new centers of conflict. The Cold War bloc alliances were loosening, but a new international framework was not yet in place. It was an uncertain era in international politics.

In these domestic and international circumstances, Chinese diplomacy developed in two distinct phases. During the first, from mid-1953 to mid-1956, while the PRC pursued national economic development, the Chinese leadership focused on strengthening national security and promoting a peaceful external environment. During the second, from mid-1956 to mid-1958, Chinese policymakers, observing the changing international situation, assessed whether or not tension between the two blocs, and between China and the United States, could be reduced, and how China could play a more important role in international politics.

The first phase was marked by Zhou Enlai's active role in formulating China's foreign policy. Among Chinese leaders, Zhou excelled in his understanding of international affairs and multilateral diplomacy, and he was able to combine the struggle against imperialism and colonialism with more flexible policies. At the Geneva Conference in 1954, Zhou promoted the Indochina peace agreement, enhancing Chinese border security and enabling China to establish direct contact with Britain and France. He also contributed to the success of the 1955 Asian-African conference in Bandung, Indonesia, where his proposal to "seek common ground while reserving differences" promoted consensus-building and helped to expand Chinese influence not only with its neighbors but throughout the Third World.

China also tried to reduce international tension and promote cooperation by issuing Five Principles of Peaceful Coexistence, first proclaimed by Zhou in 1954: mutual respect for sovereignty and territorial integrity, mutual nonaggression, noninterference in each other's internal affairs, equality and mutual benefit, and peaceful coexistence. These principles were initially designed to apply to relations with neighboring countries, such as India and Burma, but China also applied them in its relations with other Asian and African countries and with Western and socialist countries.

China's policy of peaceful coexistence was inseparable from its leaders' assessment of the United States as the greatest threat to Chinese security. They realized, however, that this threat was gradually diminishing, that the United States had interests that conflicted with those of its allies, offering China opportunities for diplomacy. Just before the end of the Korean War, Zhou Enlai had pointed out that "the most outstanding international conflict today is that between peace and war" and that Chinese policy was premised on "the courage to practice peaceful coexistence and peaceful competition among countries of different systems." He added that "the U.S. threat of war may ... deepen its rift with Western Europe and no country in Asia, the Middle East, and North Africa wants to follow it."[1] On July 7, 1954, at an expanded meeting of the Politburo following the conclusion of the Geneva Conference, Mao Zedong observed that "the general international trend reveals that America is quite isolated," and faced conflicts both at home and abroad. "It is not impossible to deal with countries like the United States to our advantage." He added, "We are no longer able to shut our door against outsiders even if we wanted to. Now, things are looking up in our favor. We must walk out [into the international arena] of our own accord."[2]

Although the United States had given no indication that it was prepared to change its China policy, Chinese leaders took the initiative. During the Geneva Conference, when Zhou Enlai was informed through the British chargé d'affaires in Beijing that the U.S. delegation intended to deal with the issue of Americans detained in China, he used the opportunity to establish contact with the United States, offering to conduct direct negotiations with U.S. diplomats. The two sides met four times between June 5 and June 21.

Beijing took this initiative because it believed that China should not miss any opportunity to ease U.S.-China tensions and because it hoped that by adopting a more moderate foreign policy, it would drive a wedge between the United States and its allies. Most important, in the aftermath of the Korean War and the wars in Indochina, Chinese leaders made every effort to prevent the continuation of the Taiwan issue. Before and after the Geneva Conference, Taiwan had been widely publicizing its negotiations with the United States over a "mutual defense treaty," a development that alarmed the Chinese leadership. At an expanded meeting of the Politburo, Chairman Mao said that Taiwan would be a long-term issue between China and the United States, and that China's immediate objective should be to prevent the United States from signing the treaty with Taiwan. It should use propaganda as well as diplomatic gestures, including negotiating with Washington over the issue of foreign residents in China.[3]

Mao was worried that if Washington and Taiwan signed the treaty, protracted Sino-American tension would result, and that "it would be difficult to seek any room for reconciliation." In these circumstances, in late July the Party Central Committee decided that "Taiwan must be liberated," and in

August the Party launched a nationwide propaganda movement. To increase pressure on the United States and to indicate China's unrelenting position, the People's Liberation Army (PLA) started shelling Jinmen on September 3, 1954. On February 13, 1955, the PLA liberated Dachen and the surrounding islands. The aim of the shelling was twofold: to eliminate the Kuomintang (KMT)'s largest military base for carrying out sabotage in the coastal areas of Zhejiang Province using the tactic of "making a feint to the east and attacking the west." The longer-term strategic consideration was to dramatize the Taiwan issue in order to prevent a perpetual separation of the two sides of the Taiwan Strait.

The shelling of Jinmen did not mean that Mao Zedong opposed improving relations with the United States. Before the bombing, in a meeting with a British Labour Party delegation, he remarked that China would like to coexist peacefully with countries having different social systems. He emphasized that China included the United States among these countries and "expected that it would adopt the same policies of peaceful coexistence." He also suggested that Britain persuade the United States to "move the Seventh Fleet away and leave Taiwan alone."[4] China seemed to be practicing contradictory policies, seeking friendlier relations with the United States while simultaneously increasing pressure over the Taiwan issue, but Mao believed that the two policies were consistent. If the United States continued to expand its cooperation with Taiwan and to consolidate the island's separation from the mainland, thus undermining Chinese sovereignty and intervening in its internal affairs, then U.S.-China relations would further deteriorate, and China would have to adopt even more hostile policies.

Mao Zedong argued that the relationship between mainland China and Taiwan was different from that between the two Germanys, the two Koreas, or the two Vietnams. China was one of the Allies during the Second World War and one of the victorious powers after the war. The lines of partition in Germany, Korea, and Vietnam were drawn by international conferences and embodied in international treaties, whereas the separation of mainland China and Taiwan had never been governed by any international agreement.[5] While signaling to the United States China's interest in peaceful coexistence, Mao used the shelling of Jinmen to demonstrate that China's policy over Taiwan was unrelenting, confident that it served China's long-term objectives.

As a result of China's limited power, however, the bombing of Jinmen revealed only China's determination, and it neither forced the United States out of the Taiwan Strait nor averted the long-term separation of the two sides of the Strait. Objectively speaking, the shelling hastened, if it did not cause, the signing of the U.S.-Taiwan "Mutual Defense Treaty." Taiwan thus became a fundamental issue at the core of the confrontation between the United States and China, and the major obstacle to better Sino-American relations.

The shelling of Jinmen reflected the belief among Chinese leaders that a demonstration of power would avoid an appearance of weakness and be an effective way to achieve a more relaxed relationship with the United States. After the shelling ended, Zhou Enlai again promoted an improvement in relations. At the Asian-African conference at Bandung, he proposed U.S.-China negotiations, which led to the Sino-American ambassadorial-level talks that began on August 1, 1955. Bilateral relations between the two parties, once threatened by grave tension, became friendlier.

Because Chinese leaders viewed China's pressure as the impetus for the opening of these talks, they had high expectations. The day before the negotiations were to begin, Zhou Enlai, as a token of sincerity, passed a message to the Indian Ambassador to China indicating that China would release detained American pilots ahead of schedule. He also noted China's hope that the Geneva meetings would enable the Chinese and American foreign ministers to sit down together in negotiations on the "relaxation of tension over the region of Taiwan."[6]

But the differences between the two sides remained huge, and Chinese optimism soon vanished. The Chinese side believed the negotiations should focus on Taiwan but also discuss other substantive issues, such as cultural relations between the two countries, and that the two foreign ministers should meet in direct talks. The U.S. side, however, was interested only in the question of the Americans detained in China and in a guarantee that China would not use force against Taiwan.[7] Sino-American ambassadorial negotiations quickly became extremely difficult and protracted.

Yet, in spite of its frustration, China persisted in its policy goals until the end of 1956. It continued to hope that it could break the stalemate to achieve U.S. concessions on Taiwan as well as mutual assurances that neither party would use force against the other. In August 1956, when reviewing the political report of the Eighth Party Congress, Mao Zedong inserted the following text: "For the sake of peace and construction, we are willing to establish friendly relations with all countries in the world, including the United States."[8] During the Party Congress in September, he modified that statement, saying that it would be better to establish diplomatic relations with the United States upon completion of the Second Five-Year Plan and after admission to the United Nations. China planned to "clean up its house" before inviting visitors. It had not yet completed its socialist reforms or built up a solid industrial base, so that diplomatic relations with the imperialist powers would only cause China more trouble. Mao also pointed out that China's doors would remain open and that in a few years the United States, West Germany, and Japan would all come to do business with China.[9]

Chinese optimism soon diminished. From the early months of 1957, Chinese leaders increasingly sensed that Washington had no intention of improving relations and was determined to pursue its "two-China conspiracy." They also believed that the United States was threatening China by strengthening American control over the countries and regions around it. They thus abandoned their effort to improve U.S.-China relations and embarked on a policy of fighting relentlessly against U.S. imperialism. In September 1957, Chairman Mao reported that China's policy toward Western countries was "now to fight against them."[10] Then, at the end of the year, Sino-American ambassadorial negotiations were interrupted by a U.S. attempt to lower the diplomatic level of the talks. Secretary of State John Foster Dulles also stated repeatedly that the United States would adhere to its three principles toward China: nonrecognition of the People's Republic of China, opposition to China's admission to the United Nations, and a trade embargo. This reiteration of U.S. policy made Mao all the more determined to emphasize the role of struggle in China's U.S. policy.

But reemphasizing the importance of struggle was not simply a change in China's U.S. policy; it signaled a larger shift in China's overall foreign policy in response to U.S. persistence in its policy of containment and isolation as well as other factors. Beginning in 1956, a series of important international events prompted the Chinese leadership in general, and Mao Zedong in particular, to rethink Chinese foreign policy on major international issues. That February, in his report to the Twentieth Congress of the Soviet Communist Party, Khrushchev condemned Stalin, sending a shockwave throughout the socialist bloc, including China. Later that same year, Poland and Hungary experienced political instability. Signs of division in Sino-Soviet relations also began to emerge, and by the end of the year, relations were at a turning point.

Mao Zedong made two comments on Khrushchev's secret report. First, he said, it "disclosed the facade," meaning that it showed that the Soviet Union, the Soviet Communist Party, and Stalin had not always been correct in everything, thus abolishing any possibility of blind faith in the Soviet Union. Second, the report "went too far," meaning that it made serious mistakes in both content and methodology.[11] The ensuing instability in Poland and Hungary confirmed China's doubts about Khrushchev's leadership. Although the Chinese leadership made different assessments of the two incidents—Beijing regarded the Polish crisis as the consequence of the Soviet Union's protracted chauvinism and the Hungarian crisis as a conspiratorial activity incited by imperialism and Hungarian counterrevolutionaries[12]—neither incident reflected well on Khrushchev's leadership credentials.

At the Moscow conference in November 1957, with the assistance of the Chinese Communist Party, the crisis in the socialist bloc seemed to be over, but the reputation of the Soviet Communist Party as the leader of the communist bloc had been severely damaged. To protect the unity of the socialist camp, Mao Zedong maintained that socialist countries should continue "to be led by the Soviet Union," although he wanted to abandon the Soviet model and explore China's own way of building socialism. Chinese leaders also wanted to play a greater role in the socialist camp. The Chinese Communist Party criticized the Soviet Communist Party for not treating brother countries as equals. It opposed Khrushchev's total negation of Stalin's contributions and disagreed with Moscow's suggestion that some capitalist countries could become socialist by way of "peaceful transition." Nor did it agree that "peaceful coexistence" should be the socialist guiding principle, a reflection of recent changes in Chinese foreign policy.

Eastern European turbulence coincided with instability in the Middle East. In July 1956, Egypt regained sovereignty over the Suez Canal. At the end of October, Britain and France launched hostilities against Egypt but soon backed down because of a lack of U.S. support, Soviet threats, and opposition from a number of other countries. If the Bandung Conference showed that nationalist countries had become part of the international political scene, the outcome of the Suez conflict demonstrated the determination of those countries to fight against imperialism. At that time, China had just established diplomatic relations with Egypt and showed deep concern over developments in the region.

Although China had limited interests in the Middle East, as well as limited influence, Chinese leaders considered the region an important indicator of the international situation. Mao Zedong believed that the emergence of Third World nationalist countries would lead to changes in world power and accentuate conflict among imperialist countries. At the end of 1957, Mao returned to the phrase "the intermediate zone" and reconsidered his proposition that "the middle way leads to nowhere." He now maintained that the nationalist countries could remain outside the two camps and "take a neutral position."[13] Thus, following the Suez crisis, assisting the Asian and African countries in their struggle against imperialism became an increasingly important element of China's foreign policy.

Despite these conflicts, socialism was full of vigor in the mid-1950s. In the struggle between the two camps, the socialist camp was gaining the advantage, and many Asian and African nationalist countries were moving toward socialism. Socialism seemed to be creating economic miracles; according to statistics, the Soviet economy was growing at a rate double that of the major Western countries and triple that of the United States. In 1957, the Soviet Union became the first country to launch a man-made satellite into space. Meanwhile, China completed its Ffirst Five-Year Plan ahead of schedule and entered its best period of economic development since the founding of the PRC.

Mao Zedong was encouraged by these developments, but he was not sure whether capitalism in decline would be willing to coexist peacefully with socialism or whether it would go to war in a desperate attempt to survive. He wondered whether it was still advantageous for the developing socialist countries to take the initiative and persist in the policy of relaxation or whether they should adopt a less cooperative foreign policy and pressure the imperialists to change theirs. After much contemplation of the international situation, from the winter of 1957 to the autumn of 1958, Mao Zedong came to three conclusions.

First, Mao described the international situation as "now at a turning point," "the east wind taking over the west wind." Socialism was assuming an overwhelmingly advantageous position in terms of its popularity, its population, and its scientific achievements. The Western world was "abandoned forever."[14] Second, in terms of East-West relations he said, "the West is more afraid of us." East-West tension was "not totally without merit to us," but rather "more harmful to the Western countries." NATO was on the defensive and "would attack only when socialism is crumbling down."[15] Third, regarding the relationship of communism, imperialism, and nationalism, "communism and nationalism are more similar to each other," but the United States was "concentrating on dominating the intermediate zone." The U.S. leadership was very aggressive and was "now attacking nationalism."[16]

But Mao Zedong overestimated the superiority of socialism over capitalism and depicted international relations simplistically. His idiosyncratic conclusions persuaded him that world peace was possible. Yet he also believed that revolutionary forces should not yield to the imperialists and should not be afraid of a world war against imperialism. Convinced that power in the international arena, as well as within the socialist bloc, must be backed by strong economic might, he initiated the "Great Leap Forward." It was his conviction that in fifteen years the Soviet Union would be more advanced than the United States and that the Chinese economy would surpass the British economy. By then, socialism would be "invincible throughout the world" and the world would enjoy lasting peace. He also believed that in a mere four years, by 1962, China's steel production would catch up with that of the United States. "By then we will certainly be more confident when negotiating with the Americans."[17]

In launching the "Great Leap Forward" in 1958, Mao announced that Chinese diplomacy should cast off conservative thinking. In June, when the Ministry of Foreign Affairs met to consider the international situation, it reaffirmed the correctness of post-1949 diplomatic policies but identified a rightist and conservative tendency in dealing with some specific issues. In China's relations with socialist countries, for example, there was not enough criticism or argument against some revisionist positions; in its relations with nationalist countries, there was insufficient struggle and the line between socialists and nationalists was blurred; in its relations with imperialists, there was too much impractical fantasy about prospects for cooperation.

At the meeting, Chen Yi, who had succeeded Zhou Enlai as foreign minister at the beginning of that year, conveyed a critical message from Mao. Mao criticized the Ministry for speaking in favor of the United States on the release of all eleven American prisoners before the start of the Sino-American ambassadorial-level negotiations in 1955. Mao also characterized the February 1958 Sino-Japanese agreement on the long-term barter trading of steel as a mistake in principle, pointing out that to approve of initiating contacts with the Americans at the 1954 Geneva Conference was not in conformity with his thoughts. He said that China's original policy was good, and that instead of developing diplomatic relations with the United States, China should have persisted in its struggle against the United States. Chinese policy toward the United States demonstrated whether or not the Chinese people had truly risen to their feet, and the Chinese people should not forget the long history of imperialist invasion of China. He further argued that China should take advantage of U.S. containment and the economic embargo policy to close its doors and concentrate on self-reliant socialist development.[18] After hearing Mao's criticism, the Foreign Ministry changed its policy. Henceforth, China's diplomacy could be summarized as "expose Yugoslavia and consolidate socialism; fight the United States and bring down imperialism; and isolate Japan and win over nationalist countries."[19]

The new diplomatic strategy determined by Chairman Mao abandoned the practical policies based on the Five Principles of Peaceful Coexistence for highly unrealistic policies full of revolutionary dynamism and romanticism. Diplomacy became a tool to serve the international political struggle, while socialist development was carried out behind closed doors. In the interest of safeguarding sovereignty and territorial integrity, and of winning over nationalists and fighting against revisionists, opposing American imperialism once again became the predominant task of Chinese foreign policy.

Confrontation with the Two Superpowers (1958–1967)

In 1958, following the launching of the Great Leap Forward, China confronted both the United States and the Soviet Union simultaneously. China's dual-adversary policy lasted for ten years, coming to an end in 1967, at the height of Cultural Revolution. During that decade, the international situation continued to follow the three trends of the mid-1950s. Superpower relations experienced slow changes, while escalating Sino-Soviet conflict, and conflict within the socialist bloc itself, exerted the greatest influence on the overall international situation.

The Chinese leadership had not intended to confront the two superpowers at the same time. China's dual-adversary policy was the unintended outcome of interactions between China, the United States, and the Soviet

Union and of changes in China's external environment and domestic politics.

Like a Beijing opera, which often begins with wildly beating gongs and drums, China's diplomacy during this period was vigorous and bustling. As it had four years earlier, the People's Liberation Army started shelling Jinmen on August 23, 1958, signaling China's decision, in the context of the Great Leap Forward, to adopt a tougher policy toward the United States. Later that same day, Mao Zedong revealed the twofold purpose of the shelling to a meeting of the Politburo Standing Committee: the shelling was intended to support the Arab people in their struggle against American imperialism and to determine whether Jinmen and Mazu were included in the U.S.-Taiwan Mutual Defense Treaty. Mao thus made it clear to the Chinese central leadership that the decision to shell Jinmen reflected his overall strategic judgment.

After a month and a half of artillery action, Chinese leaders decided to delay the recovery of Jinmen. On October 5, Mao Zedong ordered a two-day halt to the shelling and personally drafted the October 6 message to Taiwan compatriots that was issued in the name of Defense Minister Peng Dehuai. Once the nature of the Taiwan issue had changed from one of military conflict to one of political and diplomatic conflict, the crisis ended.

The shelling of Jinmen affected U.S.-China relations in several ways. First, it established the pattern of China's struggle against the United States, which Chairman Mao characterized as his "noose" policy: since the United States poked its nose into everything, it put a noose around its own neck, and this would ultimately benefit the struggle of the world's people against it. Second, during the crisis, Mao established the principle of avoiding direct military conflict with the United States: "We use ... brinkmanship policy to oppose U.S. brinkmanship policy."[20] Third, after the crisis, Chinese leaders concluded that the date for solving the Taiwan question is "still far away." Both Taiwan and the mainland opposed "two Chinas," but Chiang Kai-Shek did not possess the strength to counter the mainland and China could not yet liberate Taiwan.[21] Fourth, the shelling deadlocked Sino-American relations. In mid-September, during the Chinese shelling, although the Sino-American ambassadorial talks had resumed, the United States showed no sign of compromise. In response, China adopted a "package" solution as its negotiating position, insisting that "other issues would not be dealt with before the Taiwan question is solved."[22] Thereafter, the ambassadorial-level talks merely served as a channel for maintaining contact between the two sides. In his meeting with Field Marshal Montgomery of Britain in May 1960, Mao said, "The current situation is neither division because of hot war nor peaceful coexistence; it is the third kind, namely cold war coexistence."[23] This was Mao's assessment of both Sino-American relations and the international situation.

The shelling of Jinmen also had an important impact on Sino-Soviet relations. Before the shelling, China and the Soviet Union had contended over Moscow's proposal for cooperation in carrying out two projects. In the spring of 1958, the Soviet Union proposed that it construct a military long-wave radio station on Chinese territory at the expense of both governments. Soon after, it also proposed a joint Sino-Soviet fleet. Mao was outraged, considering the Soviet proposals attempts to infringe on Chinese sovereignty. As he later recalled it, China and the Soviet Union fell out with each other in 1958 because China could never accept Moscow's attempt to control it militarily.[24]

Responding to Mao's fury, Khrushchev secretly visited China at the end of July to assuage PRC concerns. Although the two sides managed to reduce tensions, they did not discuss the Taiwan issue, and Moscow was unprepared for the shelling of Jinmen a few weeks later. Despite its dismay, the Soviet Union publicly supported China and promised to send technical troops. Nevertheless, Khrushchev no longer trusted Mao's reliability, concerned that Chinese policies might be the catalyst for war between the Soviet Union and the United States.

Khrushchev thus considered terminating the Sino-Soviet nuclear cooperation agreement of October 1957 and refusing China a sample nuclear bomb. On June 20, 1959, on the grounds that it was negotiating with the United States and Britain on a partial nuclear test ban treaty, Khrushchev met with President Eisenhower at Camp David, near Washington, D.C. In September, Soviet leaders informed China of their decision to postpone transferring the sample atomic bomb, along with the relevant drawings and materials, and advised Beijing that resumption of the program depended on the course of Sino-Soviet relations over the next two years.[25] Chinese leaders were enraged that, to appease imperialism, Moscow had reneged on its obligation to a fraternal socialist country. They now understood that Sino-Soviet relations would continue to deteriorate.

The rifts between the Chinese Communist Party and the Soviet Communist Party, which had been only partially visible for a number of years, emerged fully at the June 1960 Bucharest meeting of Communist parties. Khrushchev made a sudden, comprehensive attack on the Chinese Communist Party. The Chinese delegation immediately distributed a written declaration strongly criticizing Khrushchev by name. In July, the Soviet Union recalled all Soviet experts working in China, abruptly violating a series of Sino-Soviet agreements. The conflict reached the point of no return in October 1961 at the Twenty-Second Congress of the Soviet Communist Party. And early in 1962, at the anniversary celebration of the Sino-Soviet Treaty of Friendship, Alliance, and Mutual Assistance held in Beijing, the Soviet ambassador to China maintained that because the Soviet Union faced possible attacks from its enemies, it could only provide aid to "friendly socialist countries."[26] Moscow now considered the Sino-Soviet alliance expendable.

The role of the United States in the developing Sino-Soviet conflict should not be overlooked. By the early 1960s, the policies of China and the Soviet Union toward the United States had diverged. The Soviet Union sought U.S.-Soviet détente and cooperation on such major issues as nuclear arms control. In response, China tried to unite countries to oppose "U.S.-Soviet domination of the world." This strategy became China's fundamental diplomatic posture.

Although the Cold War continued to dominate superpower relations, U.S.-Soviet détente contributed to Sino-Soviet conflict. Whenever U.S.-Soviet relations became strained, during the Berlin crisis at the end of 1958 or the Cuban Missile Crisis of 1962, for example, Sino-Soviet tensions relaxed somewhat. Whenever a new round of U.S.-Soviet relaxation began, Sino-Soviet tensions worsened. The United States tried to exacerbate Sino-Soviet differences by offering Moscow cooperative relations, while Moscow attempted to manage China through its cooperation with the United States. In July 1963, just as the Chinese Communist Party and the Soviet Communist Party were meeting in Moscow, the Soviet Union, the United States, and Britain began negotiations on a partial nuclear test ban treaty, also in Moscow. The Soviets clearly intended that these negotiations, in their timing and content as well as their location, would support their efforts to pressure Beijing into accommodating Soviet interests. Sino-Soviet negotiations ended without agreement, and the conflict erupted in a public controversy in which the role of the U.S. factor was characterized by the phrase "fighting against imperialism must go along with fighting against revisionism."

As the Sino-Soviet conflict escalated, China abandoned its pursuit of more relaxed Sino-American relations. Although President John F. Kennedy made several small gestures of reconciliation toward China after taking office in 1961, offering, for example, to sell grain to China under favorable conditions, and Assistant Secretary of State Averell Harriman took the initiative incontacting Chen Yi at the second Geneva Conference, Chinese leaders did not reciprocate. The American side had failed to suggest any compromise on the Taiwan issue, and the ambassadorial-level talks had achieved no real progress. Beijing believed that it was premature to try to improve Sino-American relations.

Nevertheless, Chinese leaders paid great attention to every U.S. gesture, and Mao often instructed them to report to him on U.S. foreign policy and Sino-American relations. After Edgar Snow visited China in 1960, Zhou Enlai observed that the United States had allowed Snow to return to America. This, Zhou believed, showed that Kennedy was different from Eisenhower: "he wants to see reality and to acquire some materials about China through a variety of means."[27]

At the beginning of the 1960s, Sino-American relations were generally tranquil. In July 1961, at the second Geneva Conference, agreements on the question of Laos were signed. At their meeting in November 1961, neither Mao nor Ho Chi Minh thought it likely that the United States would send troops to Vietnam. What most concerned Vietnamese leaders were the prospects for Sino-Soviet reconciliation.

Simultaneous conflict with the two superpowers led China to assume a passive position. From 1962, the situation on China's borders began to deteriorate rapidly. Threats came from four directions: in South Vietnam, the United States had launched special actions against the Vietnamese insurgency; along the southeast coast, Chiang Kai-shek was actively preparing to counterattack the mainland; in the Yili and Tacheng regions of Xinjiang, the Soviet Union encouraged over 60,000 Chinese citizens to cross the border to the Soviet side; and in Tibet, Indian troops crossed over the MacMahon line and invaded Chinese territory.

These developments heightened Chinese apprehension, but the two most dangerous threats eased quickly. At the Sino-American ambassadorial-level talks in May and June, the Chinese side learned that the United States did not support Chiang's saber-rattling and that Washington had compelled him to promise not to attack the mainland without U.S. consent. Then, in a quick operation on October 20, Chinese troops initiated defensive actions along the Sino-Indian border, withdrawing immediately from Indian territory after achieving victory and punishing the invaders. Having reduced tensions with India and over Taiwan, Chinese leaders now believed that the major threat to its security occurred along the southwest border, where the United States was intervening in the Vietnam War. Although the Sino-Indian conflict aggravated Sino-Soviet relations, it was unimaginable that the Soviet Union would launch an armed invasion into China. China still considered the United States its main external security threat.

In early 1962, Wang Jiaxiang, head of the International Liaison Department of the CCP, argued that China's national security was in serious jeopardy and that Chinese diplomacy was fundamentally in error. In a series of proposals to the Central Committee, Wang emphasized again and again that China's diplomacy should "seek an environment of lasting peace for China's construction of socialism." China should pay attention to the appropriate tactics in the international struggle; it should "combine advance with retreat, offense with defense, struggle with conciliation, delay with solution." Chinese aid to other countries should "be based on our actual capability." What worried him most was the possibility that China might be forced into a conflict like the Korean War while also facing attacks on opposing flanks. Since Sino-Soviet relations had seriously deteriorated, China must avoid becoming the sole target of American imperialism and guard against the possibility that the Soviet Union might benefit from a Sino-American conflict.[28]

Wang Jiaxiang's proposals were bold and correct, penetratingly pointing out China's diplomatic requirements. But Mao Zedong erroneously thought that Wang's views revealed the influence of revisionism within the Chinese Communist Party and ignored his justified concerns over China's policy toward the Soviet Union and the United States. Mao criticized Wang's views as "making concessions to imperialism, revisionism, and counterrevolution while reducing support to the world struggle." Subsequently, Mao's subordinates did not dare to suggest changes in Chinese foreign policy.

Despite China's strategic vulnerability, Mao remained optimistic. He said that imperialist countries would begin to stir up significant conflicts with each other and that conflict between France and the United States, Britain and the United States, and Japan and the United States had already begun to intensify. In the latter part of 1962, he concluded that rapid changes had taken place in the international situation and that international forces were regrouping themselves. The forces of revolution had long contended with the world counterrevolutionary alliance headed by the United States. Now the imperialists, the reactionary forces of different countries, and the revisionists were closing ranks within their counterrevolutionary alliance. The main focus of the clash of interests was not in Europe or North America but in Asia, Africa, and Latin America. The policy toward the socialist countries adopted by Britain and the United States was not one of armed invasion but of peaceful evolution.[29] Henceforth, Mao devoted his attention to launching internal class struggle and external antirevisionist struggle. Meanwhile, he frequently received leftist representatives from the three continents, expounding on his theories and China's revolutionary experience. He also increased Chinese aid to Third World countries.

During the first half of the 1960s, China strengthened its diplomatic relations with "the middle area," trying to offset the strategic threat from the two superpowers. Mao divided the middle area into two parts: one, the economically backward countries in Asia, Africa, and Latin America; the other, mainly the countries of Western Europe and Eastern Europe. In Mao's view, both parts "were against control by the United States, and the problem for the Eastern European countries was to fight against control by the Soviet Union."[30] After Charles de Gaulle took office in 1958, France increased its independence from the United States, and this policy shift caught the attention of Chinese leaders. China and France slowly began to approach each other, and the end of the Algerian war in 1962 removed one of the major obstacles to improved relations. Following secret negotiations in 1963, in 1964 China and France established diplomatic relations. It was an important breakthrough in China's relations with Western countries. China and France opposed control by the superpowers, and their establishment of diplomatic relations broke through ideological barriers.

In order to strengthen China's relations with Asian and African countries, Zhou Enlai visited thirteen countries on these two continents at the end of 1963 and the beginning of 1964. He achieved some results, and China's prestige among Asian and African countries increased. China failed to attract significant support, however, for its simultaneous opposition to both superpowers.

In 1964, expanded U.S. intervention in the Vietnam War further exacerbated Sino-American tensions, posing a direct threat to China's southern border. To prevent further escalation of the war and to protect Chinese territorial security, the Central Committee of the Chinese Communist Party took measures in four areas: adjusting its strategic principles, strengthening its comprehensive war preparations, offering large-scale military assistance to Vietnam, and signaling to the United States its interest in avoiding direct Sino-American hostilities.

In June of that year, Mao reconsidered his strategic estimate that China should prepare for war along only its southern border while resting secure along its northern border. He now concluded that, since China's enemies would come from all directions, China should prepare for war on all fronts and remain vigilant, deciding on its main offensive and defensive directions according to the strength of its enemies. He also proposed that China "sit firmly on the bottom" by emphasizing basic industry, "grip the two fists" by developing agriculture and the defense industries, and strengthen construction of the "third front" by focusing on industrial development in the interior provinces.

The 1964 Tonkin Gulf Incident further heightened Chinese concern that the Vietnam War might spread to Chinese territory, and in October Mao instructed the country to prepare for a large-scale, or even an atomic, war. At the beginning of 1965, as the Vietnam War escalated, Chinese leaders decided to support Vietnam in the fighting, declaring, "we will send our personnel when needed by the Vietnamese and fight with them" to a successful end. At the same time, Zhou Enlai asked foreign leaders to convey four points to the United States: First, China would not take the initiative in provoking an anti-U.S. war; second, China would certainly live up to its word and carry out the international obligations it had undertaken; third, China was well prepared; fourth, if the United States shelled China, China would respond without any geographic limit.[31] In April, China and Vietnam signed an agreement covering Chinese deployment of support troops; in all, China sent 320,000 soldiers to Vietnam. On June 16, in the context of these war preparations, Mao proposed to the Politburo Standing Committee that China now give priority to national defense, followed by agriculture and industry.

As the war in Vietnam intensified and Chinese security deteriorated, the Soviet Union actively sought further cooperation with the United States, and the two sides achieved some progress toward détente. U.S. escalation of the Vietnam War not only strained Sino-American relations, it exacerbated

Sino-Soviet tensions, leading to a final split between the Soviet and Chinese Communist parties.

In February 1965, the Soviet Union proposed that the Democratic Republic of Vietnam and China sponsor an international conference on the Indochina issue to resolve the Vietnam War peacefully. Chinese leaders rejected the proposal, believing that it was a Soviet attempt to help the United States disengage from Vietnam and that any vacillation would benefit the United States. In March, the Soviet Communist Party organized a "consultative meeting for the representatives of the communist parties and workers' parties." Seven communist parties, including the Chinese Communist Party, refused to participate, the *People's Daily* and the editorial department of *Red Flag* criticizing the Moscow meeting as a serious step that publicly split the international communist movement. In March 1966, the Chinese Communist Party refused Moscow's invitation to participate in the Twenty-Third National Congress of the Soviet Communist Party. China and the Soviet Union had become adversaries.

China's struggle against superpower hegemony culminated in simultaneous hostility toward the Soviet Union and the United States. What most concerned Chinese leaders now was the possibility that the two superpowers would conspire to start a war against China. On March 19, 1965, Mao put a question to some foreign friends: "Would it be possible that they could resort to annihilating us by war? We are prepared for this. We are also prepared should the Soviet Union and the United States cooperate, and India, Japan, the Philippines, South Korea, and Chiang Kai-shek go with them."

On September 29, Chen Yi held a press conference to signal China's determination to resist superpower aggression. A series of commentaries and new slogans appeared in Chinese newspapers and magazines. A January 5 *People's Daily* editorial had put forward the slogan of "world revolution" and the task of three "againsts," calling on the people to "resolutely fight against imperialism, counterrevolutionaries in all countries, and modern revisionism headed by the United States" and to "make more and greater contributions to the noble cause of world revolution, human progress, and world peace." In September, the article "Long Live the Victory of the People's War," published under the name of Lin Biao, put forward the question of "the path for world revolution." The article held that "today's world revolution" aimed to besiege "the world cities" in North America and Western Europe through "the world country" in Asia, Africa, and Latin America. On November 11, a joint *People's Daily* and *Red Flag* editorial argued that the main feature of the "current world situation is that the world is undergoing great upheaval, great division, and great reorganization as international class struggle is increasing. The world people's revolution movement is developing vigorously, while imperialist and all the other counterrevolutionary and decadent forces are desperately putting up their death-bed struggle. Different political forces in the world are experiencing radical division and reorganization."

Chinese leaders issued these statements in reaction to external threats in order to deter aggression. They also hoped to enhance the confidence, courage, and determination of the Chinese people against imperialism, revisionism, and counterrevolution. Viewed from another angle, however, these slogans were put forward because of the growth of radical ideology at home and an incorrect assessment of the international situation. They reflected the willingness of the Chinese leadership to encourage the peoples of Asia, Africa, and Latin America to use the Chinese experience of revolution in their respective struggles and thus shape a new world revolution.

With the beginning of the Cultural Revolution in 1966, promoting "world revolution" became the principal objective of Chinese diplomacy, and proletarian internationalism became its guiding principle. The Eleventh Plenary Session of the Eighth Central Committee, held in August 1966, proclaimed that the international situation is "at present in a new age of world revolution" and that "imperialism is heading for total collapse, while socialism is heading for victory throughout the whole world." The session criticized the leadership of the Soviet Communist Party for conspiring with imperialism and counterrevolutionaries, led by the United States, to form a "new holy alliance against China."[32] In his Message of Congratulations to the Fifth Congress of the Albanian Party of Labor on October 26, Mao asked that "All Marxist-Leninists of the whole world unite to overthrow imperialism, modern revisionism, and counterrevolutionaries. A world without imperialism, capitalism, and exploitation must be established."[33]

Chinese diplomacy was caught up in the chaos of the Cultural Revolution, when political, economic, cultural, and other links between China and the outside world were almost completely shattered. The summer of 1967, when Beijing lost control over diplomatic policy completely, was the nadir, leading Mao to instruct Zhou Enlai to check extremist radical activities and reestablish control. Eventually, the disorder in Chinese foreign policymaking began to ease.

During the period from 1958 to 1967, confrontation between China and other countries worsened. The initial cause was strong pressure from the

Soviet Union to bring China under its foreign policy control. At the same time, American escalation of the war in Vietnam moved China and the United States to the edge of hostilities. China overreacted to these trends, so that a vicious circle of external pressure and Chinese reaction developed.

Under Mao Zedong's leadership, Chinese officials made grave errors in judgment. They overestimated the possibility of U.S.-Soviet cooperation on China and underestimated U.S.-Soviet conflict; they overestimated the possibility of war and revolution and underestimated the possibility of peace and development. These errors exacerbated the contemporary radicalism of Chinese diplomacy and weakened the underlying Five Principles of Peaceful Coexistence. The creed that "revolution could not be exported" was no longer followed, although aid to other countries was beyond China's means. The slogan "down with imperialism, revisionism, and counterrevolutionaries" undermined a united international front as China's foreign policy came to reflect the development of a "left tendency" in its own domestic politics rather than developments in international politics.

However, despite serious deviations and errors in China's foreign policy during this period, the struggle of Chinese leaders to safeguard national sovereignty and territorial integrity should be also recognized. Although they might have avoided escalated Sino-Soviet tension, there is no reason to believe that they could have eliminated conflict, nor is there any reason to assume that reconciliation between China and the United States could have been achieved any earlier, since a realistic opportunity never presented itself. Moreover, its simultaneous confrontation with both superpowers enabled China to develop an independent position during the Cold War, perhaps the greatest diplomatic achievement of those years. At the same time, despite continuing Sino-American hostility, Chinese leaders acted cautiously to avoid direct military confrontation with the United States.

Developing New Strategic Options (1968–1970)

Between 1968 and 1970, international politics entered a period of adjustment. A series of factors contributed to changes in the bipolar structure of the U.S.-Soviet relationship and an emerging shift toward multipolarity. Neither the United States nor the Soviet Union now had sufficient strength to dominate the world as they had during the earlier Cold War period. These years also marked the first time that China, no longer acceding to being a passive object of changing superpower relations, took an active part in strategic global readjustments.

Of the two superpowers, the United States was the first to recognize the need to rethink foreign policy. Washington faced no greater foreign policy dilemma than the Vietnam War, a prolonged conflict that had incurred heavy financial and human losses and produced a profound social and political crisis. Upon taking office in early 1969, President Richard M. Nixon initiated a radical readjustment in American foreign policy to offset Washington's strategic retrenchment. Meanwhile, taking advantage of America's preoccupation with the Vietnam War to expand its own military strength, the Soviet Union went on the offensive, trying to compete with the United States in strategic regions around the globe. At the same time, Chinese leaders were also reevaluating PRC foreign policy. Cultural Revolution diplomacy had isolated China from both the Soviet Union and the United States and undermined its relations with many other countries. After restoring domestic order, Mao turned his attention to China's strategic situation.

Trilateral relations among China, the United States, and the Soviet Union underwent fundamental changes between the late 1950s and the late 1960s. From China's perspective, the Soviet Union had replaced the United States as the greatest threat to Chinese security. When Leonid Brezhnev took over the Soviet Communist Party in 1964, the Soviet Union began deploying significant military reinforcements along the Sino-Soviet border. In early 1966, Moscow signed a Treaty of Friendship and Mutual Assistance with Mongolia, putting additional pressure on China. The situation along the border deteriorated further during the course of the Cultural Revolution. In early 1968, Sino-Soviet conflict developed in the area of Qilixin Island, on the Chinese side of the main channel of the Ussuri River. This encounter was the prelude to large-scale armed conflict along the Sino-Soviet border. As Sino-Soviet border tension intensified, the Soviet Union invaded Czechoslovakia, heightening Chinese apprehension. Chinese leaders considered the Soviet action "the most brazen and typical demonstration of power politics," which revealed that the Soviet leadership had assumed the mantle of the Czarist Empire, pursuing social-imperialist aggression against China.

Then, in March 1969, Chinese and Soviet troops engaged in a large-scale armed encounter on Zhenbao Island. Soon border conflict spread to other areas as tension increased along the entire length of the border. During the next few months, the Soviet Union sent over twenty diplomatic delegations

to the countries and regions surrounding China seeking support from
Southeast Asian countries for establishing an "Asian Collective Security
System." In the latter half of the year, the Western press reported rumors of
Soviet plans to strike at China's nuclear weapons base.

Washington's inability to defeat the Vietnamese insurgency, meanwhile,
demonstrated that the United States had no intention of challenging
Chinese security interests. As the United States prepared to withdraw from
Vietnam and focus its resources on the growing Soviet threat to its security,
the U.S. threat to China faded. The United States also recognized the strategic significance for Chinese security of the Sino-Soviet conflict and of
China's growing independence in international politics. These changes
presented China and the United States with new diplomatic imperatives and
an opportunity to renew Sino-American relations.

Even during the chaos of the Cultural Revolution, Mao had followed
America's international situation. After reading an article by Richard Nixon,
entitled "Asia after Vietnam," in the October 1967 issue of *Foreign Affairs*,
he thought it possible that the United States could shift its China policy.
Nixon, who was preparing for the U.S. presidential election, had written,
"Taking the long view, we simply cannot afford to leave China forever out-
side the family of nations, . . . There is no place on this small planet for a bil-
lion of its potentially most able people to live in angry isolation." Mao asked
Zhou Enlai and other Chinese leaders to read Nixon's article.[34] On November 25, less than three weeks after Nixon won the 1968 presidential election,
China's chargé d'affaires to Poland sent a letter to the U.S. ambassador to
Poland suggesting a meeting of Sino-American ambassadorial-level talks on
February 20, 1969. Nixon responded in his January 20, 1969, inaugural address, declaring, "We seek an open world . . . in which no people, great or
small, will live in angry isolation." Mao not only read Nixon's address himself but instructed that it was "Approved for distribution. Nixon's address
should be published." Thus, through the *People's Daily* commentary "A Desperate Confession—On Nixon's Inaugural Address and the Shameless
Praise of the Soviet Revisionist Renegades Group," Nixon's subtle message
reached a large audience in China.[35]

Nonetheless, relations between the United States and China did not
improve immediately. On February 19, China canceled the Sino-American
ambassadorial-level meeting because a diplomat in the Chinese embassy in

Holland had defected and was taken to the United States by the Central Intelligence Agency. The Vietnam War continued to expand. During the first quarter of 1969, U.S. troops in Vietnam increased from 500,000 to 543,000, a number close to the ceiling set by the Johnson administration. U.S. planes and naval vessels frequently intruded into China's territorial waters and airspace, eliciting harsh Chinese warnings. Official statements on both sides remained hostile. After the Ninth National Party Congress in April, PRC commentary continued to criticize the anti-China U.S.-Soviet conspiracy.

But behind the polemics, Chinese and American leaders were prepared to improve relations. In December 1968, Chen Yi submitted a report on the international situation. Although he was no longer engaged in diplomatic activities and had "stepped back," he followed the international situation closely and remained concerned about Chinese national security. The most significant aspect of his report was its statement, "The global strategy of American imperialism is still to take North and South America as its rear base, to tightly hold Western Europe, and to make use of the Soviet revisionists and Eastern Europe against China (but never giving up subversive activities in the Soviet Union and some other countries), and to quench fires in Asia, Africa, and Latin America. It is wrong to assume that American imperialism is making a strategic shift to the East and that it will give up or downplay Europe simply because it invaded Vietnam." Chen also said that it was wrong to assume that there was no conflict between the Soviet Union and the United States, and that American imperialism would give up the attempt to subvert the Soviet Union and Eastern Europe because the United States shared with the Soviet Union its conflict with China.[36] Chen's view was obviously different from the views expressed in Chinese newspapers and government documents, which overemphasized unremitting hostility toward China on the part of both the Soviet Union and the United States.

On February 19, 1969, Mao asked Chen Yi to take charge of a study of the international strategic situation. Seeing this as an opportunity, Zhou Enlai ordered Chen to invite Ye Jianying, Nie Rongzhen, and Xu Xiangqian to discuss the international situation several days later, on February 23. He said that they should not be bound by any popular views on international politics and that they should help him grasp the strategic situation. Because they were esteemed Chinese marshals with strategic insight, he also instructed that they submit proposals to the central leadership.

Premier Zhou was frustrated by Chinese propaganda and internal reports. Hoping to end China's diplomatic isolation and create a new strategic situation, he invited his old comrades-in-arms to reassess the international situation and, in a domestic environment in which "ten thousand horses are all muted," to present some fresh opinions. Zhou also directed other related departments to make further studies of U.S. policy trends in order to determine Washington's strategic objectives and to identify opportunities for establishing contact with the United States.[37]

From March 1 to October 18, the four marshals held 25 seminars on the international situation and submitted four reports (March 18, March 28, July 11, and September 17) to the central leadership, which put forth three major conclusions. First, they concluded that "for American imperialism and Soviet revisionism, the real threat lies between themselves," that the United States and the Soviet Union were "diametrically opposed to each other and both intend to scramble for the possessions of the other side. The real conflict of interest lies between themselves. Their struggle is frequent and intense." Therefore, "it is highly unlikely that American imperialism and Soviet revisionism will launch a large-scale war of aggression against China, either separately or jointly." Second, the marshals argued that the United States and the Soviet Union still took Europe as their strategic priority, but "American imperialism . . . regards China as a 'potential threat,'" while "the Soviet Union treats China as its leading enemy, so it is a greater threat to China's security than American imperialism." Third, they concluded that within the trilateral relationship," the United States tries to take advantage of the contradictions between China and the Soviet Union, and the Soviet Union tries to take advantage of the contradictions between China and the United States. So we should intentionally take advantage of the contradictions between the United States and the Soviet Union."

Referring to a passage from the historical novel *Romance of the Three Kingdoms*, Ye Jianying commented, "When the three kingdoms of Wei, Shu, and Wu during ancient times were engaged in a tripartite confrontation, the strategic principle pursued by Zhuge Liang of Shu, to 'ally with Wu in the east and resist Wei in the north,' can serve as a reference."

So that China could gain a favorable position in the triangular struggle, in mid-September the four marshals proposed to the central leadership that Beijing choose an opportune time to accept the American offer to resume the Sino-American ambassadorial-level talks, a "tactical action [that] may achieve strategic success." Chen Yi told Zhou Enlai that after resuming the ambassadorial-level meetings, China should take the initiative and suggest holding a Sino-American meeting at or above the level of ministers to solve fundamental bilateral problems. China should not set preconditions or demand that the United States accept Chinese positions. Merely holding a U.S.-China summit would be a strategic action. American imperialism could benefit, but China would gain an even greater benefit. Chen Yi observed that this would be an "unconventional" initiative, but to the United States, it might be a welcome one.[38]

In short, the marshals' strategic report proposed reducing Sino-American conflict by making use of U.S.-Soviet conflict, striving to open up Sino-American relations in order to unite against the Soviet threat. It took far-sightedness and extreme courage to make these proposals when the Cultural Revolution was still in full swing and the Indochina war was still escalating. No one knew what Chairman Mao was thinking when he read these reports—it was said that he did not utter a single word—but he had asked the four marshals to restudy this issue, which showed his willingness to hear original ideas. As subsequent developments revealed, the marshals' reports to Mao and Zhou served as a basis for important decisions on opening up Sino-American relations.

In the latter half of 1969, the trilateral relationship among China, the Soviet Union, and the United States entered a highly complicated and subtle stage. China and the United States were developing new strategic concepts, but neither was prepared to take dramatic steps. Meanwhile, U.S.-Soviet competition remained at a high level. Moscow and Washington held negotiations over a strategic arms control agreement and European security issues but failed to reach any agreement. Moscow was apprehensive that the United States might upset the U.S.-Soviet strategic balance by taking advantage of the Sino-Soviet conflict to improve relations with China.

On September 11, 1969, Zhou Enlai met with Soviet Premier Aleksei Kosygin at the Beijing airport. Mao and Zhou believed that the meeting would help to ease tension along the Sino-Soviet border and that China should use it to restore relatively normal border relations with the Soviet Union and to make moderate use of the U.S.-Soviet controversy.[39] The meeting resulted in an understanding between the two countries: Moscow and Beijing agreed to take temporary measures to halt border hostilities, to maintain the status quo along the border, and to resume negotiations over the border issue.

When they resumed talks with the Soviet Union, Chinese leaders explicitly put this new round into a trilateral framework. The Central Committee of the Chinese Communist Party believed that both the upcoming late October boundary negotiations between China and the Soviet Union and the early November U.S.-Soviet arms control talks would be protracted. Both the United States and the Soviet Union would try to gain the advantage and exert pressure on the other over the issue of China. Even as it engaged in Sino-Soviet boundary negotiations, the Soviet Union agreed to hold arms control talks with the United States and publicized its "progress" in the negotiations in an attempt to upstage the United States and gain bargaining chips. But the Soviet willingness to talk to the United States was also designed to put pressure on China.

Given these triangular dynamics, Mao Zedong and Zhou Enlai cautioned Chinese negotiators to be vigilant and "keep a card up their sleeve" from the very beginning of the new round of Sino-Soviet boundary negotiations. Moreover, at Zhou Enlai's suggestion, and with Mao Zedong's approval, the Central Committee decided to determine the right timing for restoring the talks in Warsaw. By making use of contradictory U.S. and Soviet positions, China would have a better knowledge of U.S. intentions on rapprochement and gain leverage over the Soviet Union during the boundary negotiations.[40]

Following the meeting between the Chinese and Soviet leaders and the resumption of Sino-Soviet boundary negotiations, the Nixon administration stepped up its revamping of its China policy, and Beijing responded positively. On January 20 and February 10, 1970, China and the United States held sessions of the Warsaw talks. This time, however, the dialogue was different from the previous 134 ambassadorial talks. After months of mutual signaling, Beijing and Washington now revealed their readiness to improve relations. On the Taiwan issue, the United States said that it welcomed "a peaceful settlement" worked out and agreed to by Chinese on both sides of the Taiwan Strait. China adopted an equally flexible attitude, declaring that it no longer adhered to a "wholesale" approach to Sino-American relations and dropping its demand that a resolution of the Taiwan issue precede any discussion of other issues. Representatives of both sides expressed a desire to improve bilateral relations on the basis of the Five Principles of Peaceful Coexistence and an interest in holding talks at a higher level, including a visit to Beijing by an American special envoy. The U.S. representative also assured China that the United States would not cooperate with Soviet efforts to weaken China or support Soviet use of the Brezhnev doctrine against China.

After the United States supported the coup d'état against Prince Norodom Sihanouk of Cambodia in the spring of 1970 and subsequently invaded Cambodia in May, China canceled the 137th meeting of the Sino-American ambassadorial-level talks scheduled for May 20, 1970. On that day, Mao Zedong issued a statement strongly condemning U.S. aggression and calling on "people all over the world to unite and defeat the American aggressors and all their running dogs." Only after U.S. forces had pulled out of Cambodia and Washington had signaled its interest in restoring the rapprochement process, did the negotiations recommence.

On July 10, 1970, Nixon endorsed diplomatic recognition of China. Soon, the Chinese side also made an unusual gesture: Zhou arranged for Mao Zedong to meet with Edgar Snow at the Tiananmen rostrum on October 1, China's National Day, signaling Mao's personal support for rapprochement and his personal involvement in the negotiations. On December 18, in his study in Zhongnanhai, Mao Zedong asked Snow to convey a message to Washington: "If Nixon comes to Beijing, I'm ready to talk with him. It's all right if the talks succeed, and if they fail, it's all right, too."[41] Before Snow had an opportunity to convey the message, China and the United States had established clandestine communications via the "Pakistani" and "Romanian" channels, and the pace of rapprochement quickened.

The Thirty-First World Table Tennis Championship in Nagoya, Japan, in March and April 1971 offered an unexpected opportunity for a breakthrough. Glenn Cowan, an American player, mentioned that he would like to participate in the International Friendship Invitation Tournament to be held in Beijing after the Nagoya tournament. Although the Ministry of Foreign Affairs proposed that China not offer an invitation, on the last day of the World Championship Mao Zedong made an extraordinary decision: to invite the U.S. table tennis team to join the other four national teams competing in Nagoya for a visit to China, and to use the people-to-people exchanges between China and the United States as a prelude to official bilateral relations. He suggested that China roll the "small ball" of Ping-Pong to move the "big ball" of the Earth. Shortly thereafter, Premier Zhou received a note from President Nixon about the final details of Kissinger's secret visit to Beijing.

In the context of these dramatic developments, the Politburo held extensive discussions on China's negotiating position for the forthcoming secret meeting in Beijing. It made an in-depth assessment of possible scenarios and developed various approaches and responses so that Chinese diplomats would be prepared for the negotiations as they unfolded. In the process, it established eight principles to guide its dealings with the United States, in particular, over the issue of Taiwan and Indochina:

1. A deadline should be set for all U.S. armed forces and military installations to be withdrawn from Taiwan and the Taiwan Strait area. This was the key issue in restoring Sino-American relations. If this could not be agreed upon in principle beforehand, Nixon's visit might be postponed.

2. Taiwan was Chinese territory. Liberating Taiwan was China's internal affair, and it would not tolerate outside interference. China had to guard judiciously against Japanese militarism in Taiwan.

3. China would try its best to liberate Taiwan by peaceful means and do a conscientious job in dealing with Taiwan.

4. China strongly opposed efforts to create "two Chinas" and "one China, one Taiwan." If the United States wanted to establish diplomatic relations with China, it must recognize the People's Republic of China as the sole legitimate government representing China.

5. Unless the . . . three principles [in points 1, 2, and 4 above] were fully realized, China would conclude that it would be premature to establish diplomatic relations but that a liaison office could be set up in both capitals.

6. China would not initiate the discussion of membership in the United Nations. If the U.S. side did so, China could explicitly state its total rejection of the "two Chinas" or "one China, one Taiwan" arrangement.

7. China would not initiate the discussion of Sino-American trade. If the United States did so, China might agree to negotiate, but only after a complete U.S. troop withdrawal from Taiwan was confirmed.

8. The Chinese government maintains that U.S. armed forces should withdraw from Indochina, Korea, Japan, and Southeast Asia to ensure peace in the Far East.[42]

Aside from reaffirming China's consistent position on these issues, these eight principles embodied three noticeable changes from China's previous policies. First, while demanding that U.S. troops withdraw from Taiwan,

China no longer insisted that the United States sever diplomatic relations with Taiwan as a precondition for exchanges between the Chinese and U.S. governments; second, while continuing to stress that liberating Taiwan was China's internal affair, China now also stressed its interest in resolving the Taiwan issue through peaceful means; third, China considered the idea of establishing liaison offices in both capitals. These three changes reflected China's commitment to improving Sino-American relations and its willingness to adopt a flexible and constructive negotiating position.

On May 29, the Politburo completed a report based on the May 26 discussions and forwarded the report to Chairman Mao for his approval. In order to adapt the whole Party to such a monumental change in China's U.S. policy as quickly as possible, on December 18, 1970, the Central Committee transmitted "the minutes of the talk between Mao Zedong and American friend Snow" down to Party branches at the grassroots level. In addition, from June 4 to June 14, the Central Committee convened a national working conference, attended by various competent government agencies, which held a thorough discussion of Sino-American relations and explained the significance of improving them.

Mao approved Zhou Enlai's response to Nixon's earlier note, which stated that Chairman Mao Zedong would welcome a visit to China by President Richard Nixon and that Premier Zhou Enlai would welcome Dr. Henry Kissinger to China for a secret preliminary talk to make necessary arrangements in preparation for President Nixon's visit.[43] A historic breakthrough in Sino-American relations was imminent, one that would change not only their bilateral relationship but, more important, global politics.

For twenty years following the establishment of the People's Republic of China, the key factor in the long confrontation between China and the United States had been each country's concern about its respective national security interests. Yet at the end of the 1960s, national security interests became the major incentive for the United States and China to strive for rapprochement. Likewise, although the impact of ideological differences and contrasting social systems on international politics cannot be overlooked, during the Cold War similar Chinese and Soviet ideologies and social systems failed to prevent Sino-Soviet conflict, and during the Cultural Revolution, when China struggled "against imperialism and revisionism," differences in ideology and social systems did not prevent China and the United States from developing cooperative relations.

But as China's Cold War diplomacy also reveals, foreign policy is not the mechanistic outcome of strategic circumstances. China's dual-adversary policy, its self-imposed global isolation, and its dire strategic situation in 1969 did not reflect policy imperatives imposed by strategic circumstances or by superpower policies. Rather, they reflected foreign policy decisions amid a wide range of other choices. Mao Zedong preferred one set of policy options; in 1962, Wang Jiaxiang proposed alternative policy choices.

The importance of leadership and prudent policymaking during the Cold War underscores their even greater importance for the post–Cold War era. In the aftermath of the Cold War, when strategic imperatives have been reduced and the range of policy choices has expanded, cautious leadership and responsible policy must play an even greater role to support national interests and ensure that ideology and domestic politics do not lead to costly policy errors.

CHAPTER THREE

Over the Volcano

The United States and the Taiwan Strait Crisis,

1954–1955

Ronald W. Pruessen

GENEVA, JULY 1955. In the midst of a summit conference that seemed to augur well for a relaxation of Cold War tensions in Europe, participants regularly cast troubled eyes toward the still explosive potential of Asian conflicts. Discussing ongoing problems over Jinmen (Quemoy), Mazu (Matsu), and other islands in the Taiwan Strait in particular, U.S. Secretary of State John Foster Dulles told Anthony Eden that "we might be said to be living over a volcano."[1]

Eden—and much of the world—would have known exactly what Dulles meant. By the time of the Geneva summit, Washington, Taipei, and Beijing, for close to a year, had been openly and dramatically jousting over control of dozens of small islands stretching out along some four hundred miles of the China coastline. Most of the islands were contained in three clusters: Dachen was the northernmost, Mazu and White Dog part of a central cluster, and Jinmen the largest of the southernmost group.[2] In 1954, all were still controlled by Chiang Kai-shek, in spite of the fact that his Nationalist government's bastion was at least one hundred miles from any of them. Chiang had been eager to retain the offshore islands as jumping-off points for a return to the mainland—and as useful bases for harassment and intelligence gathering in the interim. Many Washington leaders in the later Truman and early Eisenhower years had been dubious about the real value of the tiny outposts, but a general sense of Chiang's value to the United States had led to tolerance toward his continuing military buildup on these islands. During the more frustrating moments of the Korean War, in fact, there had even been American encouragement—and aid—for raids and other operations that diverted some Chinese Communist resources.[3] When provocative acts continued, even in the aftermath of the 1954 Geneva Conference, Beijing moved to correct at least some of the leftover anomalies of the civil war. Shelling of Jinmen, just four miles distant from the mainland and actually within the confines of Amoy harbor, began on September 3, 1954.

Over the following nine months, Washington tried to rally allies behind diplomatic efforts to keep the offshore islands out of Communist hands— and rattled nuclear sabers to emphasize that diplomacy was only a first alternative. From his capital in Taipei, Chiang ordered wide-ranging bombing operations against his old adversaries and regularly promised an imminent invasion of the mainland. Beijing, for its part, alternated pregnant diplomatic pauses with military operations of its own. Although none of these actions had induced a full-scale eruption of the volcano by mid-1955, there had been any number of moments in which sparks and smoke had provoked fear that it might. Nor was there any reason to believe that the volcano would remain indefinitely quiescent. Indeed, a furious eruption again threatened in 1958.[4]

By themselves, the dramatic tensions of the 1954–55 Jinmen-Mazu crisis make for an interesting story. More important, however, the patterns of behavior evident in that story offer important insights into the evolving overall relationship between the United States and the People's Republic of China by highlighting the dire and dangerous pass to which the two nations had come and the long road they would have to travel before more normal interaction would be possible.

The focus here will be on American policies during the 1954–55 Taiwan Strait crisis, with primary attention to two fundamental components: the perceptions of Washington leaders and the policies that emerged from those perceptions. In both cases, there are nuances and complexities that merit attention beyond those evident in the existing literature. With respect to Washington's perceptions of Beijing, for example, a catalog of standard "Cold War" components should be expanded to include the United States' appreciation of the ways in which the PRC's behavior was that of a traditional and ambitious nation-state. The complexities of American policies, on the other hand, emerge primarily from the conflicted impulses of high-level leaders. What initially meets the eye when White House or State Department behavior is examined is a genuine desire to deal with an unwelcome problem through moderate means, with an emphasis on the virtues of "deterrence" strategy as opposed to war. On closer examination, however, it becomes clear that American moderation was both fragile and limited. Eisenhower and Dulles, in particular, were never able to cease doing battle with the more aggressive voices around them, both in Washington itself and farther afield. In fact, the president and the secretary of state were never able to totally avoid their own personal attraction to behavior that was far from moderate.

One particular facet of the conflicted U.S. policies toward the offshore islands is especially revealing: the enormous variation in measurements of "moderation," if attention is paid to goals rather than methods. With respect to the latter, Eisenhower and Dulles maintained a reasonable measure of control, and self-control, although not nearly as definitively as some analysts would suggest. In determining the objectives of the United States in the Taiwan Strait, however, it is hard to see how Washington could have been much more ambitious. There was an extremism in American goals that is easily overlooked in discussions of specific strategies like "deterrence." This extremism regularly strained, and even threatened to obliterate, the moderation that initially figured in Washington's choice of methods for dealing with the offshore island problem.

If a measure of extremism is evident in U.S. policy goals, some attention should be paid to its sources, and here the story is more complex than might at first be imagined. There is a temptation, for example, to overemphasize "Cold War" atmospherics in explaining any strident or melodramatic aspects of American actions. Who would doubt the psychological relevance of a prolonged sense of crisis throughout the 1940s and 1950s—or of a sense of both ideological embattlement and crusading responsibility? Attention should also be paid to other sources, however, especially older ones. Traditional "Great Power" ambitions, in particular, can be seen at work in the Eisenhower administration's perceptions of Asia and its evolving policies toward the region.

Complex Perceptions

Any appreciation of the complexities of U.S. policies should begin at the most basic level: the perceptions that served as a foundation for the delineation of goals and the selection of strategic and tactical options. What did

Eisenhower and Dulles see when they looked at their counterparts in Beijing? What conclusions did they reach about the key characteristics and sources of PRC behavior?

Many might wonder whether there is any need to belabor the question of American perceptions during the Jinmen-Mazu crises. Did not Eisenhower and his associates link Beijing's behavior to an overall preoccupation with the proverbial "international communist conspiracy"? Did not Washington believe that the masterminds of the Kremlin were using their Chinese lackeys to foment trouble and sap the strength of the United States, and did they not see restraint of those lackeys as one more element in a grand "containment" policy?

Some signs of such Cold War clichés are certainly present. Dulles's earliest reactions to the emergence of the PRC, for example, were as crude as any heard at the time. "Mao Tse-tung is nothing but a puppet," he charged in 1951, and Beijing's critique of various Washington policies was "a parrot-like echo of what the Soviet Union has said." Building on a plan devised by Stalin some twenty-five years earlier, Dulles said, the Chinese Communists were being used as the "spearheads" of the "Soviet Communist policy of inciting peoples of South Asia and the Pacific to violent revolution."[5] Such descriptions imply, of course, that Moscow was the real nerve-center of Asian problems and crises, that, as Dean Acheson once put it, the Chinese were really only the "second team" in the area.

Early thoughts like these rematerialized in the mid-1950s. Dulles's first public pronouncement about PRC shelling of Jinmen, in early September 1954, decried the "danger that stems from international communism and its insatiable ambition."[6] During a National Security Council (NSC) session a few weeks later, discussion of the tense situation in the Taiwan Strait sent several other policymakers scurrying toward capacious old clichés. Eisenhower, for one, bemoaned the way "the Communists, by making faces and raising hell, can tie down U.S. forces." But he was determined not to let them get away with this, he said. "If we are to have general war he would prefer to have it with Russia, not China. Russia can help China fight us without getting involved itself, and he would 'want to go to the head of the snake.'"[7]

As Eisenhower administration records become increasingly available to scholars, however, it is clear that Cold War crudities were not nearly as pervasive as once thought. Behind closed doors, in particular, some American policymakers began to appreciate complexities and subtleties once assumed to have surfaced only in later decades. One striking example is revealed in the way Washington leaders privately discussed the so-called "Sino-Soviet split" long before it had become a common topic of public debate. Even prior to his tenure as secretary of state, Dulles was fascinated by the prospect of encouraging any inherent strains between Moscow and Beijing. "My own feeling," he wrote Chester Bowles in early 1952, "is that the best way to get a separation between the Soviet Union and Communist China is to keep pressure on Communist China and make its way difficult so long as it is in partnership with Soviet Russia. Tito did not break with Stalin because we were nice to Tito. . . . If China can win our favors while she is working closely with Moscow, then there is little reason for her to change."[8] By the end of 1953, Dulles believed he saw some signs of progress on this front. Having witnessed the cautious Soviet approach to Chinese dilemmas in the closing phase of the Korean conflict, among other things, he told Winston Churchill and Anthony Eden that "we were justified in believing that there was strain" and that it "may eventually give us an opportunity for promoting division between the Soviet Union and Communist China in our own common interest."[9] From his vantage point in Moscow, Ambassador Charles Bohlen expressed similar thoughts: "The Soviet Union is being very careful in its relationship with China," he had concluded by February 1954. "I would say that the Russians are attempting to exercise a restraining influence on the Chinese based on their fear of being involved in serious difficulties through Chinese action in Southeast Asia or elsewhere."[10] As excellent studies by David Allan Mayers, Gordon Chang, and others have now shown, Dulles and his colleagues devoted much thought to pursuing this "opportunity" during the next several years.[11]

Deliberations throughout the first offshore islands crisis certainly rvevealed a constant appreciation of the intricacies of Sino-Soviet relations. By mid-1955, in particular, Eisenhower and Dulles believed that important changes were under way in Moscow and that a real possibility existed for the beginning of détente and at least a de facto end to the Cold War in Europe.[12] No such prospect seemed to beckon in Asia, however, because the leaders of the still youthful Chinese Communist regime were seen as more determinedly revolutionary than their Soviet counterparts. In an early 1956 meeting with the secretaries of Defense and the Treasury, for example, Dulles commented on Moscow's apparent commitment to "policies of nonviolence." In contrast, "as regards Communist China," he argued, "he felt the risk was greater than from Soviet Russia and that we could not assume that fighting might not break out in any one of three danger spots—Taiwan, Vietnam, or Korea."[13] Under these circumstances, Eisenhower and Dulles almost invariably assumed—in private, at least—that Moscow was actually worried about the dangerous potential of Beijing's behavior in the Taiwan Strait. They concluded, in fact, perhaps picking up on Bohlen's earlier thoughts, that the Soviets might actually help with efforts to moderate Chinese behavior.[14] During a meeting in Vienna, in May 1955, Dulles told Vyacheslav Molotov that "he hoped the Soviets would exercise restraint" on Beijing and asked for ideas on what "could be done towards a peaceful solution." The same subject came up for discussion at the Geneva summit conference two months later. There, as Dulles put it to the Senate Foreign Relations Committee, he asked Molotov to do what he could to induce caution in his Chinese "buddies."[15]

There is a reverse side to this coin of Sino-Soviet contrast and conflict, one that has received less scholarly attention but which is of special importance for understanding the long-term nature of U.S.-PRC relations: implicit in the desire to play on, and even exacerbate, the tensions between Moscow and Beijing was a clear U.S. perception of the PRC as an independent actor in Asian or international affairs. The very sentence structure of a 1953 "NSC Staff Study of U.S. Policy toward Communist China" suggests that this cognitive tilt is already developing: "The elements of the problem to which the U.S. must address itself are: (a) the present and prospective capabilities—political, economic, and military—of Communist China; (b) present and prospective Chinese Communist intentions toward non-Communist Asia and the West; (c) the nature and prospects of the Sino-Soviet connection."[16]

Realization that the Chinese Communists were playing an independent role in the Jinmen-Mazu crisis and in other situations served as a foundation for further speculation about the nature of that role. If Beijing was not simply acting as catspaw for some global conspiracy, then why was it acting as it was? This was a question Washington policymakers also spent a good deal of time discussing, and their answers provide another glimpse of the sometimes surprisingly sophisticated analysis of the 1950s.

John Foster Dulles and other senior figures in the Eisenhower administration repeatedly returned to a basic conclusion: the People's Republic of China was an ambitious and dynamic state determined to become the predominant power in Asia. They believed, in fact, that the very birth of the PRC had triggered a regional earthquake. As one NSC statement put it in 1953, "The emergence of a strong, disciplined, and revolutionary communist regime on mainland China has radically altered the power structure in the Far East. With the minor exceptions of Hong Kong and Macao, American, Japanese, and European power and influence has [have] been abruptly extruded from the whole vast area between the Amur, the Himalayas and the Gulf of Tonkin."[17] Aftershocks were compounded by what was seen as Beijing's determination to add more and more power to its mainland base. There was early agreement that the "long-range objective" of the PRC was "the elimination of Western power and influence from the area and the extension of its own."[18] Dramatic entanglements in Korea and Indochina were interpreted very much in this context. As Dulles put it to Molotov during the February 1954 Berlin foreign ministers' conference, Beijing was "running amuck, recklessly seeking to show off its strength and extend its power," threatening to produce "by one step after another . . . a chain of events which would have a result none of us wanted."[19]

If Beijing was indeed thrusting outward, why was it doing so? The answers offered by Eisenhower, Dulles, and others were not as unimpressive as the old clichés might suggest. What is particularly striking in the deliberations of the middle and late 1950s is that U.S. leaders were intellectually capable of separating melodramatic "Cold War" presumptions from a more traditional, realpolitik analysis. A secret NSC policy statement approved in November 1953, for example, offers a telling contrast to simplistic public rhetoric. Most noteworthy is its sensitivity to the multiple motives of Chinese Communist leaders, since it places significant emphasis on the "nationalist" view, as well as on the ideological drives in Beijing. An annexed study pointedly concludes that "the Chinese Communist leaders are Chinese as well as Communists." A detailed survey of intentions regarding neighboring states and more distant parts of the region incorporates discussion of a variety of economic, military, and political interests, as well as a "psychology of fear" resulting from "traditional Chinese suspicion and fear of the outside world." There is even a striking declaration of the fact that "many of these specific foreign policy objectives of the Peiping regime . . . would be shared by any strong, independent, nationalistic Chinese government."[20] An extended portion of this study deserves inclusion here since its item-by-item analysis demonstrates a capacity for reasoned calculation not always associated with 1950s foreign policymaking. It is especially noteworthy that "Cold War" and ideological factors occupy a relatively minor position in the "framework of foreign policy objectives" attributed to Beijing:

a. For both security and prestige reasons, Peiping is anxious to restore Chinese sovereignty over all historically Chinese areas with the possible exception of Outer Mongolia. This aim was largely accomplished with the conquest of the Chinese mainland, including Tibet, and with the establishment of at least a temporary modus vivendi on the Sino-Soviet Asian frontier which recognized Chinese sovereignty in these areas. However, Taiwan remains in the hands of the U.S.-supported National Government; Hong Kong remains British; Macao remains Portuguese; and the naval base of Port Arthur remains under Soviet military control. Ultimately, the Chinese Communists will hope to regain full sovereignty over all those areas. . . .

b. Beyond the historically Chinese areas, Peiping apparently feels it has preeminent security interests in certain border areas, particularly North Korea, North Burma, and Northern Vietnam. Peiping would presumably go to considerable lengths to prevent the establishment of strong Western military forces in these areas. . . .

c. In Southeast Asia, Peiping's interest is two-fold. Like any Chinese government, it is interested in cultivating the sizeable Chinese minorities, whose status reflects on China's prestige and who are a useful source of trade and foreign exchange, as well as potential instruments for present and future Communist operations in these areas. As a leader of Asian communism, Peiping is interested in expanding its influence among Southeast Asian Communist movements and in providing these with aid and guidance.

d. In Northeast Asia, Peiping's interest is to insure the safety and potential for future expansion of the North Korean regime and to attempt to neutralize the threat of Japan.[21]

This kind of analysis of Chinese Communist behavior, already taking shape in 1953 and early 1954, provided the backdrop to many deliberations over the Jinmen-Mazu problem. Tension in the Taiwan Strait became just one more example of what Washington interpreted as Beijing's aggressive grand strategy. A National Intelligence Estimate circulated in November 1954, for example, prefaced its discussion of pressing offshore island matters by reminding policymakers of important basics—most of which had no inherent or exclusive connection to notions of "communist" expansion per se: "We believe that Communist China seeks: primarily to carry out rapid industrialization of its economy and modernization of its military establishment and, for this purpose, to obtain greater Soviet assistance; to increase

Chinese Communist influence over Communist movements in Asia; to gain an acknowledged position as a world power and as the leader of Asia; to gain control of Taiwan."[22]

Complex Policies

The perceptions and analytical skills of the Eisenhower administration were more complex and sophisticated than conventional wisdom would suggest. Does this mean that resulting U.S. policies toward the PRC and the "offshore islands" controversy were more nuanced and impressive than once imagined? Yes—and no.

On the one hand, it is possible to say that Eisenhower and Dulles used an orderly and essentially efficient decision-making process in deliberations on the Taiwan Strait crises and that they also sincerely hoped to use moderate tools, rather than large-scale military engagement, to achieve U.S. objectives. On the other hand, however, a close examination of month-to-month developments makes it clear that there were important countervailing tendencies in both process and policies. The president and the secretary of state regularly experienced difficulties in controlling the more extreme voices around them, in Washington and elsewhere. Perhaps more important, they also demonstrated an increasing tendency to succumb to the more aggressive impulses inherent in their own ways of thinking.

Previous assessments of the Eisenhower years have suggested that a rather lazy, golf-playing grandfather was perched precariously atop an anarchic administration, that the general did not always know, or particularly care, what his lieutenants were doing. In the area of foreign policy, for example, it was often assumed that John Foster Dulles was really in charge. More recently, a small flood of articles and books has effectively demonstrated that Eisenhower could be a potent "hands on" president. Behind the scenes, it is now argued, he carefully monitored a well-oiled machine and diligently checked the behavior of subordinates who knew they were subordinates. Secretary of State Dulles is now said to have been carefully deferential toward the president yet still subject to an occasional tug on the reins that clearly tied him to the White House.[23]

Administration records during the 1954–55 Jinmen-Mazu crisis certainly suggest that Eisenhower presided over a carefully constructed and orderly foreign policy-making process. One example of its essential efficiency can be drawn from the early weeks of the crisis. This was a difficult period for the administration's policy-making system, which still proved capable of moving along effectively. Not only was Eisenhower himself away in early September, on vacation in Colorado, but so too were those senior cabinet members likely to be most concerned with the sparks flying in the Taiwan Strait. Secretary of State Dulles was in Manila, about to begin the conference that would produce the Southeast Asia Treaty Organization (SEATO). Secretary of Defense Charles Wilson was following his boss's example and taking a short breather from the capital summer.

Nonetheless, in Washington the machinery of analysis and decisionmaking immediately moved into gear. The acting secretaries at State and Defense kept both their immediate superiors and the president informed about breaking developments and oversaw early deliberations within their respective departments. The Joint Chiefs of Staff (JCS) began meeting on the first day of PRC shelling, and overnight the Central Intelligence Agency (CIA) produced a "Special National Intelligence Estimate" about the offshore islands.[24] These separate gears quickly began to mesh as Defense, State, and JCS leaders consulted together on September 7,[25] and the CIA carried on its usual coordinating role within the group known as the Intelligence Advisory Committee (IAC), weaving together the collective wisdom of intelligence analysts from almost every interested department.[26]

The shift to interagency efforts was designed to be the middle stage of an inherently hierarchical process. Preparatory work within individual compartments formed the base of a policy-making pyramid, while joint ad hoc consultation was a step closer to policy formalization. Further up the pyramid were the more de jure collective deliberations of the National Security Council and, at the pinnacle, the president's own decisions. The upper levels were reached fairly quickly in September 1954, as was usually the case with serious problems. A preliminary skeleton meeting of the NSC was held on September 9 and a full complement, including the just-returned secretary of state, gathered around Eisenhower in Denver three days later. Although such a hierarchical structure was not always rigidly in place in the Eisenhower years, it was usually more than a theoretical schema, and it was explicitly recognized as operational as the Taiwan Strait crisis unfolded. As early as September 7, the minutes of a meeting between State and Pentagon representatives record that "there was general discussion of pros and cons of U.S. participation leading to the agreed opinion that the decision is one for the President with the benefit of a meeting of the NSC on this subject."[27]

The structure and control evident in the deliberative aspects of the decision-making process had their counterparts in actual policies. In the offshore islands controversies, two substantive attributes deserve to be acknowledged, although their problematic nature also deserves recognition: Eisenhower and Dulles genuinely desired to avoid extreme measures in dealing with the crises and were willing and able to maintain tactical flexibility when tensions proved extended and obstreperous.

The moderate impulses in the words and policy preferences of both the president and the secretary of state are often striking. In private discussions especially, time and again each emphasized his determination to avoid war with Beijing. As early as September 1954, Eisenhower was saying "he did not believe that we could put the proposition of going to war over with the American people at this time. The West Coast might agree, but his letters from the farm areas elsewhere constantly say don't send our boys to war." Dulles certainly did agree. Because war "would probably lead to our initiating the use of atomic weapons," he said, disastrous consequences were likely to flow: "Outside [Syngman] Rhee and Chiang," he told the NSC, "the rest of the world would condemn us, as well as a substantial part of the U.S. people."[28]

Such anxiety about the dangers of war continued. On a later occasion, for example, Dulles reconfirmed his determination to avoid "getting sucked into" a war over the offshore islands: "public opinion throughout the free world would be against the United States if we went to war with Communist China over these offshore islands. The effect in Japan would be extremely bad. In short, if one paid any attention to the repercussions outside the immediate area concerned, it was plain that the price we would have to pay to defend the islands was too high. The Chinese Communists would win the sympathy of all our allies, and there would be devastating repercussions both in Europe and in Japan." World opinion aside, he argued at another point that holdings like Jinmen were too insignificant to justify costly exertions. He could not accept Chiang Kai-shek's contention that their loss would cripple Nationalist dreams of "returning to the mainland," for instance, because "after all, they did not have very much real hope of realizing such an objective" in the first place. Nor would any loss of "morale" be "fatal" to the protection of Taiwan itself. The "true defense" of the Nationalist bastion ultimately depended on "the deterrent power represented by the massive retaliatory capacity of the United States," and here the retention of a

Jinmen had no actual relevance.[29] Eisenhower could be even more terse in his protestations. "All the pressure was on the side of peace, peace, peace," he said at one point. "By and large," he believed, "it was better to accept some loss of face in the world than to go to general war in the defense of these small islands."[30]

In the atmosphere of the mid-1950s, however, avoiding extreme measures was no easy matter. It required, as Dulles put it, "difficult and delicate" operations.[31] The president and the secretary of state were surrounded, at least in part, by groups and individuals who were pressing for more aggressive responses to PRC actions, and holding reasonably steady in the face of such pressures demanded arduous efforts. Republican Party fire-breathers like California Senator William Knowland steadily swiped at any Eisenhower administration inclination toward moderation. Even worse were the harangues and maneuvers of Chiang Kai-shek and other Nationalists. Taipei's frequent independent military operations were particularly troublesome. Eisenhower and Dulles regularly complained about each of these sources of discomfort. Knowland, Eisenhower once quipped, "has no foreign policy except to develop high blood pressure whenever he mentions the words 'Red China.'"[32] Looking across the Pacific in the fall of 1954, the secretary of state described Jinmen as "a powder keg" and explicitly bemoaned the fact that "Chiang . . . was in a position to start a conflict which could develop into world war three." The problems caused by Nationalist behavior, the president later agreed, showed "the difficulty of trying to carry out U.S. policy when we were in the hands of 'a fellow who hasn't anything to lose.'"[33]

Although it was not easy to deal with extremists at home and abroad, neither the president nor the secretary of state believed it impossible. Dulles and his assistants spent an enormous number of hours on the diplomacy of Capitol Hill–State Department relations, for example, and often managed to secure a genuine measure of cooperation from Republicans and Democrats alike.[34] And although he found the task unpalatable, Eisenhower was sometimes prepared to be personally tough with congressional leaders. During one November 1954 session at the White House, the president told Senator Knowland that his advocacy of a "blockade" of "Red China" was just too "risky." "That is a step toward war; if you do that, then the next question is, are you ready to attack? Well, I am not ready to attack."[35] Even the stubborn and wily Chiang Kai-shek could be "managed"—to a degree. Perhaps the single most important example was Washington's use of a U.S.-Taiwan defense treaty to limit Nationalist aggression. Negotiated in the middle of the 1954–55 crisis, the treaty was seen as a way to simultaneously support and control Chiang. In words sometimes used to describe the value of NATO with relation to the potential power of Germany, a military alliance could become a tool for containing danger through an embrace. As Dulles put it throughout the negotiations with Taipei, the United States was interested in nothing beyond "a purely defensive treaty": "We are not going to defend our partner while our partner attacks." And as he reported to Eisenhower when the agreement was initialed, "the result . . . stakes out unqualifiedly our interest in Formosa and the Pescadores and does so on a basis which will not enable the Chinese Nationalists to involve us in a war with Communist China."[36]

If the attempt to restrain Taipei is one example of moderation during the Jinmen-Mazu crises, equally important was the strong belief of both Eisenhower and Dulles that deterrence rather than grand-scale military action would be the best way to restrain Beijing. Over and over again, implicitly and explicitly, they supported policies that signaled U.S. power and confirmed U.S. determination as a way to dissuade the PRC from risking war. This crisis clearly demonstrated the deterrence logic at the heart of "brinkmanship."

From the first days of the crisis, the Eisenhower administration hoped to persuade Beijing to tame its aggressive campaign by using two tools: first, by involving the United Nations (U.N.) in Taiwan Strait issues, and second, by encouraging Chinese Communist fears about the nature of a U.S. response. These comprised what Dulles called a "two-pronged operation."[37] Eisenhower and Dulles regarded the U.N. as a weapon in their arsenal of available policy options, and in the 1954–55 offshore islands crisis, the secretary of state almost immediately suggested a move in this direction. His initial thought was to obtain a Security Council "injunction to maintain the status quo" in the Taiwan Strait by invoking U.N. Charter language authorizing steps to nip "incipient aggression" in the bud.[38] In the months ahead, other possibilities were contemplated, ranging from an outright U.N. condemnation of the PRC's behavior to enlisting the aid of Secretary General Dag Hammarskjöld as a mediator. In all circumstances, the use of what Dulles called "the U.N. expedient" was intended to supplement the traditional and unilateral power of the United States with the psychological and political prestige of the international organization in the hope that expressions of world opinion—or at least a substantial portion of world opinion—would have a valuable restraining effect on the PRC.[39]

Not that anyone assumed international pressure alone would suffice. If Beijing's leaders were to be effectively deterred, Eisenhower and Dulles both firmly believed, the direct application of U.S. power would certainly be required. This was especially evident in the earlier months of the crisis, when the administration displayed an ambiguity about U.S. policies as a way to intimidate Beijing. As Vice President Richard Nixon phrased it during an NSC meeting, "We should play poker in order to keep the Communists guessing."[40] In practice, however, this translated into a purposeful vagueness about whether Washington was actually committed to defense of the offshore islands. Neither Eisenhower nor Dulles really wanted to undertake definite ongoing responsibilities for positions that might be no more than "a bunch of rocks," as the secretary of state once described Mazu.[41] On the other hand, a more precise expression of the limits of U.S. determination would only serve as a green light to the PRC and gravely affect Nationalist morale. If Beijing's policymakers were kept in the dark about U.S. intentions, the reasoning went, they might fear the worst and limit their assault, resulting in deterrence of the Chinese Communists without an actual expansion of U.S. commitments. Dulles had exactly this game plan in mind when negotiating the U.S.-Taiwan defense treaty. In spite of Chiang's desire to rope Washington into formal obligations toward the offshore islands, Dulles set out to "fuzz up" the treaty language as far as geographical particulars were concerned. Any "U.S. action specified," he explained to the NSC, "would not be specifically limited to an attack on Formosa and the Pescadores, but would leave open to U.S. determination whether or not to construe an attack on the offshore islands as an attack on Formosa itself." "Fuzzy language" would "maintain doubt in the minds of the Communists as to how the U.S. would react to an attack" and in the process perhaps decrease the very possibility.[42]

As the offshore islands crisis continued, Eisenhower and Dulles occasionally considered making a more precise U.S. commitment— biting off formal new responsibilities in order to make deterrence more effective. In January 1955, for example, Dulles thought new PRC moves against Dachen might require correspondingly new U.S. steps. Clarifying U.S. determination over Jinmen and Mazu—via a congressional resolution—might have "a stabilizing effect" by persuading Beijing "that we have reached the point that we are not going to retreat more." As Dulles put it to congressional leaders during a White House meeting: "One of the dangers leading to war comes from miscalculation. A country that has gained one objective after another becomes too ambitious, goes too far and war is the result. That could result here if we don't quickly make out what we are prepared to do. Up to the present time we have been covering this situation by hoping the communists will be deterred by uncertainty. They are probing and will continue to probe to find where we will stop them. Our position has deteriorated and this step must be taken."[43]

In this situation, in fact, Washington ultimately decided to adhere to public imprecision as the preferable alternative. In the end, common sense seemed to dictate caution about making too great a show of a U.S. commitment to dangerous locations. With memories of Dienbienphu in mind, Eisenhower and Dulles decided that "it would be best not to nail the flag to the mast by a detailed statement respecting our plans and intentions on evacuating or holding certain of these islands."[44] Aside from the potential value of this approach in terms of the permanence of U.S. obligations along the coastline of the PRC, it was assumed that strictly private assurances to Chiang would make it easier to deal with leaders in allied countries such as Great Britain, where serious doubts existed about the course of American policy in this area.

As for concern about the nature of the signals being communicated to Beijing, Washington remained confident in the effectiveness of the indirect approach. As far as Eisenhower and Dulles were concerned, it was enough for the United States to act on rather than against its antagonist in this situation. In the end, the assumption seems to have been that awesome American power would force Beijing to pay the kind of attention it needed to pay and that this would yield the desired shifts in Chinese behavior. "The Chinese Communists didn't want to 'get tough with us in a big way' at this time," the secretary of state told his NSC colleagues. Why? Because, as he explained in a speech to the Foreign Policy Association in February 1955, both Beijing and Moscow respected the "immense destructive power" of the U.S. nuclear arsenal. The possible unleashing of such power spurred anxiety, to be sure, "but the very fact that it is frightening means that even the most reckless will pause before taking action which would bring modern weapons into play. During these days the Soviet and Chinese Communists are probing deeply the intentions of the free nations. But we need not feel worried or despondent, for what the despots will discover from their probing ought to restrain them."[45]

One other at least partially related element of Washington's moderate approach to the offshore islands crisis deserves attention: the openness to using diplomatic concessions as a way of coaxing Beijing's cooperation and compliance. Although this proved a very thin thread in the overall fabric of U.S. policy, that it existed at all is noteworthy.

What is involved is some interest, particularly on Dulles's part, in what was referred to even in the 1950s as a "two Chinas" policy. When the secretary of state sought to enlist London's assistance in mobilizing an initial U.N. maneuver (an injunction to preserve the status quo in the Taiwan Strait), he highlighted the wide-ranging benefits of defusing explosive tensions. The Security Council's assistance, Dulles argued, might allow the beginning of "a far reaching negotiation which might lead to some solution of the present chaotic F[ar] E[astern] position." Although political and morale problems would prevent too hasty a movement, such negotiations might even lead to "territ[orial] adjustments" involving Jinmen and other Nationalist bases.[46] Dulles repeatedly emphasized the need to move slowly because of the political sensitivity of the issues in the United States and Taiwan, but he also repeatedly pointed to the way even small initial steps could prove to be a "mustard seed" over time. In one later conversation with Eden, for example, he emphasized how an expanded U.N. role could encourage "a general pacification" in Asia. There was "an opportunity of separating Formosa and the Pescadores from the mainland," he suggested, and all sorts of benefits might flow if this were achieved. An "early relaxation of the China embargo" was certainly one possibility: "in the course of time," there might even be an American "acceptance of two Chinas, both of which might be members of the United Nations Assembly."[47]

Methods and Goals

Eisenhower, Dulles, and other U.S. leaders of the 1950s regularly prided themselves on their ability to shape controlled and moderate foreign policies. Dulles's notorious 1956 interview in *Life* magazine, whose statement of the concept of "brinkmanship," aroused controversy, is a case in point. "You have to take chances for peace," he said, but you must also know how to maintain balance on the edge of the abyss. "Some say we were brought to the verge of war" in Korea, Indochina, and the Taiwan Strait: "Of course we were brought to the verge of war. The ability to get to the verge without getting into war is the necessary art."[48]

Dulles's self-confident bravado, which would certainly have been endorsed by the president, at least in private, has prompted varying reactions during the years since the 1950s.[49] Both then and now, some have seen a penchant for "going to the brink" as one of the clearest examples of a capacity for dangerous excess during the Eisenhower years, while others have emphasized the importance of the president's ultimately steady hand. Robert Divine, in particular, has actually used the offshore islands crises as key examples of brilliantly nuanced presidential leadership: "Eisenhower not only determined American policy throughout the crisis, but carried it out to a successful conclusion. He took Dulles's concept of massive retaliation and refined it. . . . When the crisis became most serious, he used a measured nuclear threat to warn the Chinese without insulting them or provoking them. The beauty of Eisenhower's policy is that to this day no one can be sure whether or not he would have responded militarily to an invasion of the offshore islands. . . . It is a tribute to his leadership that he was able, as he finally allowed himself to boast in his memoirs, to thread his way 'with watchfulness and determination, through narrow and dangerous waters between appeasement and global war.'"[50]

Fuller access to the archival records of the 1950s suggests the appropriateness of a substantial measure of skepticism about both Eisenhower's and Dulles's actual level of control. As a counterpart to the current discussion, it is useful to consider two limitations: first, the neat routines of Eisenhower's hierarchical policy-making system did not always translate into thorough control from the top of the pyramid, and second, the calm moderation in resulting policies often proved fragile or deceptive.

A closer examination of the United States' deliberative decisionmaking process reveals several loopholes or weak links. One is its tolerance for Chiang Kai-shek's sometimes devious unilateralism. What is involved here goes beyond the difficulties inherent in restraining an ally or client whose behavior was almost invariably more rapidly aggressive than Washington desired. In and of itself, it was a serious complication for Eisenhower and Dulles, and their conceptualization of a mutual defense treaty as an inhibiting tool makes it clear that they were aware of the problem. Yet they regularly gave Chiang a measure of latitude that could only have limited their own control capabilities.

The United States, for example, made a crucial last-minute concession during treaty negotiations. Taipei began insisting that the need for "joint agreement" on offensive operations would not apply to Nationalist interceptions
of "enemy shipping" and the so-called "port closure policy" against Amoy
and other communist centers. Initially, U.S. representatives argued that this
caveat would be impossible to accept: "this Government does not want to be
in a position of having no control over offensive action against Communist
shipping which would provoke retaliation and lead to war." But Dulles
decided to go along. On November 23, the day the new treaty was actually
initialed, he agreed that "the circumstances under which shipping might be
interfered with were so varied it was not possible to cover all cases by a blan-
ket agreement." In spite of long-term problems in this area, he contented
himself with a verbal reference to an essentially vague alternative procedure:
"If interception activities seemed likely to provoke retaliation, the U.S. Government would expect joint consultation."[51]

Another weak link in Eisenhower's decision-making structure was closer
to home: the president could not rely on the full cooperation of his military
subordinates. Admiral Arthur Radford, chair of the Joint Chiefs of Staff,
seems to have engaged in maverick behavior regularly during the offshore
islands crisis, with a measure of assistance from other Navy personnel in the
Pacific. Even during the first week of the crisis, Radford was not averse to
single-handedly nudging the policy process in directions not yet authorized
by putting his own particular spin on an endorsed maneuver. After the State
Department agreed to guarantee a steady flow of supplies to Chiang, for
example, the admiral tacked his own rather leading injunction onto the
action cable sent to the Commander in Chief of U.S. forces in the Pacific
(CINCPAC): "It is expected that ChiNats will utilize military equipment
which we have furnished in an effective and aggressive manner in connection
with operations in defense of Quemoy."[52] The admiral also winked at confidential Pentagon reports of American activities in the Taiwan Strait, some
of which clearly went beyond the bounds that Eisenhower and others
seemed to be taking for granted. For example, although a decision had been
made on September 4 to evacuate U.S. personnel from Jinmen immediately,
Radford did not bother to secure presidential approval for delayed implementation. On September 8, six officers and four enlisted men were still
there, and a whole new "ground observer team" was to arrive the next day.
The Military Assistance Advisory Group (MAAG) in Taipei was also

"coordinating ChiNat proposed naval and air actions to include reconnaissance" and offering "tng [training] and logistical assistance to meet emergency."[53] Such local initiatives, unreported to Eisenhower, put Americans very close to the thick of things—and to danger.

Hints that the military was following its own agenda continued to emerge as the first offshore islands crisis unfolded. While Dulles was attempting to line up support for a U.N. role, any number of U.S. leaders were eager to restrain Chiang, who displayed a penchant for large-scale retaliatory assaults against the mainland coast. As early as September 13, 1954, Ambassador Karl Rankin had urged a "tapering off" of "Nationalist attacks" in response to a lull in Communist shelling, suggesting that "this is a matter which conceivably could represent the difference between a continuation of the present situation and the involvement of our country in open war with Red China."[54] Rankin believed Taipei was being urged on by American military leaders, and he was almost surely right. Admiral Felix Stump (CINCPAC) did make a formal request to MAAG in Taipei to try to prevent "a prolonged continuation" of "aggressive" Nationalist measures.[55] But as Chiang's forces kept flying and firing, military leaders declined to make more emphatic moves. In fact, when a concerned State Department officer queried the Pentagon on September 22, he was told that "CINCPAC advice is being adhered to" by Chiang. At an NSC meeting two days later, Admiral Radford shunted aside the suggestion that the renewal of Communist bombing "was the direct result of continuing Chinese Nationalist military action." He too insisted that Chiang "had generally followed the advice we had given."[56]

Were Eisenhower and Dulles simply careless in these areas of the foreign policy-making process? Did their apparent tolerance for Chiang's aggressive moves or their inattention to the near insubordination of Radford and others reflect the difficulties of supervising a global power's vast operations, in which some details would inevitably fall between the cracks? Perhaps. It is also possible, however, that an inclination on the part of allies and colleagues to turn a blind eye to certain actions was the result of their own limited devotion to moderation. Both Eisenhower and Dulles showed signs of more forceful and demanding impulses even before the offshore islands crises actually began, and these signs increased as tensions persisted.

In the summer of 1954, for example, extensive deliberations about NSC 5429, "Current U.S. Policy in the Far East," took place in Washington. In retrospect, it is hard to see how the dramatic and wide-ranging initiatives called for in this game plan could be made to fit within a framework of genuine U.S. moderation. NSC 5429 begins by identifying Beijing as the key source of America's serious challenges in Asia, although it also includes a nod toward the PRC's "close working relations with the Soviet Union." A survey of the troubled state of affairs in every country from India to Japan precedes a prodigious catalog of "courses of action." The initial emphasis is on straightforward military measures, and a specific reaffirmation of the American commitment to defend, among other locations, "the Pacific offshore island chain" and South Korea. The expanding relevance of collective security arrangements is also obvious: existing ties with Australia and New Zealand (ANZU.S.) were now to be supplemented with a Southeast Asia Treaty Organization and a mutual security treaty with the Republic of China; on the horizon, it was hoped, was a "Western Pacific collective defense arrangement including the Philippines, Japan, the Republic of China and the Republic of Korea, eventually linked with the Manila Pact and ANZU.S."

But traditional military measures were only part of the story. Efforts to counter "subversion" in many places, including Indonesia, were to be expanded. This could involve "effective information, cultural, education and exchange programs" or "psychological activities" or "all feasible covert means." In addition, expansive economic campaigns would also be mounted, some broadly conceived ("an economic grouping by the maximum number of free Asian states, including Japan and as many of the Colombo Powers as possible"), some more precisely focused (efforts to encourage economic growth in India and Southeast Asia and to ease the flow of private capital). Finally, there were to be aggressive moves "to weaken or retard the growth of the power and influence of the Asian Communist regimes." Here the focus was twofold; on the one hand, the United States would continue to refuse to recognize the PRC or allow it a seat in the U.N.; on the other, the United States would use overt and covert means to "create discontent and internal divisions within each of the Communist-dominated areas of the Far East, and to impair their relations with the Soviet Union and each other, particularly by stimulating Sino-Soviet estrangement."[57]

The final version of NSC 5429, it is worth noting, was approved only in December 1954, midway through the first offshore islands crisis. By itself, this would indicate the way in which more ambitious and aggressive impulses could serve as a counterpoint to the self-conscious Eisenhower-Dulles preference for a moderate course. Increasingly, in fact, their cooler inclinations seemed to weaken as frustrating situations remained unresolved. The option of deterrence, as opposed to war, received continued emphasis, but the kind of U.S. pressure thought necessary to restrain what was seen as a particularly obstreperous Beijing was steadily intensified. By February 1955, to cite only the most dramatic example of escalating deterrence calculations, Eisenhower and others had clearly begun to flirt with the possible use of nuclear weapons.

Through the fall of 1954, the president and his key advisers had been inclined to emphasize the utility of essentially political pressures on Beijing. Mobilizing U.N. support for freezing the status quo in the Taiwan Strait had seemed one promising route, especially in tandem with the negotiation of a mutual defense pact designed to restrain the Nationalists. But Beijing chose not to be as fully deterred as Washington desired at just this point. In late November, a group of U.S. soldiers captured during the Korean War were tried and sentenced for espionage, a move that set blood boiling in the American media and Congress and within the Eisenhower administration. To make matters worse, in January, Beijing began a new military operation designed to seize control of Dachen, the northernmost of the offshore islands and the least tenable of the Nationalist outposts. Both the president and the secretary of state were actually somewhat relieved to see them go, but the contretemps hardly suggested that U.S. policies to date had succeeded in taming the PRC's more aggressive impulses.

Under these circumstances, Eisenhower and Dulles clearly started to move in a more extreme direction. They persuaded Congress to approve a blank check "Formosa Resolution" that gave advance authorization for whatever military measures the president would deem appropriate. At least in part, the president and the secretary of state saw this kind of congressional declaration as another demonstration to Beijing of U.S. determination—one more turn of the deterrence screw. It is also clear, however, that they were growing more alarmed about PRC actions and more open to serious speculation about crossing the line between political and military pressure. Dulles conducted a tour of Asian trouble spots in late February and early March, and returned to Washington in a somewhat harried state of mind. As he put it to the NSC, "the question of a fight for Formosa [was] . . . a question of time rather than a question of fact." What he had seen in

Indochina, Thailand, and elsewhere had persuaded him that "Communist probing will go on, and there will perhaps be no definite answer until the United States decides to 'shoot off a gun' in the area." And what a gun he had in mind. Although he thought "general war" would probably not be necessary, he did advocate careful preparation of public opinion for "the tactical use of atomic weapons." As he reported at a meeting of the NSC, "Conversations he had with our military people in the area . . . had pretty well convinced him that atomic weapons were the only effective weapons which the United States could use against a variety of mainland targets, particularly against Chinese Communist airfields which they would use to attack Formosa, against key railroad lines, and gun emplacements. Accordingly, Secretary Dulles thought that very shortly now the Administration would have to face up to the question of whether its military program was or was not in fact designed to permit the use of atomic weapons. We might wake up one day and discover that we were inhibited in the use of these weapons by a negative public opinion."[58]

Nor, as the 1954–55 Taiwan Strait crisis continued, was Dulles the only high-level policymaker in danger of losing control of his temper. Eisenhower likewise, for all his traditional reputation as a mellow, golfing grandfather and for all his revised reputation as a cool and masterly chief executive, also revealed flashes of impulsive pugnaciousness. As early as August 1954, a month before the initial shelling of Jinmen, the president was speculating that a Communist fleet of junks "might make a good target for an atomic bomb."[59] During the fall NSC meetings, he indulged in freewheeling, rather chilling speculations about how a conflict might proceed. On one occasion, he "speculated on the type of war we might have to undertake if the Chinese Communists did attack Formosa itself. It might so happen that they would concentrate their forces in such a way that the United States would be in a position to deliver a massive attack . . . with such effect that we could sit back for a couple of years without necessarily following up our blow."[60]

Comments like these help explain why Eisenhower found it quite easy to accept Dulles's advice about the need to publicly reemphasize the nuclear component of the "New Look." It was the president himself who grabbed headlines when he told a March 16, 1955, news conference that tactical nuclear weapons would surely be used in the event of a war in the Far East: "In any combat where these things can be used on strictly military targets and for strictly military purposes, I see no reason why they shouldn't be used just exactly as you would use a bullet or anything else."[61]

The moderate nature of U.S. policies toward the first offshore islands crisis becomes increasingly questionable if attention is shifted from methods to goals. With respect to methods, a case can at least be made for Eisenhower's and Dulles's moderate preferences, as opposed to their actual behavior over time. With respect to Washington's overall objectives, however, it is hard to imagine a seriously credible counterpart. Throughout the 1950s, in fact, the Eisenhower administration sought ends so extreme as to defy any notion of calm moderation. This lack of alignment between the goals the president and the secretary of state sought and the ends they wanted to use to achieve them generated steady bouts of discomfort and frustration. It also contributed more generally to the prolongation of serious U.S.-PRC tensions.

Clearly, Eisenhower and Dulles were unwaveringly committed to the "containment" of the PRC. In many discussions, this would not be seen as a token of extremity but as evidence of temperance. But measurements and definitions are crucial here. Just how did Eisenhower and Dulles envision the scope and scale of containment?

As the events and crises of the 1950s demonstrate, Washington consistently sought to create a regional Asia Pacific structure in which American advantages would be maximized while China's role and opportunities would be drastically curtailed. The Eisenhower (and Truman) administration's approach to Korea all through the 1950s reveals no sense of impropriety about deep involvement in territories along the very borders of the PRC. Dulles, for one, recognized as early as mid-1950 that Beijing was sharply sensitive about U.S. or even South Korean activity so close to Manchuria, but even several years of brutal battle did not lead him to consider more than minimal concessions in this respect. (By 1953, that is, he had told Syngman Rhee to give up hope of securing control of the very northernmost province of his divided country.) Dulles spoke of "neutralization" as a long-range possibility for Korea, but the term was essentially misleading, since it was defined as "a unified and neutral Korea under a substantially unchanged ROK [Republic of Korea]."[62]

The American response to developments in Indochina also demonstrates U.S. hopes in Asia. Despite the experience in Korea and the fact that more territory directly along the border of the PRC was involved, U.S. expectations were hardly modest. Regular resistance to the course of negotiations in

Geneva in mid-1954, an arm's length attitude toward the resulting accords, and intensifying unilateral relations with the Saigon regime, among other developments, make it clear that Washington was quite prepared to take over France's role as outside policeman in this sector of Southeast Asia.

The 1954–55 Taiwan Strait crisis offers important additional testimony to the sweep of U.S. intentions concerning the PRC. On the one hand, Washington's adamant position on retaining various offshore islands mirrors the insensitivity to Beijing's fears and desires first evident in 1949–50. On the other, it seems fair to say that in this case, insensitivity reached especially striking heights. North Korea's proximity to Manchuria is similar, but there is something almost uniquely provocative about the U.S. demand for ongoing control of an island situated within a major PRC harbor, which was precisely the relationship of Jinmen to Amoy. (As a *New Republic* editorial put it at the time, Jinmen "bears about the same relation to Communist Amoy as Staten Island to New York."[63]) At the same time, the islands in contention were indisputably Chinese territory. The British and other governments clearly recognized this fact and refused to give the United States the same support on this issue that they had during the preceding Korean and Indochina controversies. Washington's refusal to back away from Jinmen and Mazu, and its exclusive attachment to Chiang Kai-shek's regime in Taipei, thus amounted to a stubborn, ongoing form of meddling in a civil war that much of the rest of the world considered long over.

There is other evidence of an Eisenhower-Dulles propensity to avoid coming to terms with an end to the Chinese civil war. This is certainly one of the messages implicit in their adamant resistance to establishing normal diplomatic relations with the PRC while yet maintaining a hostile but still "routine" connection with Moscow. "It is one thing to recognize evil as a fact," Dulles said in early 1954: "It is another thing to take evil to one's breast and call it good."[64] But the secretary of state (like the president) was either unable or unwilling to imagine the existence of a point at which engagement could exist without implying admiration of Beijing. At the 1954 Geneva Conference, indeed, if stories of Dulles's refusal to shake hands with Zhou Enlai are true, it seems that America's breast was to be literally kept at arm's length from evil.

The impact and the implications of the United States' "nonrecognition" policy are also striking in the course of the offshore islands crises. During the extended 1954–55 confrontation, Eisenhower and Dulles placed Beijing outside their active diplomatic arena. For months on end, although the secretary of state invested enormous energy into his efforts to defuse tensions, these efforts always involved a process of acting on rather than with Beijing. Dulles ran a grueling triangular course that included difficult negotiations in Washington, London, and Taipei—when a four-cornered model, at the least, might have been more sensible.

All in all, if the Eisenhower administration was committed to a "containment" policy toward Beijing, it was a particularly stringent version of that policy. The established U.S. stance toward Moscow by and large accepted the existence of a Soviet sphere of influence in Eastern Europe, but with respect to the PRC, not even its harbor waters were considered inviolable by U.S. leaders.

Why were Eisenhower and Dulles committed to absolute containment? Why did they incorporate such an extreme into their Asian policy? As with other aspects of American behavior during the first offshore islands crisis, there are both familiar and less familiar explanations. On the one hand, for example, "Cold War" factors are obviously relevant. U.S. leaders demonstrated an obvious tendency to consider problems like these within the context of the great struggle between the "Free World" and "Communism"—what Admiral Radford referred to as "the big show."[65] At the beginning of the first crisis, Dulles publicly castigated the "insatiable appetite" of "international communism," while the president privately warned of the possible need to strike at "the head of the snake" in the Kremlin.[66]

Such perceptions shape policy goals in various ways. There is a potential psychological correlation, for example, a tendency for melodramatic images to generate melodramatic fears, and for extreme anxieties in turn to spawn extreme responses. But Cold War atmospherics could also have more pedestrian effects. McCarthyism fed off public preoccupations with the "international communist conspiracy" and then became a steady, countervailing force to the influence of more moderate inclinations. With respect to "Red China" issues, in particular, Eisenhower and Dulles were always sensitive to the way "Old Guard" Republican and "China Lobby" pressures could limit their freedom to maneuver. It would be "politically impossible" to quickly adopt a "two Chinas" policy for the U.N., Dulles told Anthony Eden at one point. This was a question "charged with emotionalism which would have domestic political repercussions."[67] For Eisenhower and Dulles, both the GOP right wing and the China Lobby could serve as convenient scapegoats in explaining policy stubbornness to allies uncomfortable with U.S. views, but the constraints of domestic political realities were never totally imaginary or irrelevant.

On the other hand, Cold War calculations and impulses tell only part of the story. Other factors were invariably involved. The aggressive nature of U.S. ambitions toward the PRC were significantly affected by what might be termed non–Cold War and pre–Cold War factors. One of the most striking examples is the 1950s and 1960s relevance of a deeply rooted American yearning for predominant power in the Asia Pacific region. Eisenhower and Dulles clearly reflected impulses that long preceded the beginning of the Cold War and the emergence of the PRC.

There is little question that Eisenhower and Dulles thought of Jinmen and Mazu in broad, regional terms. One need only recall the president's famous domino metaphor, first enunciated to describe the wide-ranging implications of the 1954 crisis in Indochina.[68] The same kind of logic figured in Dulles's comments on the fate of the offshore islands. In January 1955, in making a case for what became the "Formosa Resolution," he described Chinese Communist "probing" for the Senate Foreign Relations Committee: "I am absolutely convinced that if this probing does not lead to some clear and strong and united reaction on the part of our country . . . then they will press further and further, and then the situation will disintegrate. Then I think we will be faced with the clear alternative between . . . a general war with China . . . or an abandonment of the entire position in the western Pacific."[69]

Geographical particulars were often laid out even further. In one NSC discussion, Dulles said that if the Nationalists did not retain at least "the bare bones of Quemoy," the United States would "be faced with a very serious situation all the way from Tokyo to Saigon." And again, during a meeting with congressional leaders at the White House, he argued that Chiang Kai-shek's collapse in the face of Communist aggression "would so jeopardize our offshore defenses that it would really be a matter of time before we would be forced back to Hawaii or the West Coast."[70]

The geographical sweep of Eisenhower's and Dulles's concerns had its counterpart in the range of American interests that seemed at stake in the Asia Pacific region. In the middle of the Taiwan Strait crisis of 1954–55, for example, the president tried to explain the intensity of his anxiety to a skeptical Winston Churchill: "It is clear that our vital interests can be seriously damaged by operations that she [PRC] is capable of carrying out against the weaker territories lying along the boundaries of her territory. . . . Here I shall not outline the importance to the western world of Japan and the island chain extending on to the southward, as well as the bits of mainland on the Pacific that still remain in the possession of the free world. The moral, political and military consequences that could follow upon the loss of important parts of this great chain are obvious to both of us and to the staffs that work for us in the military, economic and diplomatic fields."[71]

It is precisely these multifaceted definitions of U.S. interests in the broad Asia Pacific region that focus attention on the importance of historical roots. Neither Eisenhower nor Dulles was, after all, the first American leader to be powerfully attracted in this fashion. Even in the nineteenth century, U.S. awareness of varied riches on the far side of the Pacific was evident. From the days of "jackal diplomacy" (when Americans scurried for advantage in the wake of the British lion's rampages of the 1840s) to the efforts to use the Hawaiian islands and the Philippines as steppingstones or "hitching posts" in the 1890s, there were those who wanted to make the United States a powerful force in the region.[72] As Theodore Roosevelt, a self-styled "expansionist," explained shortly before his White House years, "In the century that is opening, the commerce and command of the Pacific will be factors of incalculable moment in the world's history." The seat of the greatest empires "ever shifts from land to land, from sea to sea," he said, and steady westward movement would mean that the United States as a Pacific power would be able to follow in the footsteps of Rome and Britain. Many others, from missionaries to businessmen and philosophers, elaborated on the logic of Asian ambitions. The rhetoric was often ripe. Henry Adams, friend to many Washington leaders, wrote of the desirability of the Pacific becoming "like an inland sea": if the United States could dominate the Chinese market, in particular, it would become a "greater seat of wealth and power than ever was England, Rome, or Constantinople." The industrialist and banker Chauncey Depew fully agreed. American farmers and manufacturers could deal with an "emergency" of vast surplus production, he advised, by treating "the Pacific as an American lake."[73]

In the twentieth century, although the ability of the United States to breathe real life into earlier ruminations greatly increased, thanks to expanding American wealth and the shifting fortunes of other players, the logic behind the desire to expand power in the Asia Pacific region remained perfectly consistent. By 1935, for example, Secretary of State Cordell Hull was pointing to the exceptional promise of such expansion: "As our own population becomes more and more dense, as the struggle for existence in this country becomes more intense, as we feel increasingly the need of foreign markets, our definite concern for open markets will be more widely felt among our people and our desire for and insistence upon free opportunity to trade with and among the peoples of the Far East will be intensified. For in that region lie the great potential markets of the future."[74]

The tendency to tie Asian economic opportunities to high priority American needs only intensified in the later 1930s. During those years, Japan sought to build its own economic preserve in China and Southeast Asia. The ongoing economic depression in the United States and a sharpened sense of the integrated nature of the global economy produced a hostile reaction among Americans. In 1937, Commerce Secretary Daniel Roper insisted that the United States was not "prepared to abandon our share in the commerce of the Far East."[75] By 1940, a State Department memo argued that further Japanese success in building its "Greater East Asia Co-prosperity Sphere" would yield major problems by "our loss of Chinese, Indian and South Seas markets (and by our loss of much of the Japanese market for our goods, as Japan would become more and more self-sufficient) as well as by insurmountable restrictions upon our access to the rubber, tin, jute, and other vital materials of the Asian and Oceanic regions."[76]

Knowledge of its historical roots (and routes) suggests that the 1954–55 Taiwan Strait crisis should be viewed as a revealing moment in the Cold War and as an episode of relevance to the broader history of twentieth-century international relations. In both cases, important facets of U.S. foreign policy deserve more attention than they have received in previous analyses.

With respect to Cold War dynamics, for example, careful study of mid-1950s tensions over the offshore islands helps to illuminate the complexity of Eisenhower administration policymaking. At the most basic level, the president and some of his key advisers moved, if awkwardly and inconsistently, toward a more sophisticated reading of Asian developments than is often imagined: their perceptions reveal increasing awareness of the PRC as an independent and essentially traditional "Great Power." U.S. policies based on such perceptions were also more subtle and nuanced than was once believed. Eisenhower, for example, oversaw an orderly deliberative process and worked with key advisers like John Foster Dulles to maintain a substantial measure of control and moderation as the crisis gathered steam. Nevertheless, in a perfect demonstration of the layer-upon-layer complexity of mid-1950s policymaking, it is important to avoid overstating the attributes. The president and the secretary of state were sometimes more capable of congratulating themselves for moderation and control than of achieving it, particularly when it came to delineating the specifics of their "containment" approach toward Beijing.

Ironically, the extreme nature of Washington's desire for containment underscores the logic of placing the 1954–55 Taiwan Strait crisis within a broader historical context. U.S. intentions were clearly related to the pre–Cold War experiences of a "Great Power" whose ambitions in the Asia Pacific region had been gathering force for more than a century. Having surpassed the power of Great Britain and dealt with the independent clout of Japan, among other things, Americans were unwilling to calmly accept what American policymakers like Eisenhower and Dulles saw as the dangerous pretensions of an upstart such as the PRC. Under such circumstances, conflict was inevitable, and even a modicum of relaxation would come only after the scale of America's appetite in Asia was reduced by the tragedies of the 1960s.[77]

CHAPTER FOUR

"A Thorn in the Side of Peace"
The Eisenhower Administration and the 1958
Offshore Islands Crisis

Robert Accinelli

"HISTORY DOES NOT REPEAT ITSELF," Mark Twain once wrote, "but sometimes it does rhyme." The two confrontations between the United States and the People's Republic of China (PRC) during the 1950s over the Nationalist-held offshore islands bear out the truth of this observation. From the perspective of top American leaders at the time, the second crisis, from late August to late October 1958, while by no means simply a replay of the earlier contest from September 1954 to April 1955, echoed that initial encounter in significant respects. During both episodes, senior officials in the Republican administration of Dwight D. Eisenhower, led by the president and Secretary of State John Foster Dulles, determined that the United States could not remain indifferent to the Chinese Communist challenge in the Taiwan Strait, and they made preparations to intervene militarily, possibly with nuclear weapons, to protect the Nationalist government's coastal possessions if circumstances so required. At the same time, they tried to deter the Chinese and find a satisfactory peaceful exit from the crisis while coping with a difficult Nationalist ally and the troubling domestic and international repercussions of their actions.

The striking similarities between the two crises from the U.S. standpoint have not escaped scholarly notice. Yet recent studies of the Eisenhower administration's conduct during the second episode, in 1958, have failed to give close attention to a crucial dimension of American decision making common to both incidents, namely, the Taiwan factor.[1] As in 1954–55, so in 1958, American policymaking was shaped in fundamental ways by the perceived U.S. stake in Taiwan and the preservation of a viable and friendly Nationalist government as well as by the necessity not just to support but to constrain the exiled regime of Chiang Kai-shek. Eisenhower and Dulles, together with other high-level civilian and military officials, were convinced that the loss of Jinmen (Quemoy) or the other larger offshore islands to the Chinese Communists by the threat or use of force would have dire consequences for the Nationalist government and thus for the security of Taiwan and the noncommunist Far East. This was the dominant consideration behind the Eisenhower administration's decision to chance a military collision with the PRC over what were otherwise considered to be militarily insignificant and vulnerable parcels of territory along the south China coast. American leaders believed that the foremost goal of Mao Zedong and his comrades, when they attempted to put a military stranglehold on Jinmen in late August, was the eventual takeover of Taiwan and the ultimate undoing of the U.S. strategic position in the western Pacific. American officials resolved to assist the Nationalists in resupplying Jinmen and defending it if necessary with U.S. air and naval forces, while trying to induce the Communists to stop the fighting and keeping a rein on Nationalist military actions that might incite a larger conflict.

Sticking to this course as the crisis unfolded, Eisenhower and Dulles became increasingly worried about the mostly negative reaction of domestic and world, and especially allied, opinion to the apparent U.S. readiness to risk war over Jinmen. The president himself very much wanted to avert a brawl with China on Chiang Kai-shek's behalf, and he shrank from the prospect of having to use nuclear weapons to secure these offshore island bases. When the urgency of the Chinese threat to Jinmen faded, in late September, Eisenhower and Dulles publicly dissociated themselves from Chiang's extreme position toward his fringe possessions but without reversing the secret provisional U.S. commitment to the islands' defense. In October, as the Chinese allowed the crisis to wane, Dulles crafted a new approach to Chiang to put the Nationalist government on a firmer footing with

American and international opinion while fostering the conditions for the informal stabilization of the Taiwan Strait and a de facto two-China situation. In devising this approach, he sidetracked an ambitious proposal put forward by the president that included the removal of most, if not all, of the Nationalist forces from the islands. Following negotiations in Taipei in late October, Dulles and Chiang issued a joint communiqué, which won wide acclaim in the United States and abroad but represented only a modest advance toward the secretary of state's goals.

During the three-year period that separated the two offshore islands crises, the Eisenhower administration remained hostile to the PRC and persisted in its hard-line policy of military containment combined with diplomatic and economic ostracism. The United States was unyielding in its opposition to diplomatic recognition of the Beijing government and China's admission to the United Nations; in 1957, while Washington resigned itself to a relaxation of the harsh multilateral trade restrictions imposed on China during the Korean War, it retained its own strict economic embargo. That year the State Department foiled a Chinese invitation to American journalists to visit their country by refusing to extend reciprocal rights to Chinese correspondents. The Sino-American ambassadorial talks that had commenced in Geneva in August 1955 produced no enduring improvement in relations and soon bogged down in a sterile ritual that ended with an indefinite suspension in December.[2] Intelligence analysts consistently depicted a China that was mistrustful, antagonistic, and bent on the ultimate goal of a communist Asia, though unlikely to court a military conflict with the United States.[3]

The reverse side of this tough anti-PRC stance was the U.S. role as patron and protector of Chiang Kai-shek's stranded regime. In early October 1957, the National Security Council (NSC) put its seal on NSC 5723, "U.S. Policy toward Taiwan and the Government of the Republic of China," which replaced an existing policy statement approved in January 1955, during the first Sino-American confrontation over the offshore islands. In essential respects, the new policy paper faithfully followed the old: NSC 5723 reaffirmed the strategic value of Taiwan and the Penghus as vital links in the U.S. island security chain in the Far Pacific, the Taipei government's role as a "focal point of the free Chinese alternative to Communism," and the contribution of the Nationalist armed forces to the defense of Nationalist-controlled territory as well as to overall U.S. military strategy in East Asia.

The new policy document likewise mandated the continuation of a broad range of domestic and international support for America's Chinese ally.[4]

As was well understood in both Washington and Taipei, the security of Taiwan, together with the internal viability and international standing of the Nationalist government, was critically dependent on U.S. aid and backing. By the same token, the success of American objectives relating to Taiwan and China required that Chiang Kai-shek's regime remain politically stable and reasonably effective and cooperative. The United States and the Taiwan government were locked in a classic patron-client relationship, the one exercising its influence from a position of dominance, the other from a position of inferiority, yet each needing the other to sustain its own interests and objectives. The relationship between the two was close but sometimes tense; divergent perceptions and priorities gave rise to distrust and suspicion on both sides. In Eisenhower's view, Chiang was a valuable but troublesome ally who had to be handled gingerly and guardedly.[5]

In managing the uneasy relationship with the Generalissimo and his associates, the most vexing problem Eisenhower and his advisers faced was how to maintain the good will and viability of the marooned Nationalist government, while at the same time pursuing the stabilization of the Taiwan Strait and a de facto two-China situation in which both sides would restrain their mutually aggressive designs without renouncing their territorial claims. The first objective required that U.S. officials show sympathy for the preeminent Nationalist goal of mainland recovery, while the second demanded that, when necessary, they curb or discourage provocative policies and courses of action by Chiang and his loyalists toward their enemies across the Taiwan Strait. A persistent dilemma for American leaders was how to constrain the Nationalists and stabilize the Strait without calling into question the Chiang government's principal source of domestic legitimacy, its mainland aspirations.

The deliberations in the National Security Council preceding final approval of NSC 5723 touched on two sensitive matters directly connected to the psychological outlook and political stability of the Nationalist government: the mission of the Nationalist armed forces and the U.S. posture toward the offshore islands. During a discussion of the first question, Eisenhower and Dulles strongly endorsed preserving and supporting an offensive mission for the Nationalist armed forces in order to sustain the morale of Chiang Kai-shek and his displaced mainland followers. The secretary of

state bleakly predicted that if the Nationalists lost hope of a victorious return to their lost homeland, "the United States would lose the whole show
in the Far East. We simply could not afford to permit the Chinese Nationalists to think we believe that a Communist China was a permanent feature
of history."[6] Although NSC 5723 contained an unambiguous reassertion of
an offensive mission for Chiang's armed forces, it did not signify a readiness
to underwrite his bellicose liberationist schemes. The document stipulated
that the development of the Nationalist military establishment's offensive
capability "should be directed primarily toward, and limited by, what is
deemed necessary to maintain the position and morale of the GRC [Gov-
ernment of the Republic of China]." American officials were instructed to
show "friendship for the GRC and the Chinese people, while avoiding any
implication of an obligation to guarantee the former's return to power on the
mainland."[7] Eisenhower and Dulles harbored no illusions that Chiang's
prospects for recovering his lost territory were bright. Intelligence analysts
found no evidence of unrest on the mainland that might endanger Communist control.[8] Still, the president and his chief foreign policy adviser held it as
an article of faith that authoritarian regimes were inherently unstable, and
they allowed for a possible future upheaval in Chiang's former domain that
might serve his revanchist goal. "What happened in Hungary and Poland
could conceivably happen in Communist China," Dulles told the NSC.
If there was a blow-up on the mainland, Nationalist troops might find the
opportunity for which they had been waiting.[9]

   During the 1954–55 crisis, Dulles had attempted to steer Chiang away
from a strategy of counterattack and toward a more patient, less belligerent
strategy of opportunism that hinged on a major uprising against Communist
rule.[10] Although the Nationalist supremo refused to budge on his strategy,
in the aftermath of the crisis he did put greater emphasis on fomenting and
exploiting unrest on the mainland to lay the groundwork for direct military
intervention. He and his subordinates importuned U.S. officials for a more
proactive attitude toward ending Communist domination across the Taiwan
Strait.[11] During a visit to Taipei by Under Secretary of State Christian
Herter and special State Department envoy James P. Richards in September 1957,
the Generalissimo called their attention to the decline in morale on Taiwan because of dimming expectations for a return to the mainland and submitted a proposal to train and equip 13,000 parachutists as the initial phase of an
ambitious plan to intensify guerrilla activities behind Communist lines.

Washington subsequently agreed to train and equip a regiment in parachute jumping and guerrilla warfare but refused to adopt the strategic concept behind the Nationalist leader's grandiose plan. The State Department also informed Chiang, much to his chagrin, that any employment of these special forces was subject to the restrictive understanding in the exchange of notes that had accompanied the signing of the U.S.-Taiwan mutual security treaty in December 1954.[12] That understanding gave Washington a virtual veto over all Nationalist military action other than that carried out in emergency self-defense, and it served as a highly useful diplomatic instrument in keeping Chiang's armed forces in check, thereby promoting stabilization in the Taiwan Strait.

Following approval of NSC 5723, the Eisenhower administration provided the Nationalist armed forces with only a modest offensive capability, as it had in the past, while defining their mission as primarily defensive.[13] Still peddling a strategy of patient opportunism, Dulles counseled Chiang, during a brief sojourn in Taipei in March 1958, that it was "within the realm of possibility" that events such as those that had shaken the Communist regimes in Poland and Hungary might occur in mainland China but that he should not "throw away such an opportunity through premature action based more on hope than on realism."[14] At this time, the United States apparently frowned on, and even withheld its covert support for, Nationalist infiltration of the mainland. In April, Everett Drumwright, the newly appointed U.S. ambassador in Taipei, reported to the State Department that to the best of his embassy's knowledge, the Nationalists did not have any mainland guerrilla bases and had stopped trying to organize resistance in early 1955. "I gather that the United States retired from practically all activity in this field," the ambassador noted, "and that there is no existing directive authorizing U.S. agencies to encourage and support infiltration and build-up activities on the mainland. Indeed, our current directives (which I have not had an opportunity to examine) apparently are directed to stopping the Chinese [Nationalists] from engaging in infiltration activities on the mainland."[15]

The issue of the offshore islands, like the question of an offensive mission for the Nationalist armed forces, was inseparable from the joint problems of Nationalist morale and regional stability. In the case of the offshore islands, however, it was Chiang who held the upper hand. NSC 5723 contained a reformulation of existing policy that reflected the broad discretionary authority, granted to the president by the Congress under the

January 1955 Formosa Resolution, to utilize U.S. military forces in the Taiwan area. Its updated language stipulated that the chief executive could order U.S. forces to assist the Nationalists in protecting the offshore islands from Chinese Communist attack whenever he judged "such action to be required or appropriate in assuring the defense of Taiwan and the Penghus."[16] If fighting were again to erupt there, this provision gave Eisenhower considerable latitude in deciding whether, when, and how to intervene militarily. Because the provision merely codified authority that the president already possessed, however, it excited little comment in the National Security Council. Yet an observation by John Foster Dulles is noteworthy, because it offers a preview of the American response to the second crisis that lay just nine months ahead. Contending that the "defense of the off-shore islands was now so complete and so integral a part of the defense of Taiwan that it was not to be compared to the fluid situation of three years ago," he concluded that as matters now stood, the United States could not permit the loss of Jinmen and Mazu (Matsu) in the event of an all-out Communist assault.[17]

The secretary's assertion revealed that the United States, more than ever before, remained hostage to Chiang Kai-shek's determination to retain a secure grip on the Nationalist island enclaves. At the height of the first offshore islands crisis in April 1955, Chiang had flatly rejected a deal for evacuating his troops from Jinmen and Mazu in exchange for a U.S. naval blockade of part of the south China coast and other inducements, an offer made by Admiral Arthur Radford, then chairman of the Joint Chiefs of Staff (JCS), and Assistant Secretary of State for Far Eastern Affairs Walter Robertson during a secret visit to Taipei. Within five months of the fruitless Radford-Robertson mission, the Nationalist president dispatched an additional division to Jinmen and another two battalions to Mazu, increasing the total number of troops to over 100,000. The JCS acquiesced in the transfers after deciding that they were acceptable within the terms of a provision in the December 1954 exchange of notes delimiting such redeployments from Taiwan.[18] Although Nationalist military strength on the island complexes did not increase appreciably from September 1955 to August 1958, seven of the twenty-one divisions in the Nationalist army were located there when the second crisis began.[19] By overloading the islands with troops and committing himself to protecting his front-line positions at all costs, Chiang did all he could to make the defense of the islands essential to the defense of Taiwan.[20]

The possible loss of Chiang's forces on the islands to enemy attack had undeniable military implications for the defense of Taiwan. Yet the primary and irreplaceable deterrent against a successful Chinese Communist assault on the Nationalist abode was U.S. air and naval might. Chiang and his subordinates had elevated the offshore islands, the last pieces of indisputably Chinese territory they controlled, into symbols of their implacable resistance to their Communist foes and their paramount goal to one day return in victory to the mainland. The fate of the islands was therefore enmeshed with the prestige and legitimacy of the Nationalist government and with the morale of Chiang's loyalists.

American officials remained keenly aware of the politico-psychological dimension of the Nationalist military commitment to the islands after the 1954–55 crisis had passed.[21] In fact, a preoccupation with morale was a notable feature of the stance taken by American officials toward Taiwan. Intelligence analysts warned that a marked erosion of morale, particularly among the exiled mainlanders who held sway over the indigenous Taiwanese, could generate divisive, defeatist tendencies that would subvert the island's stability. Intelligence experts and policy planners maintained that the Chinese Communists, apparently recognizing their inability to gain control of Taiwan by force because of U.S. military opposition, were resolved to achieve their goal by nonmilitary methods aimed at reducing the will of their uprooted compatriots across the Strait to resist. Washington kept on the alert but detected neither worrisome slippage in morale nor threats to internal order.[22]

Although the 1958 crisis did not erupt until late August, American intelligence had already spotted signs of renewed conflict. On August 7, Central Intelligence Agency (CIA) director Allen Dulles warned the NSC that the situation in the Taiwan Strait was "heating up." Over the next several weeks, the intelligence community continued to keep a watchful eye on the islands. On August 27, the CIA head reported that the Chinese could undertake "decisive operations" against the islands "without much intelligence warning."[23]

The disturbing developments in the Taiwan Strait put decision makers in Washington on guard as they considered how best to warn off the Chinese and respond to a possible interdiction or invasion. There was near unanimity at the highest echelons of the government that the United States could not permit the Chinese to capture the islands by threat or use of force. Both civilian and military officials acknowledged that these tiny bits of land had scant intrinsic military value, either as defensive sentinels against an invasion of Taiwan or as springboards for a Nationalist offensive against the mainland. Yet there was also a strong consensus that the United States could ill afford to turn its back on the islands, leaving the 100,000 troops installed there to the mercy of the Communists, because of the damaging impact such inaction would have on morale on Taiwan. Though other considerations, such as the desire to uphold American credibility and avoid appeasement, contributed to the determination to safeguard the islands, the decisive motivation arose from a profound anxiety that forfeiture under duress would discredit Chiang's authority and deliver Taiwan into the hands of the Chinese Communists, setting off a chain reaction of Communist successes throughout East Asia.

On August 12, just before his departure on a ten-day visit to New York for an emergency session of the United Nations General Assembly over a still simmering crisis in the Middle East, Secretary of State Dulles consulted for the first time with Eisenhower about the disquieting conditions off the south China coast. Sensing that the president had not yet adequately grasped what was at stake, Dulles reminded him that the Nationalists had "closely integrated" Jinmen and Mazu into the defense of Taiwan; he predicted that if these outlying positions succumbed to Communist attack "morale [on Taiwan] would crumble and Chiang's control would be lost." Eisenhower agreed that "the key point is an evaluation of morale, since physically the islands would not help the Chinese Communists against Formosa [Taiwan]."[24]

The Joint Chiefs of Staff assigned little military value to the islands but did underline their politico-psychological significance and their connection to the fate of Taiwan and the U.S. strategic position in the Far East. In consultation with State Department officers, the JCS recommended that U.S. forces assist the Nationalists, as required, to protect their coastal territories from a successful blockade or a major assault. In either of these two eventualities, JCS plans called for the use of tactical nuclear weapons, first against airfields near Jinmen but soon progressing to military targets deep inside China and as far north as Shanghai if the Communists did not relent. In the latter stage, the military chiefs expected that the Soviet Union would retaliate with nuclear strikes against Taiwan and possibly Okinawa and elsewhere. "In other words," the JCS chair, General Nathan Twining, soberly commented, "if it is our national policy to defend the Offshore Islands, then we must face the possible ultimate consequences of that policy."[25]

In gauging the consequences of defending the offshore islands with nuclear weapons, military and civilian leaders could draw on a special intelligence estimate on the use of nuclear weapons in a limited war in the Far East completed a few weeks earlier. In the event of an extensive U.S. nuclear response to an invasion of the offshore islands, analysts expected the Soviets to retaliate with their own nuclear attacks at least against Taiwan and the Seventh Fleet but possibly other targets. At the same time, limited and localized U.S. nuclear strikes might perhaps avoid Soviet atomic reprisal and compel the Chinese to abandon their invasion. Yet whatever the scope of a U.S. nuclear assault on China, intelligence experts predicted a highly unfavorable reaction among neutral nations, most Asian countries, and many American allies.[26]

The question of U.S. military intervention to protect the offshore islands brought top decision makers face to face with the thorny issue of whether their defense was worth the using of atomic weapons. The nuclear question required that American leaders measure the anticipated consequences of a Nationalist defeat in the islands against the probable military and political results of U.S. nuclear intervention. The use of atomic weapons, even against limited and localized aggression, was sanctioned under the New Look national security policy first introduced by the Eisenhower administration in 1953 and most recently reaffirmed by the president and his National Security Council advisers in late July 1958. The central component of the New Look, the strategy of massive retaliation, emphasized nuclear weaponry and air power as the principal military means of deterring and defending against aggression. From the inception of the New Look, however, massive retaliation had aroused doubts and provoked opposition in military and civilian circles within the administration because of its overreliance on nuclear firepower. The problem of whether or not to deploy nuclear weapons in a limited war became especially contentious in the last years of the administration. Indeed, its thinking about limited war was clouded by disagreement and uncertainty. During a review of basic national security policy in the spring and summer of 1958, John Foster Dulles and a majority of the joint chiefs argued for more military flexibility in dealing with the contingency of limited war, yet Eisenhower overruled any significant departure from

massive retaliation. But despite an unwavering endorsement of massive retaliation over the years, the president was far from enamored of nuclear weapons and
left himself free to decide on their use in a local war on a case-by-case basis.[27]

Though voicing no reservations about nuclear intervention to fend off a
Chinese offensive during the prelude to the crisis, Eisenhower was disturbed
and disgruntled that the United States might have to run to the rescue of
Chiang Kai-shek's troops. Since the concluding phase of the first Taiwan
Strait crisis, he had personally felt that the Nationalists would be better off
abandoning the islands, or at least treating them as expendable outposts
to be manned by modest garrisons.[28] Disapproving of the Generalissimo's
stubborn insistence on staking so much, militarily and symbolically, on strategically inconsequential parcels of real estate, he complained that "we are
being shoved into something that we do not think is correct because of
someone else's intransigence" and that "this is when the American public and
press say that the U.S. has a vacillating policy." Despite his evident frustration with the predicament now before him, the president saw little choice
but to hold open the option of military action to prevent the islands and
their defenders from falling to the Chinese Communists.[29]

As Eisenhower and his advisers reacted to the danger signals flashing in
the Taiwan Strait, they considered whether to try to ward off further menacing military moves by the Communists through either a private or a public
warning. Various Nationalist interests pressured for a public statement, one
declaring that the United States regarded an attack on Jinmen and Mazu as
a threat to Taiwan or deploring such an assault as disturbing to the peace of
Asia.[30] The JCS advised against announcing any U.S. intention to defend
the islands, preferring instead to follow the practice of "'keeping them [the
Chinese] guessing'" first adopted during the initial 1954–55 crisis.[31] Dulles
favored a strong public statement that would put Beijing on notice about
U.S. intentions. The president, however, inclined toward a deterrence strategy that relied more on ambiguity; like the JCS, he reasoned that this was
the best way not just to give pause to the Chinese Communists but to
restrain Chiang Kai-shek, who, under the umbrella of guaranteed U.S. protection, might provoke a larger conflict with his opponents. Further, Eisenhower wanted to retain his flexibility in responding to Chinese maneuvers
and, in any event, felt constrained by the Formosa Resolution to refrain
from any unequivocal advance commitment to defend the islands.[32]

In the end, the president gave his approval to a public statement by Dulles that kept U.S. intentions under wraps yet also intimated a willingness to resort to military countermeasures. In a well-publicized August 23 letter to Thomas Morgan, acting chair of the House Foreign Affairs Committee, the secretary of state stressed that, since 1954, the ties between the offshore islands and Taiwan had "become closer and their interdependence has increased" and that it would be "highly hazardous" for anyone to assume that a Chinese Communist attempt to conquer the islands could be a "limited operation." Although the letter contained no nuclear saber-rattling of the kind that had frightened the American public and the Western allies during the earlier crisis, its language subtly hinted at a readiness to use atomic weapons.[33]

The day after the release of the Morgan letter, Chinese artillery rained 41,000 rounds on Jinmen and its satellite islands, igniting a full-fledged crisis. Within two days of this furious bombardment, Eisenhower and other ranking officials (except for John Foster Dulles, who was at his vacation retreat on Lake Ontario) had mapped out a muscular course of action in response to the more combative Chinese move. The president quickly ordered a build-up of U.S. air and naval strength in the Taiwan area, additional equipment for the Nationalist armed forces, and, most important, preparatory measures to convoy Nationalist supply ships to the principal offshore islands and to defend these positions from a major attack, using atomic weapons if he, as the chief executive, so authorized.[34]

Striking a comforting note, the intelligence community concluded that the main purpose behind the step-up in Beijing's military pressure was to test American and Nationalist intentions and that the Chinese were unlikely to hazard an assault on a principal offshore island as long as they were convinced that the United States might intervene. Intelligence experts believed that neither the Chinese nor Soviets wanted to risk a major war with the United States.[35]

Senior officials in Washington coupled their resolve to compel the Chinese to stand down with an equal determination to constrain the Nationalists from exacerbating a volatile situation. On August 27, Chiang Kai-shek sent Eisenhower an urgent message painting a gloomy picture of the Communist threat to Jinmen and intimating that he could not defer a defensive response for much longer. Militarily and politically, he asserted, the Jinmen and Mazu island groups were "inseparable from Taiwan itself." He asked that the president in effect invoke the Formosa Resolution, initiate convoying of

Nationalist supply vessels by U.S. warships to the two island complexes, and broaden the authority of the head of the United States Taiwan Defense Command to make on-the-spot decisions about U.S. military assistance in defense of the islands without consulting Washington.[36]

The president and many of his advisers greeted Chiang's message with suspicion and exasperation. They felt that he wanted to ensnare the United States in the islands for his own ends and resented the fact that, after unwisely placing a large proportion of his troops on these peripheral territories, he had now come "'whining'" to Washington. Nevertheless, Eisenhower was unprepared to let the Nationalists fend for themselves and suffer the loss of their island possessions. He therefore ordered U.S. naval vessels to escort Nationalist supply ships en route to Jinmen, but only in international waters outside an area within three miles of the Chinese shoreline. In addition, he authorized new operational instructions for U.S. forces in the Taiwan area that outlined a three-phase response to Chinese military action in the islands and the Taiwan Strait. Under this contingency plan, which was kept secret from the Nationalists, the United States would stick only to convoying and only as long as the Chinese did not attempt to overwhelm any of the main islands; if the Chinese launched a major assault, a second phase would begin, in which American forces would join in the defense of the islands and hit enemy artillery positions and local airfields in the vicinity. In the third phase, if the Chinese carried the battle to international waters near Taiwan and the Penghus, "United States forces would extend action as appropriate." It was not anticipated that atomic weapons would be used until this final phase. Eisenhower was reluctant to resort to nuclear countermeasures during the invasion phase because of the international outrage that would follow.[37] Although he had refused to depart from the New Look's massive retaliation strategy a month earlier, the president shied away from a decision to pull the nuclear trigger to defend the islands.

As Secretary of State Dulles discovered after his return from vacation on September 1, the joint chiefs were far from sanguine about successful non-nuclear counteraction against a sustained invasion attempt. At a JCS briefing, Dulles learned that to beat back such an all-out assault, tactical atomic weapons would be needed to take out coastal batteries and air bases, and that there was a real danger of enlarged hostilities with China and possibly even the Soviet Union. The implications of this JCS assessment for the massive retaliation policy were obvious. As he told the chiefs, "If we shrink from using nuclear weapons when military circumstances so require, then we will have to reconsider our whole defense posture. In dealing with this crisis we were facing some tough questions."[38] In an ironic twist, Dulles seemed less hesitant than the president to march to the nuclear brink, despite his own reservations about the massive retaliation strategy. It is interesting to note that for a time during the first Taiwan Strait crisis, Dulles had similarly subordinated his doubts about this strategy to the demands of a fearless stand against a Chinese military thrust.[39]

As American military power was being mobilized in the Taiwan Strait, the Eisenhower administration's staunch policy evoked widespread anxiety, skepticism, and opposition within and outside the United States. By early September, a "substantial segment" of articulate U.S. opinion was critical of the administration's war-risking position, convinced that the coastal islands were not worth shedding American blood over.[40] Likewise, a study of foreign opinion by the United States Information Agency forecast that an "adverse world-wide reaction" would follow U.S. intervention to protect the islands.[41] Public sentiment in some countries with close ties to the United States, such as Japan and Britain, was overwhelmingly against intervention and profoundly fearful of the possible use of nuclear weapons.[42] The U.S. ambassador in Tokyo reported that domestic revulsion against the employment of atomic weapons to protect the islands might oblige the Japanese government to demand the withdrawal of U.S. forces from Japan or, at the very least, to request that they stop using Japanese bases for operations in the Taiwan Strait.[43] From London, Prime Minister Harold Macmillan informed Eisenhower that while his "overriding concern" was to avoid the appearance of an Anglo-American split over what to do in the islands, he would need to "steer" at opinion home if the United States and China should clash.[44]

Despite the worrisome direction of much national and international opinion, the main preoccupation of Eisenhower and Dulles in early September was to help the Nationalists while also harnessing them, and to spook the Chinese into backing down or, at the least, carrying their military plans no further. Although Dulles appreciated the seriousness of the Chinese military move against Jinmen, he still regarded it as essentially a probing operation, probably agreed upon by Mao and Soviet leader Nikita Khrushchev when they had met in Beijing in late July. He speculated that Mao, emboldened by Khrushchev's

trumpeting of Soviet military prowess, had chosen to embark on a more adventurous course in the Strait, with his ally's approval, to test American resolve.
Convinced that the timing and origins of the crisis were explainable in such
terms, Dulles gave no consideration (nor did the president) to the possibility
that Beijing might have been stimulated or provoked to turn up the temperature
in the Strait by perceived American intransigence and hostility.[45]

Dulles believed that to achieve effective deterrence, the Chinese had to
understand that the United States would intervene to repel a major attack
against Jinmen. The secretary's thoughts again turned to the device of another public statement to scare off Mao and his comrades. On September 4,
Dulles huddled with Eisenhower at Newport, Rhode Island, where the
president was on vacation. In a memorandum prepared in consultation with
State Department and Pentagon officials, he spelled out the rationale for
robust U.S. action to prevent the loss of Jinmen through blockade or amphibious assault and examined the possible repercussions of using nuclear
weapons. The fall of Jinmen, Dulles argued, would have a "serious impact"
on the authority and military capability of the Nationalist government It
would expose Chiang's regime to subversion and/or military action likely to
bring to power a government that would eventually endorse union with
Communist China. Not only would a Communist takeover greatly boost
Beijing's prestige and influence in Asia while depreciating that of the United
States, it would also "seriously jeopardize the anti-Communist barrier" in
the western Pacific. Within a few years, the secretary predicted, much of the
region would gravitate toward or fall within the Sino-Soviet orbit, with
results "more far-reaching and catastrophic" than those that had ensued after
the Communist victory on the Chinese mainland.

Turning from this nightmare scenario to the nuclear issue, Dulles acknowledged that using nuclear weapons risked an enlarged conflict and
would likely produce a strong international backlash. However, he also
emphasized that conventional weapons alone would probably not suffice to
beat off a determined Chinese attack on Jinmen.[46] In going over the memorandum with the president, the secretary stressed that "if we will not use
them [nuclear weapons] when the chips are down because of adverse world
opinion, we must revise our defense setup."[47] For Dulles the crisis was a test
of how far the Eisenhower administration was prepared to go in practice to
carry out the massive retaliation strategy in a case of local aggression.

Following the Newport meeting, Dulles issued another warning to Beijing through a press statement that amounted to a barely disguised threat: the United States would take up arms if necessary to block the Communists from ousting the Nationalists from Jinmen by force. Falling just short of a definite commitment, the statement nonetheless conveyed the unmistakable impression that the United States was prepared to fight, exactly the message Dulles wanted to send the Chinese. He reinforced that impression in off-the-record remarks to reporters, which had the effect of making the administration's military intentions even more transparent, despite the thin veil of ambiguity.[48] The next day, the *New York Times* carried the headline "U.S. Decides to Use Force If Reds Invade Quemoy" and the *Washington Post*, a front page announcement that "Ike Pledges Aid for Quemoy."[49]

Available Chinese sources suggest that the Eisenhower administration's massive show of military power and menacing rhetoric prompted Mao and his associates to reassess their course of action in the Taiwan Strait. Though scholars still dispute exactly why the Chinese Communist Party (CCP) leadership decided to put pressure on Jinmen, there seems to be general agreement that Mao was not bent on a military duel with the United States. Following the Newport statement, although the Chinese continued shelling Jinmen, they refrained from air bombardment and similar military actions that might touch off combat with U.S. forces. At the same time, the CCP Politburo elected to seek a resumption of the suspended Sino-American ambassadorial talks as soon as possible in order to reopen the only direct channel of discussion with Washington. On September 6, in a public statement reiterating Chinese policy in the Taiwan Strait, Premier Zhou Enlai announced that Beijing was prepared to accept a U.S. offer made in early August to restart the talks.[50] The White House swiftly issued its own statement welcoming the resumption of the talks, and Eisenhower saw to it that this official response was unmistakably positive.[51] Taken together with other signs of Chinese caution, Beijing's decision to restart the ambassadorial talks reinforced the view within the intelligence community and among senior decision makers that Mao and his lieutenants were reluctant to get into a military scrape with the United States.

No sooner had Beijing made its conciliatory gesture than Khrushchev followed with a harsh letter to Eisenhower on September 7, in which he condemned U.S. intrusions in the Strait and declared that the Soviet Union would consider an attack on the PRC an attack on itself. Despite its threatening tone, the letter seems to have been intended less to intimidate the United States than to win favor with the Soviet Union's chief ally through its unflinching public expression of support. Behind the scenes, however, Kremlin leaders were disturbed by the PRC's unilateral provocation. The crisis over Jinmen further strained the already brittle Sino-Soviet alliance.[52]

Among top American policymakers and intelligence analysts the prevailing view was that the Sino-Soviet alliance remained firm, if not friction-free, and that Moscow had backed the Chinese Communist ratcheting up of tension in the Strait. Dulles maintained that the two Communist giants were pursuing a larger strategy, exerting pressure at multiple points around the world, to spread out U.S. armed forces. Both he and Eisenhower were certain that Sino-Soviet complicity in the crisis had as its goal the expulsion of the United States from Taiwan and the rest of Asia.[53] Despite such perceptions of collusion between Moscow and Beijing, the president and secretary of state showed no sign that they took Khrushchev's fist-waving rhetoric at face value. Intelligence experts offered reassurance that the Kremlin's principal objective was political and that it did not want Chinese military ventures to result in hostilities with the United States that could raise the issue of Soviet military intervention. There was no evidence of Soviet military preparations at this time.[54] Moscow reacted mildly when Eisenhower refused to accept a second, more intemperate letter sent on September 19 in which Khrushchev again blasted U.S. interference in the Taiwan area.[55] Dulles speculated privately that the Soviets had problems with the Chinese Communists similar to those of the United States with Chiang Kai-shek, and that they too were reluctant to exert excessive pressure on their ally for fear of untoward consequences.[56] Nonetheless, the secretary suggested to the British that they nudge the Soviets to urge restraint on Beijing. Eisenhower, too, in a stiff reply to Khrushchev's first letter, called on him to use Moscow's diplomatic influence for peaceful ends in the Taiwan Strait.[57]

On September 15, after a hiatus of nine months, the Sino-American ambassadorial talks restarted in Warsaw in the spotlight of international publicity. Over the next eight weeks, Jacob Beam, the U.S. ambassador to Poland, and Wang Bingnan, the Chinese ambassador, met in ten unproductive sessions. The two sides remained far apart, unable to bridge their opposing views of how to bring about peaceful conditions in the offshore islands and the Taiwan Strait. American proposals focused on an immediate informal cease-fire followed by steps to end "provocative" activities between the offshore islands and the mainland and to lessen tension in the surrounding area; Chinese proposals essentially demanded that the United States abandon its protection of the Nationalist government and withdraw its forces.[58] In designing the American approach, which was consistent with the goals of an informal stabilization of the Strait and a de facto two-China situation, Dulles left the door open to an unspecified form of demilitarization that would leave the offshore islands under Nationalist control. Yet he acknowledged the daunting problem of "how to get Chiang Kai-shek to disengage without fatal implications on Formosa."[59] In pursuit of informal stabilization in the Strait, Dulles had to reckon not just with the Chinese Communists but with the Nationalists and the psychologically deflating perils of a pullback from the offshore islands.

As it was, the Nationalists were distressed that the United States had even consented to resume the ambassadorial talks, which they had always viewed with anxiety and suspicion. Despite assurances from Washington that they would be consulted on all matters affecting their rights and interests, they remained deeply skeptical of the purpose and usefulness of the discussions between an indispensable ally and a detested enemy.[60]

In truth, Dulles and his State Department aides were almost certain that Chinese Communist intransigence would prevent the Warsaw talks from getting anywhere. Even so, they saw considerable advantage in prolonging the Sino-American dialogue in order to curry the support of domestic and international opinion, to build a record that would place the blame for any failure to reach a peaceful accommodation on the Chinese Communists, and to provide a diplomatic cover for the Chinese to limit, reduce, or cease their military activities. Dulles judged that the most promising resolution lay in a unilateral Chinese decision to turn down the temperature in the offshore islands, just as they had after Zhou Enlai's invitation to enter into direct talks with the United States in April 1955. Anticipating that the resumed bilateral discussions would fail to yield a diplomatic solution to the problem of who should control the islands, Dulles still thought they had merit as a means to an informal cease-fire. The fact that Zhou Enlai had offered to recommence the talks reinforced his belief that the Chinese would avoid a showdown if the United States was resolute, and that they would probably let the crisis die down once they realized that their Berlin-type blockade of Jinmen would miscarry.[61]

Throughout most of September, the Communist siege of Jinmen remained unbroken, much to the frustration and concern of American civilian and military officials. On September 6, U.S. destroyers began to escort Nationalist resupply convoys from Taiwan to a point three miles off Jinmen. The Chinese did not open fire on these U.S. warships, even though they ventured into what the PRC two days earlier had claimed were territorial and not international waters. Nationalist vessels attempting to land supplies on Jinmen, however, were attacked by torpedo boats and shelled by shore batteries. The first eight U.S.-escorted convoys met with little or no success in offloading supplies. At the start of the convoy operations, local U.S. military authorities estimated that Jinmen had enough provisions and ammunition for about thirty days.[62] The joint chiefs quickly grew impatient. Faulting the Nationalists for their ineptitude, the chiefs suspected that they were deliberately attempting to draw the United States into a conflict with the Chinese Communists or to force Washington to approve air bombardment of mainland artillery emplacements. More willing to give the Nationalists the benefit of the doubt, Dulles blamed their ineffective performance on inexperience and difficult conditions.[63] Nevertheless, he recognized that the success of the resupply effort was essential in thwarting the Chinese Communist military initiative and convincing the CCP leadership to take the crisis off the boil.[64]

The Nationalists were straining at the bit to retaliate against mainland targets, and American decision makers exerted themselves to ensure that they abstained from any unapproved unilateral military actions against Communist territory. Such countermeasures might incite the Communists to crank up the level of hostilities and thus pull the United States into the fighting. The State Department also fretted that any Nationalist military retaliation that appeared to be a provocation would work to the propaganda advantage of the Communists in the forum of world opinion. Chiang Kai-shek and other Nationalist officials made no secret of their discontent when Washington refused to consent to attacks by their air force against enemy shore batteries and airfields. Chiang took umbrage at constant reminders by American representatives of the restrictive understanding on Nationalist military action in the 1954 exchange of notes.[65] As the crisis lengthened and the interdiction remained unbreached, the Nationalists grew more and more restive, increasing the danger that they might strike at the mainland without Washington's approval.[66]

With no end to the crisis in sight, despite the Warsaw talks, the Eisenhower administration's apparent readiness to do battle with China over the offshore islands continued to agitate and alarm many foreign observers. Articulate public opinion within western allied countries, such Britain, Canada, Australia, and New Zealand, overwhelmingly rejected the notion that the islands were worth a war, and government leaders in these nations made their own concerns known in Washington. Reports in the American press gave an overall impression of a "critical—even hostile—attitude" among major allies and in Asia, not only to American military action in the offshore islands but to U.S. China policy in general.[67] Events at the United Nations further highlighted the negative international response to Washington's hard-line China policy. The Jinmen issue surfaced briefly at the start of the General Assembly's regular session on September 16 and soon became entangled in the debate over the renewal of the moratorium procedure used by the United States and its supporters since 1951 to prevent consideration of the question of Chinese representation. Although the Assembly voted on September 23 to renew the moratorium arrangement, the majority was the smallest yet recorded.[68] Reporting on this outcome by phone from New York, U.N. ambassador Henry Cabot Lodge, Jr., remarked glumly to Dulles that "they [the United States] got through but it was the roughest one we have ever had. The Quemoy thing dominated everything. No one made a speech on our side." In a follow-up letter to the secretary, Lodge explained that the apparent U.S. commitment to Jinmen "deeply perplexes representatives of governments here" and had caused them to wonder whether the United States had been "dragged into following policies which are not in our own best interests." He speculated that neutralizing disaffection over the coastal islands within the United Nations might help to arrest the alarming decline of support for the United States on the Chinese representation question.[69]

On the domestic scene, the administration's course of action in the Taiwan Strait was also a lightning rod for controversy and debate. To bolster public approval, Eisenhower spoke to the nation in a radio-TV address on September 11, and Dulles followed with a major speech in New York on September 25. Both men insisted that for the United States to retreat in the face of threatened aggression in the Strait was unacceptable, but they also expressed a preference for diplomatic measures to ensure, in Eisenhower's words, that the "offshore islands will not be a thorn in the side of peace." In justifying their firm stand, they invoked the Munich analogy, drew a parallel between Jinmen and Berlin, and emphasized the necessity of safeguarding Taiwan and resisting a Sino-Soviet challenge. The secretary of state also alleged that by seizing Jinmen and Mazu, the Chinese probably hoped to "destroy the prestige and authority" of the Nationalist government and take control of Taiwan by "subversive coup." [70] This was the only public reference during the crisis to what was in fact their paramount motive for standing up to the Chinese in the islands. To broadcast it loudly, the secretary feared, would itself undercut Chiang's regime and strain its relations with the United States. [71]

Despite their weighty appeals to the American public, Eisenhower and Dulles failed to muster broad endorsement for possible U.S. military intervention. State Department compilations of domestic opinion showed that a preponderance of the elite and mass public looked with doubt or outright disfavor on a fight with China over the islands. They preferred a nonviolent resolution through the Warsaw talks or the United Nations and neutralization or demilitarization of the islands. Intermixed with such sentiments was criticism of Chiang's obdurate attitude and calls for a reappraisal of the U.S. relationship with his regime. [72] A Gallup poll reported on September 26 that 91 percent of a survey sample of informed citizens wished to turn the off-shore islands issue over to the United Nations before resorting to military intervention, and that 61 percent considered it a "good idea" to neutralize Taiwan itself by placing it under U.N. guardianship. The same poll showed that opinion was almost evenly split over the use of atomic weapons against Chinese Communist military forces and installations if the United States were to go to war over the offshore islands. [73]

Although the Formosa Resolution granted the president broad authority to take defensive action in the Taiwan Strait, Eisenhower and Dulles remained mindful of congressional opinion and of how lawmakers would react to a decision in favor of military intervention. The second crisis in the islands had broken out just as the 1958 midterm election campaign was getting into swing, when Congress was not in session. This complicated the administration's task in trying to garner support for its policy among leading legislators, although the State Department undertook to keep key congressmen and senators across the country informed about military and diplomatic developments. [74]

The offshore islands controversy acquired something of a partisan coloration when a contingent of influential Democratic legislators and party notables took issue with the administration's war-risking policy. In a bare-knuckle indictment published in the *New York Times* on September 7, former secretary of state Dean Acheson accused the administration of chancing a military bout with Communist China over issues "not worth a single American life." Dissenting from this conclusion, Acheson's former boss, ex-president Harry S. Truman, backed Eisenhower's actions in a statement released to the press a week later. Yet most Democrats who spoke out on the offshore islands issue were more in sympathy with Acheson's views. These critics included such prominent senators as William J. Fulbright, Mike Mansfield, John F. Kennedy, and Theodore Green, the chair of the Foreign Relations Committee.[75] In a private letter to Eisenhower on September 29, Green voiced his "deep concern" that events in the Far East "may result in military involvement at the wrong time, in the wrong place, and on issues not of vital concern to our own security, and all this without allies either in fact or in heart."[76] The next day, Dulles privately lamented that the administration was having difficulty getting the country to understand the "real issues" in the crisis, particularly "during an election time when the Democrats are vigorously at work to confuse the issues."[77] The partisan dimension of the controversy was bound to unsettle both the secretary and the president, who had striven, since taking office, to depoliticize China policy.

The unfavorable currents in world and national opinion preyed on Eisenhower, and he increasingly desired to find a way out of the disturbing predicament in the offshore islands.[78] Although the president saw the necessity of holding firm, he also took pains to ensure that the United States appeared open to a peaceful solution. Privately, he had gnawing misgivings about coming to blows with China over the islands simply because Chiang had stubbornly staked so much of his armed strength and his prestige on them.[79] At the same time, he had no stomach for using atomic weapons just to keep the islands out of the grasp of the Chinese Communists. In a conversation with Selwyn Lloyd, the British foreign secretary, on September 21, he disclosed that "if nuclear weapons were going to be used [in any situation], it would have to be an all-out effort rather than a local effort." He did not "plan to use nuclear weapons in any local situation at the present time."[80] In pulling back from the nuclear precipice, Eisenhower was setting a limit on the implementation of the New Look's massive retaliation strategy for defensive purposes in local conflicts.

Searching for a way to disentangle the United States from the offshore islands, the president was attracted to the notion of a quid pro quo arrangement by which the Generalissimo would remove all or most of his troops in exchange for an amphibious lift capability. In the last two weeks of September, Eisenhower brought up the possibility of a deal in several meetings with Dulles and with General Twining. Such a bargain, he reasoned, might appeal to Chiang by allowing him to retrieve his forces without losing face, since in compensation he would gain an improved ability to strike at the mainland in the event of a major upheaval.[81] As the amphibious lift deal revealed, Eisenhower's preferred solution to the problem still involved, as it had since the last months of the 1954–55 crisis, Chiang's voluntary decision to treat the offshore islands as lightly defended, dispensable outposts or to quit them entirely. If Chiang were to choose either of these options, the loss of the islands would no longer threaten a demoralizing military and psychological defeat, and the United States itself could safely disengage. By removing the islands as "a thorn in the side of peace," Eisenhower's amphibious lift deal would also achieve the administration's twin goals of informal stabilization of the Taiwan Strait and a de facto two-China situation. In late September, the president looked favorably on a possible secret mission to Taiwan by John J. McCloy, the highly regarded former high commissioner for Germany. Although Eisenhower was convinced that "the amphibious lift [deal] was the key to getting Chiang out of his difficulties," it is unclear whether he intended that McCloy actually present this idea to the Nationalist leader. In any case, the mission never got off the ground because McCloy, after talking to Dulles, declined to go to Taiwan. In explaining his decision to the secretary, McCloy noted that his inclination was to ask for more concessions from Chiang than Dulles was considering and that he did not "really know yet how far you want him [Chiang] to go in view of the somewhat uneasy position he holds on Taiwan."[82]

As Eisenhower knew, Dulles did not always see eye to eye with him on how best to resolve the dilemma.[83] He showed no enthusiasm for the amphibious lift idea, and he was skeptical about whether Chiang would willingly give up the only unquestionably Chinese territory still under his authority. The secretary had not forgotten the failure of the Radford-Robertson mission to dislodge the defiant Nationalist leader from the islands three years earlier. As for resorting to drastic coercive methods, such as cutting off aid, to strong-arm Chiang into evacuating the islands, he predicted that this approach would generate rancorous anti-American resentment on Taiwan and perhaps trigger a suicidal attack against the mainland. Although Dulles was far from keen about an amphibious lift deal, he regarded the overconcentration of troops on the islands as a "monstrosity."[84]

The secretary still expected that the crisis would subside once the Chinese Communists were convinced they could not win Jinmen by interdiction alone. Prospects for a cease-fire brightened near the end of September, when Washington received the encouraging news that the convoy escort operations had at last proven successful. Enough supplies were now getting through to the Jinmen islands to support them for an extended period. This favorable development, together with the fact that Nationalist pilots, flying U.S. Sabre jets equipped with recently supplied heat-seeking Sidewinder missiles, had established air superiority in the Taiwan Strait, greatly heartened the Nationalists and relieved pressure for retaliation against the mainland.[85]

The improved conditions in the Strait gave Dulles and Eisenhower an opportunity for a more public demonstration of flexibility. At a much-noticed press conference on September 30, Dulles questioned the soundness of the inordinate Nationalist troop commitment on the islands, adding that it would be "foolish to keep these large forces" there if a "reasonably dependable" cease-fire came into effect. Meeting with reporters two days later, Eisenhower stated that "as a soldier" he did not think "it was a good thing to have all those troops on the offshore islands."[86] In so disclosing their private reservations about the overconcentration of troops, the two men put a more moderate face on American policy. However, their revelations represented less a reversal of basic policy than a tactical shift. Eisenhower and Dulles still regarded the loss of the islands by either the threat or the use of force as intolerable, and both still adhered to an approved policy sanctioning direct military intervention to prevent this from happening. Despite the president's unhappiness with the status quo in the islands and his preference for an amphibious lift deal, he made no move to alter the existing secret decision to keep the islands out of the embrace of the Chinese or to revise the public impression that the United States would oppose a forceful seizure. At his September 30 press conference, he reemphasized that the United States would not back down in the face of force in the Taiwan Strait. On October 5, in a public reply to

Senator Green's letter of September 29, he affirmed his discretionary authority under the Formosa Resolution to take military action in the islands. He also repeated the line taken by the administration since the early days of the crisis that the goal of the Chinese after they had scooped up the islands was to lay hold of Taiwan and to expel the United States from the western Pacific.[87]

This new display of flexibility served two tactical purposes. One was to put publicly announced U.S. policy in a better light at home and abroad. Concerned about the negative cast of domestic and international opinion, the two men felt a need to inject a larger measure of suppleness into that policy. Dulles and his aides wanted to ensure the believability of a U.S. claim to reasonable and peaceful intentions should the crisis take a turn for the worse and the moment for direct U.S. military intervention draw nearer; this was particularly necessary in view of the anticipated involvement of the United Nations in the dispute.[88] Dulles had also concluded that the domestic and international reaction against what appeared to be a needlessly hazardous U.S. posture was jeopardizing the administration's entire pro-Nationalist policy. The impression shared by much of the American press, many members of Congress, and most of the nation's allies was that the United States was "being dragged into a world war by Chiang [Kai-shek]" because of its seemingly rigid attachment to his entrenched position in the islands. Dulles's comments to reporters on September 30 were intended to counter that impression "in order to prevent our whole China policy from being swept overboard."[89]

A second motive for a display of flexibility was to offer the Chinese an incentive to give up their blockade and let the fighting subside. Following Dulles's press conference, the State Department instructed Ambassador Jacob Beam to suggest to the Chinese at the Warsaw talks that if the fighting quieted down, they could "expect de facto cessation of harassments from [the] offshore islands and probably considerable troop reductions." Dulles and his advisers anticipated that the next two to three weeks would tell whether the Chinese would move toward a cease-fire because their interdiction by artillery bombardment and small naval craft had faltered or would instead clamp down harder on Jinmen by launching air attacks.[90]

Eisenhower's and Dulles's candid remarks were well received at home and among Western allies. Administration critics applauded what they viewed as a significant policy shift toward a more temperate position. Administration supporters endorsed the more adaptable attitude toward the size of the Nationalist garrisons, even while insisting that U.S. policy remain opposed to appeasement or concessions under duress. Less encouraging, from the perspective of both the White House and the State Department, was a persistent current of outspoken American opinion favoring settlement of Taiwan's political status, perhaps in the form of independence or U.N. protection.[91]

Against this backdrop of widespread approval, news reached Washington that the Chinese had proclaimed a seven-day cessation of their bombardment of the islands starting on October 6, on condition that the United States halt its convoy protection. Rejecting Chiang Kai-shek's admonition to ignore the announcement as a treacherous stratagem to divide the United States and his government, the State Department and Pentagon quickly opted to suspend U.S. naval escorts.[92] On October 12, when the Chinese declared that they would hold their fire for a further two-week period, Dulles informed Eisenhower that "it would be hard for them [the Chinese] to start again."[93]

Eisenhower acted immediately to turn the attention of his top civilian and military advisers toward a long-term resolution of the offshore islands problem. Taking the unusual step of writing a "strong letter" to Dulles, he again recommended consideration of his amphibious lift deal. Such an arrangement, he submitted, would eliminate the danger of U.S. involvement in "a severe battle under unfavorable conditions near the Chinese coastline," improve Chiang's capability to intervene on the mainland if and when such an opportunity arose, and put the Nationalist government in a "better position before world opinion," thereby ensuring a stronger U.S.-Nationalist alliance "because of a unified public opinion at home." In the letter, Eisenhower also revealed that he had recently mentioned his idea to Nationalist ambassador George Yeh, who had seemed receptive. In view of the Chinese cease-fire, the president thought the moment right to present the idea to Chiang in secret, possibly through Yeh.[94]

Clearly Eisenhower had decided to push hard for a voluntary Nationalist pullback. On the same day he sent his letter, he told Dulles in a phone conversation that he wanted to "do everything we can to make it possible for this guy [Chiang Kai-shek] to get off the hook." Dulles could see that Chiang might be tempted by the additional paratroopers but was nonetheless dubious that the Nationalist leader would agree to a deal. Eisenhower, too, was less than confident that Chiang would accept but saw good reason to go ahead anyway.[95] In asserting his presidential leadership, Eisenhower carried his still skeptical secretary of state along with him.

As Dulles knew, his press conference suggestion that the Nationalists had overloaded the islands with troops had provoked an angry reaction. Chiang bristled at the notion of relocating even a small number of his soldiers.[96] Spurred on by the president, the secretary and the JCS nonetheless focused on specific inducements that might persuade the Nationalist president to reconsider. On October 10, they discussed a package prepared by military planners, which the JCS chief, General Twining, characterized as "good-sized and expensive." The package included not just an amphibious lift for 25,000 to 30,000 troops but other military and economic incentives intended to convince Chiang to reduce his forces by two-thirds. The JCS plan did, however, allow the Generalissimo to use the amphibious lift to reinforce these island outposts in a military emergency, which ran counter to Eisenhower's hope of turning them into lightly defended positions. Without passing judgment on the JCS package, Dulles conceded that some troop reduction might be feasible, although he and the military chiefs were unanimous that a durable cease-fire was a precondition for any scale-back of Chiang's forces.[97]

In a draft talking paper he prepared on October 13 for comment by a few trusted State Department subordinates, Dulles situated the problem of the offshore islands in the larger context of the foreign policy objectives the United States shared in common with the Nationalist government. These objectives could be served, he contended, by an informal armistice in which provocations on both sides ceased and "some appreciable reduction of [Nationalist] forces" occurred. Without mentioning the JCS package, he suggested that the Nationalists could acquire some amphibious mobility to assist a "substantial organized resistance movement" on the mainland or to redeploy troops to the islands in an emergency.[98]

On October 14, Dulles obtained Eisenhower's permission to make a stopover in Taipei on his return from an upcoming trip to Rome. After hearing his secretary of state's outline of the pros and cons of consultations with Chiang Kai-shek, the president declared that it was important to "show positive action" during the two-week cease-fire extension just announced by the Chinese. The record of this meeting is silent on whether the discussion included an amphibious lift deal, the JCS package, or any other plan to lure

Chiang into a troop reduction. Dulles cautioned the president not to expect a change in the Nationalist attitude toward the offshore islands or their defense.[99]

Before his departure, Dulles gave further thought to the purpose of his visit and settled on a plan of action well short of the far-reaching change for which Eisenhower yearned. In conversations with State Department assistants, he said that he was going to Taipei not to swing a deal for troop reduction but to persuade Chiang to recast his government's role to be more in tune with American and "free world" opinion. What he had in mind was to reshape the Nationalist regime's stated mission and restore its reputation as a respected symbol of "free China." He would leave the actual task to Pentagon representatives, but he acknowledged that "thinning" the large garrisons would "evoke a widely favorable response, which would help swing public opinion toward the GRC and might promote de facto peace arrangements."[100]

Absent from Dulles's plan of action was the president's amphibious lift deal. The record does not show whether Eisenhower followed up on his proposal after he had turned it over to the State Department and the Pentagon or whether he raised any objection when Dulles instead favored his own approach. Why the president apparently remained so passive after his initial burst of decisiveness is unclear. Perhaps it was a result of inattention stemming from his habit of delegating responsibility to subordinates; or he might have concluded that his quid pro quo would not work without a reliable cease-fire, which he and his advisers viewed as a necessary precondition for substantial troop reduction. Whatever the reason, in the absence of Eisenhower's firm support of the amphibious lift deal, the secretary of state was left free to pursue a more modest agenda. Never partial to the president's scheme, Dulles no doubt also realized that it played into Chiang's military proclivities and therefore jarred with the more peaceable spirit he hoped to infuse into the Nationalist cause. The secretary of state's success in turning aside Eisenhower's proposal was consistent with the pivotal role he played throughout the crisis in framing issues and plotting the American course of action.

Dulles's arrival in Taipei on October 21 marked the start of grueling negotiations in which he and Chiang Kai-shek were the principal participants. On October 23, they issued a joint communiqué, for the most part an innocuous declaration of common aims, but also a statement on two extremely sensitive issues. Regarding the first, the Nationalist mainland mission, Dulles had tried to convey to Chiang the sense that it was in his government's own best interests to emphasize its role as a symbol and a guardian of traditional Chinese culture. Warning that its bellicose reputation had contributed to a dangerous decline in political support among "free world" nations, Dulles also underscored the "imperative need" to win popular endorsement for the Eisenhower administration's pro-Nationalist policy among allied nations and the American public. Dulles encouraged Chiang to concentrate on fostering an armistice in the Chinese Civil War, meanwhile waiting for the time when a major revolt on the mainland would give him an opening to realize his liberationist ambitions.[101]

Under pressure from Dulles, Chiang agreed to a self-denying statement in the joint communiqué that represented a significant modification of the Nationalist military counterattack strategy. The communiqué stated that the "principal means" the Nationalist government would rely to regain the mainland would be the implementation of "Sun Yat-sen's three people's principles (nationalism, democracy, and social well-being)" rather than the use of force.[102] This reformulation harmonized with Dulles's belief that a more peaceful image would improve the regime's political standing in the "free world" and better ensure support among the American public for a pro-Nationalist policy. The reformulation was likewise consonant with the less aggressive strategy of patient opportunism the secretary of state had first urged on Chiang during the earlier offshore islands crisis, and with his dual aims of bringing about informal stabilization of the Taiwan Strait and a de facto two-China situation. At the same time, the redefinition kept alive the goal of mainland recovery so prized by the Nationalist regime, which Washington deemed essential to the preservation of morale and political stability on Taiwan.

On the other significant issue, the offshore islands, the joint communiqué enunciated no new departures. Stating that "under present conditions the defense of the Quemoys, together with the Matsus, is closely related to the defense of Taiwan and Penghu," the communiqué reiterated what Dulles had said in his public letter to Senator Morgan before the crisis flared up[103] and contained no hint of any troop reduction. Privately, however, Chiang Kai-shek conceded a willingness to cut back on the size of his garrison on Jinmen. Dulles had advised him that it was unwise to identify the "whole fate of Free China . . . with the holding of a few square miles of real estate in a highly vulnerable position." He also made sure that Chiang understood the human cost of defending Jinmen with tactical nuclear weapons. Employing such devices in ground bursts against Communist artillery emplacements, he disclosed, would kill millions and probably contaminate Jinmen itself with radioactive fallout.[104] While still in Washington, Dulles had attended a briefing by nuclear experts that underlined the high civilian casualties anticipated in using tactical atomic weapons against Communist positions.[105]

In separate talks during Dulles's stay on Taiwan, a U.S. military team headed by Army Chief of Staff General Maxwell D. Taylor made progress in reaching an understanding with Nationalist military leaders for troop reduction on Jinmen. As a result of continuing negotiations after Dulles and Taylor departed, on November 17, Major General L. L. Doan, the commander of the U.S. Military Assistance Advisory Group on Taiwan, and General Wang Shu-Ming, Chief of the General Staff, signed an agreement that provided for a removal of no less than 15,000 men, including one infantry division, from the Jinmen islands complex by June 30, 1959. The Doan-Wang agreement contained no provision for an amphibious lift, but it did obligate the U.S. to transfer additional heavy artillery and armor to the offshore islands.[106] Shifting at least some troops from the islands to Taiwan was a definite concession to the American viewpoint, but even so, a large number of soldiers remained, preserving the Nationalist government's military and psychological investment in the islands.

At an off-the-record press briefing before returning to Washington, Dulles gave reporters an upbeat assessment of the results of his Taipei visit. Putting his own spin on the mission passage in the joint communiqué, he claimed that it was "in effect a renunciation of the use of force," and that this put the Republic of China in the same category as the Republic of Vietnam, the Republic of Korea, and the Federal Republic of Germany, states divided by communism but which desisted from the use of force for reunification. The secretary boasted that his discussions with Chiang had laid a basis for "what might be regarded as a sort of de facto armistice, if there was any sort of willingness on the Communist side to have a de facto armistice."[107]

A Chinese Communist announcement on October 25 that the shelling of Jinmen would resume on odd-numbered days sent the unequivocal message that CCP leaders were uninterested in a de facto armistice in the Taiwan Strait. Still, what Dulles described as the "rather fantastic statement" by the Chinese confirmed the prevailing view in Washington that their objective in the islands was now clearly political and propagandistic rather than military.[108] As the secretary had predicted, Beijing had ended the crisis by allowing it to fade away.

The joint communiqué received a warm reception both in the United States and abroad. In praising Dulles's achievement, American commentators singled out the declaration on the nonuse of force. A sizable number, however, voiced qualms and reservations about the absence of any sign of a more moderate U.S. or Nationalist position with respect to the offshore islands.[109]

In briefing the National Security Council on the outcome of his trip, Dulles struck an optimistic note. He was certain that Chiang was "converted to the idea that renunciation of the use of military force to retake the mainland was a sound course of action." Noting that the Nationalist president had agreed in principle to some contraction of his garrison on Jinmen, he predicted that "if we could achieve a genuine cease-fire in this area, an even greater reduction in Nationalist forces . . . could occur, and that even their eventual demilitarization was possible." Overall, he anticipated that "our problems with Chiang Kai-shek in the future would be much more manageable than in the past."[110]

But Dulles overestimated his accomplishments in Taipei and what they portended for the future. The ink on the communiqué was hardly dry when Nationalist officials started to complain that overseas Chinese in the United States and elsewhere had reacted negatively to the reformulated mission and that outside Taiwan the mistaken impression had taken hold that the declaration renounced the use of force to regain the mainland under all circumstances. The State Department, while acknowledging that the declaration did not preclude the use of force in self-defense or in case of a large-scale uprising on the mainland, tried to steer the Nationalist government away from any amendment or interpretation of the communiqué by an exchange of notes or other such device. It would be a "catastrophe," diplomats in Washington warned, for the Nationalist government to undercut the "extremely favorable" reaction to the communiqué in the United States and the "free world" with statements that appeared to qualify its "clear meaning" or that indicated disagreement between their two nations.[111] Although the Nationalists refrained from attempting to amend or interpret the communiqué through a formal device, the practical meaning of the declaration on the nonuse of force remained a source of tension and discord between

Washington and Taipei. In a letter to Eisenhower in early November, Chiang Kai-shek interpreted the declaration in a manner that suggested backtracking on his part. Dulles immediately saw to it that the Generalissimo was set right.[112] Nevertheless, the Americans and the Nationalists remained at odds over the concrete application of the declaration.[113] Through most of the remainder of the Eisenhower years, the Nationalists tried unsuccessfully to overcome Washington's reluctance to support paramilitary operations to organize anticommunist resistance on the continent.[114] After the conclusion of the Doan-Wang agreement, Chiang showed no further inclination to reduce his troop complement on the offshore islands. As it was, the Nationalists complied with the Doan-Wang agreement only under pressure and after much foot-dragging.[115]

Like the earlier 1954–55 crisis, the 1958 Sino-American confrontation in the offshore islands concluded without a clash of arms. Recent studies of the Chinese role in the crisis have agreed that caution and flexibility characterized Mao's calculations in dealing with the United States. For their part, even as they flexed America's military muscle and asserted its interests in the Taiwan Strait, Eisenhower and Dulles similarly demonstrated restraint and adaptability in pursuing their deterrence strategy. Despite pressure from Taipei, they refused to approve military countermeasures by the Nationalists that might further enflame the crisis and spark fighting between the U.S. and the Communist mainland. A retrospective report by American military authorities on Taiwan concluded that during August and much of September, the Nationalists had deliberately exaggerated the urgency of their need for support of their offshore islands garrisons in order to further enmesh the United States.[116]

Eisenhower and Dulles also tried to keep open a path to a peaceful resolution. The United States immediately took up the Chinese offer to resume the ambassadorial talks and withdrew naval protection from Nationalist resupply convoys after the first Chinese cease-fire announcement. Although Dulles placed no confidence in a peaceful settlement through negotiations, one reason he welcomed the Warsaw talks was that they might allow the Chinese to defuse the confrontation without loss of face. Once the blockade of Jinmen had been broken, the secretary and the president publicly distanced themselves from Chiang Kai-shek's massive troop deployment on the islands, a tactical ploy intended in part to facilitate a Chinese decision to let the crisis abate. Privately, Eisenhower showed more boldness and flexibility

than Dulles in looking for an escape hatch, although it seems highly unlikely
that the offer of an amphibious lift or even the bigger JCS package of
inducements could have enticed Chiang into wholesale retreat from the
islands. Significantly, by early October, Mao and his top-level comrades had
themselves decided that the Nationalists were best left in control of the
islands in order to frustrate Washington's two-China designs and retain a
reliable instrument for increasing tension in the Taiwan Strait when it
served their advantage.[117]

Despite Eisenhower's attachment to the New Look's massive retaliation
strategy and his approval of JCS plans for nuclear retaliation in the Taiwan
Strait, the president was hardly a nuclear hawk during the crisis. Even Dulles backed away from his initial readiness to face up to the consequences:
His harrowing description to Chiang of the human cost of nuclear intervention revealed his own doubts about the massive retaliation strategy in this
situation. Before leaving for Taipei, the secretary agreed that the NSC Planning Board should prepare a study on the lessons of the crisis that would
stress the need to develop greater conventional military capability.[118] Down
to the end of his administration, Eisenhower and his policy advisers debated
the use of atomic weapons in a limited war in the offshore islands. [119]

While the crisis underscored the hazards of nuclear retaliation in the
Taiwan Strait, it also reinforced the conviction in policy-making circles that
the Chinese took the threat of armed conflict with the United States seriously. A State Department memorandum setting out the "Ten Principal
Conclusions and Lessons Deriving from the Taiwan Crisis" declared that
the recent confrontation had "demonstrated that the Chinese Communists
respect firmness backed up by strength."[120] When he was asked by Prime
Minister Macmillan why the Chinese had backed off in the islands, Eisenhower opined that "they had just gotten tired of it, and saw no way to bring
about any great result without the likelihood of bringing us into full-scale
war against them." [121]

Despite the Chinese backdown, the crisis impressed on Dulles the extent
to which the administration found itself on the defensive, domestically and
internationally, over the offshore islands issue. While the 1954–55 crisis had,
in his view, been "agonizing enough," the most recent encounter had strained
relations with Congress and foreign governments almost to the breaking
point. Anticipating that the United States would be hard-pressed to win
support for the defense of the islands in any renewed crisis, he apparently

contemplated taking the issue to the United Nations if another threatening situation arose.[122]

Throughout the crisis, the overriding concern of senior American officials was the perilous process of demoralization and destabilization on Taiwan that the surrender of Jinmen would set in motion, with grim consequences for the Nationalist refuge and the U.S. security structure in the Far Pacific. It was this sense of ominous threat, which in retrospect appears much exaggerated, that convinced American leaders to risk war over territory so close to the China coast whose intrinsic military value they considered negligible. That assessment grew out of a hard-line policy toward the PRC that represented the most militant manifestation of America's global containment strategy during the Eisenhower years. The subjective doctrine of national security, which guided U.S. administrations during the Cold War, could be stretched to include peripheral areas whose direct salience to U.S. core interests was limited or nonexistent.[123] In the case of the offshore islands, American policymakers perceived their defense as vital to U.S. security primarily because of their politico-psychological connection to the preservation of a pro-American political order on Taiwan, a key strategic strongpoint in the western Pacific. Applying the domino theory and the bandwagon concept, policymakers were fearful that if Taiwan was destabilized and the island forfeited to the Chinese Communists, other friendly nations in the region would soon enter the orbit of the Sino-Soviet bloc. Dreading such a chain reaction, they extended the boundaries of national security to the offshore islands, in the process overcommitting the United States to a periphery whose protection risked an unwanted military clash with China and possibly the Soviet Union.

Deemed dangerously mistaken by many allies as well as by a preponderance of American and world opinion, such overcommitment exposed the Eisenhower administration to intense domestic and international criticism, which acted as a constraint on its decision making. Mounting disapproval of the administration's war-risking conduct on behalf of an intractable and belligerent Nationalist regime unreconciled to its defeat on the mainland contributed to Eisenhower's aversion to the use of nuclear weapons and his attraction to an amphibious lift deal; to his and Dulles's tactical shift at the cusp of September and October; to the secretary of state's effort in Taipei to refurbish the image of Chiang Kai-shek's government by redefining its mission; and to negotiation of the Doan-Wang agreement for downsizing the

Jinmen garrison. As the crisis unwound, the president and secretary of state both came to recognize that the furor over the islands not only hampered their assertive stance toward these contested territories, it weakened their ability to sustain their overall pro-Nationalist policy.

The crisis did not, as one historian has contended, mark a "watershed" that divided a previous "aggressive" U.S. policy along China's southern flank from a new, "totally defensive posture."[124] Despite its sympathy for the Nationalists' liberationist goal, the Eisenhower administration had never endorsed the strategy of counterattack, had deliberately endowed the Nationalist armed forces with only a modest offensive capability, had erected various formal safeguards against independent military action, and had curtailed its covert support for Nationalist incursions against the mainland. The joint communiqué was merely the further extension of an existing policy of restraint without squelching Nationalist hopes for a return to their lost territory.

Despite the difficulties and risks of the 1958 crisis, U.S. policy toward the offshore islands (including the option of military intervention) remained essentially unchanged for the remainder of Eisenhower's term of office. After the death of John Foster Dulles in April 1959, his successor, Christian Herter, initiated no new departures in the Taiwan Strait. Following a State Department review in the summer and early fall of 1960, Herter reaffirmed existing policy and rejected any attempt to persuade the Nationalist government to forsake the islands. Eisenhower never again took up his amphibious lift scheme or gave thought to any other plan to achieve a substantial troop reduction. The subject of the islands did not even come up in the president's conversations with Chiang Kai-shek during a visit to Taiwan in June 1960.[125] When Eisenhower left the White House, the two sides in the unfinished civil war still squared off against each other just a few miles off the south China coast, and the offshore islands remained a tinderbox for Sino-American confrontation.

CHAPTER FIVE

Tension across the Taiwan Strait in the 1950s

Chinese Strategy and Tactics

Gong Li

TAIWAN AND THE PENGHU ISLANDS (the Pescadores) have been China's territory since ancient times. Historical textual research reveals that the prehis-
toric culture on Taiwan shared common origins with that on the mainland
of China. Contact between Taiwan, the Penghu Islands, and the mainland
was established centuries ago, and many inhabitants moved from the coastal
regions of the mainland and settled on Taiwan. Chinese feudal governments
appointed officials, set up effective administration, and stationed soldiers on
Taiwan as early as the Song and Yuan dynasties.

On April 17, 1895, following the Sino-Japanese War of 1894–95, Japan
forced the Chinese Qing government to sign the unequal Treaty of Shimonoseki, which ceded Taiwan and the Penghu Islands to Japan. But the treaty
also stated that Taiwan and the Penghu Islands had been China's territory,
and under China's effective administration, before China was defeated and
forced to cede them to Japan. The people of Taiwan launched a ceaseless
struggle against Japan's forced occupation of the islands. On December 9,
1941, after the anti-Japanese war broke out, the Chinese government announced, in its statement declaring war on Japan, "All treaties, agreements,
and contracts concerning relations between China and Japan are hereby
abolished."[1] This surely included the unequal Treaty of Shimonoseki. The

Cairo Declaration, signed by the heads of the governments of China, the United States, and Great Britain on December 1, 1943, stated that "all the territories Japan has stolen from the Chinese, such as Manchuria, Formosa, and the Pescadores, shall be restored to the Republic of China."[2] This document made clear that the American and British governments formally promised to support restoration of China's sovereignty over Taiwan and the Penghu Islands. The Potsdam Declaration of July 26, 1945, reiterated this understanding: "The terms stated in the Cairo Declaration are to be carried out."[3] Soon thereafter, the Soviet Union also joined the Potsdam Declaration, which then became an important international agreement, acknowledged by the four major powers, with irrefutable legal effect in relation to the Taiwan issue.

On September 2, 1945, in its Instrument of Surrender, Japan stated that it would "accept the provisions set forth in the declaration issued by the heads of the governments of the United States, China and Great Britain on 26 July, 1945, at Potsdam, and subsequently adhered to by the Union of Soviet Socialist Republics."[4] This statement clearly encompasses the provision of the Cairo Declaration, reiterated in the Potsdam Declaration, that Taiwan should be returned to China. After the surrender of Ando, commander of Japan's Tenth Army and its governor of Taiwan, Taiwan and the Penghu Islands were returned to China, not only legally but as a matter of fact.

For this reason, ever since the Chiang Kai-shek leadership retreated to Taiwan, China has been determined to liberate Taiwan and reunite the country.[5] In order to prevent certain countries from trying to treat the "two Chinas" as a fait accompli by separating Taiwan from the mainland, Mao Zedong, on the eve of the founding of the People's Republic, immediately put forward two principles for establishing diplomatic relations with non-socialist countries: First, such countries must sever relations with the Kuomintang (KMT) government; second, PRC delegates would be sent abroad to establish diplomatic relations, "the final result depending on the negotiations,"[6] to maintain the position of "one China."

By signing the Cairo Declaration and the Potsdam Declaration, the United States acknowledged that Taiwan should be returned to China. But with the gradual collapse of the KMT on the mainland, the American government began to consider a policy of separating China's mainland from Taiwan. President Truman formally approved a new policy toward Taiwan that aimed to "deny Formosa to the communists" and to prevent "Formosa from falling under Communist control." The policy also stipulated that such goals were to be reached through diplomatic and economic means rather than through the use of American military force to "defend" Taiwan.[7]

But the situation in China developed faster than the American government had expected. By the end of 1949 the United States realized that if it did not use force to defend Taiwan it would have to accept the reality of giving up Taiwan. On January 5, 1950, President Truman stated that "Taiwan has been handed back to Generalissimo Chiang. The United States and its allies have acknowledged in the past four years that China has sovereignty over that island." The president's statement said that the United States "has never had any wild ambition to seize it. At the present time, the United States has no intention of using armed forces to intervene in the current situation. The United States has no plan to follow any course that might involve the United States in the Chinese civil war." The statement also declared that "the American government has no plan to offer military aid or advice to the Chinese army in Taiwan" but that it would only "continue to carry out the economic aid plan of the Economic Cooperation Agency according to current legal rights."[8] Although Truman suggested that the United States recognized that Taiwan belonged to China, his statement remained ambiguous. First, by "returning Taiwan to China," Truman meant returning it to the KMT, not to New China. Second, in a later version of the statement, following "the United States has no intention of obtaining special rights or establishing military bases," the key words in the original draft, "or make Taiwan break from China," were deleted. Third, before the statement that "the United States has no intention of obtaining special rights or establishing military bases," the qualifying phrase "at the present time" was added. Such alterations were intentional and foreshadowed later changes in policy. In addition, many officials within the administration were unwilling to "let Taiwan fall into the hands of Communists,"[9] and they continued to press their cause. Therefore, Truman's statement that the United States would not use armed force to intervene or become involved in China's civil war was unreliable.

On June 27, 1950, scarcely half a year later and following the outbreak of the Korean War, Truman announced, "The determination of Taiwan's status must wait for the restoration of peace in the Pacific region, the signing of a peace treaty with Japan, or is to be subjected to the consideration of the United Nations."[10] He also ordered the U.S. Seventh Fleet to the Taiwan

Strait. The Taiwan issue thus evolved from an internal Chinese issue into a serious dispute between China and the United States. Direct U.S. intervention increased the difficulty of Taiwan's liberation, and China postponed it. On June 30, 1950, the Central Committee of the Chinese Communist Party (CCP) relayed its new policy to the Chinese People's Liberation Army (PLA): "China's attitude is to denounce the American invasion of Taiwan and intervention in China's internal affairs. Our plan is to continue to demobilize the army, strengthen the construction of the navy, and delay the liberation of Taiwan."[11] Later, the CCP Central Committee adopted the "resist U.S.-aid Korea" policy, a shift in the strategic focus of the PLA from southeast to northeast China.

To China, it was intolerable that the United States should use its armed forces to intervene in Taiwan and in China's internal affairs. The Chinese government never wavered on matters such as sovereignty, independence, and territorial integrity. China put off its plan to liberate Taiwan because of the interference of the United States, but its long-term goal of recovering Taiwan was unshakable.

In his speech at the Eighth Session of the Central People's Government Committee, on June 28, 1950, Mao Zedong pointed out that "The U.S. invasion in Asia can only arouse broad and determined resistance among the people of Asia. Truman said on January 5 that the United States would not intervene in Taiwan. Now he himself has proved he was simply lying. He has also torn up all international agreements guaranteeing that the United States would not interfere in China's internal affairs. It has been beneficial to the people of China and Asia to see revealed the true colors of American imperialism."[12]

On the same day, Premier Zhou Enlai declared, "The fact that Taiwan belongs to China can never be altered no matter what obstructionist tactics American imperialism may adopt. This is not only a fact of history but has been confirmed by the Cairo Declaration and the Potsdam Declaration, as well as the conditions following the Japanese surrender. The people of our country will be united as one to fight to the end to liberate Taiwan from the hands of American invaders."[13]

The United States ignored China's warnings. It not only sent armed personnel to Taiwan as "advisory teams" and "investigation groups" and supplied Taiwan with large amounts of war materiel, but also secretly agreed with Chiang Kai-shek to set up an "American Military Liaison Group to Taiwan" to "jointly defend" Taiwan. There were three factors that caused the United States to intervene in Taiwan and become more deeply mired in the issue. First, the United States had for a long time maintained close relations with the Kuomintang, adopting it as its ally in defending U.S. interests in the Far East and thus believing that it had a moral duty to support the Kuomintang. Second, the United States took New China as a strategic threat, so that Taiwan's important geographic position made it a crucial link in the crescent-shaped blockade encircling China. Third, due to its anti-communist Cold War ideology, the United States was unwilling to let Taiwan fall into the hands of the Communists. As a result, the United States increasingly interfered in the Taiwan issue, causing sharp antagonism between itself and China.

China's Strategic Intent in Bombarding Jinmen

Relations between the United States and Taiwan became closer after the Korean cease-fire. In August 1953, the United States and Taiwan held their first joint military maneuver involving naval and air force units. In September, the United States and Taiwan authorities signed an "Agreement on Mutual Military Understanding," which stipulated that the United States would be responsible for reorganizing, training, monitoring, and equipping the Kuomintang army and that, should hostilities occur, all orders to move KMT troops should be agreed upon in advance by the United States. The area covered by the agreement included Taiwan, the Penghu Islands, Jinmen (Quemoy), Mazu (Matsu), and Dachen.[14]

In early 1954, when the Geneva Conference met to settle the Korean and Indochina conflicts, the United States held talks with Taiwan authorities toward signing a "Mutual Defense Treaty." This situation alarmed Chinese leaders, who believed that the United States intended to legalize its interference in China's internal affairs and further threaten China's safety by creating a military front in the Taiwan Strait. It was inevitable that China would react. On July 7, 1954, at an expanded Politburo meeting, Mao Zedong analyzed the international situation. He observed that on the whole, the situation was much improved and that

the United States is quite isolated. Its isolation will continue even after the problems in Southeast Asia and Indochina. Now many states in the British Commonwealth, France, countries in Southeast Asia, Canada, Mexico and some countries in South America do not like the United States, so the situation is quite good. Not only is it now impossible for us to shut the door, but in addition, the situation is quite favorable to us. We need to go out . . . to dissolve the unity among the imperialists. There are pro-U.S. factions in all countries, in England, France, India, Burma . . . but there are differences in their attitudes toward the United States. For example, Churchill and Eden are not as pro-American as their minister of finance. So there are such contradictions in all states. We should unite with those anti-American and less pro-American factions. [15]

Mao further asserted that "there are contradictions even in America. Eisenhower, [Walter Bedell] Smith, and the finance and defense secretaries do not agree to fight a war, but Dulles, [William] Knowland, [Richard] Nixon, and [Arthur W.] Radford are more risky. So, even in a country such as the United States, we can do some persuasion." He argued that "one particular problem with America is the Taiwan issue. . . . The Taiwan issue cannot be solved in a short time. We should do something to eliminate the possibility of America signing a treaty with Taiwan and do some propaganda work. We should blame America for intending to seize Taiwan and Chiang Kai-shek for being a traitor. On the other hand, we should adopt a posture of making contacts with American citizens, with the objective of forcing the United States not to sign a treaty with Taiwan. I think both England and France are against America signing a treaty with Taiwan because they could not derive any benefit from it."

Those at the Politboro meeting, after careful deliberation, agreed with Mao's view that the Taiwan issue was worth special attention. If the United States and Chiang Kai-shek were to realize their plot, Sino-American relations would remain tense for a long time, and "it would be more difficult to seek relaxation or any change." [16] To prevent the United States and the KMT from establishing a military and political alliance, and the Taiwan issue from reaching an impasse, the CCP Central Committee decided to carry out a large-scale propaganda campaign. Mao explained that "after the Korean War we failed to put forward to the people of the whole country this task in time (we lost about half a year's time). We failed to take the necessary military, diplomatic, or propaganda measures or to carry out effective work on this task. This is not proper. If we fail again to put this task forward now and remain idle, we will have made a serious political mistake." [17]

In accordance with the instructions of the Party's Central Committee and Chairman Mao, China began to emphasize the theme of "liberating Taiwan." The *People's Daily* ran an editorial on July 23, 1954, reaffirming that Taiwan was China's territory and that the Chinese people were determined to liberate Taiwan. On August 1, in a speech commemorating the twenty-seventh anniversary of the founding of the PLA, Zhu De, the commander-in-chief of the

PLA, stressed the Chinese people's determination to liberate Taiwan and stated that no foreign country would be allowed to interfere in China's internal affairs. On August 2, Premier Zhou Enlai also stated that Taiwan was China's territory and that the Chinese people would surely liberate Taiwan. On August 6, in response to the news that the United States was trying to organize a "Southeast Asia Defense Group" that would include Taiwan, Mao issued these instructions: "To Premier Zhou: Both your report and the joint statement of the parties should make comments on this issue."[18]

On August 11, in a speech at the Thirty-third Meeting of the Central People's Government Committee, Zhou Enlai denounced the United States for "redoubling its efforts to instigate and support the traitorous Chiang Kai-shek clique to carry out increasingly disruptive and destructive wars along the coastal regions of the mainland, to actively restore Japanese militarism, and to step up its plan to organize a "Pacific Anti-Communist Alliance," as well as other invasion alliances in Southeast Asia and the Middle East, to create new tension in Asia." Zhou added that "the Government of the People's Republic of China declares once again that Taiwan is China's sacred and inviolable territory. We will never allow the United States to invade it or let it be put into the trusteeship of the United Nations. The liberation of Taiwan is a matter of China's sovereignty, and no other country will be allowed to interfere. All the so-called treaties signed by the United States and the traitorous Chiang Kai-shek clique entrenched in Taiwan are illegal and null and void. Should any foreign invaders dare to prevent the Chinese people from liberating Taiwan, or dare to violate China's sovereignty and territorial integrity, or dare to interfere with China's internal affairs, they shall have to bear all possible consequences of their aggression."[19]

Even as it launched a massive propaganda offensive, China also passed signals to the United States through diplomatic channels, trying to persuade the Eisenhower administration not to adopt hostile policies. During his meeting with a delegation of the British Labour Party on August 24, 1954, Mao criticized U.S. policy toward China and asked Great Britain to try to persuade the United States to make a fresh start on the Taiwan issue and adopt a wiser attitude. Mao said he hoped that friends in the British Labour Party would persuade the Americans, first, to remove their Seventh Fleet from the area and leave Taiwan alone, because Taiwan was part of China; second, not to engage in work on the Southeast Asia Treaty, as this ran counter to history, and that it would be better to draft a peace treaty; third, not to arm Japan, because arming Japan to counter China and the Soviet Union would only result in harming the United States itself and other countries in the southwest Pacific. Such a move would be tantamount to "lifting a rock only to drop it on one's own foot"; and fourth, not to arm West Germany, since that would also have undesirable consequences, "lifting another rock to be dropped on one's own foot."[20]

In coordination with the Party's political offensive, in August 1954 the CCP Central Committee issued an order to the East China Military Command to shell Jinmen, and the PLA accordingly did so on September 3 and 22. China's intention was to puncture the arrogance of the Kuomintang army and to focus world attention on the Taiwan issue, thus demonstrating, through a show of force, the determination of the People's Republic of China to liberate Taiwan. Militarily, China was not prepared to seize Jinmen but used the shelling as a tactical move to allow the PLA to concentrate its forces along the Zhejiang coast. China's military objectives were limited, but it aimed for strategic, political, and diplomatic results.

The shelling of Jinmen aroused heightened tension within the U.S. government. Lacking information about the attack, the United States believed that the PLA intended to seize Jinmen and perhaps launch an attack on Taiwan. U.S. military officials suggested that additional U.S. troops be sent to defend Jinmen and that the navy and the air force be deployed on surprise attacks against Chinese harbors and airports. President Eisenhower decided against this course, however, because he thought the risk would be too great. The United States tried its best to persuade Chiang Kai-shek to give up Jinmen and Mazu, but he flatly refused, insisting that his army's morale would decline badly should it withdraw from the islands and that Taiwan would, as a result, be in jeopardy.

While the United States and Chiang Kai-shek were occupied with Jinmen and Mazu, China directed its front-line forces against KMT-occupied islands along the Zhejiang coast. The PLA began shelling Dachen on November 1, 1954, and dispatched naval vessels to the sea east of Zhejiang Province, sinking the Kuomintang's destroyer *Taiping*. Kuomintang troops stationed on Dachen found themselves in a precarious situation.

The United States and the Taiwan authorities stepped up negotiations over the "Mutual Defense Treaty," which they signed on December 2, 1954. It stipulated that the United States would "continue and develop" Taiwan's armed forces, and that "joint actions" would be taken in case "the territory of any signatory state" suffered an "armed attack." The treaty covered Taiwan and the Penghu Islands but could be extended to cover "other territories agreed upon" by both sides.[21] It revealed the U.S. intention to "divide the Strait to rule," but it did not clearly indicate whether it covered the defense of Jinmen, Mazu, and other islands along the Chinese coast.

To express China's firm position that it would never recognize the "Mutual Defense Treaty," the CCP Central Committee and Chairman Mao decided to pursue action in two areas. Zhou Enlai would draft a government statement denouncing the so-called treaty and would make diplomatic efforts in parallel with the military efforts to liberate Dachen. The PLA planned a breakthrough by seizing Yijiangshan, an offshore base of Dachen. To allow for unforeseen circumstances, Mao thought the attack on Yijiangshan should try to avoid a head-on confrontation with U.S. troops. His instructions, issued on December 11, 1954, and based on the operation plan submitted by the East China Military Command, stated: "Please consider whether the present is opportune for an attack on Yijiangshan island as U.S. troops have been holding large-scale maneuvers on the sea to the east of Zhejiang Province."[22]

The Chinese People's Liberation Army, waiting for an opportune time, attacked Yijiangshan on January 18, 1955: about 1,000 Kuomintang troops stationed there were wiped out, and the United States was forced to withdraw its naval vessels. Now Dachen was in range of PLA fire.

President Eisenhower was surprised by the incident and reacted immediately, urging the United Nations to "mediate to cease the war along China's coastal line" and, at the same time, threatening China with war. He asked the U.S. Congress to empower him to "safeguard the safety" of Taiwan and the Penghu Islands by using American troops "when necessary." As for the islands along China's coastline, Eisenhower asked Congress to allow him to "clarify the situation," and if actions taken by China on these islands were "part of or preparatory steps in attacking Taiwan and the Pescadores," he would have the authority to use American troops.[23] On January 25 and 28, 1955, respectively, the U.S. House and the U.S. Senate both passed resolutions to approve Eisenhower's requests. Large numbers of U.S. troops were then dispatched to Taiwan, posing a military threat to China. The United States also signaled that it would use nuclear weapons.

But the American side overlooked a simple fact: the People's Republic of China was born through gunfire. Most Chinese leaders had been well tested in battle and could not be intimidated by threats of war. Mao Zedong, in particular, was not shaken by these threats, believing that the United States was merely engaging in nuclear blackmail. Mao made it clear in the speech he delivered when the first Finnish ambassador to the People's Republic presented his credentials that the main threat of a world war and the main threat to China were from bellicose elements in the United States: "They have invaded Taiwan and the Taiwan Strait and wanted to launch an atomic war. We have two principles: first, we don't want war, and second, we shall firmly strike back should anyone invade us. We have been educating our Party members and our people according to these principles. American nuclear blackmail cannot intimidate the Chinese people. We have a population of six hundred million and nine million six hundred thousand square kilometers of territory. The atom bombs owned by the United States cannot wipe out all the Chinese people."

Mao said that even if the United States had more powerful atom bombs that could strike China and penetrate into the earth, it would not mean much to the universe, though it might be considered to be a big event in the solar system. "We have an old saying," he observed, "millet plus rifles. The United States has planes plus atom bombs. But if the United States should launch an aggressive war against China by using its planes plus atom bombs, China would eventually win with our millet plus rifles. The whole world will support us."[24] While making known its resolve in the face of U.S. military threats, China adopted a prudent attitude to prevent escalation. The Military Affairs Commission under the CCP Central Committee ordered the PLA to postpone the attack on Dachen but to continue heavy aerial shelling of the island.

Because U.S. intimidation failed to pressure China into abandoning the shelling, and China ignored the "mediation" effort of the United Nations, the United States declared, on February 5, 1955, that it would "help" Kuomintang troops withdraw from Dachen. Secretary of State John Foster Dulles informed Soviet Foreign Minister Vyacheslav Molotov about this decision in advance, hoping that the Soviet Union might persuade the Chinese side not to attack KMT troops during their withdrawal. The East Zhejiang Province front command of the Chinese People's Liberation Army had planned to strike the enemy when they retreated, but taking the international situation into consideration, on February 2 Mao ordered Peng Dehuai not to open fire on the port or places around it when Chiang Kai-shek's troops withdrew, whether U.S. battleships were involved or not. He had decided to allow the enemy to withdraw in safety.[25] By February 12, the 25,000 KMT troops on Dachen and the 18,000 inhabitants who lived there had withdrawn under a U.S. Navy escort. The next day the PLA occupied Dachen, the nearby Yushan islands, and Poshan island. Thus, all the islands in east Zhejiang Province were liberated.

Through the shelling of Jinmen and the liberation of the islands along the Zhejiang coast, China reaffirmed its commitment to liberating Taiwan, wiped out the KMT's dangerous strongholds along the coast, and tested the resolve of the United States and the Taiwan authorities. In addition, the Taiwan Strait crisis aroused the attention of many countries.

China's Efforts to Ease the Tension across the Taiwan Strait

China sowed seeds of dispute between the United States and the Taiwan authorities by bombarding Jinmen. The United States had tried to persuade Chiang Kai-shek either to give up Jinmen and Mazu and "divide the Strait to rule" or to hand the Taiwan issue over to the United Nations. But Chiang stood firm in his resolve never to retreat from Jinmen and Mazu. On March 23, 1955, when Great Britain tried to persuade him to give up Jinmen and Mazu, he stated that the United States should not agree with the British position. Whether or not the United States took part in the defense of Jinmen and Mazu, it should not attempt to force the Kuomintang to give up the islands: "We shall not yield under any pressure, but will fight to the end, till the last man. It would be a mistake for anyone to think that we are prepared to withdraw from Jinmen and Mazu simply because we withdrew from Dachen."[26]

Although it was dissatisfied with Chiang's position, the United States could not wash its hands of the KMT. Eisenhower was compelled to declare that "In order not to damage the morale of free China or dash their hopes, the United States is determined to help with the defense of Jinmen and Mazu to consolidate the position of Taiwan and the Pescadores."[27] But U.S. policy immediately aroused opposition from the majority of its allies. Canadian Foreign Minister Lester Pearson, for example, declared that Canada would not enter into any war for the coastal islands. One columnist observed that, "with the exception of Generalissimo Chiang Kai-shek, all of us allied countries think this is a wrong war fought at a wrong time in a wrong place."[28] Conflict between the United States and its allies, and between the United States and Chiang Kai-shek, was increasing.

Observing the situation, the CCP Central Committee and Chairman Mao decided to take advantage of the discord and proposed talks with the United States to ease tension in Asia, especially with regard to the Taiwan Strait. The *People's Daily* ran an editorial on March 7, 1955, which argued that no country would tolerate another country occupying its territory and supporting rebellious cliques to launch wars. If another country occupied Long Island in the United States and supported anti-American activities there, it argued, the United States would not tolerate it. In other words, the United States should put itself in China's position and respect China's right to liberate Taiwan. The editorial concluded with a call for an international conference, with the participation of China, the United States, Great Britain, the Soviet Union, India, Burma, Indonesia, Pakistan, and Ceylon, to discuss easing tension across the Taiwan Strait and safe-guarding peace.

At the Bandung Conference then in session there were many calls for an easing of tension in the Far East. To show its sincere desire for peace and to dispel doubts in certain Asian and African countries, China authorized Zhou Enlai to suggest the possibility of peaceful liberation of Taiwan if the United States withdrew its forces from Taiwan and the Taiwan Strait. On April 23, in a meeting of the heads of the eight delegations to the conference, Zhou declared that "the Chinese people and the American people have always been on friendly terms. The Chinese people do not want to fight a war against the United States. The Chinese government is willing to sit down and enter into negotiations with the government of the United States to discuss how to ease the tension in the Far East, especially the tension in the Taiwan region."[29] This statement evoked a positive reaction worldwide, and many countries expressed hope that the United States would accept China's proposal. India's representative to the United Nations, Krishna Menon, made a special trip to China to mediate. China welcomed him and reaffirmed its policy.

In a discussion with Indonesian Prime Minister Ali Sastroamidjojo on May 26, 1955, Mao Zedong further reiterated that China was willing to sign a peace treaty with the United States: "We want to strive for a peaceful environment that will last as long as possible, and this is both desirable and possible. If the United States is willing to sign a peace treaty, the duration can be fifty or even a hundred years. But I do not know if the United States is willing. I think you will not disagree that now the main problem is the United States."[30] In addition, China released four American pilots it had been holding in custody. These proposals and unilateral offers clearly showed China's interest in easing Sino-American tensions.

In response to the positive reception of China's proposals in the international community and to the impact of China's position on U.S. public opinion, the Eisenhower administration gave serious consideration to China's proposal for talks. It also wanted to probe China's intentions and hoped to be able to resolve the issue of American citizens and espionage agents who were being held in custody in China. Thus, on July 13, through Great Britain, the United States proposed that the two sides hold talks in Geneva at the ambassadorial level. China replied on July 15, also through Great Britain, that it was willing to hold such talks.

The Chinese side attached great importance to the U.S.-China talks and set up a special group to give guidance to the delegates taking part. To further signal its conciliatory stand, China declared unilaterally, before the talks started, that the Chinese Supreme Military Court would free eleven American agents in detention on July 31, 1955, before the end of their sentence. From the very beginning, however, the ambassadorial-level talks that opened the next day in Geneva encountered trouble. China believed these talks should stress the Taiwan issue and pave the way for further talks at higher levels. It wanted to discuss substantive issues like the lifting of the American ban on trade with China and the exchange of journalists. But the United States' sole objectives were the release of Americans held in China and obtaining China's commitment that it would not use force against Taiwan. After much negotiation, China and the United States agreed to two agenda items: first, the issue of "returning citizens of both sides to their own country," and second, "other substantive issues in dispute by the two sides." The second agenda item could include any issue in Sino-American relations either side wanted to raise.

On September 10, 1955, after fourteen grueling sessions, China and the United States recognized the rights of citizens in each other's country to return to their own country—the only agreement reached through the Sino-American talks at the ambassadorial level— and a number of citizens were able to realize their wish of returning to their own country. As Zhou Enlai would later remark, it was important that China had brought back Qian Xuesen, and that this alone made the talks worthwhile and valuable.[31]

About the second agenda item, China raised two issues on September 14: lifting the ban on trade with China; and preparing for Sino-American talks at higher levels. But the American side again created complications, first on the issue of the return of citizens and then on the issue of China's "giving up the use of armed force to achieve the country's goals," thus interfering in the Taiwan issue, which was China's internal affair. The Chinese delegate stressed that since it had been China's consistent policy not to resort to military force in solving disputes between China and the United States, it had proposed the U.S.-China talks, but that this policy did not apply to China's internal affairs, specifically, whether China would use peaceful or military means to liberate Taiwan. This question, he insisted, could not be considered in the Sino-American talks. The only Taiwan issue that could be discussed was a U.S. commitment not to use force against China and to withdraw its armed forces from Taiwan and the Taiwan Strait.[32] But the United States insisted that it would not discuss any other issues until China accepted the American proposal on "the mutual agreement not to resort to armed force." It was thus impossible to reach any additional agreements.

By 1955, while advocating peaceful talks with the United States, China had also begun to formulate new policies toward Taiwan. In April, during a visit to Burma, Zhou Enlai told Premier U Nu that China "may adopt peaceful means to liberate Taiwan." On May 13, at the Fifteenth Plenary Session of the Standing Committee of the National People's Congress, Zhou declared that the PLA might adopt two possible ways to liberate Taiwan— through war or through peaceful means— and that the Chinese people would strive toward peaceful means if conditions allowed.[33] This was the first time that Chinese leaders had publicly suggested the possibility of a peaceful liberation of Taiwan, and it marked a major change in China's policy. On July 30, Zhou further declared that the possibility of a peaceful liberation would increase if the United States did not interfere in China's internal affairs. If possible, the Chinese government was willing to negotiate with Taiwanese authorities over concrete steps toward unification.[34]

In an interview with Cao Juren, a former journalist from the KMT's Central News Agency, on July 16, 1956, Zhou Enlai unequivocally proposed a third period of cooperation between the Chinese Communist Party and the Kuomintang. He pointed out that they had already experienced two periods of cooperation: the first enabled the National Revolutionary Army to win the Northern Expedition, and the second led to the victory of the Anti-Japanese War. Why couldn't there be a third period of cooperation? The Taiwan issue was China's internal affair, and all patriots were of one family. China did not demand that Taiwan surrender but proposed only that it hold talks on an equal footing. As long as there was a united government, all the other issues could be arranged jointly through negotiations.[35] In an October 4 interview with Cao Juren, Mao Zedong said that everything would be settled if Taiwan broke off its relationship with the United States and returned to the motherland.

Chiang Kai-shek rejected these proposals, more concerned about preparations for a "counterattack" against the mainland. To determine whether the Chinese Communist Party was setting up a smoke screen to hide preparations for an attack on Taiwan, however, Chiang sent Song Yishan, a Hong Kong Chinese, to Beijing to probe Chinese intentions. In April 1957, Song Yishan went to Beijing through Guangzhou, where he met Zhou Enlai and held talks with Li Weihan, head of the Department of United Front Work of the Central Committee of the Chinese Communist Party. The Communist Party proposed that peaceful reunification could be achieved through talks on an equal footing: Taiwan would be an autonomous region with a high self-governing status under the central government; Taiwan's affairs would remain under the leadership of Chiang Kai-shek, and the Chinese Communist Party would not interfere with his authority; the Kuomintang could send its delegates to Beijing to take part in the administration of the whole country. China did insist, however, that U.S. military forces withdraw from the Taiwan Strait.

To publicize China's position, Chinese leaders began a propaganda campaign promoting a third period of cooperation between the Chinese Communist Party and the Kuomintang. On April 16, 1957, Zhou Enlai held a banquet for Voroshilov, chair of the Supreme Soviet of the U.S.S.R., at the Beijing Hotel. When he introduced Wei Lihuang, a former KMT general, to the guests, he recalled the two prior periods of cooperation between the Kuomintang and the Chinese Communist Party. Mao Zedong, who was also present, said that the Chinese Communist Party was preparing for a third such period,[36] the first time Chinese leaders had publicly raised the issue of a third period of cooperation between the Communist Party and the Kuomintang. On April 17, the *People's Daily* ran Mao's words in a front-page banner headline.

When he returned to Hong Kong, Song Yishan submitted a report to the Taiwan authorities describing the achievements of his Beijing trip and his thoughts about it. The content of the report was fairly objective, yet Chiang Kai-shek was unmoved. The Eighth Congress of the Kuomintang, convened later that year, in October, maintained the task of "counterattacking the mainland" and characterized the Chinese Communist Party's proposal for peaceful talks as a "conspiracy of the united front," which aimed to "overturn Taiwan and the bases in its outer islands by political means." From that point on, KMT military harassment and sabotage along the mainland coastline escalated. Beijing's peace proposal thus met with setbacks, and cross-strait tension intensified.

The Decision to Bombard Jinmen for the Second Time

In November 1957, the U.S. Seventh Fleet held a large-scale military maneuver in the waters around Taiwan. In conjunction with these U.S. exercises, 110,000 Kuomintang troops held a maneuver, called "Kunyang," throughout Taiwan. In May 1958, the United States combined its seventeen military aid agencies on Taiwan, including the "Military Advisory Group" and the "United States Headquarters of Coordinated Defense of Taiwan," under a single authority, the "Headquarters of the U.S. Army Stationed in Taiwan to Aid the Taiwan Defense." The Taiwan authorities assigned one-third of their ground forces to the islands off Taiwan and increased harassment and sabotage against the mainland from bases in Jinmen and Mazu. These measures challenged Mao Zedong's patience, and he began to think of new ways to push the Taiwan issue to the forefront of world attention.

Coinciding with these events, the United States sparked a conflict in the Mideast. On July 15, 1958, U.S. troops landed in Lebanon to support the Chamoun administration in the name of "defending Lebanon's sovereignty." Mao used this opportunity to achieve several international and domestic objectives. On July 17, the Taiwan authorities proclaimed special martial law on the grounds that "the current situation in the Mideast is explosive." As a show of support for the Mideast people's struggle and to oppose U.S. interference in China's internal affairs, the Central Committee of the Chinese Communist Party and Mao Zedong again decided to shell Jinmen and Mazu. Mao wanted to strike a punitive blow against the KMT and probe just how far the United States would go to defend Taiwan. Mao explained that China was shelling Jinmen in support of the Arab people and to thwart American designs in Taiwan. The United States had been bullying China for many years, so why shouldn't China make the United States suffer when it had the opportunity?: "We didn't wrong the United States by saying it created tension across the Taiwan Strait. The United States has several thousand troops stationed in Taiwan in addition to its two air force bases. The Seventh Fleet, the largest U.S. [fleet], has been cruising around the Taiwan Strait from time to time. The United States has another large navy base in Manila. [Chief of Naval Operations Arleigh A.] Burke said not long ago [on August 6] that U.S. troops were ready to disembark and fight in the Taiwan Strait at any time, just as they did in Lebanon. This is proof."[37] At this time China was just about to launch the "Great Leap Forward." Mao believed that it was dangerous for the Chinese masses to live in fear of conflict from day to day and discouraging to the enthusiasm necessary for this effort. Thus, another factor in his decision to begin the shelling was his interest in heightening the people's initiative to expedite economic development.

On July 17, 1958, the CCP Central Committee gave orders to prepare to shell Jinmen and to deploy air force units in Fujian. The Chinese air force was soon ready to engage the KMT air force in order to seize control of the airspace over the Fujian coast, and Chinese naval and artillery reinforcements had also reached their positions. The timing of the shelling was carefully chosen, and the date had been changed several times as Mao closely coordinated China's military action with its political and diplomatic struggles. On July 27, in a letter to Peng Dehuai and Huang Kecheng, who were in charge of the work of the Central Military Commission, Mao pointed out that "It seems appropriate to wait for a few days before shelling Jinmen. Do not strike for the time being but wait to observe the situation. Do not strike whether they are relieving their garrison or not. Take the offensive when they attack us unreasonably. It will take time to settle the Mideast issue. Why should we be in a hurry, since we have plenty of time? We shall hold back for the time being, but we shall surely strike some day." Mao Zedong further pointed out: "Put politics in command, make repeated deliberations, and the result will be truly favorable."[38] His purpose was to combine the shelling of Jinmen with the settlement of the Taiwan issue and with support for the anti-American struggle of the people in the Mideast. He wanted to coordinate policies so that each situation would support the other. Later, in a letter to Zhou Enlai, Mao again pointed out that operating from a strategic commanding height to sweep down irresistibly was the necessary pattern for China's diplomatic struggles.[39]

After a period of observation and preparation, Chairman Mao made the final decision to shell Jinmen at the Beidaihe Conference. On August 21, he summoned Ye Fei, commander of the Fujian front, to report on the preparations for the shelling. Peng Dehuai and Lin Biao were also present. According to Ye Fei's later account of events, Mao listened to the report and then suddenly asked, "Will Americans get killed if you use so many artillery pieces?" Because there were American advisers down to the level of KMT troop battalions, Ye Fei replied, "Oh, it's possible that they will get killed." After thinking for a while, Mao asked "Can it be done so that no Americans will be killed?" Ye Fei replied, "Chairman, some killing is inevitable." Mao said nothing but announced that the meeting would be adjourned for further consideration. Lin Biao took the opportunity to write Mao a note, suggesting that he ask Wang Bingnan to inform the United States of the imminent shelling through the Sino-American talks in Warsaw, but Mao brushed aside Lin's suggestion. At the next day's meeting he said to Ye Fei: "All right then. Strike according to your plan."[40] As Ye Fei recalled, Mao attached great importance to relations with the United States and had tried to avoid a head-on confrontation. He only made up his mind to strike when he saw that it would be inevitable. Mao then asked Ye Fei to remain in Beidaihe to take part in the command. A telephone line was set up to connect the Fujian front with Ye's room in Beidaihe, enabling Ye to keep Mao up to date on the situation.

On August 23, under Mao Zedong's direct command, the PLA began shelling Jinmen. Within a few minutes, the whole island was engulfed in flames and many KMT positions were destroyed. Over thirty thousand shells fell on Jinmen in just under an hour and a half, and approximately 600 KMT troops were killed or wounded. Neither the United States nor Chiang Kai-shek had expected that the PLA would strike Jinmen at that time. Zhao Jiaxian, vice commander of Jinmen defense, Liu Mingkui, chief of staff, and Zhang Jie, vice commander of the air force, were killed. When the shells hit, Hu Lian, commander of Jinmen defense, and Yu Dawei, "defense minister" of the Taiwan regime, who had come to Jinmen for an inspection, were returning to headquarters. They were almost killed.

According to Mao's plan, the objective of the first round of the shelling was to probe U.S. intentions while maintaining ambiguity about whether the PLA would land on Jinmen, since the decision to occupy the island would depend on U.S. policy. As Mao said, "The purpose of the bombardment was not to reconnoiter Chiang Kai-shek's defense but rather to reconnoiter and test the determination of the Americans. The Chinese people dared to break ground where the god Taisui presides—to defy the mighty. In addition, Jinmen and Mazu, and even Taiwan, had always been China's territories."[41]

The shelling lasted for ten days. Then, on September 3, Mao gave the order to stop the shelling for three days. He wanted an opportunity to observe the reactions from the different sides. The next day China declared that the breadth of its territorial waters was twelve nautical miles. Although the United States and other Western countries did not recognize this declaration, they did not risk challenging it. The shelling signaled Chinese determination and discouraged the United States from intruding into China's declared territorial waters.

The first round of bombardment not only gained the military advantage of a surprise attack, it also achieved China's political goals. Three days before, the United Nations had passed a resolution calling for American and British troops to withdraw from Lebanon and Jordan. China used the bombardment over Jinmen to demand that American troops withdraw from Taiwan and that Kuomintang troops withdraw from Jinmen and Mazu. This attracted the attention of the international community. Mao said, "We will strike if you don't retreat. If Taiwan is too far to strike, we can strike Jinmen and Mazu. This will surely shock the world, not only the American people and the Asian people, but also the European people. The Arab world will be happy, and the majority of the people in Asia and Africa will sympathize with us."[42]

As expected, the shelling of Jinmen shocked the world. The United States was all the more nervous and hurriedly dispatched over one hundred battleships and two hundred planes to reinforce its armed forces in the Taiwan Strait. Its strategic focus quickly shifted from the Middle East to the Far East. On August 27, President Eisenhower had reaffirmed that the United States would not abandon its "responsibility" to use its armed forces to prevent China from liberating Taiwan. On September 4 he authorized Secretary of State Dulles to state that the United States would extend the scope of its defense from the Taiwan Strait to Jinmen and Mazu, and made it known that the United States had made corresponding military arrangements, thus threatening China with U.S. intervention. But later, in a memorandum, Dulles revealed that the United States would not give up the prospect of peaceful negotiations over the offshore islands.

Mao believed that the United States would now slip into the "noose" of Jinmen and Mazu, that it was ready to undertake responsibility for all of Taiwan, the Penghu Islands, Jinmen, and Mazu: "So far so good, as he

[Dulles] fell into the trap. We can now give him a kick whenever we feel like it. So we have the initiative, while the Americans have landed in a passive position."[43] Mao observed that "U.S. imperialism" was "making a noose to hang itself," an observation that became the guideline of China's struggle against the United States. On September 4, the Politburo Standing Committee analyzed the situation and decided that China would not land on Jinmen immediately but would employ the "noose policy," as Mao had suggested, that is, it would make Taiwan the noose it could pull tight to exert pressure on the United States.

At the fifteenth Supreme State Conference, on September 5, 1958, Mao Zedong pointed out that U.S. imperialism had occupied China's territory of Taiwan for nine years and had recently dispatched its armed forces to invade Lebanon. The United States had established hundreds of military bases in many countries. China's territory Taiwan, Lebanon, and all the American military bases abroad were nooses around the neck of U.S. imperialism. It was none other than the United States itself that had made the nooses and placed them around its own neck by handing the rope end of those nooses to the Chinese people, the Arab people, and all peace-loving people of the world. The longer U.S. imperialists stayed in these places, the tighter the nooses would be. U.S. imperialism had been creating tension all over the world as it tried to invade and enslave the people of various countries. It thought tension favored its interests, but tension mobilized the people of the whole world to rise against the U.S. invaders. Mao further asserted that the U.S. monopoly capitalist group would be put to death by hanging if it insisted on pursuing invasion and war. All the lackeys of the United States would meet with similar fates.[44]

Before the shelling began, China had informed the Soviet Union of its plans through Soviet military advisers in China, but it did not raise the issue when Khrushchev visited China at the end of July 1958. Khrushchev, apparently unaware of China's intention, was surprised by the shelling and worried that it would escalate into a confrontation between the Soviet Union and the United States. On September 5, Khrushchev made a personal telephone call to Sudarikov, the Soviet counselor to Beijing, asking him to inform Zhou Enlai that the Soviet Union planned to send Foreign Minster Andrei Gromyko to Beijing for talks. That evening, Zhou met Sudarikov and reported that China did not plan to liberate Taiwan immediately but intended only to punish KMT troops and prevent the United States from creating "two Chinas." He assured the Soviet Union that "China would shoulder the consequences by itself should anything go wrong and that China would not "drag the Soviet Union into war." Zhou asked Sudarikov to convey China's intentions to the Central Committee of the Soviet Communist Party. Reassured by the report, Soviet leaders decided to give China the necessary support.

Gromyko arrived in Beijing on September 6. He told Zhou Enlai that the Soviet Union agreed with Chinese policies. China and the Soviet Union exchanged drafts of a Chinese government statement and of Khrushchev's letter to Eisenhower. At six-thirty that evening Gromyko met with Mao. He told Mao that the Soviet Central Committee agreed to China's stand, policies, and measures, as conveyed in Sudarikov's report of his conversation with Zhou. Gromyko thought Khrushchev's letter to Eisenhower would act as a dose of wake-up medicine to the United States and have the effect of a cold bath. Mao said that the United States should have taken a bath long before, because the weather had been too hot. Gromyko later recalled in his memoirs that Mao wanted the Soviet Union to "adopt all kinds of means to strike" at U.S. troops should they invade China's hinterland. But according to the recollections of several Chinese officials who were also present, Mao made no such request and certainly did not suggest that the Soviet Union should use atom bombs to wipe out invading U.S. troops.[45]

Khrushchev sent his letter to President Eisenhower on September 7, after the Sino-Soviet consultations. He appealed to the United States to act cautiously, advising it not to take lightly steps that might bring about irremediable consequences. His letter stressed that China was not isolated, but had faithful friends who would help China whenever China was invaded.[46]

After more than twelve days of shelling, the KMT supply line to its troops on Jinmen island was cut off. Troops on the islands repeatedly sent emergency reports to Taiwan asking for aid. Chiang Kai-shek asked American warships to provide escort, trying to drag the Americans into the fray. Although the United States was reluctant to intervene, it had no alternative. On September 7, the U.S. navy and the KMT navy formed a joint force to escort supplies to the island: U.S. warships sandwiched KMT warships in the middle of the formation, thus protecting Chiang's forces from the PLA.

Now that PLA action might lead to Sino-American hostilities, the front command in Fujian asked Mao Zedong personally for instructions. Mao gave the order to strike as planned, but only at Chiang Kai-shek's warships. China should not fire against U.S. vessels, even if U.S. warships first opened fire on Chinese vessels.[47] This order aimed to test the role of the U.S.-KMT "Mutual Defense Treaty" and to determine how far U.S. troops would intervene in the crisis. Thus, after the U.S.-KMT joint fleet had entered Liaoluowan harbor in Jinmen and started unloading, the PLA began intensive shelling of Chiang's warships and of the wharves in Liaoluowan. Unexpectedly, U.S. warships did not return fire, but turned to flee toward Taiwan, leaving KMT warships and transportation ships behind. This proved that the United States would not readily enter into direct military confrontation against the PLA on behalf of KMT interests, although it had signed the "Mutual Defense Treaty" with Chiang Kai-shek.

In addition to testing U.S. commitment to the KMT through military conflict, Mao Zedong decided to restore the U.S.-China ambassadorial-level talks, which Washington had unilaterally suspended. He "put on a military play and a scholarly play at the same time," forcing the United States back to the bargaining table to explore new ways out of the Taiwan issue. On September 6, the United States welcomed China's proposal, an action to which Mao attached great importance: "We fought this campaign, which made the United States willing to talk. The United States has opened the door. The situation seems to be no good for them, and they will feel nervous day in and day out if they don't hold talks with us now. OK, then let's talk. For the overall situation, it is better to settle disputes with the United States through talks, or peaceful means, because we are all peace-loving people."[48]

In order to facilitate the talks, Mao summoned Wang Bingnan before he returned to Warsaw, and emphasized that persuasion should be used when the talks resumed. He suggested that Wang point out that both the United States and China are big countries and ask why the United States would want to throw itself against the six hundred million Chinese people for the sake of Taiwan, whose population is less than ten million. What good would it do the United States to pursue its present policies? Mao Zedong advised Wang Bingnan to rack his brains and remain modest and prudent, and not to use the belligerent language China adopted in the talks in Panmunjom in Korea or to offend American national sentiments. The Chinese people and the American people are both great peoples, and the two peoples should be friendly with each other. Mao also instructed the Xinhua News Agency to disseminate a report about Wang's return to Warsaw, stating that Wang had finished his consultation at home.[49]

Following the tests imposed by the shelling and the agreement to reopen the Warsaw talks, Mao concluded that the United States wanted to defend Taiwan, but not necessarily Jinmen and Mazu. It might want to give up Jinmen and Mazu in return for China's recognition of Taiwan's existing status. As expected, the United States retreated when its threats not only failed to coerce China to abandon its Taiwan policy, but also risked war with China for the sake of Jinmen and Mazu. Its policy shifted from "brinkmanship" to that of "extricating itself." By giving up Jinmen and Mazu, the United States now wanted to induce China to agree to its "cease-fire" proposal and to acquiesce to the fait accompli that the United States would retain its forces on Taiwan.

On September 30, 1958, Dulles set off a trial balloon at a press conference. He said that because there seemed to be a reliable "cease-fire," it would be "foolish" for the KMT to maintain so many troops on Jinmen and Mazu. To force Chiang Kai-shek to withdraw, Dulles stated that the United States "bears no legal responsibility to defend the coastal islands" and "did not want to shoulder any obligation of this kind. Today we have no such obligations."[50] Dulles's speech caused a great rift between the United States and Chiang Kai-shek. The next day, October 1, Chiang told reporters from the Associated Press that he was opposed to reducing the troops stationed in the coastal islands and to any change in the position of these islands. He pointed out that Dulles's speech was "only a unilateral statement," which the Taiwan authorities "had no obligation to abide by."[51] The Taiwan "foreign ministry" repeatedly stated that Taiwan would resolutely defend Jinmen and Mazu and would protect its troops stationed there.

Change in Strategic Policies toward the United States and Chiang Kai-shek

The differing positions of the United States and Chiang Kai-shek on the question of Jinmen and Mazu attracted China's attention. On October 3, the Politburo Standing Committee began a series of meetings to discuss the Taiwan situation and possible countermeasures. Mao held that China had fulfilled its reconnaissance mission and now had to decide its next moves. China and the KMT held a common view of Dulles's policies: both opposed "two Chinas." Neither the KMT nor China wanted to give up the option of using force—Chiang remained committed to a "counterattack" against the mainland, and China would never give up Taiwan. Mao further observed that China could not liberate Taiwan for a fairly long period, and even Dulles recognized that there was not much substance to Chiang's counterattack plan.

In this context, Mao stated that the pressing issue for China was what to do about Jinmen and Mazu. Chiang was not willing to withdraw from them and China was not necessarily determined to liberate them. What if China should let Chiang keep Jinmen and Mazu? Because Jinmen and Mazu are not far from the mainland, if China allowed them simply to hang there, half alive, it could use them to maintain contact with the Kuomintang and to deal with the Americans. China could shell them whenever the situation called for it. It could tighten the noose whenever tension was needed and loosen the noose whenever relaxation was needed. As soon as China began shelling the islands, Chiang Kai-shek would ask the Americans for assistance, causing them to become nervous that Chiang would involve them in a crisis. On the other hand, failure to recover Jinmen and Mazu would not affect China's socialist construction. KMT troops in Jinmen and Mazu alone could not cause much harm to Fujian. But if China recovered Jinmen and Mazu or if the United States forced Chiang to withdraw from the islands, China could no longer use them to manage the United States and Chiang Kai-shek, and the "two Chinas" would become a fact.[52]

After much discussion, the Politburo Standing Committee agreed with Mao's analysis. China would continue shelling Jinmen and Mazu without attempting a landing. It would cut off supply lines without killing them completely. This would leave the islands in Chiang Kai-shek's hands and prevent the United States from extricating itself, putting China in a better position to fight against the U.S. policy of "two Chinas." The shelling of Jinmen would be carried out intermittently, sometimes with concentrated fire and other times with slack fire. However, large-scale propaganda would continue, establishing that the Taiwan issue was China's internal affair, that the shelling of Jinmen was the continuation of China's civil war, and that no foreign countries would be allowed to interfere.

To implement the new tactics, Mao Zedong sent Peng Dehuai and Huang Kecheng a telegram on October 5 instructing them that "our army is not to fire a single shell on the 6th and 7th whether or not there is an escort by American airplanes or warships; we won't fire back even if the enemy opens fire on us first. We'll remain quiet for two days, watching before deciding what to do next."[53] On October 6, the *People's Daily* published an

"Announcement to Taiwan Compatriots." Although the author was reported to be Chinese Minister of Defense Peng Dehuai, Mao had drafted it himself. The "Announcement" declared that the shelling of Jinmen would stop for seven days so that Chiang Kai-shek's navy could transport supplies, with the precondition that there would be no U.S. escort. The "Announcement to Taiwan Compatriots" was of great significance. It took full advantage of the contradictions between the United States and Chiang Kai-shek, reminding Taiwan authorities of China's righteous national cause, pointing out that the two sides agreed that there was only one China, and proposing to settle the internal confrontation through talks. The shelling thus entered a new phase: political and diplomatic struggle became primary, while military struggle became secondary. This dual policy proved an effective means of conveying political information while the two sides of the Taiwan Strait were cut off from each other.

China's new tactics were well received in international opinion. Some newspapers even said that this was a sign of dramatic changes in relations between the two sides of the Taiwan Strait, or even between the United States and China. The United States tried to claim that China's temporary halting of the shelling was in fact PRC acceptance of its "cease-fire" proposal. Under this pretext, the U.S. State Department announced, on October 8, 1958, that the U.S. navy would stop its escorts in the Taiwan Strait. But the KMT strongly opposed this shift in U.S. policy. Its "foreign minister," Huang Shaogu, declared that Taiwan would not withdraw from the islands or agree to let the islands remain neutral. He assailed what he called the "trade" of "international politicians." The Taiwan authorities also charged that China's "Announcement to Taiwan Compatriots" was a "trick" played by the Chinese Communists.

At this new stage in the conflict, Mao instructed that China focus its efforts on the Kuomintang. He suggested that the *People's Daily* publish an editorial directed at Chiang Kai- shek, but one that would also put the United States in a difficult position. The resulting editorial elaborated on China's Taiwan policy, making it clear that it was not a trick and that the CCP was once again reaching out to the KMT. It also tried to sow discord between the United States and Chiang Kai-shek by pointing out that it was no easy thing to live under someone else's roof and that "being aboard the American ship" was not a reliable position. The editorial then went on to criticize the so-called cease-fire put forward by Dulles and asked the Americans to "pass five tests," namely, to (1) stop escorting Chiang's ships; (2) stop violating

China's territorial air and sea; (3) stop military provocation and threats of war; (4) stop interfering with China's internal affairs; and (5) withdraw all American armed forces from Taiwan and the Penghu Islands. Mao himself examined the final proof of the editorial and rewrote the last paragraph: "It seems that the whole issue has to be watched and tested, and it will take a long time to finally settle the issue. Imperialism is, after all, imperialism, and reactionaries are, after all, reactionaries. Let's wait and see how they will react!"[54] The editorial, entitled "Let's Wait and See How They Will React," was published on the first page of the October 11 issue of the *People's Daily*.

To further resist U.S. efforts to create "two Chinas" and to give Taiwan authorities an opportunity to consider a peaceful settlement of the issue, the PRC stopped shelling Jinmen for another two weeks, allowing civilians and troops on Jinmen to obtain sufficient supplies to remain on the island. In this way, China could realize its objective of using Jinmen and Mazu to connect the two sides of the Taiwan Strait. On October 13, 1958, Mao issued an order to this effect, under the name of Peng Dehuai, defense minister of the People's Republic of China, to the PLA at the Fujian front. The order stated that China's tactics were not a ploy, but were directed against the United States. It continued, "The Americans want to have a hand in the issue of China's civil war. They make themselves a laughingstock by calling for a cease-fire. What right do they have to talk about this issue? Whom do they represent? Nobody at all. Do they represent all the American people? China and the United States did not declare war on each other, so there is no war between the two countries to be halted. Do they represent the Taiwan people? The Taiwan authorities haven't given them any certificate of appointment. The leaders of the Kuomintang were firmly opposed to the talks between China and the United States." The order then reiterated that reunification of the motherland was China's internal affair and no foreigner had any right to interfere: "The United States must not provide an escort in the seas around Jinmen, and any escort will be immediately attacked. This order is to be strictly carried out!"[55] The order was also published on the front page of the October 13 issue of the *People's Daily* to deepen understanding of the central leadership's strategic intentions among the broad masses and the PLA troops at the Fujian front.

On October 17, the CCP Central Committee distributed an internal Party circular, which analyzed the situation and outlined China's next steps. Its four main points were as follows:

1. The statement of October 6 and the order of October 13 drew a distinct line between internal and international issues and shattered the scheme of the "cease-fire" put forth by the United States, thus blocking the pathways of international interference and widening and deepening the conflicts between the United States and Chiang Kai-shek.

2. This struggle had further revealed the true colors of the United States as a paper tiger, which did not dare to risk a large-scale war: "As the United States failed to intimidate us but has entered into a noose of its own making, it is now eager to adopt policies to extricate itself from Jinmen and Mazu, with the aim of permanently occupying Taiwan and the Penghu Islands, and carrying out the scheme of 'two Chinas.' Now we have shattered its intention to free itself by that very noose. We insist on liberating Taiwan, the Penghu Islands, Jinmen, and Mazu all together and are opposed to the American scheme of giving up Jinmen and Mazu in exchange for Taiwan and the Penghu Islands. We propose to have direct talks with the Taiwan authorities, but will not talk about the so-called cease-fire put forth by the United States."

3. There existed between the United States and Chiang Kai-shek many misgivings as well as certain agreements. "What we are doing now is to widen the gap between the United States and Chiang Kai-shek, to pin down the United States by taking advantage of the fact that Chiang Kai-shek does not want to withdraw from Jinmen and Mazu. We would rather let Taiwan, the Penghu Islands, Jinmen, and Mazu remain in Chiang's hands a little longer than allow them to be taken away by the United States."

4. The liberation of Taiwan, the Penghu Islands, Jinmen, and Mazu is an arduous and complex task. At present the United States will not withdraw its troops from the Taiwan region and Chiang Kai-shek will not immediately agree to have peaceful talks. "It is to our advantage that Chiang's troops continue to remain in Jinmen and Mazu. Because the initiative to go on fighting or stop fighting or talk is in our hands, the United States will continue to be in a passive position and the conflicts between the United States and Chiang Kai-shek will deepen. And sooner or later there will be changes inside the Chiang Kai-shek clique. We can then take advantage of the situation to accelerate the construction of the country and strengthen our defense capacity. We shall totally discredit the United States and create favorable conditions to liberate Taiwan, the Penghu Islands, Jinmen, and Mazu all together."[56]

The United States was in a very passive position as it became increasingly mired in the crisis. On October 19, Secretary of State Dulles and Secretary of Defense McElroy went to Taiwan to pressure Chiang Kai-shek to withdraw from Jinmen and Mazu, using the pretext that a "cease-fire" was in effect. But the next day, the PLA resumed its shelling of Jinmen in retaliation against renewed U.S. naval escort of KMT ships. Thus, the Taiwan authorities once again had a valid reason not to withdraw, and Dulles remained frustrated in his efforts to pressure Chiang to give up Jinmen and Mazu and thus freeze the situation across the Taiwan Strait. The U.S.-KMT joint communiqué reaffirmed that Jinmen and Mazu were closely related to the defense of Taiwan and the Penghu Islands. But under American pressure, the KMT reluctantly agreed to stop its propaganda about "counterattacking the mainland" and changed its rhetoric, stating that the major way to "restore freedom to the people on the mainland" was to "realize Doctor Sun Yat-sen's Three Principles of the People, and not through force."

The mainland and Taiwan agreed that there was only one China, but sharp differences now existed between the United States and Chiang Kai-shek. Renewed PLA shelling assisted Chiang's resistance to U.S. pressure. But the *People's Daily*, which had not grasped the changes in Chinese policy, published an editorial entitled "Nobody but Himself to Blame," arguing that the United States and Chiang Kai-shek were collaborating against China. The CCP leadership criticized the editorial for stressing unanimity between the United States and Chiang Kai-shek.

On October 21, at a meeting of the Politburo Standing Committee, Mao pointed out that "This time Dulles quarreled with Chiang Kai-shek, which in a sense reflects the fact that we have been aiding Chiang Kai-shek in resisting the United States. Our delay of the liberation of Taiwan set Chiang's mind at ease, enabling him to ask for independence from the Americans. We will not land in Jinmen, but neither do we agree to the so-called cease-fire proposed by the United States. This will incite Chiang to quarrel with the United States. Our principle during the past month was striking but not landing, cutting off but not killing. We shall follow the same principle now, but a little more leniently on the cutting off, so as to support Chiang in resisting the United States."

Those in attendance at the meeting supported Mao's judgment. Zhou Enlai held that as the "cutting off" could be somewhat lenient, the "striking" could likewise be somewhat lessened. Mao agreed, suggesting that China could simply declare that it would strike only on odd days and not even days, and only the wharf and the airport, not fortifications or houses. These would be small-scale strikes, or perhaps not even actual strikes. Militarily, this might seem to constitute something of a joke. There was no historical precedent for it, either in China or abroad. Yet, Mao argued, this was a political battle, and political battles are fought this way.[57]

On October 23, the U.S. State Department published an interview Dulles had given to a BBC reporter a few days earlier, on October 16. On the one hand, Dulles said that "Communist China" did exist and that the United States was willing to deal with it, but on the other hand, that the "Republic of China" was a "factual political entity." Dulles continued to press for a "two China" solution, but neither side of the Taiwan Strait supported him.

The Party's Central Committee and Mao Zedong watched the latest developments in U.S.-KMT relations closely. To expose U.S. schemes and to try to persuade Chiang Kai-shek to reduce Taiwan's dependence on the United States, the People's Daily published the "Second Announcement to Taiwan Compatriots," drafted by Mao Zedong under the name of Minister of Defense Peng Dehuai. As the "Second Announcement" pointed out, "The affairs of the Chinese people can be settled only by the Chinese themselves. We can give the matter further thought and discuss it later if it proves to be difficult to settle in a short time. The American politician Dulles likes to poke his nose into others' business and wants to have a hand in the historical dispute between the Communist Party and Kuomintang, and thus impose his will on the Chinese. This is against the interests of the Chinese people and for the interests of the Americans. They meant first to isolate Taiwan and then turn Taiwan into a trust territory. If you defy him, he will adopt the most vicious means."

The "Announcement" declared to Taiwan that the U.S.-KMT joint communiqué was merely a piece of paper, with no legal effect. It argued that Taiwan could easily "break away from it as long as you have the determination. There is only one China in the world, never two Chinas, and we share this same view. The Chinese people, including you compatriots in Taiwan and all the overseas Chinese, will never allow the United States to realize its scheme of creating "two Chinas." Ours is an epoch full of hope, when all patriots have many possible situations. There is no need to be afraid of imperialists. Of course we don't mean to ask you to break away from the Americans all at once. It is unrealistic to expect this. We only hope you won't succumb to American pressure and depend on the whims of others. Otherwise you will risk losing your sovereignty and your homes, and you will be thrown into the sea. We harbor no evil intention but mean you good, and we are sure you will understand us some day."[58]

Henceforth, the conflict over Jinmen became a political battle. There was no shelling on even days, and the shelling on odd days was aimed at beaches rather than at troop positions or living quarters. Chiang Kai-shek's troops returned fire against mainland beaches. The PLA stopped the shelling for three days for New Year's and other festivals. Chiang's troops reciprocated. There developed a kind of tacit CCP-KMT agreement to shatter the U.S. scheme to draw a line down the Taiwan Strait and separate Taiwan from the mainland. As Mao Zedong pointed out to Lin Ke, his secretary of international affairs, on October 26, "Now our principle is to aid Chiang to resist the United States and strongly oppose the scheme of 'two Chinas.' It would be equivalent to joining the United States to bring pressure on Chiang if we did not shell Jinmen when Dulles came to Taiwan. Our bombardment over Jinmen shattered the United States' scheme and upset its plan."[59] The shelling of Jinmen had become a form of political communication between China, the United States, and Chiang Kai-shek.

China and the United States had each adopted "brinkmanship" policies during the two Taiwan Strait crises. Each side tested the other but neither went over the brink. The CCP Central Committee and Chairman Mao had assessed U.S.-KMT relations and concluded that the "Mutual Defense Treaty" between the United States and Chiang Kai-shek was mainly defensive and was being used by the United States to hold Chiang in check rather than to free him. Because the United States was not willing to enter into direct military confrontation with China, it wanted to extricate itself from Jinmen and Mazu. But Chinese leaders understood that the new U.S. strategy harbored a more evil intent: to separate Taiwan completely from the mainland in order to create "two Chinas" or "one China, one Taiwan." China thus decided to maintain the status quo and to handle the liberation of these two islands with the liberation of Taiwan as a whole.

The two crises established Chinese and U.S. policies toward the Taiwan issue. Once China had established its intention to safeguard the unity of the country, it was no longer necessary to carry out large-scale military actions, even as Jinmen and Mazu were left in KMT hands. On this basis, China greatly reduced its armed forces. From 1958 to 1959, the total number of Chinese troops dropped to 2.4 million, the lowest since the founding of the People's Republic. Defense expenditure also fell to the lowest proportion of the national budget since 1949. The crisis also established the pattern of limited U.S. aid to Chiang Kai-shek, which compelled the KMT to be content with its rule over Taiwan.

The shelling of Jinmen had a positive effect on mainland-KMT relations. The two sides avoided warfare and reached a tacit agreement to resist U.S. policy by mutually insisting that there was only one China. In March 1959, the Taiwan "foreign ministry" stipulated that in external relations, the mainland should be referred to as "the administration of the Communist Party" rather than as "red China" or "Communist China," and that Taiwan should be referred to as the "Republic of China," rather than as "free China." These changes in wording aimed to oppose international acceptance of "two Chinas."

On May 22, 1960, presiding over a meeting of the Politburo Standing Committee, Mao Zedong discussed Chinese policy toward Taiwan. He asserted that China preferred that Taiwan remain in the hands of Chiang Kai-shek and his son, rather than in the hands of the Americans, and that China could wait to recover Taiwan. Mao instructed that Taiwan would be allowed to maintain its own way of life even after it returned to the motherland. He observed that even fish living in water are adapted only to local conditions. He also said that China would welcome Chiang to come to the mainland when the United States no longer wanted him, and that his arrival on the mainland would be a great contribution and would signal the defeat of the United States. At times Mao asked visitors to China to convey to the Taiwan authorities that Chiang should not fear that China would join the Americans to make him suffer. Using the metaphor of a tree, he said that if Chiang Kai-shek should link up with the branch of the mainland and break away from those branches interlocked with the United States, he would still have his own roots and be able to maintain his own ways. As for his troops, Mao said that Chiang could keep them. "I would not force him to cut his army or to simplify his administration; he would be free to practice the Three Principles of the People."

Zhou Enlai summed up Mao's statements as "one guiding principle and four policies." The guiding principle was that Taiwan must return to the motherland. The four policies were the following: (1) After Taiwan returned to the motherland, Chiang Kai-shek would retain power to decide all military, political, administrative, and personnel matters, except for diplomatic power, which should be handed back to the central government; (2) the central government would appropriate money to him to aid in military and political management and construction; (3) there was no hurry for social reform in Taiwan, which could be settled through negotiations; and (4) neither side should send people to undermine the other's unity.[60] Although China's proposals to win over the Taiwan side were not successful, they had far-reaching influence on relations between the two sides of the Taiwan Strait.

The crux of the Taiwan issue lies in U.S. military intervention and interference in China's internal affairs. To thoroughly settle this issue, it remains necessary that the United States change its policy. But the United States continues to underestimate the highly sensitive Chinese national sentiment regarding sovereignty and territorial integrity, a sentiment formed through centuries of defending itself against foreign invasions. The United States continues to miscalculate that China will give tacit consent to the so-called fait accompli of "two Chinas" or "one China, one Taiwan."

During the 1950s the United States stressed the use of peaceful means to settle the Taiwan issue and tried to obtain a promise from the Chinese side that it would "relinquish the use of force." But this required China to accept the fact of U.S. military involvement in the Taiwan issue and U.S. interference in China's internal affairs. The Chinese held that "the international dispute between China and the United States over the region of the Taiwan Strait and the liberation of China's own territory by the Chinese People's Liberation Army are cases of a completely different nature." The former could be settled only when the United States gave up its invasion and interference and withdrew all its armed forces from Taiwan, while the latter was China's internal affair. "The Chinese people have the irrefutable right to liberate their own territory in any proper time frame and with whatever appropriate means, and no foreign countries are allowed to interfere."[61] The differing Chinese and U.S. policies on the vital issue of Taiwan have had a far-reaching impact on Sino-American relations from the 1950s to the present.

CHAPTER SIX

Steering Wheel, Shock Absorber, and Diplomatic Probe in Confrontation
Sino-American Ambassadorial Talks Seen from the Chinese Perspective

Zhang Baijia and Jia Qingguo

AMBASSADORIAL TALKS between China and the United States during the Cold War ranged over a fifteen-year period and solved few if any substantive problems. As an instrument of diplomacy, however, they played an important role in stabilizing and moderating the relationship between the two countries by providing a channel for contact. The two governments found the talks useful for different reasons and thus adopted different policies. A review of their views and their behavior is helpful in understanding Sino-American relations during this period and the policies the two countries developed toward each other. To enhance this understanding, this essay focuses on the views and actions of the Chinese government and demonstrates that its assessment of the usefulness of the talks evolved over time.

At the beginning, the Chinese government greatly hoped that it might be able to improve relations with the United States by taking a conciliatory position. But from mid-1956, faced with an uncompromising U.S. attitude on substantive issues, the Chinese government gave up any hope of improving relations through secret negotiations. Instead, it turned directly to the American public and the Taiwan authorities in hopes that they might pressure the U.S. government to make concessions in the negotiations. This approach, however, did not get very far either, and as a result, the ambassadorial talks went on, but with little substance. The American attempt at the end of 1957 to reduce the level of the talks met with China's strong opposition and in part paved the way for the outbreak of the second Taiwan Strait crisis in 1958, which eventually brought the two sides back to the negotiating table. At that point, the Chinese government began to view the talks more in terms of a shock absorber, a function that appeared to be quite useful in 1962, when the two countries cooperated to thwart the attempt by the Taiwan authorities to stage large-scale military attacks against the mainland. By the end of the 1960s, as China's domestic and international situation deteriorated, improving relations with the United States became increasingly important. Under these circumstances, Chinese leaders began to view the ambassadorial talks as a way to probe U.S. intentions toward improving relations.

Throughout the 1950s and 1960s, China attached great importance to the ambassadorial talks, although its reasons for doing so varied over time. At first, they were an opportunity to redirect China's relationship with the United States, then they served as a crisis-management mechanism, and finally, they were a way to gauge and assess the possibility of rapprochement with the United States.

Unexpected Gains: Contacts at the Geneva Conference

The first official bilateral contacts between China and the United States began at the Geneva Conference in 1954, when officials of the two sides entered into talks on the question of removing restrictions on Chinese and American nationals in returning to their respective countries. China regarded the holding of the talks as an unexpected gain. In the words of Ambassador Wang Bingnan, who participated on the Chinese side, through the talks the two countries established "a bridge over the great divide between them."[1] The bridge might be a narrow one and prove dangerous to walk on, yet it allowed useful contacts during years of intense hostility between the two countries.

When the Korean War ended, in June 1953, many wondered whether China and the United States could walk out of the shadow of confrontation. Now that they were no longer at war with one another, what should each side do? China's answer to this question was quite simple: it could at last turn its attention to its other problems, which were both numerous and daunting. Internally, large-scale economic development and socioeconomic reforms, delayed by the war, were just beginning. The ambitious domestic economic and social programs of the Chinese Communist Party required it to accomplish miracles, despite the threat of an intense, even violent, reaction from within Chinese society.

China's foreign policy objectives reflected its domestic priorities. In external affairs, Beijing's primary objectives were to build and maintain a peaceful and stable international environment and expand China's diplomatic relations, which had been greatly constrained by the Korean War. These policies would enable China to devote its resources to economic construction. In addition, looking beyond the immediate horizon, China needed time to make preparations to recover Taiwan, a task that had been postponed by the Korean War. China's policy priority toward the United States was to dismantle the program of U.S.-imposed political isolation and economic sanctions, but this could only be achieved if China could improve its relationship with the United States.

In the immediate aftermath of the Korean armistice, Chinese leaders believed it possible to reduce Sino-American tensions. From their perspective, the existence of the People's Republic of China (PRC) was a reality. Whether Washington legally recognized the PRC or not, it had to acknowledge reality and ultimately deal with the Chinese leadership. As Chairman Mao Zedong explained, the Chinese mainland had a population of six hundred million, whereas Taiwan's population was less than ten million. This fact could not be changed. It would be foolish for the United States to make an enemy of six hundred million people on the mainland for the sake of relations with fewer than ten million people on Taiwan.[2]

The United States likewise faced the question of how to handle its relationship with China amid a number of pressing policy issues. The end of the Korean War posed a series of problems that were both old and new. As the Korean War ended, many countries began to demand that the United Nations restore China's seat in the organization. What position should the United States adopt on this question? What should Washington do if other countries wished to accord China diplomatic recognition? Should the United States itself seriously consider diplomatic recognition of China? How should the United States cope with its allies' demand to relax Western trade sanctions against China? Should it respect China's international rights and privileges?

Washington continued to maintain a rigid position on all these issues. Although some Americans began to entertain the idea of recognizing China, believing that the real interests of the United States would be better served by driving a wedge between the Soviet Union and China,[3] the U.S. government was not prepared to alter its established China policy: it continued to oppose diplomatic recognition of the Chinese government and China's admission to the United Nations, to prevent China's efforts to recover Taiwan, and to maintain the current level of trade sanctions against China.

Despite Washington's extreme policy of containment, establishing some form of contact between the two countries, both of which were great powers, was a matter of necessity, not choice. Each country had an interest in managing the confrontation to avoid any unintended escalation of tensions and further costly conflict. In addition, both had important overlapping interests and needed a mechanism for coordinating their policies. This was one lesson of the Korean War: without an effective mechanism for conducting diplomacy, Sino-American miscommunication had occurred, contributing to the escalation of the conflict. It was against this complex historical background that the process of ambassadorial talks began to unfold.

The Geneva Conference, held between April and July 1954, provided China with an opportunity for active participation in world affairs in its great power capacity. Prior to the conference, at a meeting of the Secretariat of the Central Committee, Zhou Enlai had suggested that "We should adopt a policy of active participation in the Geneva Conference and enhance our diplomatic and international activities." China could use these negotiations to undermine the U.S. policy of "blockade, trade ban, and military expansion and preparation to promote relaxation of international tension."[4] Zhou hoped that China's participation would help China improve its foreign relations, promote greater understanding of New China among more countries, and promote the establishment of diplomatic relations between China and these countries.[5] Judging from the information made public in China, the primary objective of the Chinese delegation at the conference was to improve China's international environment by making full use of the differences between the United States, Britain, France, and other Western countries in order to seek a satisfactory solution of the Korean problem and prevent American intervention in Indochina. Perhaps Mao Zedong and

Zhou Enlai also considered the possibility of seeking improved relations between China and the United States; if such were the case, however, it was not reflected in their previously developed objectives.

The China-U.S. confrontation at the Geneva Conference is by now well known. Dulles's stiffness contrasted sharply with Zhou Enlai's flexibility. The often-told story that Dulles refused to shake Zhou Enlai's extended hand might not have occurred, but it does suggest the true state of the relationship between the two countries at the time.[6] But an opportunity for contact between the two sides appeared suddenly, and a shrewd Zhou Enlai grabbed it.

During the latter part of May, American officials working through the Soviet Union and Britain to request release of Americans imprisoned in China for various crimes expressed the view that some aspects of U.S. policy toward China were unrealistic. When he learned of this, Zhou immediately called a meeting to consider the question. He said that China should not refuse to establish contact with the United States. At a time when relations between the two countries were extremely tense, and U.S. policy toward China extremely hostile and rigid, China could make use of Washington's interest in obtaining the release of imprisoned Americans to establish a channel for contact. Accordingly, the Chinese delegation informed the British chargé d'affaires that, since both China and the United States had sent delegations to the conference, issues involving the two countries should be handled through direct contacts between the two delegations rather than through a third party. Taking the initiative, on May 27, the spokesperson for the Chinese delegation held a press conference concerning unreasonable detention of Chinese residents and students by the U.S. government. He also expressed the view that China was willing to hold direct talks with the United States on this question.[7]

From the Chinese perspective, the most important question was whether this would lead to the establishment of a direct channel of contact with the United States. The Chinese delegation tried to anticipate problems that might arise in the talks and to assess U.S. objectives. On June 3, Zhou Enlai cabled Mao Zedong, Liu Shaoqi, and the Chinese Communist Party Central Committee. He reported that the Chinese delegation had already replied to the British, to the effect that China and the United States could meet directly through an introduction by British officials: "If the United States agreed to the talks, we should meet them in accordance with our established policy and decide where to hold talks in the light of the meeting."

During the talks, the Chinese side should first raise the question of the Chinese students who were prohibited from leaving the United States. At the same time, China should also inform the American side that the Chinese handling of the cases of Americans who had violated Chinese laws would be different from its handling of the cases of other Americans in China.[8]

On June 4, Humphrey Trevelyan of the British delegation introduced the Chinese and American representatives to each other—the chief Chinese representative was Wang Bingnan, and the chief U.S. representative U. Alexis Johnson, both of ambassadorial rank—after which the two sides engaged in preliminary discussions. The two diplomats subsequently held two rounds of formal talks. On June 11, following these meetings, Zhou Enlai cabled the Central Committee as well as the Ministry of Public Security and Ministry of Foreign Affairs, to explain China's negotiating position: First, China should raise the issue of the protection of the rights and interests of Chinese residents and students living in the United States; it should point out that forced detention of Chinese students violated international law and humanitarian principles, and demand immediate restoration of their freedom to leave the United States and return to their motherland; second, with regard to Americans detained in China, China should permit them to write letters to their family members, inform the United States about the death of three Americans, and make public the crimes of detained American air force personnel; third, should Washington change its policy on Chinese students in the United States and permit them to return to China, China might then consider permitting a few Americans to leave China or, depending on the circumstances, expel a few of the Americans detained for committing crimes. These decisions would be subject to the situation and the timing, since the moment was not yet ripe for taking such action.[9]

The third and fourth round of talks were held during the latter part of June. During these talks, the United States insisted that Chinese detention of Americans was illegal but that the U.S. ban on the return of Chinese students to China was consistent with American law. It thus refused to consider the two issues together. In addition, the United States took every precaution to avoid creating the impression that agreeing to enter into talks with Chinese officials in any way constituted U.S. diplomatic recognition of the Chinese government.[10] Under these circumstances, the talks could not make any progress. On July 21, the Geneva Conference ended. In order to maintain contact, China and the United States agreed to hold consular-level talks beginning September 2. Although the initial talks in Geneva produced few if any significant results, the establishment of official contacts between the two countries had far-reaching historical significance.

The Taiwan Problem: The Main Theme of the Talks

In some respects, the impetus for the Sino-American ambassadorial talks was the outbreak of the first Taiwan Strait crisis in 1954. At the same time, however, the Taiwan problem was also the critical factor that prevented the two countries from achieving substantive results.

In July 1954, the Central Committee decided that China must liberate Taiwan. This decision simply reconfirmed China's strategic objective; it did not call for immediate action. Nothing in the available evidence shows that China planned to use force in 1954 to take over Taiwan. The most plausible explanation for continued Chinese patience is that the Chinese leadership did not believe that China had the military capability to achieve this goal.

Despite China's interest in domestic economic development and its full awareness of the unfavorable military balance of power in the Taiwan Strait, Chinese leaders decided to shell the offshore islands. This decision reflected three considerations. First, the Kuomintang (KMT) authorities had stepped up their effort to reach a "Mutual Defense Treaty" with the United States.[11] Second, stabilization of the Korean and Indochina situations had shifted world attention to the Taiwan question, and inaction would give rise to the perception that China was prepared to accept the permanent separation of Taiwan from China. Beijing had taken note of British Prime Minister Winston Churchill's recent suggestion that the United Nations establish a trusteeship over Taiwan.[12] And third, benefiting from U.S. military assistance, Taiwan authorities had strengthened Taiwan's defense capabilities and had increased their harassment and sabotage activities against the Chinese mainland.[13]

In this context, Chinese leaders hoped that public reconfirmation of its determination to liberate Taiwan would help prevent the signing of the "Mutual Defense Treaty" between the United States and Taiwan and the permanent separation of the mainland and Taiwan. Mao argued that "we should destroy the chances of the United States to conclude the treaty with Taiwan. We should think of ways to achieve this objective, including enhancing our propaganda. . . . On the diplomatic front, we should also make gestures, such as contacts with overseas residents. Our objective is to put pressure on the United States so that [it] will not conclude the treaty with Taiwan." Mao maintained that "U.S. conclusion of the treaty with Taiwan . . . would mean a permanent deadlock, at least a very long deadlock."[14] In addition, Chinese leaders also wanted to use the Taiwan issue to inspire enthusiasm among the Chinese people for national economic construction and to promote the enhancement of China's national defense capabilities.[15] In August, a large-scale Taiwan-liberation propaganda campaign swept over the Chinese mainland. Then, on September 3, 1954, the People's Liberation Army (PLA) began shelling Jinmen.

This was the first time the Chinese government had expressed its determination to achieve national reunification in such strong terms. Nonetheless, the shelling of Jinmen failed to prevent the conclusion of the U.S.-Taiwan mutual security treaty. On the contrary, it removed any lingering American hesitation, ironically expediting the treaty signing and moving the U.S. Senate to pass the treaty with unusual speed in February 1955.[16] Meanwhile, the People's Liberation Army followed its own plan to take over KMT-controlled islands along the coast of Zhejiang province and to clear out the KMT's most important strongholds, from which their troops conducted harassment and sabotage activities against the mainland.

The first Taiwan Strait crisis put Sino-U.S. relations in a state of extreme tension. In retrospect, it is clear that neither China nor the United States wished to get involved in a new war. As time passed, however, the likelihood of direct military conflict loomed ever larger, even though, despite the lack of an effective communication channel, the two sides made various efforts to relieve the increasing tension. Having demonstrated its determination to reunify the country, the Chinese government adjusted its policy to reduce the tension. On April 23, 1955, at the Asian-African conference, Zhou Enlai announced that "the Chinese people are friendly to the American people. The Chinese people do not want to have a war with the United States of America. The Chinese government is willing to sit down and enter into negotiations with the United States government to discuss the question of relaxing tension in the Far East and especially the question of relaxing tension in the Taiwan area."[17] This unexpected announcement had a worldwide impact. Following Zhou's speech, Dulles said that the United States would not exclude the possibility of negotiating with China. Tension in the Taiwan Strait began to decrease.

Before China launched the 1954-55 Taiwan-liberation campaign, Mao Zedong had expressed the idea that China wanted to ease tension with the United States. He told a visiting delegation from the British Labour Party that China wished to coexist with countries having different political systems and stressed that this "also included the United States."[18] As China's subsequent shelling of Jinmen indicated, however, the Taiwan issue, securing China's right to national reunification, was more important than improved China-U.S. relations. Chinese leaders could not tolerate the interference of any foreign country in China's national reunification efforts and were firmly opposed to any attempt to create "two Chinas" or "one China and one Taiwan." In its efforts to improve its foreign policy relationship with the United States, China found itself in a Catch-22 situation: as long as the United States maintained its policy of supporting the Taiwan authorities, China could not meaningfully improve its relations with the United States; as long as China could not improve its relations with the United States, it could not resolve the Taiwan problem. This situation haunted Sino-American relations throughout the 1950s and 1960s.

Despite this dilemma, in order to open negotiations with the United States, Zhou Enlai quickly formulated China's negotiating policy and on April 30 submitted a report on the Taiwan issue to the CCP Central Committee. The report stressed that the Taiwan issue contained two interrelated but substantively different issues. The relationship between China and the Chiang Kai-shek clique is an internal issue. The relationship between China and the United States is an international issue. The Chinese people's actions to liberate Taiwan would not result in world tension, just as the liberation of the mainland and the offshore islands did not lead to heightened tension; on the contrary, the completion of China's reunification would contribute to world peace. However, U.S. intervention made it likely that an international war could break out at any time in the Taiwan area. Thus, the current problem was first to identify ways to ease and eliminate tension there. To do this, China and the United States should sit down and negotiate. China and the United States were not at war, so there was no question of a cease-fire. The U.S. proposal for a cease-fire was intended to cut a deal: Washington wanted to exchange the withdrawal of Chiang Kai-shek's troops from Jinmen and Mazu for the Chinese people's abandonment of their demand for, and their actions toward achieving, Taiwan's liberation. This was something, Zhou insisted, that China absolutely could not agree to under any circumstances.

Only when the United States abandoned its aggression and intervention and withdrew all of its military forces from the Taiwan Strait could China peacefully liberate Taiwan and complete China's reunification.[19]

In mid-May, Krishna Menon, the Indian ambassador to the United Nations, visited Beijing to mediate the China-U.S. talks. In his meeting with Menon, Zhou Enlai emphasized three points. First, reducing tension would require efforts on both sides. If the United States would pressure the KMT to withdraw its troops from Jinmen and Mazu, China would consider foregoing any attacks against these islands during the withdrawal and take them over peacefully. However, this was in no way meant to suggest that China would agree to Dulles's so-called cease-fire or to abandoning its liberation of Taiwan in exchange for U.S. pressure on the KMT clique to withdraw from the islands. Nor did it mean that China would recognize the legitimacy of the U.S. occupation of Taiwan and the "two-Chinas" arrangement.

Second, China and the United States should also take measures to ease tensions over other issues. For its part, the United States ought to do two things: lift the trade ban against China and permit those Chinese students and other Chinese residents in the United States who wished to return to China to do so. China could also do two things: on the question of Americans serving jail sentences for their crimes in China, including airmen and residents, China was willing to reconsider their cases in accordance with Chinese legal procedures and, in light of the crimes committed and their behavior in prison, decide whether to release them or expel them; China would also permit American groups and individuals friendly to China to visit China. Although such permission should be granted on an equitable basis, China was willing to take the first step. China wanted to allow Americans to come to China to see whether China was friendly toward them or hoping to wage war against them.

Finally, China was willing to negotiate with the United States and with the KMT authorities. Although the two sets of negotiations were related, they were of two different kinds. The first was international, and its purpose to persuade the United States to give up intervention and withdraw its troops from Taiwan and the Taiwan Strait. The second was domestic and should cover both a cease-fire between China's Central People's Government and KMT authorities and China's peaceful reunification.[20]

On May 26, Zhou Enlai met with the British chargé d'affaires, Humphrey Trevelyan. During their meeting, Zhou further elaborated on China's policy toward negotiations with the United States, maintaining that the central theme of Sino-American negotiations was to reduce and eliminate tension in the area of the Taiwan Strait. As to the specific format of the negotiations, however, Chinese leaders had not reached a final decision. While China agreed to, and would support, a ten-country conference like that proposed by the Soviet Union—the number of participating countries could be greater or fewer—and China and the United States could also conduct direct negotiations sponsored by other countries, under no circumstances would Beijing agree that the Taiwan authorities could attend. However, the Chinese government would not refuse to conduct direct negotiations with the Taiwan authorities; on the contrary, it was willing to do so. There were two ways to solve the Taiwan problem, through peaceful means or through war. If possible, China would try to liberate Taiwan peacefully. Chinese leaders sought to conduct both international and domestic negotiations, either simultaneously or in any sort of sequence. As Zhou explained, the two kinds of negotiations were related to each other but should not be entangled.[21]

In mid-July, through British mediation, China and the United States agreed to upgrade the consular-level talks previously held in Geneva to the ambassadorial level. China attached great importance to these forthcoming talks. The Chinese Ministry of Foreign Affairs set up a special supervisory group, headed by Zhang Hanfu and Qiao Guanhua, both senior diplomats who worked closely with Zhou Enlai, to provide guidance to Chinese negotiators. Zhou served as director of the group and Qiao Guanhua was in charge of specific operations. On the eve of the talks, Zhou appeared to be quite optimistic about the prospects for improved relations with the United States. As he told the Indian ambassador to China, China hoped the ambassadorial-level talks would pave the way for further talks between the foreign ministers of the two countries and that the United States held similar expectations. He said China also hoped that such talks would enable the foreign ministers to negotiate a relaxation of tension in the Taiwan area.[22]

The Sino-American ambassadorial talks began on August 1 in the League of Nations building in Geneva. The chief Chinese representative was Wang Bingnan, then China's ambassador to Poland; his American counterpart was U. Alexis Johnson, then U.S. ambassador to Czechoslovakia. In order to create a positive atmosphere for the talks, the Chinese delegation first announced Beijing's decision to release eleven detained American airmen before the completion of their sentences. The U.S. representative welcomed this gesture. Then the two sides reached agreement on two agenda items: the first concerned permission for residents to return to their own countries, the second, various technical disputes.

In his memoirs, Wang Bingnan wrote that significant differences on agenda and policy objectives existed from the very beginning. The Chinese side believed the talks should concentrate on the Taiwan problem, preparations for direct talks between Secretary of State Dulles and Foreign Minister Zhou Enlai, the establishment of cultural ties, and other substantive issues. The U.S. side, however, was interested only in getting back the Americans detained in China and compelling China to promise not to use force against Taiwan. In the end, in order to get the talks started, the Chinese side agreed to discuss the question of the return of the civilians first and then move to other matters.[23]

From August 4 to September 10, the two sides discussed the return of civilians. After much effort on the Chinese side and fourteen rounds of talks lasting 40 days, the two sides finally reached an agreement on the issue—the only agreement the two sides ever reached during fifteen years of ambassadorial talks—which required the two sides to announce it separately. These initial ambassadorial talks clearly revealed that the United States had made every effort to maintain its position of nonrecognition of the People's Republic of China as an independent government with full sovereign powers. Even on specific issues, its position reflected extreme caution to avoid giving the rest of the world any opportunity to imagine that the United States might offer China any degree of diplomatic recognition.

Deadlock in the Ambassadorial Talks

In mid-September, as the talks entered the second stage, China still hoped they could lead to improved relations with the United States. Wang Bingnan forcefully raised the issue of the U.S. trade embargo and preparations for ministerial-level talks between the two countries. He repeatedly pointed out that only through talks between foreign ministers could China and the United States address serious problems, such as U.S. withdrawal from Taiwan and the easing of tension in the Taiwan area. The foreign ministers could also discuss establishing cultural exchange programs, trade relations, and other matters. However, the United States adopted a very negative attitude and continued to raise problems over the first agenda item, deliberately avoiding any discussion of substantive issues. Its primary objective was to tie

China to the negotiating table in order to stabilize the situation in the Taiwan Strait.[24] As a result, the talks moved very slowly.

Beginning in October, the two sides discussed the U.S. demand that both sides guarantee not to resort to force on the Taiwan question. Washington maintained that the United States had the right to unilateral or collective defense in the Taiwan area and that it would not consider holding talks between foreign ministers until China announced that it would not use force against Taiwan. The Chinese held that any statement by China and the United States on the nonuse of force should not constitute any degree of recognition of the legitimacy of U.S. occupation of Taiwan or of its interference in the Taiwan question; the means China used to solve the Taiwan problem, whether peaceful or not, should not be the subject of discussion in the bilateral talks; and the two sides should hold ministerial-level talks if they were to reach an agreement on a statement on nonuse of force. Since their positions were very far apart, deadlock ensued.

Explaining China's position during the second phase of the ambassadorial talks, Wang Bingnan wrote in his memoirs: "In retrospect, it was impossible for the U.S. to change its China policy at the time. Under the circumstances, we went directly at the Taiwan question, which was the most difficult, least likely to be resolved, and most emotional. It was only natural that the talks could not get anywhere. The question is whether we could avoid this problem and deal with other problems first. Personally, I think that under the historical circumstances of the time, we had no choice but to make the U.S. concede on this key issue. Once progress was made on this issue, we could make progress on other issues. Otherwise, it would be difficult for us to discuss other issues." Wang also explained China's negotiating tactics in the context of U.S. intransigence on the Taiwan issue:

During the negotiation, we should take a tit-for-tat approach. In this way we could boost our morale and dampen the U.S. government's spirit. Having suffered long-term oppression and humiliation at the hands of the Western powers before the founding of the PRC, the people of the new China were on their own feet and must not appear weak again in front of the Western powers. That is the intense feeling the Chinese people had at the time. If we ignored this historical fact and single-mindedly sought for breakthroughs in the talks, we would have sacrificed principle, hurt the feelings of the Chinese people, and even damaged the unprecedented trust the Chinese people had in the government. If that had happened, we would have committed what Chairman Mao called "serious political mistakes."[25]

As the ambassadorial talks continued to go nowhere, Chinese leaders believed they had developed a better understanding of Washington's real objectives. In June, at the Third Plenary Session of the National People's Congress, Zhou Enlai pointed out that China would not oppose issuing a declaration with the United States on the question of mutual renunciation of the use of force. However, "the United States attempted to obtain a declaration that was only in its favor. It wanted to maintain the status quo of U.S. occupation of Taiwan and continue to obstruct the Chinese people's efforts to liberate Taiwan." Zhou explained that when Washington "realized that it could not obtain such a declaration, the United States attempted to indefinitely prolong the talks in order to freeze the status quo of the Taiwan situation. This is the reason why the Sino-American talks have thus far failed to reach an agreement."[26]

Confronted with such a situation, China tried to identify its own alternatives. In the same month, in briefing the Indian ambassador to China on the Sino-American talks, Zhou said that the United States had two alternatives: one was to reach an agreement with China and the other was not to reach an agreement and let the talks drag on. China also had two alternatives: one was to reach an agreement and the other was to let the talks drag on. However, China had freedom to maneuver. If the second alternative served its interests, China would continue to play the game. If it hurt China's interests, China could refuse to play along at any time. This was China's view on the prospects for Sino-American ambassadorial talks.[27] Obviously, China no longer hoped that the talks would lead to a breakthrough in China-U.S. relations.

With the ambassadorial talks deadlocked, the Chinese side attempted to break the deadlock through other means. One was China's decision to invite American journalists to visit China. At the beginning of August 1955, when the ambassadorial talks were just getting under way, the Chinese government approved the visit to China of eight American journalists. But the U.S. State Department issued a statement soon after, declaring that the United States prohibited American citizens, including journalists, from visiting China. A year later, in early August 1956, the Chinese government unilaterally announced the lifting of its ban on visits by American journalists. It cabled fifteen important American news agencies and invited them to send journalists to China for month-long visits. The Chinese move helped weaken U.S. news censorship on China. During the following year, the U.S. media put considerable pressure on the State Department to allow visits to China. A few American journalists even ignored the ban and went to China. In addition, American youth representatives attending a world youth celebration in Moscow also found their way to China. Nevertheless, Dulles still managed to resist demands to lift the ban for a year.

The following year, however, Dulles was compelled to adjust U.S. policy: the State Department announced that the United States would allow 24 American journalists to visit China. But by now, China had changed its own policy. On August 17, 1957, the *People's Daily* carried an editorial condemning Washington for manipulating the journalist question. On September 12, in the ambassadorial talks, Wang Bingnan made a journalist-exchange proposal and demanded reciprocity from the United States.[28] Chinese leaders now wanted Chinese journalists to be allowed to visit the United States.

Wang Bingnan's new position at the ambassadorial talks in part reflected the leftward swing under way in Chinese domestic politics. Under Mao's leadership, China was pursuing more ideologically inspired economic and political policies with a greater emphasis on class struggle. But the harder line also reflected China's growing impatience with American policy, including Dulles's public reaffirmation that Washington would not recognize the Chinese government as the legal government of China.[29]

In August 1956, the Chinese side suggested discussions of the U.S. trade embargo against China and that both countries take active steps to eliminate obstacles to trade between them. From September to December of the following year, the Chinese side made a succession of proposals promoting travel and cultural exchanges, encouraging journalists' exchange visits on an equal and mutually beneficial basis, and offering legal assistance on a reciprocal basis. Chinese leaders hoped that these proposals would move the talks forward and improve relations between the two countries. However, the United States stuck to its excuse that because the two sides had not reached an agreement on "mutual renunciation of the use of force" and because some American prisoners in China had not been released, Washington could not consider China's proposals. Meanwhile, as a result of the active efforts of Walter Robertson, the U.S. assistant secretary of state on Far Eastern affairs, the United States decided to downgrade the status of the talks. On December 12, 1957, when the U.S. side informed China of its decision to appoint Edwin Martin, a first secretary at the American embassy in London, to serve as the U.S. representative to the ambassadorial talks, the Chinese side protested and the talks were suspended.[30]

Crisis Management: A New Role for the Talks, 1958–1962

Mao Zedong had retained some interest in the possibility of improving relations with the United States for several years, but by 1958 this was no longer the case. Early in that year, Mao told Chen Yi, China's new foreign minister, that he had instructed Chinese diplomats to make contact with Americans officials during the Geneva Conference in 1954, but that this instruction had not been consistent with his usual line of thinking. Now, Mao said, it appeared that his usual line of thinking had proved to be superior, that is, that China should insist on waging struggle against the United States and refrain from developing relations with the U.S. government.[31] In the context of the domestic economic and political radicalism that is reflected in the overambitious, ideologically inspired policies of the Great Leap Forward, it seemed that Chairman Mao was no longer interested in maintaining a peaceful international environment.

On August 23, 1958, the PLA once again began to shell Jinmen. Meanwhile, Wang Bingnan was recalled back to China to report on developments in the ambassadorial talks. Mao Zedong, Liu Shaoqi, and other top Chinese leaders listened to his report. At a time when China and the United States had little contact, and tension in the Taiwan Strait was mounting, the ambassadorial talks played a uniquely important role in informing Chinese leaders about U.S. intentions and foreign policy. Indeed, on September 4, Secretary of State Dulles, with Eisenhower's authorization, issued a statement threatening to expand the U.S. defense line in the Taiwan Strait to include Jinmen, Mazu, and other Chinese offshore islands. At the same time, Dulles also indicated that the United States would not abandon its hope for peaceful negotiations. At the meeting of the Standing Committee of the CCP Politburo on the same day, Mao proposed that China should resume the ambassadorial talks as a concerted effort in the struggle on the Fujian front. "There should be scenes of talks and war at the same time," he said.[32]

On September 6, Zhou Enlai issued a statement condemning the serious war provocations by the United States. He announced that since the United States had already appointed an ambassadorial representative for the talks,

China was ready to resume. China and the United States viewed these talks as a way to control any further escalation of the crisis and to prevent direct military confrontation.

During preparations for the new round of talks, Chen Yi instructed Wang Bingnan that he should not try to resolve the various issues one by one. Rather, from now on the Chinese side should insist on an "all or nothing" principle: if the Taiwan problem could not be resolved, then China would not discuss other issues.[33] On September 13, two days before the talks, Mao Zedong instructed Zhou Enlai that "during the first three or four days or the first week of the Warsaw talks, we should do some reconnaissance work. Do not reveal our bottom line. The U.S. side will not reveal its bottom line either. They will conduct some reconnaissance on us too." Zhou Enlai replied that he had already passed the instruction on to Wang Bingnan: "We will try to deal with the American side to make it reveal its bottom line first."[34] To Chinese leaders, who had just been through the bitter experience of negotiating with the Americans, the direct aim of their participation in the talks was no longer to seek improved China-U.S. relations but to restore the channel of contact to facilitate their assessment of U.S. intentions.

On September 15, when the ambassadorial talks resumed in Warsaw, the new American representative was Jacob Beam. Although like China, the United States wanted to restore the talks, its intention was to use the negotiations only to stabilize the explosive situation in the Taiwan Strait. It did not entertain any idea of compromise with China on substantive issues. Instead, it not only demanded that China agree to an immediate cease-fire but claimed that the United States would not tolerate military aggression against its "ally's territories." Upon receipt of the report on the talks, Zhou Enlai decided that during subsequent rounds, Chinese negotiators should "adopt an active and offensive policy." Thus, China put forth a counterproposal demanding that the United States withdraw all of its troops from Taiwan, the Penghu archipelago, and the Taiwan Strait.[35] At the end of September, U.S. negotiators proposed a draft statement, but the Chinese side rejected the proposal after concluding that there was nothing new in it. Henceforth, the talks dragged on without substance, as each side talked only to please itself.

During the second Taiwan Strait crisis, the question that most concerned Chinese leaders was whether or not the United States planned to compel Chiang Kai-shek to remove his troops from the offshore islands. Zhou Enlai paid close attention to U.S. statements at the ambassadorial talks in order to determine Washington's intentions. On September 30, in response to journalists' questions, Dulles said that the United States had no obligation to defend the offshore islands, nor did it wish to assume such an obligation. This statement received much attention from Chinese leaders, and a Politburo meeting concluded that the United States wanted to create "two Chinas." Zhou said that Dulles wanted China to renounce the use of force to liberate Taiwan; in exchange, the United States was most likely prepared to demand that Taiwan abandon its aspirations to "recover the mainland" and that it withdraw its troops from Jinmen and Mazu. Zhou's assessment was consistent with what China had learned about U.S. intentions during the ambassadorial talks, where the United States was especially straightforward about its intentions,[36] and this conclusion led Mao to decide not to attack Jinmen and Mazu. He preferred that Chiang keep KMT troops there, since that would make it more difficult for the United States to perpetuate the division of Taiwan and the mainland.

From the end of the second Taiwan Strait crisis to the Kennedy administration, Sino-American relations remained frozen. The ambassadorial talks made little progress—a few Americans still served their prison terms in China, and the two sides continued to stick to their respective policies. During the late 1950s and early 1960s, Washington considered adjusting its policy of nonrecognition of Beijing and let it be known that it was willing to entertain the idea of simultaneously recognizing Beijing and Taipei. However, although Washington considered such a move a reflectiion of greater flexibility in its China policy, Beijing considered this U.S. probe with a sense of apprehension and opposition. American recognition of the PRC on the basis of such "flexibility" was worse than its existing policy of nonrecognition. At least the current U.S. policy acknowledged that there was only one China, whereas the new policy would essentially be a two-China policy that could very well lead to Taiwan's permanent separation from the mainland. Thus, although the United States made a few new proposals on such issues as the exchange of journalists and U.S. grain sales to China on preferential terms, Chinese negotiators adhered to the "all-or-nothing" principle and ignored U.S. overtures.

Despite the absence of serious China-U.S. negotiations and concrete progress, during the Kennedy administration the ambassadorial talks played a crucial role in averting another major Taiwan crisis. In 1962, China faced a precarious international environment. The Sino-Indian border conflict was escalating, and Moscow was tilting toward India just as Sino-Soviet relations were deteriorating. Meanwhile, China's domestic economy was still recovering from the devastating effects of the Great Leap Forward. As China's strategic situation deteriorated, tension once again developed in the Taiwan Strait.

At the end of May 1962, Wang Bingnan was on vacation in China when Zhou Enlai called him in for a meeting to discuss the situation in the Taiwan Strait. Shortly thereafter, Zhou asked him to cut short his vacation and return immediately to Warsaw: the Central Committee had concluded that Chiang Kai-shek was eager to launch military attacks against the mainland, but that he still faced some difficulties in carrying out his plan. The key factor that would influence his actions now was American policy. Yet Chinese leaders remained uncertain about whether or not the United States would support a KMT military offensive. They decided that China should try to persuade the United States to use its influence to constrain Chiang. Zhou asked Wang to go back to Warsaw and look for an opportunity to determine U.S. intentions.[37]

Upon his return to Warsaw, Wang Bingnan made an appointment with Ambassador John Cabot, the current American representative to the ambassadorial talks, on the pretext of having tea together. On June 23, when Cabot arrived at the Chinese embassy, Wang told him that he would like to call the tension in the Taiwan Strait to the attention of the U.S. government. He pointed out that Chiang Kai-shek's preparations for attacking the mainland were made with U.S. support, encouragement, and cooperation and warned that the United States must bear full responsibility for Chiang's adventurous actions and their serious consequences.

Cabot responded that he would report Wang's concerns to Washington, but he also reassured him that under the circumstances, the United States would never support Chiang in launching military attacks against the Chinese mainland. He reported that Chiang was under obligation to the United States not to launch such a military attack without prior U.S. agreement. Cabot also said that the United States did not want a world war and would make every effort to prevent this from happening. He assured Wang that publicly and by its actions, the United States would dissociate itself from any Taiwan attack. He also suggested that if Taiwan took military action against the mainland, the United States and China might cooperate by continuing to hold the ambassadorial talks to restore peace. Wang's report on this conversation provided the Central Committee with important information as it formulated China's response to Taiwan's preparations for war.[38]

In mid-1964, Wang Bingnan was recalled from Warsaw and appointed vice minister of foreign affairs. Summarizing his nine-year experience in the talks, he wrote, "In a sense, the ambassadorial talks constituted [a form of] relations between the two countries under the historical circumstances. In some respects, such a relationship represented even more contact than that between some countries that had diplomatic relations. If there had not been ambassadorial talks, it would have been more difficult to find an appropriate occasion to express some of our views. Whenever a major international event occurred, both China and the United States could state their positions and express their views, enabling each to appreciate the other's attitude and actions. Therefore, although the two sides had little other contact, they understood each other quite well."[39]

The Last Mission: A Probe for Change

In mid-October 1964, China exploded its first atomic device. Meanwhile, the news from Moscow was that Khrushchev, whom China had blamed for ideological "revisionism" and for instigating the Sino-Soviet conflict, had been ousted. China's international prestige and strategic circumstances seemed to be improving. Moreover, during the following year, the atmosphere of the ambassadorial talks also underwent some subtle changes. For the first time, Chinese and American negotiators exchanged views on the question of limiting and banning nuclear weapons. It appeared that the talks had thus begun to assume some meaning. But the escalation of American intervention in the Vietnam War blocked progress in Warsaw. From the Chinese perspective, the height of the Cultural Revolution (late 1965-early 1969) was no time to consider improved relations with "American imperialists." On the contrary, not only was the Vietnam War becoming an important bilateral issue, but at this time Chairman Mao was preoccupied with "continuing the revolution" inside China.

As the 1960s progressed, changes in China's domestic politics and strategic circumstances, including changing superpower relations, created conditions that encouraged Chinese leaders to reassess Beijing's policy toward the United States. Simultaneously, changes in U.S. security circumstances encouraged Washington to reevaluate its China policy. In these changing international circumstances, the China-U.S. ambassadorial talks finally assumed major significance in the improvement of U.S.-China relations.

In March 1966, at the 129th meeting of the talks, China received a message from the Johnson administration. China's chief negotiator at this time was Ambassador Wang Guoquan and the U.S. representative was Ambassador John Gronouski. Gronouski took the initiative to speak first. He said that the United States was willing to develop bilateral relations with "the People's Republic of China." Until that moment, the United States government had never addressed China by its official name. Wang Guoquan communicated this change in U.S. policy to Beijing, but because China was just then on the eve of the Cultural Revolution, his report did not receive sufficient attention from, or timely study by, Chinese leaders. As Wang Guoquan wrote in his memoirs, "We lost a favorable opportunity to give Sino-American relations a timely push. It must be a regretful thing in the history of diplomacy."[40]

After the 133rd ambassadorial meeting, in June 1967, Ambassador Wang Guoquan was recalled home to participate in the Cultural Revolution, and subsequent talks could not be conducted at the ambassadorial level. China's chargé d'affaires to Poland, Chen Dong, led China's delegation to the 134th meeting on January 8, 1968. Thereafter, however, the 135th meeting was repeatedly postponed.

While the ambassadorial talks stalled, triangular relations between China, the Soviet Union, and the United States experienced fundamental changes. Factors favoring Sino-American rapprochement assumed greater significance for both Washington and Beijing. For the United States, Soviet efforts to narrow the nuclear gap were creating nuclear parity between the two superpowers. Superpower parity, in turn, accorded China a critical role to play in the global strategic balance of power. It thus became a strategic imperative for the United States to seek improved China-U.S. relations in order to improve its strategic position in relation to the Soviet Union. In addition, heightened Sino-Soviet tension, especially in the aftermath of the Soviet invasion of Czechoslovakia and in the context of Sino-Soviet border clashes, created an opportunity for the United States to explore possibilities for rapprochement with China. Finally, increasing American casualties in Vietnam had produced overwhelming domestic political pressure for an early end to U.S. intervention. Because China was a major supporter of Vietnamese resistance, a successful U.S. withdrawal would require at least tacit Chinese cooperation.

Improved relations with the United States would also benefit China. At the height of the Cultural Revolution, under the influence of leftist ideology, China developed confrontational relationships with both the Soviet Union and the United States. Its strategic situation could not have been worse. Moreover, the domestic chaos and violence of the Cultural Revolution had significantly crippled China's domestic political order and economic viability. At this juncture, improved relations with the United States would help to reduce the imminent military threat posed by the Soviet Union and gain China much-needed time to restore domestic order and economic growth. Moreover, U.S. reconsideration of its role in Vietnam suggested that the U.S. threat to China was declining. It was against this background that the Chinese leaders began to consider the Sino-American ambassadorial talks as a useful instrument to probe the possibilities for improved relations with the United States.

On November 25, 1968, Chen Dong sent a letter to U.S. Ambassador Walter Stoessel proposing that the 135th meeting of the ambassadorial talks be held on February 20, 1969. The U.S. side agreed. The next day, the spokesperson for the Chinese Ministry of Foreign Affairs raised the issue of the talks and again explained the two principles the Chinese government had adhered to in the negotiations: the U.S. government should promise to withdraw all military forces from Taiwan and the Taiwan Strait, and it should agree to the five principles of peaceful coexistence. The foreign ministry spokesperson said that if the United States was not going to change its previous behavior, the ambassadorial talks would produce no results, no matter which administration came into office in the United States.[41] This statement reflected China's initiative over resuming the talks, but it was also an appeal to the incoming Nixon administration for improved Sino-American relations. China delayed this meeting, however, after the defection of a Chinese diplomat in Holland to the United States.

Chinese leaders continued to seek favorable opportunities to resume the ambassadorial talks. In June 1969, Lei Yang was appointed as China's chargé d'affaires in Poland. Before his departure, Zhou Enlai instructed him to look closely at the development of Sino-American relations, in particular, for signs of change in U.S. policy and behavior, and to report back on anything significant. Zhou also stressed the need to ensure that the Warsaw channel did not break down. Before Lei Yang left for Warsaw, he carefully went through the archives of the ambassadorial talks and other written materials on Sino-American relations.[42]

In early September, a Romanian Party and government delegation visited China. The Romanians told Chinese leaders that during his recent visit to Romania, Nixon had clearly and unreservedly expressed a desire to seek ways to normalize relations with China. Zhou Enlai responded that the key problems included Taiwan and China's seat in the United Nations, and if the United States wished to solve these problems, a channel already existed, the Warsaw talks.[43] In mid-November, Nixon sent word through Pakistan expressing his hope of establishing the highest possible level of secret contacts. On November 16, Zhou sent a letter to Mao Zedong suggesting that China "should pay attention to the behavior of Nixon and Kissinger."[44] He subsequently told a Pakistan friend that if Nixon wished to establish contacts, he could use the official channel.[45]

On the evening of December 3, 1969, at a fashion show held in the Yugoslav embassy in Poland, an interesting scene occurred: the American ambassador chasing two Chinese diplomats. The Chinese diplomats were not, as many have believed, chargé d'affaires Lei Yang and his liaison officer; in fact, one was the newly appointed second secretary Li Juqin, and the other, the embassy translator Jing Zhicheng.[46] The incident nevertheless reflected the U.S. sense of urgency about resuming the ambassadorial talks. That night, Zhou Enlai received a report on the incident from the Chinese embassy and reported it immediately to Mao Zedong. Zhou said excitedly, "We have found the door; it is time to knock on it, and here is the knock."[47] After obtaining Mao's agreement, Zhou acted on it the first thing the next morning. He approved the report by the Ministry of Foreign Affairs on the release of two Americans arrested for illegally entering Chinese waters and instructed that the American ambassador to Poland be informed of the decision, signaling that the ambassadorial channel was still open.

On December 10, Ambassador Stoessel visited the Chinese embassy in Warsaw, and the following day, the Chinese chargé d'affaires returned the visit to the U.S. embassy. These visits were the first for both officials. On December 12, Zhou Enlai passed on to Mao Zedong three cables concerning the meetings between Lei Yang and Stoessel, stating that in terms of Sino-American contacts, China should wait for a while to see how various parties reacted before deciding on a response.[48] That same day, Zhou told the Pakistan ambassador to China that Nixon could make use of the Warsaw channel; the United States did not need to play games to communicate with China. Beijing wanted to see how effective the Warsaw channel could be.

In terms of relations with the United States, Zhou said that China's positions were that the United States should withdraw all military forces from Taiwan and the Taiwan Strait area and adhere to the five principles of peaceful coexistence.[49]

Zhou Enlai still harbored considerable doubt about Nixon's intentions and thus approached resumption of the ambassadorial talks with great caution. Taiwan had been the key problem in the earlier Sino-American talks, but the United States had then had little to say on the issue. For China, a resolution of the Taiwan problem could not be avoided, because it was the precondition for normalization of Sino-American relations. At the end of December, after careful consideration by Mao and Zhou, the Chinese government approved resumption of the Warsaw talks.

The 135th round of ambassadorial talks convened on January 20, 1970. Both sides expressed a desire to improve relations and raised the possibility of higher-level meetings. The two sides also decided not to continue to use the meeting place provided by the Polish government but instead to rotate the meetings between their respective embassies.

On February 12, Zhou Enlai presided at a Politburo meeting to discuss the revision of the Ministry of Foreign Affairs' cable to Lei Yang in Warsaw and the speech of the Chinese representative at the 136th meeting of the ambassadorial talks. Zhou believed that the next ambassadorial meeting "was an important opportunity and step." The original wording of the Chinese representative's speech read: "If the U.S. government wishes to send a ministerial-level representative or a special envoy of the American president to Beijing to explore the fundamental problems in Sino-American relations, the Chinese government is willing to consider it." Zhou suggested changing "consider" to "receive." After the meeting, he explained that "consider" did not carry much weight, while "welcome" would appear to be too enthusiastic. "Receive" lay somewhere in between the two and was therefore more appropriate. Then he sent the draft speech to Mao and Lin Biao for approval. Mao soon approved it.[50] On February 20, Lei Yang duly informed the U.S. delegation that if the United States wished to send a ministerial-level representative or a special envoy of the U.S. president to Beijing to explore the basic principles of Sino-American relations, the Chinese government was willing to receive the representative.

On March 20, China's embassy in Pakistan passed on to Beijing a message President Nixon had asked the Pakistan president to convey to the Chinese government. The U.S. message explained that, as is usually the case, the White House could not avoid speculation by American newspapers on the nature of the Warsaw talks. The difficulty lay in the official nature of this kind of diplomatic channel. Under these circumstances, the message explained, it would be difficult for the White House to maintain freedom of decision and diplomatic silence, because too many people outside the embassy could see what was going on. Therefore, the United States "was prepared to open a direct channel from the White House to Beijing if Beijing also agreed to this. No one outside the White House would know of the existence of such a channel and under the circumstances the White House would be in a position to make decisions in complete freedom." On March 21, Zhou Enlai wrote, "Nixon wishes to adopt the method of the Paris negotiations and to ask Kissinger to conduct secret contacts."[51] Mao and Zhou spent some time considering the merits of holding Sino-American negotiations in Beijing. They even wondered whether such talks could be held in mid-April of that year.[52]

The U.S. invasion of Cambodia led to China's decision to postpone the 137th meeting in Warsaw, and ultimately, this meeting never took place. After U.S. military forces had left Cambodia, China and the United States expedited the rapprochement process through other channels, including arranging for Kissinger's secret visit to Beijing. Although the United States had not yet expressed any new views on the Taiwan question, Zhou Enlai had good reason to believe that if Nixon sent Kissinger to China, Kissinger would be prepared to adopt a new position on the Taiwan question.

Between July 9 and 11, 1971, Henry Kissinger, President Nixon's special assistant on national security, made a secret visit to Beijing. During the visit Zhou Enlai and Kissinger agreed that Nixon would visit China before May 1972. They also decided that Paris would serve as a secret channel for future contacts and that the Warsaw channel had finished its historic mission. The Sino-American ambassadorial talks officially ended.

Questions on Policy Continuity and Decision Making

In retrospect, this analysis of the evolution of China's perspective on the ambassadorial talks gives rise to two sets of questions, one related to the continuity of China's Taiwan policy and the other to the nature of its foreign policy decision-making process during the 1950s and 1960s. Was there strong continuity in China's Taiwan policy? If so, how should one interpret the policy shifts in 1958 and in the late 1960s and early 1970s? Was China prepared to accept a partial solution of the Taiwan problem before 1958, as it did in the 1970s? In terms of decision making, who made the key decisions in China's foreign policy during the 1950s and 1960s? What was the role of Zhou Enlai and his subordinates? To what extent did they operate under political constraints?

On the surface, China's policy toward Taiwan appears to have been fluid from 1949 through the 1970s and the U.S.-China rapprochement. It seemed to alternate between demanding a total solution of the Taiwan issue from 1958 to the late 1960s and accepting a partial, if nonetheless temporary, solution during the mid-1950s and again in the late 1960s; between stressing military "liberation" of Taiwan before the late 1970s and emphasizing peaceful reunification after the late 1970s.

But beneath this apparent fluidity in Chinese policy there has been strong continuity. China has never abandoned its claim or its resolve to recover Taiwan, although at times other pressing interests have required that Beijing adjust its tactics, including the method and the pace of unification. Yet, given the fact that national reunification has been portrayed as such a core national interest, it is highly unlikely that any Chinese leader has ever entertained the idea of sacrificing Taiwan for other interests. China's Taiwan policy has been flexible only insofar as short-term tactics have changed in response to immediate circumstances.

Thus, Chinese leaders were willing to accept a partial solution of the Taiwan problem in the mid-1950s because they believed such a move would contribute to rapprochement with the United States, which would in turn facilitate rather than impede unification. This was also the case in 1972, 1979, 1982, and 1998.[53] Because the United States has been Taiwan's principal supporter and protector, improved China-U.S. relations would leave the Taiwan authorities more vulnerable and susceptible to China's pressure for reunification. It is reasonable to speculate that had Chinese leaders concluded otherwise, China-U.S. rapprochement in the early 1970s and subsequent cooperation would not have occurred.

Although the available evidence does not permit a comprehensive review of China's foreign policy decision-making process, the history of the ambassadorial talks and the Taiwan issue do allow broad consideration of its major characteristics during the first two decades of the People's Republic. First, Mao's unrivaled importance in shaping and making key foreign policy decisions is obvious. His charisma, built up over the history of the Chinese

Communist Party, and his interest in broad strategic deliberations that cut through the boundaries separating domestic and international affairs granted him unrivaled foreign policy authority over all other leaders, including Zhou Enlai. This was especially evident in China's decision in 1954 to launch the Taiwan-liberation campaign, a decision made while Zhou Enlai was on his way back from the Geneva Conference. Zhou, the apparent chief overseer of China's foreign policy, was barely, if ever, consulted. Indeed, he was criticized for failing to address the Taiwan question once the Korean War ended.[54]

Second, the Chinese policymaking underlying the ambassadorial talks reveals that despite Zhou Enlai's limited authority in comparison to Mao, he still played a major role in developing and influencing foreign policy decisions. As the chief custodian of China's foreign and domestic policy, he developed his own share of charisma, a loyal following, especially in the Ministry of Foreign Affairs, and direct knowledge of Chinese diplomacy and international affairs. He was an important force in policy implementation and in shaping China's overall foreign policy agenda.

Third, from the early days of the People's Republic, Chinese leaders developed special institutional arrangements for managing major diplomatic undertakings, such as the Sino-American ambassadorial talks. These special task forces monitored and guided concrete negotiations in order to provide timely reports from policy specialists to senior leaders, including the Politburo, and thus to facilitate the leadership's control over diplomacy. Such institutional arrangements have proved useful in cutting through bureaucratic red tape and in bringing qualified personnel together to focus on pressing policy issues.

Finally, domestic political considerations have weighed heavily in the foreign policy-making process. Previous ideological and political decisions established the unalterable domestic context of foreign policymaking and imposed important limits on the policy options available. The China-U.S. ambassadorial talks reflect this process. Political necessity made it necessary for Chinese leaders to adhere to such principles as national sovereignty and reunification. On such questions, not even Mao was immune from political considerations. It was against this backdrop that Mao cautioned against flexibility on the Taiwan question in the ambassadorial talks, warning that it could lead to "serious political mistakes."

CHAPTER SEVEN

Dialogue of the Deaf?

The Sino-American Ambassadorial-Level Talks,

1955–1970

Steven M. Goldstein

OVER NEARLY FIFTEEN YEARS (August 1955 to February 1970), the United States and the People's Republic of China (PRC) held 136 meetings at the ambassadorial level. The talks began in Geneva and moved to Warsaw in 1958. Until the recent declassification of United States archives pertaining to 134 of the 136 meetings, researchers have relied largely on inferences from public documents and clues from insiders in analyzing the content of these meetings.[1] The release of the transcripts of the talks, the instructions to the American delegation, and State Department memos now provide a basis for a richer and more nuanced picture. This discussion, based on these new materials, is intended primarily to reconstruct the course of the talks.

Background to Negotiations

Any understanding of the United States' posture in the early stages of the talks must begin with John Foster Dulles, who was clearly the major, but not the only, force shaping China policy. Explanations of Dulles's policy toward the PRC, as in the case of his foreign policy in general, have become more complex in recent years. Earlier explanations proceeded from his presumed image of a global Manichean struggle with communism. This, it is argued, led Dulles to reject any notion of compromise with "Communist China" and to tie the fate of American policy to the internationally isolated and provocative Republic of China (ROC). According to this view, Dulles's policy toward the mainland was merely to contain and, if the occasion arose, contribute to the fall of a regime that, by 1957, he depicted as temporary.[2]

Subsequent studies have presented a less ideological (even pragmatic) Dulles who was as much, if not more, responsive to political pressures than to his own ideological blinders. According to this view, the Secretary of State's options in taking the initiative toward Beijing were constrained by external factors: residual anticommunist sentiment from the McCarthy era, pressure from such groups as the "Committee of One Million," and scrutiny by the politically influential anticommunist, pro-Taiwan forces in Congress. Although he sought to mobilize more flexible constituencies, the strength of these political forces was always present in his calculations.[3]

Dulles was sensitive to pressures emanating from the international environment as well. European allies of the United States, in particular Great Britain, perceived his commitment to Taiwan and hostility toward the mainland as both unrealistic and liable to lead to unnecessary conflict in Asia. Moreover, the British and the Japanese were growing increasingly unwilling to pay the costs of the economic embargo imposed on the mainland during the Korean War.[4]

However, the primary international pressure on American policy came from the ROC. Taiwan was central to the Eisenhower administration's Asia policy. Its existence, under American protection, was essential to maintaining the belief in Asia that the mainland juggernaut could be stopped and that the United States would stand by its anticommunist friends. When crises developed in the Taiwan Strait in 1954–55, and again in 1958, such considerations played a major role in shaping American policy.[5]

Thus, although Dulles could be tough with Taiwan, ignoring its opposition to the ambassadorial talks, carefully supervising its military activities, and extracting a pledge not to use force as the primary means for returning to the mainland, the ROC could not be ignored. Taiwan's needs had to be heeded, not only because of its supporters in the United States, but also because any threat to morale resulting from American policy might undermine the island's stability and the determination of anticommunist forces in Asia or, more ominously, provoke a desperate Taipei to spark a confrontation with the mainland that would involve the United States.

To the Table: Rocky Beginnings, Crisis in the Strait, and the Spirit of Bandung

The first post-Panmunjom talks between the PRC and the United States took place in the waning hours of the Geneva Conference on Korea and India. The issue that provided the stimulus for these talks was the detention and imprisonment of American citizens on the mainland. In May 1954, the British delegation offered to act as a broker in arranging meetings between the two countries, and on June 5, U. Alexis Johnson, the American delegation coordinator, met with his PRC counterpart Wang Bingnan.

Over the next six or seven weeks, Johnson and Wang met four more times in Geneva. The meetings, which were formal and stilted, focused on the issue of detained citizens and did substantively little more than permit discussion of the status of nationals in each country. The PRC pressed for evidence that its nationals could leave the United States, while the Americans sought and received specific information on the names and the current status (alive, imprisoned, on trial, etc.) of its citizens.[6]

The reasons for the stilted nature of the talks are obvious from the State Department record. On the PRC side, there was a clear preoccupation with issues of sovereignty and mutual equality. Wang denied that American prisoners in the PRC could be treated as ordinary nationals and allowed to leave. Truly sovereign states, he argued, need not account to others for those who are tried and convicted in accordance with local laws. In a similar vein, Wang also asserted the PRC's right to inquire after its citizens in the United States.[7]

These arguments were anathema to Washington. Any acknowledgment of these demands would increase the PRC's diplomatic standing. This, it was believed, would weaken the U.S. position in Asia, anger and demoralize Taiwan, and incense the island's supporters in Washington. Indeed, the simple fact of continuing the negotiations could give the impression that some recognition was being accorded to the mainland. Thus, when on June 21, Wang suggested a joint communiqué asserting the right of the "'law abiding' nationals and students" of their respective countries to leave and noted that Beijing would designate a "third party" to represent its interests in the United States, the American side broke off the talks.[8] Until June 1955, PRC

and American consular officers in Geneva held occasional desultory meetings about this issue, but by spring 1955 the talks were simply expiring.

The stimulus for the resuscitation of the Sino-American talks came from
the Taiwan Strait crisis of 1954–55. In September 1954, amid talk of a possible U.S. mutual defense treaty with the ROC, the Southeast Asia Treaty
Organization (SEATO)—which did not include Taiwan—was inaugu-
rated in Manila. The PRC's response was to begin shelling Jinmen.
In December 1954 the treaty was signed and in February 1955 the "Formosa
Resolution" gave the president the option of extending it to the offshore islands. By March 1955, the conflict had intensified. Eisenhower and Dulles
were putting the United States on a collision course with the PRC. Administration officials spoke publicly of the mainland's growing aggressiveness and
of the possible use of nuclear weapons.[9]

At the Bandung Conference in April 1955 a breakthrough occurred.
Zhou Enlai declared a willingness "to sit down and talk with the United
States regarding the relaxation of tensions in the Far East, and especially in
the Taiwan area."[10] The initial American response, drafted by the White
House, represented a virtual rejection of Zhou's offer. The statement
insisted that "free China . . . [would have to participate] as an equal in any
discussions regarding the area" and that the PRC could show its good intentions by declaring a cease-fire as well as releasing American airmen and
"others being held unjustly." The next day, Secretary of State Dulles was
more receptive. While the United States would not discuss the "rights" or
"claims" of the ROC in its absence, it could certainly discuss a cease-fire or
even Beijing's renunciation of force as a way "to satisfy their claims and their
ambitions."[11]

Preparations for the talks, conditioned by political pressure at home and
from Taiwan, went slowly. By the end of May, several nations had offered to
facilitate the process.[12] Dulles was eager for the talks to go forward. For example, when Zhou Enlai declared that the PRC could use either peaceful
means or military means to achieve the "liberation of Taiwan," the Secretary
of State drafted but never sent a personal letter to Zhou seeking "discussions" to follow up on his statement.[13]

By the end of May 1955, momentum was growing. Beijing released four
American flyers. Zhou Enlai indicated a willingness to talk with the United
States on "international" questions, while insisting that Taiwan, as a domes-
tic matter, could not be discussed.[14] The approaching four-power Geneva

summit in July 1955 provided further impetus. Dulles was concerned that the Soviets might press for the PRC's inclusion. Moreover, given the uneasy calm prevailing in the Taiwan Strait, he believed direct talks were the "minimum needed to preserve [the] de facto cease fire."[15]

In early July, the United States sent messages through third parties indicating that it was ready to talk with the PRC at the ambassadorial level about matters of "direct concern" that "did not deal with the rights of third parties" (i.e., Taiwan). It proposed that questions about "citizens in each of our countries" be discussed and that "further progress" on that question could lead "to discussion of other topics which the Chinese Communists might want to suggest."[16] On July 25, 1955, it was announced that meetings would be held to solve the question of the "repatriation of civilians who desire to return to their respective countries and to facilitate further discussions and settlement of certain other practical matters now at issue between both sides."[17]

Genuine Negotiations: The "Agreed Announcement" (August–September 1955)

A day after the July 25 announcement, Dulles stressed the fact that the talks did not imply recognition and would not "prejudice the rights of our ally, the Republic of China." After a surprisingly brief comment on U.S. nationals on the mainland, he emphasized that the United States "hope[d] to find out" if the PRC would "accept the concept of a cease-fire" in the Strait as part of a mutual pledge to renounce the use of force other than for self-defense. Dulles added that the United States would listen to whatever Beijing wanted to bring up to resolve peacefully those issues that "directly involve[d]" the two countries. He did not rule out a future meeting with Zhou Enlai.[18]

U. Alexis Johnson, the American representative to the Geneva talks, was given his detailed instructions on July 30. Although he was authorized to meet socially with the PRC delegation, the instructions insisted that the talks not "involve diplomatic recognition." He was not to discuss any questions that touched on the rights of the ROC. The instructions noted that the first purpose of the meetings was to resolve the issue of repatriation and that Johnson should seek "immediate authorization for US civilians [and members of the military] to return to the US." Although he was not "to promise any concessions for their release," he was authorized to mention that their release "might facilitate" a less restrictive policy on U.S. citizens going to the mainland. He was instructed, "at whatever times you deem appropriate," to raise the desire of the United States that the PRC be "prepared to abandon force to achieve its ambitions." He was also told to respond to claims that this was a domestic matter by emphasizing the defensive nature of the U.S.-ROC treaty and contending that any attempt to destabilize divided countries could threaten world peace.[19]

The priority given to repatriation was essential in justifying the talks, but it was misleading. Although it provided a link to the earlier meetings and made the talks politically acceptable, it was not Dulles's primary concern in initiating them. His focus was the need to escape the Eisenhower administration's predicament in the Strait area.[20] This might be achieved by a pledge to renounce force, but it could also be gained by simply keeping the PRC tied to the negotiating table. As long as the United States could keep the PRC talking, Dulles believed, conflict in the Taiwan Strait would be avoided. Dulles told Johnson in conversation that he would be "happy if you [Johnson] are sitting there three months from now."[21]

THE NATURE OF THE REPATRIATION ISSUE

The repatriation issue grew out of the confrontational turn that Sino-American relations had taken after the Communist victory. Restrictions were placed on the departure from the United States of certain technical personnel and students of Chinese nationality who, particularly after the Korean War, were viewed as possessing knowledge that could damage American national interests. Beyond these comparatively few Chinese (Johnson places their numbers at less than 200), other Chinese aliens, mostly students, were free to return to the mainland. On the mainland, during the last days of the civil war and the subsequent conflict in Korea, approximately forty to fifty U.S. citizens, who were charged with economic crimes, espionage, and so on, had been imprisoned or detained. The Eisenhower administration had sought their release since 1954.[22]

The central difficulty in solving the repatriation issue was apparent almost from the outset: for any settlement to be reached, both sides would have to yield on fundamentally nonnegotiable issues. For Beijing, the issues were national sovereignty and validation of the claim that the Chinese Communist Party would restore China's national dignity as an equal nation-state after decades of imperialist humiliation. It might agree to review the cases, but it would never agree to an immediate release or to setting a date for release in response to foreign demands.[23] It insisted on equal treatment for Chinese aliens in the United States and the right, as their international protector, "to entrust [a] third country of [the PRC's] own choice [to] take charge of affairs of nationals [of] each country."[24]

The PRC's refusal to set a timetable for the release of the Americans made a mockery of one of the administration's principal rationales for the talks but, if agreed to, would surely provoke the Republican right. Similarly, to acknowledge that the PRC could entrust the affairs of Chinese nationals in the United States to a third party would not only suggest an acknowledgment of the legitimacy of the new government but also slight the ROC, angering an already suspicious Taipei.[25]

Thus, the repatriation issue pitted the pride of a newly successful revolutionary state against the fundamental domestic and international priorities of a major world power. There was little likelihood of compromise. Surprisingly, however, an agreement was reached. And even more surprisingly, it was reached because Secretary of State Dulles made a major concession.

NEGOTIATIONS FOR AN "AGREED ANNOUNCEMENT"

The deadlock in the talks came early. From the beginning, Washington was clear: it would accept nothing short of the departure from China of all those Americans who wished to leave, regardless of whether or not they were criminals under PRC law. For the reasons discussed earlier, Beijing would make no such concession. By mid-August the most the PRC had offered was to announce that the cases of some of the Americans wishing to leave had been "reviewed" and that the rest would be reviewed in the future. If an agreement on repatriation were reached, the status of those reviewed cases would be made public.[26] In his cable, Johnson noted that although in this context, "review" probably meant release, some Americans would remain despite any agreement. Acknowledging that leaving some citizens behind would be distasteful, he suggested that it was equally awkward to effect the detention of those who could leave by insisting on the release of all Americans. Johnson proposed the acceptance of the release of some citizens and then a move to other matters, reserving the right to raise the issue again.[27]

Dulles was uncompromising. He instructed Johnson that it was "essential to hold tenaciously to our basic position on return of all detained nationals."

With the PRC side insisting that this was their final offer, the talks approached a deadlock. Cables went back and forth between Washington and Geneva regarding calling a recess or even breaking off the talks. [28] Ambassador Johnson, however, taking the initiative, sought an alternative to Dulles's "all or nothing" stance. He asked permission to "explore possibility release some now with commitment to release remainder within definite time limit." Dulles agreed, noting that a word such as "promptly" might be used to limit the time frame, but only if it was tied to a specified period "such as two or three months." Dulles had not blinked, but he had winked. [29]

The PRC responded by upping the ante. Wang then maintained that decisions would be made according to the nature of each case, but that consideration would also be given to the "state of relations between our two countries." [30] Johnson once again pressed Washington to compromise in the interest of those Americans who might be allowed to leave. On September 2, Dulles yielded, authorizing wording for a settlement whereby both sides recognized the right of nationals from each side to return to their respective countries, and declared that the two countries had "adopted, and will further adopt appropriate measures so that nationals could *expeditiously* [emphasis added] exercise their right to return." After demanding the release of all Americans, Dulles ultimately conceded that he would accept the immediate release of some and of the rest in a predetermined period, settling for the undefined term "expeditious." [31]

On September 10, 1955, an "agreed announcement" was finally issued, which declared that each ambassador had informed the other of the conditions and that India and Great Britain would be "invited" by the PRC and the United States, respectively, to make representations for, and provide funds to, any citizens who "were encountering obstruction in departure." [32] The first—and only—agreement that was to come out of the talks had been reached.

The Settlement: Solution or Problem?

After both sides had settled on the wording, Wang Bingnan provided the names of twelve Americans in the PRC who could leave, but Johnson once again failed to get a date for the release of the remaining Americans. Still, even the staunchly anticommunist assistant secretary of state for Far Eastern Affairs, Walter Robertson, was pleased. He was "amazed" and felt "we had just about written our own ticket as far as the phraseology went." [33]

He had little reason to be pleased. The United States had stood firm on questions that touched on recognition and had gained concessions on the wording that defined the PRC's role vis-à-vis the Chinese in the United States, but it had yielded on its initial nonnegotiable demand that all citizens be allowed to leave. The "agreed announcement" left some American citizens in limbo. No matter how the U.S. side chose to define "expeditiously," the PRC side had made no commitment whatsoever about a specific time for the release of the remaining prisoners and, more important, had also made it clear that future repatriations would depend on improvements in bilateral relations. The agreement was clearly a gamble.

Even as the "agreed announcement" was being made, Dulles was setting a course that would ensure that the gamble would be lost. Johnson was instructed to limit the frequency of the meetings to twice a week and to narrow their scope to "implementation and details and progress in carrying out [the] agreed announcement." He was not to get into the "substance" of any new agenda items until all Americans had been released. Should the PRC show signs of carrying out the agreement in "good faith," discussions on possible subjects for future talks could begin; otherwise, Johnson was instructed to recess the talks.[34] The potential for deadlock was obvious: even as the PRC was insisting that the future resolution of the repatriation issue would depend on an improvement in relations, the United States was insisting that any improvement in relations would depend on the resolution of the repatriation issue.

Johnson sensed this problem immediately, but State Department discussions did not address it.[35] Policymakers might have been so closely focused on the recognition issues that they failed to see the problem, or they believed that Beijing would release all the Americans. What is more likely, however, is that Dulles had other objectives in mind when he compromised. The first is suggested by comments within the State Department that the agreement could be a public relations "club" with which to beat Beijing.[36] By refusing to go ahead on recognition until the repatriation issue was settled, the administration could deflect domestic and foreign (particularly ROC) criticism of the weak "agreed announcement." It could also use Beijing's nonimplementation of the agreement to expose its bad faith to those pressuring Washington for a more flexible policy. A second objective in compromising and then provoking a deadlock would serve Dulles's original intent: to keep the PRC at the negotiating table in order to preserve the calm in the Taiwan Strait.

When the talks entered the next stage, it was apparent that this strategy was more likely to lead to their termination. The "agreed announcement" was hardly a victory for Washington—it neither assured the return of all Americans nor provided a basis for extending the talks.

The Taiwan Quagmire: The End of Sino-American Negotiations (October 1955–July 1956)

The July 25, 1955, announcement had identified only one topic: repatriation. Others issues were designated simply as "certain other practical matters now at issue between both sides." These issues came to be known as "item two," and it was originally agreed that their content would be negotiated, although it was clear from the beginning that this would be a difficult process. What negotiators had not anticipated was that the repatriation question would be settled inconclusively, leaving the United States reluctant to move on to any new topics. Thus, before discussions on the next topic could begin, the negotiators had to agree on whether to move on at all.

GETTING PAST REPATRIATION

The administration had assumed, somewhat cynically, that reaching an imperfect agreement would have its benefits. As preparations for the second stage of the talks began, its strategy was to use the incomplete implementation of item one to slow the momentum toward consideration of item two, while prolonging the talks and building a case for the United States as the aggrieved party. Johnson was told "to keep him [Wang] so busy reporting on the progress of the departure of the Americans" that he could not raise other issues. [37]

For much of September 1955, this was what happened. At the first meeting after the "agreed announcement," Wang proposed that the talks move on to the "US blockade and embargo" and to "preparations for 'negotiations at a higher level' on easing and elimination of tensions in the Taiwan area." Angered by the immediate American refusal, Beijing made two public announcements condemning the U.S. position. In private, Wang argued that the repatriation issue had been settled and that the PRC would not allow further stalling. The American side soon realized that the stalling game could not last and that preparations for discussion of item two had to begin. [38]

On September 28, the American side was authorized to agree to a pre-liminary discussion of future topics. By early October, the "renunciation of use of force in the Taiwan area" had become not only an American priority for the next stage of the talks but a precondition for moving on. It was pro-posed that each side be prepared to set aside conflicting claims and declare that they "will not resort to the use of force in the Taiwan area except defen-sively." Such declarations would "make it appropriate for us to pass on to the discussion of other matters with a better hope of coming to constructive conclusions."[39] Anticipating PRC pressure to discuss this issue at a "higher level" (a foreign ministers' meeting), the American side held that the two ambassadors could negotiate the issue adequately in their talks. The United States considered the question of higher-level talks a procedural issue that could come up only after negotiations on this first question were completed. Finally, Johnson was instructed to keep the repatriation issue on the agenda.[40]

Wang Bingnan of course resisted attempts to keep the prisoner issue on the agenda, arguing once again that it was a closed issue. His reaction to the proposal to discuss renunciation of force, however, was more complex. The PRC, he said, "fully endorsed [the] principle [of] no recourse to force or threat of force in international relations," but the U.S. proposal to deal with this question in the context of Taiwan was unacceptable. This was "Chinese territory." The PRC could not agree to renounce the use of force on its own territory; rather, it was up to the United States to remove its forces from Chinese territory. Still, the PRC was willing to continue talks on the "tense situation in the Taiwan area," but only at a foreign ministers' meeting. The ambassadorial meetings could prepare for such a conference, but the next substantive issue should be a discussion of the economic embargo.[41] Despite Wang's warning that the Taiwan question was too complex and sensitive to be handled at the ambassadorial level, the United States continued to insist.[42]

THE TAIWAN MORASS

From October 8, 1955, to July 26, 1956, thirty-five meetings (almost 25 per-cent of the total number of sessions) were devoted primarily to the "renun-ciation of force" issue. Six draft agreements were tabled—three by each side. For nearly six months each side sought a second "agreed announcement"—and failed. The prisoner issue still intruded on the talks, but it was largely a sidebar to the fruitless discussions over Taiwan, which ended in deadlock.

The American proposals of November 10, 1955, and of January 12 and April 3, 1956, were relatively uniform in content. In its first statement, Washington proposed that both sides first "recognize" that the use of force to achieve "national objectives" was not in accord with the U.N. Charter or international law; that "renunciation of the threat or use of force" was essential to settling "disputes or situations which lead to a breach of the peace"; and that "without prejudice to the pursuit of each side of its policies by peaceful means they have agreed" to the following identical statements: "In general and with particular reference to the Taiwan area, the People's Republic of China [the United States] renounces the use of force, except in individual and collective self-defense."[43]

The American draft of January 12 was much the same. It omitted the introductory sections, but the core declaration expressed a determination that disputes would be settled "through peaceful means" and that "without prejudice to the inherent right of collective and self-defense, they would not resort to the threat or use of force in the Taiwan area or elsewhere." Washington's final April proposal simply reorganized and reiterated these basic ideas.[44]

The PRC draft statements were more varied. The draft of October 27, 1955, stated that both sides "agree that they should settle disputes between their two countries by peaceful means without resorting to the threat or use of force." This was followed by a statement that a foreign ministers' meeting had been agreed upon to "negotiate a solution of the question of easing and eliminating the tense situation in the Taiwang [sic] area." The December 1, 1955, draft simply affirmed the peaceful resolution of disputes (without reference to Taiwan) and declared that the ambassadorial talks would continue.[45]

On May 11, 1956, the PRC proposed an announcement whereby, "without prejudice to the principles of mutual respect for territorial integrity and sovereignty and non-interference in each other's internal affairs," both sides would announce their determination to "settle disputes . . . in the Taiwan area through peaceful negotiations," adding, "The two ambassadors should continue their talks to seek and to ascertain within two months practical and feasible means for the realization of this common desire, including the holding of a Sino-American conference of the foreign ministers and to make specific arrangements."[46]

The essentials of Washington's position are clear. It was not seeking any resolution of the merits of either side's case with respect to the Taiwan question. All it sought was a mutual commitment to renounce force in the

Taiwan area while retaining the right of self-defense. Each of the American proposals specify the "Taiwan area" (including the Strait) as well as the right of self-defense and make no mention of higher-level talks. If accepted, Dulles's goal of an extended cease-fire in the Strait would thus be reached without compromise.[47]

The fundamentals of the PRC drafts reflect the interplay of two elements: Beijing's quest to hold a meeting at the foreign minister level and the rock-bottom principle that the Taiwan question was a purely domestic matter. The first two draft proposals remain within the boundaries defined by these elements. In the first , the PRC agrees to continue to hold discussions at the ambassadorial level on the renunciation of force, but without specifying the "Taiwan area." The second draft includes the phrase the "Taiwan area" but also the commitment to a foreign ministers' meeting. The final draft combines these two with a pledge to discuss the renunciation of force in the Taiwan area at the ambassadorial level but on the condition that higher-level talks follow within two months. The choice was up to the United States. If the United States wanted to discuss Taiwan, there would have to be a foreign ministers' meeting or, as Wang briefly suggested, a meeting with a "presidential representative." If Washington refused, then any announcement would remain at the general level of international disputes.[48]

Absent from Beijing's proposals was any willingness to include a renunciation of force and any mention of the American right of self-defense in reference to the "Taiwan area." This was a part of China and the conflict across the Strait was a domestic affair. While Wang asserted that the PRC sought a peaceful resolution, he added that, like any sovereign country, the PRC would never make any pledges to an outside power about how a domestic matter might be settled. The ROC was a "puppet government," not an international actor. It could not conclude treaties with another country. Thus, the Mutual Defense Treaty of 1954 had no validity and the presence of American forces in the Taiwan area constituted an act of aggression and occupation. By its simple presence in the Taiwan area, the United States was using force. Any pledge not to use force in the future would require an American military withdrawal. The United States could not claim a right to self-defense on Chinese territory any more than the PRC could do so in San Francisco. Thus, to discuss the renunciation of force under existing conditions would be to freeze an unacceptable status quo and continue China's humiliation by imperialist forces.[49]

As this summary suggests, an insurmountable chasm separated the two sides. If Washington agreed to the international variant of the PRC's proposals, the "domestic issue" of Taiwan would probably, by definition, be excluded. And in view of the assurances that had been given to both the U.S. Congress and Taipei, a foreign ministers' meeting was politically impossible for Washington. Moreover, even if it agreed to the variant mentioning the "Taiwan area" and a foreign ministers' meeting, there was no assurance that the "domestic issue" of Taiwan would be seriously discussed. In a worst-case scenario, the Eisenhower administration feared paying an unimaginable political price for a statement that mentioned "the Taiwan area," only to find that peace in the cross-Strait conflict was either taken off the table as a domestic issue or stabilized for a mere two months.[50]

Beijing had its own worst-case scenario. Wang Bingnan repeatedly maintained that there was absolutely nothing in the American proposals for the PRC. If the PRC were willing to sacrifice essential nationalist credentials and agree to a renunciation of force that included Taiwan and the Strait, it would be acquiescing to the status quo with no assurance that the United States would continue the talks. The American side was demanding a unilateral concession that the civil war had ended short of a total CCP victory and with a part of China still occupied by imperialism.[51]

The future of the talks was not bright. To move forward, one side or the other would have to give in on a fundamental principle. Faced with a deadlock, U. Alexis Johnson, in Geneva, sought a way out. Although in the talks he toed the hard State Department line, in his cables to Washington he sought compromise. In particular, he strongly recommended accepting Beijing's December 1 proposal pledging that both sides simply renounce the use of force in settling disputes. Johnson noted that this would keep the talks going without mentioning a foreign ministers' meeting and would make it difficult for the PRC to "justify" any attack on Taiwan. A U.S. rejection of the statement, he noted, would damage America's public image.[52]

Dulles would not be moved. Noting that there was little chance of a breakdown at this point, he instructed Johnson to return to the demand that the repatriation issue be solved before serious discussions of other questions could proceed. Dulles reminded Johnson that one goal of the talks was to keep the PRC talking.[53] In response, the PRC publicly charged the United States with stalling. The United States responded in kind. By May 1956 both sides' proposals and much of the substance of their arguments were public knowledge.[54]

In Washington, the deadlock and Beijing's public charges raised two concerns. The first was that the PRC would simply end the talks. From the transcripts it appears that Beijing never made a direct threat, although there were indirect suggestions that Washington took seriously. In general, however, the assessment was that Beijing would not break off the talks and that the unyielding American position could be maintained. Still, Washington did prepare drafts of press statements, and even a White Paper, should a break occur.[55]

The second concern was Beijing's proclivity to go public in response to American intransigence and the danger that a breakdown in the talks would bring greater public visibility to the process. This meant that over time, the substance and timing of Washington's proposals became as much a response to putative public judgment as to the PRC's proposals. Indeed, at one point Johnson noted that a good public record was clearly being achieved at the expense of the Americans being held in the PRC.[56]

The deadlock over the renunciation of force led to much public airing of the substance of the talks but not to breakdown. The deadlock, however, marked the effective end of negotiations to resolve the serious issues separating the two sides. The sessions increasingly became mere polemical exchanges, each side posturing as much for public consumption as for mutual edification. From the summer of 1956 until December 1957, when they were suspended, the talks moved away from substantive discussions, circling back on themselves and drifting aimlessly.

Talks in Search of a Topic: Prisoners, Trade, and Citizen Exchanges (July 1956–December 1957)

Since Secretary of State Dulles was not keen on leaving the prisoner issue in limbo and moving on to item two, when he did agree to move on to keep the talks going, he instructed that the prisoner issue be revisited throughout the negotiations on the renunciation of force, further poisoning the negotiating environment.

Sino-American differences over repatriation were straightforward. Wang maintained that the issue was closed—that it would be resolved by the PRC's legal system and was being used by Washington to prolong the talks. He argued that the United States was still detaining Chinese citizens, and if repatriation stayed on the agenda, the PRC might insist that all these cases be considered. Under such conditions, Wang noted sarcastically, the talks could go on for hundreds of years.[57] Of course, going on for "hundreds of years" was exactly what Dulles and his colleagues wanted. Continually raising the issue would allow Dulles to respond to congressional pressure while reaping the public relations benefits of highlighting Beijing's perfidious behavior.

The bitter discussions over repatriation, which served as a contretemps to the negotiations on the renunciation of force, concerned relatively few issues. The first was also the most basic: were prisoners covered under the repatriation agreement? Wang argued that they were not; the American side insisted that they were.[58] Even the record of the discussions leaves the real answer shrouded in ambiguity. Although it is true, as Washington contended, that the statement covered all citizens and included the term "expeditiously," it is also true that the PRC made it clear throughout the August 1955 talks that prisoners would be released on a schedule set by Beijing. As we have seen, the United States had knowingly agreed to an ambiguous formula.

In his correspondence with the State Department, Ambassador Johnson argued against giving the prisoner issue continued prominence. It would open a "can of worms," he claimed, and do little to gain their release. Beijing had clearly stated that further releases would depend on progress in Sino-U.S. relations. Johnson suggested that getting entangled in the prisoner issue would retard progress and so delay their return.[59] However, Washington refused to yield. The delegation was instructed to continue to press the issue.

Following its initial protests, the PRC shifted to a strategy of resistance and turned the issue against the Americans. From January through June 1956, giving tit for tat, Wang protested against obstacles to the departure of Chinese citizens from the United States; he asked to be given the names of all Chinese in the United States in reciprocation for the earlier list the PRC had given the Americans; he submitted the names of those whose departure was allegedly being obstructed; and he made oblique inquiries about the status of those who were imprisoned. The United States responded by denying that any obstructions existed and flatly refusing to supply a list of Chinese nationals. A steady stream of separate inquiries from Beijing followed, producing a morass of problems that ranged from misspelled names to trying to locate individuals undergoing treatment in mental institutions.[60]

In late February 1956, when Johnson was told that Dulles was considering the release of some imprisoned Chinese "dopedealers" in an attempt to break the deadlock, he opposed the idea. The release of American prisoners, he argued, had nothing to do with similar treatment being accorded to Chinese in the United States. What was needed was progress in Sino-American relations, such as an agreement on the renunciation of force and a promise to schedule a foreign ministers' meeting.[61] Still, Washington pursued the issue thinking it was setting a trap for the PRC negotiators. Johnson was instructed to draw Wang out on the prisoner question and then to announce suddenly that all Chinese prisoners in the United States would have the option of being deported. Johnson reported to Washington that he was "delighted . . . to throw him [Wang] into a spin." It seemed that the United States had cornered the PRC while winning a victory in the court of public opinion. However, India refused to take part in the plan and Beijing was indifferent. The ploy failed.[62]

After the deadlock on the renunciation of force, the State Department was not inclined either to move on to new issues or to take the initiative on the two questions that remained deadlocked. A credible American position had been established, and it would stand pat. Wang seemed ready to extend the talks through the summer, and Johnson was instructed to lengthen the interval between them and told that no new proposals would be forthcoming. The public relations flank was covered. Dulles could return to his initial strategy—stall and maintain an unofficial cease-fire.[63]

Beijing, however, seemed wise to Dulles's stalling strategy and called the Eisenhower administration's bluff. At the August 9, 1956, meeting, Wang turned to the embargo question.[64] In this and the presentations that followed, he argued for a new approach that would endeavor to address less controversial issues, such as the embargo and cultural exchange, and put aside the larger ones that had earlier deadlocked the talks.[65]

Dulles was prepared to elicit Beijing's specific complaints about the embargo, apparently reasoning that if allied pressure was going to force change, it might be useful to use the unavoidable changes as a bargaining chip in the talks.[66] However, there would be no extended discussions, since this would only exacerbate the already strained relations with the allies. In his instructions for the July 26 meeting, Johnson was told that he could "lead Wang to disclose just what he had in mind" on the trade embargo, but that there must be a "meaningful agreed announcement by parties renouncing force before trade embargoes can be usefully discussed." Johnson pursued this line throughout the summer.[67]

In reality, the American position was even more rigid. From the ambassador's confidential correspondence, it is clear that even if by some remote chance Beijing did meet American demands on the renunciation of force, there would still be no movement on the embargo issue. Instead, the prisoner issue would be revived.[68] The United States would not accept the PRC's demand that it put aside earlier issues. Deadlock again loomed.

The PRC, however, was not quite finished. On August 5, representatives of U.S. news organizations were invited to visit China. Dulles rejected their request for permission to go. In his instructions for the August 9 meeting, Johnson was told to inform Wang that Americans would be allowed to travel to the mainland only when all of the prisoners were released. The State Department believed that this would assure that "maximum leverage will be exerted on them to release Americans."[69] The intention was to frustrate the step-by-step approach and keep the focus on the previous two issues.

It should come as no surprise, then, that subsequent meetings were sterile and desultory. They went around in circles, the PRC raising the two new issues (the embargo and cultural exchanges), the American side returning to the earlier items, Wang dismissing these and returning to the embargo, and so on. Washington's response to this deadlock was similar to that of the previous February: its primary concern was whether Beijing would break off the talks and, if a break occurred, whether the U.S. posture at the talks put it in the best possible light. In general, the assessment was that the PRC was not ready to terminate the talks but that, were they to do so, Washington was in a good position from a public relations point of view. No initiative would be taken to break the deadlock.[70]

When, in January 1957, Ambassador Johnson expressed his frustration and suggested that the value of the talks should be reconsidered "at a high level," Walter McConaughy replied that the message had been passed on to Dulles, who recalled that he had warned Johnson he might be at the talks for two years. McConaughy added that the talks were "serving the purpose he [Dulles] had in mind." The United States would continue to "beat them [the PRC] at their own game by out-sitting and out-talking them."[71] The primary goal—to tie the PRC down at the talks—remained.

The talks, characterized by senseless, almost spiteful, bickering, dragged on until the fall of 1957. During the final months, some new issues did surface, but given the bitter tone of the discussions, the new issues simply tightened the deadlock. The most significant of these was the question of travel to the PRC by the American press. Media pressure on the administration to allow such travel developed in the spring of 1956, and in July Dulles agreed that "a limited [10–15] number" of correspondents, chosen by the press, could travel to the mainland. There would, however, be "no reciprocity, with Chinese Communists sending news representatives here."[72] Wang Bingnan rejected the proposal and introduced a draft statement whereby both countries "agreed to give permission, on an equal and reciprocal basis, for correspondents." Johnson, in turn, rejected this proposal: the U.S. would not agree beforehand to any notion of reciprocity.[73] The PRC protested, but it did not test the uncertain American position, nor did it even bother to raise the issue at the November 14 meeting, and it quickly became, as Johnson noted in a letter, "dead on all sides."[74]

The desultory manner in which both sides approached the question of the exchange of correspondents reflected the toll the previous year had taken on each side's commitment to the talks. This toll was also apparent in discussions of the appointment of a new representative to replace Ambassador Johnson, who was scheduled for reassignment. Within the State Department, three alternatives had been proposed: to appoint a new ambassador to the talks (possibly Karl Rankin, formerly ambassador to the ROC, soon to be transferred to Yugoslavia); to move the talks to Warsaw and designate the ambassador there, Jacob Beam; or to lower the talks to the first secretary level, with Edwin Martin (a frequent participant in the Geneva talks) commuting from London.

Although Johnson favored continuing the talks at the ambassadorial level (but not with Rankin, whom, he said, Beijing perceived as pro-ROC), Washington had other ideas. Here was an occasion for expressing dissatisfaction with the failure to resolve the prisoner or renunciation of force issues and with a recent statement by Zhou Enlai that the United States was seeking to establish relations with the PRC under the rubric of a "two-China" policy.[75] In his instructions for the final meeting of the year, Johnson was told to inform Wang that, in future, Edwin Martin would represent the United States. The State Department further specified that the proposal for a change in the level of representation should only come after "a strong statement of U.S. disappointment" with Beijing's posture at the talks. It was essential that Wang "perceive [the] connection" between the PRC posture and Washington's "unwillingness to continue at the ambassadorial level." Judging that Beijing was unlikely to end the talks, Washington instructed

Johnson to leave open the possibility of a future return to the ambassadorial level but to be unyielding should the PRC reject the current proposal or threaten a break.[76]

Johnson clearly enjoyed springing this surprise on an unprepared Wang. The PRC ambassador's spontaneous response to the news of Martin's designation was to suggest that the change in the level of the talks involved "a change in the nature of the talks and the nature of the problems to be settled will be influenced." He refused to approve a press announcement that set January 9, 1958, as the date for the next round, suggesting instead that the announcement note Johnson's transfer and state that the talks were "suspended" and that the "procedure for future talks" would be agreed upon by both sides. In the end, the statement simply said that the meeting had taken place and that the date for the next meeting would be announced.[77]

In fact, as subsequent events show, "suspension" was a more accurate description. Bickering over the resumption of talks continued until August 1958, when another crisis brought the negotiators back to the table, this time in Warsaw.

The 1958 Jinmen-Mazu Crisis: Did the Talks Really Make a Difference? (August–December 1958)

On August 23, 1958, the PRC began shelling the islands of Jinmen and Mazu from Fujian province.[78] Although Beijing's ultimate military objective was not clear, the immediate result of the attack was an artillery blockade. By the end of August, the United States had deployed a huge task force to the Taiwan Strait area, and on September 4, for the first time, Secretary of State Dulles made a public U.S. commitment to the defense of the offshore islands. On September 6, as American naval vessels escorted ROC supply ships to the international waters around the islands and provision of military supplies was increased, Zhou Enlai offered to reconvene the talks in Warsaw. However, the military situation remained tenuous, and the possibility of an escalation in U.S. support of the ROC substantial. At the end of the month, the U.S. military declared that the blockade had been broken, dramatically lessening the danger of American intervention. In early October, Beijing declared a cease-fire, which was followed by a symbolic, alternate-day shelling of the islands. During a Dulles visit to Taipei later that month, Chiang Kai-shek was pressured into agreeing to a joint communiqué declaring that the U.S.-ROC treaty was "defensive in character" and that Taipei would not use force as the "principal means" to achieve the "restoration of freedom" on the mainland.[79]

It is difficult to define the relationship between the Sino-American talks and the easing of the crisis. In the view of most analysts, the simple fact of Zhou Enlai's call for a resumption of the talks was a definitive indication that the PRC sought to ease the crisis. In his classic study of the talks, Kenneth T. Young goes further, however, suggesting that the ten sessions held during September–November 1958 "justified the twelve years of talks" and that the meetings in Warsaw "played a useful part in controlling and calming the crisis."[80] Young argues that for the first time, the United States came to the table ready to negotiate "earnestly and resourcefully" to reach "mutually satisfactory arrangements," only to be frustrated by Beijing's intransigence.[81] In their memoirs, the U.S. and PRC ambassadors present much less expansive views, suggesting that the talks played a negligible role during the crisis and, in fact, contained very little in the way of new proposals.[82] The diplomatic record is more supportive of their position than of Young's.

BACK TO THE TABLE

After the December 1957 suspension, Dulles's impatience with the talks intensified. When it seemed that the PRC might release the American prisoners in January 1958, Dulles feared that if the U.S. returned to Warsaw the "only things left to talk about . . . [would be] those subjects which the Communists insist upon." Dulles added that Johnson's transfer was "a plausible opportunity to break off the talks and that if we do not take advantage of this opportunity we may be in for trouble."[83] He was not interested in seeing the talks become a vehicle for resolving issues in Sino-American relations because of the "trouble" that would result from foreign and domestic political pressures.

However, when the prisoners were not released, interest in restarting the talks was rekindled.[84] The PRC was to be notified that Washington was ready to resume. Although there was "little enthusiasm" in Washington for more talks, they were seen as a useful way "to keep before the world" Beijing's failure to release all prisoners as agreed.[85] On June 30, before such a message could be delivered, the PRC issued a statement charging the United States with stalling and giving Washington fifteen days or else Beijing would "consider . . . that the United States has decided to break up the Sino-American ambassadorial talks." At a news conference, Dulles replied that the United States would not abide by the "15 day ultimatum" but would pursue its earlier inquiries about the talks. On July 17, Ambassador Jacob Beam in Warsaw approached the PRC, and preparations were made for renewed monthly talks.[86]

Although the shelling of the islands did not begin until August 23, by the first week of August Washington was turning its attention to the Taiwan Strait, where, in the words of a CIA report, "the situation . . . was 'heating up.'" Although Dulles had told Secretary of Defense Neil McElroy that an approach to the PRC through diplomatic channels might at that point be "interpreted as a sign of weakness," when Zhou Enlai announced that Beijing was ready to resume talks, Washington quickly agreed.[87]

Two days later, Dulles held a meeting at the State Department to map out strategy. The administration did not want to appear to be "panting for the resumption of the talks," but it still considered them a better forum than the U.N. Dulles mused about gaining the neutralization of the offshore islands in exchange for recognition of ROC sovereignty over Taiwan and the Penghu Islands, but there is little indication at this meeting of any belief that the talks could deal with such real issues. Still, the certain failure of U.S. proposals was not really important, since the United States was only seeking "to improve our negotiating posture in the eyes of the world." Echoing the past, one participant added that the "purpose . . . was to string the talks out as much as possible."[88]

Washington approached the Warsaw talks of 1958 with the same objectives it had espoused earlier. Despite Dulles's public statement that there was "quite a lot to negotiate," the United States was returning to the table only reluctantly and with few expectations that anything would be resolved.[89] In the instructions for the first meeting, scheduled for September 15, Jacob Beam was told to emphasize the need to avert a widening of the conflict and, while reserving the right to raise previous issues (for example, prisoners and missing servicemen), to press for an "informal cease-fire" followed by a discussion of ways to end provocations and ease tensions. However, Beam was also informed that Washington was "under no illusions that Chinese Communists will use Warsaw talks for anything we would regard as constructive." With the usual expectation that the PRC would publish the record of the talks, Beam was told to ensure that his presentation emphasized an "open constructive" approach, refuted charges that the United States was the aggressor, and included a "carefully worded statement of support for position and dignity" of the ROC.[90]

Crisis Negotiation or Playing to Public Opinion?

The first meeting in Warsaw took place on September 15, 1958, at a site provided by the Polish government—the Mysliweicki Palace—after the PRC refused to meet at the Swiss embassy and the United States refused to meet at either the U.S. or the PRC embassy. As Ambassador Jacob Beam notes in his memoirs, the choice of that site, undoubtedly bugged, meant that Washington was "inviting participation by third (Polish) and presumably fourth (Soviet) parties."[91] This was of interest to the American side, since it was directing its arguments as much toward world opinion as to the PRC representative.

The talks on the situation in the Taiwan Strait took place at ten meetings held between September 15 and November 11, 1958, at intervals ranging from three days to almost two weeks. Despite Dulles's pessimism about their usefulness, the talks in Warsaw were a port in an ever-growing storm. As Dulles told Beam in an "eyes only" letter on the eve of the first meeting, "our basic objective is to bring about quickly a cessation of hostilities." Otherwise, Washington would have to resort to "desperate measures" in the Taiwan Strait.[92]

When the two sides finally met, Wang declined the opportunity to speak first, and Beam took the initiative.[93] Following instructions, he made a very brief reference to the prisoner issue and then passed on to the Strait crisis. Depicting PRC actions as an unacceptable attempt to achieve "territorial changes . . . through use of military force," Beam asserted that, given its defense treaty with Taiwan, the United States could not "stand idly by." Washington's position was that there should be an "immediate cease-fire in Taiwan Strait area," followed by discussions related to "terminating provocative activities and easing of tensions."

Predictably, Wang rejected this proposal, using arguments from the previous year that stressed the domestic nature of the conflict, the illegality of the Sino-American treaty, and American responsibility for the crisis. He then presented an uncompromising, even hostile, draft of an "agreed announcement" in which Beijing would reassert its claim to the offshore islands and Taiwan; the United States would agree to withdraw its armed forces; the PRC would agree to allow KMT troops to evacuate without pursuit; the PRC would pledge to strive to liberate Taiwan and the Penghu Islands "by peaceful means and will, in a certain period of time, avoid using force" should such an evacuation take place; and both sides would agree on the need for freedom of navigation. Beam dismissed the document as one that "involves surrender."[94]

The United States and the PRC had picked up where they had left off in 1957. The exchanges at this first meeting set a rigid pattern that would once again deadlock the talks, the PRC side insisting on American cessation of provocations (soon to become withdrawal) as the prerequisite to talks and the American side insisting on the need for a cease-fire before there could be any discussion of the status of forces. But the discussions never moved beyond empty exchanges on the nature of the dispute (domestic or international), the nature of the ROC government (puppet regime or sovereign state), and which side presented the greatest danger to peace in the area (American occupation or PRC aggression).[95]

In contrast to 1955–57, when the talks followed a crisis, this round occurred in the midst of a crisis. To retreat now would have an even greater impact on perceptions of the United States and the PRC in Asia. At the same time, the ROC and the American embassy in Taipei were pressing for a quick end, since the talks were damaging morale on the island. Should concessions be made, morale could collapse or, even worse, it might provoke Taipei to engage in an act of desperation that would ignite a Sino-American conflict.[96]

With war jitters growing at home and abroad, the United States could not appear rigid.[97] As past experience had demonstrated, much of the substance of the talks would be subject to public scrutiny. Now only the Soviet Union and Poland were listening; eventually the world might even become a party.[98] As the deadlock became more apparent, the possibility that the venue might shift to the U.N. increased. If the two sides could not reach an agreement, at least the United States could establish a good record for subsequent international discussions.

The lengthy American counterproposal of September 30, 1958, stated the positions of both sides on the Taiwan area, noted the support of the Soviet Union for the PRC position and the American treaty obligation to the ROC, and recognized that this was an "international dispute and threat of force which endangers international peace and security." On this basis, the United States proposed that the PRC "suspend hostilities," that it would be ready to pursue such remedies as mediation or judicial settlement, and that both sides refrain from "harassment or provocations."[99]

There was of course no way that Beijing would accept any such proposal. Wang rejected it out of hand as a "deceitful proposal that can never be realized," just as Beam had rejected the uncompromising PRC draft at the start of the talks. However, as Beam noted in a cable to Washington, the draft could also serve as the basis for a later "presentation to the UN or to [the] public." And it was no coincidence that on the same day this presentation was being made in private, Dulles spoke publicly of the possibility of a withdrawal from the offshore islands and a drawing down of American forces. In characteristic fashion, Dulles personally drafted a proposal that left little room for compromise at the negotiating table, laying the groundwork for a public position of moderation.[100]

This trend had accelerated when Washington received the news on September 29 that the blockade of Jinmen had been broken and that the resupply of the island's garrison was assured. The sense of crisis that had shaped the American approach at the beginning of the talks had now passed. In the instructions for the October 4 meeting (again personally drafted by Dulles), Beam was told that with the successful resupply of the garrison, Beijing would soon realize the impossibility of taking Jinmen. It was important to keep the talks going as either a "cover or [an] excuse" for the mainland to cease hostilities, or, if the PRC resumed hostilities, to create a "Warsaw record" for seeking U.N. action, which would precede consideration of any action that went "beyond conventional weapons."[101]

On October 5 (Washington time), PRC Defense Minister Peng Dehuai announced a suspension of military activities "on the Fukien front" and declared that the offshore islands could be resupplied as long as the United States did not resume its escort activities. The first scenario, it seemed, was becoming more likely. In his instructions for the October 10 meeting, Beam was told that the announcement had "changed [the] negotiating picture for [the] time being at least" and that he should work toward gaining an indefinite extension of the cease-fire and some sense of U.S. actions that might provoke Beijing to resume hostilities.[102] He was also instructed to press for reconsideration of the American proposal and to question Wang on whether the Warsaw talks had any meaning for the PRC, since despite its rejection at the talks, Beijing had announced a cease-fire.

Washington's hopes that the talks might prolong the cease-fire evaporated when the two sides met. Refusing to discuss the cease-fire, Wang maintained that the proposal had not been directed at the United States. Beam was not a representative of the "Chiang clique," and his attempt to initiate discussions was an attempt to internationalize the issue. Only an American withdrawal could pave the way for further negotiations. The talks were back at square one. Washington once more turned to public relations. By early December 1958, the deadlock was as unrelenting as ever.[103]

The record from the American side suggests that there is little justification for any claim that the Sino-American talks might have played a role in calming the 1958 Strait crisis or that Washington used the talks to take any bold new initiatives. Here again, any real resolution would have required a radical change in one side's fundamental foreign policy outlook. The American side was not prepared to accord greater standing to the PRC or to weaken its ties with Taiwan; similarly, Beijing was not ready to yield on the nature of Taiwan or on the U.S. relationship to Taiwan. Most likely, Wang Bingnan was receiving instructions similar to those received by Jacob Beam.

Following these intense but largely insignificant discussions, the meetings became desultory. Although Christian Herter replaced a dying John Foster Dulles in early 1959, the U.S. posture changed little, and the PRC side made it clear that no other questions could be meaningfully addressed until the irreconcilable differences over Taiwan were resolved. Washington's attempts to focus on other issues were rebuffed by Beijing, suggesting that their roles in the earlier stages of the talks had reversed.[104] By the end of 1960, both sides were marking time, waiting for a new American administration.

Kennedy, Johnson, Vietnam, and the Cultural Revolution (1960–1970)

By the end of 1960 there had already been 102 meetings. The intervals between them had varied from two or three days during the repatriation talks, to weekly or biweekly during much of 1956, to monthly in 1957, and to every three days to two weeks during the crisis of 1958. Thereafter, the intervals were erratic: monthly, bimonthly, once (1968), five times a year (1964), and none at all (1969).

Their irregular nature provides clues to the distinctive quality of the final 34 meetings. In the first place, although certain topics recurred, there was no unifying agenda, sustained dialogue, or exchange of proposals as before. Negotiators dealt with issues as they emerged. Second, the infrequency of the meetings contrasts sharply with the frequency of the dramatic developments—such as the PRC's invasion of India, the Sino-Soviet conflict, the Cultural Revolution, the war in Vietnam— that had a profound impact on U.S.-PRC relations, although to be sure, these events do help to explain the erratic schedule of the meetings. However, the contrast between the declining importance of the talks and the gravity of the events suggests that major developments were taking place outside the talks. During these years, the Warsaw talks not only became less important in shaping Sino-American relations, they also became less reflective of the totality of United States policy toward China.

THE KENNEDY YEARS

As a candidate, John F. Kennedy had criticized the decision to defend the offshore islands, a stance that reflected the broader policy goal of disentangling the United States from the Chinese civil war. This became the core of the Kennedy administration's China policy. However, it was intended more to create greater distance from—and to maintain greater control over—the actions of the ROC than to seek rapprochement with the PRC.

The Taiwan question had vexed the Eisenhower administration, complicating relations with allies and nearly causing a confrontation with the mainland. After eight years, John Foster Dulles had finally concluded that in securing interests in Asia, the ROC was as much a part of the problem as a solution. Ironically, the secretary of state made significant progress toward securing from the ROC what he could not obtain in the talks with the PRC: a renunciation of force and a less belligerent posture in the Strait. The Kennedy administration completed this process of bringing Taipei under control.[105]

Since the end of the Eisenhower administration, Chiang Kai-shek had been pressing for the supplies and training he needed to mount large-scale cross-Strait operations. These demands continued into early 1962, when they became particularly intense (and public) due to the ROC's perception of PRC instability in the wake of the Great Leap Forward. As a crisis atmosphere developed in the Strait, Washington pressured Chiang into postponing any major military operations. By early 1963, postponement had become termination. Washington told the ROC that American support would be restricted to economic aid and a firm commitment to the defense of the island. Other than small raids, the United States would not "acquiesce in military action against the China mainland." Taipei complained bitterly but to no avail.[106]

Although the policy of disentangling from the Chinese civil war meant seeking greater distance from the ROC, there was little inclination in Washington to move closer to the PRC. The major reason was Kennedy's concern about the impact of such a policy on public opinion, in particular the danger posed by lingering elements of McCarthyism. China policy would be a matter for his second term.[107] This attitude was reinforced by international developments. Growing instability in Asia, particularly in Laos and Vietnam, and the expected PRC detonation of a nuclear device contributed to the sense of a China threat. The administration was also sensitive to the impact a change in China policy would have on the shaky Soviet-American détente and saw in Beijing's attack on moderate Soviet policies a confirmation of its view of China as dangerous.[108]

It is thus not surprising that the Kennedy administration did not take the initiative to revive or refocus the mired Warsaw talks. For the most part, there was little movement on the issues that had deadlocked the negotiations. However, what sets the Warsaw talks during the Kennedy administration apart from those held earlier was a willingness to broaden the scope of the issues under discussion to include contemporaneous problems. In some cases, there were no real exchanges on these questions, simply propaganda blasts from the PRC side. This was the dominant response to questions such as U.S. relations with India or policy in South Vietnam or South Korea. In other cases, however, such as Laos, U.S. concerns about threatening PRC postures, or alleged incursions by American ships into PRC territorial waters, there was an actual exchange of views and constructive requests for clarification.[109]

During the course of the talks, the Kennedy administration debated the advisability of offering assistance in the form of food and medicine to China in the wake of the Great Leap Forward.[110] However, the issue was moot, since Wang Bingnan refused to discuss the sending of food parcels, even by private individuals, and the United States refrained from pressing this sensitive issue further. However, such restraint was not present in its handling of the Sino-Soviet dispute. The American side confronted Beijing with its own

harsh rhetoric and made comparisons between PRC statements and conciliatory Soviet policy.[111]

It is interesting that, although the administration taunted the PRC over
the Sino-Soviet dispute, it did seek to engage it on one of the issues at the
center of that dispute—control of nuclear weapons. At the first meeting in
Warsaw, Jacob Beam was instructed to note that the American proposal at
the disarmament talks provided for the accession of additional states and to
seek the thoughts of Beijing.[112] When the test ban treaty was finally signed,
however, the PRC's response was condemnatory. It did not go beyond
a public call for total disarmament and a proposal for the creation of a
nuclear-free zone in Asia, one that could be realized by a U.S. withdrawal of
atomic weapons from the area,[113] a not-so-subtle attempt to return to the
Taiwan issue. The ploy failed, but the issue remained very much on the
table. Despite the new restraints on Taiwan's mainland operations, the PRC
watched for signs of intensifying military activity in Taiwan with considerable concern. In the course of the meetings, the PRC complained about
American support for U-2 flights and demonstrated a detailed knowledge of
visits to the island by American civilian and military officials as well as ROC
military exercises.[114]

However, the most substantive intrusion of the Taiwan question
occurred during the crisis of mid-1962, when it seemed that the military
build-up on both sides of the Strait might bring renewed conflict. Although
many within the administration felt that the PRC was securing a defensive
position, the possibility of mainland provocation remained. Both eventualities were covered in a special meeting, requested by the PRC, in Warsaw. At
the meeting, John Moors Cabot, the new American ambassador, informed
Wang "that US government had no intention of supporting any GRC
[Government of the Republic of China] attack on Mainland under existing
circumstances . . . [and that] the GRC committed not to attack without our
consent." However, in the event that the PRC's actions proved to be offensive and not defensive, Cabot warned his counterpart of the "serious danger
US forces would be involved." Finally, he stressed that if Taipei did attack, it
would be "without support of US" and that Washington hoped that the
Warsaw talks would continue despite such a development.[115]

This was a remarkable exchange for three reasons. First, in contrast to
the 1958 Taiwan Strait crisis, the talks apparently did play a role in defusing
the situation. Second, and reflecting its growing impatience with Chiang

Kai-shek, the Kennedy administration offered to continue the talks with the mainland despite possible conflict. Finally, the "special meeting" was one of seven such meetings, initially proposed by the PRC, that took place during these years and briefly showed some promise of becoming a second, more informal and informative channel.

After an earlier meeting on June 29, 1961, Wang asked Beam to join him for a cup of coffee. Their informal discussions covered a range of issues, from Laos to the U.N. Although there were no revelations or breakthroughs, the discussions were more spontaneous than the formal meetings. In a very closely held "eyes only telegram," the State Department gave Beam somewhat lukewarm encouragement to pursue such meetings (even if they should take place at either embassy) and to explore new topics under the pretext of securing ideas for his forthcoming reassignment to Washington.[116] There were further meetings, but in the end, with the exception of the June 1962 meeting on the Taiwan Strait, these informal talks never became a genuine "second channel" for more open discussion.

THE JOHNSON ADMINISTRATION

In the early years of the Johnson administration, officials continued to see the PRC as a major threat to American interests in Asia. Because of concern about Beijing's nuclear weapons, discussions of a preemptive strike, begun in the Kennedy administration, were continued.[117] During these years, however, there was more to China policy. Paradoxically, precisely because of the war in Vietnam, proposals made at the highest levels of government were more innovative than at any time since 1949, yet this policy fermentation was imperfectly reflected in the Warsaw talks. The infrequency of the meetings (only fifteen between 1964 and 1968) made sustained discussions very difficult and dampened the value of the talks as a reliable channel of communication. However, there is still much to be learned from the record of the meetings.

From the Gulf of Tonkin incident in the summer of 1964 until the end of the Johnson administration, policy toward the PRC (and, by extension, the U.S. posture at the Warsaw talks) was driven by three considerations: to head off Beijing's intervention in the Vietnam War; to ameliorate the negative impact of the war on domestic and world opinion; and to lay the groundwork for policy toward a post–Cultural Revolution PRC. However,

as we shall see, priorities changed over time, the last becoming more prominent as the Cultural Revolution unfolded.

In the aftermath of the Gulf of Tonkin incident and the retaliatory
bombing of North Vietnam, James Thomson suggested to McGeorge
Bundy that the United States call a special meeting in Warsaw to clarify the
limited purposes of the bombing and to state that Washington's goal was
neither to destroy North Vietnam nor to attack China. Only by using such
a channel, Thomson argued, could "misinterpretation and miscalculation" be
avoided. It was ultimately decided that, rather than call a special meeting,
America's Vietnam policy would become a leading topic in Warsaw.[118]

The overwhelming majority of the discussions concerned with Vietnam,
however, were simply restatements of the public positions of each side.[119]
Although detailed discussions of specific incidents took place, there is only
one example in the records of the Warsaw talks of mutual signaling. This
was a direct and stern warning from the PRC that "disastrous developments
were in store for the US" if it "linked up Chinese civil war with its war of
aggression" by introducing ROC troops into Vietnam.[120] The more important question, of course, was how to determine other conditions that might
provoke PRC intervention, yet here, the transcripts show neither direct
discussions of this topic nor unique signals that differed from public statements. If such signals existed, it would appear that they were communicated
via channels outside the talks.[121]

Washington used the Warsaw talks in more subtle ways to lessen Beijing's sense of threat arising from American actions in Vietnam. In a memo
to Undersecretary of State George Ball in December 1965, William Bundy
noted that the United States should "balance" its intention of a continued
commitment to Taiwan with steps to "indicate to the Chinese that we still
seek to avoid a major confrontation." He proposed that the United States
offer a broad menu of initiatives that would include the admission of PRC
journalists, liberalized travel, and a joint examination of incidents involving
American forces in the areas around China. In January 1968, the American
side offered a long list of possible areas of cooperation (everything from satellite communications to joint scientific research to arms control talks).[122]

Other, more dramatic gestures were made outside the talks or considered
within the Johnson administration. For example, in the spring of 1966, Vice
President Hubert Humphrey made remarks suggesting a new flexibility in
policies toward Beijing. Both James Thomson and Robert W. Komer (then

acting special assistant for National Security Affairs) argued that the administration should seize on these remarks, as well as on a more supportive public opinion, to take new initiatives toward improving relations with the PRC.[123] By summer, the administration was considering new approaches to the question of representation at the U.N. and to relaxing trade restrictions, and President Johnson called publicly for a "free flow of ideas and people and goods" to China.[124]

The most notable example of this new thinking came in June, when the White House drafted, but did not send, a letter to Zhou Enlai proposing that talks be held at the foreign minister level. The letter was considered for submission at that month's Warsaw meeting but withdrawn at the last moment because some thought that in view of the situation in Vietnam, it might make the United States look weak. However, John Gronouski, the new American ambassador, was given the letter and told that its submission would be reconsidered "as circumstances change."[125]

Although Secretary of State Dean Rusk showed only lukewarm support for these initiatives, the more important factor in slowing the momentum was the development of the Cultural Revolution over the summer and fall of 1966. The times were unpropitious for major new American diplomatic initiatives.[126] Indeed, the Warsaw meetings thereafter (a total of only three) were characterized by the dress ("Mao suits") and rhetoric of the Cultural Revolution. Still, the Johnson administration continued to send signals of openness and nonhostility. Gronouski was instructed to do all he could to keep the talks going, and the State Department seemed ready to raise their level, if considered necessary, to accomplish this purpose.[127] Despite repeated rebuffs, the American side continued to present expansive agendas in Warsaw and to signal flexibility publicly.[128]

It is probable that this continuing posture of openness was intended to reduce the danger of PRC intervention in Vietnam by projecting a benign, nonthreatening image of the United States. But as American involvement in Vietnam deepened between 1965 and 1967, so too did political opposition at home and unease abroad. In the eyes of many, the Johnson administration's posture was a return to the rigid, anticommunist days of the 1950s. From almost the beginning of the escalation in Vietnam, administration officials realized that public opinion, the war, and China policy were interrelated: a firm anticommunist posture in Southeast Asia would disarm conservative critics, but it would also make possible a more flexible American approach to the PRC, which in turn would demonstrate that the United States opposed Communist aggression, not communism.

And so, as domestic opposition to the war grew, so did the administration's tendency to see shifts in its China policy as a way to blunt opposition to its Vietnam policy. This was especially clear during Washington's brief flirtation with a démarche toward China in the spring of 1966 described earlier. Moreover, one also has the sense that the administration's constant and imperative instructions to Warsaw to avoid a breakdown of the talks were related to its concern that a break would provoke even greater domestic criticism.[129]

There was yet another intended audience for the U.S. posture in Warsaw, which, it was expected, would receive the message more directly: the Soviet Union. In late 1965, Ambassador Gronouski reported to Washington that an embassy official had picked up radio broadcasts of the talks, and there was some discussion of moving their venue. In the end, Secretary of State Rusk decided that there was perhaps "some benefit in letting the Poles and Russians know about the contents of our talks at the present time." Indeed, rather than move them, Rusk decided that they would remain where they were, since it was possible that Beijing was also adjusting its presentation for the Russians![130]

The final audience for U.S. China policy was the future leaders of the PRC. The outbreak of the Cultural Revolution in the summer and fall of 1966 considerably lowered administration expectations of any change in the PRC's international behavior. In the ensuing years, Washington followed events on the mainland closely for any hint that the political climate was becoming more amenable to change or that a new leadership was emerging. As one State Department official put it in late 1968, policy toward the PRC should be prepared for either a changed attitude by the current regime ("post-Maoist" but not "post-Mao") or a future, less radical leadership (a "true change of dynasty").[131]

In anticipation of the latter eventuality, administration officials spoke of the Warsaw talks as serving an "educational" function.[132] There was little expectation that the views of the current Chinese representatives would change. However, there was a hope not only that the record sent back to Beijing might have some influence on inner-party debates but that it might also provide both a general signal of openness to future leaders and a list of specific proposals that could form the basis for reconciliation. With this in mind, the administration was careful not to propose anything at Warsaw that, if rejected by current leaders, might limit the options of future PRC leaders.[133]

This was especially the case in the period from December 1968 to early January 1969, when it appeared that events in China might take a moderate turn. Indeed, two weeks before Richard Nixon's inauguration, Walt Rostow sent a memo to President Johnson saying that there were "faint signals" from China and suggesting that it might be wise to respond with a small change in trade policy. This, Rostow argued prophetically, would open options for Johnson's successor.[134]

As is well known, the Nixon administration continued the talks for two more sessions. During the 135th session, held on January 20, 1970, the United States signaled its readiness "to consider sending a representative to Peking for direct discussions with your officials or receiving a representative from your government in Washington" to discuss subjects raised at the session "or other matters on which we might agree."[135] At the 136th, and final, meeting held the following month, the PRC accepted this proposal. From that point on, major American initiatives toward—and negotiations with—Beijing took place outside the ambassadorial talks.

Did the Talks Really Make a Difference?

In his memoirs, Henry Kissinger suggests that the Geneva/Warsaw talks were of little significance. The meetings were, in his judgment, "sterile" and "could not point to a single accomplishment." Kissinger depicts the talks as frozen on the issue of Taiwan and guided by American policymakers who "considered China as a brooding, fanatical, and alien realm difficult to comprehend and impossible to sway." In his view, the breakthrough in relations with Beijing came when the Nixon administration bypassed the Warsaw talks and the conservative State Department that managed them, and changed the basic issue from Taiwan to geopolitical questions, that is, the Soviet threat.[136]

Kissinger's assessment has played an important role in shaping the manner in which subsequent historians have presented the course of Sino-American relations since 1955. For many, this relationship is best depicted as "before Kissinger" and "after Kissinger." Before Kissinger, American policy was based on unreasonable and unbending support for the ROC and uncompromising hostility toward the PRC. Reaching a crescendo during the Vietnam War, this rigid rejection and demonization of Beijing came to an end only after the sudden and dramatic initiatives of the Nixon administration. To put it another way, the oft-told story of U.S. China policy depicts an abrupt transition from the hostile containment policy of the 1950s to the diplomacy of the 1970s. The middle years are relegated to relative obscurity.

This chapter joins the work of scholars such as Rosemary Foot, who have questioned the validity of this view by exploring the subtle changes in the context and substance of U.S. policy previous to the Nixon administration. In Foot's view, Kissinger did not cut the Gordian knot of U.S.-PRC relations in one sudden stroke; rather, he built upon a legacy of changes in perceptions and policy that preceded his stewardship.

Kissinger's assertion that the talks were "sterile" and devoid of a "single accomplishment" is justifiable only if one judges them simply on the basis of their stated purpose. To do so, however, is to miss other subtle but important aspects. The stated purpose of the talks from 1955 to 1957 was to solve major issues in Sino-American relations through negotiation. Yet, in this respect, beyond a terribly flawed August 1955 agreement on repatriation, the American side simply could not compromise, or perhaps even seriously negotiate, any of the principal issues needed to settle the larger problems related to the tensions in the Taiwan area.[137] In fact, the achievement of the agreement on repatriation actually narrowed Washington's options in the talks. Because of domestic political considerations, the issue of repatriation had to be given prominence well after the settlement, increasing PRC intransigence on the prisoner issue and intensifying the confrontational posture taken by each side.

If it was obvious at this early stage that the talks could barely address much less solve major problems, why did Dulles pursue them? The answer lies not in their publicly stated purposes but in the State Department record, which offers clues to what the decisionmakers themselves intended. In this respect, clearly Dulles saw the primary goal of the talks as simply talking: as long as Beijing was at the negotiating table, he reasoned, it would not provoke conflict, thus contributing to a de facto cease-fire in the Taiwan Strait and providing stable conditions for a "divided country" solution. Second, the talks were a useful lightening rod for neutralizing domestic and international criticism of the Eisenhower administration's China policy as excessively anticommunist and pro-ROC. Third, as the stalemate at the negotiating table increasingly provoked both Washington and the PRC to publicize the contents of the talks, Dulles realized that the content could serve much the same purpose—provided that it succeeded in portraying the United States as the aggrieved but reasonable party. At times, in fact, the American negotiating posture was intended to establish just such a record rather than to solve bilateral problems. Finally, it is reasonable to infer that the talks also played some role in Dulles's policy of keeping a tight rein on the ROC by suggesting that any overaggressiveness on Taipei's part might provoke a deal with the PRC behind its back.[138]

These factors motivated the Eisenhower administration to devote considerable time and energy to bilateral talks that were going nowhere. The fact that their usefulness lay in realms other than negotiating and settling difficult questions with the PRC became apparent once again during the Jinmen-Mazu crisis of 1958. Dulles apparently believed that, although the talks could not play a major role in managing a dangerous crisis, they could be refashioned into an important part of Washington's public relations campaign. Faced with a choice of future actions ranging from U.N. intervention to the possible use of nuclear weapons, Washington carefully crafted a record that would, if revealed, demonstrate moderation and an exhaustive effort to reach a peaceful solution.

During the Kennedy and especially the Johnson administrations, this pattern became more obvious. The infrequency of the talks, along with such complicating factors as the Sino-Soviet dispute, the Cultural Revolution, and the Vietnam War, rendered major agreements virtually impossible. Even attempts at "small steps" in resolving minor issues failed. With the exception of the cross-Strait crisis in 1962, there is no evidence that the talks made a significant contribution to either managing or exchanging information on bilateral issues.

By the end of the Johnson administration, however, American policymakers were aggressively pursuing the talks to propose suggestions for joint cooperation to the PRC. The reasons are obvious. The fact of the talks was again considered to be a useful corrective to growing opposition, at home and abroad, to the war in Vietnam and the administration's militant anticommunist image. For reasons ranging from their impact on Soviet perceptions of American policy (via wiretaps), to their calming message to Beijing on American intentions in Vietnam, to their part in preparing an agenda for future relations between the two countries, Washington considered their substance to be important.

Another legacy of the talks is what might be called their "latent function," their "unintended or unrecognized" contribution to the management of U.S.-PRC relations.[139] As others have suggested, the talks gave the American side an increased familiarity with the PRC's negotiating style and a greater knowledge of Beijing's positions on various issues.[140] However, their most important unintended consequence was their role in stimulating Washington to rethink, and in some cases to test, its policies in negotiations with the PRC. The need to provide information and instructions to the delegation in Geneva/Warsaw compelled the State Department to devote considerable time to trying to understand the foreign policy of the PRC. As the record from 1955 to 1968 amply demonstrates, preparations for the talks were occasions for fresh thinking about ways to engage Beijing.

This latent function brings us to the final issue at hand—assessing the relationship of the talks to the Kissinger-Nixon initiative of 1971. The Geneva/Warsaw talks helped to stimulate a policy legacy that would play an important, if subtle, role in laying the foundation for the Nixon initiative. Kissinger attributes to policymakers an inflexible, distorted view they simply did not have. His depiction of the 1971 initiative as a revolutionary reversal of Cold War policy does not square with the historical record. The process, as Rosemary Foot suggests, was more evolutionary, with American policy undergoing important changes in the 1960s. As James Thomson has noted, the thinking of these years left a rich set of policy options that could be drawn upon later.[141]

Is there evidence that the 1971 initiative drew on the groundwork of the previous years? About this, there are only suggestions, even in the Kissinger memoirs.[142] Not until State Department documents for the post-1968 period are released will we be able to address this question adequately. Currently available records, however, allow some speculation. Most analysts emphasize that the PRC's willingness to hold substantive talks with the United States in 1971 reflected the growing importance, in the judgment of China's leader, of the Soviet threat relative to the issue of Washington's ties with Taiwan. The record of the Geneva/Warsaw talks would suggest, however, that from its perspective, Beijing was not setting aside the Taiwan issue at all when it agreed to follow up on the Kissinger initiative. Rather, Mao Zedong and Zhou Enlai might have believed that Washington had made the concessions necessary for moving on to other issues. Beijing might have seen the Kissinger visit of 1971 and the Nixon visit a year later as meeting the preconditions it had established in the Geneva talks for discussion of any other issues in the relationship: the United States had raised the level of the talks, it had committed to eventual military withdrawal from Taiwan, and it had pledged formal recognition of the PRC in Nixon's second term. Following this line, one can further argue that a major reason Beijing slowed down the relationship after 1973 was the lack of movement in U.S. policy toward Taiwan. Thereafter, the PRC again leaned toward its earlier stance at the Geneva/Warsaw talks, which maintained that any further progress would depend on an end to Washington's relationship with the ROC.

We end with a paradox. If Kissinger had not dismissed the legacy of the Warsaw talks so quickly, he might have been more sensitive to how his visit appeared to Beijing, less likely to believe that contemporary geopolitics would trump PRC demands of the previous fifteen years, and, most specifically, more aware of the importance of addressing the Taiwan question during the formative years of the new U.S. relationship with the People's Republic of China.

CHAPTER EIGHT

The Johnson Administration, China,
and the Vietnam War

Robert D. Schulzinger

China—like Germany in 1917, and like Germany in the West and Japan in the East in the late 1930s—looms as a major power threatening to undercut our importance and effectiveness in the world and, more remotely but more menacingly, to organize all of Asia against us.

—Robert S. McNamara, 1965

[The Chinese Cultural Revolution of 1966] led to China's withdrawal from active involvement in international affairs for more than a decade. But, blinded by our assumptions and preoccupied with a rapidly growing war, we—like most other Western leaders—continued to view China as a serious threat in Southeast Asia and the rest of the world.

—Robert S. McNamara, 1995

CONCERNS ABOUT CHINA played a major role in U.S. decision making during the Vietnam War. The United States fought in Vietnam in part to contain and compete with the People's Republic of China, but the administration of Lyndon B. Johnson pursued a complex, often contradictory policy toward the PRC during the war. U.S. officials believed that China sought to reduce the influence of the United States in Southeast Asia. At the same time, by sending messages through diplomatic channels, the United States recognized and sought to encourage Chinese caution. As the United States first escalated its military involvement in the war and later sought negotiations to end the fighting, American planners often considered what China might do. On the one hand, advocates of U.S. participation based the U.S. role on the need to counter the influence of the PRC not only in Asia but among revolutionary movements around the world. On the other hand, once they had made the commitment to fight in Vietnam, U.S. officials constantly tried to avoid provoking China into sending in its own forces, as it had done during the Korean War.[1]

Tactically, the Johnson administration was successful in limiting the war to avoid direct Chinese intervention, yet these tactical skills did not translate into a successful Vietnam policy. Before 1967, the administration often overestimated the danger China posed to U.S. interests. These exaggerated fears of the influence of the revolutionary doctrines of Mao Zedong probably encouraged the United States to involve itself more deeply in Vietnam than leaders would otherwise have considered worthwhile.

This chapter is divided into three parts: a discussion of the escalation of the Vietnam War; an account of 1966, the year of stalemate; and an analysis of the last two years of the Johnson administration, when the United States reassessed the nature of the threat now posed by a China in the throes of Cultural Revolution. From 1963 to 1965, U.S. officials did not waver in their view that China was a threat to American interests in Southeast Asia. The United States fought in Vietnam in part to counter that perceived threat. When the Cultural Revolution convulsed the country, beginning in 1966, American officials initially believed that China would become more unpredictable and possibly more dangerous. In 1967 and 1968, however, the continuing turmoil helped spark new thinking among American policymakers: China seemed to have turned inward, becoming less threatening to its neighbors and possibly ready for détente with the United States.

China and the Escalation of the Vietnam War, 1964–1965

In its first six months in office, the Johnson administration faced a deteriorating situation in Vietnam. The United States had helped General Duong Van Minh overthrow the government of Ngo Dinh Diem in November 1963 in the hope that a new military regime would wage war more aggressively against the Vietcong fighters of the National Liberation Front (NLF). Events soon dashed these optimistic expectations. The Minh government lasted barely three months. Its replacement, led by General Nguyen Khanh, took office in late January 1964. For the rest of the year, the United States watched in horror as the Khanh government failed to gain popular support or to pursue the war against the NLF more effectively.

From its earliest days, the Johnson administration looked for ways to bolster the morale of the South Vietnamese government. Within two weeks of taking office, Johnson characterized the situation in Vietnam as "our most critical military area." He urged the Defense and State departments and the CIA to move quickly to shake up the personnel in Saigon.[2] Secretary of

State Dean Rusk told Ambassador Henry Cabot Lodge that Johnson wanted "our effort in Vietnam be stepped up to the highest pitch."[3] He perceived a loss of momentum since the coup and bewailed the fact that "we as a government were not doing everything we should" in South Vietnam. Concern that the situation there had not improved significantly since the coup permeated official Washington. Staff members who had backed the plan to remove Diem grumbled about his successors, who had difficulty organizing a new government, thereby slowing the war effort.[4]

In December 1963, most of Johnson's advisers agreed that the United States needed to do more to boost the sagging morale of the government in South Vietnam. The only dissent came from Mike Mansfield, the majority leader of the Senate and a long-time Diem supporter. Mansfield had grown increasingly disillusioned with Diem and had warned Kennedy against excessive U.S. involvement in Vietnam.[5]

Some of Mansfield's uneasiness arose from his concern about provoking Chinese intervention in the war. He thought that current efforts to secure a victory over the Vietcong in South Vietnam might "in time, involve U.S. forces throughout Southeast Asia, and finally throughout China itself in search of victory. What national interest in Asia would steel the American people for the massive costs of an ever-deepening involvement of that kind?" Instead of heading for this kind of war, with inestimable costs in morale, Mansfield favored a truce in Vietnam leading to peace throughout Southeast Asia—a neutralized Vietnam and a Southeast Asia less dependent on U.S. aid and support, not so directly under U.S. control, and not cut off from China but not under Chinese domination either.[6]

Mansfield's cautions might have found a more sympathetic reception in the Johnson administration had American officials not perceived a growing PRC threat, largely because of the worsening Sino-Soviet split. American officials had been following the situation since 1961, but by the time the Johnson administration was poised to make the fateful decisions that would escalate American involvement in Vietnam, a consensus on the effect of the dispute on Chinese foreign policy had emerged. China now challenged the Soviets for preeminence among revolutionaries in the underdeveloped world. It consistently denounced the Soviet Union for what its leaders characterized as "revisionism"—a cowardly acquiescence to Western, especially American, domination. The Chinese had intensified their denunciation of the Soviet Union in the wake of the tentative steps toward arms control taken in

Washington and Moscow in 1963. But what did this new militancy mean for China's relations with its neighbors and with the United States? A series of National Intelligence Estimates predicted that Chinese rhetoric would become increasingly warlike and that China would look for low-cost ways to assist revolutionary and nationalist movements in Southeast Asia. Beijing would be supportive of Asian revolutionaries, but it would also be restrained. Paradoxically, American officials reasoned that the chasm between the Soviet Union and Beijing also meant that Washington was in a better position to avoid a direct military confrontation with China than it had been during the Korean War. China realized that the split with Moscow reduced the prospect of material aid from the Soviet Union. "The Chinese have thus far shown a marked respect for U.S. power," a National Intelligence Estimate noted in mid-1963. "We don't expect them to change this basic attitude."[7]

Rebutting Mansfield's views, Secretary of Defense Robert S. McNamara explained that the U.S. commitment in Vietnam was part of the Cold War competition with the Soviet Union and China. A communist-dominated Vietnam would weaken the U.S. position in the rest of Asia and "indeed other key areas of the world." McNamara believed officials in other regions threatened by communist insurgencies considered the U.S. reaction to the war in South Vietnam "a test of U.S. firmness and specifically a test of U.S. capacity to deal with `wars of national liberation.'" He concluded that the stakes for the United States in preserving an anticommunist South Vietnam "are so high that . . . we must go on bending every effort to win."[8] That clinched it for Johnson. Neutralization of Vietnam, as Mansfield advocated, was set aside as a viable policy option.

Over the next six months, the position of the Vietcong in the countryside grew stronger and the morale of the Khanh government sank lower. Officials in Washington were convinced that a communist victory in South Vietnam would have a dramatic effect throughout Asia. In June 1964 the CIA estimated that the major impact of a Democratic Republic of Vietnam (DRV) victory, "aside from the immediate joy in the DRV over achievement of its national goals, would be upon Communist China, both in boosting its already remarkable self-confidence and in raising its prestige as a leader of World Communism." The CIA concluded that a Communist victory in South Vietnam would validate the PRC's claim that the United States "is a paper tiger, and that local insurgency can be carried through to victory without undue risk of precipitating a major international war."[9]

American officials monitored the Chinese response during the incident of August 4, 1964, in the Gulf of Tonkin. National Security Adviser McGeorge Bundy minimized the threat posed by Chinese air power in the DRV. Euphoric that President Johnson had been persuaded to seek congressional approval of a resolution supporting the use of force in Southeast Asia, something the National Security Adviser had been urging for the previous two months, he said, "General [Curtis] LeMay [Air Force chief of staff] doesn't think in terms of the enemy, does he? He assumes they won't be there." This was one of the few times during the Johnson administration's deliberations over Vietnam that officials made light of potential Chinese intervention.[10]

Initially, the CIA concluded that the retaliatory air strikes ordered by Johnson would not trigger an immediate Chinese military response. The PRC, however, was preparing its population for possible later fighting. An editorial in the *People's Daily* stated that "aggression by the U.S. against the DRV means aggression against China." The United States had "lit the flames of war" in Indochina. The PRC would "not sit idly by" as the United States attacked the DRV and asserted its "right" to help the North Vietnamese.[11] As Allen Whiting of the State Department's Bureau of Intelligence and Research later noted, this phraseology recalled Chinese warnings in 1950, during the Korean War, against moving U.S. troops toward the Yalu River.[12]

Yet the CIA considered it noteworthy that the PRC had underscored the role of the Vietnamese in defending themselves. Indeed, in their relations with the North Vietnamese, the Chinese consistently stressed that they would act according to their own interests. The North Vietnamese could expect help, but they themselves bore the burden of the war. U.S. officials took heart that Chinese commentary on the Gulf of Tonkin air raids "avoids any firm Chinese commitment to action and indicates war can still be avoided if U.S. leaders `come to their senses.'" Within a few days, the CIA's assessment of China's intentions turned more pessimistic. The Chinese were likely to increase the aid they sent to North Vietnam, although they would probably still not confront U.S. forces directly. A member of the Central Committee of the Communist Party told a rally on August 9 that China was "determined by practical deeds to volunteer aid."[13]

At their regular monthly meetings in Warsaw, Wang Guoquan, the Chinese ambassador to Poland, told his American counterpart, John Moors Cabot, that the United States had fabricated the second attack in the Tonkin Gulf "as a pretext to flagrantly launch an armed attack on the DRV." He warned the

United States that it was "playing with fire" and promised Chinese support to the DRV.[14]

In the aftermath of the U.S. air raids over North Vietnam, China offered further verbal and material support to the DRV. Premier Zhou Enlai asked the leaders of the DRV to "investigate the situation, work out countermeasures, and be prepared to fight." On a more material level, China sent some fifteen to seventeen MiG-15 and MiG-17 jets to the Hanoi area and promised to train DRV pilots. China also moved four air divisions and one antiaircraft division to the southern Chinese provinces bordering the DRV.[15]

Following the Tonkin Gulf Resolution, the administration continued its effort to determine China's intentions in the Vietnam War. In September 1964, the Joint Chiefs of Staff sponsored Sigma II-64, an interagency political military game designed to predict China's strategy in the war and determine the plausible strategy it might follow if the war intensified. The gamers' scenario proved accurate in broad outline, although some of the details were fanciful. They projected increasing Republic of Vietnam (RVN) activities against the Vietcong and the DRV during the fall and winter of 1964–65. They foresaw increasing Vietcong troop levels, reinforced by the introduction of additional People's Army of Vietnam (PAVN) forces. They believed that the political situation in South Vietnam would remain shaky, and that Premier Khanh would do little to stiffen the war effort. In the winter of 1964–65, the PRC would introduce MiGs flown by volunteer pilots into North Vietnam. Army of the Republic of Vietnam (ARVN) forces, supported by U.S. air power, would suffer a serious defeat in a major ground engagement in December. On Christmas day, the Vietcong would shell Saigon for thirty minutes. Facing an increasingly grave situation, in February 1965 the United States would take the fateful step of Americanizing the war. The president would send a Marine expeditionary force and air lift an Army brigade to Thailand. The United States would also commence sustained bombing of industrial and military sites in North Vietnam.[16]

The participants in the game then determined likely PRC moves. They concluded that the primary Chinese objective was the security of mainland China but that the PRC would also want to eliminate the U.S. presence and U.S. influence in Southeast Asia. It would hope to avoid direct confrontation with the United States. Provided that the United States sent only a modest force of about six divisions (approximately 120,000 soldiers), the PRC would not directly confront the United States with ground forces as it had in Korea. Should the United States bomb China or should the government of the DRV appear to be on the point of collapse, then China would enter the war.

The results of the war game disappointed the participants, but the experience of the simulation helped Defense Department planners determine the likely impact of U.S. actions. They concluded that the DRV and the PRC were willing to match any American escalation and that there was little the United States could do to bolster the standing of the Khanh government. The summary of the game's results insisted that the participants had played out the worst case and that the "future viewed through Red colored glasses undoubtedly is less than rosy."[17]

In fact, the game presented a fairly accurate prognosis of the way the Vietnam conflict unfolded. The United States eventually sent about five times more troops to Vietnam than the Sigma II-64 players had contemplated. But policymakers persisted in their efforts to keep the conflict from escalating as it had in Korea. They held a clear idea of what would and would not provoke the Chinese to enter the war. They expected the PRC to come into the war if it were threatened directly or if the DRV seemed likely to crumble under the weight of American attacks. The PRC would give material aid to the DRV, but it would not itself fight to assure the success of the revolutionaries in the South.

The weakness of the Khanh government conformed to the projections of the game players. In mid-September 1964, Johnson met with his principal Vietnam advisers to determine their next step. Most wanted to see increased American military involvement in the war. They worried, however, that Khanh's inability to encourage the ARVN to fight harder made late 1964 a particularly inopportune time to send additional U.S. combat forces. As long as the South Vietnamese government was inept, they believed, such a move might backfire and make the Saigon authorities all the more dependent on the United States. Johnson, as he often did when his advisers outlined a series of unappealing choices, once interrupted the proceedings to ask if it "was worth all this effort." The answer, an emphatic yes, rested partly on the need to deter China. Chairman of the Joint Chiefs Earle Wheeler, Director of Central Intelligence John McCone, and Secretary of State Dean Rusk all agreed that "if we should lose South Vietnam, we would lose Southeast Asia. Country after country on the periphery would give way and look toward Communist China as the rising power of the area."[18]

The desire to contain China figured prominently in the Johnson administration's decision in 1965 to escalate U.S. participation in the war. In January, Assistant Secretary of State William P. Bundy attributed Hanoi's increasing confidence that it would prevail partly to the increased aid it had recently received from the PRC.[19] Yet the collaboration between the PRC and the DRV added to the danger of a direct confrontation between the United States and the PRC. As Johnson's advisers urged him to attack North Vietnam, the president repeatedly questioned whether such actions risked Chinese ground or air attacks on U.S. forces. In February, the CIA decided that the ongoing Chinese military buildup near the border with the DRV was defensive. The Chinese government "hopes to avoid a direct confrontation with US forces, and the steps it has taken are probably calculated in part to back up threatening propaganda aimed at deterring the US from actions that would bring it face to face with Communist China."[20] But the intelligence commuity warned that China might take real steps to convince the United States of how seriously it took sustained bombing of the DRV. Most likely would be the introduction of additional "volunteers" into the DRV. Less likely, according to a Special National Intelligence Estimate, was the possible introduction of large-scale combat units into North Vietnam or Laos.[21] The CIA noted with satisfaction that China's protest at the introduction of U.S. Marines at Danang "raises no new threats."[22]

Indeed, in April Liu Shaoqi of the Chinese Communist Party Central Committee met Le Duan and Vo Nguyen Giap, top leaders of the DRV Communist Party. Liu said that China would provide volunteer pilots and engineering troops. It would "do our best to provide you with whatever you need and whatever we have." He added, "You have the complete initiative" in requesting aid from China. In the following months, however, the Chinese drew back from providing the DRV with a blank check. It was clear that this aid was meant not to prevent the United States from escalating the war but to deter it from going too far. China saw benefits from growing U.S. involvement in the Vietnam War as long as that involvement did not directly threaten Chinese territory. China would not commence a Korea-style ground war unless the United States invaded the North or attacked China directly.[23]

CIA Director McCone told Johnson he thought Chinese air attacks unlikely, given the PRC's limited air capability. The greater possibility was Chinese ground intervention, but this was not probable. McCone believed that the Chinese would not directly enter the fighting so long as the United States limited its attacks on North Vietnam to air raids and did not undertake ground invasion. The air strikes should begin in the South and gradually work their way to the North, avoiding the Chinese border region.[24]

As the Joint Chiefs of Staff recommended the sustained bombing of North Vietnam (code name Rolling Thunder), they weighed the risks of Chinese intervention. Like the CIA, the Chiefs believed there was small likelihood that the Chinese would use their airplanes against the United States. The Chinese would be reluctant to become directly involved in the fighting. "As the number and severity of U.S. attacks against the DRV increase," however, China "probably would feel an increased compulsion to take some dramatic action to counter the impact of the US pressures. There is a fair chance that Beijing would introduce limited numbers of Chinese ground forces as 'volunteers' into North Vietnam . . . intending to raise the specter of further escalation."[25]

A few of Johnson's advisers opposed Rolling Thunder on the grounds that it might spread the danger of war to China. Senator Mike Mansfield, increasingly concerned about the risks of a wider war, considered potential Chinese intervention a primary reason to avoid escalation. National Security Adviser McGeorge Bundy replied that the administration was aware of the risks but aimed to "keep the risk of that involvement as low as possible." Yet, although the United States wanted to minimize the risk, it could not reduce it to zero, since the principal aim of U.S. policy was to "defeat Communist aggression in Southeast Asia."[26]

Other dissent came from within the administration. Undersecretary of State George Ball, who for over a year had expressed misgivings about escalation, and Ambassador-at-large Llewellyn E. Thompson, a former ambassador to the Soviet Union, argued that sustained bombing of North Vietnam risked a Korea-type war with China. They claimed that U.S. objectives in the Vietnam War were excessive, since Washington required Hanoi to call off the insurgency in the South, and that course in their view amounted to unconditional surrender. China would see such a North Vietnamese capitulation as a defeat, "since it would mean the collapse of the basic Chinese ideological position which they have been disputing with the Soviets." Ball and Thompson warned that Rolling Thunder would itself place Beijing "under great pressure to engage the United States on the ground as well as in the air." In the end, China's decision to escalate to full-scale war with the United States depended on whether they could count on Soviet support. Given the Sino-Soviet tensions of the preceding six years, a rapprochement between Beijing and Moscow over Vietnam seemed unlikely. But Ball and Thompson thought the "costs of such [Chinese] intervention [so] tremendous," the United States should not take the risk entailed in sustained bombing of the North.[27]

Vice President Hubert Humphrey also considered the danger of Chinese war plane attacks on U.S. bombers if they approached the Chinese border. We should not "repeat the mistake of the Korean War," he warned. He thought the public saw ominous parallels between current events in Vietnam and what had happened twelve years earlier, in Korea. Even worse, he noted, "the chances of success are slimmer" now than in Korea: "if a war with China was ruled out by the Truman and Eisenhower administrations alike in 1952–3, at a time when we alone had nuclear weapons, people find it hard to contemplate such a war with China now." Once China sent planes into the war, "Beijing's full prestige will be involved, as she cannot permit her Air Force to be destroyed." Humphrey foresaw air engagements with the Chinese escalating into ground warfare between the United States and China throughout South Vietnam. In that case, the Soviet Union might be under enormous pressure to honor its military alliance with China. The nightmare of a U.S.-Soviet war might become real.[28]

Yet Johnson rejected Humphrey's advice to be cautious in proceeding with additional troops and air attacks. Like most of his advisers, the president believed that the stakes for the United States in Vietnam were too high to allow an NLF victory. They also believed they could manage any Chinese threat. Former president Dwight D. Eisenhower advised Johnson that the risks of Chinese intervention were tolerable and that he should worry less about what China might do if the United States escalated the bombing of the North. He doubted they would intervene in strength simply to help the DRV. If they did, however, Eisenhower was ready for a major war. Recalling his own experience in ending the Korean War, he recommended that the United States threaten its own retaliation against China, should China decide to fight in Vietnam. If the Chinese mounted a major ground offensive, Eisenhower recommended "hit[ting] them at once with air, picking out the key points along their support routes." Again recalling Korea, the former president said he would threaten China with atomic weapons if necessary: "if we were to use tactical nuclear weapons, such use in itself would not add to the chances of escalation."[29]

Johnson paid more attention to the projections of the CIA in calculating the Chinese response to further U.S. escalation. The Agency's estimates were consistent: China would complain about U.S. military actions against the DRV, and it was likely to encourage the DRV to resist the United States more strongly. Increased air raids against North Vietnam were unlikely to cause either the DRV or China to want to negotiate an end to the war. "Beijing—like Hanoi—has no desire for any agreement except on Communist terms." But U.S. bombing of the North would not in and of itself bring China directly into the war. The DRV and PRC were enormously patient. Introduction of additional U.S. ground forces would encourage the DRV and the PRC to step up the insurgency and send North Vietnamese troop reinforcements to the South. According to the CIA assessment, DRV and PRC leaders "would likely count on time being on their side and try to force the piecemeal engagement of U.S. troops under conditions which might bog them down in jungle warfare, hoping to present the U.S. with a de facto partition of the country."[30]

Faced with what they considered to be the imminent collapse of the government of South Vietnam, the Johnson administration went forward with the bombing of North Vietnam in February and March of 1965, calculating that Chinese objections to bombing would not bring Chinese forces directly into the war. In that sense, Allen Whiting concluded in 1975, "Chinese deterrence was a prominent failure." Yet Chinese concerns weighed heavily on the minds of American officials as they decided on which locations in the North to bomb and when, and Whiting observed that "deterrence was a partial success in determining both the pace and the limits of escalation."[31]

In mid-1965, the communist officials engaged in Vietnam—the DRV, the NLF, the PRC, and the Soviet Union—believed that their forces would eventually prevail.[32] Their confidence reduced the likelihood that China would come into the war in force. The CIA concluded that "as long as the Communists think they are winning in South Vietnam it is unlikely that Chinese Communists or Soviets will intervene with substantial military forces of their own, in combat." Moreover, the PRC would not send ground troops, as they had in Korea, even if it appeared that the United States and its South Vietnamese allies were winning in the South or if U.S. air strikes damaged the industrial and military sectors of the North. But the Chinese *were* likely to fight if the United States invaded North Vietnam in strength. They would probably escalate to something nearing full-scale war if the

United States bombed their fighter bases in South China, and they would certainly fight the United States if its ground forces invaded North Vietnam and approached the Chinese border.[33] U.S. military leaders and Secretary of Defense McNamara concurred that China would intervene to prevent the destruction of the DRV authority, but probably not to prevent a DRV/Vietcong defeat in the South.[34]

In deciding to send over 100,000 ground troops to fight in South Vietnam, Johnson also took into account direct warnings about the PRC's attitude toward American escalation. Many of these warnings arose during the regular talks between the U.S. and Chinese ambassadors to Poland.[35] U.S. Ambassador John Moors Cabot characterized Wang Guoquan, his Chinese counterpart, as "loud, tendentious, impolite and arrogant, virtually spitting out his accusations, often with finger wagging." Yet other American officials considered these tirades more theatrical than threatening. The Chinese denounced the Americans, explained that they would most surely lose in Vietnam, and repeated their statement that the "Chinese people will not sit idly by and we know how to deal with your aggression." But Ambassador Wang did not say that China would come into the war if the United States sent ground troops into the North to attack China directly.[36]

Shortly after Rolling Thunder began, Wang taunted the Americans, saying "your defeat in South Vietnam is a foregone conclusion." In April he went further: "If you choose to fight on there," he said, "the end of Nazi Germany and the Japanese militarists is a lesson for you to learn." He rejected President Johnson's call for negotiations and a promise of billions of dollars to redevelop the Mekong River valley. American calls for unconditional talks were, he said, a pretense to "legalize your aggressive actions." The proposed aid was nothing so much as a forlorn attempt to "buy over the Vietnamese people with a few stinking dollars so as to save yourself from your ultimate doom." He repeated Zhou Enlai's promise to "send [the] South Vietnamese people all their needs, including arms," and "[their] own men when [the] South Vietnamese people wanted them."[37]

The official Warsaw talks served the important function of allowing each side to learn the other's position on Vietnam.[38] By 1966 the United States and China both understood the extent and the limits of the fighting in the war, how far the Americans would and would not go, and how much aid the Chinese would provide to the DRV. The Americans had learned to distinguish between Chinese bluster and realistic threats. The Chinese, for their part, understood what the Americans meant when they said they did not want a wider war that would include China.

The United States paid more attention to the comments of Foreign Minister Chen Yi. On May 31, Chen told the British chargé d'affaires in Beijing that China would not provoke war with the United States, but that "what China says counts." China is prepared for war with the United States and "if the United States bombs China that would mean war and there would be no limits to the war." Assistant Secretary of State for Far Eastern Affairs William P. Bundy thought Chen displayed toughness regarding the resolve of the DRV. Chen also drew a line for the United States. If it limited its attacks to the air over the DRV, did not approach China, and did not directly attack China, the PRC would not come into the war. But China would "go all the way if it did come in[to the war.]"[39] Zhou Enlai repeated these Four Points in an April 1966 interview with a correspondent from the Karachi newspaper *Dawn* and reiterated them to Simon Malley, an American journalist working for the Tunisian-based journal *Jeune Afrique*, in April 1967.[40]

China's likely reaction to American escalation figured prominently in the high-level U.S. government deliberations of July 1965 over sending an additional 100,000 soldiers to South Vietnam. Among the assumptions underlying the Joint Chiefs of Staff recommendations for additional ground forces was the prediction that "China and Russia will not intervene with armed forces, overtly or covertly, so long as there is no U.S./Government of Vietnam land invasion of North Vietnam."[41] The State Department agreed that the Chinese "expect to use subversion and infiltration of supplies to achieve their objectives, and not direct military force unless their own immediate lines of defense are threatened."[42]

At one point in the July discussions, President Johnson asked Army Chief of Staff General Harold Johnson to go on record defending the Joint Chiefs' assessment. The president asked, "If we come in with hundreds of thousands of men and billions of dollars, won't this cause [China and Russia] to come in?" General Johnson said he did not think so. The president replied "MacArthur didn't think they would come in [to Korea] either." To which General Johnson replied that the situation was different. The president persisted that he had to "take into account that they will" send their troops into the fighting. The generals present assured the president that if the United States maintained the limits on its attacks, China would not enter the fighting in force. President Johnson framed three stark alternatives:

"1. Sit and lose slowly. 2. Get out. 3. Put in what needs to go in." Since the first two were unacceptable to such strong believers in containment, and Chinese intervention seemed unlikely, Johnson decided to send an additional 100,000 troops to Vietnam.[43]

The desire to dampen China's revolutionary ardor was at least as strong a motive as the hope of avoiding Chinese intervention in the war. As Senator Russell Long (D.-La.) told Johnson in explaining his support for the commitment of more troops, "if a nation with 14 million [the DRV] can make Uncle Sam run, what will China think?"[44] Secretary of Defense McNamara characterized the 1965 escalation as part of "a long run United States policy to contain Communist China. China—like Germany in 1917, and like Germany in the West and Japan in the East in the late 1930s—looms as a major power threatening to undercut our importance and effectiveness in the world and, more remotely but more menacingly, to organize all of Asia against us."[45] McNamara denounced Chinese Defense Minister Lin Biao's speech "Long Live the Victory of People's War," in which he called for the revolutionaries of the developing world (the countryside) to surround the capitalist states (the developed world). McNamara characterized Lin's work as "a program of aggression . . . that ranks with Hitler's *Mein Kampf*."[46]

In fact, a Rand Corporation analysis of "Long Live the Victory of People's War!" reached a conclusion very similar to that of the 1964 CIA study of Chinese intentions after the Gulf of Tonkin episode. In both cases, analysts noted their belief that caution would likely characterize the Chinese response to American escalation. The Rand study considered "Long Live the Victory of People's War!" an admonition to the DRV that they bore the major burden of the fighting. Lin Biao understood that "the United States wants the war confined to South Vietnam, just where Beijing also wants it fought."[47]

As Walt Rostow, who was not directly involved in the 1965 decisions to Americanize the war (he did not become national security adviser until February 1966), later argued, U.S. officials believed that by using proxies in North Vietnam and Indonesia, China was trying to squeeze Southeast Asia in a giant pincer move. My own reading of the contemporary documents has turned up no evidence that U.S. officials explicitly linked Chinese actions in Vietnam to the future of either Indonesia or other island states of Southeast Asia. (American decisionmakers did, of course, express more generalized fears about China's growing prestige in East and Southeast Asia.)[48]

Stalemate, 1966

The Americanization of the war in late 1965 averted an immediate victory by the revolutionaries in the South. The United States and China understood the limits beyond which a Korea-style confrontation between the two powers was inevitable. But by the winter of 1965–66, the Johnson administration faced the unsavory prospect of stalemate. McNamara warned that "we will be faced in early December with a military standoff at a much higher level [600,000 troops], with pacification still stalled, and with any chance of military success marred by the chance of an active Chinese intervention."[49]

Looking for a way out of the morass of Vietnam, the United States stopped bombing North Vietnam for 37 days. Realizing that there would be no movement toward peace talks while the bombing continued, some of Johnson's advisers believed that a pause might encourage the North to explore negotiations on terms acceptable to the Americans. One group reviewing the bombing policy concluded, in the fall of 1965, that "it would be difficult for any government, but especially an oriental one, to agree to negotiate while under sustained bombing attack."[50] National Security Adviser McGeorge Bundy endorsed the idea of a pause as a potential prelude to a cease-fire: if the North rejected a proposal for a cease-fire, "the international political rewards are very great indeed."[51]

Johnson dispatched several high-level envoys to Europe, the Soviet Union, and Asia to explore the possibility of peace talks with the North. The results were not encouraging. By the end of January 1966, most of the president's advisers believed that North Vietnam did not want to negotiate anything other than the terms of the American withdrawal from Vietnam and urged a resumption of bombing. Again, the likely Chinese reaction played a major part in their thinking. This time, however, they believed that it would send the wrong message to Beijing if the United States did *not* bomb. Both countries comprehended and mutually agreed on the extent of and limits to U.S. intervention. Bombing up to but not beyond the PRC-DRV border was acceptable to the Chinese, as were American ground troops fighting in South Vietnam. Only a ground or air assault into or near China would provoke Beijing to a Korea-style attack.

But it was this very mutual acknowledgment of the ground rules of the fighting in Vietnam that made Johnson's senior advisers reluctant to introduce any changes that would appear to offer an unreciprocated advantage to the PRC. Secretary of Defense McNamara, one of the most vociferous advocates of the bombing pause, thought that the United States should be ready for more peace moves, but the experience of the previous month had made him doubt that the North wanted to negotiate. In the meantime, he said, "unless we resume bombing, we will give the wrong signal to Hanoi, Beijing and our own people." Secretary of State Dean Rusk concurred, carefully distinguishing the present situation from the catastrophic Chinese intervention during the Korean War. He recalled being with MacArthur "when he made the mistake about China coming in." But this time was different, he assured the president. The United States had moved slowly and had carefully avoided coming close to China with either bombers or troops. Rusk feared that "If we don't resume" the bombing, "China will think a sanctuary has been approved and they can do more than ever." Johnson should carefully control the bombing targets to avoid giving the Chinese an excuse to intervene.[52]

Dissenters from the prevailing view favoring a resumption in the bombing thought that China still might take offense at U.S. bombing of the DRV, even if the bombs did not hit beyond or even near the Chinese border. NSC staff member Chester Cooper pointed out the "serious risk that we will become involved with Communist China through its joint air defense support of Hanoi." But it was George Ball who offered the most frightening prospect: "the bombing of the North cannot win the war, only enlarge it." The war would be won or lost in the South. Indeed, "sustained bombing of North Vietnam will more than likely lead us into war with Red China—probably in six to nine months." The United States needed to do what it could to make an independent peace with Hanoi. The more it bombed the North, the more dependent on China the DRV would become. In these circumstances, Ball concluded, Hanoi fell "under pressure from China to do more" against the United States. In Hong Kong, the major U.S. "listening post" for determining events inside the PRC, Edward Rice, the U.S. consul-general, also worried that "the risk that we will get into a war with Communist China would be substantially increased by our extending intensified attacks to the Hanoi-Haiphong area."

But these views were in the minority. More of Johnson's lieutenants agreed with presidential adviser Jack Valenti's recommendation that the bombing resume on what he called "a surgical basis," but as before, avoiding, "if we can, any target that summons up a direct response from the Chinese Communists."[53] The Joint Chiefs of Staff argued that continuing restraint might actually increase the odds of Chinese intervention, "by encouraging gradual responses on the part of the Chinese Communists."[54]

The United States resumed the bombing of North Vietnam on January 31, 1966. Afterward, U.S. officials continued to express concern about what China might do. Their anxiety was deepened by growing evidence of the internal upheaval of the Cultural Revolution. On the one hand, American analysts considered China's leaders to be "hardshell, deepwater Marxists," who believed on some level that war with the United States was inevitable, and had prepared the Chinese for just such a war in 1965 and 1966. These preparations consisted of dispersing important industrial sites, moving old people out of some cities, and publicly talking about war with the United States. Chinese Foreign Minister Chen Yi was also reported to have said that China's army was "just waiting for the word" from Ho Chi Minh before crossing the border to help his forces.[55] Chen warned that "it is up to the U.S. president and the Pentagon to decide whether the U.S. wants a big war with China today. . . . Should the U.S. imperialists invade China's mainland, we will take all necessary measures to defeat them."[56]

On the other hand, American analysts also noted that China's planners thought the war was going well for the Communist side at the present level of Chinese aid to the DRV. The Chinese opposed a negotiated settlement, because the present course of the war, they believed, validated their calls for "armed revolutionary struggle." The Chinese Foreign Minister hoped "the Vietnam war would continue and would keep the United States involved." He said that "the war was to the Chinese advantage. If it grew, there was a possibility that China and the United States would fight each other." At present, though, Chen wanted to avoid war until China was better prepared. To that end, the Chinese had subtly changed the conditions under which they would send fighting forces to the DRV. Previously, they offered help "if Hanoi calls for it." Now they said, "If both Hanoi and Beijing agree on the necessity for such aid, China will take steps to provide it." The Americans understood that a rift between the DRV and the PRC had occurred. In the future, Hanoi would have to rely more on its own initiative in fighting the Americans. While U.S. officials did not believe that the divisions between Hanoi and Beijing made it easier for the South Vietnamese and the Americans to prevail, these divisions did reinforce the growing perception that the Vietnam War was not going to turn into another Korean War in which China and the United States would fight one another.[57]

The Impact of the Cultural Revolution, 1966–1968

In 1966 and 1967, American officials puzzled over the implications of the Cultural Revolution.[58] Its domestic turmoil left no clear guide to what China might do. The experience over the previous several years had encouraged American officials to believe that the Chinese conducted their foreign policy on the basis of a rational calculation of the threats against them, and that the limits established in the fighting over the past several years were therefore likely to persist. Yet the Chinese seemed to be behaving irrationally at home. Might not the frenzy extend beyond China's borders?

Secretary of State Dean Rusk seemed to be of two minds. Sometimes he held out a hand of friendship, predicting that eventually China would become a great power that "would be expected to have close relations—political, economic, and cultural—with the United States." On other occasions the Secretary of State raged at the danger posed by "one billion Chinese armed with nuclear weapons."[59] Lower-level U.S. China experts also thought that the Cultural Revolution held both short-term perils and long-range opportunities. China's domestic upheaval might lead to an apocalyptic engagement in Vietnam. Many American analysts believed that China saw "the conflict in Vietnam as a test case which must be won to vindicate Chinese pretensions to the ideological leadership of the Communist world."[60]

In mid-1966 the United States stepped up its bombing of North Vietnam's oil supplies, prompting intensified Chinese calls for "joint [PRC and DRV] blows" against the United States. Edward Rice, the U.S. consul-general in Hong Kong, thought that Chinese leaders had such a profound sense of international isolation, they could behave irrationally.[61] They feared attack from nearly every outside power—Japan, India, and even the Soviet Union—in collusion with the United States. Rice believed that Mao, "as is the way with aging men," saw echoes of the past in the present situation, and that the United States was acting the way Japan had acted in 1937. "Given the way he is deified," Rice wrote, this fear of encirclement had penetrated to many other high Chinese government officials. Most worrisome of all for the United States, Mao might actually half welcome a U.S.-Nationalist Chinese invasion of the mainland, "believing his two old enemies could, before he dies, be drowned in the sea of Chinese manpower once they were sucked inland." Internally, a war with the United States would enable Mao to crush his "revisionist" opponents. The same, Rice thought, might also be true for some of the more moderate, Soviet-leaning officials within the DRV, who had expressed worry that Vietnam was relying too heavily on the PRC for aid.[62]

The CIA noted that renewed Chinese threats came at a time when China wanted to show how tough it was in comparison with the Soviet Union, yet in practical terms, the Cultural Revolution had so disrupted life in China that going to war was nearly impossible. The CIA also noted that the predominant theme of the Cultural Revolution had been "that the main enemies are inside China."[63] Analysis of official party communiqués reinforced the view that China was preoccupied with internal problems. Party condemnations represented the "same old thing, long said in Warsaw and in the public press." China continued to promise aid to the revolutionaries in Vietnam, but the tenor of its promises seemed to be mostly defensive.[64]

Amid internal upheaval, PRC officials could still offer subtle signals to make certain that the United States avoided attacking China from the air. In February 1966, for example, a high Chinese official asked a member of the Japanese trade office in Beijing to pass a warning on "to the Japanese foreign office." If "the U.S. bombs China," during its air war on Vietnam, "unfortunately the U.S. is out of reach" of Chinese retaliation. "We are not able to return the blow. However it is not impossible for us to reach Japan." American analysts agreed that this threat was designed to "push Japan toward a neutralist position and use Japan to restrain the scope of U.S. action" in Vietnam.[65]

In the end, U.S. officials decided that China's policy on potential war with the United States over Vietnam remained what it had been since 1964. China would certainly go for a Korea-style war if the United States invaded North Vietnam or if the DRV seemed to be on the verge of collapse. Short of that, however, China would continue its present course of verbal denunciation, warning the United States not to go further and providing noncombatants to the North Vietnamese. In mid-1966 the CIA estimated that China had approximately 25,000 to 45,000 military personnel, including anti-aircraft troops, engineers, construction crews, and other support groups, in North Vietnam. The CIA believed that in the coming years such support was likely to grow.[66] According to Chen Jian's recent research in Chinese sources, however, these figures are actually somewhat low. Chen estimates that during the war, about 320,000 Chinese anti-aircraft and engineering troops served in North Vietnam. In the peak year of 1967, he calculates that 170,000 Chinese troops were present in Vietnam.[67]

Some mid-level U.S. government officials believed that the Cultural Revolution presented an opportunity for the United States in East and Southeast Asia, since a weakened China enhanced U.S. standing. China's domestic troubles actually reduced the likelihood that it would participate in the Vietnam War. A joint Defense-State Department long-range study of the U.S. position in East and Southeast Asia concluded in 1966 that over the next decade, the United States should try to move away from a strategy of "close containment," that is, of actual military conflict on the mainland of Asia, and toward a strategy of "remote containment behind buffer zones." But this policy was a long time in the future. "For a good part of the [next] decade, and possibly longer," the planners concluded, "close-in containment must be the preferred strategy in East and Southeast Asia."[68]

Alfred Jenkins, the NSC staff member directly in charge of China policy, thought that at present, Mao Zedong was "semi-demented," and that China represented, for the time being, "the world's toughest and perhaps most urgent problem." The United States was, in turn, China's great problem. But after the turmoil in China reached a climax, Jenkins believed that the two powers might achieve a new understanding, even a rapprochement. Over the long term, the United States could bring China back into "the community of nations on an acceptable basis." At present, "paranoid, provincial, prophetic zealots" were in charge in China, but their day would pass. Even these radicals, led by Mao and Lin Biao, "while preaching belligerence, have acted more cautiously where foreign adventure is concerned." Jenkins perceived signs that "the masses are tiring of constant revolution." In preparation for that day, he advocated a new, "radical" path toward Vietnam. He decided that the Vietnam War was unwinnable. Indeed, "if we came anywhere near `winning' in Vietnam ... that could mean World War III."[69]

Jenkins's analysis presented a remarkably accurate forecast of U.S. Asian policy during the administration of Richard Nixon.[70] Although Jenkins advocated that the United States keep fighting in Vietnam for the time being, he thought that over the next several years it should look for a way out. Like Nixon and National Security Adviser Henry Kissinger after 1969, Jenkins thought the United States should gradually diminish the importance of the war for U.S. relations with East Asia: "Vietnam is for the foreseeable future unsolvable unless it is first sort of walked away from." He considered it bad for long-term U.S. interests for the Chinese "to continue to believe that we are implacably hostile."[71]

Some of that hostility came from Secretary of State Dean Rusk, about whom Jenkins used language extraordinary for a subordinate: "Entre nous," he wrote National Security Adviser Walt Rostow, "while I believe the Secretary to be one of the greatest in our history, on China his style scares me. He is so orderly and judicial and a sheaf of other virtues, that he wants all the returns in before he moves. On China we are not going to get as many returns as we want; and inaction is an act watched by mainlanders."[72] Jenkins advised Rusk to downplay China's role in Vietnam when the secretary spoke publicly about U.S.-Chinese relations: "playing up Beijing's role in Vietnam tends to give the Chinese Communists greater leverage in world opinion [than they might otherwise enjoy]."[73]

On July 12, 1966, in a nationally televised address, President Johnson tried to point the way toward a new China policy. He decried China's isolation, which, he said, the PRC had brought upon itself. He reiterated the calls made by the U.S. representatives to the Warsaw talks for scholarly and cultural exchanges between the United States and China. He called for improved relations between China and the United States after the war in Vietnam ended. Although the Chinese initially rebuffed U.S. overtures to improve relations in the areas of trade and cultural exchanges, the U.S. proposals laid the groundwork for later détente.[74]

John Gronouski, the U.S. representative at the Warsaw talks with the PRC, elaborated on the president's themes. Like John Moors Cabot, his predecessor at the talks, he assured the Chinese that the United States did not want to maintain bases in Southeast Asia after the war ended. The United States would even accept a neutral South Vietnam, if that was what the South Vietnamese chose. Not above using the sort of needling customarily employed by the Chinese ambassador in his denunciations of U.S. policy in Southeast Asia, Gronouski said that "it is in its opposition to any resolution in Vietnam which is not achieved by violence and war that your government has found itself isolated from the overwhelming majority of people and governments in the world."

A few months later, Gronouski repeated his contention that the Chinese refused to believe any protestations of friendship from the United States. They saw any U.S. efforts to strengthen ties to other nations in Asia or East Asia as threats to China. "You continue to speak of the U.S. as threatening your country," Gronouski told Wang Guoquan. "Your leaders continue to talk of the U.S. as planning to attack or invade your territory." Once more

Gronouski held out the hope of greater cultural cooperation between the United States and the PRC. He looked forward to Chinese help in arranging peace in Vietnam. "In our view," he said, "peace in Vietnam does not mean the domination of any one country over Vietnam. It need not mean one country's victory and another's defeat."[75]

In 1967 the Johnson administration confronted China publicly, but U.S. officials also perceived that the period of greatest danger in Sino-American relations had passed. In that year also, Secretary McNamara became deeply disillusioned with the war in Vietnam and increasingly concerned about the danger of a nuclear arms race with the Soviet Union. Yet, although he publicly opposed deployment of a large and expensive antiballistic missile system against the Soviets, he did endorse a "thin" ABM system to defend against a missile attack from the PRC.[76] At the same time, more officials within the Johnson administration, including McNamara, thought that the threat from China had diminished and considered Chinese criticism of U.S. Vietnam policy ritualistic. Some Americans even believed that the Vietnam War was having a curiously counterproductive influence on U.S.-East Asia relations. The New China News Agency claimed that "the Johnson administration was scared out of its wits" by the large antiwar march on the Pentagon in October, but National Security Adviser Rostow dismissed this report as a typical PRC complaint.[77] From Hong Kong, Consul-General Rice sent word that U.S. bombing of North Vietnam actually had the effect of intensifying the Cultural Revolution.[78]

Some of the Johnson administration's thinking on improving relations with China made its way into the press. Alfred Jenkins noted with appreciation how much a *Wall Street Journal* editorial of November 1967 mirrored his own views on U.S. China policy. With the Cultural Revolution and the Vietnam War going on, the editorial stated, the current U.S. policy of attempting to isolate China made sense. Sooner or later, however, Maoist revolutionary fervor in China would ebb. "The U.S. interest is to nudge future generations of Chinese leadership toward moderation in foreign policy." The *Journal*, like Jenkins, recommended cultural exchanges, lifting travel restrictions, and ending the trade embargo as tangible first steps in improving U.S.-Chinese relations, even while the war in Vietnam continued.[79]

In the last year of the Johnson administration, the United States made tentative moves toward improved relations with China. While the Vietnam War raged on, earlier fears that it would expand into a direct confrontation between the United States and China no longer had the same salience as in 1965 or 1966.

Both countries understood that the United States would not permit an NLF/ DRV victory in the South and that China would not permit the destruction of the DRV or an attack on its own territory. Short of those two outcomes, catastrophic for one side or the other, the United States and China would not fight each other. U.S. war gaming exercises throughout 1968 revealed that Beijing would not get into a large-scale conflict with the United States "short of threat to its territory or threat to the existence of a neighboring communist state."[80]

Looking ahead to what would happen in China after the Cultural Revolution, the Johnson administration believed that Vietnam was important, but less so than it had been. As long as the United States was not humiliated in Vietnam, Mao's radicalism would not be vindicated. NSC staff member Alfred Jenkins believed that in the near but not immediate future, the United States might make significant overtures to China: the embargo could be lifted or at least modified and the United States could quietly drop its objections to China's membership in the United Nations. In the short run, however, Jenkins thought the United States should keep "our future options open . . . by keeping relatively quiet while mainland China is trying to sort itself out."[81]

In February 1968, President Johnson met with eight prominent Asia experts. Despite their differences of opinion on U.S. participation in the Vietnam War, they agreed, in the words of Lucian Pye of the Massachusetts Institute of Technology, that "we must look beyond Vietnam to China, the really big problem." Johnson agreed. He seemed bemused that the Vietnam War had not aroused more public passion against all communists. He thought this presented an opportunity to improve relations with China, but for the time being he was preoccupied with Vietnam.[82] The obsession with Vietnam persisted for the remainder of Johnson's last year in office. The war went on, despite Johnson's announcement that he would not run for another term and his efforts to open peace talks. It remained for his successor to reduce the war's importance and make a dramatic move toward improved relations with China.

Assessment

The Korean precedent hovered over the deliberations of American officials as they calculated their moves in Vietnam. The Korean War had preceded the major events of the Vietnam War by only twelve to fifteen years, well within the professional lives and memory of many top Johnson administration decisionmakers. While looking for a way to improve relations with

China, Alfred Jenkins of the NSC staff criticized Mao for living in the past and depending on historical analogies to guide the present. The Vietnam War did not resemble the Japanese invasion of China in 1937 (the analogy Consul-General Edward Rice believed Mao had misused); Korea provided a more accurate model. Insofar as American policymakers properly applied lessons learned in Korea, they kept the Vietnam War from escalating into a conflict in which both sides were armed with nuclear weapons.

The Johnson administration had a clear view of what was likely to provoke the Chinese into intervening in the war and took care to avoid it. As the historian Qiang Zhai's research in Chinese sources for the crucial years 1964–65 has shown, the PRC warned that it would enter the war if attacked or if the viability of the government of the DRV was threatened.[83] Intelligence professionals and their political superiors carefully calibrated American actions to avert possible Chinese involvement . At the same time, U.S. estimates of China's difficulties during the Cultural Revolution also proved accurate. Watching the PRC's turmoil unfold and its isolation increase, Americans found it less threatening to Asia's stability and prosperity. This more relaxed view of China served to undermine one of the principal reasons for initial U.S. involvement in the war: the potential Chinese threat. As the war and the Cultural Revolution both continued, some Johnson administration officials explored possible ways to improve relations with China afterward. As they thought more about the potential gains from better relations and détente with China, they came to believe that Vietnam was far less important to the United States than the planners who had originally pushed for U.S. involvement had believed.

By *The Irony of Vietnam: The System Worked*, the title of their classic 1979 study of U.S. decision making during the Vietnam War, Leslie Gelb and Richard K. Betts meant that each part of the decision-making process performed its function as intended—offering an acceptable range of options based on good information. The final product, however, was catastrophic.[84] The Johnson administration's calculations about China offer a special case of this disappointing judgment. On one level, the Johnson administration performed well by assessing what China was likely to do, developing its own policies in ways that minimized the dangers of a larger war, and signaling to the Chinese its intention to avoid a Korea-style confrontation. On the strategic level, however, American planners failed to draw the most important lesson: containing the PRC was not a good enough reason for fighting a war in Vietnam.

CHAPTER NINE

Redefinitions: The Domestic Context
of America's China Policy in the 1960s

Rosemary Foot

THE 1960S WERE CRITICAL YEARS for the United States, for China, and for their bilateral relationship. Both societies experienced a crisis of identity during this period that in a number of areas has never been entirely resolved for either party. In 1963 U.S. citizens had to come to terms with the assassination of a young and promising president, and then, in 1968, with the killings of two other significant, representational political figures, Robert Kennedy and the Reverend Martin Luther King, Jr. The civil rights movement entered its most active phase and forced a reappraisal of the myth of America as a land of equal opportunity, a land tolerant of diversity and pluralist rather than elitist in nature. Questioning of the domestic order interacted with and reinforced doubts about America's conduct abroad. The war in Southeast Asia, and especially the way in which it was prosecuted, became morally repugnant to many inside and outside the country.[1] The evidence of a serious rift between China and the Soviet Union led to a questioning of the ends for which the war was fought. The domestic consensus crumbled alongside the consensus on foreign policy that had come into being after Pearl Harbor, which had been reinforced by the seemingly implacable Cold War divide and had held firm until this turbulent decade.

These years were no less traumatic for the Chinese. The Beijing leadership rejected the international reference group—the Soviet-led socialist bloc—that had served to provide the new regime with a vital sense of belonging and legitimacy. China began to give greater weight to an alternative identity as a Third World radical socialist state, self-reliant in nature and a model to be emulated by other revolutionary nationalists.[2] That rejection of the Soviet Union and its allies destabilized China's border areas, eventually resulting in military clashes with its northern neighbor and sharpening disputes among and with communist parties throughout the world. In addition, by 1960 the PRC's self-reliant development path, exemplified by the Great Leap Forward, had proven itself to be a disastrous failure, producing a famine of major proportions. If China's political cadres discreetly came to question Mao's supposed infallibility in 1966, with the onset of the Great Proletarian Cultural Revolution, the whole party political structure was to come under attack and be fatally damaged. The attempted coup in 1971 by Mao's chosen successor, Lin Biao, at a time of dramatic reorientation in China's external relations that culminated in the visit of President Nixon to China in February 1972, capped this era of insecurity and chaos.

This chapter focuses on the United States in this troubled decade of the 1960s and its efforts to redefine its relationship with the People's Republic of China (PRC). It will examine the domestic aspects of America's China policy, including the views of the mass public, the attentive or informed public (at most, some 15 percent of the population), and especially the views of the policy elites with direct access to top decisionmakers. Attention will be paid to the perceptions and preoccupations of those at the top charged with determining China policy, a remarkably stable group over the years 1961 to 1969. Presidents Kennedy and Johnson both had Dean Rusk as their Secretary of State; Secretary of Defense Robert McNamara served for seven years; and there were only two National Security advisers, McGeorge Bundy and Walt Rostow.[3]

As I have suggested, it is valuable to bear in mind the broader societal context in which these opinions were formed and to take account of the fact that China policy was being reevaluated during a time of domestic uncertainty and questioning. Doubts about America's own polity and the country's inability to extract itself from the conflict in Vietnam led the politically involved or aware to question whether those in the highest offices in Washington knew best in any area of policy. A reexamination of China policy was one important means of voicing those doubts and a significant factor in the search for a redefinition of what America stood for in the eyes of its citizens and its friends and allies overseas. The manner in which this discourse over China was conducted may well have helped to steady certain beliefs Americans held about themselves at a time when antiwar and civil rights activists had forced a fundamental self-questioning.[4]

Expectations of a Kennedy Presidency

The advent of a new administration raised high expectations among America's allies as well as the informed U.S. public of a change in policy toward the PRC. Of course it was not only China policy that was thought likely to change. President Kennedy's campaign pledges and his inaugural speech promoted images of movement and innovation that were deemed likely to have consequences in all areas. The torch had indeed been passed to a new generation, taken from the allegedly tired, the old, the sick, the inflexible and given to the vigorous, the daring, the young. Where China policy was concerned, new appointees and the presidential candidate himself were hinting strongly, in public and private, that revisions were in the offing. In a speech delivered in June 1960, John Kennedy argued cautiously for improved communications with the mainland via the test ban talks in Geneva.[5] Secretary of State designate Dean Rusk told the British ambassador to Washington in December 1960 that he considered America's current U.N. recognition policy for China to be "unrealistic" and that he would like to see the new administration get itself "off the hook" on it.[6] Adlai Stevenson, subsequently appointed as Kennedy's U.N. ambassador, went somewhat further in a *Foreign Affairs* article published in January 1960. He called for an end to Beijing's exclusion from the United Nations, although he coupled this with the need to hold U.N.-supervised elections in Korea and to achieve self-determination for Taiwan. In his view, China, "with a quarter of the world's population, would be more accountable to world opinion than as an outcast."[7]

Other midlevel appointees among the White House staff and in the State Department were also expecting a policy environment that was receptive to new ideas, either out of necessity or because those in the policy-making circles believed the time was ripe. Robert W. Komer of the National Security Council (NSC) staff wrote in blunt terms to his superior, McGeorge Bundy, in March 1961: "Let's face it; China problems may not wait for careful, leisurely review. . . . Hence, as I see it, we should prod State to get started pronto on broad-scale rethinking exercise." Edward Rice, a China specialist and member of the Policy Planning staff, prepared a long and detailed paper in 1961 outlining several possible policy initiatives toward Beijing.[8] The State Department's monthly survey of press and public opinion had reported in January 1961 that the tendency here too was "to anticipate a 'more flexible' United States posture during the Kennedy Administration."[9] And in the U.S. Congress, developments in 1959 had given some small signs that a more permissive era might soon begin. Staunch defenders of Chiang Kai-shek (Jiang Jieshi), such as Senators Alexander Smith and William F. Knowland, were out of office, and in May 1959, Senator Clair Engle, Knowland's replacement, made a speech decrying the "Maginot line response" to China and advocating instead limited contact, including a reciprocal exchange of news representatives, trade on the same basis as that with the Soviet Union, prevention of Chinese Nationalist attacks against the mainland, and Sino-American negotiations at a level higher than that of ambassador.[10] Congress went further on the issue when Senator Alexander Wiley, the incoming chair of the Senate Foreign Relations Committee, commissioned a special study on China policy. The report, produced by the private research organization Conlon Associates and largely penned by Professor Robert Scalapino, also recommended greater flexibility in U.S. dealings with the PRC. Surprisingly, neither the Engle speech nor the Conlon report occasioned much in the way of comment, even though the latter attracted the critical attention of the anti-PRC lobbying organization "the Committee of One Million,"[11] suggesting that the executive branch did have a degree of latitude in this area of policy if it should choose to exercise it. As the noted China expert Professor John K. Fairbank put it in a speech two weeks after Kennedy's victory, this electoral success "presumably marks the burial of the unreal and divisive issue of 'Who lost China?,'" an issue that in the 1950s had damaged the lives and careers of many of those who had chosen to study and work on this part of Asia.[12]

Moreover, the Kennedy era reorganization within the Department of State appeared to open new channels for communicating fresh ideas about the China problem. In November 1961, Averell Harriman was brought in as Assistant Secretary of State for Far Eastern Affairs, replacing the Dulles-era appointee and staunch opponent of the Beijing regime, Walter P. McConaughy. Harriman recruited two newcomers to the bureau, Edward Rice and Robert Barnett, both of whom favored a change in policies. Chester Bowles, a key Kennedy adviser, whose first appointment was as Undersecretary of State, joined with the others to form a critical mass of those willing to contemplate new ways of dealing with the PRC. Finally, and significantly, in December 1961 a "Mainland China Affairs" desk was hived off from "Republic of China Affairs," suggesting opportunities for promoting a Beijing perspective on events.

This general sense among middle-level bureaucrats that change in policy might prove possible (although, as will be shown below, it suffered a number of significant setbacks in 1962 and 1963) continued through to the Johnson era. For those in the administration eager to revise Washington's China policy, such as Robert W. Komer, the scale of Lyndon Johnson's election victory in 1964 meant that the president had been given an opportunity to demonstrate greater flexibility toward China, particularly because the strong electoral mandate had come at a time when policy toward Vietnam had also toughened.[13] This argument was based on the belief that toughness on Vietnam reduced the likelihood that political opponents would revive the damaging "Who lost China?" debate and deflected accusations of Democratic "appeasement" of the Asian communist enemy. Firmness in Vietnam, even if coupled with a softening toward China, would also dissuade Asian communists from assuming that U.S. resolve was weakening. Expectations were one thing, however; effecting a change in China policy was quite another.

Bureaucratic Initiatives

In the Kennedy and Johnson years, a number of administration officials discussed a variety of policy initiatives, mainly concerning recognition of the mainland and other means of enhancing communication between the two societies and governments. In broad terms, it came to be accepted that the United States should move away from the Dulles/Eisenhower policy of "containment with isolation" toward "containment without isolation," phrases that the noted academic A. Doak Barnett had first coined in the Senate hearings on U.S.-China policy held in March 1966. There was, however, an important middle stage that emphasized the conditional aspects of this policy: China would have to learn to behave before it could be rewarded and thereby become less isolated, lessons the Soviet Union had learned after the Cuban missile crisis.[14] The call for modified containment was also based on another explicit change in the argument: that the Chinese Communist regime itself, despite the vulnerabilities through which it would pass in the 1960s, was not "a passing phase" but was here to stay, at least for the medium term if not longer.[15]

International factors not within the remit of this chapter prompted certain of the bureaucratic initiatives, such as the growing realization in Washington that U.S. policies toward China, largely deemed unacceptable and unworkable by even close allies, undermined the U.S. leadership role in the international community. Events within China itself gave impetus to other policies, including its rift with Moscow and its explosion of an atomic device in 1964. The rift provided opportunities for exploiting the erstwhile allies' relationship and undercut the public argument of a fearful monolithic communist world; and the nuclear development promoted a belief that China, for all its obvious material weaknesses, could, if it was sufficiently determined, channel its resources into policy areas that disturbed the global order. This prompted some to argue that Beijing had to be drawn into international discourse on such fundamental matters as nuclear arms control.

The actual initiatives contemplated covered the matter of U.N. recognition; the opening of trade—at one end of the spectrum at a level comparable to that with the Soviet Union and at the other, minimalist end, trade in humanitarian areas such as pharmaceuticals or food; authorized travel to China by, for example, U.S. news representatives, medical personnel, and scholars; the involvement of China in arms control negotiations; and Chinese Nationalist evacuation of the offshore islands, together with explicit assurances that the United States would not support any attempt by the Taiwan authorities to use military means to reestablish their rule on the mainland. Many of these suggestions had been made in Edward Rice's remarkable 1961 paper, which largely set the agenda for those searching throughout the 1960s for a means to improve relations with the PRC. Time and again its recommendations were revived and repackaged, although it was only late in the Johnson administration and in the early Nixon period that many came to fruition.[16]

This discussion concentrates on the fate of U.N. recognition, trade, and travel issues in view of their importance and centrality in the deliberations of the Kennedy and Johnson administrations. However, it is worth noting that, although it did not prove possible to persuade Chiang Kai-shek's government to quit the offshore islands, this policy was modified in one aspect: in 1962 the Kennedy administration made it plain to the Nationalists and the

Communists that it would never support a Chinese Nationalist attack on the mainland—a strong indication that the administration realized it had to live and deal with two Chinas.[17]

U.N. RECOGNITION

The U.N. recognition policy forced its attention on Kennedy at an early stage in his administration. The United Nations had been steadily changing its political complexion. In 1960 alone, fifteen African states plus Cyprus were admitted to the world organization, and it was not thought likely that they could be persuaded to support the so-called moratorium procedure, which since 1951 had served to block U.N. debate on the issue of Chinese representation. In light of this realization, the president and his top officials considered two options for the 1961 U.N. session: a two Chinas or successor states' resolution—that is, the General Assembly would affirm the continuing membership of the Republic of China while also supporting membership for Beijing; or the use of Article 18 (2) of the U.N. Charter, whereby "important questions," such as matters of admission of new members, would require a two-thirds majority of the membership to agree to a change.[18] The first suggestion was not pursued assiduously, however, because it was thought to be too dangerous a path. Discussions among the president, the secretary of state and America's U.N. ambassador suggested that none of them expected either China or Taiwan to accept such a solution anyway. But most important, Ambassador Stevenson said, was not to report "for domestic consumption that the purpose of the exercise is to keep the Chinese Communists out of the UN." If that came out, the administration would appear hypocritical, and the international disapprobation it was already experiencing over its determined exclusion of Beijing would reach new heights. At the same time, if the real purpose was not to be explained to likely domestic critics, such as former President Eisenhower, and the broad outlines of the U.S. plan leaked, then a different kind of trouble would surface. As President Kennedy put it, "political dynamite" was "locked up in this issue."[19]

In that he was quite correct. When details of this policy were inevitably leaked, the former vice president, Richard Nixon, spearheaded a campaign to destroy it, and the Senate passed a resolution, 76 votes to nil, calling on the administration not simply to support the Nationalist government in the United Nations but to support Chiang's regime as the "representative of China."[20] Not surprisingly, in July Dean Rusk recommended the "important question" (IQ) route: it represented "the best tactic to use since it offered us a reasonable chance of getting a clear, blocking one third." Even though the president recognized that this was "too transparent a blocking measure" and that a more attractive proposal ought to be sought, this IQ formula came to be seen as the best the United States could devise at this stage.[21]

However, this course of action produced new difficulties. The support of African states for the "important question" device depended partly on Chinese Nationalist agreement to U.N. representation for the Mongolian People's Republic. Chiang Kai-shek was not reconciled to the independence of that country and threatened to veto its application for membership. But if he did so, the Soviets had threatened to veto the application of Mauritania, which in turn would cause the French African states to turn against Taiwan. Although the United States pressured Taiwan to accept such linkages, Kennedy assumed that the only thing that would ensure Nationalist cooperation over Mongolia was the guarantee of a U.S. veto of any resolution recommending U.N. membership for the PRC.[22]

Despite the promised veto and the tightening of the bond between Washington and Taipei, the arguments for dual representation gathered pace over the remainder of the decade. In 1961, Ambassador Stevenson, in a statement to the U.N. General Assembly designed to bolster support for Taiwan, pointed out that the Chinese Nationalist government's effective control extended over "more people than does the legal jurisdiction of two-thirds of the Governments represented here."[23] This appealed to the British, the Japanese, and the Canadians, among others, Japan arguing, for example, that although it supported the principle of universality and was aware that the PRC was in effective control of the mainland, the Nationalists were in "solid and effective control of Taiwan and the adjacent islands."[24] Stevenson's own statement, therefore, perhaps inadvertently, had given an important boost to the dual representation idea.

Undersecretary of State Chester Bowles seemed ready to take up the idea within the administration. At first he recommended tying U.S. opposition to the PRC's entrance into the United Nations more closely to Beijing's refusal to accept the independence of Taiwan, but in April 1962 he went further, suggesting that Washington publicly forgo opposition to Beijing's membership provided the PRC accept Taiwanese representation.[25] That was too much too soon, as far as Kennedy and Rusk were concerned; their preference was to let a number of allied states make that argument.

With French recognition of the PRC in January 1964 and China's atomic test in October, international support for China's entry quickened.[26] The Johnson administration, like its predecessor, felt under pressure to respond. Although there was no vote in 1964 on the matter of representation because of a funding crisis affecting U.N. peacekeeping operations, in 1965 an Albanian resolution to seat the PRC and expel the Nationalists produced a tie vote and a belief within the Johnson administration that in the following year it would gain a simple majority—still short of the two-thirds majority needed but of symbolic significance nonetheless. In response to these expectations, in 1966 Washington once again explored a "two Chinas" solution, as well as the more cautious option of a resolution to set up a study committee to examine the question of representation. In speeches in Chicago and California that spring, Assistant Secretary of State for International Organization Joseph Sisco, and the new U.S. ambassador to the United Nations, Arthur Goldberg, both attempted to draw attention away from PRC exclusion and toward the prevention of the Republic of China (ROC)'s expulsion. Meeting on May 6 with a skeptical Dean Rusk and with Assistant Secretary of State for Far Eastern Affairs William Bundy, Sisco and Goldberg also recommended supporting countries such as Canada, which were ready to argue openly for two Chinas at the 1966 U.N. General Assembly session.

Despite these promising developments, however, at a meeting between Canadian and U.S. officials Ottawa demonstrated that it was some way ahead of a U.S. administration still thinking in terms of a two Chinas initiative and of setting up a study committee to consider the matter. Canada was prepared to recommend PRC entry into the Security Council immediately, leaving the Nationalists in the General Assembly. In a personal letter to Canadian Foreign Minister Lester Pearson, an angry Rusk wrote: "If your resolution is introduced, we shall not merely have to oppose it, but [shall] have to go to great lengths to see that it is defeated by the heaviest possible margin." To further ensure Canadian compliance, Rusk warned: "I need not underscore the seriousness of such a split between our two nations."[27] Undoubtedly alarmed by these developments, the Johnson administration plumped for the more cautious of the two options: the establishment of a study committee that would make recommendations to the 1967 session.

At that session, however, the study committee resolution was rejected, but so too was the Albanian motion, clearly a result of the deterioration in Chinese Communist relations with a number of countries as the Cultural

Revolution entered its most violent phase.[28] It was not until 1970 that Albania's resolution gained a simple majority, with both Canada and Italy voting in favor of it even as they continued to support the IQ resolution. The Nixon administration responded, publicly accepting what Bowles had first advocated in 1962: that the PRC should be represented but not at the expense of the expulsion of the Taiwanese. In 1971, America's U.N. ambassador, George Bush, offered an extension of this position, arguing, close to Ottawa's idea of 1966, that the PRC should hold the Security Council seat but both Chinas should be represented in the General Assembly. Despite much political lobbying at the United Nations, the IQ resolution failed, apparently much to the astonishment of the U.S. delegation. When Bush rose on a point of order to attempt to remove the Albanian resolution clause calling for the expulsion of the Republic of China delegation, this too was blocked. Once the IQ resolution was overturned, the Chinese Nationalists declared that they would no longer "take part in any further proceedings of the General Assembly," which left the way open for the Albanian text. It passed by the healthy majority of 76 to 35 with 17 abstentions.[29]

TRADE

The Kennedy and Johnson administrations were equally tortuous in their deliberations and timid in their approach on the trade issue. Between 1950 and 1952 the trade embargo imposed on China had steadily tightened until it was firmer than that against the Soviet Union and Eastern Europe, a distinction that caused considerable difficulty between the United States and its major allies.[30] Thus, in his 1961 paper, Rice had suggested putting trade with China on the same basis as that with the Soviet Union and, in the context of China's disastrous Great Leap agricultural policies, had made a special plea for modifying the embargo on food grains and medicines. In early April 1962, as a result of discussions in State and between Harriman and Rusk, the secretary of state put four recommendations to the president: that shipments of medicines to all destinations go under general license; that it be made known that no licenses would be denied for private gift shipments of food or food grains to China; that Ambassador Wang at the Warsaw talks be asked about the rumor of Chinese interest in the purchase of U.S. grains and, if true, the reasons for this interest before China had exhausted the possibility of meeting its needs from other suppliers such as Canada and Australia; and that it be suggested to such suppliers that they should consider the leverage their supplies of grain might provide in deterring "deeper Chinese Communist external involvement at the expense of the free world."[31]

By May this highly qualified document, with its mix of motives, had not progressed. Bowles pressed President Kennedy to state, at his May 23 press conference, that the United States stood ready "to offer substantial food shipments to Communist China" in response to "the spectacle of Chinese suffering." He also told the president he lamented the fact that Washington had failed to develop a contingency plan to deal with the possibility of food sales or grants and that the issue had not been raised in discussions in Warsaw.[32] Kennedy's remarks on the subject, in response to a question asked at a meeting with the headquarters staff of the Peace Corps, were grudging: U.S. policy was "to do nothing on the food until there is some indication that the Chinese Communists desire it." The reaction of China's foreign minister, Chen Yi, to such proposals was unequivocal: "American traders, Rusk, and President Kennedy say they will supply China with food if China makes a gesture, but we will never make any gesture to this bid."[33]

Although the food issue lost its centrality as China slowly recovered from its disastrous famine, those officials sympathetic to the idea of relaxing trade controls continued to press for the sale of grain and pharmaceuticals. In a clear rejection of the "China must behave first" approach, James Thomson, a China specialist on the National Security staff, argued in a memorandum to National Security Adviser McGeorge Bundy in November 1964 that Beijing had "no intention of 'shaping up' in terms of taking tension-relieving initiatives with us, either now or in the foreseeable future." Instead, what they were doing was making it look as though it was the United States that was isolated in its approach to the PRC rather than Beijing, which, through its own actions, was responsible for this isolation. Would it not be better, therefore, Thomson inquired, for the United States, which had always sought "the 'domestication' of Communist China," to go for "modified containment—plus subversion . . . [through] the careful use of free world goods, people, and ideas?"[34] It was a phrase that eventually, in a slightly modified form, made its way into President Johnson's nationwide television and radio address on Asian policy, delivered on July 12, 1966, in which he stated that the United States had "also learned that the greatest force for opening closed minds and closed societies is the free flow of ideas and people and goods."[35] Thomson regarded the inclusion of these words as something of a triumph and a breakthrough, modest though it was. (He later intimated that they might have inadvertently slipped through the bureaucratic vetting process.)[36]

With the president now on record as favoring increased contact, including trade, this seemed the moment to try once again to relax specific controls. Thomson proposed, as the "result of the first interagency review of the complete China trade picture since the outbreak of the Korean War": "(a) general licensing of relevant transactions for those categories of U.S. citizens now entitled to travel to Communist China, (b) an end to the special bunkering controls that have been in effect for 16 years, and (c) preparation for unilateral relaxation of trade controls (subject to the President's approval) with initial focus on two-way trade in foodstuffs, non-war related pharmaceuticals, and art objects."[37] In March 1967, Assistant Secretary of State William Bundy again recommended that foodstuffs be placed under general export-import license as well as medical supplies for use in combating epidemics. However, only the ban on medical products was lifted, and it took until February 1968 before Rusk would recommend other minor trading steps to the president that included not only foodstuffs, but also fertilizer, insecticides, and farm machinery.[38]

The advent of the Nixon administration saw these ideas finally put into place. In 1969, Nixon lifted the ban on travel to the PRC, removed a previously imposed ceiling of one hundred dollars on tourist purchases, and signed an order allowing foreign subsidiaries of American firms to trade with the PRC. In April 1971 the administration adopted the boldest of the initiatives on offer when it finally announced the ending of the embargo on trading in non-strategic goods.[39] U.S. trading practices toward China at last came into line with those toward the Soviet Union and with the policies its leading allies had long followed.

TRAVEL

Obviously trade and recognition were the two most important signals of fundamental change in the U.S. relationship with the PRC. However, the matter of travel to the mainland also absorbed a great deal of bureaucratic effort in the 1960s. This matter of travel, with its wider relevance to the rights of freedom of movement and expression, became a point of serious contention in the Eisenhower administration. In 1957, during the Sino-American ambassadorial negotiations in Geneva, China first offered (but later rescinded its pledge) to allow U.S. news representatives to visit the

PRC, a suggestion that stirred considerable interest in the American media. The administration's initial response had been to threaten to revoke the passports of those Americans who attempted to make such a trip. Over the following weeks, however, it was forced to relent to a degree and agreed to permit American journalists to travel to China, although it would not offer reciprocal visas to Chinese holding PRC passports. As Arthur H. Sulzberger of the *New York Times* had argued, he could not "escape the feeling the Administration [was] abridging the freedom of the press and using the press as an instrument in its diplomacy."[40]

Left unresolved at the close of the Eisenhower era, the issue stayed on the agenda for the following two administrations. Rice's 1961 paper had also recommended the lifting of the passport ban to allow news representatives and scholars to visit the PRC. According to James Thomson, approximately twice a year, from 1961 until January 1964, a proposal on travel would make its way from the Bureau of Far Eastern Affairs to the Secretary of State, there to wither through neglect. In August 1965, however, Dr. Paul Dudley White, the renowned heart specialist and Eisenhower's personal physician, injected new life into the debate when he offered himself as a possible means to break the travel ban to a country he wanted to visit.[41] McGeorge Bundy got behind this travel package and managed to persuade the president to give oral authorization for issuing unrestricted passports to medical personnel and scientists. It took until December 1965 to obtain final written clearance, despite clear media and congressional approval of such a course of action, but it was a breakthrough nonetheless, and thereafter the categories of those permitted to visit became steadily wider. Indeed, according to a memorandum dated December 1, 1966, which argued in a qualified way for the removal of all restrictions on travel to China, there were already "literally tens of thousands of individuals" in the United States who could qualify for a visa.[42] In May 1968 (the same month the PRC unilaterally suspended the ambassadorial talks—now held in Warsaw—stating that there was "nothing to discuss at present"), the administration took a further step by offering to allow Chinese journalists to come to the United States to cover the presidential election campaign.[43]

It was Nixon who finally removed all aspects of the travel ban, and in 1970 the State Department validated more than a thousand U.S. passports for travel to China. Only three Americans received travel visas, however, and no Chinese applied for entry to the United States, hardly surprising in light of contemporary political conditions within China itself.[44] During the previous two Democratic administrations there had been opportunities for "ideas, people, and goods" to begin to work their presumed magic on Chinese authorities and the Chinese citizenry. In each of these policy areas, however, only the most timid of the options had been recommended, and a number of bureaucrats believed their best efforts had largely been wasted.

Explaining Policy Developments

It is necessary to explain why these small policy changes were enacted but even more necessary to explain why they were so modest—why the bureaucracy labored so long and hard to bring forth what amounted to a mouse or two.[45] I have referred to the public and private expectations of change in China policy during the Kennedy and Johnson eras and provided evidence to show that several midlevel U.S. officials were willing to argue persistently for a modification in Washington's approach. (I would give the "persistence award" to Edward Rice, who moved on to become U.S. Consul General in Hong Kong from 1964, Chester Bowles, James Thomson, Robert Komer, Roger Hilsman, and Edwin Reischauer.) Reischauer, in his valedictory cable from his ambassadorial post in Tokyo in August 1966, provided one of the most eloquent expositions of the whole period, explaining why America's policy needed to be altered. From the perspective of his own posting, Reischauer described "Japanese unease at being linked to a China policy which they consider . . . basically unrealistic and not in Japan's long-range interests." In his judgment, it was "the most serious problem that now exists in U.S.-Japanese relations," and he added, correctly, that "Japan is not the only country in which we pay a price for our present stand," that the United States paid "something of a price in practically every other of our major industrialized allies [sic] and in many other countries throughout the world." Such allies were similarly distressed, he wrote, by the U.S. pretense that the "twelve million people on Taiwan and not the seven hundred million in continental China, represent the great historical political entity known as China."

Moreover, it was a claim that prevented Taiwan from recognizing reality, encouraged dangerous behavior among America's Asian allies, damaged regional solidarity in Southeast Asia, and stood in the way of building broad multilateral support for the U.S. role in that region. In a clear rejection of the "China must behave first" line of argument, Reischauer stated that it was in fact this attitude that undercut any Chinese readiness to seek a rapprochement; at fault was "the callous pretense on the part of the world's greatest power that China does not really exist or that, if it does exist, it is so depraved or so unstable or so inconsequential that it should be barred from world society." In his view, nothing but good—as much for America's interests as for its reputation—would come from a policy that showed respect for Chinese nationalism. Such respect would be demonstrated by U.S. support for Beijing's representation in the United Nations, a pledge of noninterference in its domestic affairs, and an expressed willingness to live in peace with the country. What was fundamentally required, he wrote, was a "redefinition of our attitude toward Peking." Shortly thereafter, in a memorandum to the president, Robert Komer, an Asia specialist on the White House staff, directly associated himself with this "compelling" argument.[46]

Thus, respected figures in the bureaucracy, including those with direct access to the president, were willing to make strong arguments in support of a modified containment policy, and from a variety of perspectives. Reischauer made his case almost on moral, and certainly on reputational grounds. But in other parts of the bureaucracy, it was plain that change had become acceptable because the dangers of dealing directly with China had lessened. Whereas in the 1950s the Eisenhower administration had feared that trading with or recognizing the PRC would contribute to the power and prestige of a regime bent on challenging the postwar regional and international order the United States had set out to establish, after 1962, given the Sino-Soviet rift and the failure of the Great Leap Forward, many considered China to be facing a period of severe, possibly prolonged weakness. Its level of technology was deemed "very backward," it suffered from a shortage of "well-trained scientists in the middle and upper brackets of competence," and it was an overpopulated country struggling to feed its people on a restricted land base.[47] In these circumstances, it was hardly a socioeconomic model for other developing countries to emulate, and in this sense it represented less of a threat to American conceptions of order than it had during the more confident days of the 1950s. Richard Madsen has captured this modification in perception effectively and succinctly, describing it as a gradual shift from the "Red Menace" view of China to the myth of China as "troubled modernizer." In this latter guise, Beijing was becoming, for some officials at least, far less of a challenge to the core values of American society, an outcome that was especially significant when antiwar and civil rights demonstrators were gathering in their thousands on America's streets to proclaim that the administration's own behavior betrayed these values.[48]

Beyond the bureaucracy, public opinion surveys in early 1961 indicated that the mass public were also ready for changes in policy toward the PRC. However, poll results were often difficult to interpret, especially for the cautious, the politically insecure, or those who wanted above all to appear tough and uncompromising. Moreover, the mass public still continued to view the Chinese Communist regime with considerable distaste. In 1963, 47 percent of those polled saw China as the greatest threat to world peace, compared with 34 percent for the Soviet Union; by 1967 this figure had risen to 71 percent, compared with 20 percent for the Soviet Union.[49] There were also pluralities against China's admission to the United Nations—65 percent in September 1961 and 67 percent in December 1965.[50]

Nevertheless, on closer examination the polls did show areas of flexibility in mass opinion that could have been built upon, and on some issues they demonstrated a clear desire to accept the need for improved relations provided there was strong leadership in this direction from the president. These attitudes were shaped by three main factors: the growing realization that the Chinese Communist regime was a hard fact of life that had to be accommodated and, after China's 1964 explosion of an atomic bomb, one that would be ignored at America's peril. It was also plain, in relation to U.N. representation and trade, that few of America's allies willingly followed its lead on these matters, and that some, such as Britain and France, had forged their own particular policy stances.[51]

Polls in the 1960s demonstrated this presidential room for maneuver. For example, a Gallup Poll in 1962 showed 48 percent in favor of shipping food to the Communists and 43 percent against; and in late March 1966 (unlike the poll results noted above), 56 percent said they would favor U.N. admission for the Communists if this action would help in reducing tensions in East Asia, a phrase that obviously triggered consideration of how best to reduce or end U.S. involvement in the Vietnam War.[52] A Harris Poll in June 1966 showed that 55 percent favored admitting both Chinas to the U.N., with 45 percent against, and 92 percent thought the United States should stay in the United Nations if the PRC were to be admitted.[53]

A Council on Foreign Relations (CFR) book published in 1966 but based on a survey of opinion conducted during May and June 1964 was particularly revealing about the potential for a presidential role. When respondents were asked, for example, "suppose the President suggested visits between Americans and people from Communist China," or suggested "the exchange of ambassadors," or that "we talk over problems of Asia with Communist China," then 73 percent, 51 percent, and 71 percent, respectively, pronounced themselves to be in favor of such action. They did not support selling wheat to China, however (47 percent against and 43 percent for), or U.N. entry (53 percent against), but that last figure needs to be compared with the one given previously, which shows a plurality in agreement when entry is linked to the resolution of tension in East Asia. James Thomson, in arguing for moves to "domesticate the Chinese Communist revolution," pointed to the CFR text as indicating a "high degree of public tolerance for coexistence with Communist China." [54]

Congressional activities in the Johnson era also provided further support for change in China policy. Following Assistant Secretary Roger Hilsman's speech on China in San Francisco in December 1963, the pro-Chinese Nationalist lobby, the "Committee of One Million," sent a rebuttal of its contents to every member of Congress, but on this occasion was unable to generate criticism in either that body or the media.[55] Many of the stalwarts of the China bloc—men such as Walter Judd, Alexander Smith, and William F. Knowland—who had linked their arguments with those of Joseph McCarthy in the 1950s and caused such difficulty to the State Department and to Democratic administrations in particular, no longer had their platforms in Congress. On the contrary, it was now the U.S. Congress that was taking the lead in shaping a new attitude and a new approach to Beijing. In March 1965, a House subcommittee of the Foreign Affairs Committee, headed by Clement J. Zablocki, issued a report on the Sino-Soviet rift that recommended "at an appropriate time, consideration to the initiation of limited but direct contact with Red China through cultural exchange activities with emphasis on scholars and journalists." In the Senate, William Fulbright, as chair of the Senate Foreign Relations Committee, was a key figure in helping to build a climate in which rational discussion of China policy could take place. He spoke critically of the inflexibility in current policy in March 1964 and received some twelve thousand letters in response, two-thirds of which were favorable.[56] In March 1966, he was instrumental in organizing televised Senate Hearings on American policy.

It was at those Hearings that several Asian specialists developed the theme of "containment without isolation," urging trade in nonstrategic goods and movement toward eventual diplomatic and U.N. recognition.[57] Moreover, the view of China that emerged at the Hearings promoted its image as "troubled modernizer" rather than simply the "Red Menace." In testimony before the Senate Foreign Relations Committee, for example, General Samuel B. Griffith described China, except in regional terms, as a "paper tiger" that would be unable to project conventional military power beyond its borders for ten to twenty years. In a book published the following year, he argued that in many important areas, such as aircraft, chemicals, electronics, and computer technology, China was far behind the West, and he quoted China's then foreign minister, Chen Yi, who had said in September 1965 that it could take "30–50 years" to make up this lost ground.[58]

Vice President Hubert Humphrey quickly endorsed this modified containment policy in an appearance, at the time of the Senate Hearings, on NBC's *Meet the Press*, and as I noted earlier, President Johnson was emboldened in his nationwide address on Asian policy in July to advocate increased contact between the two societies, stating that "lasting peace [could] never come to Asia as long as the 700 million people of mainland China are isolated by their rulers from the outside world."[59] A year later, Congress' Joint Economic Committee urged a reevaluation of U.S. trade policies toward China,[60] and Richard M. Nixon, that staunch anticommunist, whose political following had been built on the harshness of his attacks on Democratic administrations for being "soft on Communism," published an article in *Foreign Affairs* advocating a change of stance. As Nixon put it, "Taking the long view, we simply cannot afford to leave China forever outside the family of nations, there to nurture its fantasies, cherish its hates, and threaten its neighbors. There is no place on this small planet for a billion of its potentially most able people to live in angry isolation."[61]

Various interest groups also made known their support for improving the level of communication between Washington and Beijing. Representative Charles O. Porter of Oregon, who in June 1959 had proposed a trade mission to China, cofounded with Ernest Nash in San Francisco a "Committee for a Review of Our China Policy." This committee began its activities with a request for U.S. permission to sponsor a trade delegation to the Chinese trade fair in Guangzhou in October 1963.[62] The Quakers also became active on the matter of China policy, the San Francisco American Friends Service Committee (AFSC) asking Cecil Thomas, its associate peace secretary, to organize a regional conference.

That first conference, held in December 1964, was deemed a considerable success. It was put together with the energetic help of Professor Robert Scalapino of UC Berkeley's political science department, a supporter of the Johnson administration's Vietnam War policy and the main author of the 1959 Conlon report. Further conferences were to follow, garnering widespread support from business, labor, academic, and religious groups, and gaining the plaudits of the mass media. The San Francisco office of the AFSC also charged Thomas with responsibility for developing what came to be called the National Committee on U.S.-China Relations, officially founded in June 1966. Two other such organizations would be established in the late 1960s and early 1970s: the Committee on Scholarly Communication with Mainland China and the National Council on U.S.-China Trade. As Madsen reports, the middle-class and middle-aged had begun to make their views known on the China question, no longer fearful of being labeled unpatriotic or, worse still, of being called un-American. Moreover, they began to make those arguments in a cool and dispassionate manner, in doing so affirming that "diversity was safe, not something that threatened to fragment the liberal republic. It was safe because it was rational, comprising nothing more than the different opinions of professional experts; because it was deferential to the prestigious elites who had lent their names to the gathering; and because it was blessed by an assemblage of religious and civic bodies whose patriotism had been demonstrated for a long period of time."[63]

This dispassionate discussion of China policy provided the necessary encouragement for the policy steps ahead. Presidential hopefuls Richard Nixon and Hubert Humphrey obviously felt emboldened enough to offer more for the future, both promising in their election campaigns that they would stretch out a hand to the PRC. But if this elite was no longer so fearful of the political consequences, at least after late 1963, if Congress was actively promoting a change in policy, if the quality media were suggesting a reexamination, if the mass public displayed somewhat contradictory views but were obviously receptive to presidential leadership on the matter, and if America's allies and the nonaligned countries were urging new policies on the two administrations, why were the policies that were implemented relatively minor? It is difficult to be conclusive here, in part because on a number of issues the reasoning must be inferential. The explanation seems to lie in three main areas: with the PRC itself, with other foreign policy priorities, and within the U.S. executive branch.

Explaining the Minor Nature of the Revisions

President John F. Kennedy began his term in office acutely aware of the narrowness of his electoral victory and the need to prove to his potential domestic critics, and to himself, that he could be tough with foreign opponents.[64] He also had a particular dislike for the Chinese Communist regime, and here the Beijing leadership did not help matters, staging a "Hate America" week in the summer of 1960 and sharpening its ideological animus in order to establish new revolutionary credentials after its split with the Soviets.

Even as a senator, Kennedy had been fearful of China, concerned that in a race with democratic India, for example, Beijing's form of government and economy might win. In a speech in February 1959, he described New Delhi as the "hinge of fate in Asia," the "one great counter to the ideological and economic forces of Red China," and the "testing ground for democracy" throughout the region.[65] By the time Kennedy took office, India ranked as the world's largest recipient of U.S. economic assistance.

Not surprisingly, therefore, his administration continued to support New Delhi and gave it considerable material assistance during the Sino-Indian border war of 1962. Here was direct evidence of Beijing's ability to make trouble with a country administration advisers, including those who supported a change in China policy, either had great affection for (as with Chester Bowles, a former ambassador to New Delhi) or wanted to move closer to. As Robert Komer stated, the war provided "a golden opportunity for a major gain in our relations with India," a goal that Kennedy had sought to reach since the beginning of his presidency.[66]

China also appeared to demonstrate its capacity for aggressive behavior during the Cuban missile crisis of October 1962. To members of the Kennedy administration, its bellicose rhetoric over Cuba seemed designed to demonstrate that China, rather than the revisionist Soviet Union, represented the major challenge to U.S. imperialism. One consequence was that Khrushchev in turn felt compelled to take a more militant stance or risk losing the support of other key socialist allies, an interpretation encouraged by the efforts of Anatoly Dobrynin, the Soviet ambassador to Washington, who brought out this reasoning in explaining Khrushchev's policy toward Cuba.[67]

Kennedy was also particularly concerned about China's developing nuclear capacity, and he, and others within the administration, believed that

Moscow was similarly concerned: "There is little doubt that Moscow's desire to inhibit Communist China's acquisition of nuclear weapons has been one important reason why the Soviets have seriously entertained the idea of a supervised nuclear test ban."[68] As China moved closer to exploding an atomic device, the president made it clear within the administration that he regarded such developments as "intolerable to the United States and to the West" and that some form of action against it should be prepared "unless they [the Chinese] agreed to desist from further efforts in this field." In one of Kennedy's most chilling public speeches on China, he described it thus: "700 million people, a Stalinist internal regime, nuclear powers, and a great determination of war as a means of bringing about its ultimate success." The United States faced, he said, "potentially a more dangerous foe than any we faced since the end of the Second World War."[69] After speeches like this, it was hardly surprising that the American public came to view China as the greatest threat to world peace or that both the Kennedy and Johnson administrations should decide to attempt to exploit this coincidence of interest with Moscow and find ways jointly to prevent the further development of China's nuclear capacities.[70]

This particular intolerance of the Chinese Communists made it logical to support the continuation of the old Dulles/Eisenhower policies, but so too did developments in Sino-Soviet relations, of which the nuclear question was but one source of tension. The Sino-Soviet rift forced its attention on even the most skeptical within the Kennedy administration, although as Walt Rostow put it at a meeting in January 1962, no one knew "what to do about it."[71] But some knew, up to a point. At that same meeting, Charles Bohlen, the noted Soviet specialist, said that the Russians had "become the Mensheviks, while the Chinese are Bolsheviks." This kind of reasoning— that the Chinese were a greater source of international instability—spawned a policy designed to move closer to the comparatively more cautious and reasonable Moscow at Chinese Communist expense. The enactment of such a policy obviously undercut the arguments of those seeking rapprochement with Beijing but seemed to fit better with Kennedy's preferences.

Domestic politics also reinforced the president's predilections. Certainly Kennedy's own campaign rhetoric served to constrain his options: for example, his charge that the Eisenhower administration had been lax in its dealings with the Communist world and had allowed Moscow to open up a "missile gap" restricted room for movement. Such rhetoric, together with his narrow electoral victory, made him especially vulnerable to Republican countercharges should he display any flexibility toward the Chinese Communists. I have already noted his concerns in 1961 about the "political dynamite" concealed behind the U.N. representation for China issue and former Vice President Nixon's obvious willingness to exploit the matter. Kennedy informed the British in April 1961 that former President Eisenhower had told him he "would feel it necessary to return to political life if the Chinese communists were admitted to the United Nations," a remark Dean Rusk repeated to his British counterpart during that April summit. This expectation also resurfaced as a political constraint during the Johnson era.[72]

Rusk's own apparent rigidity on the issue of China policy is partly explained by his proclivity to carry out the wishes of his president rather than to innovate. But it is also true that the secretary of state did not believe the Chinese had earned any modification in the U.S. approach, a belief he clung to well into the Johnson era. As Rusk's biographer, Warren I. Cohen, has argued: "The Chinese championed a different world order and a militant behavior that Rusk feared would mean chaos, war, and, in a nuclear world, the destruction of civilization." The secretary questioned whether reinforcing such behavior could truly serve the interests of peace and argued that first the Chinese needed to be tamed.[73]

Despite occasional evidence of tactical flexibility, Rusk's stonewalling on a variety of issues and his subordinates' attempts to bypass him in certain areas are evident from several of the documents available from this period. Alfred Jenkins, an NSC staff member, has been most revealing of the mood of the time. In a memorandum to Walt Rostow, he confided: "Entre nous: While I believe the Secretary to be one of the greatest in our history, on the one issue of China his style scares me. He is so orderly and judicial and a sheaf of other virtues, that he wants all the returns in before he moves. On China we are not going to get as many returns as we want."[74] An exasperated James Thomson referred on several occasions to "resistance at the top of the Department even to these minimal steps [on trade relaxation]."[75] Thus, the slow pace of change in China policy during these years is partly explained by the role and personal beliefs of key individuals such as Kennedy and Rusk.

There are also other matters of style and personality to consider. Of Rusk it has been said that, although he could express forthright views in a crisis, he "never pursued any sustained policy initiative of his own." When he came to serve in the Johnson administration, he found himself working with a president who lacked a foreign policy agenda and was fearful of making mistakes. Johnson "therefore put the highest priority upon following the consensus of his senior advisers and never chose an alternative that they would have rejected."[76] Thus, while there may have been a raft of initiatives available, a new structure within the State Department, new personnel brought into play, and a more tolerant domestic environment, these were not enough. As Thomson put it in a memorandum to Bundy in January 1966, central to the neglect of a strategy designed to undermine Beijing's hostility was the "communications gap between the working level of China specialists on the one hand, and the highest levels of government on the other. To my knowledge, neither President Kennedy nor President Johnson had occasion in office to focus at any length on the problem of Communist China's domestication. . . . In the absence of an Ambassador to Peking, or a China advocate on the 7th floor of State, our opportunity to explore and exploit a multiple strategy in regard to mainland China has been let pass."[77] With no figure at the highest levels ready to think through U.S. China policy and play an advocacy role, decisions were basically tentative and piecemeal. In the absence of hard evidence of "good behavior" on the part of the Chinese, it was difficult for the policy of "containment without isolation" to fully establish itself.

In his memorandum to Bundy, Thomson also drew attention to the tendency of the Johnson administration to view China through the lens of the Vietnam War. This was also true during the Kennedy era as developments in Southeast Asia began to encroach on Kennedy's agenda, and with that encroachment came the belief that Hanoi's gains in Indochina would strengthen China's influence.[78] But it was in the Johnson era that the Vietnam War truly began to shape and constrain most other issues, including China policy. As Nancy Tucker has put it, "for the President the Vietnam War defined policy in Asia."[79]

The Johnson administration at first depicted Vietnam as a Chinese-inspired war of national liberation, a model of warfare that was presumed to have resonance elsewhere in the developing world, and one which the United States had a duty to attempt to defeat. In the early stages of the Vietnam conflict, China was seen to be behind the fighting and thus the major actor in preventing a negotiated settlement: it was therefore difficult to move toward rapprochement with such a regime, even though some officials continued to advocate this course. Later, as U.S. involvement deepened,

Johnson and many of his officials became almost entirely preoccupied with the progress of the war and had little time or energy for other issues. Antiwar demonstrations, beginning in the spring of 1965, grew in intensity, as the numbers of young men sent to fight in this frightening, alien land increased.

In an attempt to bolster the international legitimacy of U.S. actions in Vietnam, Johnson had insisted that U.S. allies be pressed to help with the war effort. Taiwan (and South Korea) offered troops, and although U.S. advisers persuaded Johnson not to accept uniformed men, the Chinese Nationalists did supply small units for covert action, aircrews to fly transport and espionage missions, and technical maintenance teams. Taipei also set up training programs for South Vietnamese forces and offered its territory to U.S. forces as a staging area for operations.[80] Taiwan and South Korea thus used "Vietnam as hooks by which to link Washington to their distinct agendas,"[81] further compounding the difficulty of introducing more positive elements in policy toward Beijing.

If the time-honored as well as newly formed links with Taiwan were a matter of constraint, the United States detected no signs that China was itself ready to deal with the United States. Anti-Americanism was a very useful means of reinforcing Beijing's revolutionary legitimacy in the wake of its split from Moscow and of demonstrating its purity in comparison with the revisionist and accommodationist Soviet Union. With the onset of the Cultural Revolution in 1966, there was little evidence that the Chinese leadership wished to have diplomatic contact with any state, let alone the Americans. As Rostow argued in February 1968, although there was something of a change of dynasty taking place on the mainland, the Maoists still found it convenient to have the United States "in the devil's role." In his perception, "it takes two to play some games, and Peking does not see it in its interest to play, just now."[82]

Rapprochement at Last

That Washington was still waiting for China to reciprocate with some positive moves of its own is evident from Rostow's statement. True, this requirement was strongest during the Kennedy period and had lessened over the course of the Johnson administration, as shown by the movement on the trade and travel issues as well as by the minor shifts in the argument on the U.N. representation question. Nevertheless, only in the Nixon era do we witness the full implementation of the approach Reischauer had advocated in 1966 (ironically, to do it, Nixon and Kissinger virtually bypassed the State Department).

Nixon seems to have been particularly interested in a change of approach toward the PRC, as shown by his 1967 *Foreign Affairs* article, his campaign statements on building bridges, and his steps, immediately after his inauguration, to let it be known through private channels that he would be reexamining China policy. As further confirmation of his early interest, in 1996 Senior Minister Lee Kuan Yew revealed that during Nixon's Asia travels in 1967 he found himself in a serious and sustained discussion with the U.S. president about China, "his main interest" and obviously a topic more engaging to him than Vietnam. Lee met Nixon again in 1969, 1970, and 1971, and on each occasion China was the main item in their conversations.[83] From 1969, therefore, at last one individual at the very highest level of government was interested in China policy and ready to take up the initiatives developed in previous administrations. As noted earlier, in 1969 Nixon moved swiftly to modify the travel and trade ban, to allow his secretary of state, William Rogers, in August to signal interest in opening a dialogue, and, crucially, in November to terminate regular Seventh Fleet patrols in the Taiwan Strait. His administration also moved toward a dual representation policy at the United Nations. In his first foreign affairs report to Congress in February 1970, Nixon described the Chinese as a "great and vital people" having the "longest unbroken history of self-government in the world." A year later, he modified the approach in another symbolic area, referring to the Beijing government as the "People's Republic of China," and in July 1971 he described it as becoming, within his lifetime, one of the "five great economic superpowers"—a statement that caused enormous excitement among the Beijing leadership.[84]

The Nixon administration was clearly more sensitive to Chinese nationalism than previous administrations and decided to push ahead with new policies even though it had no assurance that the Chinese were fully ready to reciprocate. As advocates of balance-of-power and realpolitik approaches to international relations, Nixon and Rogers surely expected the Chinese to reciprocate at some early date as a consequence of the militarization of their conflict with the Soviet Union.

The boldness that had been lacking was now present: advocates of a change in China policy included the president himself, and his national security adviser went along willingly. A Republican with strong anticommunist credentials, Nixon had less residual fear of a domestic political backlash and regarded a shift in approach as in line with much elite and mass opinion. In order to be certain, however, he initiated efforts to woo potential domestic critics, holding bipartisan briefings on his plan to visit China with Republican senators Barry Goldwater, John Tower, Paul Fannin, and Strom Thurmond; and Democratic senators Robert Byrd, James Eastland, Russell Long, and Herman Talmadge. Former congressman Walter Judd, at one time a key figure in the "China bloc" in Congress and still active in the "Committee of One Million," was to be treated with "firmness" but if possible not "alienated." [85]

The Nixon administration was fortunate that potential domestic critics had by now lost their power, but it also benefited from the fact that China's association with the hostilities in Vietnam had significantly diminished. Moreover, America's own decision to withdraw from Vietnam sidelined this issue as a source of difficulty between the two countries. The rapprochement was supposed to encourage Beijing to pressure Hanoi into negotiating a final settlement and provide a way to moderate the American sense of failure associated with withdrawal. In addition, in the face of a stronger Soviet Union, improved relations with Beijing would be a new way to contain Moscow and promote détente with the Soviets.

Given these shifts in the domestic and external environments, the raft of initiatives that Edward Rice had first drawn up in 1961 and the arguments that James Thomson and Edwin Reischauer, among others, had so assiduously promoted could at last come into their own. Ironically, where once the PRC had been projected as the cause of domestic conflict over U.S. Asian policy, with rapprochement its role would be redefined in ways that would help to heal those wounds. Contact with a state once described as dangerous and irrational reinforced the belief that rationalist solutions could still bear fruit.

CHAPTER TEN

Changes in China's Domestic Situation
in the 1960s and Sino-U.S. Relations

Li Jie

FROM THE TIME of the Tenth Plenary Session of the Eighth Central Committee of the Communist Party of China in 1962 to the start of the Cultural Revolution in early 1966, Chairman Mao Zedong adhered more closely to a "leftist" cycle stressing class struggle, so that extreme "leftism" threatened to engulf the country. It was against this domestic political backdrop that Sino-U.S. relations evolved from Cold War hostility through the first thaw in relations at the end of the 1960s to the 1972 visit to China by Richard Nixon. These developments in China's foreign affairs and internal politics seem paradoxical. What was the interrelationship between the course of domestic "leftism" in China and the evolving moderation in Chinese foreign policy? What were the domestic factors contributing to the shift in Chinese policy toward the United States and to China-U.S. rapprochement?

The Origins of Sino-U.S. Conflict and China's Early Diplomacy

Between 1949 and 1956, the Chinese leadership reached three strategic decisions that affected Sino-U.S. relations. The first was to "lean to one side"—the side of the socialist bloc—and not to be impatient in developing relations with the United States. China had made active efforts to develop

Sino-U.S. relations until the founding of the People's Republic of China (PRC).[1] But once Mao had judged that U.S. enmity toward China was unlikely to change and that the United States would not accept an equal relationship, he adopted the "lean to one side" policy to break the U.S. blockade.[2] The second concerned Taiwan. China called for a third round of Kuomintang-Communist cooperation and peaceful unification, while opposing internationalization of the Taiwan question and the "two Chinas" or "one China, one Taiwan" schemes. The third decision concerned membership in the United Nations. Because Beijing's resumption of China's seat in the United Nations would involve a protracted struggle, Mao and the Central Committee decided to be patient while working actively with all sides to regain it.

After the establishment of the PRC, the Chinese leadership faced internal and external pressures: internal pressure because of opposition from the bourgeoisie and the intelligentsia, who had been influenced by British and American culture, and external pressure because of the U.S. containment policy and its economic blockade of China. In Mao's view, internal and external pressures interacted, so that Chinese domestic objectives were reflected in China's foreign policy toward the United States. The "lean to one side" policy, for example, resolved the debate over foreign policy and paved the way for domestic socialist development.[3] Similarly, Mao thought that China should "not be eager to develop relations with America," not only because of U.S. hostility but because he wanted to consolidate political power in China. In Mao's words, China needed "to sweep the house before inviting guests."[4]

Taiwan policy also reflected domestic policy. The liberation of Taiwan was one aspect of the strategic aim of "liberating the whole of China" and consolidating political power. But after consolidating power on the mainland and deciding to focus on industrialization, the most important domestic consideration would be establishing a peaceful environment. Hence, in 1955 China announced its policy of peaceful resolution of the Taiwan problem. After China started shelling Jinmen in 1958, Chinese leaders adopted an even more moderate Taiwan policy, in part reflecting their focus on economic and political difficulties following the Great Leap Forward. In a conversation with foreign guests, Mao said that "the Taiwan problem is very complicated. It involves both internal and international problems. Because it involves the United States, it is an international problem. An international problem can only be solved by peaceful means, and not by force." He argued that the Chinese "demand that the Americans withdraw from Taiwan. They will not do it, so we will have to wait. We will wait for as long as they will take to withdraw. We shall not be the first to start a war with the United States, of this the comrades may rest assured. With regard to Chiang Kai-shek, Taiwan is an internal problem. Does this mean that it must be solved by force? The answer is also no." He observed that "there are two ways to solve an internal problem, by peaceful means or by military means. Some people have mixed up the international and the internal problems involved in the Taiwan issue."[5]

From 1949 to 1956, Chinese leaders, concentrated on restoring and developing the economy, so that foreign policy, under the principle of "lean to one side," was quite flexible. Influenced by developments in Poland and Hungary and the anti-rightist struggle in China, however, Mao changed the policy line at the Eighth Party Congress in 1958, insisting that class struggle remained the main contradiction of domestic society. Soon, domestic policy shifted to emphasizing quick results. Then, in 1959, the campaign to oppose the "right-deviationist thinking" of Marshal Peng Dehuai unfolded.

These developments affected Chinese foreign policy. Under the banner of opposing imperialism, China abandoned compromise and stressed struggle against the United States; under the banner of maintaining heightened vigilance against the danger of a new world war, China stressed the danger of war. A lack of understanding of the emergence of coexisting Cold War tensions and détente led to an overemphasis on the advantages of heightened tension. However, through the end of the 1950s, these policy errors had yet to cause serious damage to Chinese interests.

Domestic Radicalization in the Early 1960s and Sino-U.S. Relations

From the early 1960s, China's domestic economic and political situation and the international environment deteriorated significantly. Domestically, the Great Leap Forward ended in a disastrous defeat that led to economic decline and famine. Although this produced greater pragmatism in domestic and foreign policy,[6] the dominant trend soon moved in the opposite direction, reflecting a major change in Mao Zedong's political thought and the rapid development of leftist ideology.

The defeat of his economic policies and the break with the Soviet Union led Mao to stress class struggle and the two-line struggle within the Party and to abandon economic development in favor of "taking class struggle as the guideline." The Tenth Plenary Session of the Eighth Central Committee in 1962 marked the introductory stage of Mao's leftist guiding ideology.[7] Following the meeting, China launched the socialist education movement throughout the country. In foreign policy, Mao rejected Wang Jiaxiang's suggestion in 1962 that China develop a more moderate policy toward the United States, the Soviet Union, and Third World "reactionaries,"[8] the *"san he yi shao."*[9] To Mao, revisionism had begun to appear in China under Soviet influence. He charged that *"san zi yi bao"*[10] was the domestic program of the Chinese "revisionists" and that *"san he yi shao"* was their international program. These alleged policy deviations proved the correctness of the Moscow Declaration of 1957: "the influence of capitalism is the domestic source of revisionism. Submitting to pressure from imperialism is the foreign source of revisionism."

The international environment was also deteriorating. While the United States continued its policy of containment, ideological differences inspired rivalry between China and the Soviet Union. Mao had once said to an aide that he could allow neither America to blockade China nor the Soviet Union to bully China. Rather, he said, "it seems that I have to fight on two lines, as Lu Xun once said, that is, to fight against America on the one hand and the Soviet Union on the other."[11] At the same time, heightened tension also characterized relations between China and its neighbors, including its border dispute with India.

ANXIETY OVER STATE SECURITY

From the mid-1950s, as Beijing pursued the Five Principles of Peaceful Coexistence, the situation along China's borders stabilized. Mao believed that China could maintain a peaceful international environment for fifteen or twenty years, possibly longer, and Chinese leaders thus concentrated on economic development and the peaceful resolution of international disputes. As early as 1950, Mao Zedong declared that "a new World War can be prevented."[12] With the acceleration of domestic development, he argued that "détente is beneficial to the peoples of both socialist and capitalist countries."[13] Thus, he praised Zhou Enlai's diplomacy at the 1954 Geneva Conference.

But in November 1957, at a meeting of representatives of Communist and Workers' parties in Moscow, Mao Zedong became overly optimistic. He argued that "the international situation has reached a new turning point" and that "the current situation is characterized by the east wind prevailing over the west wind, that is to say, the forces of socialism are in a position of overwhelming advantage over the forces of capitalism." In order to substantiate his thesis, he recounted ten major events that had taken place recently in the international scene.

Mao's leftism intensified in the 1960s, when the Soviet Union turned from an ally to a rival, so that China faced two external adversaries and a new domestic threat from revisionism. Because the Soviet Union was linked to China ideologically, Soviet influence in China could not be eliminated simply by ideological remolding. For Chinese leaders, especially Mao, the growing external threat from the Soviet Union created an internal domestic threat.

In 1958 the Soviet Union demanded that a "long-wave station" and a "joint-command submarine fleet" be established in China. This was not a simple issue. The nucleus of the question was whether China should possess its own nuclear weapons or whether it should rely on the Soviet "nuclear umbrella." Chinese leaders feared that, because China was an "Asian member" of the Warsaw Treaty Organization, cooperation with Soviet proposals would involve it in the conflict between the United States and the Soviet Union and compromise China's interests by promoting strategic dependency. The Soviet proposal also revealed that Moscow would not treat China as an equal power and did not want China to develop nuclear weapons.

In June 1959, to punish Chinese independence and improve relations with the United States before Khrushchev's impending U.S. visit, the Soviet Union canceled its 1957 agreement to transfer new defense technologies to China and refused to provide China with a model of the atomic bomb and related blueprints. After the U.S.-Soviet summit at Camp David, Khrushchev hurried to China to teach Mao and other Chinese leaders a lesson. In these circumstances, Mao feared that the easing of U.S.-Soviet tension would damage China's interests.

These developments in Sino-Soviet relations prompted Chinese leaders to reevaluate Chinese security. They concluded first that the Sino-Soviet alliance no longer provided an unconditional guarantee to China in its struggle with the United States. On the contrary, Moscow might now use the alliance as a bargaining chip to reduce tension with the United States. Second, China would not receive Soviet "selfless aid" for economic development, since Moscow would use Chinese dependence on such aid to pressure it into becoming an obedient member of Moscow's "big family." Third, as their foreign policies and security interests diverged, China questioned whether Soviet leaders had become "revisionists" and the Soviet Union another

"Yugoslavia."[14] In two articles and an April 1960 speech entitled "Long Live Leninism," Chinese leaders questioned Soviet domestic and international policies.[15] Although on the surface these documents seemed to criticize Yugoslavia, they were in fact critical of Soviet policy since the Twentieth Congress of the Soviet Communist Party. Moscow retaliated by publicly criticizing Chinese delegates to the June 1960 Bucharest conference of communist parties. Then, in July, Moscow withdrew its experts from China and suspended economic aid, trying to compel Beijing to bow to Soviet pressure, as Warsaw Pact members had done. This is what Nikita Khrushchev referred to as "synchronizing watches."[16]

The ensuing polemics between China and the Soviet Union pushed Sino-Soviet relations to the brink. Moscow gradually increased its military strength along the Sino-Soviet border and instigated separatist incidents in minority areas along China's northwest border. In May 1962, the Soviet consulate promoted a rebellion by ethnic minorities in Xinjiang. The Soviet Union also cooperated in a nuclear blockade against China by signing the Nuclear Test Ban Treaty with the United States and Britain in 1963.

The growing Soviet threat also reached within China. Over time, a thousand and one ties had been formed between the Soviet and the Chinese communist parties and disentangling them was all but impossible. Fear of Soviet ideological subversion contributed to Mao's decision to initiate the strategic task of "combating and preventing revisionism." On September 29, 1962, Mao pointed out that "all revisionism abroad or domestic will have illicit relations with foreign states. Our comrades doing work in international relations should pay attention to this."[17] The ninth article in the open letter of the Soviet Central Committee published on July 14, 1962, quoted Mao on the prerequisites of China's successors: "special vigilance should be paid to intriguers and careerists such as Khrushchev, preventing such elements from seizing leadership of all levels of the Party and government." Chinese foreign policy and the Socialist Education Movement both reflected Mao's twin strategic objectives of "combating revisionism" internationally and "preventing revisionism" domestically.

Compared to the Soviet threat, the U.S. threat was much simpler. It came primarily from southern Vietnam and then, only from the outside. Hence, no matter how fierce the fighting in Vietnam, the threat was far less than that during the Korean War, which gave Mao some leeway in managing Sino-American conflict. Mao paid greater attention to the war after the

Gulf of Tonkin incident in August 1964, when U.S. forces entered into battle in southern Vietnam and bombed northern Vietnam.[18] In this situation, China declared that "any U.S. encroachment on the Democratic Republic of Vietnam is an encroachment on China, and the Chinese people will never sit idly by without lending a helping hand." Mao was primarily worried about two things. First, if the United States sent troops to northern Vietnam, China would face the threat of war because Vietnam bordered China.[19] Second, after the war escalated, the post-Khrushchev leadership tried to expand Soviet influence to Indochina by providing aid to Hanoi.[20]

In this context, although China gave full support to Vietnam's struggle against U.S. aggression, it also tried to contain the conflict. First, China tried to avert U.S. troop intervention in northern Vietnam. In March 1963, Pakistani Foreign Minister Zulfikar Ali Bhutto told Zhou Enlai and Chen Yi in Beijing that Pakistan was willing to serve as a bridge between China and the United States. Thus, after the Tonkin Gulf incident, when Zhou Enlai met with the Pakistani president, Mohammad Ayub Khan, on April 2, 1965, Zhou asked, "When Your Excellency President visits the United States, if the United States asks you what China is going to do, you can tell the United States the following three points: 1. China will not take the initiative to provoke a war with the United States; 2. The Chinese people mean what they say; 3. China has made preparations."[21] Although Mohammad Ayub Khan postponed his visit to the United States and thus failed to pass the three-point message on to the American side, events compelled China to open communications with the United States. On April 10, 1966, when Zhou Enlai met with the *Pakistani Dawn* correspondent Ijaz Hussain, he made an important addition to the three points: "If the war is fought, there will not be a boundary line." He also said, "You come by air. Why cannot we go by land?" On May 10, the main points of this conversation were published in the *People's Daily*.

Regarding aid to Hanoi, China distanced itself from the Soviet Union by opposing "joint action" or a "united front." From December 1964 to February 1965, when Moscow proposed a meeting of the Warsaw Treaty Organization and Asian socialist countries to consider "joint action" on aid, China rejected the proposal. In April 1965, when Premier Aleksei Kosygin proposed a summit meeting of Soviet, Vietnamese, and Chinese leaders, China also rejected this proposal. China did agree to permit and coordinate the transit of aid from the Soviet Union to Vietnam and to provide free transportation, but it opposed an airlift across Chinese airspace and any establishment of bases and military depots on Chinese territory.[22] China could not prevent Moscow from expanding its influence in Indochina, but because Mao rejected both "joint action" and a "united front," and refused to give Moscow an "air corridor" over China or bases and military depots in China, the Soviet Union did not supplant Chinese influence. Thus, when the United States sought to withdraw from Vietnam in the 1970s, it had to appeal to China.

China also faced a threat off its southeast coast. In 1962, Chiang Kai-shek called for "mounting a counterattack against the mainland" and sent armed agents to harass China's coast. Mao ordered heightened combat readiness, and tension mounted. Fortunately, Chinese and U.S. leaders were able to cooperate. On June 23, 1962, in his meeting with Wang Bingnan, China's ambassador to Poland, John Moors Cabot, the U.S. ambassador to Poland, stated that under present circumstances, the United States would not support Taiwan's attack on the Chinese mainland and would distance itself from such an attack. He suggested that if Taiwan should take such action, the United States and China might cooperate by continuing their talks to restore the peace.[23]

Nonetheless, in the latter half of 1962, Mao faced the possibility of simultaneous large-scale invasions by the United States and the Soviet Union. He told the Vietnamese defense minister, General Vo Nguyen Giap, that "in the past few years, we did not give much thought to how the imperialists might attack us. Now we will have to think it over."[24] Subsequently, Mao frequently raised the possibility that the Soviet Union and the United States would jointly attack China, one from the north and one from the south, and assessed whether Moscow or Washington posed the greater threat.[25] On January 17, 1964, in a meeting with Anna Louise Strong, Frank Coe, Sol Adler, Israel Epstein, Sidney Rittenberg, and others, Mao noted a commentary in the American press stating that, for the immediate future, the Soviet Union was America's major enemy but that China would be America's long-term enemy. Mao remarked that because imperialists are pragmatists, they place secondary importance on long-term issues and noted that the tendency of imperialists to look down on China was a good thing and to China's advantage. Mao also doubted that the United States was preparing to fight a third world war.[26]

Mao understood that the U.S.-Soviet conflict was the paramount global contradiction. In January 1964 he told Vietnamese leaders, "We see a rule in this: Whenever the Soviets need to strike a political bargain with the United States, they do something to harass us. Their aim is to show the Americans that they are not friendly with China but are friendly with America."[27] On September 17, 1965, he remarked to Japanese visitors: "We must admit that there is a contradiction between the United States and the Soviet Union, and this contradiction can never be resolved."[28]

Mao reached these important conclusions prior to launching the Cultural Revolution. At this time, he also further developed his theory of the "intermediate zone." He posited that two intermediate zones (also known as the two "Third Worlds") lay between the United States and the Soviet Union: "The first Third World refers to Asia, Africa, and Latin America, and the second Third World refers to a group of countries where capitalism is highly developed, mainly represented by the Western European countries, some of which are even imperialist countries themselves. These countries oppress others on the one hand while on the other they are oppressed by the United States, and contradictions exist between them and the United States."[29] The struggle between control and resistance to control, he argued, had weakened the strength of the two great powers and diverted their attention, giving China room to maneuver even as it faced enemies on two sides. Mao thus formulated a strategic guideline for China that used these contradictions to win over the many and isolate the few, and to defeat the enemy one by one. He also gradually shifted the emphasis from anti-imperialist and antirevisionist struggles to the struggle against revisionism.

Anxiety over the Domestic Political Situation

In the early 1960s, concluding that a "capitalist restoration" was taking place in the Soviet Union, Mao Zedong reevaluated the political situation within China and shifted China's domestic focus from economic construction to class struggle. After the anti-rightist struggle of 1957, Mao and the Central Committee raised the proposition that the major contradictions in Chinese society were the struggle between the proletariat and the bourgeoisie and between the socialist and capitalist roads.[30] Although economic development remained the central concern, the guiding ideology of economic policy now reflected the "leftist" deviationist mistake of trying to advance too quickly. As a result, the Great Leap Forward ended in disastrous failure, causing serious economic difficulties from 1959 to 1961.

While Mao allowed Liu Shaoqi, Zhou Enlai, Chen Yun, and other leaders to readjust the economy, he shifted his focus from economics to politics, and further, to polemics with the Soviet Union. The year 1962 was a crucial one. In January and February, an Enlarged Work Conference of the Central Committee (also known as the "Conference of Seven Thousand Persons"), at which economic policy was the central question on the agenda, convened in Beijing. On January 30, speaking to the conference, Mao made some self-critical remarks regarding the Great Leap Forward. However, he also called for heightened vigilance against the emergence of "capitalist restoration" in China, as had happened in the Soviet Union. That summer, at the Party's Beidaihe working conference, Mao unexpectedly changed the agenda, demanding that the conference discuss the class situation and the contradictions between classes.[31] A month later, at the Tenth Plenary Session of the Eighth Central Committee, discussion of these three topics continued. One paragraph of the communiqué, in Mao's own handwriting, reflected the radical changes under way in Party policy: "The Tenth Plenary Session of the Eighth Central Committee points out that in the entire historical period of proletarian revolution and proletarian dictatorship, in the entire historical era of transition from capitalism to communism (which will take several scores of years or even more), there exist the class struggle between the proletariat and the bourgeoisie, and the struggle between the socialist road and the capitalist road." The communiqué also insisted that China emphasize class struggle and the danger of a capitalist restoration, "so that we shall have a relatively clear recognition of this problem and have a Marxist-Leninist line."

Here, Mao was not only expounding his theory, he was also directing it against definite targets and calling for concrete measures. He was targeting "the wind of darkness," "the wind of returning to individual farming," and "the wind of reversal of verdicts." The "wind of darkness" referred to the economic assessment made by Liu Shaoqi, Chen Yun, and others at the "West Building" conference in February 1962, which was even more pessimistic than that made at the Seven Thousand Persons work conference. Liu bluntly reported that "the central work conference did not talk about the full difficult situation. Many problems were not presented, out of fear of exposing all that was dark! What is there to fear if the real situation is presented?"[32]

But Mao disagreed. He believed that the economy had hit bottom and that an upturn was imminent. In a speech to the Beidaihe conference on

August 6, he said, "Now, some comrades take the situation as all darkness and no brightness. Hence, some are ideologically confused and can see no prospect and have no confidence."[33] On August 9 he said, "For two years, since the later half of 1960, everyone has talked about darkness and not brightness. When I toured the country, I revealed a few of my opinions on the problem of darkness and brightness, putting forward a topic. In these two years, it was legal to talk about difficulty and darkness, and illegal to talk about brightness."[34] This was a criticism of Liu's speech at the Seven Thousand Persons meeting, which argued that China's troubles were "three parts natural calamities and seven parts man-made disasters." Liu had no choice but to make a self-criticism at the Beidaihe conference.

The "wind of returning to individual farming" referred to the policy of "farming with fixed household output quotas with each household on its own," which Liu Shaoqi, Chen Yun, Deng Xiaoping, Deng Zihui, and other leaders had been advocating for areas facing extreme hardship since the 1960s. In July, they sent their suggestions to Mao. He severely criticized their proposal, however, arguing that it is a matter of "whether we are working for socialism or for capitalism." Connecting the "wind of darkness" with the "wind of returning to individual farming," he argued that by claiming that everything is dark, Liu and others have proved that socialism does not work and therefore advocate individual farming.

The "wind of reversal of verdicts" was a reaction to the reexamination of wrongful verdicts and the rehabilitation of people falsely charged in the 1957 anti-rightist struggle. Deng Xiaoping was responsible for carrying out this policy. In the course of his reexamination and rehabilitation, Peng Dehuai wrote a letter to the Central Committee and Mao Zedong appealing some of the charges against him, including those of maintaining secret ties with a foreign government and organizing an anti-Party clique. Mao responded that rehabilitating Peng was out of the question. He also criticized the policy of reexamination and rehabilitation.[35] He said that "the recent wind of reversal of verdicts is wrong, and the struggle against deviations to the right must not be negated, with all charges dismissed." At Beidaihe, he again criticized this policy. Three years later, his opposition was further reflected in his criticism of the historical drama *Hai Rui Dismissed from Office*.[36] Mao's opposition to the three "winds" led him to focus on class struggle at the Tenth Plenary Session of the Eighth Central Committee. The "struggle to combat and prevent revisionism" had become an urgent task requiring immediate attention. Then, in 1963, China launched the Socialist Education Movement. Party leaders at all levels, including Liu Shaoqi, actively participated.

The Soviet factor played an important role in Mao's decision to "combat and prevent revisionism" and to emphasize class struggle. On the one hand, his conclusion that the Soviet Union had "turned revisionist" led him to shift the focus of domestic efforts toward "combating and preventing revisionism" and to concentrate on class struggle. On the other hand, combating and preventing revisionism forced a corresponding readjustment in China's foreign policy. The Socialist Education Movement and the escalating Sino-Soviet polemics, begun simultaneously in 1963, reflected this interrelationship. Similarly, Sino-Soviet polemics also had foreign and domestic policy objectives. Externally, it was used to proclaim to the international community China's position on important policy issues and its opposition to Soviet foreign policy, in an attempt to win friends and isolate the Soviet Union. Internally, the polemics supported the Socialist Education campaign by distinguishing between what was revisionist and what was socialist and through this kind of ideological education unifying understanding, consolidating the ranks, and eliminating Soviet influence.

For Mao, the Soviet threat involved intangible as well as tangible factors; it was a question not simply of external pressure and armed invasion but of revisionist thought infiltrating China and recruiting "agents." Indeed, the domestic threat was even more dangerous than the external threat. At the Tenth Plenary Session of the Eighth Central Committee, Mao alleged that it would be better for Chinese "right deviationists" to change their name to Chinese "revisionists."[37] He believed that the danger of revisionist thought infiltrating the Chinese Communist Party and recruiting "agents" far exceeded the danger of the imperialist "peaceful evolution" strategy. Thus, Sino-Soviet contradictions were sharper and more profound than those between countries possessing different social systems and ideologies.

China Joins the Ranks of the Nuclear States

In the early 1960s the Soviet Union and the United States gloated over China's economic difficulties. But by 1963 economic decline had ended, and in 1964 China embarked on a program of economic growth. In addition, on October 16, 1964, China carried out its first atomic test, breaking the nuclear monopoly of the United States, its allies, and the Soviet Union, and joining the ranks of the nuclear states.

China's nuclear explosion legitimated Mao's domestic policies. In the immediate aftermath of the Great Leap Forward, he faced great political pressure, as is reflected in his self-criticism at the expanded central working conference. But in little more than a year, the domestic situation had undergone tremendous change: agricultural output was growing and excavations at the Daqing oil field had been successful, alleviating China's petroleum shortage. Thus, after three years of difficulties, the prospect of "leaping forward" on all fronts again emerged. Mao Zedong, after experiencing frustration and depression, again felt elevated. The nuclear test also reflected positively on Mao's foreign policy, raising China's international strategic position and proclaiming the bankruptcy of the U.S. policy of containment and blockade. The test also broke through Moscow's technological blockade, revealing that China could survive and develop without the help of the Soviet Union.

On January 15, 1955, at an enlarged meeting of the Secretariat of the Central Committee chaired by Mao Zedong, China decided to develop its nuclear industry.[38] In March, at the National Party Conference, Mao announced that China had started "a new historic period of work on nuclear energy."[39] The Central Committee set up a three-member group consisting of Chen Yun, Nie Rongzhen, and Bo Yibo to take charge of the nuclear energy industry. In November 1956, the Third Ministry of the Machine-Building Industry (later renamed the Second Ministry of the Machine-Building Industry), was created to administer the nuclear industry.

In the first few years of China's nuclear program, Beijing counted on Soviet assistance. But as Sino-Soviet relations deteriorated, all hope of such help evaporated. Following the Soviet cancellation of the nuclear sharing agreement, the Central Committee stepped up nuclear research. On July 18, 1960, after listening to a report by Li Fuchun in Beidaihe, Mao remarked, "It is very good that Khrushchev refuses to let us have the highest technologies. If he had let us have them, it would be hard to repay the debt. Now we must steel ourselves to work on the highest technologies ourselves."[40] On November 3, 1962, he approved a report by the Second Ministry of the Machine-Building Industry, which proposed that the first atomic test take place by mid-1965.[41] Although the economy faced serious difficulty, and research for the atomic bomb required huge expenditures from a tight budget, the consequences of failure would have been unthinkable. Mao focused on national defense and international struggle, in particular the struggle against the Soviet Union.

Research for the atomic bomb promoted comprehensive technological development, which contributed to unprecedented growth in China's overall strength and in its ability to resist the U.S. blockade and U.S. containment. The nuclear test also proved that the United States could no longer isolate China. Washington now believed that to restrain China, it not only had to cooperate with Moscow, it also had to allow China to join the world community. On March 13, 1966, Vice President Hubert Humphrey called for containing but not necessarily isolating China. Indeed, Mao had always insisted that China wanted the bomb for political, not military purposes. In May 1963, he remarked to a New Zealand delegation: "We do not yet possess an atomic bomb or a hydrogen bomb. However, we wish to develop and manufacture such weapons. Even when we do make them, compared with the United States and the Soviet Union, we won't even have one-tenth what they have. We don't wish to win a war by using atomic and hydrogen bombs."[42]

China's nuclear test shook Western countries. It presaged the end of the old world order, from which China was excluded, and the birth of a new order requiring China's participation. Yet, at this very moment, an upsurge of leftist thought overwhelmed China, throwing it into self-imposed isolation.

WANG JIAXIANG'S PROPOSALS

A primary issue for Chinese policymakers in the early 1960s was how to reduce international pressure on China. In 1962, Wang Jiaxiang, the head of the International Liaison Department of the Central Committee, considered ways of alleviating tension in China's foreign relations and thus enabling Beijing to focus on its domestic problems. At about the time of the Seven Thousand Persons Conference, he held several meetings at his home with leaders of the Party's International Liaison Department. These confidential, "closed door" discussions included deputy ministers Liu Ningyi, Wu Xiuquan, Zhao Yiming, Xu Li, and Xiong Fu, General Secretary Li Qixing, Zhang Xiangsan, Deputy General Secretary Wang Li, and He Fongxi, Wang Jiaxiang's political secretary. The participants supported Wang's proposals and offered various suggestions.

On February 27, Wang Jiaxiang wrote a letter to Zhou Enlai, Deng Xiao-ping, and Chen Yi advocating changes in Chinese foreign policy. Wang also sent the letter to Central Committee members Liu Ningyi and Wu Xiuquan seeking their support. He then prepared two documents for internal use in the International Liaison Department. The first was entitled "On the Question of Support to Other Countries in Their Struggle against Imperialism and for National Independence and People's Revolutionary Movements—Seek Truth from Facts, Act According to One's Capability," the second, "On the Open Views of Mass Organizations in Our Country on Certain International Issues." On June 29 Wang submitted the second report to the Central Committee and included the first document as an appendix.

In these documents, Wang argued that the propaganda banners of peace and anti-imperialism should be appropriately balanced; if China trumpeted only anti-imperialism, the peaceful nature of its foreign policy would be weakened and blurred. With the strategic aim of achieving a long-lasting, peaceful international environment that would enable China to build socialism and step up its economic development, he proposed a government statement proclaiming that China's foreign policy had always been one of peace. On the question of war and peace, Wang suggested that "the danger of a world war must not be overstressed to such an extent that the possibility of preventing world war is diluted. We must not say only that 'So long as imperialism exists, war is inevitable,' because the possibility of preventing a world war exists."[43] Regarding nuclear war, he argued that "it is of course wrong to make propaganda only about the terrors of nuclear war without mentioning that a nuclear war may be prevented by a people's struggle." He also insisted that China should not try to reassure the masses "simply by saying 'we are not afraid.'" He believed that fear of war was common in Europe, and that Chinese propaganda should acknowledge the destructive nature of nuclear war. He similarly argued that China should adopt a positive stance toward disarmament, rather than say only that "total disarmament is an illusion" or that "our aim in supporting the disarmament proposal is only to expose the enemy."

Wang Jiaxiang also proposed several changes in Chinese policy toward the great powers. On the issue of China's Soviet policy, he suggested that China guard against Khrushchev's reaching a compromise with the United States and breaking with China. At meetings of international communist parties, he maintained that it was not appropriate for us to push ourselves forward and to take the lead (owing to the domestic situation, generally speaking, it is not appropriate for us to push forward in foreign affairs). Rather, China should avoid raising any reference to differences and provoking disputes with the Soviets. If the Soviet Union instigated disputes, China should invite a united front with fraternal parties, seeking common ground while reserving differences and adhering to the principle of mutually refraining from imposing one's own opinions upon others. In its relations with Western countries, including the United States, Wang argued that China should adhere to the principle of peaceful coexistence between countries of different social systems and that it was incorrect to claim that "peaceful coexistence is impossible given the existence of imperialism." He also said that to avoid a Korea-type war in Indochina, China should avoid receiving the brunt of the U.S. offensive in Vietnam.

On the issue of the Sino-Indian border, Wang suggested that China "should try to break the deadlock" and that "Nehru is not China's enemy." He further argued that in the larger international struggle, China should maintain the initiative, "combining advance with retreat, attack with defense, struggle with conciliation, delay with solution," and not simply struggle to the end without letup. Regarding foreign aid, he advised that China "be realistic and settle for what is practical, and act in accordance with our capabilities."

Wang directed his criticism at erroneous foreign propaganda and at Mao Zedong. His differences with Mao involved fundamental questions of international strategy and diplomacy: the estimate of the danger of a world war, China's policy toward the international peace movement, its management of Sino-Soviet relations, its basic posture toward the United States and other Western countries, its appraisal of and policy toward national independence and national liberation movements, and the use of diplomatic flexibility to promote a positive Chinese image in complex and changing international circumstances. Wang sought to ensure a favorable international environment for economic advancement by reducing tension, eliminating misunderstanding of China's domestic and foreign policies, and exploiting diplomatic opportunities.

CRITICISM OF WANG'S PROPOSALS

Various Party leaders supported Wang's suggestions. Moreover, his objectives corresponded with Mao's preferences in the 1950s and with the foreign policy guidelines of the Eighth National Party Congress. But by the early 1960s, Mao had turned his attention from economics to politics. "Combating and preventing revisionism" had become his foremost priority. Instead of accepting Wang's proposals, he criticized them harshly, characterizing them as "the three moderations and the one reduction." After this, Wang found it impossible to continue as a foreign policy leader.

On May 22, 1963, in his talk with V. G. Wilcox, general secretary of the New Zealand Communist Party, Mao said, "In our Party there are some who advocate 'the three moderations and the one reduction.' They say we should be more moderate toward the imperialists, more moderate toward the reactionaries, and more moderate toward the revisionists, while toward the struggle of the peoples of Asia, Africa, and Latin-America, we should reduce assistance. This is a revisionist line." He also said that "for a short time in the first half of 1962, a minority of comrades went out of their senses, and that the Moscow Conference [the World Disarmament Conference of July 1962] was an example of this."[44] At the Moscow Conference, Chinese delegates, acting on guidelines developed by Wang and others that called for a "low-key" posture, expressed support for disarmament. Wang suggested that China raise the banner of peace and argued that "it is not in accord with the Marxist strategic viewpoint to talk about supporting national liberation movements and not world peace, and to put aside the peaceful forces that would make us able to win over many more allies." Thus, in accordance with the guidelines, the Chinese delegation promoted "peace" and supported "disarmament."

Kang Sheng later complained to Mao Zedong about Wang's policy package, characterizing it as the "three moderations and one reduction." Reflecting Kang's report, Mao said, "We committed a mistake at this conference, and adopted a policy of not . . . showing our colors prominently. We were criticized . . . by our friends from Asia, Africa, and Latin America. Our Korean comrades also criticized us. Only Khrushchev welcomed our stand. That was why we hurried to make a self-criticism."[45] He added, "Later, at the Tokyo Conference, we took the line of giving tit-for-tat and not yielding an inch of ground. We made a good showing at the conference. This is a piece of experience in the international struggle."[46]

At the preparatory meeting for the Tenth Plenum of the Eighth National Party Congress, Wang made a self-criticism before delegates from the northwest, referring to Mao's criticism and taking responsibility for alleged mistakes. Later, at a meeting called by the Foreign Affairs Office of the State Council, Wang was again criticized, although he did not attend. Wang made a further self-criticism at the Tenth Plenum. As he later recalled, "I thought my mistake was a grave one. So I asked several comrades responsible for the work of the International Liaison Department to come to me and criticize me. In addition, I asked a few comrades to draft a self-criticism for me to be read at the Tenth Plenum." He recalled that "I wrote a letter to Chairman Mao, saying I would like to hear his instruction on my mistakes. After a short interval, the Chairman's secretary telephoned, asking me to go to Chairman Mao." At that time, this signaled that Mao was prepared to be lenient. When he arrived at Mao's living quarters, "Chairman Mao asked me what did I want to talk to him about. I said: I would like to make a self-criticism on the mistake I made at the Moscow Disarmament Conference. The Chairman said: it was not necessary to raise your problem to the Standing Committee, nor to make a self-criticism at the plenum. Some deputy ministers of the International Liaison Department had some complaints. . . . You just need to promote mutual understanding with them."[47]

But in reaction to the "three moderations and one reduction" policy, Mao advocated "three struggles and one more": that China should struggle against the imperialists, the revisionists, and the reactionaries of all countries, and that more assistance should be given to anti-imperialist, revolutionary, and Marxist-Leninist political parties and factions. He added that "three moderations and one reduction" was Khrushchev's slogan, and "three struggles and one more" was China's slogan.[48]

Mao's criticism of Wang and his assessment of domestic political change strengthened his "leftist" deviationist tendencies. He observed a connection between the "three moderations and one reduction" and what he called the "three selfs and one contract" (more small privately farmed plots for peasant households, more free markets with prices determined by the buyers and sellers, more enterprises with profit and loss borne by the management, and farms contracted to households at fixed output quotas), alleging that the former was the international program of some Party members and the latter, their domestic program. He labeled the two policy packages the "revisionist line," indicating that Chinese "revisionism" acted in concert with the Soviet Communist Party and that there were "people of the Khrushchev type" at the center of the Chinese Communist Party.

As a result of Mao's attack on the Party leadership, China lost an important opportunity to adjust its foreign policy. Thereafter, following the escalation of Sino-Soviet polemics and the unfolding of domestic mass political movements, "leftist" deviationist views of international affairs increasingly dominated policymaking. This trend created an overly pessimistic estimate of the danger of world war and foreign invasion, promoted propaganda aimed at the Soviet Union and the United States, and encouraged foreign policy rigidity. It also led Chinese policymakers to exaggerate China's global role, thus promoting policies that exceeded national capabilities. China was also overly optimistic about the world revolutionary situation and the centrifugal tendencies among Western countries, which contributed to excessive idealism in its foreign propaganda.

Despite his tit-for-tat position and his inflexibility in relations with the Soviet Union and the United States, Mao maintained a certain degree of pragmatism, particularly about Sino-American relations. On January 30, 1964, in a discussion with French legislators, Mao said, "After we solve the Taiwan problem, we will resume diplomatic relations with America."[49] On June 30, in an interview with a delegation of Chilean journalists, Mao said that he would welcome a visit to China by American journalists. He said, "Someday normal relations between the two countries will be resumed. In my view, it will take another fifteen years. Because fifteen years have already passed, in another fifteen years it will be thirty years. If that is not enough, then it may take several years more."[50] On January 9, 1965, Mao met with American journalist Edgar Snow. When Snow asked him if there was any hope for improved Sino-American relations, Mao replied, "In my view, there is hope, but it will take time. But there may not be any hope during my lifetime. I soon will go to visit God. Perhaps you may have the chance to see that day." He added, "Due to historical reasons, the two countries will come to each other, but it requires waiting. Someday it will happen." When Snow said, "I don't think there will be war between China and America," Mao responded, "Maybe you are right."[51] In another discussion with Snow, he said that he would like to swim in the Mississippi River before he was too old,[52] implying that he hoped he would live to see normalization of Sino-American relations. As early as the 1960s, Mao understood that the major threat to China came from the Soviet Union and that there were corresponding prospects for U.S.-China cooperation.

The Transformation of Opposites: Internal Forces Promoting Reconciliation

During the second half of the 1960s, internal problems caused by the Cultural Revolution occupied most of Mao's time and energy, but he also kept a close watch on international politics. At this time China's periphery was becoming more stable. In the Soviet Union, Leonid Brezhnev, who had just replaced Khrushchev as Party leader, was focusing on domestic problems. In the United States, the Johnson administration was sinking deeper into the Vietnam War and encountering domestic antiwar feeling, which restrained its international capabilities. India's defeat in its border clashes with China cautioned it against further challenges. To the east, Japan was occupied with economic growth. A rare quiet had even fallen on the Taiwan Strait: the Kuomintang faced a sensitive succession from Chiang Kai-shek to his son Chiang Ching-kuo, and unable to "counterattack against the mainland," Taiwan occupied itself with internal affairs. In these circumstances, Mao could focus on domestic affairs and combat "revisionism appearing at the Center."

From "Great Disorder under Heaven" to Loss of Control in Foreign Affairs

In 1966 and 1967, Mao Zedong accomplished almost nothing in foreign affairs, devoting himself instead to the Cultural Revolution. He relied on mass mobilization to expose the "dark side" of leaders at various levels of the Party and the government and to sweep away "persons of the Khrushchev-type in China" who "take the capitalist road." He believed he could control the movement and attain "great order under heaven" through "great disorder all over the land." But the Cultural Revolution exceeded Mao's expectations and his control, and social upheaval followed.

In August 1966, the Red Guard movement and the "great link-up" engulfed the whole country. Many leading cadres were "pulled out" and "struggled against," and the extreme leftist thinking expressed by the slogans "suspect all" and "strike down all" spread throughout the Party. When Mao supported the "January storm" of Shanghai in 1967, the movement to "wrest power" from the bottom spread throughout the country. "Rebel factions" then split into two antagonistic factions, each trying to wrest power from the other. At the height of the disorder these factions frequently resorted to armed violence, pushing the country to the brink of civil war.

The Cultural Revolution was disastrous for China's domestic and foreign affairs. All leading cadres in the Ministry of Foreign Affairs suffered, including Foreign Minister Chen Yi, who was frequently surrounded and attacked by "rebel factions." In Beijing, slogans and *dazibao* (big-character posters) were directed against Zhou Enlai. All but one Chinese ambassador returned home to take part in "study classes," and many were criticized or denounced at public meetings.[53] "Rebel organizations" were organized in Chinese embassies in many countries and *Quotations from Chairman Mao Zedong* and other revolutionary propaganda materials were distributed and posted in foreign capitals. Some Chinese embassy officials carried out demonstrations and distributed propaganda sheets. China's foreign policy proclaimed such theories as "the transfer of the center of world revolution" to China, Chinese communists are "the only revolutionaries," and the "export of revolution." Such activities and propaganda provoked protests from other countries, and relations with many countries deteriorated.[54] Then, in August 1967, the "rebel faction" in the Foreign Ministry, with the support of the Cultural Revolution Leading Group, announced that it had wrested power from the ministry. It then issued directives to Chinese embassies. On August 22, the office of the British chargé d'affaires in Beijing was set on fire.

Because Chinese leaders, including Mao and Zhou Enlai, were preoccupied with domestic politics, they could not oversee diplomatic operations. Foreign Minister Chen stopped conducting diplomacy, and when Chinese ambassadors were instructed to return home, Chinese diplomacy ceased altogether. All that was left was propaganda emphasizing opposition to reactionaries in all countries and support for the anti-imperialist and anti-revisionist struggle. Four years later, Zhou Enlai recalled that "extreme leftist thinking affected our Foreign Ministry." Had the Cultural Revolution "only produced extreme leftist ideas, they could have been . . . corrected. The problem was that some bad people made use of this opportunity to manipulate the mass movement, split the movement, and sabotage our foreign relations."[55]

While he was on an inspection tour outside Beijing, Mao read Zhou Enlai's report on rebel factions in the Foreign Ministry and on the burning of the Office of the British chargé d'affaires. He was furious. He called Wang Li's August 7 speech to the "Rebel Liaison Station" of the Foreign Ministry, which instigated the rebels to wrest power, a "big, big, big poisonous weed."[56] On August 30, he approved Zhou's report and ordered that Wang Li and Guan Feng, both members of the Central Cultural Revolution Group, be held in custody and placed under investigation. Mao thus alerted leftists that they should restrain themselves and began to bring "the great disorder under heaven" under control.

Mao issued many orders criticizing ultra-"leftist" language, blowing one's own horn, and forcing one's views on others. On March 29, 1968, on the text of a proposed statement on the twentieth anniversary of the armed struggle of the Burmese Communist Party, he wrote: "Generally speaking, we shall not interfere in the internal affairs of any foreign (Marxist-Leninist) party. How they make propaganda is their own business. We must be careful of our own propaganda and should not boast too much or say inappropriate things, which may give others the impression that we are trying to impose our views on them."[57] In a note on a draft report of the International Liaison Department, Mao wrote that "resolute and step-by-step reforms should be carried out in external propaganda."[58] On May 16, 1968, [Mao] criticized a document that called Beijing "the center of the world revolution." He insisted that "Chinese should not say such things. It is the erroneous thinking of the so-called 'making ourselves the core.'" On May 29, 1969, he noted on a Foreign Ministry document, "First of all, be careful not to force our views on others; second, do not issue propaganda that people's movements in foreign countries are influenced by China. Such propaganda will be used by the reactionaries and will be harmful to people's movements." On December 6, 1970, he called the practice of forcing one's views on others "great-nation chauvinism at home and abroad, which must be overcome."[59] Seven years after he had criticized Wang Jiaxiang for revisionist thinking, Mao issued orders reflecting Wang's suggestions. Domestic chaos had compelled him to abandon his ideological foreign policy.

THE TWOFOLD EFFORT TO ESTABLISH A NEW POLITICAL ORDER AND A NEW FOREIGN POLICY

Mao's ideological shift transformed China's diplomacy. First, Zhou Enlai again enjoyed greater status and responsibility. Ye Jianying, as vice-chair of the Central Military Commission, also assumed an important role in policy-making, especially in relation to Henry Kissinger's July 1971 visit to China.[60] Second, China restored order to the Ministry of Foreign Affairs; Chinese ambassadors gradually resumed their duties and returned to their posts,[61] while diplomatic relations between China and other countries normalized. Third, China abandoned the ultra-left practice of making enemies everywhere and developed a more comprehensive national-interest-based foreign policy. It reestablished friendly relations with developing countries and

cooperated with them in opposition to Soviet hegemony. It also consoli-
dated relations with Western countries and with Eastern European countries, including Romania and Yugoslavia.[62] Beijing took the initiative in the
campaign to return to the United Nations. Fourth, Chinese leaders reevaluated global strategic patterns and adjusted China's strategic principles, an
important step in the normalization of Sino-U.S. relations. These readjustments began in 1968, as Mao was trying to end internal political turmoil and
establish a new leadership system. The Twelfth Plenary Session of the
Eighth Central Committee and the Ninth National Party Congress in 1969
signaled Mao's efforts to initiate a new order. In the latter half of 1969,
changes in domestic politics and foreign policy accelerated.

Mao characterized the excesses of the Cultural Revolution as "strike
down all" and "all-round civil war."[63] After these excesses had peaked, in
1967, he proposed a revolutionary union and the "three-in-one combination."[64] He sent troops to support the left, the workers, and the peasants and
to exercise military control and conduct military training. He also sent
propaganda teams of workers to universities, where violent armed struggle
continued to rage. He thus moved China from "great disorder under heaven"
to "great order all over the land."[65] Revolutionary Committees were set up in all
provinces, municipalities, and autonomous regions, and when the Twelfth Plenary
Session of the Eighth Central Committee convened in October 1968, it symbol-
ized a temporary stability in national politics.

On August 20, 1968, Soviet forces moved into Czechoslovakia. Moscow
then put forward its "theory of the big socialist family" and its "theory of limited sovereignty." These developments indicated that in its relations with the
United States, the Soviet Union had ended its period of domestic and foreign readjustment and was now moving from defense to offense. They also
proved that Moscow posed an invasion threat to China. Mao believed that
the Soviet Union had become a "social imperialist" country—socialist in
words but imperialist in deeds. Hence, it was more aggressive and adventurist
than the United States, validating Mao's judgment in the mid-1960s that the
greatest threat to China's national security was likely to come from the north.

Following the Soviet invasion of Czechoslovakia, Mao frequently reassessed the possibility of a war. On October 5, 1968, in a talk with the Albanian minister of defense, he pointed out, "It seems there is still going to be
disorder all over the world because contradictions and struggles exist. The
question is what the disorder will be like. It is still hard to say." Mao believed

that there were two possibilities. One was world war, the other, local war, such as the Soviet invasion of Czechoslovakia. "We do not wish to fight a war, but if they want to fight, we will have to fight, too."[66] On November 28, Mao raised the question of the danger of a world war with E. F. Hill, chair of the Communist Party (Marxist-Leninist) of Australia. Mao believed that the current situation, neither war nor revolution, could endure for an extended period. If there was going to be a war, the Soviet Union and the United States might be the ones to start it, yet they feared nuclear war. Alternatively, such defeated powers as Japan or West Germany or Italy might start one, but Mao was doubtful. As for Britain and France, Mao did not believe that they sought war. Thus, the current, post–Second World War situation was different from that after the First World War, in which the threat of war had remained high.[67]

Mao Zedong realized the seriousness of China's diplomatic straits prior to the Ninth National Party Congress in April 1969. On March 15, he met with the members of the Cultural Revolution Leading Group and with Chen Yi, Li Fuchun, Li Xiannian, Xu Xiangqian, Nie Rongzhen, Ye Jianying, and other leaders. For the first time he admitted that "now we are isolated, and no one shows interest in us."[68] On July 13, 1970, in a meeting with a French government delegation, he said, "Countries like ours are squeezed between the two big powers," and he compared such a situation to a "sandwich." The French guests pointed out the one thing that must be prevented: united action between the United States and the Soviet Union against China. Mao appreciated this remark.[69]

Mao believed that the U.S.-Soviet struggle for spheres of influence was irreconcilable. He also saw the weakness in U.S. strategy: "The United States has taken too wide an area as its sphere of control. It wants to rule over Asia and it wants to rule over Europe, the Middle East, and Africa, in addition to ruling over its own people."[70] In America's strategic predicament, he perceived an opening for Chinese diplomacy. As he said to Zhou Enlai and other Chinese diplomats, "Of the two superpowers, we must win one over. We must not fight on two fronts."[71]

BREAKING OPEN THE CLOSED DOOR TO SINO-U.S. RELATIONS

The first important post–Cultural Revolution national security issue addressed by the Central Committee and Chairman Mao was the prevention of a large-scale invasion by the Soviet Union. The Zhenbao Island incident in 1969 pushed the danger of a large-scale armed conflict between China and the Soviet Union to the top of the leadership agenda. Soon there were reports that the Soviet Union would launch an air attack on China's Lop Nor Nuclear Test Base. China responded by shifting its strategic focus from defense in the south to defense in the north.

The Political Report of the Ninth National Congress of the CCP in April 1969 stated, "We must not ignore the danger of the United States imperialists' and the Soviet revisionists' launching a large-scale war of aggression. We must be fully prepared against their unleashing of a massive war, be prepared against their starting it at an early date, be prepared against their starting a conventional war, and also be prepared against their starting a massive nuclear war." Although the report observed that both superpowers threatened China, Mao was preoccupied with the Soviet threat. At a meeting of the Cultural Revolution Leading Group on March 15, Mao had ordered that "the Northeast, the North, and the Northwest should make some preparations. It doesn't matter if we get prepared and they don't come. With the dangerous enemy looming in front of us, it would be advantageous if we get mobilized and prepared." He also commented, "We adopt the policy of gaining the upper hand by letting the enemy strike first. Our atomic bases should be prepared against their bombardment from the air."[72]

On May 24, in a statement on the border conflict with the Soviet Union, China proposed negotiations to work out a solution. On September 11, Zhou Enlai met with Aleksei Kosygin. The two leaders agreed that "the long-pending Sino-Soviet border question should be resolved through peaceful negotiations under conditions of absence of any threats; before the solution, both sides shall adopt provisional measures to maintain the status quo of the border and avoid armed conflict." During this meeting, Zhou asked Kosygin whether Moscow would use nuclear weapons to bomb China's nuclear facilities: "You said that you want to launch a preemptive strike . . . ; if you do this, we will declare that this is war, that this is aggression, and we will resolutely put up resistance to the end. But we hope this does not happen and thus I want to tell you our position." But Kosygin did not reply and did not clarify the matter.[73] Thus, Chinese leaders remained on high alert for a Soviet attack. Several days later, on September 17, in its slogan for the twentieth anniversary of the founding of the PRC, the Chinese government declared to the world its determination to prepare for a nuclear war.[74]

Following the Zhenbao Island incident, Mao aimed to ease Sino-Soviet tensions and avoid an armed clash. But the border situation also encouraged Chinese leaders to consider whether the United States might cooperate with China to cope with the Soviet threat. To end China's two-front threat, Mao, with Zhou's assistance, sought reduced Sino-U.S. tensions and an international united front against Soviet hegemony.

On October 20, 1969, Sino-Soviet boundary negotiations began. The head of the Soviet delegation was Vice Minister of Foreign Affairs Vasily Kuznetsov, and of the Chinese delegation, Vice Minister of Foreign Affairs Qiao Guanhua. Zhou Enlai followed the negotiations closely and prepared timely reports for Mao Zedong. He also instructed the Xinhua News Agency to keep Chinese leaders informed of the attitudes of other countries toward the negotiations. He wanted a great deal of information quickly and demanded several reports each day. Chinese leaders paid especially close attention to U.S. attitudes toward the negotiations. Chinese negotiators later recalled that at each daily briefing, Zhou first inquired about U.S. reactions.[75]

Mao and Zhou realized that major changes were taking place in Sino-U.S. and Sino-Soviet relations.[76] They corrected erroneous views of U.S.-Soviet relations, emphasizing the contentious situation between the United States and the Soviet Union while opposing superpower collaboration.[77] This reflected their effort to reduce border tensions while seeking normalization of Sino-U.S. relations. China's first step to open U.S.-China relations was its November 26, 1968, proposal to Washington to resume ambassadorial-level talks in Warsaw. On November 29, Lyndon Johnson, the outgoing president, with the agreement of president-elect Richard Nixon, accepted China's proposal. Although the actual resumption of the talks was delayed, this was the first sign of détente in Sino-U.S. relations. Mao's second step toward rapprochement with the United States was to direct four Chinese marshals to assess the global order, China's strategic environment, and Sino-U.S. relations. On February 19, 1969, he proposed that Marshal Chen Yi head this group, which included Marshals Xu Xiangqian, Nie Rongzhen, and Ye Jianying. He repeated his proposal in March and April, underscoring the importance he attached to it.

The four marshals worked from March through October 1969, concluding that the contradiction between China and the Soviet Union was greater than that between China and the United States and that the contradiction between the United States and the Soviet Union was greater than that between China and the Soviet Union. They observed that a large-scale war against China was unlikely but that China should take advantage of the contradictions between the United States, the Soviet Union, and the European countries. It should resume the Sino-U.S. ambassadorial-level talks and end its stalemate with the United States as quickly as possible.

On July 21, 1969, the United States canceled certain trade sanctions against China and relaxed limitations on travel to China. In December, the United States ambassador to Warsaw, on orders from President Nixon, proposed resuming the ambassadorial-level talks. Mao quickly agreed, and on January 20, 1970, after an interruption of over two years, the talks resumed.

Mao's third step toward resumption of Sino-U.S. relations was to work toward a China visit by a U.S. leader. On July 26, 1969, Zhou Enlai received from Samdech Norodom Sihanouk a letter from Senator Mike Mansfield written at the encouragement of President Nixon. Mansfield asked to visit China to meet with Zhou and discuss Sino-U.S. relations. During this period, Nixon also signaled his interest in improved relations with China through France, Pakistan, and Romania. He stated that the United States did not support the Soviet proposal for an "Asian Collective Security System" and would not participate in any action designed to isolate China. The United States also ceased its U.S. naval patrols of the Taiwan Strait and informed Beijing of this decision in October ,through the Pakistan channel.

On November 16, 1969, Zhou gave Mao the telegram relaying Nixon's oral message conveyed by Pakistani President Agha Mohammad Yahya Khan. Then, on December 2, Zhou asked Khwaja Mohammad Kaiser, the Pakistani ambassador to China, to request that President Agha Mohammad Yahya Khan report to Nixon that the United States could use Pakistan as a channel for communicating with China.[78] On November 7, 1969, the Ministry of Foreign Affairs prepared a report proposing that China release Baldwin and Donald, two Americans who had been arrested for entering Chinese waters near Hong Kong, which Zhou submitted to Mao Zedong and Lin Biao on December 4. It said that "through discussions by the comrades of the Political Bureau in Beijing, we intend to agree to the proposal of the Ministry of Foreign Affairs about setting free the two Americans riding in a yacht. The time is the seventh day of the month or later." Mao approved the proposal immediately.[79]

During the next year, Mao encouraged progress toward rapprochement. On December 18, 1970, he told Edgar Snow that a high-level meeting was necessary to open Sino-U.S. relations. He said that Nixon "had early on written numerous letters to various people saying that he would send an envoy here, but we didn't make the letters public. We had to keep the secret! He is not interested in those talks in Warsaw, Poland, and wants to come and talk to us face to face. So, I said that if Nixon is willing to come, I am also willing to talk with him. It's all right if the talks succeed, and if they fail, it's all right, too. It's all right if we quarrel, and it's all right, too, if we don't. Whether he comes to talk as a tourist, or as the United States president, both are all right. In a word, any way he comes, it's all right."[80]

But after the United States escalated the war in Indochina by invading Cambodia, progress halted. China declared that it would not bargain over the interests of its friends and that a breakthrough in Sino-U.S. relations was impossible when Washington threatened China's security. Once the United States withdrew from Cambodia, however, progress resumed. In April 1971, Mao directed that the U.S. table-tennis team in Japan be invited to China, using the "little ball" to push the "big ball" (meaning global strategy) along. Then, from July 9 to 11, 1971, Kissinger secretly visited China, and from February 21 to 28, 1972, President Nixon visited China. The first Sino-U.S. summit meeting was held and the Shanghai Communiqué was announced.

These changes in Chinese foreign policy reflected a renewed pragmatism in China's domestic politics. In turn, the success of China's U.S. policy created a favorable external environment for easing domestic politics. It raised the position of Zhou Enlai and his allies in decision making and helped to restrain the leftist activities of Jiang Qing and others. In addition, improved U.S.-China relations fostered a pragmatic reexamination of domestic class relations and contributed to a more relaxed social atmosphere. In this context, observing the tremendous gap between China and the West in productive power and in scientific and technological levels, the Chinese people began to turn their attention away from ideological movements and toward support for Deng Xiaoping's efforts to reform China's political and economic system.

Nevertheless, China's diplomacy remained constrained by domestic politics. Because China was still immersed in the Cultural Revolution and Mao still adhered to the theory of "continuing the revolution under the dictatorship of the proletariat," foreign policy could not fully return to the path of the 1950s, when diplomacy was used to encourage domestic economic development. Although Mao seemed to support the pragmatic policies proposed by Zhou Enlai and Deng Xiaoping, radical leftists supported by Mao remained critical of these policies.

IMPORTANT CHANGES IN THE POLITICAL OBSTACLES TO SINO-U.S. RELATIONS

In the process of normalizing relations with the United States, China achieved important policy objectives. First, Washington gradually abandoned its policy of containment and its economic blockade of China. And as the Nixon administration worked to extricate the United States from Vietnam, it was acutely aware of China's strategic importance. As Nixon observed in the October 23, 1967, issue of *Foreign Affairs*, "Any U.S. policy on Asia must be closely geared to the reality of China." Mao offered a similar assessment. When Kissinger remarked to Mao, in 1971, that the United States had no favor to ask of China strategically, Mao said pointblank: "It is not true that the United States has no favor to ask of China. Neither is it true that China has no favor to ask of the United States. Otherwise, why are we sitting here together?"[81]

Second, China defeated U.S. efforts to isolate and contain it and returned to its legal seat in the United Nations. In the early 1960s, Mao had said, "For Western countries, China doesn't seem to exist, and yet it seems to be there all the same."[82] On November 20, 1970, a majority of the Twenty-fifth Session of the U.N. General Assembly voted in support of China's resumption of its seat in the U.N. On October 25, 1971, an overwhelming two-thirds majority of the Twenty-sixth General Assembly voted for China to regain its seat. Although Washington opposed the motion, it had given up its effort to isolate China.

Third, the Taiwan question underwent a major change. During his first visit to China, Kissinger said that the United States did not support "two Chinas" or "one China, one Taiwan." He said that the United States recognized that Taiwan was part of China and that it did not support Taiwan's independence. When Zhou briefed Mao on Kissinger's position, Mao said of U.S. policy, "Man has evolved from the monkey, yet with a tail. The Taiwan question will have a tail." Although the Shanghai Communiqué did not meet all of China's demands, Washington had begun to abandon its Taiwan policy.

Mao Zedong's Idealism, Domestic Factors, and Chinese Diplomacy

As China's chief policymaker, Mao Zedong challenged China's domestic order as well as its international environment. He tried to change the bipolar postwar pattern of superpower domination by strengthening China's own strategic position. Mao had always challenged the status quo—an essential characteristic that permeated his life—both in China and in the world, and his strategy thus merged China's domestic and foreign policy. His policies reflected rational considerations, but they also reflected emotion, a combination characteristic of Mao's idealism. Although this idealism enabled him to achieve military success during the revolution, during the post-1949 era of peaceful development the contradiction between revolutionary idealism and revolutionary realism remained unreconciled.

Domestically, Mao aimed to create a modern, egalitarian society in which material incentives, economic justice, and idealism coexisted. But rather than acknowledge the contradictions in his policies, he instead became suspicious that China's leaders had developed vested interests and become revisionists. Changes in the post-Stalinist Soviet Union reinforced his suspicions. He chose "to continue the revolution" rather than to accept the status quo and directed his political power against Liu Shaoqi and other "revisionist" leaders.

Mao's idealist domestic policy influenced his foreign policy. On the one hand, he accepted Lenin's thesis that this was the era of the end of imperialism and of the proletarian revolution leading to the high tide of socialist revolution. On the other hand, he had to acknowledge that in the postwar period, socialism was on the defensive and capitalism was relatively stable. He also faced the contradiction between his ambitious strategic goals and China's limited national strength.

But Mao believed that no existing order remained unchanged, and he sought a force that would shake the existing order. He found it in Third World national independence and national liberation movements, which would be the main revolutionary force in international politics, just as peasants had been the main revolutionary force in the Chinese revolution. Mao extended his theory of revolution—"surround the cities with the countryside"—to the world, and it formed the basis for the "intermediate zone" and ultimately, for his theory of three worlds in the 1970s. Mao's idealism led China in the early 1960s to support national independence and national liberation movements in the Third World as elements of the global revolutionary movement.[83] Mao opposed the bipolar postwar system established at Yalta, especially its impact on Chinese security.[84] He first struggled against U.S.-led embargo and containment policies while resisting Soviet control, but after Sino-Soviet relations deteriorated in the 1960s, China's support for national independence and national liberation movements served its efforts to seek strategic support apart from both superpowers.

But Mao's attempts to combine national independence and national liberation movements with the socialist revolutionary movement failed, and in the 1970s he abandoned them.[85] In their place, he sought a strategic international united front against Soviet hegemony.[86] Frustrated by the contradiction between idealism and reality, he finally made the realistic choice to develop a united front, although he refused to confront the contradiction between realism and idealism.[87] This denial made it possible for him to shift from strategic confrontation with the United States to strategic cooperation.

The contradiction between idealism and realism influenced Mao's perspective on war, peace, and revolution.[88] He was convinced that the only way to eliminate war was to "use war to oppose war" and that "revolution prevents war." Later, he would argue that "war leads to revolution" and that "revolution prevents war."[89] As the arms race between the United States and the Soviet Union escalated, Mao's idealism influenced his thinking on nuclear war; "If they want to fight, it will be as if an atomic bomb has been placed on top of our head. If it explodes, it will blow a huge hole from China to the United States. This earth is not so large. As far as I know, the diameter of the earth is only 12,500 kilometers or more. There is nothing so terrible if a hole is blown. By that time, I think they will be in trouble."[90]

Later, he said, "we are not afraid if half our people die. This is the worst outcome."[91] Regarding nuclear war, he had already insisted, "First, we are against it; second, we are not afraid of it."[92] Although he argued that nuclear weapons were merely a tool of the Soviet Union and the United States to intimidate other countries, he also believed that as long as there was imperialism, war would exist, and thus a new world war was inevitable.[93] Ultimately, however, as the country's political leader, he needed to promote a peaceful foreign relations environment for domestic development.[94] He needed to be realistic, and in the late 1960s, in response to the Soviet threat, Mao decided to normalize relations with the United States.

During the early 1960s, following the Tenth Plenary Session of the Eighth Central Committee in 1962 and the escalation of Sino-Soviet polemics, China opposed peaceful coexistence and revisionism. By stressing international class struggle, however, it denied itself opportunities for compromise and cooperation and attacked any country that maintained close relations with the Soviet Union or the United States as reactionary.[95] With the broadening of domestic class struggle, many contradictions among the Chinese people were handled through class struggle; with the broadening of class struggle in diplomatic relations, many middle-of-the-road forces that might have been won over were attacked indiscriminately. China thus blockaded and isolated itself.[96] But encouraged by Zhou Enlai and other leaders, and prompted by deteriorating international circumstances, Mao faced reality. He abandoned revolutionary slogans and acknowledged strategic trends and the aspirations of developing countries. He thus proposed the theory of the three worlds to correct the influence of class struggle and of "continuing the revolution" through diplomacy. Despite the theory's ideological rhetoric, China's diplomacy gradually moved from ideological struggle to the pursuit of national interests.

Maoist idealism, combined with Mao's dominant role in domestic politics, meant that throughout the entire post-1949 period, China's changing domestic policies influenced its diplomatic efforts. During the 1950s, when pragmatism dominated Mao's policy agenda, China concentrated on economic development. In this context, Chinese diplomacy aimed to ease peripheral relations and relieve international tensions. Even during the Great Leap Forward, China's domestic focus was on economic development and, through peaceful competition in international politics, on demonstrating to the world that the "east wind prevailed over the west wind."

But in the 1960s and throughout the Cultural Revolution—despite economic difficulties, Sino-Soviet conflict, and domestic social and political instability—under Mao's idealist policy guidelines Chinese leaders focused on class struggle and on "combating and preventing revisionism." The radicalization of domestic policy also radicalized foreign policy. China overemphasized the danger of war and struggled against revisionists and imperialists simultaneously, creating a "two front" situation. Its diplomacy exhibited toughness but insufficient flexibility, which undermined its ability to maneuver. In its foreign propaganda, China placed itself at the center of the world.

"Things are sure to reverse themselves when they have gone to an extreme." In the latter half of the 1960s, when Mao decided to reestablish control and correct the mistakes inspired by the slogans "strike down all" and "all-round civil war," China's diplomacy returned to moderation and pragmatism, facilitating Sino-U.S. rapprochement. However, even then, Mao's idealism was reflected in the continued interference of the ultra-leftist forces of the Cultural Revolution in diplomacy. Final change occurred only in the post-Mao era and after the Third Plenary Session of the Eleventh Central Committee, when pragmatism replaced idealism, China returned to economic development as its central task, and its foreign policy, including its policy toward the United States, focused on the national interest. Deng Xiaoping explained the importance of a national-interest-based foreign policy to post-Mao China during his meeting with Richard Nixon in October 1989, when Sino-U.S. relations confronted serious obstacles: "I appreciate very much your views that, in determining relations between two countries, each party should proceed from his country's own strategic interests. I too think that each country should proceed from its own long-term strategic interests, and at the same time respect the interests of the other. Each country, whether it is big or small, strong or weak, should respect others as equals, giving no thought to old scores or to differences in social systems and ideologies. In this way, all problems can be properly solved. But it takes courage to use this approach. So you were not only wise but courageous to visit China in 1972. I know that you are an anti-Communist, while I am a Communist. Nevertheless, in studying and handling problems, both of us place the highest importance on the national interest. In dealing with a major question like this, both of us are realistic, broad-minded, and respectful of each other."[97]

The lesson of China's policy toward the United States from the late 1950s through rapprochement in the 1970s and into the post-Mao era is clear. China's domestic policy agenda has consistently influenced China's foreign policy. When China has pursued pragmatic domestic policies, it has made economic development its foremost priority and employed a pragmatic foreign policy to promote a peaceful international environment. Such diplomacy has not only contributed to China's economic development, it has also greatly increased China's security and its influence in the world. Such was the case throughout most of the 1950s and, even more, from the late Maoist period to the present.

CHAPTER ELEVEN

Chinese Decision Making
and the Thawing of U.S.-China Relations

Gong Li

THIS ESSAY IS AN ANALYSIS of the historical process of China-U.S. rapprochement from the perspective of China's chief decision makers. It examines the decision-making process during the period of rapprochement, analyzes the factors contributing to this process, and explains the dramatic readjustment of China's U.S. policy. It then describes in detail the major policies, methods, and steps adopted by China in the process of rapprochement to transform its relations with the United States and offers a general assessment of the decision-making process regarding relations with the United States.

The Policy-Making Process during the Cultural Revolution

The Cultural Revolution, which began in 1966, disrupted domestic law and order and brought about tremendous changes in elite decision making. During the Cultural Revolution, Chairman Mao Zedong's arbitrariness increased. He would not tolerate any difference of opinion, thus undermining democratic decision making and the leadership of Liu Shaoqi and Deng Xiaoping, who had handled the routine work of the Party.[1] In effect, Mao abolished the Politburo and the Secretariat and severely weakened the Mao

Zedong-Zhou Enlai foreign policy system. As he weakened the authority of the Party leadership, Mao turned to the Cultural Revolution Leading Group as his personal cabinet. In the latter half of 1966, Cultural Revolution Leading Group meetings replaced Politburo meetings in handling major national issues.[2] Zhou was responsible for briefing Mao on the results of such meetings. Jiang Qing, the deputy leader of the group, also briefed Mao.

Within the leadership, there were pragmatists, led by Zhou Enlai, and two ultra-leftist factions, represented by Lin Biao and Jiang Qing, respectively. In the early stages of the Cultural Revolution, Zhou Enlai maintained a significant influence in foreign affairs, but leftist leaders in the Leading Group opposed his influence. As they became more influential in decision making, they intervened in Foreign Ministry affairs, using the disruptions during the January 1967 seizure of local political power. Their main objective was to topple Zhou Enlai and his Foreign Ministry supporters.

On August 7, 1967, Wang Li, an important member of the Leading Group, summoned "rebel" representatives of the Foreign Ministry to Diaoyutai,[3] where he incited them to repudiate Chen Yi, the foreign minister, and take control of the ministry. Wang said that "the general orientation of ferreting out Chen Yi is certainly right. Why cannot he be ferreted out?" He told the rebels that "Since it is a revolution on such a large scale, it will not do not to change the leadership. Why cannot the leaders be removed?" Further encouraging chaos, he said, "What is so secret and mysterious? Anything that is not favorable to the revolution will have to be done away with. Rigid stratification must be repudiated and transformed."[4] When the speech was relayed to lower Foreign Ministry officials, the ministry erupted in chaos. Then, on August 16, 1967, the rebels imprisoned vice foreign ministers Ji Pengfei and Qiao Guanhua in a basement and seized control. The rebels obeyed orders from the Cultural Revolution Leading Group without consulting Zhou Enlai or even Mao. They soon issued orders and directives to overseas embassies, causing serious repercussions.

On August 22, under the pretext of protesting persecution of patriotic Hong Kong journalists by the British-Hong Kong authority, the Foreign Ministry presented a note to the British chargé d'affaires in Beijing containing belligerent demands. That night, rebels from the Beijing Foreign Languages Institute, together with rebels from ten other organizations, demonstrated in front of the office of the British chargé d'affaires, holding a "denunciation meeting against the British imperialists for the crimes committed against China."

Immediately after the rally, knowing that the British-Hong Kong authority had failed to respond to the Foreign Ministry's note, the Red Guards broke into the office and set it on fire.

Following the takeover of the Foreign Ministry and the burning of the office of the British chargé d'affaires, Mao and Zhou stepped in to restore order. On August 25, Zhou asked Yang Chengwu to carry the minutes of Wang Li's August 7 speech to Mao, who was then in Shanghai.[5] After a briefing on August 26, Mao told Yang that "Wang, Guan, and Qi aim to damage the Cultural Revolution and are not good guys. You go and report only to the premier that they be arrested. Ask the premier to do it."[6] He wrote that Wang's speech was a "big, big, big poisonous weed." He told Yang, "Handle Qi at a later date."[7] Later that day, Yang briefed Zhou on Mao's instructions. Zhou then presided over a Central Leading Group meeting and relayed Mao's decision. Wang Li and Guan Feng were detained for examination immediately, and Qi Benyu in January 1968. The attempt by the Jiang Qing clique to control the Foreign Ministry had failed. The radical influence on foreign affairs soon declined, and Zhou Enlai once again managed policy, reporting directly to Mao and the Politburo.

To draw lessons from the chaos, Zhou proposed pinpointing and criticizing ultra-leftist ideas and rectifying discipline in foreign affairs. Mao agreed. On March 15, 1968, at a Cultural Revolution Leading Group meeting and at a talk with Chen Yi, Li Fuchun, Li Xiannian, Xu Xiangqian, and Ye Jianying, he said, "We are now isolated. No one wants to make friends with us."[8] On May 16, Mao criticized the slogan "Beijing as the center of the world revolution" and insisted that "Chinese should not say such things. It is the erroneous idea of the so-called 'making ourselves the core.'"[9] Then, on May 29, in response to a Foreign Ministry proposal concerning the dissemination of his thought and support for mass struggle in Western Europe and North America, he wrote, "First, please take care not to force our views on others; second, do not issue propaganda that people's movements in foreign countries are influenced by China. Such propaganda will be used by the reactionaries and will be harmful to popular movements."[10]

On May 1, 1969, Mao received a number of foreign envoys at the Tiananmen rostrum and conveyed to them that China sought improved relations. China's envoys, who had been recalled to China to take part in the Cultural Revolution, then returned to their posts. Chinese leaders also explained to foreign guests that the radical diplomatic acts in the summer of

1967 were the responsibility of misguided persons who had infiltrated the Foreign Ministry, and that they did not represent Chinese intentions.[11]

In April 1969, as the first stage of the Cultural Revolution came to an end, the Ninth Party Congress met and elected a new Central Committee and Politburo. This ended control by the Cultural Revolution Leading Group and restored authority to the Politburo. But because important members of the Leading Group and of Lin Biao's clique had joined the Politburo, decision making remained complicated. Thus, the Politburo's authority was much less than it had been before the Cultural Revolution, and collective leadership was significantly weakened. Moreover, although Mao rarely participated in Politburo meetings, important policy decisions still required his approval.

In this domestic political context, as the easing of China-U.S. tensions was placed on the leadership agenda, China's organizational procedures remained complex. The Foreign Ministry, policy study departments, Xinhua News Agency, and military each separately provided Mao, Zhou, and other important leaders with analyses of and policy proposals concerning diplomatic and military affairs as well as foreign agency news dispatches on the international situation and relations among the United States, the Soviet Union, and China. Despite their ideological extremism and their tendency to cater to Mao's perspectives, these materials contained relatively reliable information and were of considerable value.

Zhou Enlai, with support from his chief advisers, including Ye Jianying, Huang Hua, Zhang Wenjin, and Xiong Xianghui, was China's chief foreign policy official. He received Foreign Ministry briefings and reports, including various policy proposals. Although Zhou possessed significant authority over policy toward the United States, on major issues he would consult with the Politburo, and he frequently needed to seek Mao's ideas and approval.

Mao and Zhou were the driving forces in U.S.-China rapprochement, but they were not independent of the Politburo. The Politburo discussed major issues and developed policy options, subject to Mao's approval. During rapprochement with the United States, it convened many meetings to formulate policies and strategies. For example, in December 1969, the Politburo members in Beijing held intense discussions of the Foreign Ministry proposal to release two American tourists, who had entered Chinese territorial waters. On February 12, 1970, the Politburo convened to discuss, and consequently revise, the speech to be made at the 136th Sino-U.S.

ambassadorial-level talks, strengthening its signaling of China's interest in opening relations. On May 16, 1970, following the U.S. invasion of Cambodia, the Politburo met to discuss Foreign Ministry policy options and decided to postpone the Sino-U.S. talks in Warsaw scheduled for May 20. A month later, on June 16, the Politburo once again decided to postpone the Sino-U.S. ambassadorial-level talks. On May 26, 1971, the Politburo drew up an eight-point policy and strategy report on U.S.-China relations. On March 1, 1972, it convened to evaluate the outcome of Nixon's visit to China and made a report to Mao.

Because the Cultural Revolution had disrupted normal procedures, the initial proposal to ease Sino-U.S. tensions originated not from subordinate foreign affairs and policy study departments but from the top leadership, who instructed relevant departments to study its feasibility. The political climate of the Cultural Revolution had blocked free discussion. Diplomats, fearful of committing an ideological mistake on the sensitive issue of U.S.-China relations, did not dare to express genuine ideas. Moreover, the influence of leftist ideas had contributed to ossified thinking.

In this context, Mao and other Chinese leaders depended on Zhou Enlai, the military agencies, and the Xinhua News Agency for information and analysis. Influential materials included Zhou Enlai's report on China's participation in the Thirty-first World Table Tennis Championship; the Foreign Ministry proposal that China postpone the China-U.S. talks because of the U.S. invasion of Cambodia and that Chairman Mao issue a statement on the invasion (which was eventually drafted by the ministry, the Xinhua News Agency, and the *People's Daily* and released after receiving Mao's approval); the analysis of the international situation by the four vice-chairmen of the military commission, including Ye Jianying and Xiong Xianghui, vice director of the Second Department of the General Staff; and foreign agency news dispatches and other reference material translated in *Reference News* (*Dacankao*), edited by the Xinhua News Agency.

Regarding China's policy toward the United States, Mao laid special emphasis on strategic planning, while Zhou stressed specific planning details and operations. Although they shared a general understanding of U.S. policy, they might disagree on certain issues. One important difference between them concerned the implications of U.S.-Soviet détente for China. Zhou believed that the June 1973 Nixon-Brezhnev summit and the "Soviet American Agreement on the Prevention of War" were important events requiring special attention. Against this background, Lin Ping, head of the Foreign

Ministry's Department of North America and Oceania, conferred with Zhang Zai, head of the department's section on the United States, and Tian Zengpei, an official in the Soviet division of the ministry's Department of the Soviet Union and Eastern Europe. The result was a research article by Zhang Zai entitled "The Nixon-Brezhnev Talks: A Tentative Opinion," published in the department's internal journal *New Situations* (issue no. 135). It argued that greater U.S.-Soviet cooperation created an atmosphere in which U.S.-Soviet dominance of the world was "more conspicuous." Zhou Enlai thought highly of the article and instructed that the Foreign Ministry's *Foreign Affairs Bulletin* follow this line of thinking.

But Mao dismissed this analysis of U.S.-Soviet relations as "taking it at its face value, while failing to touch the crux of the matter." In Mao's opinion, although the Nixon-Brezhnev summit appeared successful, it concealed the essential rivalry in U.S.-Soviet relations. Furthermore, America's strategic focus had not moved eastward but remained on Europe: "The year of Europe! It is what they themselves said."[12] Thus, Mao believed that China could still use U.S.-Soviet rivalry to its advantage. As a result, when the Politburo convened to discuss the issue, Zhou Enlai made a self-criticism (*ziwo piping*) and claimed responsibility for the consequences. Then Zhou summoned his aides in the ministry and drew up the report "What is wrong with issue no. 135 of *New Situations*" and had it submitted to Mao, who accepted Zhou's assessment.

Mao and Zhou also disagreed over the Taiwan issue. In November 1973, after Kissinger's sixth visit to China, Mao, basing his thinking on unreliable briefings by the radical faction within the Politburo, thought Zhou Enlai was too soft on the Taiwan issue. The Politburo convened on several occasions between the end of November and early December to discuss the matter. Zhou was criticized. Jiang Qing and other members of the Gang of Four used this opportunity to attack Zhou, referring to the episode as "the eleventh two-line struggle." They accused Zhou of being the "chief of the wrong line," who "just cannot wait to replace Mao Zedong." Mao, after receiving a briefing on the meeting, believed that the criticism was quite necessary but argued that Jiang Qing had gone too far. He declared, "Something is wrong with what has been said on the matter." He said that Jiang's accusation regarding "the eleventh two-line struggle" was "not actually true" and that she was wrong to accuse Zhou of being too impatient. "He is not what he is accused of. In fact, it is she who just cannot wait."[13] Thus, Zhou survived the crisis.

The role of Lin Biao and the Gang of Four in easing relations with the United States was complex. On the one hand, they opposed rapprochement, contending that China should not kowtow to the "American imperialist." They also resented the increased domestic authority accorded to Zhou as a result of his importance in China's U.S. policy. According to the memoirs of Zhang Yunsheng, former secretary to Lin Biao, Lin Biao said in private that Zhou Enlai would suffer from establishing ties with Americans. When Alexander Haig visited China in 1972, paving the way for the visit by Richard Nixon, Jiang Qing directed Minister of Culture Yu Huiyong not to publicize Nixon's China trip on television. On the other hand, Lin Biao and Jiang Qing knew that the decision to relax tensions was Mao's, and that Mao had never authorized Jiang and her supporters to assume authority from Zhou for policy toward the United States. Thus, they did not dare oppose improved U.S.-China relations openly.

Nonetheless, Lin Biao and Jiang Qing did influence decision making. When discussing and implementing decisions, Zhou Enlai and other leaders were always very careful, as if walking on thin ice. Indeed, not only Zhou but also Deng Xiaoping (who replaced Zhou in negotiations with the United States after Zhou was hospitalized) encountered interference. During the 1974 campaign against Lin Biao and Confucius, for example, Jiang Qing and her allies attacked Zhou Enlai's policy of "making friends with those from afar and attacking those on the border" by comparing Zhou to Confucius. Similarly, in the 1976 campaign against Deng Xiaoping and his alleged "right-deviationist wind to reverse verdicts" policy, Jiang Qing remarked at a high-level cadre meeting that "Deng Xiaoping has gone too far in foreign affairs; [and on the Taiwan issue] Deng Xiaoping is always apple-polishing Bush." She also accused Deng of being "a traitor to China, representing the comprador bourgeoisie."[14]

International Factors in China's U.S. Policy

In the late 1960s and early 1970s, a number of important changes in China's international strategic situation encouraged Chinese leaders to adjust their policy toward the United States. By the end of the 1960s it was clear that China could no longer sustain simultaneous confrontation with the two superpowers. In the context of U.S.-China hostility, Sino-Soviet relations had deteriorated. Although objective conflicts of interests had developed, Sino-Soviet tension also reflected the impact of growing leftist tendencies in

Chinese policymaking. During this period, Mao overruled proposals made by Wang Jiaxiang, the director of the International Liaison Department of the CCP Central Committee, and others to improve China's foreign relations so that China could concentrate on domestic difficulties. But Mao maintained rigid opposition to "imperialists, revisionists, and reactionaries."[15]

In these circumstances, China held U.S.-China relations hostage to U.S. policy toward Taiwan and overreacted in its polemic assaults on the Soviet Union, leaving itself no room for maneuver. By the end of the 1960s, China faced trouble at home and abroad. Not only did its weak and deteriorating position in relation to the superpowers limit its policy options and undermine national security, but the domestic disorder associated with the Cultural Revolution disrupted relations with many countries. It was now clear to Chinese leaders that China could no longer endure hostility from both superpowers simultaneously and that it was necessary to make use of the rivalry between the Soviet Union and the United States. Mao later said, "We have to win over one of the two superpowers; we cannot wage a war on two fronts."[16]

Just as China's strategic environment began to deteriorate, strategic retrenchment in the United States relieved international pressure on China. In the late 1960s, as the United States became more deeply involved in the Vietnam War, it concluded that it had overextended itself. It thus decided to reduce its strategic commitments in Asia and to revise its strategy of preparing to fight two and a half major wars simultaneously. President Nixon's speech in Guam in 1969 reflected these changes. Meanwhile, there were other indications that Washington was easing its economic blockade and containment policies. These changes in U.S. strategy toward Asia and the ensuing shifts in its China policy reduced the U.S. threat to China from the southwest and encouraged China's interest in adjusting its own policy toward the United States.

Strategic overextension and problems in Vietnam had compelled the United States to reevaluate its China policy. American leaders now understood the importance of having "contact with . . . one quarter of humanity."[17] Moreover, in its competition with the Soviet Union, the United States thought that China could be an "asset." Nixon believed that he could rely on the U.S. relationship with China to give him a favorable position in negotiating with the Soviet Union.[18] Nixon later wrote, "The most pressing foreign problem I would have to deal with as soon as I became President was the war in Vietnam."[19] To manage its Vietnam problem, the United States would have to deal with China, since China provided crucial support to Hanoi. In Nixon's words, "The heart of the problem lay more in Beijing and Moscow than in Hanoi."[20]

In China's view, improved U.S.-China relations would assist China in countering the Soviet threat as well as in making progress on the Taiwan issue and the Vietnam War. Improved relations with the United States would also clear away obstacles to improved relations with other countries and end China's passive diplomatic position. Later, in commenting on the signing of the Shanghai Communiqué, Zhou Enlai pointed out, "This is a breakthrough in the sense that more and more countries are willing to make friends with us. And this is where China and the U.S. have gained in establishing a relationship."[21]

Yet, although the U.S. threat to China declined, Sino-Soviet tension intensified, and the Soviet Union replaced the United States as China's primary adversary. In the late 1960s, Moscow took advantage of U.S. difficulties in Vietnam to increase its military capabilities and pursue international expansion. This expansion of Soviet military power not only challenged U.S. spheres of influence but also constituted a growing military threat to China along the seven-thousand kilometer Sino-Soviet border.

As Sino-Soviet relations deteriorated, the Soviet Union provoked several border clashes and sided with India over Sino-Indian border conflicts, leading Mao to consider the possibility of a full-scale Soviet attack. In 1964, in a series of talks with Kim Il Sung, Choi Yong-gun, Baruku, and other foreign guests, Mao asked, "Will Khrushchev attack us?" and "Will he possibly send troops to occupy Xinjiang and Heilongjiang?" He concluded, "We must get ready for it."[22] But the situation only worsened throughout the 1960s as Moscow reinforced its forces along the Sino-Soviet and Sino-Mongolian borders and signed a treaty of friendship and cooperation with Mongolia, suggesting a military alliance directed against China. On January 5, 1968, Soviet troops invaded Qilixin Island on the Chinese side of the Ussuri River, causing casualties to Chinese soldiers. Four Chinese fishermen were reportedly crushed by Soviet armored vehicles, and another nine injured.

In response to these circumstances, on January 24, 1968, the CCP Central Military Commission ordered PLA units in Shenyang and Beijing "to strengthen the defense in the eastern section of the Sino-Soviet border and militarily prepare to play a supporting role in political and diplomatic struggles." The commission emphasized that "to resort to any kind of self-defense, you must see to it that courteous and peaceful means precede military actions and that counterattacks are kept within Chinese territory." It ordered border units "to choose the most politically opportune time, location, and circumstance to hit back against provocative acts of the Soviet army. To this end, you prepare beforehand, consider a number of possibilities, work out an action plan to hit in a concentrated and planned way, and try to be successful once you start."[23]

In August 1968, the Soviet Union invaded Czechoslovakia and put forward the theory of "limited sovereignty" and the "socialist family," causing heightened concern over Chinese security among Chinese leaders. China began to refer to Soviet policy as "social imperialism," suggesting that the Soviet Union had become more aggressive and dangerous, and it intensified its preparation for war.

Border tension further intensified in 1969. On January 25, the Heilongjiang provincial military command presented a plan for retaliation against Soviet provocations: "We propose that we use a force of three companies to engage in action in the Zhenbao Island area and some forces in ambush on the island proper. If the Soviet troops come to stop our patrols with armed force, the detachment in ambush would come out in reinforcement." On February 19, the PLA Headquarters of the General Staff and the Foreign Ministry endorsed the plan. In a cable to the Shenyang military area units and the Heilongjiang provincial military command, the PLA Headquarters stated, "Strictly observe the principle of waging a tit-for-tat struggle and gaining mastery by striking only after the enemy has struck, and abide by the spirit of reasonableness, advantage, and control. You will not show signs of weakness, nor will you provoke trouble. In the practical struggle, you have to render counterattacks, if any, in a concentrated and well-prepared way and finish as quickly as possible without getting tied down by the enemy."[24]

On March 2, 1969, the Soviet Union mobilized large numbers of ground forces and invaded Zhenbao Island from two directions. Chinese frontier forces ambushed the Soviet forces. On March 15, the Soviet army invaded the island for a second time and engaged Chinese border patrol forces. The Soviet army also bombarded deep within Chinese territory. Chinese frontier forces defeated three Soviet attacks. Following this encounter, the Soviet Union continued to create violent border incidents. On August 13, 1969, Soviet military forces, including ground forces with tanks, armored vehicles, and helicopters, invaded the Tielieketi Region, Yumin County, in Xinjiang Autonomous Region. They surrounded Chinese frontier guards, killing and wounding many.

As hostilities intensified, Chinese leaders reassessed the Soviet military threat. On March 15, 1969, having heard a report about the fighting in the Zhenbao Island area at a Cultural Revolution Group meeting, Mao said, "As we are confronted with a powerful enemy, it is beneficial to mobilize the people and get well prepared. We will gain mastery by striking the enemy only after it has struck."[25] On April 28, at the First Plenary Session of the Ninth CCP Central Committee, Mao commented, "We must be ready to fight in a war," further pointing out that "If you invade China, China will not fight a war on your territory. We will not fight on your land. I mean we are not to be provoked. China will not go, even if you invite it. But if you invade us, China will have to deal with you. China will see if we will be engaged in a small-scale war or a full-scale one. If it is a small one, let's just fight it on the border; if it is a bigger one, I would say we will save some space for you inside China. China is a big country. In my opinion, it [the Soviet Union] will not come in unless it gets some cheap gains. We will let the whole world see that we are fighting a just and superior war. Once it [the Soviet Union] is in, it will be quite to our advantage, since the Soviets will be trapped in a people's warfare."[26] After this, China swung into action to achieve war preparedness.

Chinese leaders overestimated the possibility of a Soviet invasion, and thus reacted excessively to Soviet provocations. Nonetheless, Soviet deployment of over a million soldiers and its full-scale expansion around the world had contributed to a U.S. and Chinese reassessment of their respective policies toward each other. The changing strategic situation within the U.S.-China-Soviet triangle and growing Soviet bilateral military pressure on the Chinese border, which led Chinese leaders to conclude that the Soviet Union had replaced the United States as China's primary threat, transformed the underlying elements of China's U.S. policy. China now understood that easing tensions with the United States was its optimum policy because it would enable Beijing to concentrate its efforts on the Soviet threat.

The Decision-making Process
during U.S.-China Rapprochement

Beijing's decision to open relations with the United States and seek rapprochment developed gradually as its perception of the United States changed. During this period, China responded to strategic movements and signals from the United States and launched its own carefully calculated trial balloons, a process subject to incremental steps as well as dramatic twists and turns.

THE DELIBERATION STAGE

In the deliberation stage, Chinese leaders reevaluated the premises underlying U.S.-China relations, relying on reference materials provided by the Xinhua News Agency and the Ministry of Foreign Affairs. Mao noticed an article, written by Richard Nixon as he prepared to run for president, in the October 1967 issue of *Foreign Affairs*. In addition to discussing a strategy for getting out of Vietnam, Nixon also launched a trial balloon regarding U.S. policy toward China: "Taking the long view, we simply cannot afford to leave China forever outside the family of nations, there to nurture its fantasies, cherish its hates, and threaten its neighbors. There is no place on this small planet for a billion of its potentially most able people to live in angry isolation."[27] After studying this article, Mao was convinced that if Nixon became president, Washington would alter its China policy, and he asked Zhou Enlai to read it.[28] Zhou understood Mao's thinking and instructed foreign affairs departments to track and analyze U.S. strategic movements carefully. On November 25, 1968, following Nixon's election victory, China informed the United States, with Mao's approval, that it was prepared to resume the China-U.S. ambassadorial-level talks in Warsaw.[29]

In December, Chen Yi, who had come under attack during the Cultural Revolution, submitted a report to the Central Committee analyzing the international situation. According to this report,

the global strategy of American imperialism is still to take North and South America as its rear base, to tightly hold Western Europe, and to make use of Soviet revisionists and Eastern Europe against China (but never giving up subversive activities in the Soviet Union and some other countries), and to quench fires in Asia, Africa, and Latin America. It is wrong to assume that American imperialism is making a strategic shift to the East and that it will give up or downplay Europe simply because it invaded Vietnam. It would be equally mistaken to conclude that there is no rivalry between the U.S.S.R. and the United States, or that America has given up its attempt to subvert the Soviet Union and other East European governments.[30]

Chen Yi argued, accurately, that America's global strategic focus had not shifted to the East and that there was no room for compromise in the

U.S.-Soviet struggle. Therefore, it was wrong to overemphasize the prospect of U.S.-Soviet cooperation against China, and China enjoyed some leeway to maneuver between the two superpowers. This argument, which coincided with Mao's opinion, was brought to the attention of top leaders.

In his inaugural address on January 20, 1969, Nixon again signaled his interest in improving relations with China: "Let all countries know that during this administration our lines of communication will be open. We seek an open world—open to ideas, open to the exchange of goods and people—a world in which no people, great or small, will live in angry isolation."[31] Nixon later revealed that China "occupied quite an important position" in this part of his speech.[32] The *People's Daily*, China's official newspaper, missed Nixon's signal. An editorial submitted to the Central Committee assailed Nixon. But Mao understood Nixon's message: "From 1949 till now, they have truly had a taste of the angry isolationist."[33] He instructed the commentators at the *People's Daily* and *Red Flag*: "Approved for distribution. Nixon's address should be published."[34] Thus, the speech received wide publicity throughout China.

Following the Zhenbao Island incident, Chinese leaders increasingly considered the Soviet Union, rather than the United States, as China's primary adversary. On March 15, 1969, Mao proposed to a meeting of the Cultural Revolution Leading Group that China make necessary preparations to counter the Soviet threat: "The northeast, north China, and the northwest should be well prepared. Once we are prepared, it won't do any harm even if an invasion does not happen. With a formidable enemy before us, preparedness will ensure security." Mao further instructed that China's "nuclear base should also get ready in case they bomb us with their planes."[35] He observed that "now that China and the Soviet Union are at war, it will be an ideal subject for America to elaborate on."[36] Lin Biao's political report to the Ninth Party Congress in April 1969 attacked both superpowers and repeatedly criticized the United States, but it also pointed out that Moscow's ultimate goal was to "organize a Tsarist 'socialist community,' namely, the colonies of social imperialism."[37]

During this period, Mao directed several Chinese marshals to prepare a report for the Cultural Revolution Leading Group on the international situation and China's defense strategy. At a meeting on February 19, 1969, he said, "International questions are fairly strange. The American and British press often say that the Soviet Union will get into trouble. The Soviet Union has staged military maneuvers without much publicity." He asked

Marshal Chen Yi to lead Marshals Ye Jianying, Xu Xiangqian, and Nie Rongzhen in a study of international questions. He twice repeated this idea, once after the Zhenbao Island incident in March and again during the Ninth Party Congress.[38]

Zhou Enlai instructed the Foreign Ministry and other departments to distribute telegrams and international reference materials to the four marshals. The group met two or three times a month. At first, the four marshals were unsure of their mission. Because Lin Biao's political report at the Ninth Party Congress had dealt with the international situation in depth, they were not clear on why Mao had charged them with the same task. Zhou explained that Mao still believed that it was imperative to study the international situation. Mao sought an analysis consistent with objective facts. Since the objective international environment was changing constantly, China's perception must also be subject to change. Zhou explained that a partial or even a total adjustment of China's outlook would be necessary and that the marshals should not tie their hands. Because of their position and their broad vision, their research could help Mao gain a good grasp of major strategic trends. He emphasized that their mission was a critical task.

From March to October 1969, Chen Yi and his team met to discuss various issues and eventually submitted reports on "The Initial Assessment of the Situation of War" and "Ideas Concerning the Current Situation" to the Central Committee and also made an oral presentation. They reported that "Soviet revisionism regards China as its major enemy. Its threat to China's security is bigger than that of U.S. imperialism. Soviet revisionism intensified tensions on the long border shared with China, launched armed invasions of China, and massed large numbers of troops. It also whipped up world opinion against China. Toward some Asian countries it used the stick and the carrot in an attempt to create an anti-China alliance to encircle China. These are all to be viewed as important steps taken by the Soviet Union to start a war against China. But to fight a major war against China, the Soviet Union has to think twice, as a great deal of difficulty still exists."

During their working sessions, the four marshals repeatedly studied the possibility of "whether China could play the U.S. card should Soviet revisionism launch a large-scale war against China." Ye Jianying said that when "the states of Wei, Shu, and Wu confronted each other [during the Warring States period], the strategic principle of Zhuge Liang [prime minister of the state of Shu] was to ally with Sun Wu in the east and attack the State of

Wei in the north. We can learn from this lesson." Chen Yi said, "We may also learn from Stalin, who signed a treaty of mutual nonaggression with Hitler." Finally, after months of discussion and analysis, Chen Yi commented that Nixon, with a strategic attempt to confront Soviet revisionism, "is eager to win over China. We should make strategic use of the contradictions between the United States and the Soviet Union. It is necessary to clear the impasse in China-U.S. relations. To this end, we will have to have corresponding tactics. I have some 'unconventional' ideas":

a. When the Warsaw talks are resumed, we may actively propose that Chinese-American ministerial or higher talks be held to discuss fundamental questions as well as other questions that exist between the two countries. We propose only the level of the talks and the topics to be discussed, without asking the Americans to accept our ideas. I think the Americans will be happy to accept this. If we don't say this, the Americans will make similar proposals, I presume. If so, we should accept them.

b. When high-level talks are conducted, the fact itself is a strategic act. That we don't make any preconditions does not mean that we change our stand on the Taiwan question. The Taiwan question can be resolved gradually at the high-level talks.

c. The Warsaw talks should not necessarily be held at a venue provided by the Polish government. They can be held at the Chinese embassy for the sake of secrecy.[39]

Such unconventional strategic analyses and policy proposals by Chen Yi and other Chinese leaders provided an important foundation for the decision to ease U.S.- China tensions.

SUBTLE TRIAL BALLOONS

On September 11, 1969, when Sino-American rapprochement was at a very tentative stage, Aleksei Kosygin, the chair of the Soviet Council of Ministers, met with Chinese leaders at the Beijing Airport after attending Ho Chi Minh's funeral in Hanoi.[40] Two days later, Zhou sent a report to Mao: "It is the first of such talks between the governments of China and the Soviet Union. We shall strive to reach . . . agreements to relax border tensions, issue diplomatic documents, and promote border talks." Mao wrote: "Approved."[41] Shortly thereafter, the Xinhua News Agency announced that the Chinese and Soviet governments would hold border talks at the vice-ministerial level in Beijing. Chinese leaders calculated that this would contribute to the U.S.

sense of urgency in improving its relations with China. On December 3, 1969, on the occasion of a fashion show at the Yugoslav embassy in Warsaw, U.S. Ambassador Walter Stoessel and his assistant tried to approach the Chinese diplomats.[42] But the Chinese diplomats deliberately avoided them, and after the last model had appeared, tried to leave quickly, with Stoessel in hot pursuit. Stoessel asked the interpreter to convey the message that he had recently met with Nixon and that the president would like to communicate with Chinese leaders on matters of vital importance.

Prior to this episode, Mao and Zhou had received messages from Washington via the leaders of France, Pakistan, and Romania. Upon receiving a message via the Pakistani channel, Zhang Tong, the Chinese ambassador to Pakistan, had responded with a very negative assessment of the U.S. initiative, but Chinese leaders disagreed. The turning point, however, was the incident in Warsaw. Before Lei Yang left for Poland in June 1969 to become chargé d'affaires, Zhou instructed him to pay close attention to developments in U.S. policy. Thus, the Chinese embassy in Warsaw immediately reported Stoessel's contacts to the Foreign Ministry. Zhou was excited to receive the telegram. He told Mao: "We have found the door; it is time to knock on it, and here is the knock."[43]

After Nixon was elected president, Chinese leaders studied American gestures closely and developed carefully calibrated responses. For example, when two American tourists capsized their motorboat in the Hong Kong sea and their lifeboat entered Chinese territorial waters, they were arrested. Then, on October 27, 1969, U.S. Consul-General Martin in Hong Kong wrote Liu Xingyuan, the chair of the Provincial Revolutionary Committee of Guangdong, inquiring about the whereabouts of the two American tourists, and Zhou Enlai personally handled the incident. The Foreign Ministry reported the inquiry to the Central Committee on November 7, observing that "This is obviously a new act on the part of U.S. Government to test our response. We suggest that we take over the matter and have the two released at the right moment." It also suggested the decision should be announced in the press and that the Chinese ambassador to Poland be informed of it. On December 4, Zhou wrote Mao and Lin Biao about the issue: "Upon discussing the issue with Politburo members living in Beijing, we tentatively agree to release the two American tourists on the yacht, scheduled for the 7th or later." Mao instructed: "Do as you see fit."[44] The two were released, one of China's first signals to the Nixon administration of its interest in improved relations. The U.S. decision to halt naval patrols of the Taiwan Strait also attracted Chinese attention.[45]

In this context, Mao approved a meeting between the Chinese chargé d'affaires in Poland and U.S. representatives in Warsaw and directed that the meeting not be kept secret. Zhou then instructed the Foreign Ministry to send a telegram to Lei Yang telling him that he should meet with Stoessel to learn more about U.S. objectives. On December 11, 1969, Lei Yang invited Stoessel to the Chinese embassy, and the U.S. side proposed a formal resumption of ambassadorial-level talks. Lei Yang immediately reported this proposal to the Chinese government. On December 12, Zhou submitted the report to Mao for approval, proposing that China "just lay it aside and wait for further response from various sides." On December 29, Zhou wrote: "Talks scheduled to resume February 20" and asked Mao for further instructions. Mao approved.[46] Lei Yang then paid a return visit to Stoessel on January 8 and reported that he was instructed to resume the China-U.S. ambassadorial-level talks. They agreed that the first round would take place on January 20, 1970, at the Chinese embassy.

To prepare for the talks, the Foreign Ministry drew up draft instructions for Lei along with a draft of his statement and submitted these drafts to Zhou Enlai for amendment. Zhou added the following instructions: "After your speech, if the U.S. reiterates that the U.S. and Taiwan have a relation based on a treaty, you should reply in such terms as 'The U.S.-ROC Treaty' is not to be recognized by the Chinese people; if the U.S. side inquires about what the higher-level talks or other channels refer to, you should reply by saying that if the U.S. government is interested, it can make a proposal or work out a solution upon mutual agreement at the ambassadorial-level talks."[47] Chinese leaders believed that since "at present, Nixon appears to be a bit more sober-minded than Brezhnev, . . . the policy of engagement is necessary."[48]

On January 20, 1970, the 135th round of the Sino-U.S. ambassadorial-level talks resumed in Warsaw. Representatives from both sides expressed their wish to improve bilateral relations. On the issue of Taiwan, Ambassador Stoessel reiterated that "the United States shall continue to maintain its friendly relations with Taipei" but stated for the first time that the United States would not prevent the Chinese themselves on both sides of the Strait from "reaching a peaceful solution." He also said that the United States would consider sending an envoy to Beijing "to conduct direct discussions with your officials or to receive a government representative in Washington." Lei Yang, the Chinese representative, demonstrated equal flexibility. Lei stated that "discussions will continue to be conducted at the ambassadorial-level talks, or . . . at higher levels or through other channels to be accepted by both parties."[49] For the first time, the two sides agreed to hold higher-level talks.

The Politburo convened on February 12 to discuss Sino-U.S. relations and concluded that the next Sino-U.S. ambassadorial-level talk "will be an important opportunity and step to take." The Politburo studied and revised the drafts of Lei Yang's instructions and his statement for the 136th round of ambassadorial-level talks. The original draft statement read, "If the U.S. Government intends to send a representative at the ministerial level or a presidential envoy to Beijing to probe into issues of principle in Sino-U.S. relations, the Chinese government would like to consider it." Following Zhou Enlai's proposal, the phrase "consider it" was changed to "receive it." Zhou argued that "because we have already agreed to take it into consideration and to discuss the issue through other channels and, further, because the U.S. side mentioned in the last talk that they would like to come to Beijing to talk to us directly, to follow the logic of this position it would be too casual to phrase it using 'consider.'" After the Politburo meeting, Zhou Enlai submitted the revised version of the texts to Mao and Lin Biao for approval. Mao instructed "Approved."[50]

Each side expressed interest in holding talks at a higher level. At the 136th round on February 20, 1970, they agreed to high-level talks in Beijing to discuss major issues. But the Vietnam war suddenly halted all progress. On April 30, 1970, Nixon announced that southern Vietnamese and American forces were invading Cambodia in search of arms depots and enemy forces. China reacted strongly. On May 3, Zhou convened a meeting of the heads of the ministries of foreign affairs and foreign trade to discuss how to support Prince Sihanouk. On May 4 the Chinese government issued a statement denouncing the U.S. invasion of Cambodia. On May 16, the Politburo met to discuss the current international situation and Foreign Ministry proposals. It decided: (1) to delay until June 20 the Sino-U.S. talk scheduled for May 20; (2) to propose that Mao issue a brief statement in support of the international struggle against the U.S. imperialists and the struggle of the People's Supreme Conference of Indochina and the Sihanouk government; and (3) to hold mass rallies and stage demonstrations in Beijing, and to invite Mao and Lin Biao to attend and Sihanouk to make a speech. Zhou then submitted a written report on the Politburo meeting to Mao, with an attachment containing the Foreign Ministry's request "to delay the 137th Sino-U.S. ambassadorial-level talk." Mao agreed.[51]

On May 18, the Chinese government formally notified the U.S. side that in view of the U.S. invasion of Cambodia and the deterioration of the Indochinese situation, "the Chinese government believes that the 137th Sino-U.S. ambassadorial-level talk scheduled for May 20 would not be appropriate to the occasion. It shall be postponed until further notice upon agreement to be reached by liaison officers on both sides."[52] On May 20, the Central Committee issued a statement in Mao's name, calling on "All people of the world unite together to defeat the aggressors of American imperialism and its running dogs."[53] Mao's statement provided moral support to the people in Indochina but avoided warnings or threats of direct Chinese intervention. Mao was similarly careful to avoid denouncing Nixon by name, in contrast to his criticism of earlier U.S. presidents. China thus left room for future contact with the United States.

In view of the Cambodian issue, contact between China and the United States was suspended, and on June 16, 1970, the Politburo decided to once again postpone the ambassadorial-level talks. Nonetheless, because China-U.S. contacts reflected each country's national interests, they had their own momentum. Following the withdrawal of U.S. troops from Cambodia at the end of June, China made a positive gesture. On July 10, before the end of his sentence, the Public Security Bureau released James Walsh, who had been arrested for espionage. It also announced that Hugh Redmond, who had been arrested for spying in 1954, had committed suicide three months earlier.[54] By releasing Walsh, China balanced its decision to reopen Sino-Soviet talks on navigation of border rivers with a positive signal to the United States. In August, Mao approved a visit to China by Edgar Snow and his wife and put Zhou in charge of the arrangements. On October 1, Mao received Snow on the Tiananmen rostrum and had his photograph taken with Snow at his side. The photo appeared on the front page of the *People's Daily* over Mao's statement that "People from all over the world, including the people from the U.S., are our friends."[55] Mao thus signaled that development of Sino-U.S. relations had the support of China's highest leaders. As he explained, "I first send off a trial balloon to test the senses of America."[56]

On October 12, Zhou submitted a proposal to Mao on the Foreign Ministry's arrangements for another meeting between Mao and Snow. Zhou wrote, "I suggest that Chairman Mao receive Snow soon." Mao responded: "Certainly, I plan to listen to him for more information on the current international situation."[57] On December 18 Mao had a lengthy conversation with Snow in Zhongnanhai and told him he hoped that "the Foreign Ministry will see to it that the American rightists, leftists, and the middle elements will all be allowed to come. Why should the rightists be allowed to come? Nixon represents the monopoly capitalists. Of course, he should be allowed to come. For you cannot resolve any problem with the leftists and the middle elements, but now we can solve the problem with Nixon." Snow asked Mao whether he thought that "China and the United States would establish diplomatic relations." Mao said, they "will have to establish diplomatic relations sooner or later. Will they have to get along without diplomatic relations for a hundred years? We have not occupied your Long Island."[58]

Mao's conversation with Edgar Snow was well calculated. In Mao's words, "After I send off the trial balloon, I have to create conditions. This is what I call reconnaissance by firing. When I fire these rounds of bullets, the opponent will not stay inactive."[59] But Mao's estimate of the United States was too optimistic. Years later, after the normalization of Sino-U.S. relations, Kissinger recalled that "Chairman Mao once passed on the message to us through Snow saying that China would like to normalize her relations with the United States, but we suspected that the message conveyed by Snow was not reliable, thus failing to make the necessary response. However, in April 1971, the Chinese side invited the U.S. Ping-pong team to visit China. So, the Chinese leaders did share with us some similarities in strategic thinking."[60]

THE DECISION THAT LED TO PING-PONG DIPLOMACY

After Mao had met with Edgar Snow and discussed visits to China by Americans, Zhou Enlai asked the Foreign Ministry to study the issue. The ministry's report pointed out that "in handling such matters as visits by Americans to China, the following principles shall be observed: our side is to take the initiative: however, the arrangement must be made step by step in a planned fashion as to who will be approved to visit China. In addition to those progressive personages friendly to China and those influential middle-of-the-roaders, some on the right who might play a positive role are also permitted depending on the situation involved. The tentative idea is to permit entry of a group of Americans (roughly 30 of them) to visit China by

1971. Generally, an entry permit will be granted based on application; if necessary, we can offer the invitation."[61]

The report also developed an initial invitation list. On February 19, 1971, Zhou commented that the list did not seem to contain enough "American rightists." He concluded that when China announced that Americans could visit China, "influential Republicans will ask to come to China. I will make other choices then."[62]

Following Mao's talks with Snow, China sent up another trial balloon on the occasion of the Thirty-first Table Tennis World Championship, to be held in Nagoya, Japan, from late March to early April 1971. The Chinese decision to participate in the championships followed repeated discussions among senior officials before Mao finally approved it. It was very controversial because there was still war in Indochina, and the government of the Kingdom of Cambodia officially requested that China oppose the participation of a team sponsored by the Lon Nol authorities, asking China to expel this team. North Korea was also worried about sending its own team to the championships, and in Japan, some right-wing groups, after hearing of Chinese participation, vowed to stir up trouble. Finally, Taiwan was also preparing to send its participants to the tournament. On March 14, Zhou Enlai directed the Foreign Ministry and the State Physical Culture Commission to hold a meeting with the Chinese Table Tennis delegation. Some participants believed that since China had already registered for the championships, failure to attend would harm its prestige; others held that since forces hostile to China were converging in Nagoya, and threats had been made against the lives of Chinese table tennis players, China's prestige would suffer if it attended. The meeting ultimately recommended to Zhou that the team not participate in the championship.

But Zhou disagreed. In a March 15 report to Mao, he proposed that "the Chinese table tennis team go to Nagoya, Japan, to take part in the Thirty-first Table Tennis World Championship. After it arrives in Japan, it will declare that it supports the stand of the Cambodian government of national unity, which does not recognize the legitimacy of the Lon Nol clique team and takes the same stand concerning the south Vietnamese renegade clique team. So far as Israel is concerned, we may consult the opinions of the United Arab Republic and Syria. If we fail, we will try to avoid competition with them. If our team goes there, it should be well prepared against all possibilities."[63] Mao, taking into account China's strategic objectives, agreed with Zhou Enlai. He wrote on the report: "Our team should go and be ready for several deaths. Of course, if there is no death, it will be still better. It is necessary to defy death and hardship."[64] The matter was settled. The Chinese Ping-pong team declared its strategy of "Friendship First, Competition Second" and was prepared to make friends in Nagoya with people from all walks of life.

Once the Chinese team had left for Japan, Mao instructed that *Reference News* be delivered to him immediately after it was published. He explained that such information was "of vital importance. It is firepower reconnaissance. Afterward, I will seek to take the initiative, make the most timely choice. Let the world see that China is not monolithic."[65]

With the increasing contacts between Chinese and American participants, and following China's invitation to other teams to visit China, the Americans said that they would also like to visit China. At a meeting of officials from the Foreign Ministry and the State Physical Culture Commission, the majority held that it was too early to invite the team to China, that journalists and statesmen should be the first to visit, overruling views that the visit would promote friendly exchanges between the people of the two countries. The draft report submitted to Zhou recommended against issuing an invitation. Zhou wrote that he "tentatively agreed," but he added in the margin: "We can ask them to leave their addresses. But we must reiterate that the Chinese people are strongly opposed to the conspiracy of 'one-China, one-Taiwan' when contacting their chief representatives." He thus left open the option of a future invitation. Acting cautiously, he also wrote "File this for approval by Chairman Mao."[66]

On April 4, Zhou Enlai presented the report to Mao. Mao considered it for two days. Meanwhile, in Nagoya, Chinese and Americans made further contacts. On April 4, reporters surrounded Glenn Cowan, a U.S. player, as he left the Chinese athletes' bus. Cowan said that the Chinese were very friendly and if he received an invitation, he would like to go to China.[67] He also held up a banner given to him by Zhuang Zedong and had photographs taken by reporters. The next day he gave a gift to Zhuang—a T-shirt with the peace sign. Zhuang said, "I am happy to receive the gift from my American counterpart."[68] All major news agencies covered the event immediately. On April 6, *Reference News* reported the media coverage by United Press International and Agence France Presse. Although it buried the stories in the middle of the issue, they caught Mao's attention. Mao commented that

"Zhuang Zedong is not only very good at Ping-pong but also quite diplomatic. This man is quite politically minded."[69] Mao then asked for reports from Nagoya four times a day.

On April 6, Mao circled the word *Chairman* on the Foreign Ministry report advising against an invitation to the American Ping-pong team, thus approving the report, and asked that it be sent back to the Foreign Ministry. But at eleven o'clock that night, having already taken his sleeping pills, Mao reversed his decision. He instructed his staff to inform the Foreign Ministry to issue an invitation to the American Ping-pong team immediately. The next morning, Zhou directed the Foreign Ministry to telephone the Chinese team leader and instruct him to make the announcement. He also worked with Foreign Ministry officials to develop a plan for receiving foreign table tennis teams, including the American team. With Huang Hua and Zhang Wenjin, he concluded that

(a) Chairman Mao has personally decided to invite the American Ping-pong team to China as a good opportunity to open up new prospects in Sino-U.S. relations. We must offer good treatment to the American team. It is such a critical task that to a large extent, it is more significant politically than as a sports event; (b) Altogether six Ping-pong teams will visit China. Though we should strike a balance among these six teams, we must put our emphasis on the U.S. team; (c) We must be warm and enthusiastic in our reception work. Since they come for contests with our players, it is natural that the matches be well organized. At the same time, we will also have to make their life here easy and comfortable. There must be some kind of organized trips to various scenic spots so that they can take a good look at the New China.[70]

On the morning of April 8, Zhou wrote on the State Physical Culture Commission report on the impending visits: "Nagoya is shocked by this sensational news, far more than by the championships themselves."[71] That evening he announced: "From today, we will take a new diplomatic offensive, which will start first with the Chinese Ping-pong team."[72] Later, Mao recalled to his close aides:

I had to take into consideration the overall situation in deciding to invite the U.S. Ping-pong team to China. This was the cherished wish of the peoples of both China and the U.S. There was simply no stopping the friendly exchange between the two peoples. You see, what happened to Cowan and Zhuang Zedong is quite natural. There were no past disputes between them; therefore there were no old scores to settle. Even if there were some misgivings or suspicions, those were purely man-made.

Are we, the Chinese and the Chinese Communists, the ferocious-looking devils we are negatively portrayed to be? . . . Thus, seeing is believing. It is easy for young people to accept new things that to a large extent are representative. After all, the People's Republic of China has been in existence for more than 20 years, and that very fact has great appeal.[73]

On April 4, "Ping-pong diplomacy" entered its heyday. In Beijing, Zhou Enlai addressed the U.S. team: "There have been constant exchanges between the peoples of China and the United States. Unfortunately, these have been disrupted for quite a long time. Your visit to China at our invitation actually opens up a new prospect for future friendship." He added: "We believe that the current friendly exchange will win the approval and support of the majority of the peoples of the two countries."[74]

Ping-pong diplomacy showed that China had shouldered the duty of improving relations with the United States. U.S. leaders understood that this, more than mere diplomatic messages, was a signal that U.S. envoys invited to China would surely step on the soil of a friendly country. Henry Kissinger praised the "whole enterprise" as "vintage Zhou Enlai," reflecting the diplomacy of China's "extraordinary premier."[75] Kissinger described the decision accurately but overlooked the role of Mao Zedong, the behind-the-scenes mastermind of Ping-pong diplomacy.

Later, in reflecting upon the episode, Zhou commented, "Sometimes, one single event can bring about strategic changes. There must be sound judgment of the proper opportunity and good command of the situation. The inevitability of things usually appears in the contingency of things. Similarly, strategic changes often express themselves in trivial details."[76] After five years of disaster inflicted by the Cultural Revolution, China used Ping-pong diplomacy to put its feelers out to the world.

DISCUSSIONS OF THE POLITBURO AND THE CENTRAL COMMITTEE WORK CONFERENCE

On May 25, 1971, Zhou Enlai called a meeting of the leaders of the core group of the Foreign Ministry to discuss a series of oral messages from the Americans. Thanks to the advances of Ping-pong diplomacy, the visit of the special envoy of the American president to China was on the agenda.

Given the important changes about to take place, it was necessary to unify national thinking concerning U.S.-China relations. Zhou Enlai, in accordance with Mao's plan, presided over a Politburo meeting on May 26,

1971. The next day, Zhou wrote to Mao that "At the meeting convened on the night of the 26th, everyone came up with certain ideas. I will draw up a report, which is subject to further amendment by other Politburo members. I will submit it to you and Vice Chairman Lin Biao for approval." Mao underlined the phrase "further amendment by other Politburo members" and added "Good if it is handled in this way."[77] Zhou then drafted "A Politburo Report on Sino-U.S. Relations," which was read by Politburo members, revised, and submitted to Mao and Lin.

The Politburo maintained that in China-U.S. talks, the Chinese side should abide by the following principles:

1. All American armed forces and special military facilities must be withdrawn from China's Taiwan province and the Taiwan Strait. It is a key question in the restoration of bilateral relations. If this cannot be agreed on in principle in advance, Nixon's visit might possibly be postponed.

2. Taiwan is China's territory, and to liberate Taiwan is China's internal affair and no foreigners should intervene. Vigilance toward the activities of Japanese militarism on Taiwan must be pursued.

3. We will try to liberate Taiwan through peaceful means, and the efforts concerning Taiwan affairs should be carried out conscientiously.

4. All activities that feature "two Chinas" or "one China, one Taiwan" will be resolutely opposed. If the United States wishes to establish diplomatic relations with the PRC, it must recognize that the PRC is the only legitimate government that represents China.

5. If the first three terms [1, 2, and 3 above] cannot be met, China and the United States will not establish diplomatic relations but rather liaison offices in each other's capitals.

6. The PRC will not actively raise the question of the United Nations. If the Americans do so, we will tell them that we will not accept the arrangement of "two Chinas" or "one China, one Taiwan."

7. We will not actively raise the trade issue. If the Americans do so, talks may be conducted under the condition that the principle of the withdrawal of American forces from Taiwan is established.

8. The Chinese government maintains that U.S. armed forces should withdraw from Indochina, Korea, Japan, and Southeast Asia to ensure peace in the Far East.[78]

This report contained many new policy positions. It demanded that American forces be withdrawn from Taiwan, but it did not persist in the precondition that the United States must end all ties with Taiwan. It stressed that the liberation of Taiwan is China's internal affair, but it also stressed that China's objective was liberation through peaceful means. The report also marked the first time that Chinese leaders accepted the idea of establishing liaison offices in Washington and Beijing.

The Politburo report recognized that Sino-American talks might fail. But whatever the results, such talks would not harm China and might even enable it to gain the initiative. If agreement could be reached during Kissinger's visit, then Nixon could visit China. If additional agreement could then be reached with Nixon, a formal agreement on normalization would most likely occur before the U.S. presidential election. On the other hand, if the Kissinger visit ended in failure, Nixon would be unlikely to visit China, but China's positive attitude would promote Nixon's rival in the election. China's priority was the incumbent, because the opposition party could not be trusted to keep its campaign promises after taking office. China assumed, however, that Nixon would be eager for the talks to succeed to increase his prospects for victory, and there was pressure on Kissinger to reach agreement.

A few Party members had misgivings about secret talks with the United States. Some feared that talks might affect the fighting will of the Chinese people in opposing U.S. imperialism. Others were concerned that talks would obstruct the anti-American imperialist struggle in Indochina and the Paris Peace talks. Still others worried that Nixon and Kissinger could not be trusted. American leaders spoke of peace while in fact remaining committed to war. Their opening to China might aim to sap China's morale in preparing for war, leading to a counterattack by Chiang Kai-shek from Taiwan or encouraging Moscow to direct its forces eastward.

The Politburo report responded to these concerns. It argued that

mass movements in the United States, which focus on the issue of the Vietnam War and racial discrimination, are gaining momentum since Nixon was elected to the White House. Some have argued that the movement is now changing from a reform-oriented movement into a revolution-oriented one. As a result, we can play two cards, one being U.S. withdrawal from Vietnam and Taiwan, the other being normalization of Sino-U.S. relations, to mobilize the broad masses in America to influence the policy of those in power and those in opposition in order to boost the morale of the people. Furthermore, there is no way to be sure that an armed revolution would break out in the United States and that people would take power, while as far as the anti-American war in Indochina and the Sino-U.S. talks are concerned, it is a golden chance to mobilize the masses and test their leadership. For instance, prior to China's Great Revolution (1924–1927), Soviet Russia on the one hand sent representatives to help Dr. Sun Yat-sen reform the Nationalist Party in order to forge an alliance between the Nationalists and the Communists, while on the other, it dispatched its ambassador to engage the Northern Warlords' government in diplomatic negotiations. What is behind the idea is that, in carrying out a diplomatic policy along that line, Lenin intended to mobilize the broad masses in China. The history of the period could be a reference point.[79]

The Chinese government conceded that the talks might undermine the anti-American war in Indochina and the Paris Peace talks by placing China in a passive position, but argued that Kissinger's visit would eventually benefit the Paris Peace talks once the issues were clarified. While U.S.-Soviet rivalry would remain focused on the Middle East and Europe instead of the Far East, progress in U.S.-China relations would promote the Paris Peace talks and U.S. withdrawal from Indochina. As for alleged U.S. deception, the Politburo argued that

the current situation is the result of the victory of our constant struggles against imperialism and revisionism. It is also an inevitable development of the fact that the U.S. has been beset with difficulties, both at home and abroad, and of U.S.-Soviet rivalry for hegemony. Even if deception does exist, we should take the opportunity to train our troops and test our fighting capabilities, as we are now in the very heyday of the Cultural Revolution with a focus on denunciation, criticism, and reform; in response, we should step up our combat readiness in case of full-scale war. Meanwhile, we can be exposed to the reactionary features [of the United States] and have the masses' consciousness raised. Conversely, if the talks produce good results, that will at least intensify the rivalry between the two superpowers so that we will enhance combat preparedness.[80]

The Politburo's analysis, although written from the leftist perspective of the Cultural Revolution, was characterized by pragmatism and insight. It was relatively accurate in its assessment that the United States' strategic focus was on Europe rather than on the Far East, that there was no prospect of armed revolution in the United States, that Sino-U.S. talks reflected American domestic and international difficulties, and that ongoing U.S.-Soviet rivalry was inevitable.

On May 29, Mao Zedong checked and approved "A Politburo Report on Sino-U.S. Talks," and Zhou then sent an oral message through Pakistan to Nixon: "We welcome Dr. Henry Kissinger as a representative of the Americans to come to China for advance secret preparatory meetings with Chinese high officials to make necessary arrangements for the visit to China of President Nixon."[81]

On June 1, 1971, the Politburo decided to convene a work conference to discuss Sino-U.S. relations and related international issues. The CCP Central Work Conference met in Beijing from June 4 through 18. When Zhou Enlai read the Politburo report at the meeting, 225 leaders from various departments discussed it, along with the minutes of Mao's talks with Edgar Snow. They also received background materials on China-U.S. relations, including a chronicle of major bilateral events, the oral messages of both countries, and the main points of speeches by American leaders. They heard special reports on various international issues, such as conditions in the United States and Taiwan, the development of the international Communist movement, the situation in the Middle East and Europe, and the status of Sino-Soviet talks. On the last day of the meeting, Zhou made a three-hour speech. He pointed out that "through the meeting, the Party, the military and all the people of China have been mobilized to show further concern about state affairs. To study and act in the spirit of the conference has become a critical task as well as important to mobilizing public opinion and challenging public thinking. It will be conducive to psychological and organizational preparedness. If we fail to seek unity of thinking, it will be impossible to talk about unity of action."

To achieve the desired the result, Zhou directed that local governments coordinate their activities with the central government and do well in their reception work: "In receiving our foreign guests, we must be courteous and neither haughty nor humble nor chauvinistic. We should also guard against ultra-leftist tendencies and the old sycophancy."[82] China's chief policymakers had thus confirmed and provided ideological support for China's new policy toward the United States.

Chinese Tactics
and the Breakthrough in Bilateral Relations

Under Mao's guidance, Zhou formed a working team to prepare materials and work out positions for the forthcoming talks. After prolonged study, they completed "On the Key Questions in the China-U.S. Preparatory Meeting" and sent it to the Politburo with an attached note: "We will persist in principles and act tactically and flexibly in the talks. We will be ready for bargaining from the American side. Whenever there are important things, we will ask for instructions from Chairman Mao, Vice Chairman Lin Biao, and the Politburo."[83] After the Politburo had discussed the report, on the evening of July 4, 1971, Mao approved it. Four days later, Kissinger arrived in Beijing.

Zhang Wenjin recalled that before the talks began, Zhou Enlai reread all of the background materials and bilateral messages and went over every major event that had taken place in the United States in the previous few weeks. He then jotted down a few main points to bring to the negotiating table.[84] During his July 9 meeting with Kissinger, Zhou emphasized that "There are disagreements between China and the United States, which, however, should be discussed and resolved in the spirit of equality." He reiterated the Chinese government position that Taiwan has been Chinese territory from time immemorial; that to liberate Taiwan is China 's internal affair; that U.S. troops must withdraw from Taiwan within a stated time; and that the U.S.-Taiwan Defense Treaty is invalid. As for Indochina, Zhou observed that "our American friends always tend to stress America's dignity and honor. Only when you withdraw all your military forces can you truly have honor and dignity."[85]

Mao was the behind-the-scenes strategist and final decision maker. On July 9, soon after the Zhou-Kissinger talks, Mao received a briefing from Zhou and other leaders and issued a few instructions. On the Taiwan question, when he heard that the United States still wanted to keep some troops in Taiwan, he said, "Man has evolved from the monkey, yet with a tail. The Taiwan question will have a tail. However, it is not a monkey, but an ape with a tail that is not too long." This shows that Mao held that, although the Taiwan question had not been completely resolved, there was progress, and the problem was not too serious. On Indochina, Mao maintained that "when the Americans wish to withdraw from Vietnam, Taiwan will not be thrown into a panic. Taiwan does not involve itself. It is Vietnam that is fighting and losing lives. We should not consider only our own interest when we let Nixon come." Mao thus placed the Vietnam question ahead of the Taiwan issue as the primary obstacle between China and the United States. Mao also said, "You should tell Kissinger that the whole world is in turmoil and the situation is extremely good. Do not always get to too concrete things. We are prepared for the United States, the Soviet Union, and Japan to carve out China. It is on this basis that we invite him to China."[86] Mao was concerned with issues of strategic importance, especially the political structure of the world and China's national security. He wished to sound out America's real intentions through high-level contacts between the two countries so that China could develop its own strategy.

On July 10, Zhou discussed China's views on international tension with Kissinger. Kissinger said, "Please rest assured that the United States wishes to have contacts with China and will not attack China. It will not collude with its allies and adversaries against China. The Chinese troops that confront the U.S. may be moved to the north or elsewhere." Zhou was reassured and responded, "The greedy Soviet Union is threatening the whole world."[87] They agreed that China and the United States would communicate via their embassies in Paris and that Nixon would visit China in the spring of 1972. Later that evening, Mao received a briefing on that day's talks. Regarding a joint statement on Nixon's visit, Mao said that "neither of us is the initiator and yet both are initiators. The communiqué will not say that I will meet him. We should learn maneuvering tactics from Zhuge Liang."[88] Mao was following the adage of drawing the bow but not discharging the arrow. That same day, the Politburo met to consider the impact of the Kissinger-Zhou meetings and made relevant arrangements.

In early October, China and the United States reached an agreement through the secret channel in Paris and announced simultaneously that Kissinger would visit China to "make basic arrangements for President Nixon's visit to China."[89] On October 17, 1971, the Foreign Ministry drafted a report proposing policy positions on international issues and the bilateral negotiations and arrangements for receiving Nixon. Zhou revised the report and then submitted it to Mao, who issued the following response on October 19: "Basically I agree. Some points are still subject to change during the talks."[90]

Kissinger initially raised the subject of a joint summit communiqué during his first meeting in Beijing. Zhou Enlai reported this to Mao, who instructed that China wait for Kissinger to present a draft. He added that if China had to present a draft communiqué, it should be a positive, rather than an unfriendly statement. The draft the United States ultimately presented employed diplomatic rhetoric to cover up bilateral differences and stressed mutual agreement with ambiguous wording, trying to highlight the achievements of the U.S. president's visit to China. Zhou was not satisfied with the draft and drafted a counterproposal for Mao's approval. But Mao had developed his own position on the communiqué: "The international situation, which I talk about repeatedly, is in a state of chaos. It is a good idea for each country to stick to its own argument. Are they not talking about peace, security, and nonhegemony? OK, let us talk about revolution, and let us talk about liberation of all the exploited nations and peoples all over the world, let us talk about strong countries, which are not supposed to bully weaker ones. If we fail to emphasize this, I do not see any point in drafting the communiqué."

Despite the inflammatory rhetoric, Mao understood that "we are just wasting our breath, because it might be difficult to have Nixon agree to liberate the exploited nations and peoples of the world." Finally, he said: "It is a good idea for each to stick to its own argument. Give them a chance to brag awhile."

Following Mao's instructions, the Chinese side developed a revised draft. The preface summarized the details of Nixon's visit to China. Then, in the first part, the Chinese side clarified its position in unequivocal terms on a wide range of important issues, and left some space for the U.S. side to strongly express its positions. The second part incorporated consensus principles and statements on Sino-U.S. relations. In the third part, each side could put forth its respective position on the Taiwan issue. The final part presented concrete proposals to improve bilateral relations. After being briefed on the revisions, Mao said: "This is an acceptable version which includes some of my figures of speech, and is thus full of vitality."[91]

After prolonged negotiations, the Chinese and American sides each made concessions. On the Taiwan question, the American side employed constructive and imaginative wording to express its stand: "The United States acknowledges that all Chinese on either side of the Taiwan Strait maintain there is but one China and that Taiwan is part of China. The United States government does not raise any objection to this position."[92] China expressed its appreciation of this formula. The Americans wanted to add that the Chinese people should attain their goal through peaceful negotiations. China did not accept this but said the issue could be left for future consideration.

In January 1972, General Alexander Haig led an advance team to China to make technical arrangements for Nixon's visit. The Foreign Ministry developed the plans to receive the team. Wang Hairong communicated further instructions from Mao on the proposed joint communiqué: "1) The original draft must be revised, as the situation in Indochina has changed; 2) The fact that the draft was too lengthy, according to Kissinger, would make Nixon feel rather embarrassed on grounds that he did not want to fly 12,000 miles to China to be lectured; 3) Since the U.S. wants to do business with us, let us just give them some *drizzle instead of heavy rain*." [93]

On January 2, Zhou Enlai convened a meeting of the core group of the Foreign Ministry along with other concerned officials to discuss the revised Foreign Ministry–prepared draft. Zhou proposed that "the wording on Taiwan must not be changed. But they [Americans] can offer different opinions in the section about the international situation."[94] On January 3, the Foreign Ministry sent two alternative drafts to the chief decision makers, one with only small changes in China's statements on the international situation, the other with larger changes.

On January 4, Haig met with Zhou to convey an oral message from Nixon and Kissinger and present a proposal regarding the joint communiqué. After the meeting, Zhou entrusted Xiong Xianghui with drafting "A Reply to the Message from the U.S. Side." Zhou submitted the draft to Mao. From January 4 to 6, Mao received briefings on ongoing developments. When Zhou mentioned that the United States' current South Asia policy aimed to gain time to strengthen Pakistan's defense capability, Mao replied: "This is good. The issue of India-Pakistan proves that the world is in a state of chaos." Zhou reported Haig's assertion that the Soviet Union had changed its strategy and was now trying to encircle China from the subcontinent. Mao rejected Haig's remarks. He said that China would adhere to the position of self-reliance, adding that "To encircle China! And to ask them [the Americans] to save China. How could China [agree with that]?" He said, "To worry about us, they are 'the cat who is crying over the death of a mouse! [i.e., shedding crocodile tears]. When they [the Soviet Union] are in Vietnam, they want to surround China from Indochina, and again, when they are in the subcontinent, the Russians want to encircle China from the subcontinent. And when Gromyko visited Japan, is it that Japan also wants to surround China? How awful is it? To worry about us? What about Taiwan, the Philippines, and South Korea? Do all those countries need its [U.S.] protection? Isn't it dangerous that China's independence and living capability should be protected by you?"

In the end, Zhou asked Mao whether additional changes should be made in the non-Taiwan sections of the draft communiqué insofar as they seemed acceptable to the United States. Mao answered, "OK, just forget it. However, if any changes are made, just change 'the people desire progress' into 'the people desire revolution.' They [Americans] are just too afraid of revolution. The more scared they are, the more we want to mention it. In fact, this communiqué fails to cover the basic issue. The basic issue is this: No matter whether it is the United States or China, neither of us could fight simultaneously on two fronts. It is OK to say that you will fight on two, three, four, and five fronts; in fact, no country can do it. Of course, it will not do any good if you work it into the communiqué"[95] Mao thus clarified the essence of Sino-U.S. rapprochement—a mutual need for strategic concentration of their forces to deal with their respective adversary.

At 11:30 on the evening of January 6, during his second session with Haig, Zhou, following Mao's instructions, responded to Haig's earlier presentation. Zhou stated that in the context of the pending Nixon visit, hostile forces would step up their efforts to sabotage the talks, but China was fully prepared. He observed that after the announcement of Nixon's visit, Moscow revealed its true aggressive face through its actions in Europe and Asia, reflected in the turmoil in the subcontinent. Regarding Vietnam, he said that there were fundamental differences between China and the United States and that U.S. policy toward Vietnam could be an unfavorable factor during the president's visit. Zhou countered Haig's discussion of Soviet encirclement of China. He said that it was surprising for China to learn from Haig that the United States is skeptical of China's "power to exist" and that the United States thought that it would "maintain" China's "independence." He asserted that no country could rely on any foreign power to maintain its independence and existence; otherwise it would be reduced to the status of another country's protectorate or colony. Zhou reminded Haig that New China was born and had grown up in constant struggle against foreign aggression and that it would continue to exist and develop on its own.

Despite these differences, Zhou assured Haig that, although relations between China and the United States had not been normalized, China would receive the president with appropriate protocol and would make the necessary efforts to guarantee that the summit would be successful. On the Taiwan issue, Zhou said that the Chinese side would try its best to consider the U.S. predicament, but that Taiwan was a strong emotional issue for the Chinese people. If Washington sincerely sought improved relations, it should adopt a positive attitude toward this critical issue. Zhou parried Kissinger's suggestion, conveyed by Haig, that the two sides agree to expand trade. He said that since relations has not been normalized, trade must remain limited and develop slowly. But both sides should look to the future, when diplomatic relations were established.[96]

During Nixon's visit to China in February, China-U.S. talks were held at different levels: Mao Zedong, as the chairman of the CCP Central Committee, and President Nixon discussed strategic issues, determining the fundamental basis for the bilateral relationship; Zhou, as premier, discussed major bilateral issues with Nixon and proposed solutions; Foreign Minister Ji Pengfei and Secretary of State William Rogers discussed technical bilateral issues; deputy foreign ministers Qiao Guanhua and Zhang Wenjin negotiated with Kissinger the terms of the joint communiqué. All major decisions were presented to Mao for final approval.

On February 21, during his meeting with Nixon, Mao emphasized that

there does not seem to be any possibility that the U.S. will invade us, or that China will invade the U.S., nor is there the least possibility, since there is no war between our two countries. You want to pull out some of your forces and send them back home, while we won't send ours abroad. What is so weird about our two countries is we just can't make it. And it has been just 10 months since we started this relationship with Ping-pong diplomacy. You proposed to start some personnel exchange and to engage us in some business dealings, which we resisted vehemently. For the past ten years, if we wanted to solve the big problem, we just clashed on small issues. Later we, including me, found out you are right. So, we just play Ping-pong.[97]

Mao had thus confirmed that there was no fundamental conflict of interest between China and the United States and that they must find new channels for improving relations.

During the next few days, Zhou Enlai held five "broad, serious, and frank" meetings with Nixon and Kissinger on normalization of relations and other international issues in the spirit of "seeking common ground while reserving differences." Four meetings were held in Beijing and one in Shanghai. Altogether, the leaders met for nearly 18 hours. Ji Pengfei and Rogers also conducted five discussions, including one in Shanghai. Meanwhile, the negotiations over the joint communiqué—difficult negotiations requiring meetings in Beijing, Hangzhou, and Shanghai that totaled 22 hours—were basically conducted between Qiao Guanhua, Zhang Wenjin, and Kissinger. Mao stayed in Beijing, but Zhou briefed him via telephone from Hangzhou and Shanghai.

In his talks with Zhou Enlai, Nixon clarified five principles related to the Taiwan issue. First, he assured Beijing that there is only one China, that

Taiwan is part of China, and that the United States would no longer say that the status of Taiwan is uncertain. Second, he affirmed that the United States would not support Taiwan independence. Third, Nixon said that Washington would do everything in its capacity to prevent Japan from interfering in Taiwan and would not support or encourage Japanese support for Taiwan independence. Fourth, Nixon insisted that the United States would support any proposal for a peaceful resolution of the Taiwan issue but that it would not support any military effort to compel Taiwan to return to the mainland.[98] Finally, Nixon assured Zhou that Washington wanted to normalize relations with China and that it would gradually withdraw its military personnel and facilities from Taiwan. But Nixon also indicated that because of political obstacles, the United States could not simply abandon Taiwan. He hoped to normalize Sino-U.S. relations in his second term. In response, Zhou Enlai pointed out that "It is a cliché that you don't want to lose your 'old friend.' In fact, quite a number of 'old friends' have been lost. There are good 'old friends' and bad 'old friends.' You should make a better choice of them. If you hope for peaceful liberation of Taiwan, we can only say we shall seek 'peaceful liberation of Taiwan,' because this is the business between us and Chiang Kai-shek."[99]

Both sides were careful not to allow differences over Taiwan to harm the new geopolitical relationship. Thus, on February 27, after prolonged negotiations, the two sides reached agreement, and on February 28, 1972, China and the United States announced the Shanghai Communiqué. It was a tremendous achievement, reflecting the concerted efforts of both countries. But the significance of the communiqué extended beyond the text and its statements of agreement and disagreement. Its deeper significance is that it reflected a mutual understanding that in the new strategic structure, each country acquired room to maneuver to pursue its respective national interests.

The Strategic Idea of a "Parallel" and the Establishment of Liaison Offices

Following Nixon's visit to China, ongoing negotiations narrowed differences and laid the foundation for further development of bilateral relations. On March 1, 1972, Zhou Enlai made a report to the Politburo and distributed a circular to leading cadres of various concerned government agencies. He reported, "Now things have been different since Nixon assumed office. This change in the situation calls for flexibility, while our basic principles remain unchanged. However, if we do not demonstrate some flexibility, we will fail to promote the realization of world peace. As for the result of the Sino-U.S. summit meeting, 1) there are no secret agreements signed; 2) we stick to principles; 3) you cannot tell which side is the winner; the Joint Communiqué will be subject to the test of practice to prove its validity."[100]

On March 7, the Central Committee issued a document for distribution to the provincial and the army commander levels reaffirming the results of the China-U.S. talks. The document advised that "all agreements still remain something on paper. Whether they will materialize depends on the practical acts of the United States." The document cautioned senior Party cadres that "opposition forces in America have been violently attacking Nixon's visit as a surrender. So, developments in the future will have twists and turns, and we must be ready for them."[101]

In accordance with Central Committee instructions, relevant departments adopted an active, yet conscientious attitude toward contacts with Americans that produced positive U.S. responses and expanded exchanges. By 1973, China's leading decision makers had concluded that the Shanghai Communiqué had been well implemented, and they observed that the United States had ended its involvement in the Vietnam War. They thus had greater confidence in the Nixon administration. Mao in particular grew attached to the concept of "a parallel," of the Chinese uniting with the Americans in the fight against the Soviet Union, which encouraged China to forge closer relations with the United States.

On January 23, 1973, the Chinese side received an oral message from the United States that Henry Kissinger wanted to visit China to discuss normalization of relations, American policy toward Southeast Asia, and the world situation. On behalf of the Foreign Ministry, Zhou Enlai drafted an oral reply welcoming the visit.[102] Kissinger arrived in China on February 15. The next day he reported to Zhou that now that the war in Vietnam had ended, America would reduce by a considerable number its military forces and equipment on Taiwan. Under these circumstances, he proposed that in order to continue discussion of outstanding issues, China and the United States replace the Paris channel with more substantial representative offices, such as liaison or trade offices, and that important and sensitive questions still be handled through the back-channel between him and Huang Hua. Zhou merely replied that "We have studied both proposals."[103] But after he briefed Mao and received his approval, China accepted the proposal and the two sides agreed to establish liaison offices.

The liaison offices were not legal diplomatic institutions, but their officials enjoyed diplomatic immunity and diplomatic privileges. In this sense, the liaison office held a higher position than a trade office. With the subsequent constant expansion of relations, China expected that the liaison office would play an ever more important role and that "diplomatic relations" between the United States and Taiwan would exist in name only.

On February 17, 1973, during a meeting in Zhongnanhai, Mao told Kissinger that China and the United States each needed a closer relationship. Clasping his hands together, he told Kissinger, "Your president, who sat here [pointing to Kissinger's chair], said that since both of us need [closer ties], we are [working] hand-in-hand." Kissinger responded, "Both of us face the same danger. We may employ different means, but our target is identical." Mao said, "That is good. As long as the target is identical, we will not do anything to harm you, nor will you do anything to harm us. We will cope with the same damned rotten egg." Mao's candid language reflected his unique style and revealed the role of the Soviet factor in China-U.S. relations. Mao then conveyed to Kissinger his concept of constructing a "parallel" against the Soviet Union: "I once told a foreign friend that it is necessary to draw a parallel embracing the U.S., Japan, China, Pakistan, Iran, Turkey, and Europe."[104] He then proposed an international united front that included the United States and China, and discussed the establishment of liaison offices.

On February 25, 1973, the CCP transmitted the Foreign Ministry's *Foreign Affairs Bulletin*, no. 12, which assured Party members that "opposition to the two superpowers," China's guiding principle in diplomacy, will "remain unchanged" for the coming decades. Nonetheless, "we must differentiate what is primary and what is secondary." The *Bulletin* advised that "the primary target should be Soviet revisionists," so that China and the United States will develop a new relationship characterized by a combination of confrontation and coalition. The *Bulletin* also reassured Party members that the establishment of liaison offices would not alter China's opposition to two Chinas. It explained that since Kissinger's visit to China in 1971, "fundamental differences" in China's international position had developed. During this period, Beijing had regained its seat in the United Nations, welcomed Nixon to China, and established diplomatic relations with Japan and West

Germany, whereas "the Chiang Kai-shek regime has been isolated by the international community." Thus, establishing a liaison office in Washington would be "conducive to expanding China's influence among the American people."[105]

On March 17, 1973, Nixon held a press conference in Washington, D.C., to announce that the United States would establish a liaison office in Beijing on May 1. Earlier, China had been advised by the White House of its intention to appoint David Bruce as director of its liaison office. On March 4. Zhou approved the message drafted by the Foreign Ministry concerning the director of China's liaison office in Washington D.C. and wrote to Mao, "The United States has appointed a senior diplomat to head the Beijing liaison office. We plan to send Huang Zhen to head the Washington, D.C., liaison office." Mao wrote a note on the message: "All right."[106] On March 29, the Xinhua News Agency announced that Huang Zhen, the Chinese ambassador to France, would head the liaison office in Washington, D.C., and that Han Xu, the director of the Protocol Department of the Foreign Ministry, would be the deputy head. On the eve of Huang Zhen's departure, Mao received him and posed a meaningful question: "Are you promoted or demoted when you are transferred from the office of Chinese ambassador in Paris to the post of the head of the liaison office in the U.S.?" Huang Zhen smiled without answering. Mao said, "The liaison office is much greater than an embassy. I think you are promoted."[107]

Preparations for the liaison offices proceeded smoothly. On April 5, Alfred Jenkins, the deputy head of the American liaison office, led the first advance team to China. On April 18, Han Xu arrived in Washington as head of China's first advance team. The previous day, the U.S. Congress had passed a bill granting Chinese liaison officials diplomatic privileges and immunity, and on April 21 Nixon signed the bill into law. The liaison offices opened officially on May 1. Despite the absence of diplomatic relations, the liaison offices performed the role of embassies, enabling the two sides to have direct, high-level contacts. It was an important step toward normalizing relations and forging a new geopolitical map of the world.

An Assessment of Chinese Policy

In the history of China-U.S. rapprochement, there are two seemingly contradictory phenomena. On the one hand, Chinese leaders' assessment of the domestic situation, that class struggle was becoming increasingly sharp, was basically wrong. But their assessment of the international situation, especially their analysis of the United States, was basically correct. Thus, China developed a more flexible foreign policy, including its policy toward the United States. Although domestic and foreign affairs are related, this contradiction between domestic and foreign policy reflects the fact that, although Mao continued the mistaken policies of the Cultural Revolution, he paid great attention to, and had a pragmatic attitude toward, national security issues. Thus, although Mao's leftist errors were systematically corrected after his death, Mao corrected his own foreign policy mistakes and achieved a major readjustment in China's U.S. policy and U.S.-China rapprochement.

Even as U.S.-China relations improved, public speeches and the media in China were full of radical polemics. On his second visit to China, Kissinger found in his hotel room a printed pamphlet proclaiming "People of the world, unite and defeat U.S. imperialism and its lackeys." Thus, China's foreign policy evolved amid revolutionary jargon—Mao said that China liked to "talk big." Chinese leaders developed these contrasting trends because they wanted to safeguard China's external revolutionary image while simultaneously developing pragmatic policies to protect national security. In his meeting with Kissinger in February 1973, Mao said, "We sometimes criticize you, and you do us. Your president called it the 'impact' of 'the power of ideas.' That is to say, 'The Communist Party, go to hell Communism, go to hell!' We then say, 'Imperialism, go to hell!' Sometimes we have to say so. If we don't say so, it will not do."[108] A superficial hard-line image, combined with policy pragmatism, characterized Chinese diplomacy.

By taking advantage of opportunities for contacts and negotiations with the United States, China brought twenty years of confrontation and mutual suspicion to an end; promoted normalization of bilateral relations and opened the road to improved relations with Western Europe, other Western countries, and Japan; increased China's diplomatic maneuvering room; and advanced its international position. These developments improved China's strategic environment by helping to contain Soviet expansion, ensure the stability of the international strategic structure, and prevent large-scale war.

China's decision to seek improved relations with the United States had a negative impact on its relationships with the Soviet Union, Vietnam, and Albania, but this was probably the price China had to pay to achieve its chief goal. Moreover, insofar as Beijing avoided war with the Soviet Union and continued to help Hanoi end U.S. intervention in the Vietnam War, Chinese leaders tried to minimize the cost of U.S.-China rapprochement.

Nonetheless, in managing China's Soviet policy, Chinese leaders adopted an excessively hard-line posture, overemphasizing the role of struggle in foreign policy. They overestimated the Soviet military threat to China's security, which limited their flexibility in formulating foreign policy and intensified their preparations for war. These miscalculations affected China's bargaining power in the triangular relations between China, the United States, and the Soviet Union. In contrast, once Nixon had visited Moscow, he was able to drink mao tai as well as vodka, enjoying a relatively favorable position in these triangular relations that contributed to some short-term reduction of superpower tensions. But because China did not adopt a flexible policy toward the Soviet Union, it could not ease Sino-Soviet tensions. Beijing's hard-line stance harmed its bargaining position vis-à-vis Washington and facilitated U.S. efforts to position itself in the U.S.-China-Soviet triangle.

Throughout this period, the politics of the Cultural Revolution concentrated all decision-making authority in the hands of one individual—Mao Zedong. Under Mao's dominant leadership, the Politburo, the Foreign Ministry, and foreign policy research institutions could not fully contribute to policymaking. This situation was not conducive to democratic and scientific decision making. It is fortunate that after 1969, Mao increasingly depended on Zhou Enlai and that, with Zhou's advice, his decisions on China's policy toward the United States were fundamentally correct. Otherwise, given Mao's overwhelming authority, the results could have been very different.

CHAPTER TWELVE

Détente and the Strategic Triangle
Or, "Drinking your Mao Tai
and Having Your Vodka, Too"

Michael Schaller

ON JULY 13, 1971, the day Henry Kissinger returned from his secret visit to Beijing, President Richard M. Nixon mused to his chief of staff, H. R. Haldeman, that in politics "everything turns around." The Chinese "made a deal with us" because of their "concern regarding the Soviets," their former ally. He (Nixon) had "fought the battle for Chiang" on Taiwan since the 1950s and had "always taken the line that we stand by the South Koreans, . . . by the South Vietnamese, etc." How "ironic" that a conservative like himself was the "one to move . . . in the other direction." Nixon predicted that U.S. rapprochement with China would "change the world balance" and "shatter old alignments." The "pressure on Japan," America's chief Asian ally since the Korean War, might even push it toward an "alliance with the Soviets." Certainly, the Soviet Union would try to redress the balance of power by "moving to Japan and India." Nixon believed it would take much effort to "reassure Pacific allies we are not changing our policy" or selling out friends "behind their backs." They must be made to understand that while there was "validity ten years ago to play the free nations of Asia against China," the United States could now "play a more effective role with China rather than without."[1]

Kissinger's secret visit to Beijing and Nixon's announcement of his own impending trip to China were elements in a larger mosaic of changes in the military, political, and economic power balance that had prevailed in East Asia since the early 1950s. In the wake of the Chinese Revolution and the Korean War, the United States had committed itself to the containment of China (and, by extension, Vietnam). The U.S.-Japan security treaty of 1951 made the Japanese home islands and Okinawa pivots of U.S. military power, and they were an essential element in this strategy. Japan's conservative political-business leadership agreed to exchange military bases for the restoration of sovereignty and privileged access to the American market. From 1951 through 1971, a combination of U.S. military spending in Japan, U.S. military procurements in Southeast Asia linked to the Korean and Vietnam wars, and increasing exports to the American consumer market served as engines driving Japan's economic growth.

Yet, by the time Richard Nixon became president in January 1969, the foundation of containment in East Asia had cracked, if not collapsed. The February 1968 Tet offensive in Vietnam shattered hopes of an American victory, destroyed the unity of the Democratic Party, and forced President Lyndon Johnson to cap troop levels and begin the search for a negotiated settlement to the war.

The war in Vietnam had also caused increasing tension between Japan and the United States. Japan, which from 1965 to 1972 earned between $1 and $1.5 billion annually from Vietnam-related spending, ran its first post-1945 trade surplus with the United States in 1965. By 1971 the imbalance exceeded a then remarkable $3 billion. The economic pressure on bilateral relations was further magnified when Japan refused to provide more than token economic aid to South Vietnam. As Secretary of Defense Robert McNamara told Prime Minister Sato Eisaku in November 1967, Americans had become "restive and unwilling to carry the burden [of defending Vietnam] themselves." The United States was "spilling blood" to defend Southeast Asia on behalf of its allies, and the American people "wanted to know why Japan, India, and Western Europe did not believe it important to contribute." Furious at Tokyo's meager support, President Johnson dismissed Sato's offer of medical supplies and radios to Saigon as mere tokens. "What I am interested in," he shouted, "is bodies."[2]

The assumptions and costs that defined the Cold War and the U.S. confrontation with China were also unsettled by the evolving military equilibrium between the U.S. and the Soviet Union and the intensification of the

Sino-Soviet split. By 1969, Nixon and Kissinger believed, the Soviets had achieved a rough strategic nuclear parity with the United States. Given the relative decline in America's international economic position, the cost of regaining strategic superiority appeared prohibitive. This combination of economic, diplomatic, and military factors—some regional, others global— prompted Nixon and Kissinger to explore new relationships with America's allies and adversaries.

In many of their public and some of their private remarks, Nixon and Kissinger highlighted the leverage Washington would gain over the Soviet Union by their opening to China. For example, in October 1971, in a memorandum to Nixon, Kissinger wrote that "we want our China policy to show Moscow . . . that it is to their advantage to make agreements with us, that they must take account of possible US-PRC co-operation. . . . The beneficial impact on the USSR is perhaps the single biggest plus that we get from the China initiative."[3]

Although leverage over Moscow might have been the "single biggest plus" of détente with China, it was by no means the sole inspiration for the policy or result of the policy. To an important degree, the opening to China grew out of the changing relationship between the United States and Japan and the impact of the Vietnam War.

In seeking détente, the United States acknowledged its inability to shoulder the burgeoning costs of containment in both Europe and Asia unilaterally. The so-called Nixon Doctrine of 1969 (reducing U.S. troops in Asia), the decision, also in 1969, to return Okinawa to Japan by 1972, the gradual removal of U.S. ground troops from Vietnam between 1969 and 1972, the opening to China begun in July 1971, the decoupling of the dollar from gold and the restriction of Japanese imports in August 1971, and the ABM and SALT treaties with the Soviet Union in 1972 were all aspects of a broader strategy designed to ensure an orderly transition as the United States entered a period of relative decline and a reduced military presence in Asia.

Background to U.S.-China Détente

As earlier chapters have shown, tentative approaches to Beijing during the Kennedy and Johnson administrations were rebuffed. American expressions of interest paled before the scale of U.S. military escalation in Vietnam and U.S. support for Taiwan. In any case, after 1966, the Cultural Revolution quickly dominated Chinese political life and made political moderates around Zhou Enlai fearful of taking any bait offered by the U.S.

In May 1968, China suspended bilateral ambassadorial talks in Warsaw, tersely commenting that "there was nothing to talk about." During the 1968 presidential campaign, Hubert Humphrey spoke of "building bridges to the people of mainland China," but the theme went nowhere. Shortly after Nixon's inauguration, Chinese officials characterized Johnson and Nixon as "jackals from the same lair."[4]

While plausible in hindsight, few observers would have predicted that Richard Nixon would pursue an opening to China more vigorously than any of his four predecessors. As vice president during the 1950s, and then as a business representative of Pepsi Cola and other multinational firms during the 1960s, Nixon traveled frequently to Asia, especially Japan. During a visit to Tokyo in March 1964, he called on Ambassador Edwin O. Reischauer. Reischauer later recalled that Nixon spoke "forcefully of the desirability of recognizing Peking, sounding for all the world like [Harvard professor of Chinese history] John Fairbank." Three years later, in an article published in the October 1967 issue of *Foreign Affairs* entitled "Asia after Vietnam," Nixon stressed the importance of America's Asian allies—especially Japan—doing more to defend themselves against "China's ambitions." Still, he cautioned, efforts to contain China should not become a permanent policy, leaving the PRC to "live in angry isolation."[5]

Shortly after his inauguration, Nixon again raised the China issue, although in a vague way. On February 1, 1969, he mentioned to Henry Kissinger, his national security adviser, that it might prove useful to encourage speculation that the administration was "exploring possibilities of rapprochement with the Chinese." Neither bothered to do more at this time than to cultivate vague rumors, presumably to prod the Soviets.[6]

During July 1969, Nixon took a lengthy trip though Asia that was timed to coincide with the Pacific touchdown of the *Apollo 12* lunar mission. On July 25, at a press briefing in Guam, he issued a rambling statement on future security policy, which his aides dubbed the "Nixon doctrine." Nixon spoke of the American "role in Asia and the Pacific after the end of the war in Vietnam." Warning against isolation, he pledged to honor existing security pacts with Asian nations and promised military aid to counter aggression. But American ground troops would not be sent to fight another Vietnam-type war. The United States would resist nuclear intimidation by the Soviet Union and China, but Asian nations would have primary responsibility for their own defense.[7]

This attitude reflected the belief of the president and many in Congress that America's allies in Europe and Asia must carry a larger share of the common defense burden. Japan, whose export surplus to the United States had grown dramatically since 1965, was singled out for special criticism. Nixon's increasing frustration with Japan, especially its refusal to resolve a textile trade dispute to his satisfaction, played an important role in the development of his policy toward Tokyo and Beijing.[8]

Between 1969 and 1972, Nixon concerned himself with two Japan-related issues: the status of Okinawa and textile quotas. During the Korean and Vietnam wars, Okinawa served as a critical U.S. logistics base. However, in view of the declining American role in Vietnam and the expected reduction of U.S. force levels in Southeast Asia, the Joint Chiefs of Staff were prepared to support Nixon's inclination to return the Ryukyu islands to Japanese control—provided the military bases remained intact—as nearly all political factions in Japan demanded. In return, Nixon pressed Tokyo to reach a "voluntary" agreement to reduce the volume of textile exports to the United States. Although the issue was comparatively minor in dollar terms, the ensuing textile dispute and related trade tensions became a source of bitter recrimination during the next two years and played a surprisingly large part in the evolution of U.S.-China détente.[9]

Despite months of negotiations, which included back channel meetings between Kissinger and representatives of Prime Minister Sato as well as a summit between Nixon and Sato in November 1969, no trade agreement was reached. When Nixon agreed to a negotiated return of Okinawa by 1972 and dropped a demand to station nuclear weapons at the remaining military bases, Sato promised to extend the bilateral security treaty for a "considerably long period of time" beyond 1970. Japan, he declared, was prepared to play a more active role in assuring the security of the Pacific. At the same time, Sato rebuffed an "offhand" remark by Nixon that he would "understand" if Japan decided to build a nuclear arsenal. In private, Sato promised Nixon he would impose export restraints on Japanese producers, and his ultimate failure to do so infuriated and embarrassed the president.[10]

On the surface, the Japanese-American relationship seemed, by the end of 1969, to be reaffirmed as the foundation of containment in Asia. In a speech to the National Press Club, Sato pledged that Japan would respond "promptly and positively" to any future American request to use the Okinawa bases for the defense of South Korea and Taiwan. (He gave Nixon secret assurances that in a crisis, the United States could base nuclear weapons on the island.) The prime minister spoke of a "New Pacific Age" with the "two great nations across the Pacific," of quite different ethnic and historical backgrounds, on "the verge of starting a great historical experiment in working together for a new order in the world." His words coincided with Nixon's call for Asian allies to shoulder more responsibility for regional security. Few Americans seemed aware that most Asians cringed whenever a Japanese leader spoke of a "new order." China charged that "American imperialists" and "Japanese reactionaries" had hatched "a new war plot."[11]

Nixon believed he had solved his domestic textile problem and secured base rights on a Japanese-controlled Okinawa. In a February 1970 report to Congress, he described the Okinawa deal as "among the most important decisions I have taken as president." In private remarks to members of Congress, Nixon predicted that Japan had shed its reluctance to involve itself in world affairs and said he "wouldn't be surprised if in five years we didn't have to restrain them," since they might become too assertive a force in the Pacific.[12]

In fact, as Sato's failure to deliver on promised trade restraints became clear, Nixon grew increasingly bitter over what he considered Japanese "arrogance." Speaking on the president's behalf in March 1970, Secretary of Commerce Maurice Stans declared that the administration had reached the "end of the line" and would support a tough quota bill being prepared by Wilbur Mills, the chair of the House Ways and Means Committee. Stans warned Kissinger and Nixon that Japan presented a comprehensive economic challenge. The textile dispute only exemplified the fact that since the Cold War began, "overriding weight . . . has been given in our policy formulation to geo-political and military factors to the subordination of economic/financial considerations." Japanese industry prospered due to a "complex set of unwritten government-business-banking relationships which determine the direction and pace of Japanese trade and investment." Stans called on Nixon and Kissinger to alter the conduct of foreign policy radically to force Japan to back down.[13] Amid such accusations of bad faith, Nixon accepted an appeal from Sato to meet at the end of October. Meanwhile, a "high American" official, rumored to be the president, told journalists that the security treaty not only protected Japan but served to "police Japan against turning communist or returning to militarism."

On October 24, Nixon and Sato discussed Southeast Asia, the Nixon Doctrine, Okinawa, environmental pollution, economic relations, and China (the president insisted that he contemplated no change in policy and would keep Tokyo "fully informed") before turning to textiles. Sato apologized for the long delay in implementing the promised restraints and pledged, at Nixon's urging, to make sure the "issue was resolved before the November 3 congressional election."[14]

But again, Sato failed to deliver. To make matters worse, in March 1971 Japanese industry officials tried to make a deal directly with Representative Mills, a Democrat. An enraged Nixon muttered darkly about "the Jap betrayal" and threatened strict quota legislation. The incident also set the stage for Nixon's "sticking it to Japan," as he later put it, in July, when he startled Tokyo by announcing that Kissinger had opened negotiations with Beijing.[15]

The China Shock and Triangular Diplomacy

Asakai Koichiro, Japan's ambassador to Washington during the 1950s, often spoke of a recurring dream. He imagined waking up to the news that the United States had abruptly recognized China without informing Japan. This scenario, dismissed by American officials as a fantasy, became known in diplomatic circles as "Asakai's Nightmare." But the events of July 15, 1971, made him seem a visionary. As Undersecretary of State U. Alexis Johnson noted, Kissinger's "passion for secrecy, combined with his contempt for the [State] Department and disdain for the Japanese, threw a devastating wrench into our relations with Japan on the question of China."

Nixon's and Kissinger's interest in opening a dialogue with China reflected deeper Cold War changes. Both men recognized that the Soviet Union had, or soon would, achieve rough nuclear parity with the United States. Instead of a costly and probably futile effort to restore military superiority, they sought to moderate Soviet behavior through economic and political incentives broadly labeled "détente." These included negotiated limits on strategic weapons, increased trade and technology transfer, and recognizing that the Soviet Union had legitimate global interests. During the first six months of 1969, Nixon and Kissinger urged the Soviets to put pressure on Hanoi to make a compromise deal with Washington to end the war. Moscow, however, seemed unwilling or unable to maneuver its ally. Instead, Soviet leaders looked to the United States for help with its much larger Communist neighbor.

In March 1969, the decade-long war of words between Moscow and Beijing erupted in a series of violent border clashes along the Ussuri River. After some initial dithering, Nixon and Kissinger recognized this schism as an opportunity to play the Communist rivals off against each other: improved ties with China could provide leverage over Soviet behavior while also influencing Chinese policies in Asia.

Following the March border clashes, the Soviet ambassador to the United Nations told American diplomats that Moscow would teach those "squint-eyed bastards" a "lesson they'll never forget. . . . We'll kill those yellow sons-of-bitches." Soviet ambassador Anatoly Dobrynin went further, telling Kissinger there was still time for the two superpowers to contain China but that "they might not have this power much longer." Ironically, Moscow's inquiries about unilateral or joint military strikes against Chinese nuclear facilities resembled U.S. feelers to Moscow in 1964.[16]

Just as the Soviets had rebuffed that earlier approach, U.S. officials now made it clear that Washington would neither join nor approve any military strike against China. In fact, the Soviet approach elicited what the Kremlin feared most: a decision by Nixon to play the so-called China card directly. In September, the president urged Kissinger to "plant that idea" [of U.S.-China reconciliation] as a way to prod Moscow. "I think that while [Soviet Foreign Secretary] Gromyko is in the country would be a very good time to have another move toward China made." With the United States in a balancing position, Kissinger later remarked, "each communist power [had] a stake in better relations with us." The leverage gained through this triangular diplomacy with Moscow and Beijing might, they hoped, hasten the end of the Vietnam War, give Washington greater influence over Japan, moderate Soviet behavior, and facilitate an orderly reduction of U. S. military power in Asia.

While Kissinger excelled at bureaucratic politics, Nixon remained the consummate domestic politician. Even as he suggested tweaking Moscow, the president told his national security adviser to cover his flanks by consulting with key Republican politicians. Nixon wanted Kissinger to speak with Senator Karl Mundt of South Dakota and Congressman Walter Judd of Minnesota, both pillars of the so-called China Lobby, to gauge their reaction to a "move in that [China's] direction."[17]

If fear of Chinese expansion initially prompted American intervention in Vietnam, a desire to bolster Chinese resistance to the Soviet Union increased the administration's determination to speed a settlement. As Kissinger elaborated, the "China initiative . . . restored perspective to our national policy." It reduced "Indochina to its proper scale—a small peninsula on a major continent." The "drama" of opening ties with China would "ease for the American people the pain that would inevitably accompany our withdrawal from Southeast Asia," an elegant way of also saying that any political backlash from "losing Vietnam" would be mitigated by approval for "finding China."[18]

In an odd symmetry, a China weakened internally by the chaos of the Cultural Revolution and threatened externally by the Soviet Union and the potential pressure of Japan sought American assistance. Lyndon Johnson's March 1968 decision to cap U.S. troop strength in Vietnam, followed by Nixon's policy of "Vietnamization," reduced Chinese fear of a Korean-style confrontation with the United States along its southern border. In marked contrast, the Soviet invasion of Czechoslovakia in August 1968 and Leonid Brezhnev's assertion of Moscow's right to intervene in any socialist country, coupled with the Sino-Soviet border clashes of 1969 and the subsequent deployment of large numbers of Soviet forces to the disputed frontier, stunned a vulnerable China.

Although the Soviet Union posed the primary military threat to China, Japan's growing wealth and assertiveness, epitomized by Prime Minister Sato's affirmation in 1969 of Tokyo's renewed interest in the security of South Korea, Taiwan, and Vietnam, raised the added specter of a rearmed, expansive Japan. Since 1950, the substantial U.S. military presence in Japan, South Korea, and Southeast Asia had provided a form of "double" containment aimed primarily at China while also ensuring a measure of American control over Japan, Taiwan, and South Korea. The retreat of American power threatened to leave China caught in a vise, between the Soviet Union on one side and Japan on the other.

Nixon's gradual withdrawal of troops from Indochina, his decision to return Okinawa and encourage Japan to play a greater role in regional security, and his pursuit of détente with the Soviet Union all diminished America's direct security role in the Asia/Pacific region. Because this retreat of American power coincided with a growing Soviet threat, Chinese strategists who had previously feared a U.S. victory in Vietnam now agonized about the possible consequences of a U.S. defeat. As Nixon and Kissinger hoped, the determination of Mao Zedong and Zhou Enlai to protect China outweighed their disdain for capitalism, their past solidarity with Hanoi, their mistrust of the United States, and their drive to regain Taiwan.

In late 1969 and early 1970, through contacts in Warsaw and elsewhere, the administration began to signal China about its desire to improve ties. As instructed by Kissinger, Walter Stoessel, the U.S. ambassador to Poland, chased down the Chinese chargé d'affaires, Lei Yang, outside the Yugoslav embassy in Warsaw, where a fashion show was in progress. "I was recently in Washington and saw President Nixon," Stoessel shouted. "He told me he would like to have serious, concrete talks with the Chinese." Lei's interpreter promised to pass on the message.

On January 20 and again on February 20, 1970, Stoessel met with Lei Yang. Declaring his hope that "today will mark a new beginning in our relationship," the American diplomat noted that Nixon sought a "reduced American military presence in Southeast Asia, which we recognize is near the southern borders of China." Moreover, although the United States would honor its commitments to Taiwan, it had no objection to any deal made between the People's Republic and the Nationalist Chinese regime. "As peace and stability" in Asia grew, the United States "hoped" to reduce its "military deployments and installations on Taiwan." To pursue these subjects in a "more thorough" way, the Nixon administration desired to send a representative to Beijing—or to receive an envoy from China. These soothing words clearly had an impact: on February 20, Lei Yang responded by telling Stoessel that "if the U.S. government wishes to send a representative of ministerial rank or a special envoy of the United States President to Peking . . . the Chinese Government will be willing to receive him." The negotiations, however, would be limited to arranging the American "evacuation" of Taiwan. Although Washington rejected this format, Stoessel stressed Nixon's "intention" to gradually withdraw U.S. forces from the disputed island as conditions warranted.[19]

For the next several months, the Nixon administration debated over how to proceed. State Department China experts, such as Marshall Green, supported contacts with the PRC but feared that Nixon and Kissinger might abandon Taiwan and other Asian allies in their rush to normalize relations with Beijing. Kissinger's response to such criticism was to shut the State Department out of most future deliberations. Beginning in April 1970, messages to and from Chinese officials were carried by intermediaries designated by Kissinger and Nixon, among them, General Vernon Walters, then serving as military attaché in Paris. He informed the Chinese ambassador that Nixon was considering sending Kissinger to China if the two sides could agree on an agenda.

These contacts ended abruptly in April 1970, when a U.S.-backed coup in Cambodia toppled the neutralist government of Prince Sihanouk. On May 1, Nixon ordered U.S. troops into Cambodia to destroy Vietcong and North Vietnamese supplies and headquarters, provoking renewed antiwar protests in the United States and a revolt among Kissinger's staff. The resignations of Tony Lake, Roger Morris, and William Watts cleared a path for General Alexander Haig and Winston Lord to rise in the NSC structure. China responded to the Cambodian incursion by canceling scheduled talks with the United States in Warsaw. Mao condemned Nixon personally for "fascist atrocities" and renewed his call for the "people of the world" to "unite to defeat the U.S. aggressors and their running dogs." Furious at Mao, Nixon spoke of sending a naval flotilla to the China coast until Kissinger talked him out of it.

For the remainder of 1970, the fallout from Cambodia, as well as resistance among some of Mao's "radical" followers, slowed further dialogue. Kissinger sent "feelers" to Beijing via officials in Pakistan and Romania, stating his hope for continued contact. Nixon underscored these gestures by lifting some of the petty restrictions on trade with China. Mao responded by releasing James Walsh, a Roman Catholic Bishop charged with espionage in 1958, from prison.

By the end of 1970, Mao moved more boldly to signal his interest in contact with Nixon. Just as he had done in the late 1930s, Mao selected American journalist Edgar Snow to get a message to the outside world. He invited Snow to celebrate October 1, China's national day, by standing beside him atop the Gate of Heavenly Peace in Tiananmen Square. Mao then granted a frank interview to Snow, his old biographer. (According to his physician, Mao labored under the illusion that Snow worked for the Central Intelligence Agency, ensuring that Nixon would receive his message!) The Chairman said he welcomed a visit by Nixon. He blamed delays on the president's obsession with secrecy and fear of a conservative backlash. He advised Nixon to defuse criticism by "trumpeting" his purpose as "win[ning] over China so as to fix the Soviet Union." Unfortunately for Mao, Snow not only lacked CIA connections, he found no immediate outlet for a report of the visit, nor did Washington show any interest in what he had to say. By the time Snow published his account of the interview in the spring of 1971, events had superseded it.[20]

Domestic politics may explain Nixon's hesitation. The president anticipated big Republican gains in the congressional election of November 1970.
To ensure this, he encouraged Vice President Spiro Agnew to denounce
Democrats as "Radiclibs," whose policies were tantamount to treason. However, the Republicans actually lost nine House seats and eleven governor-
ships and gained only two Senate seats in an outcome determined more by
local than national issues. To make matters worse, early polling data in 1971
showed potential Democratic candidate Senator Edmund Muskie of Maine
beating Nixon in the upcoming presidential race. Nixon may have feared
alienating his conservative base by doing anything that suggested abandonment of Taiwan. On December 9, 1970, Zhou Enlai reinforced Nixon's
concern by sending a message that repeated China's willingness to receive an
envoy—but only to "discuss the subject of the vacation of Chinese territories
called Taiwan."

If Nixon feared a reaction from the "right," he also had to worry about
the "left." During early 1971, several prominent Democrats, including Senator Edward Kennedy of Massachusetts and Senator Mike Mansfield of
Montana, explored how they might travel to China. Senator George
McGovern of South Dakota made improving relations with China a theme
of his presidential bid, which began in January 1971. Nixon loathed the prospect of a Democrat beating him to Beijing. He addressed the China issue
openly in a "state of the world speech" in March, which marked the first
time since 1949 that a U.S. president had called the Beijing government by
its official name, the People's Republic of China. "We are prepared," Nixon
declared, "to establish a dialogue with Peking." The United States would
oppose any Chinese attempt to dominate Asia, but it no longer wished to
"impose on China an international position that denies its legitimate
national interests." Nixon implemented his promise to seek "broader opportunities for contact" by lifting some of the travel and trade restrictions
imposed on China during the Korean War.[21]

In April, Chinese and American leaders chanced on a convenient way to
build public support for dialogue. Members of a Chinese table tennis team
playing at a tournament in Nagoya, Japan, suggested, apparently at their
own initiative, inviting their American counterparts to China. The players
were eager to accept, and Mao and Nixon quickly approved the proposal.
Although the U.S. team was hopelessly outclassed in the exhibition
matches, the encounter energized diplomacy in unforeseen ways. The

Chinese crowds' outpouring of affection toward the American athletes gave Mao and Zhou confidence to move forward, despite opposition from Lin Biao. On April 14, Zhou told the American athletes they had "opened a new chapter in the relations of the Chinese and American people."

The cascade of favorable publicity provided by TV coverage of the visit also reassured Nixon that public opinion would back his initiative. He jokingly asked aides if they had "learned to play Ping-pong yet." He was thus both flustered and irate when Spiro Agnew denounced these developments. In a critique strangely similar to Lin Biao's leftist attack on Mao for playing the America card, the vice president sharply criticized the opening toward an old enemy. In a mid-April late-night session of drinking and griping, Agnew had complained to a group of reporters that favorable press coverage of the Ping-pong tournament was virtual collusion with communism. He had seen pictures of the apartments provided in Beijing and, he snapped, liberals would call it "oppression of the poor" if the U.S. government made Americans live in such hovels. Nixon responded by resuming his efforts to dump the vice president from the 1972 ticket. Agnew, he said, was too dense to understand "the big picture in this whole Chinese operation, which is, of course, the Russian game. We're using the Chinese thaw to get the Russians shook."[22]

Seeing Ping-pong as the start of a breakthrough, Nixon boasted to Kissinger that he had already "accomplished more with China than any of his predecessors." In Oval Office banter, Haldeman worried less about a conservative backlash than about the possibility that "the Democrats are going to jump all over this" opening. To make sure no one did, Nixon urged Beijing to put off visits by any prominent Democrats.[23]

On April 27, the White House received a message from Zhou via Pakistan. It repeated the invitation to receive Nixon or Kissinger but dropped the demand that withdrawal of U.S. forces from Taiwan was a precondition and the focal point of discussion. Instead, Taiwan's status would be one of several issues raised. Kissinger described this message as "the most important communication that has come to an American president since the end of World War II."[24]

Nixon's residual fear of news leaks, of a China visit by prominent Democrats, or of a Chinese effort to embarrass him over Taiwan was put to rest on June 2. Zhou informed the White House that Mao had formally sanctioned a secret visit in which Kissinger and Zhou could freely raise "principal issues of concern" to either party. For the Chinese, this would include the "withdrawal of all U.S. armed forces from Taiwan and the Taiwan Strait area." The American side could bring its own issues to the table.

An elated Nixon characterized the invitation as the result of "fundamental shifts in the world balance of power [that] made it in both [nations'] interest to have relations." Faced by the Soviets on one side, a Soviet-backed India on another, and a resurgent Japan that could "develop [military power] fast because of its industrial base," China sought protection from the United States. Mao and Zhou still demanded that "the U.S. should get out of the Pacific" but, Nixon surmised, they really "don't want that."

As American military strength in Asia inevitably diminished, Nixon predicted that Japan would "either go with the Soviets or re-arm," two bad alternatives from China's perspective. Soon after receiving Zhou's invitation (but before Kissinger went to Beijing) Nixon predicted that with American prodding Mao and Zhou would agree that a continued U.S. military presence in Japan, Korea, and Southeast Asia was "China's [best] hope for Jap restraint."[25]

On July 9, while visiting Pakistan, Kissinger feigned stomach trouble, dropped out of sight, and flew in a Pakistani airliner to Beijing. As he and his small staff (including John Holdridge and Winston Lord) were driven to a state guest house, veteran diplomat Huang Hua asked Holdridge for assurance that the American envoy would not snub Zhou as John Foster Dulles had done at Geneva in 1954. Zhou had nothing to worry about. In the urbane prime minister, Kissinger found someone he considered a "soulmate." From his first to his last encounters with Zhou, Kissinger described his counterpart in effusive, glowing terms. At this initial meeting, the two men conferred for seventeen hours over two-and-a-half days. Kissinger later reported that after a few rounds of rote posturing, philosophizing, and light repartee, he offered Zhou the single thing he believed motivated China, "strategic reassurance, some easing of their nightmare of hostile encirclement." As proof of American good will, he provided intelligence data on Soviet military deployment along China's border. Zhou recited what Kissinger called the "Chinese Communist liturgy," demanding that the Americans abandon Taiwan, pull out of South Vietnam, and cease assisting a "militaristic Japan." But, over lunch, Zhou reportedly assured Kissinger that these minor impediments need not delay improved ties or a presidential visit. Taiwan, Kissinger asserted, was barely discussed.[26]

Kissinger's published account somewhat misrepresents the encounter. In fact, he initiated the discussion by making several important concessions on

Taiwan and other issues of concern to China. Using a script prepared by Holdridge, Kissinger declared that the United States would reduce its military presence in and around Taiwan as relations with the PRC improved and the Vietnam War ended. Meanwhile, Washington did not favor a policy of two Chinas, of one China, one Taiwan, or of an independent Taiwan, and it would oppose any attack by Taiwan against China. Finally, Kissinger confided that Nixon intended to give formal recognition to the PRC during an expected second term. These promises effectively reversed the U.S. policy toward China of the previous twenty years.[27]

In further discussions, Kissinger explained that U.S. disengagement from Taiwan would take place, but only gradually, and Zhou made much the same case for Chinese support of North Vietnam. These disagreements did not halt plans for a presidential visit. However, when Kissinger again pressed for assurances that no prominent Americans (that is, no Democrats) would be received in Beijing before Nixon, Zhou responded that this request would be granted according to the "wisdom of Mao Zedong."[28]

Once Nixon learned of Kissinger's success on July 11, he became fixated on making sure that he and not his aide received full credit for the breakthrough. He also resolved not to inform America's allies, especially Japan, of the approach to China before his public announcement on July 15. Late on July 14, General Alexander Haig, Kissinger's deputy, summoned Undersecretary of State U. Alexis Johnson to Nixon's home in San Clemente, California. When he arrived there the next day, NSC aide Winston Lord casually told him the president was about to announce on television that Kissinger had returned from China with an invitation for Nixon to visit Beijing. Johnson grew frantic that no one had alerted Japan. (Nixon had vetoed plans to send Johnson to Tokyo 24 hours before the public disclosure.) Minutes before the president's address, Johnson spoke by telephone to Japan's ambassador in Washington, Ushiba Nobuhiko. When he learned what Nixon planned, the envoy cried out: "Alex, the Asakai Nightmare has happened."

In Tokyo, three minutes before Nixon's speech, Kusuda Minoru, Sato's secretary, encountered the prime minister emerging from a cabinet meeting, which, ironically, had reaffirmed Tokyo's support for Taiwan and South Korea. Kusuda informed him of the president's action. Just a week before, Defense Secretary Melvin Laird had visited Tokyo and assured Sato that Washington contemplated "no basic change" in China policy. Now, in shock, Sato mumbled to his aide, "Is that really so?" U.S. Ambassador Armin Meyer failed to get even a three-minute warning. He learned of the China initiative while listening to Nixon's speech on the radio, as he got a haircut.

When Kissinger and Nixon "embarked on a period of rapturous enchantment with China," U. Alexis Johnson complained, they shoved "our most important ally in Asia . . . to the back burner." Although they never publicly linked their handling of the China issue to anger over Japan's trade policy and the textile dispute, Nixon and Kissinger approved journalist Henry Brandon's attribution of motive. In a book based on interviews with both men, Brandon wrote: "Angry that the Japanese government, despite its promise to do so, did not place voluntary restraints on its exports, Mr. Nixon deliberately affronted Japanese Premier Sato by giving him no hint of his new policy toward China." In August 1971 Nixon told aides that the delivery of the twin China and economic shocks was designed to give Tokyo an overdue "jolt," or, as he later put it to a biographer, to "stick it to Japan."[29]

Although most Japanese favored broader contact with China, Nixon's calculated insult stung deeply. Sato issued a statement welcoming the Sino-American dialogue "in the interests of world peace." Japan, he noted, had long favored closer ties with China. In private, Ambassador Meyer reported, most Liberal Democratic Party (LDP) leaders were "upset as hell" and doubted that "Sato could last" after the humiliation inflicted by Nixon. Although Nixon sent the prime minister a note pledging to "work closely with you on China policy," his actions mocked his promise. "I have done everything" the Americans "have asked," a tearful Sato told visiting Australian Labor Leader Gough Whitlam, but "they have let me down." Among Nixon's cabinet, only Secretary of State William Rogers, whom Nixon and Kissinger routinely ignored, expressed sympathy for Japan, suggesting that "lots of mood music" be played to soothe Sato.[30]

The impact of the Nixon shock in Tokyo was magnified by the fact that, while Washington and Beijing had been engaged in opening lines of communication, Sino-Japanese relations had deteriorated. Chinese officials voiced alarm over Japan's rapid economic growth and rising military budget. (Japanese defense spending during the 1960s and 1970s hovered near 1 percent of GNP. Rapid economic growth led to steady increases in military expenditures. Between 1960 and 1970, annual spending tripled, rising from $508 million to $1.5 billion.) They particularly disliked Sato's assertion of Japan's security interest in South Korea, Taiwan, and Vietnam expressed in the Nixon-Sato communiqué of November 1969. The Chinese press denounced "criminal plots" among counterrevolutionaries in Japan and America, the "reactionary policies of the Sato Cabinet," and efforts to rebuild the "Greater East Asia Co-Prosperity Sphere."

In April 1970, Zhou Enlai and North Korean strongman Kim Il Sung jointly declared that "Japanese militarism has revived and has become a dangerous force of aggression in Asia." They accused Sato's government of "directly serving U.S. imperialism in its war of aggression against Vietnam," of plotting, with Washington, a new war against North Korea, and of "attempting to include the Chinese sacred territory of Taiwan in their sphere of influence." Zhou announced new guidelines governing Sino-Japanese trade. China would no longer trade with Japanese companies investing in Taiwan and South Korea, manufacturing arms for the American war effort in Southeast Asia, or engaging in joint ventures with American firms.[31]

Sato urged Japanese business leaders to resist Chinese pressure, citing Nixon's assurance that Washington contemplated no change in China policy. Nevertheless, demands from business groups representing a wide spectrum of political opinion and eager to enter the largest market in Asia persuaded nearly half the members of the Diet to join the nonpartisan Parliamentarians League for the Restoration of Ties with China. But Sato resisted calls to seat the PRC in the United Nations and dismissed all hints that Washington might alter its China policy. Even when Zhou Enlai told a Japanese trade negotiator in the spring of 1971 that China and the United States might soon begin a serious dialogue independent of Japan, Sato paid no heed.[32]

Ironically, Nixon and Kissinger may have used the threat of a nuclear-armed Japan to put pressure on China to accept U.S. terms for cooperation. During Kissinger's secret trip to Beijing of July 9–11, 1971, Secretary of Defense Melvin Laird visited Tokyo. Through his own sources, including documents pilfered by Kissinger aide Navy Yeoman Charles Radford and passed on to the Joint Chiefs of Staff, Laird learned of the approach to China. (Some years later, he claimed he had passed word of this to a Japanese defense official shortly before Nixon revealed it. However, this claim contradicts the assurances he gave Sato on July 5 that Washington was *not* about to change tack.)[33]

Laird berated Japan for demanding the removal of nuclear weapons from Okinawa. Instead of inhibiting American security efforts, Laird argued, Japan should provide military assistance money to Southeast Asian countries and boost its own defense capacity, starting with the development of an ABM system to counter a future Chinese threat. He and his aides, like Nixon and Kissinger before them, hinted that Washington favored a nuclear-armed Japan. Kissinger later claimed that Laird's remarks were unauthorized and actually undermined his effort with China.[34] But in a deposition given in June 1975 to the Watergate Special Prosecution Force, Nixon contradicted Kissinger. When asked about Yeoman Radford's theft of NSC documents, the former president, as a prosecutor later told journalist Seymour Hersh, grew animated. "Radford knew everything"; he was "in on all the meetings." Nixon explained that during their initial contact with China, he and Kissinger warned that if the PRC did not agree to strategic cooperation against the Soviets on American terms, they would encourage Japan to develop nuclear weapons. In Nixon's own words, "We had these tough negotiations with China over the Mutual Defense Treaty . . . with Japan. You have to be tough. And we told them that if they tried to jump Japan then we'll jump them." What Nixon is actually reported to have said is, "We told them that if you try to keep us from protecting the Japanese, we would let them go nuclear." He boasted of "' put[ting] it to' the Chinese like someone out of Hell's Kitchen."[35]

While Nixon may have talked "tougher" in his recollection than in reality, Laird's remarks in Tokyo add credibility to Nixon's account. Laird, Kissinger, and Nixon might have played "good cop/bad cop" to encourage a more cooperative attitude in Beijing. The last thing China wanted, after all, was a nuclear-armed Japan as it tried to enlist American support against the Soviets. At least as a bargaining ploy, as we will see, Nixon encouraged Japan to develop nuclear weapons.

On July 5, 1971, four days before Kissinger's visit to China, Zhou Enlai seemed to journalist Ross Terrill to be "very agitated indeed about Japan." In an interview, Zhou accused Washington of conspiring to revive "Japanese militarism" and assisting Tokyo's acquisition of tactical nuclear weapons. The Chinese prime minister repeated this assertion after Nixon's announcement of July 15. In a discussion with journalist James Reston in August, Zhou warned that Nixon's promotion of Japanese rearmament, along with the withdrawal of U.S. forces from Indochina, encouraged the revival of Japanese militarism. He accused Japan's civilian nuclear industry of conspiring to build atomic warheads as part of a plan to dominate Southeast Asia.[36]

In the months leading up to Nixon's February 1972 visit to Beijing, Chinese propaganda and diplomatic messages suggested that aside from the Soviet buildup, nothing was more worrisome than "Japanese expansionism." Beijing accused Tokyo of planning to take advantage of America's retreat from Vietnam by asserting economic hegemony over Southeast Asia. This played into the economic and political strains between Tokyo and Washington. According to the *People's Daily*, "Japanese militarists" hoped to "make a comeback by relying on U.S. imperialism, [while] the latter strives to tighten its control over Japan economically, politically, and militarily by fastening her firmly to its war chariot." The paper warned Tokyo that the United States had no real "wish to see an independent, prosperous, and shiny Japan in Asia. Americans called Japan a `close partner'" but stood "ready to betray her at any time."[37]

Japan's ambassador in Washington, Ushiba Nobuhiko, responded to these allegations by accusing Beijing of pandering to fear of militarism to "isolate Japan" and drive a wedge between the Pacific allies. China hoped to make Washington more dependent upon Beijing for strategic cooperation against the Soviet Union. In an unusually blunt public statement, Ushiba contrasted professional diplomats such as U. Alexis Johnson and Marshall Green, who understood this ploy, with amateurs such as Nixon and Kissinger, whom China manipulated.[38]

The Second Nixon Shock and the New Economic Policy

The tears shed by Sato over Nixon's treatment reflected both a sense of personal betrayal and a belief that, having sailed loyally in the wake of America's China policy for two decades, Japan deserved better. Over the next few months Nixon hurled additional lightening bolts at Tokyo. His decision to end the dollar's convertibility into gold, force a revaluation of the yen, levy a tax on imports, and impose textile quotas—all elements of the so-called New Economic Policy—stunned Japan's leaders.

Faced in 1971 with a $29 billion balance of payments deficit and the first overall merchandise trade deficit ($2.27 billion) in nearly a century, the Nixon administration saw Japan's $3.2 billion trade surplus with the United States as a major economic threat.[39] Spokespersons for American industry told a Senate subcommittee in May 1971 that the United States was on the "brink of defeat" in a trade war. Edsel B. Ford II, head of the Ford Motor

Company, warned shareholders that the onslaught of Japanese automobile exports would inevitably transform the United States into a service economy.

Featured articles in *Time*, *Newsweek*, and *Forbes Magazine* during the spring of 1971 all used military and racial terminology to warn of the threat posed by "Japan, Inc." *Newsweek* spoke of Japan's "massive invasion of the world automobile market." *Time's* description of Japan's "business invasion" portrayed America as locked in a struggle with a "mighty industrial economy that has been shaped by Oriental history and psychology." It quoted a "member of the Nixon Cabinet" (probably Maurice Stans) as saying: "The Japanese are still fighting the war, only now instead of a shooting war it is an economic war. Their immediate intention is to try to dominate the Pacific and then perhaps the world." A Harris Poll revealed that 66 percent of American consumers favored restrictions on imports. By July 1971, congressional Democrats were calling for suspending dollar-gold convertibility and for an import surcharge in response to Japan's allegedly unfair trading practices.[40]

Nixon's personal rage toward Japan increased as Tokyo continued to balk at limiting textile exports. The issue went "far beyond a political problem affecting Southern politics" or one industry, Harry Dent, a White House aide, told the president in July. His "prestige was on the line around the country." Alexander Haig urged getting "tough with the Japanese."[41]

By July 1971, Nixon's chief economic advisers, George Shultz, the director of the Office of Management and Budget, and Treasury Secretary John Connally (who had assumed that post in March), blamed the trade and payments deficits as well as the threat to the dollar on America's trading partners. Undervalued yen, marks, and francs, they argued, made foreign goods artificially cheap in the United States and American products unnaturally expensive abroad. They proposed raising the value of the yen and mark to make dollars—and American exports—cheaper. Nixon's economic advisers also criticized the allies for imposing a variety of regulatory barriers to American exports and for refusing to pay a fair share of defense costs. Influenced by Undersecretary of the Treasury Paul Volcker and his staff, Connally urged the president to force the upward valuation of foreign currencies, impose restrictions on imports, levy an import surcharge, suspend dollar-gold convertibility, and make the allies assume a greater share of the defense burden.[42]

Pressure on the dollar increased during the summer of 1971, and on August 13, Nixon assembled his domestic political and economic advisers at Camp David. Connally dominated the agenda. The country, he warned, "can't cover our liabilities—we're broke; anyone can topple us." Only bold action would mobilize domestic support and force the upward valuation of foreign currencies. There were no options to discuss, Connally argued, since "we don't have alternatives." Delay would place the president "in the hands of the money changers." Nixon agreed to "close the gold window," levy a 10 percent surcharge on imports, impose a temporary domestic wage-price freeze, provide investment incentives to industry, and reduce federal spending.[43]

On August 15, 1971, the anniversary of "V-J" Day, Nixon told a radio and television audience (again, with no advance notification to Japan or the European allies) that "we are going to take action—not timidly, not half-heartedly, and not in piecemeal fashion." The times required "a new economic policy for the United States" to fight "unemployment, inflation, and international speculation." He stressed his determination to "protect the dollar from the attacks of international money speculators" and called on U.S. trading partners to "set straight" the values of their currencies before he dropped the import surcharge. America, Nixon proclaimed, would no longer "compete with one hand tied behind her back."

In a written directive implementing the special import surcharge, Nixon proclaimed a "national emergency," which empowered him to take action to "strengthen the international economic position of the United States" by regulating or taxing imports. This authority derived from the Trading with the Enemy Act passed by Congress in 1917 and amended shortly after the Japanese attack on Pearl Harbor. Nixon instructed his aides to publicize use of the Trading with the Enemy Act "only for textiles—i.e. Japs."[44]

Although it was only a small part of a much larger economic picture, the textile dispute continued to arouse passions in both Washington and Tokyo. Nixon threatened that unless an export restraint agreement was reached by October 15, he would impose unilateral quotas under the Trading with the Enemy Act. The threat moved Kakuei Tanaka, head of the powerful Ministry of International Trade and Industry (MITI), to confer secretly with American negotiators. Tanaka finally convinced Japanese textile firms to accept export limits, clinching a deal hours before the October deadline.[45]

Gyohten Toyoo, a Japanese finance ministry official, believed the events of 1971 convinced his colleagues that the "Nixon administration was thinking about the possibility of using Communist China as a counterweight to Japan in post-Vietnam Asia." Kissinger and Connally, the Japanese concluded, achieved a "meeting of the minds" and acted in tandem to "pull the rug out from under Japan." Just as the Nixon administration relied on triangular diplomacy to influence Soviet behavior, the Americans seemed to be "playing a kind of China card to Japan."[46]

Kissinger's remarks to his staff in late August revealed his thinking along these lines. "It was most important that we should not in our effort to re-establish good relations with Japan act so favorably towards Japan as to cause anxiety in Peking and vice versa." At the same time, "it was unwise to sacrifice a long-time friend for the sake of small advantage with a long-term opponent." China, Kissinger observed, wanted a weak Japan and still wanted the United States out of Asia. Continued U.S. "intimacy with Japan could be a good thing to dangle before the PRC." Although a "delicate line to follow ... the President felt it was extremely important."[47]

Nixon's frustration with Japan, even after the textile deal and agreement on a plan to revalue the yen, was evident in a December 20, 1971, conversation with British Prime Minister Edward Heath. The Japanese, the president complained, "are all over Asia like a bunch of lice." The opening to China, along with détente toward the Soviet Union and the gradual withdrawal of troops from Vietnam, should have allowed Washington more flexibility in its Asian policy than at any time since the Korean War. Yet the president saw a cloud around this silver lining: the challenge of finding a stable "home" for Japan in the newly emerging Asian balance. The "biggest reason" for "staying on [so long] in Vietnam," Nixon told Heath "is Japan." Despite pressure to withdraw, he prolonged the war to "reassure Asians" that the so-called Nixon Doctrine was "not a way for us to get out of Asia but a way for us to stay in."[48]

During the seven months between Kissinger's initial trip to China in July 1971 and Nixon's arrival in February 1972, Sino-American détente evolved quickly. In September-October, Mao suppressed Lin Biao's efforts to swing China back toward the Soviet Union. Kissinger visited China a second time in October and provided enhanced intelligence information on Soviet forces to the Chinese. While Kissinger was in Beijing, the United Nations voted (despite a weak American defense of Taiwan) to seat the PRC. At the end of the year, when war erupted on the Indian subcontinent, Washington and Beijing "tilted" in support of Pakistan while Moscow backed India.

As the United States and Beijing began coordinating their policies and Nixon, in San Clemente, prepared for his China visit, Japanese Prime Minister Sato made an anxious pilgrimage to see him on January 6–7, 1972. Sato admitted that the "shock of the announcement" on China the previous July "ran much deeper than the President could even imagine." Perhaps, following Nixon's upcoming visit to China, Kissinger could "stop off in Japan," providing "he didn't have a stomach ache." The president offered little reassurance. He reaffirmed the U.S. security commitment to Japan, declared his intent to expand ties to China, and promised not to abandon Taiwan. Nixon urged Sato not to "crawl" or "engage in an obvious race to Peking," that is, to upstage him. At the same time, he pressed Japan to assume greater military and economic responsibilities in Asia, even including developing a Japanese nuclear arsenal. The president also pushed for a commitment to buy more American-built jets for Japan's air force and airlines. Sato assigned MITI minister Tanaka to work on aircraft purchases (the purchases led to a scandal that in 1974 forced then Prime Minister Tanaka from office) but firmly rejected Nixon's suggestion that Japan develop nuclear weapons. Instead, Sato requested that Nixon state publicly that "the United States would not provide Japan any nuclear weapons" and that Japan had "no other recourse except the U.S. nuclear umbrella."[49]

The Nixon Visit to China

Both to minimize jet lag and maximize press coverage, Nixon's travel to China was spread over a three-day period. Notes the president prepared for himself reveal that during the journey, Kissinger suggested ways he might "bond" with Mao. The president should "treat him as an emperor" but stress that he and Mao were both "men of the people" who had "problems with intellectuals." As journalist James Mann remarked, even if Nixon secretly desired to inflict class struggle and thought reform on American intellectuals, the analogies were "preposterous."[50] The Chinese, Nixon surmised, favored meeting him to "build up their world credentials," speed unification with Taiwan, and "get the U.S. out of Asia." He hoped a summit would speed a settlement in Indochina (despite Beijing's repeated refusal to pressure Hanoi), restrain "Chicom expansion in Asia," and reduce future threats from China. Both sides wanted a more stable Asia and "restraint on U.S.S.R."

On February 21, 1971, Nixon walked down the stairway of his plane at Beijing's airport and shook the hand of Zhou Enlai. Ushered into Mao's presence a few hours later, he spoke eloquently of his own journey from anticommunism to China. What brought him to this meeting was a "recognition of a new situation in the world and a recognition on our part that what is important is not a nation's internal political philosophy. What is important is its policy towards the rest of the world and towards us." Both China and America worried about Soviet behavior and the future of Japan. Why, he asked rhetorically (and inaccurately), did the Soviets have "more forces on the border facing you" than facing Western Europe? Sino-American differences over Taiwan, Korea, and Indochina paled in comparison.

In his first private talk with Zhou on February 22, Nixon stressed their common interest in maintaining a balance of power by "restraining" Russian expansion. He promised not to make any deals with Moscow aimed at China, to treat China on an equal basis, and to keep the PRC informed about any deals between the U.S. and U.S.S.R. He promised to be wary of a Soviet design to cooperate with the United States in Europe or the Middle East to "free its hand" for expansion in Asia. Nixon assured the Chinese that he would resist "isolationist" impulses that might create an Asian vacuum for the Soviets to fill.

Nixon and Kissinger were well prepared to parry Chinese criticism of the U.S.-Japan security treaty by asking their hosts to ponder the alternative: a Japan completely uncoupled from its American anchor. "Do we tell the 2nd most prosperous nation to go it alone—or do we provide a shield?," Nixon asked Zhou. Was not a "U.S. Japan policy with a U.S. veto" less dangerous than a "Japan only policy?" Zhou had previously asked if the United States could truly control the "wild horse of Japan?" Without the U.S. security treaty and American bases on its soil, Nixon answered, the "Wild Horse would not be controlled."[51]

Nixon twice referred to Taiwan and Vietnam as "irritants" between the United States and China that could be solved gradually, perhaps through some sort of trade-off. He repeated support for "one China," of which Taiwan was a part he hoped would be peacefully reunited with the mainland. He could not make a "secret deal" that violated the U.S. commitment to Taiwan but said, "I know our interests require normalization" of relations with China following the 1972 American election.

The United States did not oppose Japanese rearmament per se, Kissinger explained to Mao and Zhou, it only hoped to prevent a "nuclear Japan." (In fact, however, six weeks earlier Nixon had explicitly urged Sato to consider developing nuclear weapons.) Only the continued presence of American bases on Japanese soil, he asserted, restrained Japan from going nuclear or from "reaching out into Korea, or Taiwan, or China." Nixon added that no one could expect Japan to remain a "military pygmy." But as long as the United States provided it with a nuclear shield, Japan would not build its own atomic arsenal or have an excuse to flex its muscles in Asia. If "we didn't have a treaty," Nixon asserted, "our remonstrations would be like `empty cannon' and the wild horse [of Japan] would not be controlled." All but calling the pact a means to contain an incipient Japanese threat, the president told Zhou that the security treaty "is in your interest, not against" it.[52]

Throughout his week in China, Nixon stated that America's alliance with Japan was in China's interest, since it "guaranteed that we would be a major factor in the Western Pacific to balance the designs of others, and would keep Japan from pursuing the path of militaristic nationalism." This held true for U.S. troops and bases in the Philippines and South Korea as well. In a remarkably nimble reversal of twenty years of Cold War rhetoric, Nixon portrayed the American base network in Asia as China's best protection against future threats from the Soviet Union and Japan. Still unpersuaded, Mao and Zhou denied hostile intentions toward Japan or South Korea, but complained that Tokyo and Seoul struck military postures that were hostile toward China.[53]

In banquet toasts on February 27, Nixon and Zhou pledged to oppose efforts by any country to establish hegemony in the Asian-Pacific region. Finessing Taiwan's status, however, presented a larger problem. In the original wording of a joint communiqué, Kissinger noted that Washington intended to honor existing commitments to Japan, the Philippines, South Korea, Australia, and New Zealand but made no reference to Taiwan. State Department officials traveling with Nixon demanded the inclusion of Taiwan. Reluctantly, Kissinger reopened discussion with the Chinese, who refused to accept such wording in a joint communiqué. Nixon finally agreed to drop references to all U.S. defense commitments in the Pacific, thereby not singling out Taiwan. The Shanghai Communiqué of February 28, 1972, affirmed both America's support for a "peaceful settlement of the Taiwan question by the Chinese themselves" and its previously stated promise to "progressively reduce" U.S. forces on the island "as tension in the area diminishes." There was "but one China," Nixon acknowledged, and "Taiwan is part of China." The communiqué contained a brief reference to America's chief Asian ally: "The United States places the highest value on its friendly relations with Japan" and would continue to "develop the existing close bonds." The Chinese repeated their opposition to the U.S.-Japan security treaty, condemned "the revival and outward expansion of Japanese militarism," and endorsed "the Japanese people's desire to build an independent, democratic, peaceful and neutral Japan."[54]

Although Nixon privately defended the security treaty—if not Japan itself—his approval of a public statement that contained these criticisms stung Prime Minister Sato. At a press conference after the release of the Shanghai Communiqué, Sato mumbled to reporters that Nixon "called this a major event of the century," then stalked out of the room. American diplomats (who themselves were largely kept in the dark by Kissinger) assured Japanese officials that Nixon made no secret deals with China and pledged that Washington would honor its Asian commitments.[55]

In the year following his visit, the China initiative appeared to help Nixon achieve three of his goals: arms control with the Soviets, a cease-fire in Vietnam, and reelection. In May 1972, Nixon traveled to the Soviet Union and signed several accords, including a long-sought Strategic Arms Limitation Treaty (SALT). Brezhnev's willingness to host Nixon in the midst of a massive U.S. bombing campaign against North Vietnam revealed Soviet determination to restore momentum to détente. The North Vietnamese, whose offensive bogged down, recognized that both the Soviets and the Chinese were now more interested in securing American favor than in speeding a communist victory in Vietnam. By October, Hanoi and Washington agreed to a draft cease-fire.[56] Kissinger's assertion that "peace is at hand" eliminated Democratic nominee George McGovern's one campaign issue. Nixon won reelection in November with 61 percent of the vote.

In February 1973, following the Vietnam peace settlement, Kissinger returned to Beijing. "The flood gates were opened," he reported to Nixon in describing the warmth with which he was received by Zhou and Mao. Instead of parking Kissinger's aircraft in a dark corner of the field, authorities permitted his "plane to taxi right up to the terminal." His photograph graced

the "top half of the *People's Daily*," and "guards saluted" the American delegation "for the first time as we entered the Great Hall and our Guest House."

In earlier trips to Beijing, the Americans thumped the Soviet threat to
spur cooperation. This time the situation appeared reversed, as Kissinger
found the Chinese "obsessed" by fears of encirclement. "The Soviet Union
dominated our conversation," he reported. It was the "centerpiece and completely permeated our talks." Mao and Zhou sounded like the former secretary of state, John Foster Dulles, demanding that the United States. initiate
efforts to "counter the Russians everywhere" by forming alliances to "prevent
the Soviets filling vacuums." The United States and the PRC could "work
together to commonly deal with a bastard," Mao declared.

Kissinger "brought up the issue of Taiwan at the very outset" of his conversation with Zhou. He "reaffirmed our intention to move toward normalization of relations," reached agreement to establish interim liaison
offices in each other's capitals, and assured Zhou "we would be prepared to
move" after the 1974 midterm congressional elections "toward something like
the Japanese solution with regard to diplomatic relations." By "mid-1976, we
were prepared to establish full diplomatic relations," Kissinger reassured his
hosts, presumably by terminating the security treaty with Taiwan.

In addition to the strident anti-Soviet tone of the February 1973 talks,
Kissinger was struck by the "major turnabout" in the attitude of Mao and
Zhou "toward Japan and the U.S." In July 1971, Kissinger recalled, Zhou
had described Japan as "fattened economically by the U.S." and about to
"expand its militarism throughout" Asia. Throughout the next year China
condemned the U.S. - Japan security treaty. Now "the Chinese . . . clearly
consider Japan as an incipient ally," which could help "to counter Soviet and
Indian designs." Zhou acknowledged the security treaty as a "brake on Japanese expansionism and militarism" and cautioned against any actions that
might drive Japan into a "situation where the Soviet Union became its ally
instead of the U.S." Mao took pains to urge Kissinger to spend more time in
Japan and to "make sure that trade and other frictions with Tokyo . . . would
not mar our fundamental cooperation." Kissinger, in turn, cautioned the
Chinese to avoid a bidding war with America to "compete for Tokyo's
allegiance," as this might encourage "resurgent Japanese nationalism."[57]

By the time he left Beijing, Kissinger's assessment of Chinese foreign policy led him to what even he recognized as a remarkable conclusion. "We are

now in the extraordinary position," Kissinger reported to Nixon, that among all nations, "with the exception of the United Kingdom, *the PRC might well be closest to us in its global perceptions.* No other world leaders have the sweep and imagination of Mao and Chou nor the capacity and will to achieve a long range policy." The U.S. and China had become "in plain words . . . tacit allies."[58]

Unlike the Chinese leadership, however, the Americans had not given up entirely on détente with the Soviet Union. Early in 1973, for example, Kissinger wrote to the president that with "conscientious attention to both capitals, we should be able to have our mao tai and drink our vodka, too." In other words, improved ties with China were still considered a spur to cooperation with, not merely countering, Moscow. Despite this hope, during the remainder of Nixon's presidency, just under eighteen months, and those of his four immediate successors, the U.S.-China relationship assumed an increasingly anti-Soviet tinge.[59]

This evolution was influenced by both domestic and foreign developments. In March 1973, Kissinger wrote to Zhou and Mao that Nixon still planned to normalize diplomatic relations and cut links to Taiwan as soon as possible.[60] Within a month, however, the unraveling Watergate coverup began to envelop the White House. Although Kissinger had no direct tie to the Watergate crimes, his patron, Richard Nixon, possessed too little political capital to expend any of it on a complicated foreign policy whose rewards were not always apparent to the American public. More pointedly, Nixon could not afford, while Congress and a Special Prosecutor weighed his fate, to alienate conservative Republicans who retained affection for Taiwan.

At the same time, the luster faded from détente. In October 1973, another round of Arab-Israeli warfare provoked a crisis when the Soviet Union threatened to send troops to bolster Egypt and Washington threatened a military response if it did so. Although a regional cease-fire reduced tensions, the resulting Arab oil boycott spiked energy prices and produced recession in the United States and Japan. These economic problems further tarnished Nixon's credentials.

With the process of normalization and the status of Taiwan on hold and with the Watergate crisis, which the Chinese found incomprehensible, hobbling Nixon, anti-Soviet rhetoric seemed the main force binding the United States and China together. Trade, of course, did not become an important factor until the 1980s. Beginning in mid-1973, Washington supplied

a growing quantity and better quality of intelligence on Soviet military matters to the Chinese. When Kissinger met with Mao and Zhou in November
1973, and during conclaves in 1974, both sides swapped tales of Soviet perfidy
and discussed ways to contain the Soviet threat against China, South Asia,
and the Middle East.[61]

Despite the frustrations on both sides, the evolving relationship between
the United States and the People's Republic that began in the early 1970s
had dramatic, if sometimes unintended, consequences for world politics.
Although both Richard Nixon and Mao Zedong were considered leading
ideologues of the Cold War, their actions largely stripped that contest of its
ideological trappings. After 1971–72, the Cold War in Asia disappeared. The
Soviet-American rivalry that continued for almost two more decades took
on a very different coloration.

The new Sino-American relationship also eased a settlement in Vietnam
and transformed ties between Japan and the United States. Although
Washington and Tokyo remained allies and trading partners, each sought
to distance itself from the other. By the early 1980s, disputes over trade and
the security treaty became increasingly common. Some of these developments may have been inevitable, yet it would be difficult to overestimate the
importance of the changes that flowed from the U.S. opening to China
begun in 1971.

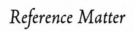

Reference Matter

Notes

Preface: Jiang Changbin

1. Harry Harding and Yuan Ming, eds., *Sino-American Relations, 1945–1955: A Joint Reassessment of a Critical Decade* (Wilmington, Del.: Scholarly Resources, 1989); Yuan Ming and Harry Harding, eds., *Zhong Mei Guanxi 1945–1955: Dui Shinian Lishi de Lianhe Pingjia* (Beijing: Beijing Daxue Chubanshe, 1989).

2. The contributors to this conference were Gong Li (Tension across the Taiwan Strait in the 1950s: Chinese Strategy and Tactics); Ronald W. Pruessen (Over the Volcano: The United States and the Taiwan Strait Crisis, 1954–1955); Jiang Ying (The Vietnam War and China's Policy toward the United States); Robert D. Schulzinger (The Johnson Administration, China, and the Vietnam War); Zhang Baijia (The Changing International Scene and Chinese Policy toward the United States, 1954–1970); Michael Schaller (U.S.-China-Japan Relations and the "Nixon Shocks"); Li Jie (Changes in China's Domestic Situation in the 1960s and Sino-U.S. Relations); Rosemary Foot (Redefinitions: The Domestic Context of America's China Policy in the 1960s). The discussants at this conference were William C. Kirby, Steven M. Goldstein, Yuan Ming, and Shi Yinhong.

3. Jiang Changbin and Robert S. Ross, eds., *1955–1971 Nian de Zhong Mei Guanxi—Huanhe Zhiqian: Lengzhan Chongtu yu Kezhi de Cai Tantao* (U.S.-China relations 1955–1971—Before détente: An examination of Cold War conflict and restraint) (Beijing: Shijie Zhishi Chubanshe, 1998).

4. Jiang Changbin and Robert S. Ross, eds. *Cong Duizhi zouxiang Huanhe: Lengzhan Shiqi Zhong Mei Guanxi zai Tantao* (From confrontation toward détente: A reexamination of U.S.-China relations during the Cold War) (Beijing: Shijie Zhishi Chubanshe, 2000). This volume includes all the papers from the first volume as well

as the following papers from the second conference: William C. Kirby (The "Two Chinas" in the Global Setting: Sino-Soviet Economic Cooperation and U.S.-Taiwan Relations in the 1950s); Robert Accinelli ("The Obstacle to Peace": The Eisenhower Administration and the 1958 Offshore Islands Crisis); Steven M. Goldstein (Dialogue of the Deaf? The Sino-American Ambassadorial Talks, 1955–1970); Jiang Ying (Mao Zedong's Diplomatic Thinking in the late 1950s); Liu Jianfei (The Impact of the China-U.S.-Japan Triangle on Sino-American Relations); Gong Li (Chinese Elite Policy Making and the Thaw in China-U.S. Relations); Zhang Baijia and Jia Qingguo (Steering Wheel, Shock Absorber, and Probe on Confrontation: Sino-American Ambassadorial Talks Seen from the Chinese Perspective); Li Jie (Mao Zedong's Challenge to the Bipolar Pattern: China's Diplomatic Work from the Late 1950s to 1976). Other contributors and discussants to the second conference were H. W. Brands, Rosemary Foot, Douglas Macdonald, Ronald Pruessen, Michael Schaller, Shi Yinhong, Michael Schoenhals, and Tao Wenzhao.

Introduction: Robert S. Ross

I am grateful to Chen Jian, Rosemary Foot, and Steven Goldstein for their helpful comments.

1. For an excellent discussion of recent Chinese works using archival materials, see Chen Jian, "Sino-American Relations in China," in *Pacific Passage: The Study of American-East-Asian Relations on the Eve of the Twenty-First Century*, ed. Warren Cohen (New York: Columbia University Press, 1996).

2. See Yuan Ming and Harry Harding, *Sino-American Relations, 1945–1955: A Joint Assessment of a Critical Decade* (Wilmington, Del.: Scholarly Resources, 1989); Michael Hunt and Niu Jun, eds., *Toward a History of Chinese Communist Foreign Relations, 1920s-1960s: Personalities and Interpretive Approaches* (Washington, D.C.: Woodrow Wilson International Center for Scholars, 1993); collaborative research by Gordon H. Chang and He Di, "The Absence of War in the U.S.-China Confrontation over Quemoy and Matsu in 1954–1955: Contingency, Luck, Deterrence?" *American Historical Review* 98, no. 5 (Dec. 1993); and the works of John Lewis and Xue Litai.

3. See, for example, Gordon Chang, *Friends and Enemies: The United States, China, and the Soviet Union, 1948–1972* (Stanford: Stanford University Press, 1990); John Gaddis, *The Long Peace: Inquiries into the History of the Cold War* (New York: Oxford University Press, 1987); John Gaddis, *We Now Know: Rethinking Cold War History* (New York: Oxford University Press, 1997).

4. For earlier and insightful Western analysis, see Robert Sutter, *China Watch: Toward Sino-American Reconciliation* (Baltimore: Johns Hopkins University Press, 1978).

5. On this point, see Jiang Ying, "Yuenan Zhanzheng yu Zhongguo dui Mei Zhengce" (The Vietnam War and China's policy toward the United States), in

1955–1971 Nian de Zhong Mei Guanxi—Huanhe Zhiqian: Lengzhan Chongtu yu Kezhi de Zai Tantao (U.S.-China Relations 1955–1971—Before détente: An examination of Cold War conflict and restraint), ed. Jiang Changbin and Robert S. Ross (Beijing: Shijie Zhishi Chubanshe, 1998). For a comprehensive analysis of China's support for Vietnam's war effort that utilizes a wide range of important Chinese documents, see Qiang Zhai, *China and the Vietnam Wars, 1950–1975* (Chapel Hill: University of North Carolina Press, 2000).

6. On the importance of Mao's domestic priorities in the 1958 crisis, see also Thomas J. Christensen, *Useful Adversaries: Grand Strategy, Domestic Mobilization, and Sino-American Conflict, 1947–1958* (Ithaca: Cornell University Press, 1997).

7. The contributions to this volume suggest that common arguments about misperceptions in policymaking—that the adversary is perceived as unresponsive to cooperative signaling and that its aggressive intentions are immutable—do not apply to the U.S.-China conflict. The classic piece on misperceptions remains Robert Jervis, *Perception and Misperception in International Politics* (Princeton: Princeton University Press, 1976).

8. On the impact of the Korean War on U.S. policy, see Yuen Foong Khong, *Analogies at War: Korea, Munich, Dien Bien Phu, and the Vietnam Decisions of 1965* (Princeton: Princeton University Press, 1992).

9. On U.S. nuclear diplomacy, see Richard K. Betts, *Nuclear Blackmail and Nuclear Balance* (Washington, D.C.: Brookings Institution, 1987); Appu K. Soman, *Double-edged Sword: Nuclear Diplomacy in Unequal Conflicts: The United States and China, 1950–1958* (Westport, Conn.: Praeger, 2000). For China's deterrence diplomacy, see Allen S. Whiting, *The Chinese Calculus of Deterrence* (Ann Arbor: University of Michigan Press, 1975).

10. On the impact of U.S.-China rapprochement on China's Japan policy during this period, see Liu Jianfei, "Zhong Mei Ri Sanjiao Guanxi dui Zhong Mei Guanxi de Yingxiang (1949–1979 nian)" (The Influence of China-U.S.-Japan triangular relations on Sino-American relations, 1949–1979), in *Cong Duizhi Zouxiang Huanhe: Lengzhan Shiqi zhong Zhong Mei Guanxi zai Tantao* (From confrontation to détente: A reexamination of Cold War U.S.-China relations), 349–66, ed. Jiang Changbin and Robert S. Ross (Beijing: Shijie Zhishi Chubanshe, 2000); Zhang Tuosheng, "China Relations with Japan" and Robert S. Ross, "U.S. relations with China," both in *The China-Japan-United States Triangle, 1972–1992*, ed. Ezra Vogel (forthcoming).

11. See, in particular, Memorandum of Conversation, by the Secretary of State, Dec. 29, 1949, *Foreign Relations of the United States (FRUS), 1949* (Washington, D.C.: Government Printing Office, 1974), *9: 467.* Memorandum of Conversation, by the Secretary of State, Jan. 5, 1950, *FRUS, 1950*, 6: 260–61. On early U.S. evaluations of the importance of Taiwan to U.S. security and the development of the U.S. commitment to the defense of Taiwan, see David M. Finkelstein, *Washington's Taiwan*

Dilemma, 1949–1950: From Abandonment to Salvation (Fairfax, Va.: George Mason University Press, 1993); Nancy Tucker, *Taiwan and Hong Kong and the United States, 1945–1992: Uncertain Friendships* (New York: Twayne Publishers, 1994).

12. On the *sanhe yishao*, see also Roderick MacFarquhar, *The Origins of the Cultural Revolution, Volume 3: The Coming of the Cataclysm* (New York: Columbia University Press, 1997), 269–71.

13. For a discussion of the 1996 confrontation, see Robert S. Ross, "The 1996 Taiwan Strait Confrontation: Coercion, Credibility, and Use of Force," *International Security* 25, no. 1 (Fall 2000): 87–123.

14. See The Taiwan Affairs Office and The Information Office of the State Council, People's Republic of China, *White Paper—The One-China Principle and the Taiwan Issue*, Feb. 21, 2000.

15. For a discussion of this period, see Ezra Vogel, ed., *The China-Japan-United States Triangle, 1972–1992* (Cambridge: Harvard University Asia Center, forthcoming).

16. For an early assessment of Chinese research materials, see Steven M. Goldstein and He Di, "New Chinese Sources on the History of the Cold War," *Cold War International History Project Bulletin*, no. 1 (Spring 1992).

1. William C. Kirby, "The Two Chinas in the Global Setting: Sino-Soviet and Sino-American Cooperation in the 1950s"

1. Xiaoyuan Liu, *A Partnership for Disorder: China, the United States, and Their Policies for the Postwar Disposition of the Japanese Empire, 1941–1945* (New York: Cambridge University Press, 1996).

2. Sergei N. Goncharov, John W. Lewis, and Xue Litai, *Uncertain Partners: Stalin, Mao and the Korean War* (Stanford: Stanford University Press, 1993).

3. Gordon Chang, *Friends and Enemies: The United States, China, and the Soviet Union, 1948–1972* (Stanford: Stanford University Press, 1990).

4. Nancy Bernkopf Tucker, *Taiwan, Hong Kong, and the United States, 1945–1992: Uncertain Friendships* (New York: Twayne, 1994).

5. See also, most recently, "Leadership Transition in a Fractured Bloc," *Cold War International History Project Bulletin*, no. 10 (March 1998); and papers presented to the Symposium on Sino-Soviet Relations and the Cold War, Beijing, October 1997. Of course, the diplomatic archives of the period are only imperfectly open in Moscow and Taipei, and in Beijing they remain altogether closed to independent research.

6. Xiang Qing, "Zhongguo gongchandang chuangli," *Zhonggong dangshi yanjiu lunwen xuan* 1: 296, cited in Arif Dirlik, *The Origins of Chinese Communism* (New York: Oxford University Press, 1989), 192.

7. *Die Komintern und die national-revolutionäre Bewegung in China: Dokumente, Band 1: 1920–1925*, hrsg. von dem Russischen Zentrum für Archivierung und Erforschung

von Dokumenten zur neuesten Geschichte, dem Ostasiatischen Seminar der FU Berlin und dem Institut für den Fernen Osten der Russischen Akademie der Wissenschaften (Paderborn (u.a.): Schöningh, 1996); *Band 2: 1926–27, Teil 1 und 2* (1997); Band 3 (2000). The best general study of CCP relations with Moscow is now Yang Kuisong, *Zhonggong yu Mosike de guanxi (1920–1960)* (The Chinese Communists and Moscow [1920–1960]) (Taibei: Dongda, 1997).

8. Second Historical Archives, Nanjing, 28 (2) 389, files on National Resources Commission and related payments to the Soviet Union through 1946. The two best sources on Sino-Soviet relations of this period are He Jun, "Lun 1929–1939 nian de Zhong Su guanxi" (Sino-Soviet relations, 1929–39), Ph.D. diss., Nanjing University, 1986; and John W. Garver, *Chinese-Soviet Relations, 1937–1945: The Diplomacy of Chinese Nationalism* (New York: Oxford University Press, 1988).

9. Academia Historica, Taiwan, NRC, file, "Ziyuan weiyuanhui jianjie," speech by Qian Changzhao of 21 Jan. 1942; Qian Changzhao, "Zhonggongye jianshe xianzai ji jianglai" (Present and future of heavy industrial development), *Ziyuan weiyuanhui gongbao* 3, no. 3 (Sept. 1942): 49–54. See also Yuan-li Wu, *China's Economic Policy: Planning or Free Enterprise?* (New York: n.p., 1946); "Sulian gongye jianshe zhi yejin" (Evolution of Soviet industrial development), *Ziyuan weiyuanhui gongbao* 3, no. 6 (Dec. 1942): 43–47; and William C. Kirby, "Nationalist China's Search for a Partner: Relationships with Germany, the Soviet Union and the United States, 1928–1942" (paper presented to the Conference on Patterns of Cooperation in Modern China's Foreign Relations, Wintergreen, Va., 1987).

10. Sun Yueqi, "Kangzhan shiqijian liangci qu Xinjiang jilue" (Record of two visits to Xinjiang during the war of resistance), *Wenshi ziliao* (Literary and historical materials) (1982), no. 84, 135–49.

11. Sun Yueqi, "Huiyi wo yu Jiang Jieshi jiechu liangsanshi" (Two or three items of my dealings with Chiang Kai-shek), *Wenshi ziliao* (1982), no. 84, 133. Or we may take the case of the Sino-Soviet Aviation Company (ZhongSu hangkong gongsi), organized on the basis of an agreement in 1939 and extended by the Nationalists for five years in 1949; see *Minguo dang'an* (Republican archives) (1995), no. 1, 31–42.

12. Extraterritorial rights were indeed relinquished for *White* Russians in China. But with the Soviet nationalization of all facets of foreign relations—economic and cultural as well as political and military—there were no "private" activities for Soviet citizens in China, who were under the authority of the Soviet embassy and therefore, the U.S.S.R. claimed, were entitled to *diplomatic* immunity. This was made more explicit in a series of agreements with Chinese governments, including one of the secret protocols of the 1950 Treaty of Friendship, Alliance, and Mutual Assistance, which went further to claim that any criminal activity of Soviet citizens in China would be dealt with by Soviet, not Chinese, courts. On the latter point, see Goncharov, Lewis, and Xue, *Uncertain Partners*, 125.

13. See Liu, *A Partnership for Disorder*, 264, and chap. 11, passim.

14. For speculation on why Mao dropped the issue that Chiang and Song had pursued at such length, see Dieter Heinzig, "The Sino-Soviet Alliance Treaty Negotiations: A Reappraisal in the Light of New Sources" (paper presented to the Symposium on Sino-Soviet Relations and the Cold War, Beijing, October 1997), 103.

15. Sun Yat-sen, *The International Development of China* (New York and London, 1922), preface, v.

16. See, for example, Second Historical Archives, Nanjing, file 28 (2) 3644, including memorandum on Sino-Soviet barter agreement of Jan. 1945; Sino-Soviet barter agreement of Jan. 19, 1946; documents on the Sino-Soviet Aviation Company Agreement of 1949 (supplementary to the agreement of 1939) in *Minguo dang'an* (Republican archives) (1995), no. 1, 31–42.

17. Deborah A. Kaple, *Dream of a Red Factory: The Legacy of High Stalinism in China* (New York: Oxford University Press, 1994), 3.

18. C. X. George Wei, *Sino-American Economic Relations, 1944–1949* (Westport, Conn.: Greenwood Press, 1997), 157.

19. See Brian Murray, "Stalin, the Cold War, and the Division of China: A Multi-Archival Mystery," *Cold War International History Project Working Paper*, no. 12 (Washington, D.C.: Woodrow Wilson Center, 1995).

20. Chang, *Friends and Enemies*, 30–31.

21. Marie-Luise Näth, "East European Sinologists Remember the First Fifteen Years of the PRC: A Balance Sheet," in *Communist China in Retrospect*, ed. Marie-Luise Näth (Frankfurt a.M.: Peter Lang, 1995), 189.

22. Goncharov, Lewis, and Xue, *Uncertain Partners*, 54.

23. John W. Garver, *The Sino-American Alliance: Nationalist China and American Cold War Strategy in Asia* (Armonk, N.Y.: M. E. Sharpe, 1997), 24, 31–32.

24. Michael M. Sheng, *Ideology and Foreign Policy: Mao, Stalin and the United States before 1950* (Princeton: Princeton University Press, 1997). For an excellent analysis, see Steven M. Goldstein, "Nationalism and Internationalism: Sino-Soviet Relations," in *Chinese Foreign Policy: Theory and Practice*, ed. Thomas W. Robinson and David Shambaugh (Oxford: Clarendon Press, 1994), 224–65. See also Niu Jun, *Cong Yan'an zouxiang shijie* (From Yanan to the world) (Fuzhou: Fujian renmin chubanshe, 1992). On the fundamental conflicts between the CCP and the United States, see also Zi Zhongyun, *Meiguo dui Hua zhengce de yuanqi he fazhan* (Origins and development of U.S. policy toward China) (Chongqing: Chongqing chubanshe, 1987).

25. For example, in nuclear matters, see Liu Xiao, *Chu shi Sulian ba nian* (Eight years as Ambassador to the Soviet Union) (Beijing: Zhonggong dangshi ziliao chubanshe), 9–10, 60–61.

26. See the transcript from the Soviet archives of Mao Zedong's conversation with P. F. Yudin, the Soviet Ambassador to China, on March 31, 1956, on the question of

the Comintern's and Stalin's China policy, in *Far Eastern Affairs* (1994), no. 4–5, 132–44. Regarding models for statebuilding, Deborah Kaple argues (in *Dream of a Red Factory*) that the adoption of a "high Stalinist" model gave the CCP even more power in society than had the CPSU.

27. Lowell Dittmer, "Socialist Reform and Sino-Soviet Convergence," in *Reform and Reaction in Post-Mao China: The Road to Tiananmen*, ed. Richard Baum (New York and London: Routledge, 1991), 19.

28. Lowell Dittmer, *Sino-Soviet Normalization and Its International Implications, 1945–1990* (Seattle and London: University of Washington Press, 1992), 10.

29. For example, Wu Xiuquan, *Zai Waijiaobu ba nian de jingli, 1950.1–1958.10* (Eight years in the Foreign Ministry: January 1950 to October 1958) (Beijing: Shijie zhishi chubanshe, 1983), 1–34. Perhaps the least politicized account of Sino-Soviet cooperation remains *Liunian lai Zhong-Su youhao hezuo gegong yu fazhan* (The stability and development of friendly cooperation between China and the Soviet Union in the past six years) (Guangzhou, 1955). A recent and balanced set of essays may be found in *Zhanhou ZhongSu guanxi zouxiang* (1945–1960) (Trends in postwar Chinese-Soviet relations, 1945–1960) (Beijing: Shehui kexue wenxian chubanshe, 1997).

30. For example, O. B. Borisov and B. T. Koloskov, *Sovetsko-kitayskie otnoshenia, 1945–1980*, 3rd ed. (Moscow: Mysl', 1980). Borisov is a pseudonym for O. B. Rakhmanin; Koloskov is a pseudonym for S. Kulik; both worked in the Central Committee of the CPSU, Rakhmanin being in charge of China policy. A more recent and (in its political assessments) evenhanded account is Iu. M. Galenovich, *"Belye piatna" I "Bolevye tochki" v istorii sovetsko-kitaiskikh otnoshenii* ("Blank spots" and "sore points" in the history of Soviet-Chinese relations), vol. 2 (1949–91) (Moscow: Institut Dal'nego Vostoka RAN, 1992).

31. RTsKhIDNI (Russian Center for the Protection and Study of Documents on Recent History), Moscow, archive of the Central Committee of the Communist Party of the Soviet Union (CPSU CC), External Political Commission, fond 17/opis 137, vol. 405, files on Sino-Soviet study commissions, lecture tours, etc., 1949–50.

32. RTsKhIDNI, Moscow, CPSU CC, External Political Commission, 17/137, vol. 406, report to Malenkov of 15 Feb. 1950 on Chen Boda; vol. 405, report of 1 June 1950 on the three-month tour of labor union delegates to China (20 Dec. 1949 to 10 April 1950); vol. 405, report of M. Abramov, Vice-Chair of Moscow City Executive Council on the delegation of city planners to Shanghai and other cities, 7 Feb. 1950.

33. RTsKhIDNI, Moscow, CPSU CC, External Political Commission, 17/137, vol. 405, report to Molotov of 27 May 1950 on the sending of teaching teams to China; vol. 406, report of 7 June 1950 on the export of Soviet horses to China; vol. 406, report to Suslov of 2 Sept. 1950 requesting fifty-one Western-style suits for Chinese comrades. (The request was granted.)

34. The short-lived era of "New Democracy" and the "Chinese NEP" of the early 1950s needs much more research. For an excellent inquiry based on Soviet archives, see Arlen Meliksetov, "'New Democracy' and China's Search for Socio-Economic Development Routes (1949–53)," in *Far Eastern Affairs* (1996), no. 1, 75–92. The quote is from the resolution of the Second Plenary Meeting of the Seventh Central Committee of the CCP (March 1949) and refers to the prospects for capitalism in a socialist China: "The existence and development of capitalism in China, the existence and development of free trade and competition, are not as limitless and unbridled as in capitalist countries, nor are they as limited and cramped as in newly democratic countries of Eastern Europe; they are specifically Chinese in form" (77).

35. Shi Zhongquan, *Mao Zedong de jianxin kaituo* (Mao Zedong's hard, pioneering road) (Beijing: Zhonggong dangshi ziliao chubanshe, 1990), 132, cited in Hua-yu Li, "Mao, Stalin, and Changing Course: Building Socialism in China, 1948–53," Ph.D. diss., Columbia University, 1997, 3.

36. Li, 11.

37. Ibid., 252. On the centrality of Mao's decisions in ending New Democracy, see Meliksetov, "'New Democracy,'" 75–92, esp. 82–83; Bo Yibo, *Ruogan zhongda juece yu shijian de huigu* (A review of some important policies and events), vol. 1, 1949–56 (Beijing: Zhonggong zhongyang dangxiao chubanshe, 1991), 234–42.

38. Kaple, viii, 11–18.

39. This was negotiated by Gao Gang in Moscow; see the account and trade statistics in Borisov and Koloskov, 30. On Soviet developmental advice before 1949, see ibid., 31–38, and, particularly, details of the 1946 "unofficial" (because Moscow still recognized the Nationalist government) trade agreement in the memoir of M. I. Sladkovskii, *Znakomstvo s Kitaem I kitaitsami* (Acquaintance with China and the Chinese) (Moscow: Mysl', 1984), 324–29. The participation of Soviet advisers in the Chinese civil war began in 1946, when 100 Soviet engineers were sent to northern Manchuria to restore the rail links with the U.S.S.R. In 1948 Soviet engineers repaired over 100 bridges and 100 miles of track that had been destroyed by the Nationalist military. See S. A. Voevodin et al., *Sotsial'no-ekonomicheskiy stroy I ekonomicheskaya politika KNR* (The socio-economic structure and economic policy of the PRC) (Moscow: Majka, 1978), 82. For his oversight of railroad repair and his aid to Lin Biao, Sladkovskii was given an Order of Lenin in Moscow in Dec. 1948; see Sladkovskii, 353. For a political and military perspective on CCP-Soviet cooperation in Manchuria after 1945, see Michael M. Sheng, "Mao, Stalin, and the Struggle in Manchuria, 1945–46: Nationalism or Internationalism?" (paper presented to the Conference on New Evidence on the Cold War in Asia, Hong Kong, 1996).

40. See Li, chap. 4.

41. Borisov and Koloskov, 52.

42. Bilateral trade increased by over 25 percent in 1953 compared with 1952. Borisov and Koloskov, 65.

43. See the excellent summary of Soviet aid in Dittmer, *Sino-Soviet Normalization*, 17–25. Under the strategic trade regime of the United States, the West refused to export to China the capital goods and military-related imports that comprised the bulk of China's imports from the Soviet Union.

44. Alexander Eckstein, "Moscow-Peking Axis: The Economic Pattern," in *Moscow-Peking Axis: Strengths and Strains*, ed. Howard L. Boorman et al. (New York: Harper, 1957), 82–83.

45. Feng-hwa Mah, "The Terms of Sino-Soviet Trade," *China Quarterly* (Jan.-Mar. 1964): 175. As Mah argued elsewhere, prices are not everything: "For China, the availability of a ready market for its exports, the existence of a reliable (at least in the 1950's) supplier of the type of producer goods it needed, the availability of Soviet credit arrangements, and the convenience of conducting foreign trade between two planned economies may be considered more important than favorable prices." Feng-hwa Mah, "Foreign Trade," in *Economic Trends in Communist China*, ed. Alexander Eckstein et al. (Chicago: Aldine, 1968), 721.

46. Mah, "Terms of Sino-Soviet Trade," 188–91.

47. Mah, "Foreign Trade," 724.

48. Eckstein, "Moscow-Peking Axis," 88.

49. L. V. Filatov, *Ekonomischeskaia otsenka nauchno-technicheskov pomoschchi sovet-skogo soyuza kitayu, 1949–1966* (An economic evaluation of the Soviet Union's scientific-technical assistance to China, 1949–1966) (Moscow: Nauka, 1980), 11–12; L. Filatov, "Cost Assessment of Soviet-Chinese Scientific and Technical Cooperation," *Far Eastern Affairs* (1990), no. 2, 111–17; L. Nikolayev and Y. Mikhailov, "China's Foreign Economic Policy," *International Affairs* 9 (1973): 45. These rosy accounts are not fundamentally challenged in the published Chinese documentation: see *ZhongSu maoyi shi ziliao* (Materials on the history of Sino-Soviet trade) (Beijing: Zhongguo duiwai jingji maoyi chubanshe, 1991). For a sober and positive assessment of Soviet technicians in development work, see Waldemar A. Nielsen and Soran S. Hodjera, "Sino-Soviet Bloc Technical Assistance—Another Bilateral Approach," *Annals of the American Academy of Political and Social Science* 323 (May 1959): 40–49.

50. Joseph Stalin, *Economic Problems of Socialism in the USSR* (New York: International Publishers, 1952), 26.

51. See Frederic L. Pryor, *The Communist Foreign Trade System* (Cambridge: MIT Press, 1963), 25.

52. Generally, see Nicolas Spulber, "The Soviet Bloc Foreign Trade System," and Raymond F. Mikesell and Donald A. Wells, "State Trading in the Sino-Soviet Bloc," both in *Law and Contemporary Problems* 24 (1959): 420–34 and 435–53, respectively; Alfred Zauberman, "Economic Integration: Problems and Prospects," *Problems of*

Communism 8, no. 4 (1959): 23–29; I. Oleinki, "Forms of International Division of Labor in the Socialist Camp," *Problems of Economics* 4, no. 6 (Oct. 1961): 56–63. On the weaknesses of socialist international integration, particularly in the Stalin years, see Charles Gati, *The Bloc That Failed: Soviet-East European Relations in Transition* (Bloomington and Indianapolis: Indiana University Press, 1990), 20. Most optimistically, see M. I. Sladkovskii, *Semiletka i ekonomicheskoe sotrudnichestvo stran sotsialisticheskogo lageria* (The seven-year plan and the economic cooperation of the countries in the socialist camp) (Moscow: Institut Mezhdunarodnykh Otnoshenii, 1959).

53. Speech of Mar. 7, 1959, quoted in Sladkovskii, 32.

54. Spulber, 424–25. Spulber notes (427) that according to a rule against price discrimination in 1951, each socialist country was to charge every other the same price for the same goods, taking into account only differences for transportation.

55. In Moscow, in the Russian State Archive of the Economy (RGAE); in Germany, in the Bundesarchiv, Potsdam, and in the Stiftung Archiv der Parteien und Massenorganisationen der DDR im Bundesarchiv, in Berlin (hereafter Stiftung Archiv).

56. Galenovich, *"Belye piatna,"* 30ff.

57. Stiftung Archiv, Berlin, IV 2/610, vol. 179, "Vermerk über die Besprechung beim Gen. Min. Präs. Tschou En-lai mit der Regierungsdelegation der DDR," 10 Oct. 1957.

58. This would also be true in the realm of scientific and technological exchange. See, for example, RGAE, Moscow, 9480/1735, files on Sino-Soviet scientific and technological agreement of 5 Feb. 1958, based on the agreement of 12 Oct. 1954.

59. Stiftung Archiv, Berlin, Nachlaß Grotewohl, Bd. 477, letter, Zhou Enlai to Otto Grotewohl, 11 Aug. 1953.

60. Yu. N. Kapelinskiy et al., *Razvitie ekonomiki i vneshneekonomicheskikh svyazey kitayskoy narodnoy respubliki* (The development of the economy and the foreign economic relations of the PRC) (Moscow: Vneshtorgizdat, 1959), 427.

61. Filatov, *Ekonomisheskaia otsenka*, 87.

62. See L. A. Schneider, "Learning from Russia: Lysenkoism and the Fate of Genetics in China, 1950–1986," in *Science and Technology in Post-Mao China*, ed. Denis Fred Simon and Merle Goldman (Cambridge: Harvard University Press, 1989), 45–65.

63. M. I. Sladkovskii, *Istoriia torgovo-ekonomicheskikh otnoshenii SSSR s Kitaem (1917–1974)* (History of trade and economic relations of the U.S.S.R. with China, 1917–1974) (Moscow: Nauka, 1974), 216, puts the proposal as emanating from Mao. The more recent work by Galenovich, *"Belye piatna,"* 50, makes Khrushchev the author and says that Mao was offended by the notion of China as a source of cheap labor for the U.S.S.R. Both accounts give evidence of a Soviet fear of Chinese designs on Siberia through Han settlement.

64. L. V. Zandanova, "Repatriiatsiaa granzhan iz Kitaia v SSSR v 1947–1960 godakh," (Repatriation of citizens from China to the U.S.S.R., 1947–1960) (Irkutsk: Irkutschkii gosudarstevennyi universitet, 1996), 183–204.

65. For a sharp, internal critique of boorish, overbearing behavior on the part of some Soviet specialists in China, see RGAE, Moscow, 9480/1724, report of M. Kudinova of 13 Nov. 1958. Such behavior may have been endemic in Sino-Soviet joint stock companies in Xinjiang; see G. Ganshin and T. Zazerskaya, "Pitfalls Along the Path of 'Brotherly Friendship' (A Look at the History of Soviet-Chinese Relations)," *Far Eastern Affairs* (1994), no. 6, 63–70.

66. New China News Agency report of 23 Dec. 1956, in *Survey of the Chinese Mainland Press* (1957), no. 1442, 41.

67. The statistics are from A. I. Arnoldov and G. M. Hovak, *Kul'tura narodnogo Kitaia* (The culture of people's China) (Moscow: Izd.Akademii Nauk SSR, 1959), 138–40. On political translations, see Wei-shung Chang, "The Impact of Soviet Dialectical Materialism on China through Translations," *Studies in Soviet Thought* 11, no. 3 (1971): 208–11. On the occasional outcry against Soviet films in China, see Galenovich, "Belye piatna," 38–39.

68. For an interesting argument in this direction, see Zhang Shuguang, "The Collapse of Sino-Soviet Economic Cooperation" (paper presented to the Conference on New Evidence on the Cold War in Asia, Hong Kong, 1996).

69. Goldstein, "Nationalism and Internationalism," 232.

70. See the remarks of National Resources Commission chair Qian Changzhao in *Ziyuan weiyuanhui gongbao* (Gazette of the National Resources Commission) 12, no. 1 (Jan. 1947): 60–62.

71. Generally, see William C. Kirby, "Planning Postwar Taiwan: Industrial Policy and the Nationalist Takeover, 1943–1947," *Harvard Studies on Taiwan* 1 (1995): 286–301.

72. On continuity of consulting arrangements, see Second Historical Archives, Nanjing, 28 (2) 50; annual reports of the National Resources Commission office in the United States; Academia Historica, Taipei, NRC files, "Gexiang jishe hetong" (Various consulting agreements) (1945–46). On basic institutions for cooperation, see Neil H. Jacoby, *U.S. Aid to Taiwan* (New York: Praeger, 1966), chap. 5; Thomas B. Gold, *State and Society in the Taiwan Miracle* (Armonk, N.Y.: M. E. Sharpe, 1986).

73. Jacoby, 31.

74. Ibid., 38–43.

75. See Marjorie Ann Walker, "The Role of U.S.-Educated Chinese in the Economic Development of the Republic of China, with Particular Emphasis on Import-Export Strategies, 1950–1965," Ph.D. diss., Washington University, St. Louis, 1996.

76. Filatov, *Ekonomisheskaia otsenka*, 14. Some 600 Soviet scientists and 500 Soviet organizations played an advisory role in the Twelve-Year Plan. L. Filatov, "Cost Assessment," 117.

77. *Gold, State and Society,* 77, argues that the "self-reliance" issue was particularly important to Chiang Kai-shek.

78. "Industrializing reformers," the term used by John Garver, is a better designation for the first group, which was no less "pro-state" than their more protectionist rivals (Garver, *Sino-American Alliance,* 238). More precise is the view of Haggard and Pang: "the difference between the 'conservatives' and the 'developmentalist reformers' was not between state intervention and free markets, but over the *nature* of government intervention." Stephan Haggard and Chien-Kuo Pang, "The Transition to Export-Led Growth in Taiwan," in *The Role of the State in Taiwan's Development,* ed. Joel D. Auerback et al. (Armonk, N.Y.: M. E. Sharpe, 1994), 68.

79. Generally, see Robert Wade, *Governing the Market* (Princeton: Princeton University Press, 1990); Alice Amsden, "The State and Taiwan's Economic Development," in *Bringing the State Back In,* ed. Peter B. Evans et al. (Cambridge: Cambridge University Press, 1985), 78–106.

80. Jacoby (*U.S. Aid to Taiwan,* 59) concludes that there was an "unusual continuity of the institutions and of their personnel, which permitted cumulative increases in their capabilities."

2. Zhang Baijia, "The Changing International Scene and Chinese Policy toward the United States, 1954–1970"

1. *Zhou Enlai Waijiao Wenxuan* (Selected works of Zhou Enlai on diplomacy), comp. Document Research Office of the CCP Central Committee (Beijing: Zhongyang Wenxian Chubanshe, 1995), 62.

2. Mao Zedong, "Tong Yiqie Yuanyi Heping de Guojia Tuanjie Hezuo" (Unite and consolidate with any peace-loving country), July 7, 1954, in *Mao Zedong Wenji* (Collected works of Mao Zedong), comp. Document Research Office of the CCP Central Committee (Beijing: Renmin Chubanshe, 1999), 6: 333.

3. Ibid., 333–34.

4. Mao Zedong, "Guanyu Zhongjian Didai, Heping Gongchu yiji Zhong Ying Zhong Mei Guanxi Wenti" (On the middle zone, peaceful coexistence, and Sino-British and Sino-U.S. relations), in *Mao Zedong Waijiao Wenxuan* (Selected works of Mao Zedong on diplomacy), comp. Ministry of Foreign Affairs of the People's Republic of China and Document Research Office of the CCP Central Committee (Beijing: Zhongyang Wenxian Chubanshe and Shijie Zhishi Chubanshe, 1994), 161–62.

5. Mao Zedong, "Zhongguo dalu yu Taiwan de guanxi butong yu liangge Deguo, liangge Chaoxian, liangge Yuenan" (The relationship between mainland China and Taiwan is different from that between the two Germanys, the two Koreas, and the two Vietnams), Oct. 2, 1959, in *Mao Zedong Wenji,* 6: 333–34.

6. *Zhou Enlai Waijiao Huodong Dashiji, 1949–1975* (A chronicle of Zhou Enlai's diplomatic activities, 1949–1975), comp. Research Office of Diplomatic History, Chinese Foreign Ministry (Beijing: Shijie Zhishi Chubanshe, 1993), 122.

7. Wang Bingnan, *Zhong Mei Huitan Jiunian Huigu* (Nine years of Sino-American talks in retrospect) (Beijing: Shijie Zhishi Chubanshe, 1985), 47.

8. Mao Zedong, "Dui Zhonggong Bada Zhengzhi Baogao Gaode Piyu he Xiugai" (Remarks and corrections on the political report to the Eighth Chinese Communist Party Congress), in *Jianguo yilai Mao Zedong Wengao* (Manuscripts of Mao Zedong since the founding of the state), comp. Document Research Office of the CCP Central Committee (Beijing: Zhongyang Wenxian Chubanshe, 1992), 6: 148.

9. Summary of Mao Zedong's talks with foreign guests, Sept. 18 and Sept. 27, 1956.

10. Mao Zedong, "Zhongguo Waijiao Fangmian de Mouxie Zhengce Wenti" (Some policy issues in Chinese diplomacy), in *Mao Zedong Waijiao Wenxuan*, 288.

11. Wu Lengxi, *Yi Mao Zhuxi—Wo Qinzi Jingli De Ruogan Zhongda Lishi Shijian Pian-duan* (Recollections of Chairman Mao—Several important events of history from my own experience) (Beijing: Xinhua Chubanshe, 1995), 4.

12. Ibid., 12–14.

13. Mao Zedong, "Tong Baxi Jizhe Ma Luojin and Du Telie Furen De Tanhua" (Talk with Brazilian correspondent Murilo Marrequin and Mrs. Maria Graca Dutra), in *Jianguo yilai Mao Zedong Wengao*, 7: 370–71.

14. Mao Zedong, "Guoji Xingshi Daole Yige Xin de Zhuanzhedian" (The international situation comes to a new turning point), Nov. 18, 1957, in *Mao Zedong Waijiao Wenxuan*, 291, 295.

15. Mao Zedong, "Zai Di 15 ci Zuigao Guowu Huiyishang de Jianghua" (A talk at the Fifteenth Supreme State Conference), Sept. 5, 8, 1958, in *Jianguo yilai Mao Zedong Wengao*, 7: 384–86, 395.

16. Ibid., 384–85, 393.

17. Ibid., 400.

18. Foundation for International Strategic Studies, comp. *Huanqiu Tong Ci Liang Re—Yi Dai Lingxiumen de Guoji Zhanlue Sixiang* (It's the same temperature around the globe: International strategic thoughts of a generation of the leadership) (Beijing: Zhong-yang Wenxian Chubanshe, 1993), 266–67.

19. Michael Hunt and Niu Jun, eds., *Toward a History of Chinese Communist Foreign Relations, 1920s–1960s: Personalities and Interpretative Approaches* (Washington, D.C.: Woodrow Wilson Center, 1992), 92.

20. Wu, *Yi Mao Zhuxi*, 90.

21. Ibid., 84.

22. Wang, *Zhong Mei Huitan Jiunian Huigu*, 71.

23. Mao Zedong, "Tong Menggemali Yuanshuai Tan Guoji Xingshi" (Talk on the international situation with Marshal Montgomery), May 27, 1960, in *Mao Zedong Waijiao Wenxuan*, 421–22.

24. Foundation for International Strategic Studies, *Huanqiu Tong Ci Liang Re*, 147–48.

25. Li Jue et al., eds., *Dangdai Zhongguo de Hegongye* (The nuclear industry in contemporary China) (Beijing: Zhongguo Shehui Kexue Chubanshe, 1987), 32–33.

26. Letters of Wang Jiaxiang to Zhou Enlai, Deng Xiaoping, and Chen Yi, Feb. 27, 1962.

27. Research Office of Diplomatic History, *Zhou Enlai Waijiao Huodong Dashiji*, 306.

28. Wang Jiaxiang, "Guanyu Duiwai Gongzuo de Yijian" (Some opinions on diplomacy), in Xu Zehao, *Wang Jiaxiang Zhuan* (Biography of Wang Jiaxiang) (Beijing: Dangdai Zhongguo Chubanshe, 1996), 553–69.

29. Minutes of Mao Zedong's meetings with foreign guests, Sept. 9 and Dec. 5, 1963.

30. Mao Zedong, "Zhongjian Didai you Liangge" (There are two middle zones), Sept. 1963, Jan. and July 1964, in *Mao Zedong Waijiao Wenxuan*, 508.

31. Research Office of Diplomatic History, *Zhou Enlai Waijiao Huodong Dashiji*, 445, 457.

32. "Zhongguo Gongchandang Di Bajie Zhongyang Weiyuanhui Di Shiyici Quanti Huiyi Gongbao" (Communiqué of the Eleventh Plenary Session of the Eighth Central Committee of the Communist Party of China), Aug. 12, 1966, in *Renmin Ribao* (People's daily), Aug. 14, 1966.

33. Mao Zedong, "Mao Zedong Tongzhi De Hedian—Zhi Aerbaniya Laodongdang Diwuci Daibiao Dahui" (Telegram of congratulations from Mao Zedong to the Fifth Congress of the Albanian Labor Party), *Renmin Ribao*, Nov. 4, 1966.

34. Foundation for International Strategic Studies, *Huanqiu Tong Ci Liang Re*, 272.

35. *Mao Zedong's Instructions on Propaganda to the Outside World*, from 1967 to Mar. 1971.

36. Foundation for International Strategic Studies, *Huanqiu Tong Ci Liang Re*, 155.

37. Xiong Xianghui, *Lishi de Jiaozhu—Huiyi Mao Zedong, Zhou Enlai jisi Wei Laoshuai* (Footnotes of history—Recollections of Mao Zedong, Zhou Enlai, and four marshals) (Beijing: Zhongyang Dangxiao Chubanshe, 1995), 177; Pei Jianzhang, ed., *Mao Zedong Waijiao Sixiang Yanjiu* (Research on Mao Zedong's diplomatic thoughts) (Beijing: Shijie Zhishi Chubanshe, 1994), 184.

38. Xiong, *Lishi de Jiaozhu*, 184–87, 197.

39. Cao Guisheng, "Xuexi Mao Zedong Dakai Zhongmei Guanxi de Zhanlue Juece" (Learn from Mao Zedong's strategic decision to open the Sino-U.S. relationship), in *Mao Zedong Waijiao Sixiang Yanjiu*, ed. Pei Jianzhang, 184.

40. Ibid., 185.

41. Mao Zedong, "Ruguo Nikesong Yuanyi Lai, Wo Yuanyi He Ta Tan" (If Nixon is willing to visit, I am willing to talk with him), in *Mao Zedong Waijiao Wenxuan*, 593.

42. Gong Li, *Kuayue Honggou—1969–1979 Nian Zhong Mei Guanxi de Yanbian* (Striding over the gap—The evolution of Sino-U.S relations from 1969 to 1979) (Henan: Henan Renmin Chubanshe, 1992), 103–4.

43. Research Office of Diplomatic History, Chinese Ministry of Foreign Affairs, comp., *Xin Zhongguo Waijiao Fengyun* (The winds and clouds in new China's diplomacy) (Beijing: Shijie Zhishi Chuibanshe, 1991), 38.

3. Ronald W. Pruessen, "Over the Volcano: The United States and the Taiwan Strait Crisis, 1954–1955"

1. July 22, 1955, PREM 11/895 (Records of the Prime Minister's Office), Public Record Office, London.

2. The northern Dachens are located more than 200 miles from Chiang's capital in Taipei but only 180 miles from Shanghai, the largest mainland city. Mazu and White Dog islands are 100 miles from Taipei but only 50 miles from Fuzhou. Jinmen, with a 120–mile perimeter, is the largest of all the offshore islands and the principal member of the southernmost cluster. This group is also the closest to the mainland, in one place a mere four miles distant.

3. One memorandum prepared for the Joint Chiefs of Staff highlighted the particular significance of Jinmen. Because the island was located within Amoy harbor, Nationalist control was seen as valuable for "psychological warfare purposes . . . commando raiding . . . intelligence gathering . . . maritime resistance development . . . sabotage and . . . escape and evasion": Memorandum for Secretary, Joint Chiefs of Staff, Sept. 7, 1954, "China-Sept. 1954" Folder, Box 7, Record Group 218 (Records of the Chairman of the Joint Chiefs of Staff), National Archives, Washington, D.C.

4. Useful surveys of the Jinmen-Mazu crises include J. H. Kalicki, *The Pattern of Sino-American Crises: Political-Military Interactions in the 1950s* (London: Cambridge University Press, 1975); Thomas E. Stolper, *China, Taiwan, and the Offshore Islands* (Armonk, N.Y.: M. E. Sharpe, 1985); Leonard H. D. Gordon, "United States Opposition to Use of Force in the Taiwan Strait, 1954–62," *Journal of American History* 72 (Dec. 1985); Gordon H. Chang, "To the Nuclear Brink: Eisenhower, Dulles, and the Quemoy-Matsu Crisis" and H. W. Brands, Jr., "Testing Massive Retaliation: Credibility and Crisis Management in the Taiwan Strait," both in *International Security* 12 (Spring 1988).

5. Ronald W. Pruessen, *John Foster Dulles: The Road to Power, 1888–1952* (New York: Free Press, 1982), 441–42, 487.

6. *Department of State Bulletin* 31 (Sept. 6, 1954).

7. Memorandum of Discussion at the 214th Meeting of the National Security Council, Sept. 12, 1954, *Foreign Relations of the United States (FRUS)*, 1952–54 (Washington, D.C.: Government Printing Office, 1986), 14: 617.

8. Dulles to Bowles, Mar. 25, 1952, John Foster Dulles Papers, Seeley G. Mudd Library, Princeton University, Princeton, N.J.

9. United States Delegation Memorandum of the Restricted Session of the Fourth Tripartite Heads of Government Meeting, Bermuda, Dec. 7, 1953, *FRUS*, 1952–54, 3: 711.

10. Charles Bohlen to Arthur Ringwalt, Feb. 27, 1954, Box 48, Record Group 59 (Records of the Department of State), National Archives, Washington, D.C.

11. Gordon H. Chang, *Friends and Enemies: The United States, China, and the Soviet Union, 1948–1972* (Stanford: Stanford University Press, 1990); Thomas J. Christensen, *Useful Adversaries: Grand Strategy, Domestic Mobilization, and Sino-American Conflict, 1947–1958* (Princeton: Princeton University Press, 1996); David Allan Mayers, *Cracking the Monolith: U.S. Policy against the Sino-Soviet Alliance, 1949–1955* (Baton Rouge: Louisiana State University Press, 1986).

12. See, for example, Ronald W. Pruessen, "Beyond the Cold War—Again: 1955 and the 1990s," *Political Science Quarterly* 108 (Spring 1993), and "From Good Breakfast to Bad Supper: John Foster Dulles between the Geneva Summit and the Geneva Foreign Ministers Conference, 1955," in *Cold War Respite: The Geneva Summit of 1955*, 253–270, ed. Günter Bischof and Saki Dockrill (Baton Rouge: Louisiana State University Press, 2000).

13. Dulles, Humphrey, Wilson meeting, Apr. 25, 1956, "Memoranda of Conversations," Dulles Papers.

14. E.g., Memorandum by the Special Assistant for Intelligence to the Secretary of State, Oct. 18, 1954, *FRUS*, 1952–54, 14: 776–77; National Intelligence Estimate, Nov. 23, 1954, ibid., 930–44.

15. Memorandum of a Conversation, Vienna, May 14, 1955, *FRUS*, 1955–57, 2: 563; July 28, 1955, hearings, *Executive Sessions of the Senate Foreign Relations Committee (Historical Series)*, vol. 7, 84th Cong., 1st sess., 1955 (Washington, D.C.: Government Printing Office, 1978).

16. Statement of Policy by the National Security Council, Nov. 6, 1953, *FRUS*, 1952–54, 14: 283.

17. Ibid., 279.

18. Study Prepared by the Staff of the National Security Council, Apr. 6, 1953, *FRUS*, 1952–54, 14: 179.

19. Dulles to Eisenhower, Feb. 16, 1954, "Berlin 1954" Folder, Dulles Papers.

20. Statement of Policy by the National Security Council, Nov. 6, 1953, *FRUS*, 1952–54, 14: 291, 294, 297.

21. Ibid., 292–93.

22. National Intelligence Estimate, Nov. 23, 1954, *FRUS*, 1952–54, 14: 934.

23. Among the most important contributions to what is generally referred to as "Eisenhower revisionism" are the following: Stephen E. Ambrose, *Eisenhower: The President* (New York: Simon and Schuster, 1984); Robert A. Divine, *Eisenhower and the Cold War* (New York: Oxford University Press, 1981); Fred I. Greenstein, *The Hidden-Hand Presidency: Eisenhower as Leader* (New York: Basic Books, 1982).

24. The Acting Secretary of Defense to the President, Sept. 3, 1954, *FRUS*, 1952–54, 14: 556–58; Special National Intelligence Estimate, Sept. 4, 1954, ibid., 563–65.

25. Memorandum of conversation by the Deputy Under Secretary of State, Sept. 7, 1954, *FRUS*, 1952–54, 14: 575–77.

26. In September 1954, the IAC members included the CIA director; the Special Assistant for Intelligence, Department of State; the Assistant Chief of Staff, G-2, Department of the Army; the Director of Naval Intelligence; the Director for Intelligence, U.S. Air Force; the Deputy Director for Intelligence, Joint Chiefs of Staff; the Assistant to the Director, Federal Bureau of Investigation; and a representative of the Atomic Energy Commission. See, for example, note to Special National Intelligence Estimate, Sept. 4, 1954, *FRUS*, 1952–54, 14: 563.

27. Memorandum of conversation by the Deputy Under Secretary of State, Sept. 7, 1954, *FRUS*, 1952–54, 14: 575–77.

28. Memorandum of Discussion at the 214th Meeting of the National Security Council, Sept. 12, 1954, *FRUS*, 1952–54, 14: 620–22.

29. Memorandum of Discussion at the 221st Meeting of the National Security Council, Nov. 2, 1954, *FRUS*, 1952–54, 14: 833–35.

30. Ibid., 836–37.

31. Memorandum of conversation by the Deputy Director of the Office of United Nations Political and Security Affairs, Oct. 26, 1954, *FRUS*, 1952–54, 14: 796.

32. Robert H. Ferrell, ed., *The Diary of James C. Hagerty* (Bloomington: Indiana University Press, 1983), 84.

33. PREM 11/867: No. 2163, Oct. 9, 1954, Public Record Office, London; Memorandum of Discussion at the 237th Meeting of the National Security Council, Feb. 17, 1955, *FRUS*, 1955–57, 2: 279–86.

34. See, e.g., Robert Accinelli, "Eisenhower, Congress, and the 1954–55 Offshore Islands Crisis," *Presidential Studies Quarterly* 20 (Spring 1990); and Anna Kasten Nelson, "John Foster Dulles and the Bipartisan Congress," *Political Science Quarterly* 102 (Spring 1987).

35. Nov. 19, 1954, Administration Series, Ann Whitman File, Eisenhower Library, Abilene, Kans.

36. Memorandum of Discussion at the 216th Meeting of the National Security Council, Oct. 6, 1954, *FRUS*, 1952–54, 14: 689–701; Memorandum by the Secretary

of State to the President, Nov. 23, 1954, Dulles-Herter Series, Eisenhower Library, Abilene, Kans.

37. Memorandum of conversation by the Deputy Director of the Office of United Nations Political and Security Affairs, Oct. 26, 1954, *FRUS*, 1952–54, 14: 794.

38. Memorandum of Discussion at the 214th Meeting of the National Security Council, Sept. 12, 1954, *FRUS*, 1952–54, 14: 620–22.

39. Memorandum of Discussion at the 216th Meeting of the National Security Council, Oct. 6, 1954, *FRUS*, 1952–54, 14: 699.

40. Memorandum of Discussion at the 214th Meeting of the National Security Council, Sept. 12, 1954, *FRUS*, 1952–54, 14: 623.

41. Memorandum of conversation, Jan. 31, 1955, *FRUS*, 1955–57, 2: 187.

42. Memorandum of Discussion at the 221st Meeting of the National Security Council, Nov. 2, 1954, *FRUS*, 1952–54, 14: 828.

43. Memorandum of conversation, Jan. 20, 1955, "White House Memoranda" Folder, Dulles Papers.

44. Memorandum of Discussion at the 233rd Meeting of the National Security Council, Jan. 21, 1955, *FRUS*, 1955–57, 2: 91.

45. Memorandum of Discussion at the 232nd Meeting of the National Security Council, Jan. 20, 1955, *FRUS*, 1955–57, 2: 69–82; *Department of State Bulletin*, Feb. 28, 1955.

46. Memorandum by the Assistant Secretary of State for European Affairs to Special Assistant to the Secretary of State, Sept. 19, 1954, *FRUS*, 1952–54, 14: 650–51.

47. PREM 11/867, Oct. 21, 1954, Public Record Office, London; Memorandum of conversation by the Assistant Secretary of State for International Organization Affairs, Oct. 18, 1954, *FRUS*, 1952–54, 14: 772.

48. James Shepley, "How Dulles Averted War," *Life*, Jan. 16, 1956, 70–78.

49. See, for example, Stephen Rabe, "Eisenhower Revisionism: A Decade of Scholarship," *Diplomatic History* 17 (Winter 1993).

50. Robert A. Divine, *Eisenhower and the Cold War* (New York: Oxford University Press, 1981), 65–66.

51. Memorandum of Conversation by the Director of the Office of Chinese Affairs, Nov. 19, 1954, *FRUS*, 1952–54, 14: 909; Memorandum of Conversation by the Director of the Office of Chinese Affairs, Nov. 22, 1954, ibid., 921; Memorandum of Conversation by the Director of the Office of Chinese Affairs, Nov. 23, 1954, ibid., 927. Several individuals working in the Office of Chinese Affairs had been urging a less-than-rigid U.S. approach to Nationalist harassment operations while precise mutual security treaty language was being debated. As Walter McConaughy put it in one memorandum, "There is a need to keep the Communists off balance, to deter their military build-up, to limit their stockpiles of jet fuel and other strategic

materials, and to make these efforts as costly as possible. The interception of Communist bloc vessels by the Chinese Nationalists has served all these purposes effectively." McConaughy to Robertson, Oct. 27, 1954, "NSC Reports and Correspondence" Folder, Box 46, Record Group 59, National Archives, Washington, D.C.

52. Joint Chiefs of Staff to the Commander in Chief, Pacific, Sept. 8, 1954, *FRUS*, 1952–54, 14: 579. See also Memorandum for Secretary, Joint Chiefs of Staff, Sept. 7, 1954, "China-Sept. 1954" Folder, Box 7, Record Group 218 (Records of the Chairman of the Joint Chiefs of Staff), National Archives, Washington, D.C.

53. Commander in Chief, Pacific to the Joint Chiefs of Staff, Sept. 8, 1954, *FRUS*, 1952–54, 14: 580.

54. National Intelligence Estimate, Sept. 14, 1954, *FRUS*, 1952–54, 14: 627.

55. Memorandum by Gerald Stryker of the Office of Chinese Affairs to the Deputy Director of That Office, Sept. 22, 1954, *FRUS*, 1952–54, 14: 657.

56. Memorandum of Discussion at the 215th Meeting of the National Security Council, Sept. 24, 1954, *FRUS*, 1952–54, 14: 658–60.

57. Note to the National Security Council by the Executive Director, Dec. 22, 1954, *FRUS*, 1952–54, 12: 1063–68.

58. Memorandum of Discussion at the 240th Meeting of the National Security Council, Mar. 10, 1955, *FRUS*, 1955-57, 2: 347.

59. Editorial Note re Aug. 5, 1954 NSC discussion, *FRUS*, 1952–54, 14: 518–19.

60. Memorandum of Discussion at the 221st Meeting of the National Security Council, Nov. 2, 1954, *FRUS*, 1952–54, 14: 834.

61. *Public Papers of the Presidents of the United States: Dwight David Eisenhower, 1955* (Washington, D.C.: Government Printing Office, 1960), 332–33.

62. Pruessen, *Dulles: The Road to Power*, 466; Draft Memorandum of Conversation, by the Secretary of State, Aug. 10, 1953, *FRUS*, 1952–54, 15: 1474–75; Draft Report by the National Security Planning Board of the National Security Council, Nov. 9, 1953, ibid., 1603.

63. *New Republic*, Sept. 20, 1954.

64. *Department of State Bulletin*, Mar. 8, 1954, 346.

65. Memorandum of Discussion at the 216th Meeting of the National Security Council, Oct. 6, 1954, *FRUS*, 1952–54, 14: 697-99.

66. See "Complex Perceptions" section of this chapter.

67. Memorandum of Conversation, by the Assistant Secretary of State for International Organization Affairs, Oct. 4, 1954, *FRUS*, 1952–54, 14: 678. For excellent discussions of the impact of "domestic politics" on the Eisenhower administration's deliberations and decisions, see Robert Accinelli, *Crisis and Commitment: United States Policy toward Taiwan, 1950–1955* (Chapel Hill: University of North Carolina Press, 1996); and Rosemary Foot, *A Substitute for Victory: The Politics of Peacemaking at the Korean Armistice Talks* (Ithaca: Cornell University Press, 1990) and *The Wrong*

War: American Policy and the Dimensions of the Korean Conflict, *1950–1953* (Ithaca: Cornell University Press, 1985).

68. Public Papers of the Presidents of the United States: Dwight D. Eisenhower, *1954* (Washington, D.C.: Government Printing Office, 1958), 381–90.

69. January 20, 1955 testimony, *Executive Sessions of the Senate Foreign Relations Committee (Historical Series)*, vol. 7, 84th Cong., 1st sess., 1955 (Washington, D.C.: Government Printing Office, 1978).

70. Memorandum of a Conversation, Department of State, Jan. 20, 1955, *FRUS*, 1955–57, 2: 62; Memorandum of Discussion at the 232nd Meeting of the National Security Council, Jan. 20, 1955, ibid., 80.

71. Eisenhower to Churchill, Dec. 14, 1954, *FRUS*, 1952–54, 5: 1499.

72. See, for example, Warren I. Cohen, *America's Response to China: An Interpretative History of Sino-American Relations* (New York: John Wiley and Sons, 1971), 13–15.

73. Howard K. Beale, *Theodore Roosevelt and the Rise of America to World Power* (New York: Collier Books, 1962), 80–81, 159, 164–65.

74. Lloyd C. Gardner, *Economic Aspects of New Deal Diplomacy* (Boston: Beacon Press, 1964), 77.

75. Dorothy Borg and Shumpei Okamato, eds., *Pearl Harbor as History: Japanese-American Relations, 1931–1941* (New York: Columbia University Press, 1973), 277.

76. Gardner, *Economic Aspects*, 145. An especially valuable discussion of the deep historical roots of post-1945 American policies in Asia can be found in Akira Iriye, *The Cold War in Asia: A Historical Introduction* (Englewood Cliffs, N.J.: Prentice-Hall, 1974).

77. For further discussion of the problems emerging from excessive U.S. ambitions in the 1950s, see Ronald W. Pruessen, "John Foster Dulles and the Predicaments of Power," in *John Foster Dulles and the Diplomacy of the Cold War*, ed. Richard Immerman (Princeton: Princeton University Press, 1990).

4. Robert Accinelli, "'A Thorn in the Side of Peace': The Eisenhower Administration and the 1958 Offshore Islands Crisis"

1. For recent scholarship on the 1958 crisis, see He Di, "The Evolution of the People's Republic of China's Policy toward the Offshore Islands," in *The Great Powers in East Asia, 1953–60*, ed. Warren I. Cohen and Akira Iriye (New York: Columbia University Press, 1990), 231–43; Gordon H. Chang, *Friends and Enemies:The United States, China, and the Soviet Union, 1948–72* (Stanford: Stanford University Press, 1990), 183–98; Shu Guang Zhang, *Deterrence and Strategic Culture: Chinese-American Confrontations, 1949–58* (Ithaca: Cornell University Press, 1992), chap. 8; George C. Eliades, "Once More unto the Breach: Eisenhower, Dulles, and Public Opinion during the Offshore Islands Crisis of 1958," *Journal of American-East*

Asian Relations 2 (Winter 1993): 347–67; Qiang Zhai, *The Dragon, the Lion, and the Eagle: Chinese-British-American Relations, 1949–58* (Kent, Ohio: Kent State University Press, 1994), chap. 9; Appu K. Soman, "'Who's Daddy' in the Taiwan Strait? The Offshore Islands Crisis of 1958," *Journal of American-East Asian Relations* 3 (Winter 1994): 373–98; Li Xiaobing, Chen Jian, and David L. Wilson, trans., "Mao Zedong's Handling of the Taiwan Straits Crisis of 1958: Chinese Recollections and Documents," *Cold War International History Project Bulletin* 6–7 (Winter 1995–96): 208–26; Thomas J. Christensen, *Useful Adversaries: Grand Strategy, Domestic Mobilization, and Sino-American Conflict, 1947–1958* (Princeton: Princeton University Press, 1996), chap. 6; Xiaobing Li, "Making of Mao's Cold War: The Taiwan Straits Crises Revisited," and Yi Sun, "John Foster Dulles and the 1958 Taiwan Straits Crisis," both in *China and the United States: A New Cold War History*, ed. Xiaobing Li and Hongshan Li (Lanham, Md.: University Press of America, 1998), 49–72, 73–95.

2. Qiang Zhai, "Dulles, Wedge, and the Ambassadorial Talks, 1955–1957," *Chinese Historians* 2 (Dec. 1988): 29–44; Rosemary Foot, *The Practice of Power: U.S. Relations with China since 1949* (Oxford: Oxford University Press, 1995), 34–35, 60–67; Qing Simei, "The Eisenhower Administration and Changes in Western Embargo Policy against China, 1954–1958," in *The Great Powers in East Asia*, ed. Cohen and Iriye, 121–41.

3. NIE 13–57, "Communist China Through 1961," Mar. 19, 1957, *Foreign Relations of the United States* (FRUS), 1955–57, 3:498, 505; NIE 13–2–57, "Communist China's Role in Non-Communist Asia," Dec. 3, 1957, ibid., 649–52; NIE 13–58, "Communist China," May 13, 1958, FRUS, 1958–60, 19: 25–26.

4. NSC 5723, "U.S. Policy toward Taiwan and the Government of the Republic of China," Oct. 4, 1957, FRUS, 1958–60, 19: Microfiche Supplement.

5. Robert Accinelli, *Crisis and Commitment: United States Policy toward Taiwan, 1950–1955* (Chapel Hill: University of North Carolina Press, 1996), 112–14, 169–70, 255–64; Nancy Bernkopf Tucker, *Taiwan, Hong Kong, and the United States, 1945–1992: Uncertain Friendships* (New York: Twayne Publishers, 1994), 36–38; Nancy Bernkopf Tucker, "John Foster Dulles and the Taiwan Roots of the 'Two Chinas' Policy," in *John Foster Dulles and the Diplomacy of the Cold War: A Reappraisal*, ed. Richard H. Immerman (Princeton: Princeton University Press, 1990), 235–62; Gordon H. Chang, "Eisenhower and Mao's China," in *Eisenhower: A Centenary Assessment*, 191–205, ed. Stephen E. Ambrose and Günter Bischof (Baton Rouge: Louisiana State University Press, 1995).

6. Memorandum of discussion, 338th NSC meeting, Oct. 2, 1957, FRUS, 1955–57, 3: 614–15.

7. NSC 5723, "U.S. Policy toward Taiwan and the Government of the Republic of China," Oct. 4, 1957, FRUS, 1958–60, 19: Microfiche Supplement.

8. "Anti-Communist Resistance Potential in the Sino-Soviet Bloc," Mar. 4, 1958, Annex C, "Communist China," *FRUS*, 1958–60, 19: 7–8.

9. Memorandum of discussion, 338th NSC meeting, Oct. 2, 1957, *FRUS*, 1955–57, 3: 613.

10. Accinelli, *Crisis and Commitment*, 171–72.

11. See, for example, memorandum of conversation, Aug. 1, 1956, *FRUS*, 1955–57, 3: 413–15.

12. Walter Robertson to Christian Herter, Nov. 15, 1957, ibid., 633–34; memorandum of conversation, Mar. 14, 1958, *FRUS*, 1958–60, 19: 11.

13. Taipei Embassy to State Dept., July 26, 1958, 793.5-MSP/7-2658, Dept. of State Record Files, Record Group (RG) 59, National Archives, College Park, Md.

14. Memorandum of conversation, Mar. 14, 1958, 611.93/3-3158, RG 59, National Archives. A different summary of this exchange of views between Dulles and Chiang Kai-shek appears in *FRUS*, 1958–60, 19: 8–12.

15. Drumwright to State Dept., Apr. 3, 1958, *FRUS*, 1958–60, 19: 12–14. Dulles later informed the Norwegian minister of foreign affairs that Nationalist raids against the mainland had declined to "negligible proportions" by August 1958, and that the Taiwan government had discontinued enforcement of its blockade against foreign shipping to mainland ports in the summer of 1957. Dulles to Halvard Lange, Dec. 12, 1958, 793.00/12-1258, RG 59, National Archives.

Taiwan did serve as a staging post for CIA-sponsored paramilitary operations in Tibet that had apparently begun in 1956: see Christopher Robbins, *Air America* (New York: G. P. Putnam's Sons, 1979), 94–101; and John Prados, *Presidents' Secret Wars: CIA and Pentagon Covert Operations from World War II through the Persian Gulf* (Chicago: Ivan Dee, 1996), chap. 9.

16. NSC 5723, Oct. 4, 1957, "U.S. Policy toward Taiwan and the Government of the Republic of China," *FRUS*, 1958–60, 19: Microfiche Supplement.

17. Memorandum of discussion, 338th NSC meeting, Oct. 2, 1957, *FRUS*, 1955–57, 3: 617.

18. Accinelli, *Crisis and Commitment*, 226–28, 244.

19. Marshall Green to Robertson, Oct. 6, 1958, Records of the Policy Planning Staff, 1957–61, Box 135, RG 59, National Archives; Taipei Embassy to State Dept., July 26, 1958, 793.5-MSP/7-2658, RG 59, National Archives.

20. Herter to State Dept., Sept. 16, 1957, *FRUS*, 1955–57, 3:604. Chiang Kai-shek told Richards that in the event of an attack on the offshore islands, he would shift his entire military force there. See Richards to Dulles, Oct. 9, 1957, ibid., 627.

21. Accinelli, *Crisis and Commitment*, 189–90, 227; Operations Coordinating Board, "Progress Report on U.S. Policy toward Formosa and the Government of the Republic of China," Apr. 11, 1956, Box 31, White House Office, Office of the

Special Assistant for National Security Affairs, Operations Coordinating Board Central Files, Dwight D. Eisenhower Library, Abilene, Kans. (DDEL).

22. NIE 43-2-57, "The Prospects for the Government of the Republic of China," Aug. 27, 1957, *FRUS*, 1955–57, 3: 586–90; Operations Coordinating Board, "Analysis of Internal Security Situation in Taiwan and Recommended Action," Annex to "Outline Plan of Operations with Respect to the Government of the Republic of China," June 12, 1957, Box 31, White House Office, Office of the Special Assistant for National Security Affairs, Operations Coordinating Board Central Files, DDEL; Operations Coordinating Board, "Taiwan and the Government of the Republic of China," Apr. 23, 1958, *FRUS*, 1958–60, 19: Microfiche Supplement. For an analysis of the impact of the U.S. fear of Nationalist demoralization on the U.S.-Taiwan alliance, see John W. Garver, *The Sino-American Alliance: Nationalist China and American Cold War Strategy in Asia* (Armonk, N.Y.: M. E. Sharpe, 1997), 84–88.

23. Excerpt from memorandum of discussion, 375th NSC meeting, Aug. 7, 1958, *FRUS*, 1958–60, 19: 42–43; excerpt from memorandum of discussion, 378th NSC meeting, Aug. 27, 1958, ibid., 87.

24. Memorandum of conference with the President, Aug. 12, 1958, ibid., 50. Four days earlier, Dulles had observed that the president might not yet have "clearly recognized" the extent to which the offshore islands and Taiwan were now integrated defensively. Memorandum of meeting, Aug. 8, 1958, ibid., 47.

25. Substance of Discussion of State-JCS meeting, Aug. 15, 1958, *FRUS*, 1958–60, 19: Microfiche Supplement. The nuclear scenario described by the JCS was drawn from a limited war study prepared that spring, which included a hypothetical conflict with the PRC over Jinmen and Mazu. See "U.S. and Allied Capabilities for Limited War Operations to 1 July 1961," May 29, 1958, Box 2, Bureau of Far Eastern Affairs, Office of the Assistant Secretary for Far Eastern Affairs, Top Secret Files of the Regional Planning Officer, 1955–63, RG 59, National Archives.

26. SNIE 199-7-58, "Sino-Soviet and Free World Reactions to U.S. Use of Nuclear Weapons in Limited Wars in the Far East," July 22, 1958, *FRUS*, 1958–60, 19: Microfiche Supplement.

27. NSC 5810/1, "Statement of Basic National Security Policy," *FRUS* 1958–60, 3: 101–3; Peter J. Roman, *Eisenhower and the Missile Gap* (Ithaca: Cornell University Press, 1995), 75–79; David Alan Rosenberg, "The Origins of Overkill: Nuclear-Weapons and American Strategy, 1945–1960," *International Security* 7 (Spring 1983): 54; H. W. Brands, "The Age of Vulnerability: Eisenhower and the National Insecurity State," *American Historical Review* 94 (Oct. 1989): 963–89; Saki Dockrill, *Eisenhower's New Look National Security Policy* (New York: St. Martin's Press, 1996), 65–71, 198–202, 236–37.

28. Accinelli, *Crisis and Commitment*, 221–26.

29. Memorandum for the record, Aug. 14, 1958, *FRUS*, 1958–60, 19: 53.

30. Drumwright to State Dept., Aug. 13, 1958, 793.00/8–1358, RG 59, National Archives; Robertson to Dulles, Aug. 8, 1958, *FRUS*, 1958–60, 19: 46.

31. Memorandum for the record, Aug. 14, 1958, *FRUS*, 1958–60, 19: 52–53.

32. Memorandum of conference with the President, Aug. 14, 1958, *FRUS*, 1958–60, 19: Microfiche Supplement; Dwight D. Eisenhower, *The White House Years: Waging Peace, 1956–1961* (Garden City, N.Y.: Doubleday, 1965), 295–96.

33. Dulles to Morgan, Aug. 23, 1958, Box 16, John Foster Dulles Papers, Chronological Series, DDEL.

34. JCS to CINCPAC (Commander in Chief, Pacific), Aug. 25, 1958, *FRUS*, 1958–60, 19: 75–76.

35. SNIE 100–9–58, "Probable Developments in the Taiwan Strait Area," Aug. 26, 1958, ibid., 81–82.

36. Chiang Kai-shek to Eisenhower, Aug. 27, 1958, ibid., 83–86.

37. Memorandum of meeting, Aug. 29, 1958, ibid., 96–99; JCS to CINCPAC, Aug. 29, 1958, ibid., 101–2; memorandum of conversation, Aug. 29, 1958, Box 10, Dwight D. Eisenhower Presidential Papers (Ann Whitman File), International Series, DDEL.

38. Memorandum of conversation, Sept. 2, 1958, *FRUS*, 1958–60, 19: 115–21.

39. Accinelli, *Crisis and Commitment*, 214–15, 221; Brands, "Age of Vulnerability," 981–84.

40. China Weekly Telegram, Sept. 3, 1958, Box 31, Records of the Office of Public Opinion Studies, RG 59, National Archives.

41. Staff Notes No. 414, Sept. 3, 1958, Box 36, Eisenhower Papers (Ann Whitman File), DDE Diary Series, DDEL.

42. "Recent Political Aspects of Taiwan Straits Developments," Aug. 31, 1958, Box 10, Eisenhower Papers (Ann Whitman File), International Series, DDEL.

43. Douglas MacArthur, II to Dulles, Aug. 30, 1958, 793.00/8–3058, RG 59, National Archives.

44. Macmillan to Eisenhower, Sept. 3, 1958, *FRUS*, 1958–60, 19: Microfiche Supplement. For discussions of Anglo-American relations during the crisis, consult Qiang Zhai, *Chinese-British-American Relations, 1949–1958*, chap. 9; Qiang Zhai, "Britain, the United States, and the Jinmen-Mazu Crises, 1954–55 and 1958," *Chinese Historians* 5 (Fall 1992): 39–44; Tracy Lee Steele, "Allied and Interdependent: British Policy during the Chinese Offshore Islands Crisis of 1958" in *Contemporary British History, 1931–61: Politics and the Limits of Policy*, ed. Anthony Gorst, Lewis Johnson, and W. Scott Lucas (London: Pinter Publishers, 1991), 230–47.

45. Memorandum of conversation, Sept. 3, 1958, *FRUS*, 1958–60, 19: 126; memorandum of conversation, Sept. 30, 1958, ibid., 303; Eisenhower, *Waging Peace, 1956–1961*, 293.

46. Memorandum prepared by Dulles, Sept. 4, 1958, *FRUS*, 1958–60, 19: 131–34.

47. Memorandum of conference with the President, Sept. 4, 1958, ibid., 130.

48. Press Release, Sept. 4, 1958, Box 7, Dulles Papers, White House Memoranda Series, Chronological Subseries, DDEL; typescript of press conference, Sept. 4, 1958, *FRUS* 1958–60, 19: Microfiche Supplement. In a conversation with Secretary of Defense Neil McElroy about the statement, Dulles remarked that the United States would help the Nationalists if they were unable to cope with a Chinese Communist attack in the offshore islands. McElroy replied that the statement "seemed to [Assistant Secretary of Defense Benjamin] Quarles and him to have that tone." See Memorandum of telephone conversation, Sept. 4, 1958, File 28, *Minutes of Telephone Conversations of John Foster Dulles and of Christian Herter, 1953–1961* (Ann Arbor, Mich.: University Publications of America, 1980), microfilm, John Foster Dulles Telephone Memoranda.

49. Marian D. Irish, "Public Opinion and American Foreign Policy: The Quemoy Crisis of 1958," *Political Quarterly* 31, no. 2 (1960): 151–52.

50. The statement by Zhou Enlai is in *Documents on International Affairs, 1958* (London: Oxford University Press, 1962), 179–82. For Chinese decision making in early September, see He Di, "Evolution of the People's Republic of China's Policy toward the Offshore Islands," 236–38; Shu Guang Zhang, *Deterrence and Strategic Culture,* 250–53.

51. White House Statement, Sept. 6, 1958, Box 135, Records of the Policy Planning Staff, 1957–61, RG 59, National Archives; memorandum of conversation, Sept. 6, 1958, *FRUS*, 1958–60, 19: 143.

52. Khrushchev to Eisenhower, Sept. 7, 1958, *FRUS*, 1958–60, 19: 145–53. For Sino-Soviet relations during the crisis, see He Di, "Evolution of the People's Republic of China's Policy toward the Offshore Islands," 242; Shu Guang Zhang, *Deterrence and Strategic Culture,* 254–56, 265–66; Qiang Zhai, *The Dragon, the Lion, and the Eagle,* 197–200; Chang, *Friends and Enemies,*, 186–87, 190–93; Christensen, *Useful Adversaries,* 233–36; Vladislav Zubok, "Khrushchev's Nuclear Promise to Beijing during the 1958 Crisis," *Cold War International History Project Bulletin* 6–7 (Winter 1995–96): 219, 226–27; Vladislav Zubok and Constantine Pleshakov, *Inside the Kremlin's Cold War: From Stalin to Khrushchev* (Cambridge: Harvard University Press, 1996), chap. 7.

53. NIEC 13–58, "Communist China," May 13, 1958, *FRUS*, 1958–60, 19: 27; Dulles to Macmillan, Sept. 4, 1958, ibid., 138; John Foster Dulles memorandum, Sept. 4, 1958, ibid., 131.

54. SNIE 100–11–58, "Probable Chinese Communist and Soviet Intentions in the Taiwan Strait Area," Sept. 16, 1958, ibid., 205–6; memorandum of conversation, Sept. 20, 1958, ibid., 243.

55. Khrushchev to Eisenhower, Sept. 19, 1958, ibid., 231–38; memorandum of conversation, Sept. 20, 1958, *FRUS*, 1958–60, 19: Microfiche Supplement; excerpt from memorandum of discussion, 380th NSC meeting, Sept. 25, 1958, *FRUS*, 1958–60, 19: 270.

56. Memorandum of conversation, Sept. 9, 1958, *FRUS*, 1958–60, 19: Microfiche Supplement.

57. Dulles to Macmillan, Sept. 12, 1958, *FRUS*, 1958–60, 19: 177; Eisenhower to Khrushchev, Sept. 13, 1958, Box 5, Dulles Papers, Draft Presidential Correspondence and Speeches Series, DDEL.

58. State Dept. to Warsaw Embassy, Sept. 13, 1958, *FRUS*, 1958–60, 19: 186; Warsaw Embassy to State Dept., Sept. 15, 1958, ibid., 190–91; Warsaw Embassy to State Dept., Sept. 18, 1958, *FRUS*, 1958–60, 19: Microfiche Supplement; Warsaw Embassy to State Dept., Sept. 22, 1958, *FRUS*, 1958–60, 19: 257; Warsaw Embassy to State Dept., Oct. 1, 1958, *FRUS*, 1958–60, 19: Microfiche Supplement.

59. Memorandum of conversation, Sept. 11, 1958, *FRUS*, 1958–60, 19: Microfiche Supplement.

60. Drumwright to State Dept., Sept. 7, 1958, 794A.5/9-758; RG 59, National Archives; Drumwright to State Dept., Sept. 13, 1958, *FRUS*, 1958–60, 19: Microfiche Supplement.

61. Memorandum of conversation, Sept. 20, 1958, *FRUS*, 1958–60, 19: 241–47; Dulles to London Embassy, Sept. 25, 1958, ibid., 272–73.

62. "Taiwan Straits Crisis: Where Do We Go From Here?," enclosed in J. Graham Parsons to Herter, Sept. 19, 1958, *FRUS*, 1958–60, 19: Microfiche Supplement; CINCPAC to JCS, Sept. 5, 1958, 793.5/9-558, RG 59, National Archives.

63. Memorandum of conversation, Sept. 12, 1958, *FRUS*, 1958–60, 19: 172–74; Substance of Discussions, State-Joint Chiefs Staff Meeting, Sept. 12, 1958, *FRUS*, 1958–60, 19: Microfiche Supplement.

64. Dulles to Beam, Sept. 14, 1958, *FRUS*, 1958–60, 19: 187.

65. Drumwright to State Dept., Sept. 1, 1958, ibid., 109–11; Dulles to Drumwright, Sept. 8, 1958, *FRUS*, 1958–60, 19: Microfiche Supplement; Drumwright to State Dept., Sept. 10, 1958, *FRUS*, 1958–60, 19: 160. The U.S. government made one exception to its refusal to concur in Nationalist retaliatory actions. American authorities conceded that the Nationalist right of self-defense encompassed the "hot pursuit" of Communist planes that attempted to bomb the Jinmen and Mazu islands. In such circumstances, Nationalist fighter aircraft defending the islands had U.S. approval to pursue the Communist planes back to their bases and attack the airfields.

66. Drumwright to State Dept., Sept. 20, 1958, *FRUS*, 1958–60, 19: 239–40; State Dept. to Drumwright, Sept. 21, 1958, ibid., 253–54.

67. C. Burke Elbrick to Dulles, Sept. 10, 1958, Box 3, Bureau of Far Eastern Affairs, Correspondence and Subject Files, 1958, RG 59, National Archives; Elbrick to

Parsons, Sept. 11, 1958, 794A.5/9–1158, RG 59, National Archives; China Weekly Telegram, Sept. 16, 1958, Box 31, Office of Public Opinion Studies, 1943–65, RG 59, National Archives.

68. United Nations, *Official Records of the General Assembly*, Thirteenth Sess., 1958–59, Plenary Sessions, 47–56, 57–82, 106–7; Foot, *Practice of Power*, 35.

69. Memorandum of telephone conversation, Sept. 23, 1958, File 28, Dulles Papers, Telephone Memoranda, DDEL; Henry Cabot Lodge, Jr., to Dulles, Sept. 24, 1958, *FRUS*, 1958–60, 19: Microfiche Supplement.

70. President Eisenhower's Radio and TV Broadcast, Sept. 11, 1958, Box 135, Records of the Policy Planning Staff, 1957–61, RG 59, National Archives; John Foster Dulles Address before the Far East-America Council of Commerce and Industry, Waldorf Astoria Hotel, New York, Sept. 25, 1958, Box 127, John Foster Dulles Papers, Seeley Mudd Library, Princeton, N.J.

71. Memorandum of conversation, Sept. 19, 1958, *FRUS*, 1958–60, 19: Microfiche Supplement.

72. China Weekly Telegram, Sept. 23, 1958 and Sept. 30, 1958, Box 31, Office of Public Opinion Studies, 1943–65, RG 59, National Archives.

73. George H. Gallup, *The Gallup Poll, 1935–1971* (New York: Random House, 1972), vol. 2 (1949–1958), 1569.

74. Memorandum of conversation, Sept. 5, 1958, Box 16, Dulles Papers, Chronological Correspondence Series, DDEL; *New York Times*, Sept. 29, 1958, 1: 6.

75. *New York Times*, Sept. 7, 1958, 3: 1–6 (Acheson); ibid., Sept. 14, 1958, 1: 5 (Truman); ibid., Sept. 7, 1958, 13: 1 (Fulbright); ibid., Sept. 13, 1958, 3: 2, 3 (Mansfield and Kennedy).

76. Green to Eisenhower, Sept. 29, 1958, Box 7, Dulles Papers, White House Memoranda Series, Chronological Subseries, DDEL.

77. Dulles to Robert Cutler, Sept. 30, 1958, Box 2, Dulles Papers, General Correspondence and Memoranda Series, Confidential Correspondence Subseries, DDEL.

78. In a conversation with Dulles on Sept. 23, 1958, Eisenhower expressed his concern that "as much as two-thirds of the world, and 50% of US opinion opposes the course which we have been following." See Memorandum of conversation, Sept. 23, 1958, *FRUS*, 1958–60, 19: 267.

79. Memorandum for the record, Sept. 12, 1958, Box 3, White House Office, Office of the Special Assistant for National Security Affairs, Special Assistant Series, Presidential Subseries, DDEL; excerpt from memorandum of conversation, Sept. 15, 1958, *FRUS*, 1958–60, 19: 161.

80. Memorandum of conversation, Sept. 21, 1958, *FRUS*, 1958–60, 19: 252.

81. Excerpt from notes of telephone conversation, Sept. 15, 1958, ibid., 196–97; memorandum of telephone conversation, Sept. 22, 1958, *FRUS*, 1958–60, 19: Micro-

fiche Supplement; memorandum of conversation, Sept. 29, 1958, *FRUS*, 1958–60, 19: 296–97.

82. Diary Notes, Sept. 26, 1958, Box 10, Eisenhower Papers (Ann Whitman), Ann Whitman Diary Series, DDEL; McCloy to Dulles, Sept. 27, 1958, *FRUS*, 1958–60, 19: Microfiche Supplement.

83. Memorandum for the record, Sept. 12, 1958, Box 3, White House Office, Office of the Special Assistant for National Security Affairs, Special Assistant Series, Presidential Subseries, DDEL.

84. Memorandum of telephone conversation, Sept. 25, 1958, File 28, Dulles Papers, Telephone Memoranda, DDEL; memorandum of conversation, Sept. 27, 1958, Box 135, Records of the Policy Planning Staff, 1957–61, RG 59, National Archives.

85. Dulles to Paris Embassy, Sept. 30, 1958, 793.5/3058, RG 59, National Archives; Jan Kalicki, *The Pattern of Sino-American Crises: Political-Military Interactions in the 1950s* (London: Cambridge University Press, 1975), 192.

86. State Dept. Press Release No. 574, Sept. 30, 1958, Box 127, Dulles Papers, Seeley Mudd Library; *New York Times*, Oct. 2, 1958, 1: 7.

87. White House Press Release, Oct. 5, 1958, Box 135, Records of the Policy Planning Staff, 1957–61, RG 59, National Archives.

88. Green to Robertson, Oct. 2, 1958, *FRUS*, 1958–60, 19: Microfiche Supplement.

89. Dulles to Drumwright, Oct. 1, 1958, *FRUS*, 1958–60, 19: 315.

90. Green to Robertson, Oct. 2, 1958, *FRUS*, 1958–60, 19: Microfiche Supplement. Nationalist "harassments" from Jinmen and Mazu included small commando raids, infiltration of agents, loudspeaker propaganda, and occasional artillery fire. Dulles did not consider these activities "very serious" but acknowledged that they might be regarded as "needlessly provocative." See Drumwright to Dulles, Sept. 10, 1958, ibid.; memorandum of conversation, Sept. 12, 1958, *FRUS*, 1958–60, 19: 169. Putting a stop to these "harassments" was not only intended as an incentive for the Chinese to leave the islands unmolested but was also consistent with previous efforts by the Eisenhower administration to keep in check unnecessarily provocative activities against the mainland. See Accinelli, *Crisis and Commitment*, 117–18, 175–76, 180.

91. China Weekly Telegram, Oct. 7, 1958, Oct. 14, 1958, Box 31, Office of Public Opinion Studies, 1943–65, RG 59, National Archives.

92. Drumwright to State Dept., Oct. 6, 1958, *FRUS*, 1958–60, 19: 332–33.

93. Memorandum of telephone conversation, Oct. 12, 1958, File 45, *Minutes of Telephone Conversations of John Foster Dulles and of Christian Herter, 1953–1961*, John Foster Dulles Telephone Conversations with the White House.

94. Diary Note, Oct. 7, 1958, Box 10, Eisenhower Papers (Ann Whitman), Ann Whitman Diary Series, DDEL; Eisenhower to Dulles, Oct. 7, 1958, *FRUS*, 1958–60, 19: 346–47.

95. Memorandum of telephone conversation, Oct. 7, 1958, Box 13, Dulles Papers, Telephone Call Series, White House Telephone Calls, DDEL.

96. *New York Times*, Oct. 2, 1958, 1: 8; Drumwright to State Dept., Oct. 2, 1958, *FRUS*, 1958–60, 19: 319–21.

97. Record of meeting, Oct. 10, 1958, *FRUS*, 1958–60, 19: 363–71.

98. Draft Talking Paper, Oct. 13, 1958, ibid., 399–401.

99. Memorandum of conversation, Oct. 14, 1958, ibid., 404–5.

100. Green to Robertson, Oct. 17, 1958, *FRUS* 1958–60, 19: Microfiche Supplement; Edwin W. Martin to Parsons, Nov. 13, 1958, ibid.

101. Memorandum of conversation, Oct. 21, 1958, *FRUS*, 1958–60, 19: 418; memorandum of conversation, Oct. 22, 1958, ibid., 424–26.

102. Joint Communiqué, Oct. 23, 1958, ibid., 443–44.

103. Ibid., 443.

104. Memorandum of conversation, Oct. 22, 1958, ibid., 431–32; memorandum of conversation, Oct. 23, 1958, ibid., 439–40.

105. Gerard C. Smith, *Disarming Diplomat: The Memoirs of Gerard C. Smith, Arms Control Negotiator* (Lanham, Md.: Madison Books, 1996), 90–91.

106. Summary record of meeting, Oct. 22, 1958, *FRUS*, 1958–60, 19: 426–27; David L. Osborn to State Dept., Nov. 25, 1958, *FRUS*, 1958–60, 19: Microfiche Supplement.

107. Taipei Embassy to United States Information Agency, Oct. 23, 1958, *FRUS*, 1958–60, 19: Microfiche Supplement.

108. Dulles to Selwyn Lloyd, Oct. 24, 1958, *FRUS*, 1958–60, 19: 451.

109. China Weekly Telegram, Oct. 28, 1958, Box 31, Office of Public Opinion Studies, 1943–65, RG 59, National Archives.

110. Memorandum of discussion, 384th NSC meeting, Oct. 30, 1958, *FRUS*, 1958–60, 19: 470–71.

111. Memorandum of conversation, Oct. 29, 1958, ibid., 463–64; State Dept. to Taipei Embassy, Oct. 30, 1958, ibid., 475–76.

112. Chiang Kai-shek to Eisenhower, Nov. 5, 1958, *FRUS*, 1958–60, 19: Microfiche Supplement; memorandum of telephone conversation, Nov. 13, 1958, Box 11, Christian Herter Papers, Telephone Calls, DDEL; Eisenhower to Chiang Kai-shek, Nov. 14, 1958, *FRUS*, 1958–60, 19: 486–87.

113. Drumwright to State Dept., May 3, 1959, *FRUS*, 1958–60, 19: 562–63.

114. See, for example, Richard Bissell to Edward G. Lansdale, Apr. 18, 1960, *FRUS*, 1958–60, 19: 656–62; ibid., 687n2. It appears that Eisenhower, shortly before leaving office, did approve a plan for Nationalist paramilitary operations on the mainland. See Chiang Kai-shek to Eisenhower, Dec. 14, 1960, ibid., 748.

115. Drumwright to Robertson, June 18, 1959, Box 1, Records of the Foreign Service Posts, Top Secret Foreign Service Post Files, Embassy Taipei, 1959–1977, RG

84, National Archives; memorandum of conversation, Nov. 21, 1960, *FRUS*, 1958–60, 19: Microfiche Supplement.

116. COMUSTDC/MAAG TAIWAN [U.S. Taiwan Defense Command/Military Advisory Assistance Group, Taiwan] Report of Taiwan-Jinmen Operations, Aug.-Dec. 1958, undated, *FRUS*, 1958–60, 19: 506.

117. Xiaobing Li, "Making of Mao's Cold War: The Taiwan Straits Crises Revisited," 66–67; Shu Guang Zhang, *Deterrence and Strategic Culture*, 261; Li Xiaobing, Chen Jian, and David Wilson, "Mao Zedong's Handling of the Taiwan Straits Crisis of 1958," 212–13.

118. Memorandum for the file, Oct. 16, 1958, Box 1, Dulles Papers, Gerard C. Smith Series, DDEL.

119. Memorandum of discussion, 462d NSC meeting, Oct. 6, 1960, *FRUS*, 1958–60, 3: 484–88.

120. "Ten Principal Conclusions and Lessons Deriving from the Taiwan Crisis," undated, *FRUS*, 1958–60, 19: 540.

121. Editorial Note [excerpt from memorandum of conversation, March 22, 1959], ibid., 553.

122. "Offshore Islands Chronology" [June 20, 1962], President's Office Files, Countries Series, Box 113A, John F. Kennedy Library, Boston, Mass.

123. The following works contain informative analyses of the role and sources of inflated threat assessments in U.S. national security policy during the Cold War: Robert J. McMahon, "The Illusion of Vulnerability: American Reassessments of the Soviet Threat, 1955–1956," *International History Review* 18 (Aug. 1996): 591–619; Robert H. Johnson, *Improbable Dangers: U.S. Conceptions of Threat in the Cold War and After* (New York: St. Martin's Press, 1994); Robert Jervis and Jack Synder, eds., *Dominoes and Bandwagons: Strategic Beliefs and Great Power Competition in the Eurasian Rimland* (New York: Oxford University Press, 1991).

124. Soman, "'Who's Daddy' in the Taiwan Strait?," 397–98.

125. Martin to Parsons, Aug. 5, 1960, *FRUS*, 1958–60, 19: Microfiche Supplement; Edward Rice to Gerard Smith, Aug. 1, 1960, ibid.

5. Gong Li, "Tension across the Taiwan Strait in the 1950s: Chinese Strategy and Tactics"

1. Zu guo she, ed., *Kangzhan Yilai Zhongguo Waijiao Zhongyao Wenxian* (Important documents since the Anti-Japanese War) (Chongqing, 1943), 71–72.

2. *Fan Faxisi Zhanzheng Wenxian* (Anti-Fascism War documents) (Beijing: Shijie Zhishi Chubanshe, 1955), 163.

3. Ibid., 299.

4. Ibid., 323.

5. Editorial, "Zhongguo Renmin Yiding Yao Jiefang Taiwan" (The Chinese people will definitely liberate Taiwan), *Xinhua*, March 15, 1949. This was the first time liberation of Taiwan was proclaimed. Chiang Kai-shek's forces had retreated to Taiwan on May 26, 1949; in July Mao Zedong suggested that the People's Liberation Army prepare to cross the sea, and quickly set up and trained its air force to try to seize Taiwan in one sweep in the summer of 1950. For details, see *Dangdai Zhongguo Kongjun* (The contemporary Chinese air force), ed. Zhou Keyu (Beijing: Zhongguo Shehui Kexue Chubanshe, 1989), 35.

6. Mao Zedong, "Guanyu Tong Miandian Jianli Waijiao Guanxi deng Wenti de Dianbao" (Telegram concerning the establishment of diplomatic relations with Burma and other issues), in *Jianguo Yilai Mao Zedong Wengao* (Manuscripts by Mao Zedong since the founding of the People's Republic), comp. Central Document Research Office of the Chinese Communist Party Central Committee, vol. 1, Sept. 1949–Dec. 1950 (Beijing: Zhongyang Wenxian Chubanshe, 1987), 193.

7. *Foreign Relations of the United States (FRUS)*, 1949, vol. 9: *The Far East and China* (Washington, D.C.: Government Printing Office, 1974), 265–67.

8. "Meiguo Zongtong Tulumen guanyu Taiwan de Shengming" (Statement on Taiwan by U.S. President Truman), in *Zhong Mei Guanxi Ziliao Huibian* (Documentary collection on Sino-U.S. relations) (Beijing: Shijie Zhishi Chubanshe, 1961), 10.

9. *FRUS*, 1949, 9: 265–67.

10. "Meiguo Zongtong Tulumen guanyu Chaoxian he Taiwan de Shengming" (Statement on Taiwan and Korea by American president Truman), June 27, 1950, in *Zhong Mei Guanxi Ziliao Huibian*, 10.

11. Xiao Jingguang, *Xiao Jingguang Huiyilu, xuji* (Memoirs of Xiao Jingguang, continued) (Beijing: Jiefangjun Chubanshe, 1988), 26.

12. Mao Zedong, "Dabai Mei Diguozhuyi de renhe Tiaoxin" (Defeat any provocation by U.S. imperialism), in *Mao Zedong Waijiao Wenxuan* (Selected diplomatic documents by Mao Zedong), comp. Ministry of Foreign Affairs of the People's Republic of China and Central Document Research Office of the Chinese Communist Party Central Committee (Beijing: Zhongyang Wenxian Chubanshe and Shijie Zhishi Chubanshe, 1994), 137.

13. Zhou Enlai, "Guanyu Meiguo Wuzhuang Qinlue Zhongguo Lingtu Taiwan de Shengming" (Statement on the U.S. armed invasion of Chinese territory on Taiwan), June 28, 1950, in *Zhou Enlai Waijiao Wenxuan* (Selected diplomatic documents by Zhou Enlai), comp. Central Document Research Office of the Chinese Communist Party Central Committee (Beijing: Zhongyang Wenxian Chubanshe, 1990), 19.

14. Li Changjiu and Shi Lujia, eds., *Zhong Mei Guanxi Erbainian* (Two hundred years of Sino-American relations) (Beijing: Xinhua Chubanshe, 1984), 184.

15. Gong Li, *Chonggou Shijie Geju—Mao Zedong yu Xin Zhongguo Waijiao* (Reconstruction of the world structure— Mao Zedong and the diplomacy of New China) (Zhengzhou: Zhongyuan Nongmin Chubanshe, 1993), 79.

16. Liao Xinwen, "Zhou Enlai yu Heping Jiejue Taiwan Wenti de Fangzhen" (Zhou Enlai and the guideline for the peaceful solution of the Taiwan problem), in *Dang de Wenxian* (Party documents), no. 5 (1994): 32.

17. Pei Jianzhang, ed., *Zhongguo Waijiao Shi: 1949–1956* (Diplomatic history of China: 1949–1956) (Beijing: Shijie Zhishi Chubanshe, 1994), 337.

18. Mao Zedong, "Guanyu Jielu Meiguo Pincou 'Dongnanya Fangyu Jituan' de Piyu" (Remarks concerning exposing the U.S. rigging up of a "Southeast Asia defense group"), Aug. 6, 1954, in *Jianguo Yilai Mao Zedong Wengao*, vol. 4, Jan. 1953–Dec. 1954 (Beijing: Zhongyang Wenxian Chubanshe, 1990), 529.

19. "Zai Zhongyang Renmin Zhengfu Weiyuanhui Di Sanshisanci Huiyishang Zhou Enlai Zongli Jian Waizhang de Waijiao Baogao" (Foreign Policy Report of Premier and Foreign Minister Zhou Enlai at the Thirty-third Committee Meeting of the Central People's Government), *Renmin Ribao* (People's daily), Aug. 14, 1954, 1.

20. Mao Zedong, "Guanyu Zhongjian Didai, Heping Gongchu yiji Zhong Ying Zhong Mei Guanxi Wenti" (On the Middle Zone, Peaceful Coexistence, and Sino-British and Sino-U.S. Relations), Aug. 24, 1954, in *Mao Zedong Waijiao Wenxuan*, 162.

21. "Mei Jiang Gongtong Fangyu Tiaoli" (The mutual defense treaty between the United States and Chiang), Dec. 2, 1954, in *Zhong Mei Guanxi Ziliao Huibian*, vol. 2 (part 2), 2051–53.

22. Mao Zedong, "Guanyu gongji Yijiangshandao shiji de piyu" (Remarks on the time to attack Yijiangshan island), Dec. 11, 1954, in *Jianguo Yilai Mao Zedong Wengao*, vol. 4, 627.

23. Han Nianlong, ed., *Dangdai Zhongguo Waijiao* (Contemporary Chinese diplomacy) (Beijing: Zhongguo Shehui Kexue Chubanshe, 1988), 74.

24. Mao Zedong, "Yuanzidan Xiabudao Zhongguo Renmin" (The Chinese people cannot be cowed by the atom bomb), Jan. 28, 1955, in *Mao Zedong Xuanji* (Selected works of Mao Zedong) (Beijing: Renmin Chubanshe, 1977), vol. 5, 136–37.

25. Mao Zedong, "Guanyu Jiangjun cong Dachendao Chetui shi Wo Jun bu Yao Xiang Gangkou Yidai Sheji de Piyu" (Remarks on the Chinese army not firing at Jiang's army as it withdraws from Dachen island), Feb. 2, 1955, *Jianguo Yilai Mao Zedong*, vol. 5, Jan.–Dec. 1955 (Beijing: Zhongyang Wenxian Chubanshe, 1991), 23.

26. *Xian Xongtong Jianggong Quanji* (Complete works of former leader Chiang), vol. 3 (Taibei: Zhongguo Wenhua Daxue Chuban Bu, 1984), 3882–83.

27. Gong Li, *Chonggou Shijie Geju*, 90.

28. Ibid., 91.

29. "Zhou Enlai Zongli Zai Canjia Yafei Huiyi de Baguo Daibiaotuan Tuanzhang Huiyishang de Shengming—Biaoshi Yuanyi jiu Taiwan Wenti yu Meiguo Jinxing Tanpan" (Statement of Zhou Enlai during the Conference of the Heads of Delegations of Eight States from Asia and Africa—Indicating China wants to negotiate with the U.S. on the Taiwan issue), in *Zhong Mei Guanxi Ziliao Huibian*, vol. 2 (part 2), 2250–51. See also *Renmin Ribao* (People's daily), Apr. 24, 1955.

30. Mao Zedong, "Heping wei Shang" (Peace above all), May 26, 1955, in *Mao Zedong Waijiao Wenxuan*, 213.

31. Wang Bingnan, *Zhong Mei Huitan Jiunian Huigu* (Nine years of Sino-American talks in retrospect) (Beijing: Shijie Zhishi Chubanshe, 1985), 56.

32. Pei Jianzhang, ed., *Zhongguo Waijiao Shi*, 348–49.

33. "Zhou Enlai Zongli Zai Quanguo Renmin Daibiao Dahui Changwu Weiyuanhui Dishiwuci Kuoda Huiyishang Guanyu Yafei Huiyi de Baogao"(Report of Premier Zhou Enlai on the Afro-Asian conference at the fifteenth enlarged conference of the standing committee of the NPC), in *Zhong Mei Guanxi Ziliao Huibian*, vol. 2 (part 2), 2264.

34. Zhou Enlai, "Muqian de Guoji Xingshi he Women de Waijiao Renwu" (The current international situation and our diplomatic tasks), July 28, 1955, in *Zhong Mei Guanxi Ziliao Huibian*, vol. 2, pt. 2, 2287. See also *Renmin Ribao*, July 31, 1955.

35. Tian Yi, "Disanci Guogong Hezuo yiyu Zuizao Jianzhu Haiwai Huawen Baokan" (The Third Cooperation of the KMT and the CCP appeared first in an overseas Chinese newspaper), *Huasheng Bao* (Voice of the Chinese), May 27, 1984, 4.

36. *Renmin Ribao*, Apr. 17, 1957.

37. Wu Lengxi, *Yi Mao Zhuxi—Wo Qinzi Jingli de Ruogan Zhongda Lishi Shijian Pian-duan* (Recollections of Chairman Mao—Several important events of history from my own experience) (Beijing: Xinhua Chubanshe, 1995), 75.

38. Mao Zedong, "Bixu Jianjue Buda Wubawo Zhizhan de Yuanze" (Firmly keep to the principle of not fighting a war without any assurances), July 27, 1958, in *Mao Zedong Junshi Wenxuan* (Selected military works of Mao Zedong), vol. 6 (Beijing: Junshi Kexue Chubanshe and Zhongyang Wenxian Chubanshe, 1993), 377.

39. Mao Zedong, "Waijiao Douzheng Bixu Gaowu Jianling, Shiru Pozhu"(A diplomatic struggle must operate from a strategically advantageous position and with irresistible force), Sept. 19, 1958, in *Mao Zedong Waijiao Wenxuan*, 353.

40. Ye Fei, "Paoji Jinmen jishi" (Report of the bombardment over Jinmen), in *Gongheguo Zhanshen Shilu* (Records of War Gods of the Republic) (Beijing: Tuanjie Chubanshe, 1993), 189–93.

41. Wu Lengxi, *Yi Mao Zhuxi*, 76.

42. Ibid., 74.

43. Ibid., 79.

44. "Mao Zedong Zhuxi zai Zuigao Guowu Huiyishang Lun Muqian Xingshi" (Chairman Mao talks on the current situation at the Supreme State Conference), *Xinhua Banyue Kan* (New China semimonthly), no. 18 (1958): 14.

45. For details, see Research Office of Diplomatic History of the Ministry of Foreign Affairs of the People's Republic of China, comp., *Xin Zhongguo Waijiao Feng-yun* (Winds and clouds in new China's diplomacy) (Beiijing: Shijie Zhishi Chubanshe, 1990), 136–37.

46. The full text of Khrushchev's letter was published in China as "Qinfan Zhongguo Jiushi Qinfan Sulian" (Encroachment of China means encroachment of the USSR), *Renmin Ribao*, Sept. 10, 1958, 1.

47. Ye Fei, "Paoji Jinmen Jishi," 192–93.

48. Liao Xinwen, "Mao Zedong 1958 nian Juece Paoji Jinmen de Lishi Kaocha" (Historical review of Mao Zedong's decision to bombard Jinmen in 1958), *Dangde Wenxian* (Party documents), no. 1 (1994): 33.

49. Wang Bingnan, *Zhong Mei Huitan Jiunian Huigu*, 72–73.

50. "Meiguo Guowuqing Dulaosi zai Jizhe Zhaodai Huishang guanyu Taiwan Haixia Jushi he Zhongmei Huitan de Tanhua" (Secretary of State Dulles at a press conference on the situation in the Taiwan Strait and Sino-U.S. talks), in *Zhong Mei Guanxi Ziliao Huibian*, vol. 2 (part 2), 2817.

51. Gong Li, *Chonggou Shijie Geju*, 96.

52. Wu Lengxi, *Yi Mao Zhuxi*, 84.

53. Mao Zedong, "Zanting Paoji Jinmen Mazu Liangdao"(Temporarily stop the bombing over Jinmen and Mazu), Oct. 5, 1958, in *Mao Zedong Junshi Wenxuan*, vol. 6, 382.

54. Wu Lengxi, *Yi Mao Zhuxi*, 87.

55. "Wo Guofangbu Mingling—Dui Jinmen Paoji Tingzhi Liangzhou" (Order of the ministry—Stop bombing over Jinmen for two weeks), Oct. 13, 1958, in *Zhong Mei Guanxi Ziliao Huibian*, vol. 2 (part 2), 2853–54. See also *Renmin Ribao*, Oct. 13, 1958.

56. *Circular by the Central Committee of the Chinese Communist Party on the Present Struggle against U.S. Imperialism*, Oct., 17, 1958.

57. Wu Lengxi, *Yi Mao Zhuxi*, 89.

58. Mao Zedong, "Zhonghua Renmin Gongheguo Guofangbu Zai Gao Taiwan Tongbao Shu"(A letter to Taiwan compatriots from the ministry of defense of the People's Republic of China), Oct. 25, 1958, in *Jianguo Yilai Mao Zedong Wengao*, vol. 7, Jan. 1958–Dec. 1958 (Beijing: Zhongyang Wenxian Chubanshe, 1992), 469–70.

59. Lin Ke, Xu Tao, and Wu Xujun, *Lishi de Zhenshi—Mao Zedong Shengbian Gongzuo Renyuan de Zhengyan* (The truth of history—Affidavits of Mao Zedong's employees) (Hong Kong: Liwan Chubanshe, 1995), 284.

60. Liao Xinwen, "Mao Zedong 1958 nian Juece Paoji Jinmen de Lishi Kaocha," *Dangde Wenxian*, no. 1 (1994): 43.

61. "Zhou Enlai guanyu Taiwan Haixia Diqu Jushi de Shengming" (Zhou Enlai's statement on the situation in the Taiwan Strait), *Renmin Ribao*, Sept. 7, 1958, 1.

6. Zhang Baijia and Jia Qingguo, "Steering Wheel, Shock Absorber, and Diplomatic Probe in Confrontation: Sino-American Ambassadorial-Level Talks Seen from the Chinese Perspective"

1. Wang Bingnan, *Zhongmei Huitan Jiunian Huigu* (Nine years of Sino-American talks in retrospect) (Beijing: Shijie Zhishi Chubanshe, 1985), 25.

2. Ibid., 73.

3. Jia Qingguo, *Wei Shixian de Hejie: Zhongmei Guanxi de Gehe yu Weiji* (The unmaterialized rapprochement: Estrangement and crisis in Sino-American relations) (Beijing: Wenhua Yishu Chubanshe, 1998), 91.

4. Document Research Office of the Chinese Communist Party Central Committee, comp., *Zhou Enlai Nianpu* (Chronology of Zhou Enlai: 1949–1976), vol. 1 (Beijing: Zhongyang Wenxian Chubanshe, 1998), 356.

5. Wang, *Zhongmei Huitan Jiunian Huigu*, 6.

6. According to Ambassador Wang, the handshaking incident never happened. See Wang, *Zhongmei Huitan Jiunian Huigu*, 21–22. However, when Jia Qingguo interviewed Ambassador U. Alexis Johnson in his Washington apartment on July 31, 1986, Johnson said he personally witnessed the incident.

7. Wang, *Zhongmei Huitan Jiunian Huigu*, 23–24.

8. Document Research Office of the CCP Central Committee, comp., *Zhou Enlai Nianpu*, vol. 1, 375.

9. Ibid., 376.

10. Jia, *Wei Shixian de Hejie*, 125.

11. Ibid., 148–49.

12. Zhang Mingyang, "Chi Wei Meiguo Qinzhan Taiwan Zhangmu de Miaolun" (Refute the fallacies that support U.S. occupation of Taiwan), *Shijie Zhishi* (World knowledge), no. 19 (1954): 14; Xie Yixian, *Zhongguo Waijiao Shi: 1949–1979* (China's diplomatic history: 1949–1979) (Henan: Henan Renmin Chubanshe, 1988), 137.

13. Jia, *Wei Shixian de Hejie*, 148.

14. Mao's speech at an enlarged meeting of the Politburo of the CCP Central Committee, July 7, 1954.

15. Document Research Office of the CCP Central Committee, comp., *Zhou Enlai Nianpu*, vol. 1, 405.

16. Jia Qingguo, "Jianxi Meitai 'Gongtong Fangyu' Tiaoyue de Dijie" (A brief analysis of the process of the conclusion of the "mutual security" treaty between the U.S. and Taiwan), *Meiguo Yanjiu* (Journal of American studies), no. 1 (1989).

17. Central Document Research Office of the CCP Central Committee, comp., *Zhou Enlai Waijiao Wenxuan* (Selected works of Zhou Enlai on diplomacy) (Beijing: Zhongyang Wenxian Chubanshe, 1990), 134.

18. Ministry of Foreign Affairs of the People's Republic of China and the Document Research Office of the CCP Central Committee, comp., *Mao Zedong Waijiao Wenxuan* (Selected works of Mao Zedong on diplomacy) (Beijing: Zhongyang Wenxian Chubanshe and Shijie Zhishi Chubanshe, 1994), 161.

19. Document Research Office of the CCP Central Committee, comp., *Zhou Enlai Nianpu*, vol. 1, 474–75.

20. Pei Jianzhang, ed., *Zhonghua Renmin Gongheguo Waijiaoshi: 1949-1956* (Diplomatic history of the People's Republic of China: 1949–1956) (Beijing: Shijie Zhishi Chubanshe, 1994), 344–45.

21. Ibid., 345.

22. *Zhou Enlai Waijiao Dashiji* (Chronology of Zhou Enlai's major diplomatic activities) (Beijing: Shijie Zhishi Chubanshe, 1993), 122.

23. Wang, *Zhongmei Huitan Jiunian Huigu*, 47.

24. Jia, *Wei Shixian de Hejie*, 208–9.

25. Wang, *Zhongmei Huitan Jiunian Huigu*, 56–57.

26. *Renmin Ribao*, June 29, 1956.

27. Document Research Office of the CCP Central Committee, comp., *Zhou Enlai Nianpu*, vol. 1, 588.

28. Jia, *Wei Shixian de Hejie*, 226.

29. John Foster Dulles, "Our Policy toward Communism in China," *Foreign Relations of the United States* (FRUS), 1955-57 (Washington, D.C.: Government Printing Office, 1986), 3: 558–66.

30. Jia, *Wei Shixian de Hejie*, 226–27.

31. Quoted in Chen Yi, "Zai Waijiaobu Dangzu Wuxuhui shang de Fayan" (Speech at a general meeting of the Party committee of the Ministry of Foreign Affairs), June 17, 1958.

32. Wu Lengxi, *Yi Maozhuxi—Wo Qinzi Jingli de Ruogan Zhongda Lishi Shijian Pian-duan* (Recollections of Chairman Mao—Several important events in history from my own experience) (Beijing: Xinhua Chubanshe, 1995), 79.

33. Wang, *Zhongmei Huitan Jiunian Huigu*, 71.

34. Jin Chongji, ed., *Zhou Enlai Zhuan* (Biography of Zhou Enlai), vol. 2 (Beijing: Zhongyang Wenxian Chubanshe, 1998), 1428.

35. Ibid., 1429; Document Research Office of the CCP Central Committee, comp., *Zhou Enlai Nianpu*, vol. 2, 177.

36. Jin, ed., *Zhou Enlai Zhuan*, vol. 2, 1431.

37. Wang, *Zhongmei Huitan Jiunian Huigu*, 86–87.

38. Ibid., 88–90; Telegram from Embassy in Poland to the Department of State, June 23, 1962, *FRUS*, 1961–63, 22: 273–75.

39. Wang, *Zhongmei Huitan Jiunian Huigu*, 93.

40. Wang Guoquan, "Wo de Dashi Shengya" (My experience as an ambassador), in *Dangdai Zhongguo Shijie Waijiao Shengya* (Experience of contemporary Chinese ambassadors), vol. 2 (Beijing: Shijie Zhishi Chubanshe, 1995), 154–55.

41. Li Changjiu and Shi Lujia, eds., *Zhong Mei Guanxi Erbainian* (Sino-American relations in the past two hundred years) (Beijing: Xinhua Chubanshe, 1984), 209.

42. Zong Daoyi, "Xin Zhongguo Waijiaoshi Ruogan Shishi Kaoding" (Examining certain facts in the history of the diplomatic history of the New China), *Dangdai Zhongguoshi Yanjiu* (Studies in contemporary Chinese history), no. 6 (1997), 108.

43. Wang Yongqin, "1966–1976 Nian Zhong Mei Su Guanxi Jishi" (Review of the relationship between China, the U.S., and the Soviet Union between 1966 and 1976), *Dangdai Zhongguoshi Yanjiu* (Studies in contemporary Chinese history), no. 4 (1997), 123.

44. Letter from Zhou Enlai to Mao Zedong, Nov. 16, 1969.

45. Wang, "1966–1976 Nian Zhong Mei Su Guanxi Jishi"; Jin, ed., *Zhou Enlai Zhuan*, vol. 2, 2046.

46. Luo Yishu, "Zai Bolan de Suiyue" (Years in Poland), *Dangdai Zhongguo Shijie Waijiao Shengya* (Experience of contemporary Chinese ambassadors), vol. 4 (Beijing: Shijie Zhishi Chubanshe, 1996), 179; Jing Zhicheng, "Waijiaoshi Shang de Yijian Qushi: Meiguo Dashi Zai Huasha Zhuizhu Wo Waijiaoguan Zhenxiang" (An interesting event in diplomatic history: What really happened when the American ambassador in Warsaw chased our diplomats), *Waijiao Xueyuan Xuebao* (Journal of the Institute of Foreign Affairs), no. 3 (1990).

47. Geng Biao, "Zhou Enlai Shi Xin Zhongguo Waijiao de Chuangshiren he Dianjiren" (Zhou Enlai was the founder and initiator of the diplomacy of the New China), in *Yanjiu Zhou Enlai—Waijiao Sixiang yu Shijian* (Study of Zhou Enlai's diplomatic thinking and practice), ed. Editorial Section of Diplomatic History of the Ministry of Foreign Affairs (Beijing: Shijie Zhishi Chubanshe, 1989), 15.

48. Document Research Office of the CCP Central Committee, comp., *Zhou Enlai Nianpu*, vol. 3, 338; Jin, ed., *Zhou Enlai Zhuan*, vol. 2, 2046.

49. Jin, ed., ibid.

50. Ibid., 2047.

51. Comments of Zhou Enlai on an oral message of Nixon passed by the Pakistan President and sent in by the Chinese Ambassador to Pakistan, Zhang Tong, Mar. 21, 1970.

52. Document Research Office of the CCP Central Committee, comp., *Zhou Enlai Nianpu*, vol. 2, 357.

53. These are the respective years, following the Sino-American rapprochement in the early 1970s, during which China obtained the following major partial solutions of the Taiwan problem: the Shanghai Communiqué, communiqué on normalization of relations between the two countries, communication on gradual phase out of U.S. arms sales to Taiwan, and President Clinton's announcement of the so-called "three nos" policy.

54. Jia, *Wei Shixian de Hejie*, 258, n. 1.

7. Steven M. Goldstein, "Dialogue of the Deaf?: The Sino-American Ambassadorial-Level Talks, 1955–1970"

1. Kenneth T. Young, *Negotiating with the Chinese Communists: The United States Experience, 1953–1967* (New York: McGraw-Hill, 1968) is the classic study of the talks, written by a former State Department official. There have also been accounts written by participants in the talks. See U. Alexis Johnson, with Jef Olivarius McAllister, *The Right Hand of Power* (Englewood Cliffs, N.J.: Prentice-Hall, 1984); Jacob Beam, *Multiple Exposure: An American Ambassador's Unique Perspective on East-West Issues* (New York: Norton, 1978); and Wang Bingnan, "Nine Years of Sino-U.S. Talks in Retrospect," trans. in Joint Publications Research Service, *China Report*, CPS-85-079 (Aug. 7, 1985).

2. The classic argument along these lines is Townsend Hoopes, *The Devil and John Foster Dulles* (Boston: Little, Brown, 1973).

3. See, for example, Hans J. Morgenthau, "John Foster Dulles," in *An Uncertain Tradition: American Secretaries of State in the Twentieth Century*, ed. Norman A. Graebner, 289–308 (New York: McGraw-Hill, 1961); and Anna Kasten Nelson, "John Foster Dulles and the Bipartisan Congress," *Political Science Quarterly* 102, no. 1 (Spring 1987): 43–64. See especially two articles by Nancy Bernkopf Tucker, "A House Divided: The United States, the Department of State, and China," in *The Great Powers in East Asia: 1953–1960*, ed. Warren Cohen and Akira Iriye (New York: Columbia University Press, 1990) and "John Foster Dulles and the Taiwan Roots of the 'Two Chinas' Policy," in *John Foster Dulles and the Diplomacy of the Cold War*, ed. Richard H. Immerman (Princeton: Princeton University Press, 1989).

4. For excellent discussions of this factor, see Rosemary Foot, *The Practice of Power: U.S. Relations with China since 1949* (New York: Oxford University Press, 1995), 54–60; and Rosemary Foot, "Search for a Modus Vivendi: Anglo-American Relations and China Policy," in *The Great Powers in East Asia*, ed. Cohen and Iriye, 143–63.

5. This argument can be found in William Bueler, *U.S. China Policy and the Problem of Taiwan* (Boulder: Colorado Associated University Press, 1971).

6. See U.S. Department of State, *Foreign Relations of the United States (FRUS),* 1952–54, 14: 462–67, 476–79.

7. Ibid., 464–72.

8. According to State Department minutes, "Johnson stated Wang raised issues beyond scope of these discussions which he not prepared discuss . . . [and] indicated his belief that further discussions between himself and Wang no longer necessary . . . [Johnson] suggested staff officers might be designated by each side for purpose passing on information." Ibid., 478.

9. For convenient summaries of this crisis, see Gordon H. Chang, *Friends and Enemies: The United States, China, and the Soviet Union, 1948–1972* (Stanford: Stanford University Press, 1990), chap. 4; and Robert Accinelli, *Crisis and Commitment: United States Policy toward Taiwan, 1950–1955* (Chapel Hill: University of North Carolina Press, 1996).

10. *FRUS*, 1952–54, 14: 506.

11. *FRUS*, 1955–57, 2: 506–9, 519–20. What was clear, above all, was that Dulles wanted only "direct" negotiations. He was "fed up with all the intermediaries," a judgment with which the president concurred. Ibid., 531–34, 605, 630–31.

12. Ibid., 534–38, 554–57.

13. Ibid., 571–72.

14. Ibid., 566–67.

15. Ibid., 563–64, 659. In his memoirs, Johnson notes that Dulles was also concerned about what might happen at a forthcoming summit in Geneva. Johnson, with McAllister, *The Right Hand of Power,* 237.

16. This wording comes from the message sent through the Indian government. *FRUS*, 1955–57, 2: 637–38. The message sent through the British government was similar, except that it used terminology referring to future agenda issues ("certain other practical matters now at issue") that found its way into the formal announcement of the talks. See ibid., 643.

17. Ibid., 678.

18. Ibid., 679–80; and *Department of State Bulletin,* Aug. 8, 1955, 220–21.

19. Dulles to Johnson, July 29, 1955, *FRUS*, 1955–57, China: Microfiche Supplement (hereafter cited as *FRUS*, 1955–57 Supplement).

20. As Dulles noted in his announcement, there were signs of a lull in the Strait. To use his words, a "pistol" to the head of the U.S. had been "laid down" by the PRC, and he was determined to see to it that it stayed that way. *Department of State Bulletin,* Aug. 15, 1955, 261. Accinelli makes the same point about Dulles's view of the talks in *Crisis and Commitment,* chap. 11.

21. Johnson, with McAllister, *The Right Hand of Power,* 239.

22. Ibid., 235.

23. Wang Bingnan insisted that "American nationals [would be] treated like all other aliens in China and accorded protection as long as they respect Chinese law. If they breach Chinese law [they would be] treated as law provides." Johnson to Secretary of State, Aug. 2, 1955; Johnson to Secretary of State, Aug. 23, 1955; Johnson to Secretary of State, Aug. 16, 1955; and Johnson to Secretary of State, Aug. 18, 1955, in *FRUS*, 1955–57 Supplement. See also *FRUS*, 1955–57, 3: 40.

24. Johnson to Secretary of State, Aug. 2, 1955, *FRUS*, 1955–57 Supplement.

25. This was no surprise, of course. From the moment the talks were announced, the Republic of China's ambassador was protesting American interference in a domestic matter as an apparent weakness in confronting the mainland. At the start of the talks, the State Department had sought to assure the ROC regarding the nature of the talks by sending a copy of Johnson's instructions to its Foreign Ministry. However, the copy omitted two key sections that would have increased suspicions on Taiwan: the permission for Johnson to meet socially with the Chinese and the suggestion that the United States might relax rules on travel to the mainland in exchange for a repatriation agreement. Dulles was not above misleading allies to avoid conflict. *FRUS*, 1955–57, 3: 22.

26. *FRUS*, 1955–57, 3: 38; and Johnson to Secretary of State, Aug. 11, 1955, *FRUS*, 1955–57 Supplement.

27. Johnson to Secretary of State, Aug. 12, 1955, *FRUS*, 1955–57 Supplement.

28. As McConaughy noted in a letter to Johnson, the secretary was not willing to settle for "half a loaf." McConaughy to Johnson, Aug. 15, 1955, ibid. About the drafting of statements justifying a break-off on the American side, see Dulles to Johnson, Aug. 17, 1955, and Johnson to Dulles, Aug. 18, 1955, ibid.

29. Johnson to Secretary of State, Aug. 18, 1955, Secretary of State to Johnson, Aug. 19, 1955, and McConaughy to Johnson, Aug. 19, 1955, ibid.

30. Johnson to Secretary of State, Aug. 20, 1955, ibid.

31. Johnson to Dulles, Aug. 24, 1955, ibid.; Dulles to Johnson, Sept. 2, 1955, ibid.

32. *FRUS*, 1955–57, 3: 85–86.

33. Johnson to Secretary of State, Sept. 6, 1955, and McConaughy to Johnson, Sept. 2, 1955, *FRUS*, 1955–57 Supplement.

34. Dulles to Johnson, Sept. 2, 1955, and McConaughy to Johnson, Sept. 2, 1955, ibid.

35. Johnson to McConaughy, Sept. 7, 1955, ibid.

36. McConaughy to Johnson, Sept. 2, 1955, ibid.

37. McConaughy to Johnson, Sept. 9, 1955, and Sept. 12, 1955, ibid.

38. Young, *Negotiating with the Chinese Communists*, 76–77. The reports of the meetings of Sept. 14, 20, and 23 can be found in Johnson to Secretary of State, Sept. 14, 1955, Sept. 20, 1955, and Sept. 23, 1955, *FRUS*, 1955–57 Supplement.

39. Hoover to Johnson, Sept. 27, 1955, and Dulles to American Embassy Prague, Sept. 30, 1955, ibid.

40. Geneva to Secretary of State, Sept. 28, 1955, ibid.

41. Ibid.; Johnson to Secretary of State, Oct. 5, 1955, ibid.

42. Johnson to Secretary of State, Oct. 5, 1955, ibid.

43. Johnson to Secretary of State, Nov. 8, 1955, ibid.

44. Dulles to Johnson, Jan. 9, 1955, and Dulles to Johnson, Apr. 16, 1955, ibid.

45. Johnson to Secretary of State, Oct. 27, 1955, and Johnson to Secretary of State, Dec. 1, 1955, ibid.

46. Johnson to Secretary of State, May 11, 1955, ibid.

47. In the meetings, Johnson made several arguments to clarify or elaborate on these assumptions: that at the moment, China was a divided country (like Germany and Korea); that the ROC was recognized internationally as a sovereign state; that, therefore, the Mutual Defense Treaty of 1954 was a valid international treaty, which justified an American presence in the area; and that for this reason, the United States would not surrender (nor did it expect the PRC to surrender) the right to "individual or collective self-defense." Examples of these arguments can be found in the following reports of meetings with the Chinese: Johnson to Secretary of State, Dec. 22, 1955, Johnson to Secretary of State, Feb. 4, 1956, Johnson to Secretary of State, Apr. 19, 1956, and Johnson to Secretary of State, May 17, 1956, ibid.

48. Johnson interpreted Beijing's mention of a presidential representative as suggesting that Beijing saw the State Department as hostile. Johnson to McConaughy, Mar. 28, 1956, ibid. Such a proposal is interesting in light of the later Kissinger trip.

49. See the transcripts of the meetings cited above, n. 47.

50. For examples of such American concerns, see McConaughy to Johnson, Jan. 16, 1955, and Dulles to Johnson, May 15, 1956, ibid.

51. See, for example, Johnson to State Department, Jan. 19, 1956, ibid.

52. Johnson to State Department, Dec. 2, 1955, ibid.

53. Still, as late as April 18, 1956, Johnson continued to argue for a reconsideration of the intransigent position on the question of self-defense. Johnson to Secretary of State, Dec. 2, 1955, Secretary of State to Johnson, Dec. 6, 1955, Secretary of State to Johnson, Dec. 7, 1955, Secretary of State to Johnson, Dec. 12, 1955, and Johnson to McConaughy, Apr. 18, 1956, ibid.

54. Young, *Negotiating with the Chinese Communists*, describes this in chaps. 3 and 4. Indeed, most of Young's analysis draws from these public statements.

55. Johnson to Secretary of State, Feb. 4, 1956, McConaughy to Johnson, Feb. 27, 1956, and Johnson to McConaughy, Feb., 22, 1956, *FRUS, 1955–57* Supplement.

56. Johnson to McConaughy, Dec. 16, 1955, ibid.

57. See Johnson to Secretary of State, Dec. 15, 1955, and McConaughy to Johnson, Apr. 30, 1956, ibid.

58. See, for example, Johnson to State Department, Jan. 12, 1956, ibid.

59. Johnson to State Department, Dec. 16, 1955, and Johnson to McConaughy, Feb. 16, 1956, ibid.

60. See, for example, Johnson to State Department, Apr. 19, 1956, Johnson to State Department, Apr. 27, 1956, and Johnson to State Department, June 8, 1956, ibid.

61. McConaughy to Johnson, Feb. 24, 1956, and Johnson to McConaughy, Feb. 26, 1956, ibid.

62. There were complications, however. Taiwan soon protested, and although this was brushed aside with unusual brusqueness, the island (much to the unhappiness of the PRC) was included as an option for prisoners seeking to return. Additional complications arose from the fact that the Indian government (undoubtedly under pressure from Beijing) refused to take part in the deportation procedures. In a cable to Johnson, Dulles noted that the American side could not exploit Wang's embarrassment too strongly lest it result in slowing the release of the Americans. There was, in other words, a growing sense that a hollow victory had been won. Dulles to Johnson, June 6, 1956, Johnson to State Department, June 8, 1956, and Dulles to Johnson, June 21, 1956, ibid.

63. McConaughy to Johnson, July 6, 1956, Hoover to Johnson, July 6, 1956, and Johnson to McConaughy, June 28, 1956, ibid.

64. In the wake of the Korean War, the United States had promoted United Nations' restrictions on trade with the PRC. Although related to the regime restricting trade with the Soviet bloc, these controls were even more restrictive, a discrepancy known as the "China differential." After the Korean War, Britain and Japan pressured for change. By August 1954, in response to a request from Tokyo, the National Security Council agreed to "release Japan gradually from its obligations" under the China differential. Growing pressure from Britain also divided the two allies in 1956–57. Finally, to further complicate matters, the Eisenhower administration was itself divided: the president favored a more open stance, while Dulles opposed it. See Foot, *Practice of Power*, 52–53, and Qing Simei, "The Eisenhower Administration and Changes in Western Embargo Policy against China," in *The Great Powers in East Asia*, ed. Cohen and Iriye, 121–42.

65. Significantly, Wang argued that at this stage, a foreign ministers' meeting would be "absolutely indispensable to solve question relaxation and elimination tension in the Taiwan area." Johnson to Secretary of State, July 26, 1956, and Johnson to Secretary of State, Aug. 9, 1956, FRUS, 1955–57 Supplement.

66. FRUS, 1955–57, 3: 125–26. See especially 126n2.

67. Dulles to Johnson, July 19, 1956, Johnson to Secretary of State, July 26, 1956, and Johnson to Secretary of State, Aug. 9, 1956, FRUS, 1955–57 Supplement.

68. *FRUS*, 1955–57, 3: 409–10, n. 3.

69. Ibid., 416–17; and Dulles to Johnson, Aug. 8, 1956, *FRUS*, 1955–57 Supplement.

70. As McConaughy reminded Johnson in an October 1 letter, it was common for the Chinese to accuse the United States of stalling and suggest that they would break off the talks. However, he added, "they are still talking . . . given the present world situation and the Chinese Communist 'peaceful posture,' . . . it would not be easy for Peiping to terminate the talks." McConaughy to Johnson, Oct. 1, 1956, ibid. In fact, Johnson had already drafted an announcement in the eventuality that the Chinese called a recess in the talks. Johnson to McConaughy, Oct. 17, 1956, ibid.

71. *FRUS*, 1955–57, 3: 466–67.

72. Ibid., 574–75. On Aug. 22, the State Department released a statement saying that twenty-four news organizations had "indicated an interest in stationing a correspondent in China" and that it would validate passports for seven months for such travel. The release stipulated that the United States would still not "accord reciprocal visas to Chinese." Ibid., 584–85.

73. Johnson to State Department, Sept. 12, 1957, *FRUS*, 1955–57 Supplement.

74. Johnson to Clough, Oct. 9, 1957, Clough to Johnson, Nov. 8, 1957, and Johnson to Clough, Nov. 14, 1957, ibid.

75. *FRUS*, 1955–57, 3: 644.

76. Dulles to Johnson, Dec. 4, 1957, *FRUS*, 1955–57 Supplement.

77. Johnson to Department of State, Dec. 19, 1957, ibid.

78. The 1958 Jinmen crisis has been the subject of innumerable studies, and this is not the place to rehash them. For a masterful summary of the various explanations of the crisis, see Thomas Christensen, *Useful Adversaries* (Princeton: Princeton University Press, 1996), chap. 6. Much of the discussion in this paragraph draws from this chapter.

79. *FRUS*, 1958–60, 19: 442–44.

80. Young, *Negotiating with the Chinese Communists*, 14, and chap. 7.

81. Ibid., 199 and 208. For examples of this argument in later works on Dulles, see Frederick W. Marks III, *Power and Peace: The Diplomacy of John Foster Dulles* (Westport, Conn.: Praeger, 1993); and Michael A. Guhin, *John Foster Dulles: A Statesman and His Times* (New York: Columbia University Press, 1972), 301–2.

82. Interestingly, in the same paragraph in which he cites Young's work, Beam asserts that the talks "played a largely peripheral and incidental role in this particular crisis." Beam, *Multiple Exposure*, 119. See also Wang, "Nine Years of Sino-U.S. Talks in Retrospect," 38–43.

83. J. N. Greene, Jr., to Walter Robertson, January 21, 1958, *FRUS*, 1958–60, 19: China: Microfiche Supplement (hereafter cited as *FRUS*, 1958–60 Supplement).

84. *FRUS*, 1958–60, 19: 6–7.

85. Ibid., 27–28.

86. Robertson to Beam, July 25, 1958, ibid.

87. *FRUS,* 1958–60, 19: 42, 127, and 155n2.

88. Ibid., 155–59.

89. Beam, *Multiple Exposure,* 122.

90. Dulles to Beam, Sept. 11, 1958, *FRUS,* 1958–60 Supplement.

91. Beam, *Multiple Exposure,* 123.

92. *FRUS,* 1958–60, 19: 187.

93. The transcript of this meeting can be found in ibid., 191–95.

94. Ibid., 190–91 and 194.

95. Ibid., 209–16. On the proposal to scale down American troops, see 198.

96. Drumright to Dulles, Sept. 13, 1958, and Herter to Drumright, Sept. 18, 1958, *FRUS,* 1958–60 Supplement. There were even CIA rumors of a campaign against the talks being promoted in the United States by the ROC. *FRUS* 1958–60, 19: 269–70.

97. *FRUS,* 1958–60, 19: 249–51, 278–81.

98. Dulles, on September 20, told a high-level meeting in Washington that he had "not the remotest idea of success at Warsaw." However, he noted, given concern among the allies and negative sentiment in the U.N. ("90%" he estimated), it was important to take a posture that would gain "support and understanding." Smith to Dulles, Sept. 19, 1958; Beam to Secretary of State, Sept. 18, 1958, *FRUS,* 1958–60 Supplement, and *FRUS,* 1958–60, 19: 245.

99. Ibid., 293–96.

100. Dulles himself admitted this; see ibid., 301, 323.

101. Ibid., 323–24.

102. Ibid.

103. Beam to Secretary of State, Oct. 10, 1958, and Warsaw to Secretary of State, Oct. 13, 1958, *FRUS,* 1958–60 Supplement. It should be noted that in talks with the Australians and the British, the Eisenhower administration denigrated the value of the talks. *FRUS,* 1958–60, 19: 394, 408–11.

104. This is Young's point in *Negotiating with the Chinese Communists,* chap. 9.

105. During the Kennedy administration's first year, a series of staff memos advocated an American withdrawal from the civil war and increased pressure on the ROC to withdraw from the offshore islands—a policy that was apparently known as "Operation Candor with the GRC." President Kennedy himself reflected the new, more impatient mood when, during a strategy session on U.N. policy, he remarked that he was sending a letter to Chiang "based on what is good for us, not what is good for Formosa." *FRUS,* 1961–63, 22: 53–54, 72–76; Arthur M. Schlesinger, Jr., *A Thousand Days: John F. Kennedy in the White House* (Boston: Houghton Mifflin, 1965), 483.

106. *FRUS*, 1961–63, 22: 359–60.

107. The locus classicus for this assertion is Rusk's report of a meeting with Kennedy early in the administration. See Dean Rusk as told to Richard Rusk, *As I Saw It*, ed. Daniel S. Papp (New York: Norton, 1990), 282–84. For a general discussion of Kennedy's China policy, see James Fetzer, "Clinging to Containment: China Policy," in *Kennedy's Quest for Victory: American Foreign Policy, 1961–1963*, ed. Thomas Paterson (New York: Oxford University Press, 1989). See also David Halberstam, *The Best and the Brightest* (New York: Random House, 1972), 104; and James C. Thomson, "On the Making of U.S. China Policy, 1964–1969: A Study in Bureaucratic Politics," *China Quarterly*, no. 50 (April-June, 1972): 221.

108. This is well covered in Chang, *Friends and Enemies*, chap. 7. See also Fetzer, "Clinging to Containment: China Policy."

109. *FRUS*, 1961–63, 22: 51–52, 231–33, 332–33, 363–65, 405–7.

110. See, for example, ibid., 25–26, 213–14, 216–17. There were never any official offers made by the United States government, although there continued to be discussions with Warsaw about presenting the idea in a "low key" way that would not make it seem like a propaganda ploy. Ibid., 231–33.

111. Ibid., 22–26.

112. Ibid., 26.

113. Ibid., 378–82.

114. See, for example, ibid., 318–20, 363–65, 392–94.

115. Ibid., 273–75. For a Chinese account, see Wang, "Nine Years of Sino-U.S. Talks in Retrospect." It should also be noted that President Kennedy revealed the gist of the American statement at a press conference a few days later. *New York Times*, June 28, 1962.

116. In particular, he was instructed to impress upon Wang the political difficulties the Kennedy administration would face in making any agreements regarding Taiwan and the benefits that might come from taking small steps in improving Sino-American relations.

117. *FRUS*, 1964–68, 30: 39–40, 94–99, on the nuclear issue. For a general assessment of China, see ibid., 168–70.

118. Ibid., 75–76.

119. Ibid., 383–86, 509–12.

120. Ibid., 135, 166. These warnings were in fact taken very seriously in Washington. Despite Chiang Kai-shek's threat to increase the size and frequency of mainland raids, a very tight rein and close watch over the activities of the ROC were maintained. See, for example, ibid., 190–91, 226–28, 391–94, 405, 507–8, 595, 612–15.

121. For example, in June 1965, a message from Zhou Enlai was passed on through the British stating the PRC's stance on the war, and in 1968 President Johnson sent a message through Prime Minister Maurer of Romania that "nothing

could be further from his mind" than going to war with China. This was undoubtedly the tip of the iceberg in back-channel communications during the Vietnam War. Zhou's message said: "(I) China would not provoke war with the United States; (II) what China says counts; (III) China is prepared; and (IV) if the United States bombs China that wd [sic] mean war and there wd [sic] be no limits to the war." See ibid., 315 and 583.

122. Ibid., 228–30, 624–29.

123. Ibid., 273–75.

124. Ibid., 293–96, 364–66, 356.

125. Ibid., 299–300, 306–8.

126. For example, ibid., 388–89.

127. Ibid., 551.

128. For example, in the last days of the administration, William Bundy made a dramatic speech in which he indicated that the United States dealt with the ROC only with respect to territories under its control; that it was willing to deal "separately" with both that government and the government of mainland China; that it did not doubt "the existence of Communist China"; and that the administration was "reviewing" the Korean War era trade embargo. Ibid., 638–41.

129. As Averell Harriman put it, such flexibility might provide help to obtain "greater credibility and more understanding of our Vietnam policy in world opinion . . . [and] be an opportunity for public rapprochement with Bill Fulbright as the instigator of the China hearings, without embracing Fulbright's softness on Vietnam." Ibid., 318. For an earlier example of such an argument, see ibid., 228–29.

Using China policy to offset domestic criticism continued to be an integral part of the Johnson administration foreign policy that found its way into the Warsaw talks. For example, when preparing the instructions for the January 1967 session, Assistant Secretary of State William Bundy argued for the inclusion of an offer to raise the level of representation at the talks should a break seem imminent, based in part on the impact of such a break on domestic public opinion. One can only assume that subsequent concerns that the talks might be broken off were also similarly motivated, at least in part, by the potential impact on domestic opinion. Ibid., 492–94 and 500–501.

130. Of course, the American public was not the only intended target for a conciliatory American posture toward China. Statements and initiatives were also intended to bolster the administration's international image and give credibility to its calls for a negotiated settlement of the war. Moreover, should either side publicize the contents of the secret talks, the public at home and abroad would see an accommodating and flexible United States, not a fanatically anticommunist one. Ibid., 254–55, 265n3.

131. Ibid., 713.

132. John Moors Cabot had spoken of the educational function in 1965. Ibid., 206.

133. The most important memos bringing together these themes were by William Bundy and Alfred Jenkins. See ibid., 645–59, 709–18.

134. Ibid., 729–30.

135. Henry Kissinger, *White House Years* (Boston: Little, Brown, 1979), 687.

136. Ibid., 684.

137. As suggested earlier, the same may probably be said of the PRC. However, that is not the topic here.

138. Of course, as noted earlier, this could not be overplayed for fear that it might provoke the ROC into hostile action vis-à-vis the mainland.

139. This is a very liberal adaptation of Robert K. Merton's distinction between manifest and latent functions. See his *Social Theory and Social Structure*, rev. ed. (Glencoe, Ill.: Free Press, 1957), 63.

140. See, for example, Young, *Negotiating with the Chinese Communists*.

141. Thomson, "On the Making of U.S. China Policy."

142. For example, Kissinger notes that the formula on Taiwan used in the Shanghai Communiqué came from a State Department planning document from the 1950s. Kissinger, *White House Years*, 783.

8. Robert D. Schulzinger, *The Johnson Administration, China, and the Vietnam War*

The first epigraph is taken from Draft memorandum from Secretary of Defense McNamara to President Johnson, Nov. 3, 1965, *Foreign Relations of the United States* (FRUS), 1964–68, 3: 514; the second, from Robert S. McNamara, *In Retrospect: The Tragedy and Lessons of Vietnam* (New York: Times Books, 1995), 215.

1. Significantly, the Johnson administration did not review U.S. policy toward China during the Chinese civil war in devising its Vietnam policy and considering the potential for Chinese intervention. The Korean precedent was so persuasive to the Johnson administration because the Chinese entry into the Korean fighting had been the greatest setback to U.S. policy in the war. Once it had become a conflict between the United States, China, and the two Koreas, the United States lost the initiative, President Harry Truman's popularity sank, and the American public became heartily disenchanted. William Stueck, *The Korean War: An International History* (Princeton: Princeton University Press, 1995), 97–106.

2. President to Maxwell Taylor, Dec. 2, 1963; President to John McCone, Dec. 2, 1963; Telephone conversation between Averell Harriman and McGeorge Bundy, Dec. 4, 1963, FRUS, 1961–63, 4: 651, 665, 579.

3. Rusk to Lodge, Dec. 6, 1963, FRUS, 1961–1963, 4: 685. Johnson was engaged in his customary hyperbole when he advocated raising American participation to the

"highest pitch." Over the next eighteen months, he continued to anguish and equivocate over the deepening commitment of U.S. forces.

4. Hilsman to Rusk, Dec. 20, 1963, ibid., 719.

5. Mike Mansfield to President Kennedy, Aug. 19, 1963, *FRUS*, 1961–63, 3: 585.

6. Mansfield to President Johnson, Dec. 7, 1963, *FRUS*, 1961–63, 4: 691.

7. "Possibilities of Greater Militancy by the Chinese Communists," Special National Intelligence Estimate (SNIE) 13-4-63, July 31, 1963. See also SNIE 13-3-61, Nov. 30, 1961; NIE 13-4-62, May 2, 1962; NIE 13-4/1-62, June 29, 1962; NIE 13-63, May 1, 1963, Box 4, NSF/National Intelligence Estimates 13-61 to 13-65, Lyndon Baines Johnson Library (hereafter LBJL).

8. McNamara to Johnson, Jan. 7, 1964, *FRUS*, 1964–68, 1: 12–13.

9. Memorandum from the Board of National Estimates to the Director of Central Intelligence, June 9, 1964, *FRUS*, 1964–68, 1: 486–87.

10. White House staff meeting, Aug. 5, 1964, *FRUS*, 1964–68, 1: 632. For Chinese responses to the Tonkin Gulf incident and the American air raids that followed, see Chen Jian, "China's Involvement in the Vietnam War," *China Quarterly* (June 1995): 365–66.

11. CIA Memorandum, The North Vietnamese Crisis, Aug. 6, 1964, Box 48, National Security File (NSF)/Vietnam, LBJL.

12. Allen S. Whiting, *The Chinese Calculus of Deterrence: India and Indochina* (Ann Arbor: University of Michigan Press, 1975), 175.

13. CIA Memoranda, The North Vietnamese Crisis, Aug. 7 and Sept. 6, 1964, Box 48, NSF/Vietnam, LBJL.

14. John M. Cabot to Department of State, Sept. 28, 1964, Box 200–202, NSF/CF: Poland, Cabot-Wang File, LBJL; Cabot to Department of State, Sept. 28, 1964, *FRUS*, 1964–68, 30: 99–100.

15. Qiang Zhai, "Beijing and the Vietnam Conflict," *Cold War International History Project Bulletin* 6–7 (Winter 1995-96): 235.

16. Summary of Sigma II-64, Sept. 8–17, 1964, Box 30, NSF/Agency File, LBJL.

17. Ibid.

18. Meeting on South Vietnam, Sept. 9, 1964, Box 1, Meeting Notes File, LBJL.

19. Bundy to Rusk, Jan. 6, 1965, *FRUS*, 1964–68, 2: 31.

20. CIA Special Report, Chinese Communists Brace for Possible Spread of Indochina War, Feb. 12, 1965, Box 244, NSF/CF: China, LBJL.

21. Special National Intelligence Estimate, Feb. 11, 1965, *FRUS*, 1964–68, 2: 248.

22. Intelligence Memorandum, Mar. 13, 1965; Also Intelligence Memoranda of Mar. 2, 7, 10, 1965; News report, Feb. 25, 1965, Box 49, NSF/Vietnam, vol. 4, LBJL.

23. Chen, 368; Qiang, 236–37.

24. Memoranda for the record, Feb. 3, 10, 1965, *FRUS*, 1964–68, 2: 130, 223.

25. Memorandum from the Joint Chiefs of Staff to the Secretary of Defense, Feb. 11, 1965, *FRUS, 1964–68*, 2: 241.

26. Mike Mansfield to President Johnson, Feb. 8, 1965; McGeorge Bundy to Mansfield, Feb. 9, 1965, *FRUS, 1964–68*, 2: 204, 209.

27. Ball to Johnson, Feb. 13, 1965, *FRUS, 1964–68*, 2: 258.

28. Memorandum from Vice President Humphrey to President Johnson, Feb. 17, 1965, *FRUS, 1964–68*, 2: 311–13.

29. Memorandum of a meeting with President Johnson, Feb. 17, 1965, *FRUS, 1964–68*, 2: 300, 305.

30. Special National Intelligence Estimate, Feb. 18, 1965; McCone to President, Feb. 23, 1965; Intelligence Memorandum, Apr. 21, 1965, *FRUS, 1964–68*, 2: 323, 361, 595.

31. Whiting, 181.

32. Chen, 371–72.

33. Briefing Paper Prepared by the Office of National Estimates, June 11, 1965, *FRUS, 1964–68*, 2: 766–68.

34. Secretary of Defense McNamara to Johnson, Dec. 7, 1965, ibid., 619.

35. Nancy Bernkopf Tucker, "Threats, Opportunities and Frustrations in East Asia," in *Lyndon Johnson Confronts the World: American Foreign Policy, 1963–1968*, ed. Warren I. Cohen and Nancy Bernkopf Tucker (New York: Cambridge University Press, 1994), 107.

36. John Cabot to Department of State, Sept. 24, 1964, Box 200–202, NSF/CF: Poland, Cabot-Wang File, LBJL.

37. John Cabot to Department of State, Mar. 1, Apr. 26, 1965, ibid.; Cabot to Department of State, Apr. 21, 1965, *FRUS, 1964–68*, 30: 165–66.

38. Kenneth T. Young, *Negotiating with the Chinese Communists: The United States Experience, 1953–1967* (New York: McGraw-Hill, 1968), 275.

39. Editorial note, William Bundy to Rusk, June 5, 1965, *FRUS, 1964–68*, 2: 700–701, 729.

40. Malley was the first U.S. reporter to go to China in two years. Thomas L. Hughes to Secretary of State, May 3, 1967, Box 241, NSF/CF: China, LBJL.

41. Intensification of Military Operations in Vietnam, July 14, 1965, *FRUS, 1964–68*, 3: 182.

42. Thompson to Rusk, July 15, 1965, ibid., 186.

43. Notes of meeting, July 22, 1965, ibid., 215, 219.

44. Congressional leadership meeting with the President, July 27, 1965, Box 1, Meeting Notes File, LBJL.

45. Draft Memorandum from Secretary of Defense McNamara to President Johnson, Nov. 3, 1965, *FRUS, 1964–68*, 3: 514.

46. Rosemary Foot, *The Practice of Power: U.S. Relations with China since 1949* (Oxford: Oxford University Press, 1995), 160; Tucker, 103.

47. D. P. Maxing and T. W. Robinson, *Lin Biao on "People's War": China Takes a Second look at Vietnam* (Santa Monica, Calif.: Rand Corporation, 1965), vii.

48. W. W. Rostow, *The United States and the Regional Organization of Asia and the Pacific, 1965–1985* (Austin: University of Texas Press, 1986), 10, 15–16; W. W. Rostow, *The Diffusion of Power: An Essay in Recent History* (New York: Macmillan, 1972), 420; Rostow interview with author, Mar. 18, 1992.

49. McNamara to Johnson, Dec. 7, 1965, *FRUS*, 1964–68, 3: 619.

50. Ibid., 53.

51. Bundy to President, Dec. 14, 1965, Box 92–94, NSF/CF: Vietnam, LBJL.

52. Meetings in the cabinet room, Jan. 22, 27, 1966, Box 1, Meeting Notes File, LBJL.

53. Cooper to Bundy, Jan. 24, 1966, Ball to President, Jan. 25, 1966, Valenti to President, Jan. 25, 1966, Box 44, NSF/NSC History Honolulu Conference; Rice to William Bundy, Jan. 11, 1966, Box 239, NSF/CF: China, LBJL; Notes of a meeting, Jan. 22, 1966, *FRUS*, 1964–68, 4: 110.

54. Joint Chiefs of Staff to Secretary McNamara, Jan. 18, 1966, *FRUS*, 1964–68, 4: 82.

55. CIA Information Report, Aug. 30, 1966, Box 240, NSF/China, LBJL.

56. Whiting, 189–90.

57. Thomas Hughes to Secretary of State, Mar. 29, 1966; CIA Information Report, Aug. 30, 1966, Box 240, NSF/China, LBJL.

58. For overviews of Johnson administration reactions to the Cultural Revolution, see Foot, 214–18, and Tucker, 103–11.

59. Thomas J. Schoenbaum, *Waging Peace and War: Dean Rusk in the Truman, Kennedy, and Johnson Years* (New York: Simon and Schuster, 1988), 454; Thomas W. Zeiler, *Dean Rusk: Defending the American Mission Abroad* (Wilmington, Del.: Scholarly Resource, 2000), 99–100.

60. Edward Rice to State Department, Jan. 7, 1965, enclosing paper "China's Major Problems Affecting U.S. Policy," Box 239, NSF/CF: China, LBJL.

61. CIA, Communist Intentions in Vietnam, July 29, 1966, ibid.

62. Edward Rice to State Department, Feb. 19, 1966, ibid.

63. CIA, Communist Intentions in Vietnam, July 29, 1966, ibid.

64. Alfred Jenkins to Bromley Smith, Aug. 13, 1966, Box 1, NSF/Alfred Jenkins Files, LBJL.

65. Edward Rice to Secretary of State, Feb. 3, 1966, Box 339, NSF/CF: China, LBJL.

66. CIA, Communist Intentions in Vietnam, July 29, 1966, Box 239, NSF/CF: China, LBJL.

67. Chen, 378.

68. China, Long Range Study, vol. 1, June 1966, 191–94, Box 245, NSF/CF: China, LBJL.

69. Alfred Jenkins to Walt Rostow, Aug. 3, Sept. 30, 1966, Box 1, NSF/Alfred Jenkins Files, LBJL; Jenkins to Rostow, Feb. 3, 1967, *FRUS, 1964–68*, 30: 515–16.

70. Robert S. Ross, *Negotiating Cooperation: The United States and China, 1969–1989* (Stanford: Stanford University Press, 1995), 17, 44–55.

71. Jenkins to Rostow, Aug. 3, 1966, Box 1, NSF/Alfred Jenkins Files, LBJL.

72. Jenkins went on to excoriate Assistant Secretary of State for Far Eastern Affairs William Bundy: "With all Bill Bundy's ability," Jenkins complained, "FE's [Far East's] fuzziness worries me. I get the impression FE's attention is nearly preempted by Vietnam." Jenkins to Rostow, Aug. 3, 1966, Box 1, NSF/Alfred Jenkins Files, LBJL. Robert McNamara later agreed that the Cultural Revolution caused China to turn inward, making it less threatening to U.S. interests in Asia than he and other policymakers had thought. McNamara, *In Retrospect*, 215.

73. U.S. Policy toward Communist China: Guidelines for Public Statements, Aug. 13, 1966, Box 1, NSF/Alfred Jenkins Files, LBJL.

74. For the background to Johnson's July 12, 1966, speech, see Tucker, 106 and Arthur Waldron, "From Non-existent to Almost Normal: U.S.-China Relations in the 1960s," in *The Diplomacy of the Crucial Decade*, ed. Diane B. Kunz (New York: Columbia University Press, 1994), 240; John Gronouski to State Department, Mar. 10, 16, Sept. 8, 1966, Box 200–202, NSF/CF: China, LBJL.

75. John Gronouski to State Department, Sept. 8, 1966; State Department to Gronouski, Jan. 3, 1967, ibid. Unfortunately, the remarks of Wang Guoquan, the Chinese ambassador at the Warsaw meetings for the years 1966–68, are still classified at the Johnson Library.

76. Deborah Shapley, *Promise and Power: The Life and Times of Robert S. McNamara* (Boston: Little, Brown, 1993), 394.

77. New China News Agency on Demonstrations, Oct. 22, 1967; Rostow to President, Oct. 23, 1967, Box 242, NSF/CF: China, LBJL.

78. Rice to William Bundy, May 27, 1967, Box 241, NSF/CF: China, LBJL.

79. "After Mao," *Wall Street Journal*, Nov. 14, 1966; Jenkins to Rostow, Nov. 15, 1966, Box 242, NSF/CF: China, LBJL.

80. Jenkins to Rostow, Nov. 16, 1968, Box 243, NSF/CF: China, LBJL.

81. Alfred Jenkins, Thoughts on China, Feb. 22, 1968, ibid.

82. The experts were Edwin O. Reischauer of Harvard University, Robert A. Scalapino of the University of California at Berkeley, Alexander Eckstein of the University of Michigan, Lucian W. Pye of the Massachusetts Institute of Technology, George Taylor of the University of Washington, Carl Stover of the National Institute of Public Affairs, and Cecil Thomas of the National Committee on U.S.-

China Relations. Memorandum on meeting of China experts with the president, Feb. 4, 1968, Box 243, NSF/CF: China, LBJL.

83. Qiang, 233–41.

84. Leslie Gelb with Richard K. Betts, *The Irony of Vietnam: The System Worked* (Washington, D.C.: Brookings Institution, 1979).

9. Rosemary Foot, "Redefinitions: The Domestic Context of America's China Policy in the 1960s"

1. For a vivid discussion of this argument, see Marilyn B. Young, *The Vietnam Wars, 1945–1990* (New York: HarperCollins, 1991), esp. chap. 10, "The War in America, 1965–67."

2. See Peter Van Ness, "China as a Third World State: Foreign Policy and Official National Identity," in *China's Quest for National Identity*, ed. Lowell Dittmer and Samuel S. Kim (Ithaca and London: Cornell University Press, 1993).

3. These officials are described in David Kaiser, "Men and Policies: 1961–1969," in *The Diplomacy of the Crucial Decade: American Foreign Relations during the 1960s*, ed. Diane B. Kunz (New York: Columbia University Press, 1994), chap. 1.

4. Such an argument is developed in Richard Madsen, *China and the American Dream: A Moral Inquiry* (Berkeley: University of California Press, 1995), 35.

5. British Foreign Office files, FO 371/148589, 17 June 1960, Public Records Office (PRO), London. The British were alert to all signs of change in China policy, hoping that America's approach would come more into line with their own.

6. FO 371/158442, 23 Dec. 1960.

7. Adlai E. Stevenson, "Putting First Things First: A Democratic View," *Foreign Affairs* 38 (Jan. 1960): 203.

8. Komer to Bundy, "Quick Thoughts on China," Mar. 1, 1961, in *Foreign Relations of the United States (FRUS)*, 1961–63, vol. 22. James C. Thomson, Jr., first discussed the genesis of Rice's paper in "On the Making of U.S. China Policy, 1961–69: A Study in Bureaucratic Politics," *China Quarterly* 50 (Apr.-June 1972): 223. The recommendations from the paper are under Oct. 26, 1961, in *FRUS*, 1961-63, 22: 162–67.

9. Leonard A. Kusnitz, *Public Opinion and Foreign Policy: America's China Policy, 1949–1979* (Westport, Conn.: Greenwood Press, 1984), 95–96.

10. *Congressional Record* (May 21, 1959), 86th Cong., 1st sess., 105, pt. 2.

11. The committee was founded in 1953 to campaign against PRC admission to the United Nations. It attacked the competence and methods of Conlon Associates. For further details, see Stanley D. Bachrack, *The Committee of One Million: "China Lobby" Politics, 1953–1971* (New York: Columbia University Press, 1976).

12. For further details, see David Caute, *The Great Fear: The Anti-Communist Purge under Truman and Eisenhower* (New York: Simon and Schuster, 1978).

13. Komer to Bundy, 23 Nov. 1964, NSF Country Files, China, China Memos, vol. 3, Boxes 237–38, Lyndon Baines Johnson Library (LBJL); *FRUS*, 1964–68, 30: 130–32.

14. Roger Hilsman's "watershed" speech in San Francisco on December 19, 1963, exhibited these aspects (Hilsman was then assistant secretary of state for Far Eastern affairs): "We hope that, confronted with firmness which will make foreign adventure unprofitable, and yet offered the prospect that the way back into the community of man is not closed to it, the Chinese Communist regime will eventually forsake its present venomous hatreds." Explaining the speech to the U.S. ambassador to the U.N., Hilsman added, "There was a need to clarify the reasons for the apparent divergence between U.S. treatment of Moscow and U.S. treatment of Peiping. As the Soviets have begun to behave more responsibly, the U.S. has become more responsive to Soviet initiatives; but with Peiping continuing to hew to a bellicose Stalinist line, we have been unresponsive to the Chinese." See Roger Hilsman, Box 1, China Policy Speech, John F. Kennedy Library (JFKL). Kennedy, in his last major public comment on China, on November 14, 1963, said in response to a question about trading with the PRC: "We are not planning on trade with Red China in view of the policy that Red China pursues. If the Red Chinese indicate a desire to live at peace with the United States, with other countries surrounding it, then quite obviously the United States would reappraise its policies. We are not wedded to a policy of hostility to Red China."

15. This was another of the main points made in Roger Hilsman's speech referred to in note 14. It was meant to demonstrate a contrast with the speech given by John Foster Dulles in San Francisco in June 1957, in which Dulles had stated: "We can confidently base our policies on the assumption that International Communism's rule of strict conformity is, in China as elsewhere, a passing and not a perpetual phase. We owe it to ourselves, our allies and the Chinese people to do all that we can to contribute to that passing." See "Our Policies toward Communism in China," June 28, 1957, in *FRUS*, 1955–57, 3: 566.

16. *FRUS*, 1961–63, 22: 162–67.

17. See Kusnitz, *Public Opinion and Foreign Policy*, 104–5. See also Wang Bingnan, "Nine Years of Sino-U.S. Talks in Retrospect," trans. in *Joint Publications Research Service* (JPRS)-CPS-85-079, Aug. 7, 1985, 49, and *FRUS*, 1961–63, 22: passim.

18. May 24 and June 15, 1961, NSF Country Files, China, Box 22, JFKL. See also Warren I. Cohen, *Dean Rusk* (Totowa, N.J.: Cooper Square, 1980), 166.

19. Memorandum of Conversation, May 24, 1961, NSF Country Files, China, Box 22, JFKL, and see *FRUS*, 1961–63, 22: 63–65.

20. Kusnitz, *Public Opinion and Foreign Policy*, 99. The British were only too aware of the significance of this wording. See FO371/158450, 1 Aug. 1961, PRO.

21. Memorandum of Conversation, July 28, 1961, NSF Country Files: China, Box 22, JFKL; and see *FRUS*, 1961–63, 22: 99–101.

22. See Sept. 5, 1961, NSF Country Files, China, Box 22, JFKL; and James Fetzer, "Clinging to Containment: China Policy," in *Kennedy's Quest for Victory: American Foreign Policy, 1961–1963*, ed. Thomas G. Paterson (New York: Oxford University Press, 1989), esp. 188.

23. U.N. General Assembly, 16th sess., 1069th meet., Dec. 1, 1961, 905.

24. For further details of the views of these countries, see verbatim reports of the 16th sess.

25. James C. Thomson Papers, Chester Bowles, 1961–63, Box 7, Apr. 4, 1962, JFKL.

26. Indeed, media opinion in many countries of concern to the United States— the U.K., Canada, France, Italy, West Germany, Japan, Brazil, Nigeria—was in favor of Beijing's entry. See Oct. 19, 1964, NSF Country Files, U.N. Charter Representation, Box 290, LBJL. For an indication of Johnson's early reaction to proposed French recognition, see the record of his conversation with Senator Richard Russell in *Taking Charge: The Johnson White House Tapes, 1963–1964*, ed. Michael R. Beschloss (New York: Simon and Schuster, 1997), 162.

27. Norman St. Amour, "Sino-Canadian Relations 1963–1968: The American Factor," in *Reluctant Adversaries: Canada and the People's Republic of China, 1949–1970*, ed. Paul Evans and B. Michael Frolic (Toronto: University of Toronto Press, 1991), esp. 117-21. Washington's record of such conversations can be found in *FRUS*, 1964–68, 30: 289–95, 301–3, 396–99, 412–14, 420–25, 455–57.

28. The impact of the Cultural Revolution seems clear from the voting pattern: the vote against the Albanian resolution stayed high in 1967 and 1968 and began to decrease only in 1969, when the worst excesses were over.

29. See U.N. Archives, DAG 1/5.2.2.13, Box 2, "Chinese Representation," Dec. 4, 1970, New York; and Rosemary Foot, *The Practice of Power: U.S. Relations with China since 1949* (Oxford: Oxford University Press, 1995), esp. 44–46. After Kissinger's July visit to Beijing, the Nixon administration had assured Taiwan that the United States would use the dual representation formula to keep it in the United Nations. However, Robert S. Ross points out that the likelihood that this policy would succeed was reduced when lobbying was delayed until Kissinger had received Beijing's assurances that the issue would not impede a Sino-American rapprochement. He also suggests that Kissinger may have desired the domestic political protection a dual representation formula afforded in the knowledge that it would not gain the necessary votes and thus would not hamper improvement in U.S.-PRC relations. See Robert S. Ross, *Negotiating Cooperation: The United States and China 1969–1989* (Stanford: Stanford University Press, 1995), 42–43.

30. For a discussion of these difficulties, see Foot, *The Practice of Power*, chap. 3.

31. Rusk to Kennedy, Apr. 4, 1962, *FRUS*, 1961–63, 22: 208–11. Chester Bowles was particularly exercised by this matter of food sales; see James C. Thomson

Papers, Chester Bowles 1961–63, "U.S. Policies in the Far East," Box 7, Apr. 4, 1962, and "Food for China" 3/62–5/62, Box 15, Apr. 16, 1962, JFKL.

32. "Food for China" 3/62–5/62, Box 15, May 23, 1962, JFKL.

33. Thomson Papers, Far East, 1961–66, Comm. China General, "China Speech material," Box 14 [undated], JFKL; and *FRUS*, 1961–63, 22: 278n3.

34. Oct. 28, 1964, NSF Country Files, China, China Memos, vol. 3, Boxes 237–38, LBJL, and *FRUS*, 1964–68, 30: 117–20.

35. See the relevant parts of the speech in *FRUS*, 1964–68, 30: 356, editorial note.

36. See Thomson's discussion of this episode in "On the Making of U.S. China Policy."

37. Thomson to Rostow, Aug. 4, 1966, *FRUS*, 1964–68, 30: 364–66.

38. Bundy to Rusk, March 29, 1967, *FRUS*, 1964–68, 30: 541–43; see also Bundy to Katzenbach, Sept. 18, 1967, ibid., 597–98 for further discussion of the relaxation of the ban on pharmaceuticals. In his memorandum to the president of Feb. 22, 1968, Rusk stated his belief that "we can take only very limited steps, since our firm posture in Asia generally remains crucial and any significant 'concessions' to Communist China would be seriously misunderstood in key quarters, not to mention the Congress." *FRUS*, 1964–68, 30: 645–46.

39. Henry Kissinger, *White House Years* (Boston: Little, Brown, 1979), 180, 191.

40. Letter to Dulles, Apr. 23, 1957, Dulles Papers, Selected Correspondence, Box 114, Seeley G. Mudd Library, Princeton University; Aug. 22, 1957, *FRUS*, 1955–57, 3: 584–85; Sept. 11, 1957, ibid., 600–601.

41. Aug. 24, 1965, *FRUS*, 1964–68, 30: 195–96.

42. Dec. 1, 1966, ibid., 3: 471–75. The memorandum noted that "To a surprising extent the American people and the Congress regard travel restrictions, not as a barometer of our feeling toward a country, but as an interference with an inherent right and freedom of American citizens" (474).

43. Nancy Bernkopf Tucker, "Threats, Opportunities, and Frustrations in East Asia," in *Lyndon Johnson Confronts the World: American Foreign Policy 1963–1968*, ed. Warren I. Cohen and Nancy Bernkopf Tucker (New York: Cambridge University Press, 1994), 107; Arthur Waldron, "From Nonexistent to Almost Neutral: U.S.-China Relations in the 1960s," in *The Diplomacy of the Crucial Decade*, ed. Kunz, 241; and *FRUS*, 1964–68, 30: 676, editorial note.

44. Waldron, "From Nonexistent to Almost Normal," 242–43.

45. This is how James Thomson characterized it.

46. White House Central Files, Confidential, Co 50–1 Formosa, Box 7, Aug. 13, 1966; and Aug. 16, 1966, NSF Country Files, China Memos, vol. 6, Box 239, both at LBJL. See also Aug. 11, 1966, *FRUS*, 1964–68, 30: 366–72.

47. These points were contained in a number of CIA reports produced between 1962 and 1967. See, for example, NSF Country Files, Box 22, various dates, JFKL; and NSF Country Files, China Cables, vol. 5, Box 239, various dates, LBJL. See, in

addition, Foot, *The Practice of Power*, esp. 207–18, for a fuller discussion and full references to documents drawn upon here.

48. Madsen, *China and the American Dream*, esp. 28–29, 35.

49. Kusnitz, *Public Opinion and Foreign Policy*, 106, 117.

50. William G. Mayer, *The Changing American Mind: How and Why American Public Opinion Changed between 1960 and 1988* (Ann Arbor: University of Michigan Press, 1992), 421.

51. For further discussion of international reaction to America's China policy, see Foot, *The Practice of Power*, chaps. 2 and 3.

52. Kusnitz, *Public Opinion and Foreign Policy*, 103, 115.

53. Hayes Redmon to Bill Moyers, July 11, 1966, Fred Panzer Files, China Hearings, Box 572, LBJL. Redmon passed this survey information on to Moyers to boost the chances that the China section of the president's July 12 speech would retain its conciliatory wording.

54. A. T. Steele, *The American People and China* (New York: McGraw-Hill, 1966), appendix, Table 16, 281–82; Thomson to Valenti, Mar. 1, 1966, *FRUS*, 1964–68, 30: 262–63.

55. Steele, 102, 225.

56. Ibid., 214.

57. See Akira Iriye, ed., *U.S. Policy toward China: Testimony Taken from the Senate Foreign Relations Committee Hearings, 1966* (Boston: Little, Brown, 1968). James Thomson's Mar. 15, 1966, report on the Hearings is in *FRUS*, 1964–68, 30: 274–75, and further discussion of the need for the administration to embrace "containment without isolation," in Harriman to Moyers, June 3, 1966, ibid., 318–19.

58. Testimony by General Samuel B. Griffith, in *U.S. Policy toward China*, ed. Iriye, 77; Samuel B. Griffith, *The Chinese People's Liberation Army* (New York: McGraw-Hill, 1967), 222–25.

59. *New York Times*, Mar. 14, 1966. Details of Johnson address in *FRUS*, 1964–68, 30: 356, editorial note.

60. Kusnitz, *Public Opinion and Foreign Policy*, 118.

61. Richard M. Nixon, "Asia after Vietnam," *Foreign Affairs* 46 (Oct. 1967). There are obvious similarities between this statement and that of Johnson in July 1966. William Bundy has argued that one should not read too much into Nixon's article, that the overall tenor of the piece was "tough and uncompromising," and that it was proposing that the time was not yet ripe for beginning a dialogue with China. Bundy also notes, however, that during Nixon's visit to Paris in February 1969, he listened "avidly" to de Gaulle's advice that the United States cultivate China. See William Bundy, *A Tangled Web: The Making of Foreign Policy in the Nixon Presidency* (London: I. B. Tauris, 1998), 17–19, 59.

62. In a White House news release, McGeorge Bundy's response to Porter was that there were "a great many factors to be considered in dealing with the problem of contacts with the Peiping regime, not the least of which has been their steadfast refusal to permit any visitors to the Mainland who are not of their own choosing." Nash was described in this release as a former deputy secretary of the International Government in Shanghai and a resident of China for more than 50 years, who in 1963 was living in Woodland, California. Thomson Papers, Comm. China General, Box 15, May 24, 1963, JFKL.

63. Madsen, *China and the American Dream*, chap. 2, esp. 33–39. In 1965 the Quakers published *A New China Policy: Some Quaker Proposals* (New Haven: Yale University Press, 1965), in which they proposed greater restraints on Taiwan to prevent its attacks on the mainland, a de facto acknowledgment that the PRC was the government of China, an end to special restrictions on trade, and entry into the United Nations.

64. One of the most helpful texts on foreign policy in the Kennedy era is Thomas G. Paterson, ed., *Kennedy's Quest for Victory*.

65. *Congressional Record*, 86th Cong., 1st sess., 1959, 105, pt. 2: 2737–38.

66. Komer is quoted in Robert J. McMahon, "Choosing Sides in South Asia," in Paterson, ed., *Kennedy's Quest for Victory*, 198.

67. Fetzer, "Clinging to Containment," 194. Dobrynin's efforts are noted in Nancy Bernkopf Tucker, *Taiwan, Hong Kong, and the United States, 1945–1992: Uncertain Friendships* (New York: Twayne, 1994), 101.

68. President's Office Files, Background Docs, G3, Vienna Meeting, Briefing Material, Box 126, May 25, 1961, JFKL.

69. Jan. 11, 1963, *FRUS*, 1961–63, 22: 339, editorial note; and see also *FRUS*, 1961–63, 8, National Security Policy; Kennedy's "Stalinist" remarks are quoted in Kusnitz, *Public Opinion and Foreign Policy*, 106.

70. Arms Control and Disarmament Agency: Disarmament, NSF Depts. and Agencies, Harriman Trip to Moscow, Box 265, June 20, 1963, JFKL. For the Johnson era, see, for example, Memorandum for the Record, Sept. 15, 1964, *FRUS*, 1964–68, 30: 94–95, and the approach by McGeorge Bundy to Ambassador Dobrynin at which the latter made clear that the Soviet government had already taken Chinese nuclear capability for granted, that such weapons "had no importance against the Soviet Union or against the U.S." and had only a "psychological impact in Asia" (Sept. 25, 1964, *FRUS*, 1964-68, 30: 104–5).

71. Thomson Papers, Far East 1961–66, Comm. China General, Box 15, Jan. 12, 1962, JFKL.

72. April 5, 1969, *FRUS*, 1961–63, 22: 42–43. Rusk also recorded this in his memoirs; see Dean Rusk (as told to Richard Rusk), *As I Saw It* (New York: Norton,

1990), 283. Rusk put it to his British counterpart as follows: "President Kennedy would wish to impress upon the Prime Minister that this was a serious political problem for the United States. Public opinion here was developing slowly but was far from the point where a change of policy would be easy. The President had been much impressed by Mr Eisenhower's warning that China was the only issue which might bring him back into politics" (FO 371/158445, 4 April 1961, PRO). A Johnson era reference to Eisenhower and the U.N. recognition issue appears at Rostow to Johnson, May 17, 1966, *FRUS*, 1964–68, 30: 303–4.

73. Cohen, *Dean Rusk*, 283–89.

74. Aug. 3, 1966, NSF Country Files, China Memos, vol. 6, Box 239, LBJL.

75. Thomson Papers, Far East, Comm. China General, Box 17, Aug. 4, 1966, JFKL; Aug. 4, 1966, *FRUS*, 1964–68, 30: 364–66. See also Thomson's memorandum for Mr. Bundy in Thomson Papers, Nat. Security Staff, McGeorge Bundy, 1964–66, Box 11, May 26, 1965, JFKL, in which he notes inaction on the State Department's travel package and on the recommendation of recognition for the Mongolian People's Republic.

76. Kaiser, "Men and Policies," 31, 12.

77. Thomson Papers, Far East, Comm. China General, Box 16, JFKL. Undated and marked "not sent," it was entitled "Some New Year's Reflections on U.S. China Policy" and was thus probably written in January 1966.

78. Fetzer, "Clinging to Containment," 182.

79. Tucker, *Taiwan, Hong Kong, and the United States*, 97.

80. Ibid..

81. Tucker, "Threats, Opportunities, and Frustrations," 99–100.

82. Exco 50-1, Formosa, Co 50-2, Box 22, Feb. 22, 1968, LBJL. For new evidence on the Chinese leadership's assessment of the United States and the Soviet Union in 1968 and 1969, see Chen Jian and David L. Wilson, "New Evidence on the Sino-American Opening," *Cold War International History Project Bulletin*, issue 11 (Winter 1998): 155–75, Woodrow Wilson International Center for Scholars, Washington, D.C.

83. Speech given at the Nixon Center for Peace and Freedom, *Straits Times*, Nov. 13, 1996. Other evidence that Nixon had shifted his views on China, and perhaps as early as 1965, is contained in James Mann, *About Face: A History of America's Curious Relationship with China from Nixon to Clinton* (New York: Knopf, 1999), 16–18.

84. Quoted in Foot, *The Practice of Power*, 105. See also Tucker, *Taiwan, Hong Kong and the United States*, 102–3.

85. See Uldis Kruze, "Domestic Constituencies in Nixon's China Policy: A New Look from the National Archives" (paper presented at the Asian Studies on the Pacific Coast Conference, Honolulu, Hawaii, June 29–2 July 2, 1989), 27–29.

10. Li Jie, "Changes in China's Domestic Situation in the 1960s and Sino-U.S. Relations"

1. Roderick MacFarquhar and John King Fairbank, eds., *Jianqiao Zhonghua Renmin Gongheguo 1949–1965* (Cambridge history of the People's Republic of China, 1949–1965) (Beijing: Zhongguo Shehui Kexueyuan Chubanshe, 1990), 277.

2. Deng Xiaoping, "Dapo Diguozhuyi Fengsuo Zhi Dao" (Break the blockade imposed by the imperialists), July 19, 1949, in *Deng Xiaoping Wenxuan, 1938–1965* (Selected works of Deng Xiaoping, 1938–1965) (Beijing: Renmin Chubanshe, 1989), 135. In this letter, Deng Xiaoping communicated Mao Zedong's decision on "leaning to one side."

3. Mao Zedong, "Lun Renmin Minzhu Zhuanzheng" (On people's democratic dictatorship), in *Mao Zedong Xuanji* (Selected works of Mao Zedong), vol. 4 (Beijing: Renmin Chubanshe, 1991), 1472–73. In the note on "the third road," which had been examined and approved by Mao Zedong during his lifetime, the road is defined as "in fact the road of British-American style bourgeois dictatorship." See Mao Zedong, "Muqian xingshi he women de renwu" (The current situation and our tasks), in *Mao Zedong Xuanji*, vol. 4, 1262, n. 12.

4. Zhou Enlai had given an explanation on this question: "The military force of imperialism has been driven out, but its economic influence for the past hundred years has been great, especially the cultural influences. Such a situation will influence our independence." See Zhou Enlai, "Women de Waijiao Fangzhen he Renwu" (Our diplomatic guidelines and tasks), Apr. 30, 1952, in *Zhou Enlai Waijiao Wenxuan* (Selected works of Zhou Enlai on diplomacy), comp. Document Research Office of the CCP Central Committee (Beijing: Zhongyang Wenxian Chubanshe, 1990), 50.

5. Mao Zedong's talk with Communist Party delegations from Latin America, Oct. 2, 1959.

6. The Seven Thousand Persons conference held in January and February 1962 is a typical example. At this conference, the pragmatic views of Liu Shaoqi, Deng Xiaoping, and others prevailed temporarily. Mao Zedong himself had to face serious difficulties and make a self-criticism.

7. On September 24, 1962, the first day of the Tenth Plenary Session of the Eighth Central Committee of the CCP, Mao Zedong said that "in a socialist country, we should recognize the existence of classes and class struggle, . . . from now on, we must remind ourselves of this every year and every month, at every plenary session of the Central Committee and at every meeting so that the whole Party heightens its vigilance and has a clear Marxist-Leninist line." See *Zhonghua Renmin Gongheguo Shilu, Dier Juan: Quzhe yu Fazhan—Tansuo Daolu de Jianxin, 1962–1965* (A faithful record of the People's Republic of China, vol. 2: Complications and

development—Hardships on the road to exploration, 1962–1965), ed. Li Chen (Changchun: Jilin Renmin Chubanshe, 1994), part 2, 745–46. Mao's secretary, Tian Jiaying, worked on the text of the speech. Later, during the Cultural Revolution, when the tenth issue of *Hongqi* (Red Flag) published an editorial commemorating the tenth anniversary of the publication of Mao Zedong's article "On the Correct Handling of Contradictions among the People" and quoted these remarks, the wording was changed to "from now on, we must remind ourselves of this every year, every month, and every day so that we can gain a relatively sober understanding of this problem and have a Marxist-Leninist line." See "Wuchanjieji Zhuanzheng xia Jinxing Geming de Lilun Wuqi—Jinian 'Guanyu Zhengque Chuli Renmin Neibu Maodun de Wenti' Fabiao Shi Zhounian" (The theoretical weapon of revolution under the dictatorship of the proletariat—Commemorating the tenth anniversary of the publication of Mao Zedong's "On the correct handling of contradictions among the people"), *Hongqi* (Red Flag), no. 10 (1967): 34.

8. Wang Jiaxiang's suggestions were included, for the most part, in the three documents prepared between February and June 1962: A Letter to Zhou Enlai, Deng Xiaoping, and Chen Yi, drafted by Wang Jiaxiang and jointly issued by Wang Jiaxiang, Liu Ningyi, and Wu Xiuquan, leading cadres of the International Liaison Department of the CCP Central Committee, on Feb. 27, 1962; the outline of "On the Question of Support to Other Countries in Their Struggle against Imperialism and for National Independence and People's Revolutionary Movements—Seek Truth from Facts, Act According to One's Capability," drafted and reviewed by him on March 31, 1962; and "On the Open Views of Mass Organizations in Our Country on Certain International Issues," drafted and reviewed by him and submitted to the CCP Central Committee by the International Liaison Department of the CCP Central Committee on June 29, 1962. See Wang Jiaxiang, "Shishi qiushi, liang li er xing" (Seek truth from facts, act according to one's capability), Mar. 31, 1962, in *Wang Jiaxiang Xuanji* (Selected works of Wang Jiaxiang), comp. Editorial Team of the Selected Works of Wang Jiaxiang (Beijing: Renmin Chubanshe, 1989), 444–45; Wang Jiaxiang, "Lue Tan dui Mouxie Wenti de Kanfa" (My opinions on some current issues), June 29, 1962, in *Wang Jiaxiang Xuanji*, 446–60.

9. *San he yi shao* refers to easing the struggle against imperialism, reactionaries, and revisionism, and reducing assistance and support to the revolutionary struggle of the peoples of Asia, Africa, and Latin America. Kang Sheng originated the phrase after making a fuss about some mistakes made by the Chinese delegation during the Moscow Disarmament Conference in the summer of 1962. Later, Mao Zedong used it.

10. *San zi yi bao* refers to an extension of plots for private use and of free markets, an increase in the number of small enterprises with sole responsibility for their own profits and losses, and fixing output quotas on a household basis.

11. Interview with Wu Xujun, Mao Zedong's nurse, Oct. 1995.

12. Mao Zedong, "Wei Zhengqu Guojia Caizheng Jingji Zhuangkuang de Jiben Haozhuan er Douzheng" (Struggle for the fundamental improvement of national finance and the economy), in *Mao Zedong Xuanji*, vol. 5, 15–16.

13. Mao Zedong, "Tong Aogong Zongshuji Xia Ji de Tanhua" (A talk with General Secretary Lance Louis Sharkey of the Australian Communist Party), Oct. 26, 1959, in *Mao Zedong Wenji* (Collected Works of Mao Zedong), comp. Document Research Office of the CCP Central Committee, vol. 8 (Beijing: Renmin Chubanshe, 1999), 97.

14. It should be pointed out that Mao Zedong had for a long time disagreed with the road taken by Yugoslavia and thought that Yugoslavia had surrendered to the Western countries, a view largely influenced by Stalin. Around 1955, Mao Zedong eased relations between China and Yugoslavia to a large extent and established diplomatic relations at the ambassadorial level. On September 24, 1956, in talking with members of the delegation of the League of Communists of Yugoslavia, who were attending the Eighth National Congress of the CCP, he said, "We did some things to hurt you because we listened to the opinions of the Cominform." However, after the League proposed its program in preparation for its seventh congress in 1958, Mao Zedong once again thought that it was attempting to split the international communist movement and opposed the Moscow Declaration of 1957. From that point, relations between the two countries, and between the two parties, once again deteriorated.

15. The two articles and the speech were: Editorial, "Liening Zhuyi Wansui" (Long live Leninism), *Hongqi* (Red Flag), no. 8 (1960); Editorial, "Yanzhe Weida Liening de Daolu Qianjin" (Forward along the path of great Lenin), *Renmin Ribao* (People's Daily), Apr. 22, 1960; and Lu Dingyi, "Zai Liening de Qizhi xia Tuanjie Qilai" (Unite under Lenin's revolutionary banner), Apr. 22, 1960, in *Lu Dingyi Xuanji* (Selected Works of Lu Dingyi), comp. Editorial Team of the Selected Works of Lu Dingyi (Beijing: Renmin Chubanshe, 1992), 643–60.

16. "Synchronizing watches" means that Chinese leaders were required to readjust their domestic and international policies in terms of Soviet domestic and foreign policies, much like setting one's watch to the same time as someone else's.

17. Mao Zedong's speech at the Beidaihe working conference of the Politburo. A portion of this speech can be found in *Mao Zedong Da Cidian* (Mao Zedong dictionary), ed. Wang Jin et al. (Nanning: Guangxi Renmin Chubanshe and Lijiang Chubanshe, 1992), 1212.

18. At that time, Mao Zedong was on a working vacation at Beidaihe. He was practicing riding a horse and planned to fulfill his long-cherished wish of conducting a survey along the Yellow River. After the Gulf of Tonkin incident, Mao Zedong abandoned this plan. (This information comes from the author's interview with Mao Zedong's guards.)

19. At the press conference for Chinese and foreign correspondents held in the Great Hall of the People in Beijing on September 29, 1965, Chen Yi said, "If the United States imperialists invade China's mainland, we shall take all necessary measures to defeat them. By that time, there will be no boundary line for the war. The boundary line is destroyed by the United States, and not by China. We are willing to abide by the boundary line. However, the United States breaks it willfully and runs amok." See *Chen Yi Nianpu* (Chronology of Chen Yi), ed. Liu Shuafa, vol. 2 (Beijing: Renmin Chubanshe, 1995), 1125.

20. On December 30, 1965, when Chen Yi replied to the questions raised by Takano Yoshi Hisa, a resident correspondent in Beijing from *Akahata*, a Japanese Communist newspaper, and talked about the Soviet Union's statement through the Western press that China had obstructed the transit of Soviet-supplied goods and aid materials to Vietnam, he said, "In fact, with regard to the so-called aid to Vietnam, the Soviet Union does not wholeheartedly help the people of Vietnam carry out the struggle against U.S. aggression and for national salvation through to the end, but attempts to make use of aid to Vietnam to control the situation in Vietnam and link the Vietnam question with cooperation between the United States and the Soviet Union. Why do they continue to vilify the Chinese people, who give all-out support to the people of Vietnam in their struggle, for no reason?"

21. Zhou Enlai, A talk with Pakistan President Mohammad Ayub Khan, Apr. 2, 1965. See Zhou Enlai, "Zhongguo Jianjue Zhichi Yuenan Renmin de Kangmei Zhanzheng" (China firmly supports the Vietnam people's war against the U.S.), in *Zhou Enlai Waijiao Wenxuan*, 440.

22. On October 5, 1966, in talks with Ion Gheorghe Maurer, chair of the Council of Ministers of Romania, Zhou Enlai said that (1) on the Vietnam question, China's position is diametrically opposed to that of the Soviet Union, and there is no joint action; (2) there will be negotiations on the Vietnam question at a certain time, but the question is conditions, opportunity, and who will have power to make decisions. Vietnam has the power to decide on negotiations; (3) so long as Vietnam invites the persons who are encouraged by the Soviet Union and the United States to put pressure on Vietnam, we shall allow them the right of transit. However, there will be an exception. If U Thant wants to go, we shall consider it; (4) If goods and materials in aid to Vietnam need to pass through Chinese territory, we shall act according to the agreement. See *Zhou Enlai Nianpu: 1949–1976* (Chronology of Zhou Enlai: 1949–1976), comp. Document Research Office of the CCP Central Committee, vol. 3 (Beijing: Zhongyang Wenxian Chubanshe, 1997), 74.

23. Wang Bingnan, *Zhong Mei Huitan Jiunian Huigu* (Nine years of Sino-American talks in retrospect) (Beijing: Shijie Zhishi Chubanshe, 1985), 89–90; "Telegram from Embassy in Poland to the Department of State," June 23, 1962,

Foreign Relations of the United States (FRUS), 1961–63, vol. 22 (Washington, D.C.: Government Printing Office, 1996), 273–75.

24. Mao Zedong, A talk with General Vo Nguyen Giap, the defense minister of Vietnam, Oct. 5, 1962.

25. For example, Mao Zedong mentioned the possibility in his talk with a Korean Party and government delegation on October 7, 1964, and in his talk with foreign specialists in China on March 19, 1965.

26. Mao Zedong, A talk with Strong, Coe, Adler, Epstein, Rittenberg, and others, Jan. 17, 1964.

27. Mao Zedong's talk with Le Duan, head of the Vietnamese delegation to the Soviet Union, during its stopover in Beijing, Jan. 30, 1964.

28. Mao Zedong's talk with a member of the political bureau and secretary of the secretariat of the Japanese Communist Party, Sept. 17, 1965.

29. Mao Zedong, A talk with Strong, Coe, Adler, Epstein, Rittenberg, and others, Jan. 17, 1964.

30. Mao Zedong, "Zai Zhonggong Bajie Sanzhong Quanhuishang de Jianghua Tigang" (Outline of speech at the third plenary session of the Eighth Central Committee of the CCP), Oct. 9, 1957, in *Jianguo yilai Mao Zedong Wengao* (Manuscripts of Mao Zedong since the founding of the state), comp. Document Research Office of the CCP Central Committee, vol. 6: Jan. 1956–Dec. 1957 (Beijing: Zhongyang Wenxian Chubanshe, 1992), 595.

31. The original agenda at the Beidaihe working conference of the Central Committee of the CCP was to discuss questions concerning agriculture, finance and trade, urban work, etc., with the agriculture questions as the focal point.

32. Bo Yibo, *Ruogan Zhongda Juece yu Shijian de Huigu* (Recollections of several important decisions and events), vol. 2 (Beijing: Zhonggong Zhongyang Dangxiao Chubanshe, 1993), 1051–52.

33. Ibid., 1074.

34. Ibid.

35. Ibid., 1091–93.

36. On December 21, 1965, in his talk with Chen Boda and others in Hangzhou, Mao Zedong said, "The crucial question is his being 'dismissed from office.' Emperor Jiajing dismissed Hai Rui from office, and in 1959 we dismissed Peng Dehuai from office. Peng Dehuai is thus Hai Rui." Ibid., 1232.

37. Ibid., 1100.

38. Li Jue et al., eds., *Dangdai Zhongguo de Hegongye* (The nuclear industry in Contemporary China) (Beijing: Zhongguo Shehui Kexue Chubanshe, 1987), 13–14.

39. Mao Zedong, "Jielun" (Concluding speech), Mar. 31, 1955, in *Mao Zedong Xuanji*, vol. 5, 143–56.

40. Gu Longsheng, _Mao Zedong Jingji Nianpu_ (Economic chronology of Mao Zedong) (Beijing: Zhonggong Zhongyang Dangxiao Chubanshe, 1993), 519.

41. In his comment, Mao Zedong wrote: "Quite good. Do as suggested. We should coordinate to do the work well." At the time, this comment amounted to an order of mobilization. For the proposed timing of the first test and Mao's comments, see Li Jue et al., eds., _Dangdai Zhongguo de Hegongye_, 47.

42. Mao Zedong's talk with V. G. Wilcox, the general secretary of the New Zealand Communist Party, May 22, 1963.

43. Wang Jiaxiang, "Zai Zhongyang Guoji Huodong Gongzuo Huiyishang de Kaimuci" (Opening speech at a working conference of international activities of the Central Committee of the CCP), Apr. 4, 1955, in _Wang Jiaxiang Xuanji_, 418, 450.

44. Mao Zedong's talk with V. G. Wilcox, May 22, 1963.

45. Ibid.

46. Ibid.

47. Wang Jiaxiang, "My Personal Record," 1968 (unpublished manuscript).

48. From a talk by Mao Zedong on May 22, 1963, in Bo, _Ruogan Zhongda Juece yu Shijian de Huigu_, vol. 2, 1154.

49. Mao Zedong, "Zhong Fa zhi jian you Gongtong Dian" (There are common points between China and France), in _Mao Zedong Waijiao Wenxuan_ (Selected works of Mao Zedong on diplomacy), comp. Ministry of Foreign Affairs of the People's Republic of China and Document Research Office of the CCP Central Committee (Beijing: Zhongyang Wenxian Chubanshe and Shijie Zhishi Chubanshe, 1994), 525.

50. Mao Zedong, "Zhichi bei Yapo Renmin Fandui Diguozhuyi Zhanzheng" (Support the oppressed people's fight against the imperialists), June 23, 1964, in ibid., 533. Mao's discussion of the "two countries" refers to China and America.

51. Mao Zedong, "Tong Sinuo Tan Guoji Xingshi" (A conversation on international issues with Snow), Jan. 9, 1965, in ibid., 548, 557.

52. Mao Zedong, A talk with Edgar Snow, Oct. 22, 1960.

53. From early 1967, except for the Chinese ambassador to Egypt, Chinese ambassadors did not stay at their posts. Between June and July 1969, after Zhou Enlai had made arrangements, fourteen Chinese ambassadors were urged to return to their posts at Chinese embassies.

54. Within four months, from May to August 1967, led by the "leftist" persons who seized power at the Ministry of Foreign Affairs, China experienced diplomatic clashes with more than ten countries. The Ministry of Foreign Affairs of the People's Republic of China presented notes to Great Britain, Mongolia, Bulgaria, India, Burma, Kenya, Czechoslovakia, Indonesia, and other countries, lodging protests or making diplomatic representations.

55. Zhou met with Burmese Prime Minister U Nu on August 7, 1971. See Zhou Enlai, "Jizuo Sichao Ganraole Zhongguo Waijiao Zhengce" (Extreme leftism has obstructed China's diplomatic policies), Aug. 7, 1971, in *Zhou Enlai Waijiao Wenxuan*, 483.

56. Chen Donglin and Du Pu, eds., *Zhonghua Renmin Gongheguo Shilu, Disan Juan: Neiluan yu Kangzheng, 1966–1971* (A faithful record of the People's Republic of China, vol. 3: Internal disorder and resistance, 1966–1971) (Changchun: Jilin Renmin Chubanshe, 1994), part 1, 307.

57. See Mao Zedong, "Duiwai Xuanchuan Buyao Qiangjia Yu Ren, 1967–1970" (Don't impose foreign propaganda on people, 1967–1970), Mar. 29, 1968, in *Mao Zedong Wenji*, vol. 8, 431.

58. Ibid., 431. This is Mao Zedong's comment on a report answering criticism by V. G. Wilcox, the general secretary of the New Zealand Communist Party, March 17, 1968. He said, "I have talked about this many times."

59. Mao Zedong, Written instructions for "Asking for Instructions for Inviting the Delegation of the Dutch Communist United Movement (Marxist-Leninist) to China," Dec. 6, 1970, published as Mao Zedong, "Bu Yaoqiu Waiguoren Chengren Zhongguoren de Sixiang" (Don't require foreigners to accept Chinese ideas), in *Mao Zedong Waijiao Wenxuan*, 591.

60. Fan Shuo and Ding Jiaqi, *Ye Jianying Zhuan* (Biography of Ye Jianying) (Beijing: Dangdai Zhongguo Chubanshe, 1995), 620, 773.

61. On June 4, 1969, Zhou Enlai told the Chinese ambassadors to other countries who were about to resume their posts that there was room for optimism but that they had to be prepared for setbacks. They should take the initiative to do diplomatic work and educate diplomatic personnel to be modest, cautious, plain-living, and neither too humble nor too pushy. He emphasized the need to be good at external propaganda work and very cautious.

62. After August 1968, China and Yugoslavia stopped their mutual criticism, and on March 17, 1969, the governments of the two countries signed an agreement on trade and repayment. In September 1970, China once again sent its ambassador to Yugoslavia, and the countries restored relations.

63. Deng Xiaoping, *Deng Xiaoping Wenxuan* (Selected works of Deng Xiaoping), rev. ed. (Beijing: Renmin Chubanshe, 1994), vol. 2, 483.

64. The "three-in-one combination" refers to the organization of the Revolutionary Committees, which took the place of government organs at all levels and was based on the principle that there should be representatives from three sides: the military, the revolutionary cadres, and the masses.

65. Mao Zedong, "Gei Jiang Qing de Xin" (A letter to Jiang Qing), July 8, 1966, in *Jianguo yilai Mao Zedong Wengao* (Manuscripts of Mao Zedong since the founding of the state), vol. 12: Jan. 1966–Dec. 1968 (Beijing: Zhongyang Wenxian Chubanshe, 1998), 71–75.

66. Mao Zedong: A talk with the Albanian Minister of Defense, Oct. 5, 1968.

67. Mao Zedong, A talk with [E. F.] Hill, chair of the Communist Party (Marxist-Leninist) of Australia, Nov. 28, 1968.

68. "Mao Zedong tong Zhongyang Wenge Pengtouhui Chengyuan de Tanhua" (Mao Zedong's talk with members of the central briefing meeting of the Cultural Revolution), Mar. 15, 1969. See *Zhonghua Renmin Gongheguo Shilu, Disan Juan*, ed. Chen and Du, part 1, 467–69.

69. Mao Zedong, "Tong Faguo Zhengfu Daibiaotuan Tuanzhang Bei Dangu de Yiduan Tanhua" (A talk with Andre Bettencourt, head of the French government delegation), July 13, 1970, in *Jianguo yilai Mao Zedong Wengao* (Manuscripts of Mao Zedong since the founding of the state), vol. 13: Jan. 1969–July 1976 (Beijing: Zhongyang Wenxian Chubanshe, 1998), 111.

70. Mao Zedong's talk with Kim Il Sung, Oct. 8, 1970.

71. Zhou Enlai, "Peitong Mao Zedong Yuejian Ji Pengfei, Qiao Guanhua, Wang Shu" (Accompanying Mao Zedong on a Visit to Ji Pengfei, Qiao Guanhua, and Wang Shu), in *Zhou Enlai Nianpu: 1949–1976*, vol. 3, 529.

72. "Mao Zedong tong Zhongyang Wenge Pengtouhui Chengyuan de Tanhua," Mar. 15, 1969, in *Zhonghua Renmin Gongheguo Shilu, Disan Juan*, ed. Chen and Du, part 2, 467–68.

73. A talk between Zhou Enlai and Aleksei Kosygin, Sept. 11, 1969; A talk between Zhou Enlai and Le Thanh Nghi and Hoang Van Hoan, Vietnam guests, Nov. 23, 1969.

74. Slogan no. 22 of "Qingzhu Zhonghua Renmin Gongheguo Chengli 20 Zhounian Kouhao" (The slogans for celebrating the twentieth anniversary of the founding of the People's Republic of China): "The people of the whole world unite and oppose the war of aggression launched by the imperialists and social-imperialists, and particularly the war of aggression using the atomic bomb as the weapon! If war takes place, the people of the whole world should eliminate the war of aggression with revolutionary war. From now on, they should be prepared for it." See *Renmin Ribao*, Sept. 17, 1969, 1.

75. Record of talk with Wang Jinqing in December 1997. At that time, Wang Jinqing worked in the Chinese embassy in the Soviet Union and was a member of the Chinese delegation for border negotiations. Later he served as Chinese ambassador to Russia. On November 16, 1969, Zhou Enlai sent a letter to Mao Zedong along with the text of the speech affirming the Chinese side's suggestions in Sino-Soviet border negotiations and the telegram about the talk between Agha Mohammad Yahya Khan, president of Pakistan, and Zhang Tong, Chinese ambassador to Pakistan, reminding Mao Zedong that "we should pay attention to Nixon's and Kissinger's actions." Zhou Enlai, A letter to Mao Zedong, Nov. 16, 1969.

76. On December 12, 1969, Zhou Enlai told Khwaja Mohammad Kaiser, the Pakistani ambassador to China, that "the Sino-Soviet border negotiations draw the attention of all the countries in the world. Sino-U.S. relations are undergoing changes. The American ambassador tried to contact us in Warsaw, and he talked with our interpreter at the fashion show in the embassy of Yugoslavia. China's positions on its relations with the United States are first, the Five Principles of Peaceful Co-existence; second, all American armed forces must withdraw from Taiwan and the areas of the Taiwan Strait. Against the background of strained Sino-Soviet relations, Chinese leaders give top priority to peaceful co-existence between the two countries of China and the United States with regard to Sino-U.S. relations. This change is meaningful." Part of this discussion can be found in *Zhou Enlai Waijiao Huodong Dashiji, 1949–1976* (A Chronicle of Zhou Enlai's diplomatic activities, 1949–1976), comp. Research Office of Diplomatic History of the Foreign Ministry (Beijing: Shijie Zhishi Chubanshe, 1993), 546; and *Zhou Enlai Nianpu: 1949–1976*, vol. 3, 338–39.

77. On November 12, 1969, Zhou Enlai told members of the Chinese Party and government delegation going to visit Algeria, that "it is very one-sided to say that the United States and the Soviet Union collaborate without mentioning their rivalry. The target of contention between the United States and the Soviet Union is the Middle East. If we see only their collaboration and not their contention, many issues cannot be explained. It is one-sided to say that there are no contradictions between the two camps." Afterward, the Chinese leaders drew the conclusion that the focus of contention between the United States and the Soviet Union was Europe.

78. A talk between Zhou Enlai and Khwaja Mohammad Kaiser, the Pakistani ambassador to China, Dec. 2, 1969.

79. Zhou Enlai, A letter to Mao Zedong and Lin Biao, Dec. 2, 1969.

80. Mao Zedong, "Ruguo Nikesong Yuanyi Lai, Wo Yuanyi he Ta Tan" (If Nixon is willing to visit, I am willing to talk with him), Dec. 18, 1970, in *Mao Zedong Waijiao Wenxuan*, 593.

81. Mao Zedong, A talk with Henry A. Kissinger, U.S. Secretary of State, Oct. 21, 1975.

82. Mao Zedong's talk with the prime minister of Somalia.

83. In November 1962, a *People's Daily* editorial declared that "the formation and expansion of the socialist system and the continued rise of national liberation movements are the main trends in the current world situation. These two great historic trends have shaken the world capitalist system so that the areas under imperialist rule have been greatly decreased and are continuing to decrease." See "Fayang Mosike Xuanyan he Mosike Shengming de Geming Jingshen"(Carry forward the revolutionary spirit of the Moscow declaration and the Moscow

statement), *Renmin Ribao*, Nov. 15, 1962. In June 1963, the *People's Daily* argued that "the national and democratic revolution in these areas [a reference to the vast areas of Asia, Africa, and Latin America] is an important part of the contemporary proletarian world revolution." See "Guanyu Guoji Gongchanzhuyi Yundong Zongluxian de Jianyi" (Suggestions on the general line of the international communist movement), *Renmin Ribao*, June 17, 1963.

84. At that time, it was not convenient for Mao Zedong to express grievances openly. On September 24, 1956, when he received the delegation of the League of Communists of Yugoslavia at the Eighth National Congress of the CCP, he openly stated that Stalin bullied China for the third time "after the Second World War ended and Japan surrendered. Stalin, Roosevelt, and Churchill held a conference and decided to give all of China to the United States and Chiang Kai-shek. At that time, Stalin did not support us, the Communists, materially or morally, and especially morally, but he supported Chiang Kai-shek. The decision was made at the Yalta Conference." See Mao Zedong, A talk with the Delegation of the League of Communists of Yugoslavia, Sept. 24, 1956, published as "Xiqu Lishi Jiaoxun, Fandui Daguo Shaowenzhuyi" (Draw a history lesson, oppose great power chauvinism), in *Mao Zedong Waijiao Wenxuan*, 253–54.

85. On Dec. 6, 1970, Mao Zedong gave written instructions on a report submitted by the International Liaison Department of the CCP Central Committee: "We do not ask all foreigners to recognize the thought of the Chinese people, only to recognize the integration of the universal truth of Marxism-Leninism with the concrete revolutionary practice in their countries. This is a basic principle." See Mao Zedong, "Duiwai Xuanchuan buyao Qiangjia yu Ren," in *Mao Zedong Wenji*, vol. 8, 433.

86. On May 20, 1970, Mao Zedong issued a statement in support of the people of Indochina in their struggle against United States aggression and for national salvation, which said that "the main trend in the world today is revolution." See Mao Zedong, "Quan Shijie Renmin Tuanjie Qilai, Dabai Meiguo Qinluezhe jiqi Yiqie Zougou" (All people of the world unite, defeat American imperialism and its running dogs), May 20, 1970, in *Mao Zedong Waijiao Wenxuan*, 584. On November 13 of the same year, when Agha Mohammad Yahya Khan, the president of Pakistan, who maintained close relations with China, talked with Zhou Enlai, he did not understand Mao Zedong's words. Zhou Enlai explained, "Here, 'revolution' is generalized to include winning and safeguarding national independence and opposing foreign invasion and interference." He emphasized that "this is more important." Actually, this was a change from the earlier view. This talk was published as "Minzu Duli Yundong zai Buduan Gaozhang" (A national independence movement continues to rise), in *Zhou Enlai Waijiao Wenxuan*, 467.

87. Shortly after the Cultural Revolution began, in 1966, Mao Zedong declared that "we are in a new, great era of world revolution." In old age, he once sighed with

deep emotion, "Can I change the world? I have no ability to do this. I only change a few places near Beijing." Quoted from Liu Yazhou, "Zhongguo Renmin Aihao Heping" (The Chinese people love peace), in *Mao Zedong Jiaowang Lu* (Record of Mao Zedong's contacts), ed. Yu Jundao and Li Jie (Beijing: Renmin Chubanshe, 1991), 456–57.

88. Mao Zedong, "Zhongguo Geming Zhanzheng de Zhanlue Wenti" (Problems of strategy in China's revolutionary war), Dec. 1936, in *Mao Zedong Xuanji* (Selected works of Mao Zedong), vol. 1 (Beijing: Renmin Chubanshe, 1991), 174.

89. On April 1, 1969, the Political Report of the Ninth National Congress of the CCP said, "Recently Mao Zedong pointed out: 'there are only two possibilities: First, war leads to revolution; Second, revolution prevents war.'" See Lin Biao, "Zhongguo Gongchandang Dijiuci Quanguo Daibiao Dahui Zhengzhi Baogao" (The political report at the Ninth National Congress of the CCP), Apr. 1, 1969, in *Zhongguo Gongchandang Jianshe Quanshu* (Complete Collection of CCP Construction), ed. Zhao Shenghui and Mu Zhe, vol. 9 (Taiyuan: Shanxi Renmin Chubanshe, 1991), 212.

90. Mao Zedong, "Tong Riben Guohui Yiyuan Fang Hua Tuan de Tanhua" (A talk with the delegation from the Japanese diet), Oct. 15, 1955, in *Mao Zedong Wenji*, vol. 6, 484.

91. Mao Zedong, "Guanyu Guoji Xingshi" (On the international situation), Sept. 5, 8, 1958, in *Mao Zedong Wenji*, vol. 7, 412.

92. Mao Zedong, "Guanyu Zhengque Chuli Renmin Neibu Maodun de Wenti" (On the correct handling of contradictions among the people), Feb. 27, 1957, in *Mao Zedong Xuanji*, vol. 5, 398.

93. With regard to the possibility of a new world war, Mao Zedong's view was gradually changing. After the war, until the 1950s, he thought that "the threat of war from the imperialist camp still exists, and so does the possibility of a third world war. However, the forces fighting to check the danger of war and prevent the outbreak of a third world war are growing rapidly. . . . A new world war can be averted." Mao Zedong, "Wei Zhengqu Guojia Caizheng Jingji Zhuangkuang de Jiben Haozhuan er Douzheng," in *Mao Zedong Xuanji*, vol. 5, 15–16. In the 1960s, after the break-off of Sino-Soviet relations, and especially when the Soviet Union was posing a threat to China, Mao overestimated the possibility of a world war. When Sino-U.S. relations were normalized in the 1970s, Mao became cautious and optimistic, but he did not change his judgment that a new world war was unavoidable. On October 6, 1984, when Deng Xiaoping met with Helmut Kohl, chancellor of the Federal Republic of Germany, Deng said, "When you visited China in 1974, you and I talked about the danger of war. Now we Chinese have slightly different views. We feel that, although the danger of war still exists and we still have to remain vigilant, the factors that can prevent a new world war are growing. Our foreign policy is to oppose hegemony and safeguard world peace." See Deng Xiaoping, "Women ba

Gaige Dangzuo yizhong Geming" (We regard reform as revolution), Oct. 10, 1984, in *Deng Xiaoping Wenxuan* (Selected works of Deng Xiaoping), vol. 3 (Beijing: Renmin Chubanshe, 1993), 82.

94. On May 26, 1955, Mao Zedong told Ali Sastroamidjojo, prime minister of Indonesia, "We want to strive for a peaceful environment that will last as long as possible, and this is both desirable and possible. If the United States is willing to sign a peace treaty, the duration can be fifty or even a hundred years. But I do not know if the United States is willing." See Mao Zedong, "Tong Yinni Zongli Shasiteluoamizuoyue de Tanhua" (A talk between Mao Zedong and Indonesian Prime Minister Ali Sastroamidjojo), May 26, 1955, in *Mao Zedong Wenji*, vol. 6, 413.

95. "Guanyu Guoji Gongchanzhuyi Yundong Zongluxian de Jianyi" (Suggestions on the general line of the international communist movement) pointed out that "we oppose the anticommunist, antipeople, and counterrevolutionary policy of the reactionaries of all countries." According to this standard, almost all those in power in developing countries taking the nonsocialist road to development might be included in the category of "reactionaries of all countries." This approach obstructed the development and consolidation of China's diplomatic relations with the countries of Asia, Africa, and Latin America. *Renmin Ribao* (People's Daily), June 17, 1963.

96. On November 26, 1979, when Deng Xiaoping met with American and Canadian guests, he said, "For a fairly long period of time since the founding of the People's Republic, we have been isolated from the rest of the world. For many years this isolation was not attributable to us; on the contrary, the international anti-Chinese and antisocialist forces confined us to a state of isolation. However, in the 1960s, when opportunities to increase contact and cooperation with other countries presented themselves to us, we isolated ourselves." See *Deng Xiaoping Wenxuan*, vol. 2, 232.

97. Deng Xiaoping, "Jiesu Yanjun de Zhong Mei Guanxi Yao you Meiguo Caiqu Zhudong" (The United States should take the initiative in putting an end to the strains in Sino-American relations), Oct. 31, 1989, in *Deng Xiaoping Wenxuan*, vol. 3, 330.

11. Gong Li, "Chinese Decision Making and the Thawing of U.S.-China Relations"

1. At the Eleventh Plenary Session of the Eighth Chinese Communist Party Central Committee in August 1966, Vice-Chairman Liu Shaoqi, who handled the daily affairs of the Politburo, and Secretary General Deng Xiaoping, who handled the daily affairs of the Secretariat, were severely criticized and removed from office.

2. Those who attended the Cultural Revolution Leading Group meetings, besides its members, included Zhou Enlai, Ye Qun (Lin Biao's representative), and leaders of the State Council and the military.

3. The Cultural Revolution Leading Group had its headquarters in Diaoyutai.

4. Wang Li's talk with the representatives of the rebels of the Foreign Ministry, Aug. 7, 1967.

5. Yang Chengwu was then chief of the general staff of the People's Liberation Army.

6. Namely, Wang Li, Guan Feng, and Qi Benyu, important members of the Central Leading Group of the Cultural Revolution.

7. Document Research Office of the Communist Party Central Committee, comp., *Zhou Enlai Nianpu: 1949–1976* (Chronology of Zhou Enlai: 1949–1976) (Beijing: Zhongyang Wenxian Chubanshe, 1997), vol. 3, 183.

8. Li Jie, "Changes in China's Domestic Situation in the 1960s and Sino-U.S. Relations," paper prepared for the International Workshop on Sino-U.S. Relations, Beijing, October 1996. (See Chapter 10 of this volume.)

9. See Mao Zedong, "Duiwai Xuanchuan Buyao Qiangjia Yu Ren, 1967–1970" (Don't impose foreign propaganda on people, 1967–1970), May 16, 1968, in *Mao Zedong Wenji* (Collected works of Mao Zedong), comp. Document Research Office of the Chinese Communist Party Central Committee, vol. 8 (Beijing: Renmin Chubanshe, 1999), 431.

10. Ibid., 432.

11. On Dec. 18, 1970, during his meeting with the American journalist Edgar Snow, Mao pointed out, "The Foreign Ministry was in a state of chaos. It was an out-of-control situation. It was the reactionaries who took over power." "Was it when the [office of the] British Chargé d'Affaires was burned?" asked Snow. Mao replied: "Yes, exactly. During the two months of July and August, there was a state of great confusion. However, it was quite an opportunity to get them exposed. Otherwise, we wouldn't know who they were!" On June 28, 1972, during his meeting with Mrs. Bandaranaike, the visiting prime minister of Sri Lanka, Mao once again remarked: "Who are the so-called leftists? It is those who set the office of the British Chargé d'Affaires on fire. Today, they want to denounce the premier, tomorrow they want to denounce Ye Jianying. Now those leftists have all ended up behind bars." Mao Zedong explained that the Foreign Ministry was then "taken over by the leftists. For almost a month and a half, the power, of which we were deprived, was taken over by the leftists."

12. A Summary of Mao Zedong's conversation with Wang Hongwen and Zhang Chunqiao.

13. On Dec. 9, 1973, after his meeting with the King of Nepal, he made the quoted remarks to Zhou Enlai, Wang Hongwen, Nancy Tang, and Wang Hairong.

14. Jiang Qing's speech, made during a meeting she convened, without authorization, with leading cadres from twelve provinces and regions, Mar. 3, 1976.

15. On May 22, 1963, during his meeting with Communist Party of New Zealand Secretary Wilcox, Mao made the following remarks in response to the suggestions of Wang Jiaxiang and others: "Some within our Party argue for 'three harmonies' and 'one reduction': seeking harmony with the imperialists, seeking harmony with the revisionists, seeking harmony with the reactionaries, and a reduction in our support for the people in Asia, Africa, and Latin America. This is a revisionist line." To counter this, Mao proposed "three confrontations and one increase": "confrontation with the imperialists, confrontation with the revisionists, and confrontation with reactionaries in all countries, and an increase in our support for Marxist-Leninist political parties and various Marxist-Leninist factions in their struggles against imperialists." According to Mao, the former was endorsed by Khrushchev, the latter by China.

16. Mao Zedong's talks with Zhou Enlai, Ji Pengfei, and others, July 24, 1972. For a record of Mao's meeting with these leaders, see *Zhou Enlai Nianpu: 1949–1976*, vol. 3, 539.

17. Henry Kissinger, *White House Years* (Boston: Little, Brown, 1979), 685.

18. Ibid., 298.

19. Richard Nixon, *RN: The Memoirs of Richard Nixon* (New York: Grosset and Dunlap, 1978), 347.

20. Ibid., 384.

21. Jin Chongji, ed., *Zhou Enlai Zhuan, 1949–1976* (Biography of Zhou Enlai, 1949–1976), vol. 2 (Beijing: Zhongyang Wenxian Chubanshe, 1998), 1110.

22. Mao's talk with Kim Il Sung on Feb. 27, 1964, with Choi Yong-gun on Oct. 7, and with Baruku on Oct. 9.

23. Li Ke and Hao Shengzhang, *Wenhua Dageming zhong de Renmin Jiefangjun* (The People's Liberation Army during the Cultural Revolution) (Beijing: Zhonggong Dangshi Ziliao Chubanshe, 1989), 318.

24. Ibid., 319.

25. Li Danhui, "1969 nian Zhong Su Bianjie Chongtu: Yuanqi he Jieguo" (The 1969 Sino-Soviet border clash: Causes and results), *Dangdai Zhongguoshi Yanjiu* (Research on contemporary Chinese history), no. 3 (1996): 48.

26. "Mao Zedong zai Zhongguo Gongchandang dijiuci Zhongyang Weiyuanhui diyici Quanti Huiyishang de Jianghua" (Mao Zedong's speech at the First Plenary Session of the Ninth Central Committee of the Chinese Communist Party), on April 28, 1969, in *"Wenhua Dageming" Yanjiu Ziliao* (Research materials on the Cultural Revolution), comp. Party History, Party Building, and Political Work Teaching and Research Office, National Defense University of the PLA, vol. 2, 1968–72 (Beijing: n.p., 1988), 336.

27. Richard M. Nixon, "Asia after the Vietnam War," *Foreign Affairs* 46, no. 1 (1968): 121.

28. During his talk with U.S. House of Representatives Majority Leader Mike Mansfield, Zhou Enlai once said, "Let me tell you a bit about our situation. It is Chairman Mao's decision to open up Sino-U.S. relations. Actually, he has read a paper written by Nixon before he won the presidential election in 1968. I wasn't even aware of it until after Mao informed us of the paper."

29. China issued a statement on Feb. 19, 1969, canceling the scheduled talk after the United States granted political asylum to Liao Heshu, a Chinese diplomat at the Chinese embassy in the Netherlands who had defected.

30. Chen Xiaolu, "Chen Yi yu Zhongguo Waijiao" (Chen Yi and China's Diplomacy), in *Huanqiu Tong Ci Liang Re—Yi Dai Lingxiumen de Guoji Zhanlue Sixiang* (It's the same temperature around the globe: International strategic thoughts of a generation of the leadership), comp. Foundation for International Strategic Studies (Beijing: Zhongyang Wenxian Chubanshe, 1993), 155.

31. Richard Nixon, "Inaugural Address," Jan. 20, 1969, in *Public Papers of the Presidents of the United States: Richard Nixon, 1969* (Washington, D.C.: Government Printing Office, 1971), 3. Also note that this section of the speech was reported in "Yipian Juemiao de Fanmian Jiaocai—Meidi Xin Toumu Nikesong de 'Jiuzhi Yanshuo'" (An excellent negative teaching example—The inaugural speech by Nixon, the new ringleader of American imperialism), *Renmin Ribao* (People's Daily), Jan. 28, 1969, 5–6.

32. For details, see Richard Nixon, "Third Annual Report to the Congress on United States Foreign Policy," Feb. 9, 1972, in *Public Papers of the Presidents of the United States: Richard Nixon, 1972* (Washington, D.C.: Government Printing Office, 1974), 221.

33. Lin Ke, Xu Tao, and Wu Xujun, *Lishi de Zhenshi—Mao Zedong Shengbian Gongzuo Renyuan de Zhengyan* (The truth of history—Affidavits of Mao Zedong's employees) (Hong Kong: Liwan Publishing House, 1995), 312.

34. Mao Zedong's Instructions on Propaganda in the Field of External Relations, Mar. 1967–Mar. 1971.

35. Li Jie, "Changes in China's Domestic Situation in the 1960s and Sino-U.S. Relations."

36. Lin, Xu, and Wu, *Lishi de Zhenshi*, 313.

37. Lin Biao, "Zai Zhongguo Gongchangdang dijiuci Quanguo Daibiao Dahuishang de Baogao" (Report to the Ninth Party Congress of the Chinese Communist Party), in *"Wenhua Dageming" Yanjiu Ziliao*, comp. Party History, Party Building, and Political Work Teaching and Research Office, National Defense University of the PLA, vol. 2, 1968–72, 324–25.

38. Wang Yongqin, "1969—Zhong Mei Guanxi Zhuanzhedian" (1969—A watershed in the Sino-U.S. Relationship), *Dangde Wenxian* (Party documents), no. 6 (1995): 78.

39. For details of the discussions of the four generals, see Xiong Xianghui, *Lishi de Jiaozhu—Huiyi Mao Zedong, Zhou Enlai ji Siwei Laoshuai* (Footnotes of history: Recollections of Mao Zedong, Zhou Enlai, and four marshals) (Beijing: Zhongyang Dangxiao Chubanshe, 1995), 173–204.

40. The Soviet side made an urgent request to the Chinese Foreign Ministry through its embassy in Beijing, and, with Mao's consent, the Chinese officially informed the Soviet Union that they would comply. Although the Chinese policy decision-making body was increasingly criticizing the Soviet drive for hegemony, it did not want out-of-control border clashes. Besides, for the Chinese, in considering a Chinese-Soviet summit meeting there was also the factor of China-U.S. relations.

41. *Zhou Enlai Nianpu*, vol. 3, 321.

42. In their memoirs, both Kissinger and Stoessel recalled that the diplomats were Lei Yang, China's chargé d'affaires to Poland, and his retinue. In fact, they were Li Juqing, second secretary of the Chinese embassy in Poland, and Jing Zhicheng, his interpreter.

43. Geng Biao, "Zhou Enlai Shi Xin Zhongguo Waijiao de Chuangshiren he Dianjizhe" (Zhou Enlai was the initiator and founder of the diplomacy of new China), in *Yanjiu Zhou Enlai—Waijiao Sixiang yu Shijian* (Research on Zhou Enlai: Diplomatic thoughts and practice), ed. Pei Jianzhang (Beijing: Shijie Zhishi Chubanshe, 1989), 15.

44. On Nov. 16, 1969, Zhou Enlai wrote Mao: "We will have to pay attention to Nixon-Kissinger intentions." See *Zhou Enlai Nianpu*, vol. 3, 334.

45. Ibid., 336–37.

46. Ibid., 338, 341.

47. Ibid., 344.

48. Zhou Enlai's talk with Khwaja Mohammad Kaiser, Pakistan's ambassador to China, Jan. 22, 1970.

49. Wang Yongqin, "Dapo Jianbing de Suiyue" (The years we broke the ice), part 1, *Dangshi Zongheng* (Review of party history), no. 4 (1997).

50. *Zhou Enlai Nianpu*, vol. 3, 348.

51. Ibid., 367. On May 17, the Politburo again met to discuss how to amend Mao's statement, drafted by the department concerned. Participants believed the statement should highlight some of the important ideas brought up by Mao during his meeting with Vietnam's Labor Party Chief Le Duan. Later, the statement went through different stages of revision in accordance with the conclusions of the Politburo meeting. On May 19, a second version amended by Zhou Enlai, Kang Sheng, and Chen Boda, was submitted to Mao for his approval.

52. See "Zhongmei Dashiji Huitan di 137 ci Huiyi Tuichi Juxing" (The 137th Sino-U.S. ambassadorial-level talk is postponed), *Renmin Ribao*, May 20, 1970, 5.

53. See Mao Zedong, "Quan Shijie Renmin Tuanjie Qilai, Dabai Mei Diguo-zhuyi Qinluezhe jiqi Yiqie Zougou" (All people of the world unite together to defeat the aggressors of American imperialism and its running dogs), May 20, 1970, published in *Renmin Ribao*, May 21, 1970, 1.

54. "Wo Zhuanzheng Jiguan Chuli Meiguo Fanren" (American criminals released by Chinese organs of dictatorship), *Renmin Ribao*, July 11, 1970, 2.

55. Quite a few writers believed that the photo and quotation were carried by the *People's Daily* on October 2, but they actually appeared in "Mao Zhuxi huijian Meiguo Youren Aidejia Sinuo" (Chairman Mao met American friend Edgar Snow), *Renmin Ribao*, Dec. 25, 1970.

56. Lin, Xu, and Wu, *Lishi de Zhenshi*, 290.

57. Mao Zedong, "Guanyu Tongyi Huijian Meiguo Zuojia Sinuo de Piyu" (Remarks on agreeing to meet the American writer Edgar Snow), Oct. 1970, in *Jianguo Yilai Mao Zedong Wengao* (Manuscripts of Mao Zedong since the founding of the state), comp. Document Research Office of the CCP Central Committee, vol. 13: Jan. 1969–July 1976 (Beijing: Zhongyang Wenxian Chubanshe, 1998), 150.

58. Mao's Dec. 18, 1970, talk with Edgar Snow is published as "Ruguo Nikesong Yuanyi Lai, Wo Yuanyi he Ta Tan" (If Nixon is willing to visit, I am willing to talk with him), in *Mao Zedong Waijiao Wenxuan* (Selected works of Mao Zedong on diplomacy), comp. Ministry of Foreign Affairs of the People's Republic of China and Central Document Research Office of the CCP Central Committee (Beijing: Zhongyang Wenxian Chubanshe and Shijie Zhishi Chubanshe, 1994), 592–93.

59. Lin, Xu, and Wu, *Lishi de Zhenshi*, 299.

60. "Jixinge zai Jinian 'Pingpang Waijiao' 25 Zhounian Zhaodai Huishang de Jianghua" (Kissinger's speech at the reception in celebration of the 25th anniversary of 'Ping-pong diplomacy'), in Zhou Xisheng, "'Pingpang Waijiao' Li Jiu Mi Xin" (The longer the time, the more meaningful the 'Ping-pong diplomacy'), *Liaowang* (Outlook weekly), no. 33, Aug. 18, 1997, 41–42.

61. Mao Zedong, "Zai Waijiaobu Guanyu Meiguo Ren Lai Hua Wenti Qingshi Baogao shang de Piyu" (Remarks on the report submitted by the Foreign Affairs Ministry concerning visits of Americans to China), Mar. 1971, in *Jianguo Yilai Mao Zedong Wengao*, vol. 13, 211.

62. *Zhou Enlai Nianpu*, vol. 3, 437.

63. Mao Zedong's Instructions on Propaganda in the Field of External Relations (1967–1971). According to Mao's instructions, Zhou Enlai's report was also included.

64. Ibid.

65. Lin, Xu, and Wu, *Lishi de Zhenshi*, 304.

66. Xiong Xianghui, "Pingpang Waijiao Lishi" (History of Ping-pong Diplomacy), *Dangshi Zongheng*, no. 10 (1997).

67. Reuters cable from Nagoya dated Apr. 4, 1971.

68. Associated Press cable from Nagoya dated Apr. 5, 1971.

69. Lin, Xu, and Wu, *Lishi de Zhenshi*, 306.

70. See Qian Jiang, *Xiaoqiu Zhuandong Daqiu: Ping-pong Waijiao Muhou* (Behind the scenes of Ping-pong diplomacy) (Beijing: Dong Fang Chubanshe, 1997), 236–37.

71. *Zhou Enlai Nianpu*, vol. 3, 449.

72. Ibid.

73. Lin, Xu, and Wu, *Lishi de Zhenshi*, 311.

74. Zhou Enlai, "Tong Meiguo Pingpang Qiu Daibiaotuan de Tanhua" (A talk with the U.S. Ping-pong delegation), Apr. 14, 1971, in *Zhou Enlai Waijiao Wenxuan* (Selected works of Zhou Enlai on diplomacy), comp. Document Research Office of the CCP Central Committee (Beijing: Zhongyang Wenxian Chubanshe, 1990), 469–75.

75. Kissinger, *White House Years*, 710.

76. *Zhou Enlai Waijiao Huodong Dashiji, 1949–1976* (A chronicle of Zhou Enlai's diplomatic activities, 1949–1976), comp. Research Office of Diplomatic History of the Foreign Ministry (Beijing: Shijie Zhishi Chubanshe, 1993), 644.

77. Mao Zedong, "Dui Zhou Enlai de Xin he Baosong Cailiao de Piyu" (Remarks on the letter and materials reported by Zhou Enlai), May 1971, in *Jianguo Yilai Mao Zedong Wengao*, vol. 13, 234.

78. Politburo Report on Sino-U.S. Talks, May 29, 1971.

79. Ibid.

80. Ibid.

81. Oral messages quoted from the appendixes to the May 29, 1971, Politburo report. On June 4, through the secret Pakistan channel, Nixon sent an oral message that he was grateful for the Chinese invitation and suggested that Kissinger arrive in Beijing on July 9. On June 11, the Chinese replied that the date was acceptable.

82. Wang, "Dapo Jianbing de Suiyue," pt. 3, *Dangshi Zongheng*, no. 6 (1997).

83. *Zhou Enlai Nianpu*, vol. 3, 467; Wang, "Dapo Jianbing de Suiyue," pt. 1, *Dangshi Zongheng*, no. 4 (1997).

84. Zhang Wenjin's words cited in Wang, "Dapo Jianbing de Suiyue," pt. 3, *Dangshi Zongheng*, no. 6 (1997).

85. Weng Ming, "Boluo Xingdong—Jixinge Mimi Fang Hua" (Operation Polo—A secret visit to China by Kissinger), in *Waijiao Fengyun—Waijiaoguan Haiwai Miwen* (The winds and clouds of diplomacy—The secret stories of overseas diplomats), ed. Fu Hao and Li Tongcheng (Beijing: Zhongguo Huaqiao Chubanshe, 1995), 62.

86. See Wei Shiyan, "Jixinge Mimi Fang Hua Neimu" (The inside story of Kissinger's secret visit to China), in *Xin Zhongguo Waijiao Fengyun* (The winds and clouds of diplomacy in New China), comp. Research Office of Diplomatic History of the Foreign Ministry, vol. 2 (Beijing: Shijie Zhishi Chubanshe, 1991), 41–42.

87. Weng, "Boluo Xingdong," 64–65.

88. See Wei, "Jixinge Mimi Fang Hua Neimu," 44–45.

89. *Renmin Ribao*, Oct. 5, 1971.

90. Wei Shiyan, "Jixinge Dierci Fang Hua" (The second visit to China by Kissinger), in *Xin Zhongguo Waijiao Fengyun*, vol. 3 (Beijing: Shijie Zhishi Chubanshe, 1994), 60.

91. Ibid., 67.

92. This statement was written into the joint communiqué without changing a word. See "Lianhe gongbao" (Joint communiqué), *Renmin Ribao*, Feb. 28, 1972.

93. See Wei Shiyan, "Heige Shuaixian Qian Zu Wei Nikesong Fang Hua Anpai de Jingguo," (The experience of Haig and his advance group in making preparations for Nixon's visit), in *Xin Zhongguo Waijiao Fengyun*, vol. 3, 72.

94. *Zhou Enlai Nianpu*, vol. 3, 505.

95. Wei, "Heige Shuaixian Qian Zu Wei Nikesong Fang Hua Anpai de Jingguo," vol. 3, 78–79.

96. *Zhou Enlai Nianpu*, vol. 3, 506–7.

97. Mao Zedong, "Xianzai bu Cunzai Zhong Mei Liangguo Huxiang Dazhang de Wenti" (Currently there does not exist the issue of war between the two countries of China and the United States), *Mao Zedong Waijiao Wenxuan*, 595–96.

98. Wang, "Dapo Jianbing de Suiyue," part 5, *Dangshi Zongheng*, no. 8 (1997).

99. Ibid.; *Zhou Enlai Nianpu*, vol. 3, 513.

100. *Zhou Enlai Nianpu*, vol. 3, 515.

101. CCP Circular Concerning the China-U.S. Joint Communiqué, Mar. 7, 1972.

102. *Zhou Enlai Nianpu*, vol. 3, 574.

103. Wang, "Dapo Jianbing de Suiyue," part 6, *Dangshi Zongheng*, no. 10 (1997).

104. Mao Zedong's talks with Kissinger (excerpts), Feb. 17, 1973.

105. Chinese Foreign Ministry, *Foreign Affairs Bulletin*, no. 12 (1973): 582.

106. *Zhou Enlai Nianpu*, vol. 3, 582.

107. Geng Biao, Ji Pengfei, Wang Youping, and Han Nianlong, "In Memory of Our Old Comrade-in-Arms Huang Zhen," *Renmin Ribao*, May 31, 1990. Also published in *Jiangjun, Waijiaojia, Yishujia: Huang Zhen Jinian Wenji* (General, diplomat, artist: Collected works in memory of Huang Zhen), ed. Yao Zhongmin, Xie Wushen, and Pei Jianzhang (Beijing: Jiefangjun Chubanshe, 1993), 301–7.

108. Mao Zedong's talk with Kissinger, Feb., 1973.

12. Michael Schaller, "Détente and the Strategic Triangle: Or, 'Drinking Your Mao Tai and Having Your Vodka, Too'"

1. Haldeman daily notes, July 13, 14, 15, 19, 1971, White House Special Files, Box 44, Haldeman Papers, Nixon Presidential Papers Project, National Archives (hereafter Nixon Project); H. R. Haldeman, *The Haldeman Diaries* (New York: G. P.

Putnam's, 1994), 318–24; Henry Kissinger, *White House Years* (Boston: Little, Brown, 1979), 762. Haldeman attended most Nixon-Kissinger meetings or discussed them with the president. His daily notes were written during these discussions. The CD/ROM and published versions of the so-called Haldeman diaries were assembled from evening summations of the day's events and are less immediate than the daily notes. The Nixon administration's National Security Files have only recently begun to open. Several researchers have utilized selective portions of the files through Freedom of Information Act requests. Among the archivally based published studies on China, see Michael Schaller, *Altered States: The U.S. and Japan since the Occupation* (New York: Oxford University Press, 1997); James Mann, *About Face: A History of America's Curious Relationship with China from Nixon to Clinton* (New York: Knopf, 1999); Patrick Tyler, *A Great Wall: Six Presidents and China* (New York: Public Affairs, 1999); William Burr, ed., *The Kissinger Transcripts: The Top Secret Talks with Beijing and Moscow* (New York: New Press, 1999); see also the memoir by John H. Holdridge, *Crossing the Divide: An Insider's Account of Normalization of U.S.-China Relations* (Lanham, Md.: Rowman and Littlefield, 1997); the president's own memoirs, Richard Nixon, *RN: The Memoirs of Richard Nixon* (New York: Grosset and Dunlap, 1978), are thin and often unreliable.

2. Memorandum dated Nov. 28, 1967, of conversation between McNamara, Sato, et al., Nov. 14, 1967, REF # 92–M-0–55(A), Lyndon B. Johnson Library (hereafter LBJL); for Johnson's remarks, see NSC File, Meeting Notes File, Box 2, F: Nov. 4, 1967, Meeting with Foreign Policy Advisers, ibid.

The Ministry of International Trade and Industry (MITI) compiled the most complete (and conservative) estimate of Vietnam-related earnings. All calculations came on top of the $340 million "base" level of U.S. procurements in Japan in 1964. They also accounted for the fact that exports to the United States and Southeast Asia were on an upward curve when escalation began. MITI data for 1965 to 1972 indicates that Japan earned at least $7 billion in "extra" sales of goods and services related to Vietnam. This included $1.77 billion in direct procurement by United States forces in Japan; $2.83 billion in indirect procurement in Japan by Vietnam and countries such as South Korea, Taiwan, and the Philippines; and almost $2 billion in additional exports to the United States made possible by war-induced shortages in American industry. For MITI data, see "Vietnam: Japan's Major Role," *Far Eastern Economic Review*, Mar. 12, 1973, 33–45; see also "Economic Benefits to Japan Traceable to the Vietnam Conflict," Nov. 9, 1967, National Security File, Country File: Japan, Box 252, LBJL; "Vietnam Special Procurement and the Economy," *Japan Quarterly* 14, no. 1 (Jan.-Mar. 1967): 13–16.

3. Kissinger, *White House Years*, 765.

4. Rosemary Foot, *The Practice of Power: U.S. Relations with China since 1949* (New York: Oxford University Press, 1995), 103; Mann, *About Face*, 16.

5. Edwin O. Reischauer, *My Life between Japan and America* (New York: Harper and Row, 1986), 264; several other diplomats, such as Marshall Green and Roger Sullivan, recall Nixon discussing a new approach to China with them in the 1960s.

6. Kissinger, *White House Years*, 169.

7. Ibid., 223–25; Tad Szulc, *Illusion of Peace: Foreign Policy in the Nixon Years* (New York: Viking, 1978), 125–27.

8. Schaller, *Altered States*, 210–44; Roger Morris, *Uncertain Greatness: Henry Kissinger and American Foreign Policy* (New York: Harper and Row, 1977), 102–3; Paul A. Volcker and Toyoo Gyohten, *Changing Fortunes: The World's Money and the Threat to American Leadership* (New York: Times Books, 1992), 64–65; I. M. Destler, Haruhiro Fukui, and Hideo Sato, *The Textile Wrangle: Conflict in Japanese-American Relations, 1969–1971* (Ithaca: Cornell University Press, 1979), 79–80.

9. As a presidential candidate in August 1968, Nixon promised textile executives that if elected he would "take the steps necessary to extend the concept of international trade agreements [i.e., quotas]" to synthetic fibers, as had been done with cotton goods. In 1969, some 2.5 million Americans worked in the textile and apparel industries, with plants located heavily in the South. This resonated with Nixon's "southern strategy," a plan to woo white Southerners away from the Democratic Party. In exchange for his pledge to limit imports, the American Textile Manufacturers Institute contributed money to Nixon's election fund and promised future donations once he delivered. Nixon singled out the textile industry as facing a "special problem which has caused great distress" to producers and wage earners alike. He demanded that Japan accept "voluntary restraints" on its synthetic textile exports, an agreement similar to the one limiting cotton goods. See U. Alexis Johnson, *The Right Hand of Power* (Englewood Cliffs, N.J.: Prentice-Hall, 1984), 544–46; Armin Meyer, *Assignment Tokyo: An Ambassador's Journal* (Indianapolis: Bobbs-Merrill, 1974), 37–43. Destler, Fukui, and Sato, *Textile Wrangle*, 66–73.

10. Destler, Fukui, and Sato, *Textile Wrangle*, 74–94, 112, 134–35; Kissinger, *White House Years*, 330–37; Wakaizume Kei, *Tasaku nakarishi o shinzemto hassu* (I would like to believe there was no other policy choice) (Tokyo: Bungei Shunjusha, 1994); Seymour Hersh, *The Price of Power: Kissinger in the Nixon White House* (New York: Summit Books, 1983), 381; John Welfield, *An Empire in Eclipse: Japan in the Postwar American Alliance System* (London: Athlone Press, 1988), 142; Morris, *Uncertain Greatness*, 104–5; Szulc, *Illusion of Peace*, 170–71; Johnson, *Right Hand of Power*, 448–50. Agreements reached prior to the Nixon-Sato summit on the issues of nuclear storage, Japan's support for the defense of South Korea and Taiwan, and use of the Okinawa bases for Vietnam operations are discussed in the following documents: "Okinawa—Preparations for Sato Visit," Winthrop and Brown to Under Secretary for Political Affairs, Oct. 28, 1969, Department of State, Freedom of Information Act (FOIA); William Rogers to Nixon, "Sato Visit—with Talking Points," ca.

Nov. 1969, Department of State, FOIA; memorandum for President from Secretary of State Rogers, ca. Nov. 1969, "Meeting with Congressional Leaders on Okinawa," Department of State, FOIA; Meyer to Secretary of State, Nov. 10, 1969, Department of State, FOIA; Johnson to Rogers, Nov. 13, 1969, "Okinawa Talking Points," Department of State, FOIA.

11. Kissinger, *White House Years*, 334–36; Meyer, *Assignment Tokyo*, 44; Johnson, *Right Hand of Power*, 546; Destler, Fukui, and Sato, *Textile Wrangle*, 139; Welfield, *Empire in Eclipse*, 246–50; for China's criticism see *Renmin Ribao* (People's Daily), Nov. 28, 1969, and *Peking Review*, Nov. 28, 1969, 28–30.

12. Kissinger, *White House Years*, 336; *Haldeman Diaries*, entry of Nov. 25, 1969 (CD/ROM version)(Santa Monica, Calif.: Sony Imagesoft, 1994); Patrick Buchanan to Nixon, "Notes from Legislative Leadership Meeting," Feb. 17, 1970, Nixon Project, National Archives, FOIA.

13. Kissinger to Nixon, "Your Meeting with Don Kendall," Apr. 13, 1970, White House Special Files (WHSF), Flanigan Files, Box 11, "Textiles," Nixon Project; memorandum of conversation, Prime Minister Sato and Treasury Secretary Kennedy, Apr. 13, 1970, Department of State, FOIA; Stans to Nixon, "Long Term Implications for the United States of Japan's Economic Growth and Potential and Policy Consequences," April 1970, with attachments by Kissinger, Flanigan, Bergsten, et al. Filed under cover memorandum by Flanigan for Nixon, June 19, 1970, WHSF, Flanigan Files, Box 11, Nixon Project; Destler, Fukui, and Sato, *Textile Wrangle*, 160–76.

14. [John] Ehrlichman to Kissinger or Gen. Haig, Sept. 21, 1970, WHSF, Peter Flanigan Files, Box 11, Nixon Project; Shultz memorandum for the files, Sept. 21, 1970, ibid.; Kissinger to Secretary of State, Commerce, et al., Sept. 25, 1970, ibid.; "The Dispensable Ally," *Far Eastern Economic Review*, Aug. 28, 1971, 21–22; U. A. Johnson for Nixon, "Meeting with Prime Minister Sato," Oct. 21, 1970, Flanigan Files, Box 11, Nixon Project; Kissinger for Nixon, "Meeting with Prime Minister Sato," Oct. 23, 1970, ibid.; Kissinger, *White House Years*, 339; Destler, Fukui, and Sato, *Textile Wrangle*, 220–22.

15. "Memorandum for the Files," Jan. 26, 1971, Peter Flanigan, WHSF, Flanigan Papers, Box 11, "Textiles," Nixon Project; Flanigan for Nixon, Mar. 9, 1971, "Meeting with Ad Hoc Textile Group," ibid.; Flanigan for Nixon, Mar. 11, 1971, ibid.; Memorandum for the Files, Mar. 12, 1971, ibid.; Meyer to Secretary of State, Mar. 12, 1971, Cable # 2238, Department of State, FOIA; Destler, Fukui, and Sato, *Textile Wrangle*, 251–74.

16. Arkady N. Shevchenko, *Breaking with Moscow* (New York: Knopf, 1985), 164; Kissinger, *White House Years*, 172–73; Anatoly Dobrynin, *In Confidence: Moscow's Ambassador to America's Six Cold War Presidents, 1962–1986* (New York: Times Books, 1995), 207; Tyler, *A Great Wall*, 60–70; Mann, *About Face*, 20–21.

17. Nixon to Kissinger, Sept. 29, 1969, WHSF, CF, Box 6, CO 34, China, 1969–70, Nixon Project, National Archives.

18. The evolution of the Nixon-Kissinger China policy is discussed in several sources. In addition to the books by Mann, Tyler, and Burr mentioned above, among the best are Robert D. Schulzinger, *Henry Kissinger: Doctor of Diplomacy* (New York: Columbia University Press, 1989), 75–101; Walter Isaacson, *Kissinger: A Biography* (New York: Simon and Schuster, 1992), 333–54; Raymond L. Garthoff, *Détente and Confrontation: American-Soviet Relations from Nixon to Reagan* (Washington, D.C.: Brookings Institution, 1985), 199–247; Robert S. Ross, *Negotiating Cooperation: The United States and China, 1969–1989* (Stanford: Stanford University Press, 1995); Hersh, *Price of Power*, 374–82; Welfield, *Empire in Eclipse*, 275–324; Kissinger, *White House Years*, 163–94, 684–787, 1049–96.

19. For published excerpts of the Warsaw talks, see Mann, *About Face*, 23–24; Tyler, *A Great Wall*, 75–77. China responded to Stoessel's initial contact by releasing two American citizens who had been seized in 1969 when their yacht entered Chinese waters.

20. Tyler, *A Great Wall*, 81–86. Allen Whiting, a former State Department China expert, tried unsuccessfully to persuade Kissinger to send him to Geneva to debrief Snow.

21. *New York Times*, Mar. 10, 1971.

22. On June 4, 1971, Agnew insisted on speaking personally to Nixon (who usually avoided his vice president) and asked, in a stunning reversal, that *he* be sent to visit China, before the president. It is difficult to know whether Agnew had come around or whether he mainly hoped to sabotage the China initiative. A startled Nixon, Haldeman reported, "told him he couldn't go." Two years later, in October 1973, Nixon helped force Agnew's resignation amid a bribery scandal stemming from the vice president's conduct while governor of Maryland. His political demise came almost as suddenly as had Lin Biao's in the fall of 1971.

23. *Haldeman Diaries*, Apr. 10, 17, 20, June 4, 1971; *New York Times*, Apr. 20, 1971.

24. Nixon, *RN*, 449–52; *Haldeman Diaries*, 307; Kissinger, *White House Years*, 687, 714.

25. Nixon comments in Haldeman daily notes, June-July, 1971, Haldeman Papers, Nixon Project; Nixon comments to Cabinet members, June 13, 1971, ibid.; Kissinger, *White House Years*, 726–27.

26. Kissinger, *White House Years*, 685, 745–50; Isaacson, *Kissinger*, 435; Hersh, *Price of Power*, 376.

27. For a more complete account of the initial Kissinger-Zhou talks than Kissinger provides in his memoirs, see Richard H. Solomon, *Chinese Political Negotiating Behavior, 1967–1984: An Interpretive Assessment* (Santa Monica, Calif.: Rand Corporation, 1995); Holdridge, *Crossing the Divide*, 57; John Holdridge, Marshall Green, and

William N. Stokes, *War and Peace with China: First-hand Experiences in the Foreign Service of the United States* (Bethesda, Md.: DACOR Press, 1994), 113, 124.

28. For more on Kissinger's initial discussions with Zhou, see Mann, *About Face*; Tyler, *A Great Wall*; and Burr, ed., *Kissinger Transcripts*.

29. Kusuda Minoru recounted these events in remarks he delivered on Mar. 11, 1996, at the Woodrow Wilson Center in Washington, D.C. Laird's assurance to Sato is contained in Meyer to Secretary of State, "Secretary of Defense Laird Visit to Japan," 4–11 July, Cable # 6522, July 6, 1971, Department of State, FOIA; Johnson, *Right Hand of Power*, 553–55; Meyer, *Assignment Tokyo*, 111–12; Quansheng Zhao, *Japanese Policymaking: The Politics Behind Politics: Informal Mechanisms and the Making of China Policy* (Westport, Conn.: Praeger, 1993), 70; Henry Brandon, *The Retreat of American Power* (Garden City, N.Y.: Doubleday, 1973), 169; *Haldeman Diaries*, entry of Aug. 16, 1971, CD/ROM version. For Nixon's boast of "sticking it to Japan," see Joan Hoff, *Nixon Reconsidered* (New York: Basic Books, 1994), 140.

30. Kusuda's remarks of Mar. 11, 1996, Wilson Center; Sato's reply to Nixon's belated message is contained in Meyer to Secretary of State, Cable # 6979, July 17, 1971, Department of State, FOIA; Haldeman daily notes, July 23, 1971, WHSF, Box 44, Nixon Project; Whitlam's account quoted in Welfield, *Empire in Eclipse*, 295.

31. *Peking Review*, Nov. 28 and Dec. 15, 1969; Apr. 10, 1970; *Renmin Ribao*, Nov. 28, 1969; Welfield, *Empire in Eclipse*, 289–91.

32. Welfield, *Empire in Eclipse*, 294.

33. Isaacson, *Kissinger*, 348; on Yeoman Charles Radford's activities, see Stanley I. Kutler, *The Wars of Watergate* (New York: Knopf, 1990), 116–19; Stephen Ambrose, *Nixon*, 3 vols. (New York: Simon and Schuster, 1987-91), vol. 2, 486–90. The Joint Chiefs and Kissinger deeply mistrusted each other. JCS chairman Admiral Thomas Moorer encouraged Radford, a naval aide to Kissinger, to copy and pass to the JCS material relating to subjects such as SALT, détente, and the secret China negotiations. Radford was eventually found out and transferred from the NSC.

34. Meyer to Secretary of State, "Secretary of Defense Laird Meeting with Sato," Cable # 6522, July 6, 1971, Department of State, FOIA; Meyer to Secretary of State, "Secretary of Defense Laird Visit to Japan," Cable # 6718, July 11, 1971, ibid.; *Japan Times*, July 10, 1971; "Old Pillars Fallen," *Far Eastern Economic Review*, Aug. 7, 1971, 49–51; Kissinger, *White House Years*, 740; Welfield, *Empire in Eclipse*, 295.

35. Hersh, *The Price of Power*, 380–81. The Watergate task force's interest in Radford focused on the White House response to his pilfering, not the foreign policy implications. The prosecutor who heard Nixon's testimony told Hersh he recalled the exchange because of Nixon's emotional response. Radford's only direct involvement with China occurred during Kissinger's July 1971 trip, but he probably had access to documents relating to earlier and later contacts. Radford's activities were

exposed at the end of 1971. In a complex power play between Nixon, Kissinger, and the Joint Chiefs of Staff, Radford was reassigned rather than prosecuted.

36. Terrill quoted in Hersh, *Price of Power*, 382; Zhou's statements to Reston quoted in "The Dispensable Ally," *Far Eastern Economic Review*, Aug. 28, 1971, 21–22.

37. Jonathan Unger, "Japan: The Economic Threat," *Far Eastern Economic Review*, Oct. 16, 1971, 49–52.

38. *Japan Times*, Aug. 15, 1971.

39. American business executives and politicians complained that collusion among Japanese politicians, bureaucrats, and business elites produced this structural imbalance. According to this view, the all-powerful Ministry of International Trade and Industry (MITI), relying on an array of formal and informal powers, coordinated a predatory trade strategy of export promotion and protection of the domestic market.

In June 1971 the Sato government approved a plan to liberalize rules on foreign trade and investment in Japan. Because the plan did not address either the textile question or yen-dollar valuation, Nixon dismissed it. See Robert C. Angel, *Explaining Economic Policy Failure: Japan in the 1969–71 International Monetary Crisis* (New York: Columbia University Press, 1991), 87–107.

40. *Time*, May 10, 1971; *Newsweek*, May 3, 1971; Welfield, *Empire in Eclipse*, 286–87; Angel, *Explaining Economic Policy Failure*, 107; *New York Times*, July 30, 1971. For the racial component of anti-Japanese and anti-Chinese attitudes among Americans, see John W. Dower, *War without Mercy: Race and Power in the Pacific War* (New York: Pantheon Books, 1986).

41. Dent to Peterson, July 13, 1971, WHSF, Peterson Papers, Box 1, Nixon Project; Haldeman daily notes, July 12, 1971, WHSF, Nixon Project; memorandum for president from Kennedy, July 16, 1971, Nixon Project, FOIA; Nixon to Sato, July 16, 1971, Nixon Project, FOIA; Peterson to President and Cabinet, Aug. 6, 1971, WHSF, Flanigan Papers, Box 11, Nixon Project; Flanigan to Peterson, Aug. 7, 1971, WHSF, ibid. Nixon's aide's warned that unless he moved immediately to impose textile quotas, American textile producers "would go to [Congressman] Wilbur Mills" and "work out a deal with him," leaving Nixon hostage to the Democrats.

42. Connally boasted to Kissinger that "you will be measured in this town by the enemies you destroy. The bigger they are, the bigger you will be." When asked by a journalist what qualified him for the Treasury post, Connally quipped "I can add." He told former NSC staffer C. Fred Bergsten that his "philosophy" of international economic policy was "all foreigners are out to screw us and it's our job to screw them first." His panache impressed Nixon so much that in July 1971 he told his staff to "figure out how the hell we can get [Vice President] Agnew to resign early" so that Connally could assume the job. Nixon called the Texan "my logical

successor." Kissinger, *White House Years*, 951; Ambrose, *Nixon*, vol. 2, 457; Hersh, *Price of Power*, 462; Angel, *Explaining Economic Policy Failure*, 117.

43. Haldeman daily notes, Aug. 12, 13, 14, 1971, WHSF, Nixon Project; Kissinger, *White House Years*, 954–55; Szulc, *Illusion of Peace*, 454–56; Ambrose, *Nixon*, vol. 2, 458–59.

44. Haldeman daily notes, Aug. 14, 1971, WHSF, Nixon Project; Destler, Fukui, and Sato, *Textile Wrangle*, 292–93.

45. Destler, Fukui, and Sato, *Textile Wrangle*, 294–99; Memoranda for the President's file, "RE: Nixon-Fukuda discussions on China, internal politics, and textiles," Sept. 10, 1971, Nixon Project, FOIA; Haldeman daily notes, Oct. 1, 2, 1971, WHSF, Nixon Project.

46. Volcker and Gyohten, *Changing Fortunes*, 80–90, 95–100; Kissinger, *White House Years*, 957–62; Szulc, *Illusion of Peace*, 461–64; Angel, *Explaining Economic Policy Failure*, 220–41, 259–60.

47. Memorandum by U. Alexis Johnson to Secretary of State, NSC SRG Meeting, Aug. 27, 1971, on NSSM 122–Japan, Record # 80714, National Security Archive. In a revealing aside, Johnson noted that NSC "discussion on economic issues was brief and inconsequential."

48. Memorandum from Henry Kissinger for Richard Nixon, "The President's Private Meeting with British Prime Minister Edward Heath," Dec. 20, 1971, Nixon Project, National Archives, FOIA.

49. Memoranda for the President's File from James J. Wickel, "Meetings with Eisaku Sato, Jan. 6–7, 1972," Jan. 7, 1972, Nixon project, FOIA; Welfield, *Empire in Eclipse*, 308; Atsushi Kusano, *Two Nixon Shocks and Japan-U.S. Relations* (Princeton: Princeton University, Center of International Studies, Woodrow Wilson School of Public Affairs, 1987), 34–35, 37–38. In news coverage and an editorial on the San Clemente meeting, probably inspired by a presidential leak, the *New York Times* (Jan. 6, and 11, 1972) criticized Sato for giving in to "Peking's pressure for change" by not standing firm enough behind Taiwan and South Korea. The *Times* also chastised Tokyo for encouraging a "kind of yen block in Asia that faintly recalls the World War II Greater East Asia Co-Prosperity Sphere" and for contemplating a self-reliant "nuclear defense." This was especially odd given Nixon's hectoring of Sato on military issues. As noted, Nixon may have encouraged Japan to build nuclear weapons in part to stir up Chinese fears and thus convince Beijing to endorse the U.S.-Japan security treaty as the lesser evil.

50. Mann, *About Face*, 13–15.

51. Nixon's Handwritten Personal Notes Regarding U.S.-China Visit, Feb. 15, 19, 22, 1972, Record #74177, 74176, 74175, National Security Archive. In these musings, the president outlined what he intended to say to Mao and Zhou

Nixon, *RN*, 560–67; Kissinger, *White House Years*, 1061–63. Full transcripts of all meetings between Kissinger and Nixon and Zhou and Mao have not been released, although extensive portions are now available. The most complete set can be found in the National Security Archive, Washington, D.C. For published transcripts, see William Burr, ed., *The Kissinger Transcripts*; extensive selections from these high-level talks of 1971–76 are printed in Mann, *About Face*, and Tyler, *A Great Wall*.

52. Nixon's handwritten notes, Feb. 19, 22, 1972, Record # 74176 , 74175, National Security Archive.

53. Kissinger, *White House Years*, 1053, 1072; Nixon, *RN*, 560–67; Szulc, *Illusion of Peace*, 521–24.

54. For the text of the Shanghai Communiqué and a discussion of its preparation, see Kissinger, *White House Years*, 1062–63, 1490–92. Neither Nixon nor Kissinger ever revealed his private assurances to Mao and Zhou concerning Taiwan. For an insightful discussion of the battle between Kissinger and State Department personnel to revise the wording of the communiqué, see Mann, *About Face*, and Tyler, *A Great Wall*.

55. Welfield, *Empire in Eclipse*, 310; in July 1972, Tanaka Kakuei became Japan's prime minister, campaigning on the slogan, "Don't miss the boat to China." In September, Tanaka traveled to Beijing and negotiated an agreement with Zhou Enlai to establish diplomatic and trade ties. China then dropped its longstanding opposition to the U.S.-Japan security treaty.

56. The Paris peace accords, finally signed in January 1973, favored North Vietnam. Both North Vietnamese and Vietcong forces could remain in South Vietnam and be resupplied. U.S. forces were to leave in ninety days. Washington could aid the Saigon regime but would almost certainly reduce assistance and lose interest once American personnel had departed.

57. For excerpts of Kissinger's conversations with Zhou and Mao, and his reports to Nixon, see Burr, ed., *The Kissinger Transcripts*, 82–117; Memorandum by Henry Kissinger for the President, "My Asian Trip," Feb. 27, 1973, Record #71724, National Security Archive; Memorandum by Henry Kissinger for the President, "My Trip to China," Mar. 2, 1973, Record #71717, National Security Archive; Memorandum of Foreign Minister Ohira's call on the President, Oct. 18, 1972, National Security Files, Nixon Project, FOIA. Nixon took credit for China's change of heart, telling Ohira that he had hammered home the point during his February 1972 visit to China that the "security treaty serves the interests of the PRC as well as the United States in maintaining peace in the Pacific." He did not repeat to Ohira what else he had said: that the treaty helped contain Japan. See Kissinger to Nixon, Meeting with Chairman Mao, Feb. 24, 1973, copy in

National Security Archive, and reports of Feb. 24 and 27, Presidents Personal File, Box 6, Nixon Project; Kissinger, *White House Years*, 1061–62, 1072, 1089, 1490–92; Henry A. Kissinger, *Years of Upheaval* (Boston: Little, Brown, 1982), 47–60.

58. Memorandum for the President from Henry Kissinger, "My Asian Trip," Feb. 27, 1973, Record #71724 (emphasis in original).

59. Kissinger, *Years of Upheaval*, 70.

60. Mann, *About Face*, 66.

61. For a partial account of Kissinger's talks with Chinese officials during 1973–75, see Burr, ed., *The Kissinger Transcripts*, 112–216, 265–321, 371–425. Nearly all these contacts focused on ways of countering perceived Soviet military and political expansionism. Soviet leader Leonid Brezhnev likewise tried to persuade Nixon to sign a pact promising military cooperation if either the United States or the Soviet Union was attacked by a third country, namely China.

Index

Harvard East Asian Monographs
(*out-of-print)

Harvard East Asian Monographs

Harvard East Asian Monographs

Harvard East Asian Monographs

Harvard East Asian Monographs

Harvard East Asian Monographs

Harvard East Asian Monographs

175. See Heng Teow, *Japan's Cultural Policy Toward China, 1918–1931: A Comparative Perspective*

176. Michael A. Fuller, *An Introduction to Literary Chinese*

177. Frederick R. Dickinson, *War and National Reinvention: Japan in the Great War, 1914–1919*

178. John Solt, *Shredding the Tapestry of Meaning: The Poetry and Poetics of Kitasono Katue (1902–1978)*

179. Edward Pratt, *Japan's Protoindustrial Elite: The Economic Foundations of the Gōnō*

180. Atsuko Sakaki, *Recontextualizing Texts: Narrative Performance in Modern Japanese Fiction*

181. Soon-Won Park, *Colonial Industrialization and Labor in Korea: The Onoda Cement Factory*

182. JaHyun Kim Haboush and Martina Deuchler, *Culture and the State in Late Chosŏn Korea*

183. John W. Chaffee, *Branches of Heaven: A History of the Imperial Clan of Sung China*

184. Gi-Wook Shin and Michael Robinson, eds., *Colonial Modernity in Korea*

185. Nam-lin Hur, *Prayer and Play in Late Tokugawa Japan: Asakusa Sensōji and Edo Society*

186. Kristin Stapleton, *Civilizing Chengdu: Chinese Urban Reform, 1895–1937*

187. Hyung Il Pai, *Constructing "Korean" Origins: A Critical Review of Archaeology, Historiography, and Racial Myth in Korean State-Formation Theories*

188. Brian D. Ruppert, *Jewel in the Ashes: Buddha Relics and Power in Early Medieval Japan*

189. Susan Daruvala, *Zhou Zuoren and an Alternative Chinese Response to Modernity*

190. James Z. Lee, *The Political Economy of a Frontier: Southwest China, 1250–1850*

191. Kerry Smith, *A Time of Crisis: Japan, the Great Depression, and Rural Revitalization*

192. Michael Lewis, *Becoming Apart: National Power and Local Politics in Toyama, 1868–1945*

193. William C. Kirby, Man-houng Lin, James Chin Shih, and David A. Pietz, eds., *State and Economy in Republican China: A Handbook for Scholars*

194. Timothy S. George, *Minamata: Pollution and the Struggle for Democracy in Postwar Japan*

195. Billy K. L. So, *Prosperity, Region, and Institutions in Maritime China: The South Fukien Pattern, 946–1368*

196. Yoshihisa Tak Matsusaka, *The Making of Japanese Manchuria, 1904–1932*

Harvard East Asian Monographs

197. Maram Epstein, *Competing Discourses: Orthodoxy, Authenticity, and Engendered Meanings in Late Imperial Chinese Fiction*

198. Curtis J. Milhaupt, J. Mark Ramseyer, and Michael K. Young, eds. and comps., *Japanese Law in Context: Readings in Society, the Economy, and Politics*

199. Haruo Iguchi, *Unfinished Business: Ayukawa Yoshisuke and U.S.-Japan Relations, 1937–1952*

200. Scott Pearce, Audrey Spiro, and Patricia Ebrey, *Culture and Power in the Reconstitution of the Chinese Realm, 200–600*

201. Terry Kawashima, *Writing Margins: The Textual Construction of Gender in Heian and Kamakura Japan*

202. Martin W. Huang, *Desire and Fictional Narrative in Late Imperial China*

203. Robert S. Ross and Jiang Changbin, eds., *Re-examining the Cold War: U.S.-China Diplomacy, 1954–1973*